Series V, No. 47

Department of Economic and Social Affairs
Statistics Division

World Statistics Pocketbook 2023 edition

Containing data available
as of 31 July 2023

United Nations, New York, 2023

The **Department of Economic and Social Affairs** of the United Nations is a vital interface between global policies in the economic, social and environmental spheres and national action. The Department works in three main interlinked areas: (i) it compiles, generates and analyses a wide range of economic, social and environmental data and information on which United Nations Member States draw to review common problems and to take stock of policy options; (ii) it facilitates the negotiations of Member States in many intergovernmental bodies on joint courses of action to address ongoing or emerging global challenges; and (iii) it advises interested Governments on the ways and means of translating policy frameworks developed in United Nations conferences and summits into programmes at the country level and, through technical assistance, helps build national capacities.

Note

Visit the United Nations World Wide Web site on the Internet:
For the Department of Economic and Social Affairs,
   http://www.un.org/esa/desa/
For statistics and statistical publications,
   http://unstats.un.org/unsd/
For UN publications, https://shop.un.org/

ST/ESA/STAT/SER.V/47
United Nations Publication
Sales No. E.23.XVII.3
ISBN: **978-92-1-259226-8**
eISBN: **978-92-1-002524-9**
Print ISSN: **2411-8915**
eISSN: **2411-894X**

Contents

World, Regional and Country profiles

Contents (*continued*)

Contents (*continued*)

Explanatory notes

The following symbols and abbreviations have been used in the *World Statistics Pocketbook*:

.	A point is used to indicate decimals.
...	Data are not available or not applicable.
~0.0	Not zero, but less than half of the unit employed.
−~0.0	Not zero, but negative and less than half of the unit employed.
%	Percentage
000	Thousands
Assist.	Assistance
Bol. Rep.	Bolivarian Republic
CIF	Cost, Insurance and Freight
CO_2	Carbon dioxide
const.	Constant
CPI	Consumer price index
Dem. Rep.	Democratic Republic
est.	Estimate
F	Females
FOB	Free on board
GDP	Gross domestic product
GNI	Gross national income
GVA	Gross value added
ISIC	International Standard Industrial Classification
ISO	International Organization for Standardization
Km^2	Square kilometres
M	Males
nes	Not elsewhere specified
pop.	Population
Rep.	Republic
SAR	Special Administrative Region
UN	United Nations
UNHCR	Office of the UN High Commissioner for Refugees
United Kingdom	United Kingdom of Great Britain and Northern Ireland
United States	United States of America
UNSD	United Nations Statistics Division
US$/USD	United States dollars

The metric system of weights and measures has been employed in the *World Statistics Pocketbook*.

The *World Statistics Pocketbook* is an annual compilation of key economic, social and environmental indicators, presented in one-page profiles. This edition includes profiles for the 30 world geographical regions and 232 countries or areas. Prepared by the United Nations Statistics Division of the Department of Economic and Social Affairs, it responds to General Assembly resolution 2626 (XXV), in which the Secretary-General is requested to supply basic national data that will increase international public awareness of countries' development efforts.

The indicators shown are selected from the wealth of international statistical information compiled regularly by the Statistics Division and the Population Division of the United Nations, the statistical services of the United Nations specialized agencies and other international organizations and institutions. Special recognition is gratefully given for their assistance in continually providing data.

Organization of the Pocketbook

The profiles are presented first with the world and its geographical regions and sub-regions, based on the M49 regional classification[1], and then countries and areas alphabetically according to their names in English. Each profile is organised into 5 sections, where relevant and/or available:

- *General information:* includes data on surface area, population and population density, sex ratio of the population, capital city and its population, national currency and its exchange rate to the US dollar, location by geographical region and the date of admission to the United Nations.

- *Economic indicators:* includes data on national accounts Gross domestic product (GDP), GDP per capita, GDP growth rate, Gross Value Added (GVA) share by industry, employment share by industry, unemployment rate, labour force participation rate, consumer price index, agricultural production index, the value of total exports, imports and the trade balance and balance of payments.

- *Major trading partners:* shows a country's main trading partners

- *Social indicators:* includes data on population (growth rates, including for the urban population), total fertility rate, life expectancy at birth, population age distribution, international migrant stock, refugees, infant mortality rate, health (expenditure and physicians), education (expenditure and gross enrolment ratios), intentional homicide rate and seats held by women in the National Parliament.

- *Environmental and infrastructure indicators:* includes data on internet users, Research & Development expenditure, threatened species, forested area, CO_2 emission estimates, energy production and energy

---

[1] See UNSD website: https://unstats.un.org/unsd/methodology/m49/

Introduction *(continued)*

supply per capita, tourist/visitor arrivals, important sites for terrestrial biodiversity protected, population using safely managed water sources and sanitation facilities and Official Development Assitance received or disbursed.

The complete set of indicators, listed by category and in the order in which they appear in the profiles, is shown before the country profile section (see page ix). Not all indicators are shown for each country or area due to different degrees of data availability.

The technical notes section, which follows the country profile pages, contains brief descriptions of the concepts and methodologies used in the compilation of the indicators as well as information on the statistical sources for the indicators. Readers interested in longer time-series data or more detailed descriptions of the concepts or methodologies should consult the primary sources of the data and the references listed in the section following the technical notes.

For brevity the Pocketbook omits specific information on the source or methodology for individual data points, and when a data point is estimated no distinction is made between whether the estimation was done by the international or national organization. See the technical notes section for the primary source which may provide this information.

Time period

This issue of the *World Statistics Pocketbook* presents data for the economic, social, environmental and infrastructure sections for three reference years - 2010, 2015 and 2023 - when available or the most recent data previous to these years, back to 2000. These instances are footnoted in each profile. For the general information and major trading partners sections the reference year is 2023 and 2022 respectively, unless otherwise footnoted.

Acknowledgement

The *World Statistics Pocketbook* is prepared annually by the Development Data and Outreach Branch of the Statistics Division, Department of Economic and Social Affairs of the United Nations Secretariat. The programme manager is Matthias Reister and Anuradha Chimata is the editor; David Carter, Mohamed Nabassoua and Kebebush Welkema provided production assistance; Joshua Kneidl provided IT support. Comments on this publication are welcome and may be sent by e-mail to statistics@un.org.

Profile information and indicator list*

General information

Region
Population (000)
Population density (per km²)
Capital city
Capital city population (000)
UN membership date
Surface area (km²)
Sex ratio (males per 100 females)
National currency
Exchange rate (per US$)

Economic indicators

GDP: Gross domestic product (million current US$)
GDP growth rate (annual %, constant 2015 prices)
GDP per capita (current US$)
Economy: Agriculture, industry and services and other activity (% of GVA)
Employment in agriculture, industry and services & other sectors (% of employed)
Unemployment rate (% of labour force)
Labour force participation rate (% of female/male population)
CPI: Consumer Price Index (2010=100)
Agricultural production index (2014-2016=100)
International trade: Exports, imports and balance (million current US$)
Balance of payments, current account (million current US$)

Major trading partners (% of exports and imports)

Social indicators

Population growth rate (average annual %)
Urban population (% of total population)
Urban population growth rate (average annual %)
Fertility rate, total (live births per woman)
Life expectancy at birth (females/males, years)
Population age distribution (0-14/60+ years old, %)
International migrant stock (000/% of total population)
Refugees and others of concern to the UNHCR (000)
Infant mortality rate (per 1 000 live births)
Health: Current expenditure (% of GDP)
Health: Physicians (per 1 000 population)
Education: Government expenditure (% of GDP)
Education: Primary, Lower secondary and Upper secondary gross enrolment ratio (females/males per 100 population)
Intentional homicide rate (per 100 000 population)
Seats held by women in the National Parliament (% of total seats)

Environmental and infrastructure indicators

Individuals using the Internet (per 100 inhabitants)
Research & Development expenditure (% of GDP)
Threatened species (number)
Forested area (% of land area)
CO_2 emission estimates (million tons/tons per capita)
Energy production, primary (Petajoules)
Energy supply per capita (Gigajoules)
Tourist/visitor arrivals at national borders (000)
Important sites for terrestrial biodiversity protected (%)
Population using safely managed drinking water sources (urban/rural, %)
Population using safely managed sanitation facilities (urban/rural, %)
Net Official Development Assistance disbursed (% of GNI of donor)
Net Official Development Assistance received (% of GNI of recipient)

* The complete set of information and indicators listed here may not be shown for each country or area depending upon data availability. The technical notes provide a brief description of each information item and indicator.

World, Regional and Country /Area profiles

Total, all countries or areas

Population (000, 2023)	7 975 105 [a,b]	
Pop. density (per km2, 2023)	61.2 [a,b]	
Surface area (km2)	130 094 010 [c]	
Sex ratio (m per 100 f)	101.1 [a,b]	

Economic indicators	2010	2015	2023
GDP: Gross domestic product (million current US$)	66 578 017	75 283 835	96 698 005 [c]
GDP growth rate (annual %, const. 2015 prices)	4.5	3.1	5.9 [c]
GDP per capita (current US$)	9 533.3	10 139.8	12 229.1 [c]
Employment in agriculture (% of employed) [d]	32.9	28.7	26.6 [c]
Employment in industry (% of employed) [d]	22.6	23.2	23.1 [c]
Employment in services & other sectors (% employed) [d]	44.5	48.1	50.3 [c]
Unemployment rate (% of labour force) [d]	6.3	6.0	5.8
Labour force participation rate (female/male pop. %) [d]	48.9 / 75.3	47.6 / 73.9	47.2 / 72.4
Agricultural production index (2014-2016=100)	88	100	110 [c]
International trade: exports (million current US$)	15 102 218	16 384 279	24 553 001 [b]
International trade: imports (million current US$)	15 275 115	16 482 346	25 244 192 [b]
International trade: balance (million current US$)	- 172 897	- 98 067	- 691 191 [b]

Social indicators	2010	2015	2023
Population growth rate (average annual %)	1.2	1.2	0.8 [a,b]
Urban population (% of total population)	51.7	53.9	55.7 [e]
Urban population growth rate (average annual %) [f]	2.2	2.0	...
Fertility rate, total (live births per woman)	2.6	2.5	2.3 [a,b]
Life expectancy at birth (females/males, years)	72.7 / 67.6	74.4 / 69.3	74.4 / 69.1 [a,b]
Population age distribution (0-14/60+ years old, %)	27.1 / 11.1	26.4 / 12.3	25.3 / 13.9 [a,b]
International migrant stock (000/% of total pop.)	220 983.2 / 3.2	247 958.6 / 3.4	280 598.1 / 3.6 [g]
Refugees and others of concern to the UNHCR (000)	...	57 959.7	104 454.3 [b]
Infant mortality rate (per 1 000 live births)	37.1	31.5	27.5 [a,b]
Education: Primary gross enrol. ratio (f/m per 100 pop.)	101.3 / 104.0	102.3 / 102.4	100.9 / 102.7 [g]
Education: Lowr. sec. gross enrol. ratio (f/m per 100 pop.)	81.3 / 83.6	84.1 / 84.3	84.3 / 84.9 [g]
Education: Upr. sec. gross enrol. ratio (f/m per 100 pop.)	58.5 / 61.0	66.0 / 67.4	68.1 / 69.3 [g]
Intentional homicide rate (per 100 000 pop.) [d]	6.1	5.9	5.8 [c]
Seats held by women in the National Parliament (%)	19.0	22.3	26.5 [h]

Environment and infrastructure indicators	2010	2015	2023
Individuals using the Internet (per 100 inhabitants)	28.5	40.0	62.6 [c]
Research & Development gross expenditure (% of GDP)	1.6	1.7	1.9 [c]
Forested area (% of land area) [d]	31.5	31.3	31.1 [g]
Energy production, primary (Petajoules)	530 045	569 897	586 995 [g]
Energy supply per capita (Gigajoules)	74	74	72 [g]
Important sites for terrestrial biodiversity protected (%)	39.1	42.2	44.3 [b]
Pop. using safely managed drinking water (urban/rural, %)	79.7 / 51.3	80.4 / 55.9	81.1 / 62.2 [b]
Pop. using safely managed sanitation (urban/rural %)	41.8 / 28.4	45.7 / 35.6	49.6 / 45.9 [b]

a Projected estimate (medium fertility variant). b 2022. c 2021. d Estimate. e 2019. f Data refers to a 5-year period preceding the reference year. g 2020. h Data are as at 1 January of reporting year.

Africa

Region	World	Population (000, 2023)	1 426 736 [a,b]
Surface area (km2)	29 648 481 [c]	Pop. density (per km2, 2023)	48.3 [a,b]
Sex ratio (m per 100 f)	99.7 [a,b]		

Economic indicators	2010	2015	2023
GDP: Gross domestic product (million current US$)	2 032 590	2 407 357	2 726 643 [c]
GDP growth rate (annual %, const. 2015 prices)	5.9	3.4	5.2 [c]
GDP per capita (current US$)	1 929.0	2 007.1	1 959.0 [c]
Employment in agriculture (% of employed) [d]	53.1	49.9	48.4 [c]
Employment in industry (% of employed) [d]	12.3	12.9	13.6 [c]
Employment in services & other sectors (% employed) [d]	34.7	37.1	38.0 [c]
Unemployment rate (% of labour force) [d]	6.5	6.7	7.1
Labour force participation rate (female/male pop. %) [d]	54.3 / 73.5	53.6 / 72.0	53.8 / 71.8
Agricultural production index (2014-2016=100)	86	101	114 [c]
International trade: exports (million current US$)	496 594	402 988	669 987 [b]
International trade: imports (million current US$)	468 435	547 529	778 689 [b]
International trade: balance (million current US$)	28 159	- 144 542	- 108 702 [b]

Social indicators	2010	2015	2023
Population growth rate (average annual %)	2.6	2.6	2.3 [a,b]
Urban population (% of total population)	38.9	41.2	43.0 [e]
Urban population growth rate (average annual %) [f]	3.6	3.7	...
Fertility rate, total (live births per woman)	4.9	4.6	4.2 [a,b]
Life expectancy at birth (females/males, years)	60.2 / 57.0	62.9 / 59.3	64.1 / 60.2 [a,b]
Population age distribution (0-14/60+ years old, %)	41.5 / 5.0	41.3 / 5.2	40.1 / 5.5 [a,b]
International migrant stock (000/% of total pop.)	17 806.7 / 1.7	22 860.8 / 1.9	25 389.5 / 1.9 [g]
Refugees and others of concern to the UNHCR (000)	...	17 067.3	37 337.9 [b]
Infant mortality rate (per 1 000 live births)	60.9	52.5	44.2 [a,b]
Intentional homicide rate (per 100 000 pop.) [d]	12.2	12.4	12.7 [c]

Environment and infrastructure indicators	2010	2015	2023
Forested area (% of land area) [d]	22.7	21.9	21.3 [g]
Energy production, primary (Petajoules)	47 355	44 326	43 879 [g]
Energy supply per capita (Gigajoules)	27	26	25 [g]

a Projected estimate (medium fertility variant). b 2022. c 2021. d Estimate. e 2019. f Data refers to a 5-year period preceding the reference year. g 2020.

Northern Africa

Region	Africa	Population (000, 2023)	259 970 [a,b]
Surface area (km2)	7 769 438 [c]	Pop. density (per km2, 2023)	33.8 [a,b]
Sex ratio (m per 100 f)	101.8 [a,b]		

Economic indicators	2010	2015	2023
GDP: Gross domestic product (million current US$)	646 437	772 568	853 806 [c]
GDP growth rate (annual %, const. 2015 prices)	5.0	3.7	6.7 [c]
GDP per capita (current US$)	3 127.4	3 390.4	3 346.0 [c]
Employment in agriculture (% of employed) [d]	29.2	26.7	23.7 [c]
Employment in industry (% of employed) [d]	24.6	24.4	26.0 [c]
Employment in services & other sectors (% employed) [d]	46.2	49.0	50.3 [c]
Unemployment rate (% of labour force) [d]	10.5	13.1	11.3
Labour force participation rate (female/male pop. %) [d]	23.1 / 72.3	23.2 / 69.4	19.9 / 67.4
Agricultural production index (2014-2016=100)	84	102	107 [c]
International trade: exports (million current US$)	165 544	108 845	223 445 [b]
International trade: imports (million current US$)	181 147	205 560	255 792 [b]
International trade: balance (million current US$)	- 15 603	- 96 714	- 32 346 [b]

Social indicators	2010	2015	2023
Population growth rate (average annual %)	1.9	2.1	1.6 [a,b]
Urban population (% of total population)	50.5	51.4	52.2 [e]
Urban population growth rate (average annual %) [f]	2.1	2.3	...
Fertility rate, total (live births per woman)	3.2	3.4	3.0 [a,b]
Life expectancy at birth (females/males, years)	71.8 / 67.5	73.2 / 68.7	73.6 / 69.1 [a,b]
Population age distribution (0-14/60+ years old, %)	32.4 / 6.6	32.8 / 7.3	32.5 / 8.5 [a,b]
International migrant stock (000/% of total pop.)	1 952.0 / 1.0	2 138.9 / 1.0	3 167.9 / 1.3 [g]
Infant mortality rate (per 1 000 live births)	29.5	25.3	21.4 [a,b]
Education: Primary gross enrol. ratio (f/m per 100 pop.)	95.5 / 100.8	98.0 / 101.5 [d]	101.4 / 103.5 [d,g]
Education: Lowr. sec. gross enrol. ratio (f/m per 100 pop.)	89.6 / 96.4	94.0 / 98.7 [d]	95.6 / 99.7 [d,g]
Education: Upr. sec. gross enrol. ratio (f/m per 100 pop.)	52.0 / 48.6	62.8 / 59.2 [d]	65.1 / 59.0 [d,g]
Intentional homicide rate (per 100 000 pop.) [d]	5.7	5.8	6.3 [c]
Seats held by women in the National Parliament (%)	13.2	24.6	20.4 [h]

Environment and infrastructure indicators	2010	2015	2023
Individuals using the Internet (per 100 inhabitants)	23.2	36.6	70.6 [c]
Research & Development expenditure (% of GDP)	0.4	0.6	0.8 [g]
Forested area (% of land area) [d]	4.4	3.6	3.5 [g]
Important sites for terrestrial biodiversity protected (%)	31.2	35.1	41.7 [b]
Pop. using safely managed drinking water (urban/rural, %)	80.6 / 57.5 [i]	81.9 / ...	81.1 / ... [b]
Pop. using safely managed sanitation (urban/rural %)	46.8 / 39.4	50.1 / 43.7	59.7 / 33.9 [b]

a Projected estimate (medium fertility variant). **b** 2022. **c** 2021. **d** Estimate. **e** 2019. **f** Data refers to a 5-year period preceding the reference year. **g** 2020. **h** Data are as at 1 January of reporting year. **i** 2006.

Sub-Saharan Africa

Region	Africa	Population (000, 2023)	1 166 766[a,b]
Surface area (km2)	21 879 043[c,d]	Pop. density (per km2, 2023)	53.4[a,b]
Sex ratio (m per 100 f)	99.3[a,b]		

Economic indicators	2010	2015	2023
GDP: Gross domestic product (million current US$)	1 386 153	1 634 789	1 872 837[d]
GDP growth rate (annual %, const. 2015 prices)	6.4	3.2	4.5[d]
GDP per capita (current US$)	1 636.5	1 682.6	1 647.7[d]
Employment in agriculture (% of employed)[e]	57.6	54.0	52.3[d]
Employment in industry (% of employed)[e]	9.9	11.0	11.7[d]
Employment in services & other sectors (% employed)[e]	32.5	35.0	36.0[d]
Unemployment rate (% of labour force)[e]	5.7	5.5	6.4
Labour force participation rate (female/male pop. %)[e]	63.3 / 73.9	61.9 / 72.7	62.3 / 73.0
International trade: exports (million current US$)	331 050	294 142	446 541[b]
International trade: imports (million current US$)	287 288	341 970	522 897[b]
International trade: balance (million current US$)	43 762	- 47 827	- 76 356[b]

Social indicators	2010	2015	2023
Population growth rate (average annual %)	2.8	2.7	2.5[a,b]
Urban population (% of total population)	36.1	38.8	40.9[f]
Urban population growth rate (average annual %)[g]	4.1	4.1	...
Fertility rate, total (live births per woman)	5.3	4.9	4.5[a,b]
Life expectancy at birth (females/males, years)	57.7 / 54.8	60.7 / 57.3	62.1 / 58.3[a,b]
Population age distribution (0-14/60+ years old, %)	43.7 / 4.6	43.2 / 4.7	41.8 / 4.8[a,b]
International migrant stock (000/% of total pop.)	15 854.6 / 1.9	20 721.9 / 2.2	22 221.5 / 2.0[h]
Infant mortality rate (per 1 000 live births)	66.2	57.2	47.5[a,b]
Education: Primary gross enrol. ratio (f/m per 100 pop.)	94.6 / 102.2	96.7 / 101.0	97.3 / 101.6[e,h]
Education: Lowr. sec. gross enrol. ratio (f/m per 100 pop.)	42.8 / 50.8	48.5 / 54.2	48.4 / 53.1[e,h]
Education: Upr. sec. gross enrol. ratio (f/m per 100 pop.)	27.2 / 34.8	30.9 / 38.1	33.0 / 37.9[e,h]
Intentional homicide rate (per 100 000 pop.)[e]	13.8	13.9	14.1[d]
Seats held by women in the National Parliament (%)	18.4	22.6	26.5[i]

Environment and infrastructure indicators	2010	2015	2023
Individuals using the Internet (per 100 inhabitants)	6.0	16.0	34.9[d]
Research & Development expenditure (% of GDP)	0.3	0.3	0.3[h]
Forested area (% of land area)	29.9	28.5	27.6[h]
Important sites for terrestrial biodiversity protected (%)	39.7	40.8	43.4[b]
Pop. using safely managed drinking water (urban/rural, %)	46.5 / 9.2	50.8 / 11.6	53.0 / 15.2[b]
Pop. using safely managed sanitation (urban/rural %)	26.6 / 16.7	28.4 / 18.0	30.5 / 19.8[b]

a Projected estimate (medium fertility variant). b 2022. c Calculated by the UN Statistics Division. d 2021. e Estimate. f 2019. g Data refers to a 5-year period preceding the reference year. h 2020. i Data are as at 1 January of reporting year.

Eastern Africa

Region	Sub-Saharan Africa	Population (000, 2023)	473 005[a,b]
Surface area (km2)	6 667 493[c]	Pop. density (per km2, 2023)	71.1[a,b]
Sex ratio (m per 100 f)	98.4[a,b]		

Economic indicators	2010	2015	2023
GDP: Gross domestic product (million current US$)	235 641	329 095	459 522[c]
GDP growth rate (annual %, const. 2015 prices)	9.4	6.0	5.6[c]
GDP per capita (current US$)	689.7	839.1	999.3[c]
Employment in agriculture (% of employed)[d]	67.7	63.9	60.4[c]
Employment in industry (% of employed)[d]	8.0	9.1	10.6[c]
Employment in services & other sectors (% employed)[d]	24.2	27.0	29.1[c]
Unemployment rate (% of labour force)[d]	4.2	3.7	4.8
Labour force participation rate (female/male pop. %)[d]	71.0 / 80.6	70.4 / 80.0	70.6 / 78.6
Agricultural production index (2014-2016=100)	87	101	119[c]
International trade: exports (million current US$)	31 652	40 742	72 150[b]
International trade: imports (million current US$)	62 688	94 477	209 241[b]
International trade: balance (million current US$)	- 31 036	- 53 735	- 137 091[b]

Social indicators	2010	2015	2023
Population growth rate (average annual %)	2.9	2.7	2.5[a,b]
Urban population (% of total population)	24.4	26.6	28.5[e]
Urban population growth rate (average annual %)[f]	4.4	4.6	...
Fertility rate, total (live births per woman)	5.2	4.7	4.2[a,b]
Life expectancy at birth (females/males, years)	60.3 / 56.7	64.5 / 59.8	66.2 / 61.0[a,b]
Population age distribution (0-14/60+ years old, %)	45.0 / 4.1	43.8 / 4.3	41.4 / 4.5[a,b]
International migrant stock (000/% of total pop.)	4 743.7 / 1.4	6 696.9 / 1.7	7 682.8 / 1.7[g]
Infant mortality rate (per 1 000 live births)	55.2	45.0	35.5[a,b]
Seats held by women in the National Parliament (%)	21.6	27.2	31.5[h]

Environment and infrastructure indicators	2010	2015	2023
Individuals using the Internet (per 100 inhabitants)	3.2	10.5	20.7[c]
Forested area (% of land area)[d]	32.5	29.7	28.9[g]
Pop. using safely managed drinking water (urban/rural, %)	46.6 / 6.2	52.4 / 8.9	53.5 / 13.5[b]
Pop. using safely managed sanitation (urban/rural %)	22.2 / 14.4	25.1 / 16.7	27.8 / 19.7[b]

a Projected estimate (medium fertility variant). **b** 2022. **c** 2021. **d** Estimate. **e** 2019. **f** Data refers to a 5-year period preceding the reference year. **g** 2020. **h** Data are as at 1 January of reporting year.

Middle Africa

Region	Sub-Saharan Africa	Population (000, 2023)	196 078 [a,b]
Surface area (km2)	6 496 820 [c]	Pop. density (per km2, 2023)	30.2 [a,b]
Sex ratio (m per 100 f)	98.9 [a,b]		

Economic indicators	2010	2015	2023
GDP: Gross domestic product (million current US$)	191 153	242 140	232 025 [c]
GDP growth rate (annual %, const. 2015 prices)	4.8	1.9	2.3 [c]
GDP per capita (current US$)	1 430.6	1 538.4	1 219.5 [c]
Employment in agriculture (% of employed) [d]	60.6	56.6	54.4 [c]
Employment in industry (% of employed) [d]	9.2	10.2	10.9 [c]
Employment in services & other sectors (% employed) [d]	30.2	33.1	34.8 [c]
Unemployment rate (% of labour force) [d]	5.7	5.9	6.4
Labour force participation rate (female/male pop. %) [d]	66.3 / 74.2	64.1 / 72.9	64.4 / 72.2
Agricultural production index (2014-2016=100)	85	100	114 [c]
International trade: exports (million current US$)	90 717	70 653	116 102 [b]
International trade: imports (million current US$)	43 623	56 081	45 038 [b]
International trade: balance (million current US$)	47 094	14 572	71 064 [b]

Social indicators	2010	2015	2023
Population growth rate (average annual %)	3.3	3.2	3.0 [a,b]
Urban population (% of total population)	45.2	47.9	50.1 [e]
Urban population growth rate (average annual %) [f]	4.4	4.3	...
Fertility rate, total (live births per woman)	6.2	6.0	5.6 [a,b]
Life expectancy at birth (females/males, years)	57.5 / 54.2	60.2 / 56.6	61.8 / 57.5 [a,b]
Population age distribution (0-14/60+ years old, %)	45.6 / 4.5	45.7 / 4.4	45.4 / 4.4 [a,b]
International migrant stock (000/% of total pop.)	2 436.8 / 1.9	3 479.9 / 2.3	3 861.6 / 2.2 [g]
Infant mortality rate (per 1 000 live births)	74.6	62.9	50.7 [a,b]
Seats held by women in the National Parliament (%)	13.5	18.1	20.8 [h]

Environment and infrastructure indicators	2010	2015	2023
Individuals using the Internet (per 100 inhabitants)	2.1	10.0	27.9 [c]
Forested area (% of land area) [d]	47.2	45.7	44.3 [g]
Pop. using safely managed drinking water (urban/rural, %)	34.3 / 2.5	37.8 / 2.9	38.7 / 2.9 [b]
Pop. using safely managed sanitation (urban/rural %)	22.8 / 14.8	22.9 / 13.1	22.5 / 11.2 [b]

a Projected estimate (medium fertility variant). b 2022. c 2021. d Estimate. e 2019. f Data refers to a 5-year period preceding the reference year. g 2020. h Data are as at 1 January of reporting year.

Southern Africa

Region	Sub-Saharan Africa	Population (000, 2023)	68 599 [a,b]
Surface area (km2)	2 650 670 [c]	Pop. density (per km2, 2023)	25.8 [a,b]
Sex ratio (m per 100 f)	95.1 [a,b]		

Economic indicators	2010	2015	2023
GDP: Gross domestic product (million current US$)	447 956	377 770	455 972 [c]
GDP growth rate (annual %, const. 2015 prices)	3.4	1.2	5.1 [c]
GDP per capita (current US$)	7 579.8	5 928.9	6 707.0 [c]
Employment in agriculture (% of employed) [d]	18.1	16.6	21.6 [c]
Employment in industry (% of employed) [d]	21.6	21.5	17.9 [c]
Employment in services & other sectors (% employed) [d]	60.5	62.0	60.5 [c]
Unemployment rate (% of labour force) [d]	22.8	22.5	28.8
Labour force participation rate (female/male pop. %) [d]	47.7 / 62.7	51.5 / 65.3	52.5 / 64.9
Agricultural production index (2014-2016=100)	91	101	114 [c]
International trade: exports (million current US$)	95 232	93 647	139 876 [b]
International trade: imports (million current US$)	97 723	104 174	131 742 [b]
International trade: balance (million current US$)	- 2 491	- 10 527	8 134 [b]

Social indicators	2010	2015	2023
Population growth rate (average annual %)	1.2	2.2	0.9 [a,b]
Urban population (% of total population)	59.4	62.1	64.1 [e]
Urban population growth rate (average annual %) [f]	2.1	2.3	...
Fertility rate, total (live births per woman)	2.5	2.5	2.4 [a,b]
Life expectancy at birth (females/males, years)	60.5 / 55.2	66.0 / 59.9	63.8 / 58.1 [a,b]
Population age distribution (0-14/60+ years old, %)	29.7 / 7.3	29.2 / 7.8	29.3 / 8.4 [a,b]
International migrant stock (000/% of total pop.)	2 352.5 / 4.0	3 477.9 / 5.5	3 125.1 / 4.6 [g]
Infant mortality rate (per 1 000 live births)	37.5	30.7	30.4 [a,b]
Seats held by women in the National Parliament (%)	33.4	33.4	36.9 [h]

Environment and infrastructure indicators	2010	2015	2023
Individuals using the Internet (per 100 inhabitants)	22.0	49.1	70.6 [c]
Forested area (% of land area) [d]	15.7	15.3	14.9 [g]
Pop. using safely managed drinking water (urban/rural, %)	86.2 / ...	83.6 / ...	80.1 / ... [b]
Pop. using safely managed sanitation (urban/rural %)	58.9 / ...	60.9 / ...	63.6 / ... [b]

a Projected estimate (medium fertility variant). **b** 2022. **c** 2021. **d** Estimate. **e** 2019. **f** Data refers to a 5-year period preceding the reference year. **g** 2020. **h** Data are as at 1 January of reporting year.

Western Africa

Region	Sub-Saharan Africa	Population (000, 2023)	429 085 [a,b]
Surface area (km2)	6 064 060 [c]	Pop. density (per km2, 2023)	70.8 [a,b]
Sex ratio (m per 100 f)	101.2 [a,d,b]		

Economic indicators	2010	2015	2023
GDP: Gross domestic product (million current US$)	511 404	685 783	725 318 [c]
GDP growth rate (annual %, const. 2015 prices)	7.6	3.5	4.2 [c]
GDP per capita (current US$)	1 635.6	1 914.1	1 733.0 [c]
Employment in agriculture (% of employed) [e]	48.9	44.4	43.2 [c]
Employment in industry (% of employed) [e]	10.7	12.2	13.0 [c]
Employment in services & other sectors (% employed) [e]	40.3	43.4	43.8 [c]
Unemployment rate (% of labour force) [e]	4.0	4.0	4.6
Labour force participation rate (female/male pop. %) [e]	57.4 / 69.2	54.0 / 66.4	53.9 / 68.6
Agricultural production index (2014-2016=100)	85	99	116 [c]
International trade: exports (million current US$)	113 448	89 100	118 413 [b]
International trade: imports (million current US$)	83 254	87 237	136 877 [b]
International trade: balance (million current US$)	30 194	1 863	- 18 464 [b]

Social indicators	2010	2015	2023
Population growth rate (average annual %) [d]	2.8	2.6	2.5 [a,b]
Urban population (% of total population)	41.1	44.5	47.0 [f]
Urban population growth rate (average annual %) [g]	4.4	4.3	...
Fertility rate, total (live births per woman) [d]	5.7	5.4	4.9 [a,b]
Life expectancy at birth (females/males, years) [d]	55.0 / 53.5	56.5 / 54.9	58.2 / 56.4 [a,b]
Population age distribution (0-14/60+ years old, %) [d]	44.1 / 4.7	44.1 / 4.6	42.7 / 4.7 [a,b]
International migrant stock (000/% of total pop.)	6 321.6 / 2.1	7 067.1 / 2.0	7 552.1 / 1.9 [h]
Infant mortality rate (per 1 000 live births) [d]	76.7	69.6	59.7 [a,b]
Seats held by women in the National Parliament (%)	11.6	14.5	18.5 [i]

Environment and infrastructure indicators	2010	2015	2023
Individuals using the Internet (per 100 inhabitants)	7.7	18.9	48.0 [c]
Forested area (% of land area) [e]	14.8	14.3	13.9 [h]
Pop. using safely managed drinking water (urban/rural, %)	40.2 / 12.6	40.8 / 15.4	41.8 / 19.6 [b]
Pop. using safely managed sanitation (urban/rural %)	20.0 / 15.9	23.0 / 17.2	27.4 / 19.0 [b]

a Projected estimate (medium fertility variant). b 2022. c 2021. d Including Saint Helena. e Estimate. f 2019. g Data refers to a 5-year period preceding the reference year. h 2020. i Data are as at 1 January of reporting year.

Americas

Region	World	Population (000, 2023)	1 037 140 [a,b,c]
Surface area (km2)	38 791 038 [b,d]	Pop. density (per km2, 2023)	26.7 [a,b,c]
Sex ratio (m per 100 f)	97.4 [a,b,c]		

Economic indicators	2010	2015	2023
GDP: Gross domestic product (million current US$)	22 029 028	25 283 652	30 618 690 [d]
GDP growth rate (annual %, const. 2015 prices)	3.4	2.0	6.0 [d]
GDP per capita (current US$)	23 570.2	25 738.7	29 723.0 [d]
Employment in agriculture (% of employed) [e]	10.5	9.6	9.6 [d]
Employment in industry (% of employed) [e]	20.8	20.9	20.2 [d]
Employment in services & other sectors (% employed) [e]	68.7	69.4	70.2 [d]
Unemployment rate (% of labour force) [e]	8.0	6.2	6.1
Labour force participation rate (female/male pop. %) [e]	53.5 / 74.3	53.0 / 73.5	53.2 / 71.6
Agricultural production index (2014-2016=100)	90	99	108 [d]
International trade: exports (million current US$)	2 551 125	2 827 588	4 060 293 [c]
International trade: imports (million current US$)	3 230 657	3 739 612	5 449 464 [c]
International trade: balance (million current US$)	- 679 532	- 912 024	-1 389 171 [c]

Social indicators	2010	2015	2023
Population age distribution (0-14/60+ years old, %) [b]	24.7 / 13.1	23.2 / 14.7	21.2 / 17.2 [a,c]
Intentional homicide rate (per 100 000 pop.) [e]	16.6	16.0	15.0 [d]

Environment and infrastructure indicators	2010	2015	2023
Forested area (% of land area) [e]	42.0	41.7	41.3 [f]

a Projected estimate (medium fertility variant). b Calculated by the UN Statistics Division. c 2022. d 2021. e Estimate. f 2020.

Northern America

Region	Americas	Population (000, 2023)	376 871 [a,b]
Surface area (km2)	18 651 660 [c]	Pop. density (per km2, 2023)	20.2 [a,b]
Sex ratio (m per 100 f)	98.1 [a,d,b]		

Economic indicators	2010	2015	2023
GDP: Gross domestic product (million current US$)	16 675 374	19 771 305	25 313 920 [c]
GDP growth rate (annual %, const. 2015 prices)	2.7	2.5	5.8 [c]
GDP per capita (current US$)	48 297.2	54 850.4	67 454.7 [c]
Employment in agriculture (% of employed) [e]	1.7	1.8	1.6 [c]
Employment in industry (% of employed) [e]	19.5	19.6	19.2 [c]
Employment in services & other sectors (% employed) [e]	78.8	78.7	79.2 [c]
Unemployment rate (% of labour force) [e]	9.5	5.5	4.7
Labour force participation rate (female/male pop. %) [e]	58.1 / 69.8	56.5 / 68.6	56.9 / 67.7
Agricultural production index (2014-2016=100)	92	97	105 [c]
International trade: exports (million current US$)	1 665 220	1 911 491	2 659 778 [b]
International trade: imports (million current US$)	2 362 932	2 736 654	3 943 384 [b]
International trade: balance (million current US$)	- 697 713	- 825 163	-1 283 605 [b]

Social indicators	2010	2015	2023
Population growth rate (average annual %) [d]	0.9	0.8	0.5 [a,b]
Urban population (% of total population)	80.8	81.6	82.4 [f]
Urban population growth rate (average annual %) [g]	1.1	1.0	...
Fertility rate, total (live births per woman) [d]	1.9	1.8	1.6 [a,b]
Life expectancy at birth (females/males, years) [d]	81.4 / 76.6	81.6 / 76.8	81.4 / 76.0 [a,b]
Population age distribution (0-14/60+ years old, %) [d]	19.5 / 18.4	19.0 / 20.5	17.7 / 23.7 [a,b]
International migrant stock (000/% of total pop.)	50 970.5 / 14.8	55 633.7 / 15.6	58 708.8 / 15.9 [h]
Refugees and others of concern to the UNHCR (000)	...	655.4	1 233.1 [f]
Infant mortality rate (per 1 000 live births) [d]	6.1	5.8	4.9 [a,b]
Education: Primary gross enrol. ratio (f/m per 100 pop.)	101.4 / 101.2 [e]	100.5 / 100.5	100.2 / 100.7 [h]
Education: Lowr. sec. gross enrol. ratio (f/m per 100 pop.)	100.6 / 101.2 [e]	100.7 / 100.5	102.4 / 104.5 [h]
Education: Upr. sec. gross enrol. ratio (f/m per 100 pop.)	92.9 / 90.7 [e]	97.8 / 96.1	99.2 / 100.7 [h]
Intentional homicide rate (per 100 000 pop.) [e]	4.4	4.6	6.3 [c]
Seats held by women in the National Parliament (%)	19.0	21.8	30.0 [i]

Environment and infrastructure indicators	2010	2015	2023
Individuals using the Internet (per 100 inhabitants)	72.5	76.1	91.9 [c]
Research & Development expenditure (% of GDP)	2.7	2.7	3.3 [h]
Forested area (% of land area) [e]	35.4	35.5	35.5 [h]
Energy production, primary (Petajoules)	88 891	104 242	112 278 [h]
Energy supply per capita (Gigajoules)	301	286	261 [h]
Important sites for terrestrial biodiversity protected (%)	36.5	37.5	38.9 [b]
Pop. using safely managed drinking water (urban/rural, %)	96.5 / ...	96.9 / ...	97.5 / ... [b]
Pop. using safely managed sanitation (urban/rural %)	88.0 / ...	89.5 / ...	91.1 / ... [b]

a Projected estimate (medium fertility variant). b 2022. c 2021. d Including Bermuda, Greenland, and Saint Pierre and Miquelon. e Estimate. f 2019. g Data refers to a 5-year period preceding the reference year. h 2020. i Data are as at 1 January of reporting year.

Latin America & the Caribbean

Region	Americas	Population (000, 2023)	660 269[a,b]	
Surface area (km2)	20 139 378[c]	Pop. density (per km2, 2023)	32.6[a,b]	
Sex ratio (m per 100 f)	97.0[a,b]			

Economic indicators	2010	2015	2023
GDP: Gross domestic product (million current US$)	5 353 653	5 512 346	5 304 770[c]
GDP growth rate (annual %, const. 2015 prices)	5.9	0.1	6.5[c]
GDP per capita (current US$)	9 084.0	8 864.2	8 100.6[c]
Employment in agriculture (% of employed)[d]	16.1	14.6	14.7[c]
Employment in industry (% of employed)[d]	21.6	21.7	20.9[c]
Employment in services & other sectors (% employed)[d]	62.2	63.7	64.4[c]
Unemployment rate (% of labour force)[d]	7.1	6.7	7.0
Labour force participation rate (female/male pop. %)[d]	50.6 / 77.2	50.7 / 76.6	50.9 / 74.1
International trade: exports (million current US$)	885 906	916 097	1 400 514[b]
International trade: imports (million current US$)	867 725	1 002 958	1 506 080[b]
International trade: balance (million current US$)	18 181	- 86 861	- 105 566[b]

Social indicators	2010	2015	2023
Population growth rate (average annual %)	1.1	1.0	0.7[a,b]
Urban population (% of total population)	78.6	79.9	80.9[e]
Urban population growth rate (average annual %)[f]	1.6	1.5	...
Fertility rate, total (live births per woman)	2.2	2.1	1.8[a,b]
Life expectancy at birth (females/males, years)	76.4 / 70.1	77.8 / 71.5	77.0 / 70.6[a,b]
Population age distribution (0-14/60+ years old, %)	27.7 / 10.0	25.6 / 11.3	23.2 / 13.4[a,b]
International migrant stock (000/% of total pop.)	8 326.6 / 1.4	9 441.5 / 1.5	14 794.6 / 2.3[g]
Refugees and others of concern to the UNHCR (000)	...	7 071.2	13 430.4[e]
Infant mortality rate (per 1 000 live births)	18.3	15.5	13.1[a,b]
Education: Primary gross enrol. ratio (f/m per 100 pop.)	107.2 / 110.6	107.0 / 109.2	105.3 / 107.2[g]
Education: Lowr. sec. gross enrol. ratio (f/m per 100 pop.)	104.2 / 100.5	108.8 / 106.6	108.6 / 105.9[g]
Education: Upr. sec. gross enrol. ratio (f/m per 100 pop.)	79.8 / 68.8	84.7 / 76.4	89.4 / 81.9[g]
Intentional homicide rate (per 100 000 pop.)[d]	23.7	22.5	19.9[c]
Seats held by women in the National Parliament (%)	22.7	27.4	35.8[h]

Environment and infrastructure indicators	2010	2015	2023
Individuals using the Internet (per 100 inhabitants)	34.7	54.3	74.8[c]
Research & Development expenditure (% of GDP)	0.7	0.7	0.6[g]
Forested area (% of land area)	48.1	47.4	46.7[g]
Energy production, primary (Petajoules)	41 849	42 429	35 067[g]
Energy supply per capita (Gigajoules)	56	57	50[g]
Important sites for terrestrial biodiversity protected (%)	36.0	38.7	40.6[b]
Pop. using safely managed drinking water (urban/rural, %)	81.6 / 45.1	82.0 / 48.8	80.2 / 53.1[b]
Pop. using safely managed sanitation (urban/rural %)	27.8 / ...	33.5 / ...	41.7 / ...[b]

a Projected estimate (medium fertility variant). b 2022. c 2021. d Estimate. e 2019. f Data refers to a 5-year period preceding the reference year. g 2020. h Data are as at 1 January of reporting year.

Caribbean

Region	Latin America & Caribbean	Population (000, 2023)	44 392 [a,b]
Surface area (km2)	225 996 [c]	Pop. density (per km2, 2023)	200.4 [a,b]
Sex ratio (m per 100 f)	97.8 [a,d,b]		

Economic indicators	2010	2015	2023
GDP: Gross domestic product (million current US$)	296 862	354 722	423 912 [c]
GDP growth rate (annual %, const. 2015 prices)	1.7	2.3	4.1 [c]
GDP per capita (current US$)	7 341.3	8 485.9	9 802.0 [c]
Employment in agriculture (% of employed) [e]	22.1	21.3	20.3 [c]
Employment in industry (% of employed) [e]	16.3	16.2	16.8 [c]
Employment in services & other sectors (% employed) [e]	61.4	62.5	63.0 [c]
Unemployment rate (% of labour force) [e]	8.1	8.0	7.8
Labour force participation rate (female/male pop. %) [e]	46.5 / 68.4	49.0 / 69.9	50.8 / 69.9
Agricultural production index (2014-2016=100)	86	99	92 [c]
International trade: exports (million current US$)	24 874	26 475	31 542 [b]
International trade: imports (million current US$)	53 245	58 007	67 909 [b]
International trade: balance (million current US$)	- 28 371	- 31 533	- 36 368 [b]

Social indicators	2010	2015	2023
Population growth rate (average annual %) [d]	0.5	0.6	0.5 [a,b]
Urban population (% of total population)	67.8	70.0	71.8 [f]
Urban population growth rate (average annual %) [g]	1.5	1.4	...
Fertility rate, total (live births per woman) [d]	2.3	2.2	2.0 [a,b]
Life expectancy at birth (females/males, years) [d]	67.6 / 63.8	75.4 / 69.5	75.9 / 69.6 [a,b]
Population age distribution (0-14/60+ years old, %) [d]	26.3 / 11.9	24.8 / 13.1	23.2 / 15.1 [a,b]
International migrant stock (000/% of total pop.)	1 338.9 / 3.2	1 501.1 / 3.5	1 605.1 / 3.7 [h]
Infant mortality rate (per 1 000 live births) [d]	38.5	30.4	26.6 [a,b]
Seats held by women in the National Parliament (%)	29.4	33.1	41.1 [i]

Environment and infrastructure indicators	2010	2015	2023
Individuals using the Internet (per 100 inhabitants)	21.2	38.0	67.1 [c]
Forested area (% of land area) [e]	33.2	34.8	35.3 [h]
Pop. using safely managed drinking water (urban/rural, %)	65.5 / ...	63.5 / ...	60.9 / ... [b]
Pop. using safely managed sanitation (urban/rural %)	42.0 / 42.6	41.6 / 43.5	40.3 / 43.9 [b]

a Projected estimate (medium fertility variant). b 2022. c 2021. d Including Anguilla, Bonaire, Sint Eustatius and Saba, British Virgin Islands, Cayman Islands, Dominica, Montserrat, Saint Kitts and Nevis, Sint Maarten (Dutch part) and Turks and Caicos Islands. e Estimate. f 2019. g Data refers to a 5-year period preceding the reference year. h 2020. i Data are as at 1 January of reporting year.

Central America

Region	Latin America & Caribbean	Population (000, 2023)	179 060[a,b]
Surface area (km2)	2 452 270[c]	Pop. density (per km2, 2023)	72.7[a,b]
Sex ratio (m per 100 f)	96.1[a,b]		

Economic indicators	2010	2015	2023
GDP: Gross domestic product (million current US$)	1 210 366	1 403 975	1 560 443[c]
GDP growth rate (annual %, const. 2015 prices)	5.0	3.4	5.7[c]
GDP per capita (current US$)	7 755.6	8 397.6	8 783.2[c]
Employment in agriculture (% of employed)[d]	17.6	16.8	15.5[c]
Employment in industry (% of employed)[d]	23.3	23.7	24.4[c]
Employment in services & other sectors (% employed)[d]	59.1	59.5	60.1[c]
Unemployment rate (% of labour force)[d]	5.3	4.4	4.1
Labour force participation rate (female/male pop. %)[d]	43.1 / 79.4	44.0 / 79.1	45.7 / 77.9
Agricultural production index (2014-2016=100)	88	99	112[c]
International trade: exports (million current US$)	336 529	426 846	635 743[b]
International trade: imports (million current US$)	366 171	464 286	719 763[b]
International trade: balance (million current US$)	- 29 642	- 37 441	- 84 020[b]

Social indicators	2010	2015	2023
Population growth rate (average annual %)	1.5	1.2	0.9[a,b]
Urban population (% of total population)	72.1	73.7	75.0[e]
Urban population growth rate (average annual %)[f]	2.1	1.9	...
Fertility rate, total (live births per woman)	2.5	2.3	1.9[a,b]
Life expectancy at birth (females/males, years)	76.8 / 70.8	77.4 / 71.4	77.4 / 70.9[a,b]
Population age distribution (0-14/60+ years old, %)	31.3 / 8.4	28.9 / 9.5	25.8 / 11.3[a,b]
International migrant stock (000/% of total pop.)	1 751.0 / 1.1	1 860.2 / 1.1	2 302.0 / 1.3[g]
Infant mortality rate (per 1 000 live births)	17.9	15.1	12.2[a,b]
Seats held by women in the National Parliament (%)	21.6	30.1	38.6[h]

Environment and infrastructure indicators	2010	2015	2023
Forested area (% of land area)[d]	37.0	36.5	35.9[g]
Pop. using safely managed drinking water (urban/rural, %)	... / 45.4	... / 48.7	... / 50.1[b]
Pop. using safely managed sanitation (urban/rural %)	28.3 / ...	38.5 / ...	53.9 / ...[b]

a Projected estimate (medium fertility variant). b 2022. c 2021. d Estimate. e 2019. f Data refers to a 5-year period preceding the reference year. g 2020. h Data are as at 1 January of reporting year.

South America

Region	Latin America & Caribbean	Population (000, 2023)	436 817 [a,b]
Surface area (km2)	17 461 112 [c]	Pop. density (per km2, 2023)	24.8 [a,b]
Sex ratio (m per 100 f)	97.3 [a,d,b]		

Economic indicators	2010	2015	2023
GDP: Gross domestic product (million current US$)	3 846 425	3 753 649	3 320 415 [c]
GDP growth rate (annual %, const. 2015 prices)	6.6	- 1.3	7.0 [c]
GDP per capita (current US$)	9 791.2	9 091.5	7 651.6 [c]
Employment in agriculture (% of employed) [e]	15.1	13.1	13.9 [c]
Employment in industry (% of employed) [e]	21.6	21.6	19.8 [c]
Employment in services & other sectors (% employed) [e]	63.4	65.4	66.3 [c]
Unemployment rate (% of labour force) [e]	7.6	7.4	8.0
Labour force participation rate (female/male pop. %) [e]	53.8 / 77.3	53.5 / 76.3	52.9 / 73.0
Agricultural production index (2014-2016=100)	89	102	110 [c]
International trade: exports (million current US$)	524 502	462 776	733 230 [b]
International trade: imports (million current US$)	448 308	480 665	718 408 [b]
International trade: balance (million current US$)	76 194	- 17 888	14 822 [b]

Social indicators	2010	2015	2023
Population growth rate (average annual %) [d]	1.0	1.0	0.6 [a,b]
Urban population (% of total population)	82.4	83.5	84.4 [f]
Urban population growth rate (average annual %) [g]	1.5	1.3	...
Fertility rate, total (live births per woman) [d]	2.1	2.0	1.8 [a,b]
Life expectancy at birth (females/males, years) [d]	77.2 / 70.5	78.2 / 71.8	77.0 / 70.6 [a,b]
Population age distribution (0-14/60+ years old, %) [d]	26.4 / 10.5	24.4 / 11.9	22.2 / 14.1 [a,b]
International migrant stock (000/% of total pop.)	5 236.7 / 1.3	6 080.2 / 1.5	10 887.5 / 2.5 [h]
Infant mortality rate (per 1 000 live births) [d]	16.3	14.1	12.0 [a,b]
Seats held by women in the National Parliament (%)	19.2	22.2	31.0 [i]

Environment and infrastructure indicators	2010	2015	2023
Forested area (% of land area) [e]	49.8	49.1	48.3 [h]
Pop. using safely managed drinking water (urban/rural, %)	82.5 / 46.8	83.7 / 51.1	82.7 / 58.0 [b]
Pop. using safely managed sanitation (urban/rural %)	28.9 / ...	33.5 / ...	39.7 / ... [b]

a Projected estimate (medium fertility variant). b 2022. c 2021. d Including Falkland Islands (Malvinas). e Estimate. f 2019. g Data refers to a 5-year period preceding the reference year. h 2020. i Data are as at 1 January of reporting year.

Asia

Region	World	Population (000, 2023)	4 722 635[a,b]
Surface area (km2)	31 033 131[c]	Pop. density (per km2, 2023)	150.6[a,b]
Sex ratio (m per 100 f)	103.6[a,b]		

Economic indicators	2010	2015	2023
GDP: Gross domestic product (million current US$)	21 128 489	26 933 005	37 498 914[c]
GDP growth rate (annual %, const. 2015 prices)	7.8	4.9	6.2[c]
GDP per capita (current US$)	5 006.1	6 040.5	7 989.0[c]
Agricultural production index (2014-2016=100)	88	100	112[c]
International trade: exports (million current US$)	5 896 164	6 827 734	10 619 006[b]
International trade: imports (million current US$)	5 459 724	6 213 020	9 755 678[b]
International trade: balance (million current US$)	436 440	614 714	863 328[b]

Social indicators	2010	2015	2023
Population growth rate (average annual %)	1.1	1.0	0.6[a,b]
Urban population (% of total population)	44.8	48.0	50.5[d]
Urban population growth rate (average annual %)[e]	2.8	2.4	...
Fertility rate, total (live births per woman)	2.3	2.2	1.9[a,b]
Life expectancy at birth (females/males, years)	73.8 / 69.0	75.6 / 70.8	75.8 / 70.8[a,b]
Population age distribution (0-14/60+ years old, %)	26.0 / 10.2	25.0 / 11.7	23.2 / 13.7[a,b]
International migrant stock (000/% of total pop.)	66 123.6 / 1.6	77 191.2 / 1.7	85 618.5 / 1.8[f]
Refugees and others of concern to the UNHCR (000)	...	28 420.7	30 447.6[b]
Infant mortality rate (per 1 000 live births)	33.2	26.6	22.2[a,b]
Intentional homicide rate (per 100 000 pop.)[g]	2.7	2.4	2.3[c]
Seats held by women in the National Parliament (%)	16.8	17.8	20.2[h]

Environment and infrastructure indicators	2010	2015	2023
Forested area (% of land area)[g]	19.6	19.8	20.0[f]
Energy production, primary (Petajoules)	234 731	260 136	274 041[f]
Energy supply per capita (Gigajoules)	55	60	63[f]
Pop. using safely managed drinking water (urban/rural, %)	75.0 / 54.1	77.1 / 61.0	79.6 / 71.5[b]
Pop. using safely managed sanitation (urban/rural %)	33.3 / 25.3	40.1 / 35.3	46.5 / 49.8[b]

a Projected estimate (medium fertility variant). b 2022. c 2021. d 2019. e Data refers to a 5-year period preceding the reference year. f 2020. g Estimate. h Data are as at 1 January of reporting year.

Central Asia

Region	Asia	Population (000, 2023)	77 040[a,b]
Surface area (km2)	4 103 000[c,d]	Pop. density (per km2, 2023)	19.6[a,b]
Sex ratio (m per 100 f)	97.9[a,b]		

Economic indicators	2010	2015	2023
GDP: Gross domestic product (million current US$)	231 077	321 586	333 699[e]
GDP growth rate (annual %, const. 2015 prices)	8.7	3.1	5.3[e]
GDP per capita (current US$)	3 632.4	4 661.3	4 396.7[e]
Employment in agriculture (% of employed)[f]	29.8	25.9	22.0[e]
Employment in industry (% of employed)[f]	21.1	22.1	24.3[e]
Employment in services & other sectors (% employed)[f]	49.0	51.9	53.7[e]
Unemployment rate (% of labour force)[f]	5.6	5.0	5.9
Labour force participation rate (female/male pop. %)[f]	50.0 / 70.2	48.5 / 69.3	46.6 / 68.5
Agricultural production index (2014-2016=100)	78	101	113[e]
International trade: exports (million current US$)	74 961	64 827	116 177[b]
International trade: imports (million current US$)	40 985	53 082	96 692[b]
International trade: balance (million current US$)	33 976	11 746	19 485[b]

Social indicators	2010	2015	2023
Population growth rate (average annual %)	1.6	1.7	1.5[a,b]
Urban population (% of total population)	48.0	48.1	48.2[g]
Urban population growth rate (average annual %)[h]	1.9	1.7	...
Fertility rate, total (live births per woman)	2.7	2.8	2.9[a,b]
Life expectancy at birth (females/males, years)	71.8 / 65.2	73.5 / 66.8	73.6 / 67.5[a,b]
Population age distribution (0-14/60+ years old, %)	29.1 / 7.1	29.6 / 7.8	31.3 / 9.3[a,b]
International migrant stock (000/% of total pop.)	5 264.9 / 8.4	5 392.8 / 7.9	5 564.0 / 7.5[i]
Infant mortality rate (per 1 000 live births)	26.2	19.9	14.8[a,b]
Education: Primary gross enrol. ratio (f/m per 100 pop.)	99.5 / 100.8	103.8 / 104.8	101.3 / 102.5[i]
Education: Lowr. sec. gross enrol. ratio (f/m per 100 pop.)	95.1 / 96.6	97.3 / 98.4	96.0 / 97.5[f,i]
Education: Upr. sec. gross enrol. ratio (f/m per 100 pop.)	80.6 / 81.9	87.3 / 88.5	91.0 / 91.9[f,i]
Intentional homicide rate (per 100 000 pop.)[f]	5.0	2.5	1.7[e]
Seats held by women in the National Parliament (%)	20.0	21.8	27.4[i]

Environment and infrastructure indicators	2010	2015	2023
Individuals using the Internet (per 100 inhabitants)	18.4	43.7	66.5[e]
Research & Development expenditure (% of GDP)	0.2	0.2	0.1[i]
Forested area (% of land area)[f]	3.1	3.2	3.3[i]
Important sites for terrestrial biodiversity protected (%)	20.7	21.1	22.4[b]
Pop. using safely managed drinking water (urban/rural, %)	87.0 / 49.3	87.7 / 60.6	88.0 / 68.1[b]
Pop. using safely managed sanitation (urban/rural %)	74.1 / 79.6	73.3 / 80.4	72.7 / 81.1[b]

a Projected estimate (medium fertility variant). b 2022. c Calculated by the UN Statistics Division. d 2017. e 2021. f Estimate. g 2019. h Data refers to a 5-year period preceding the reference year. i 2020. j Data are as at 1 January of reporting year.

Eastern Asia

Region	Asia		Population (000, 2023)	1 663 200 [a,b]
Surface area (km2)	11 560 456 [c]		Pop. density (per km2, 2023)	141.1 [a,b]
Sex ratio (m per 100 f)	103.0 [a,b]			

Economic indicators	2010	2015	2023
GDP: Gross domestic product (million current US$)	13 712 623	17 889 125	25 691 483 [c]
GDP growth rate (annual %, const. 2015 prices)	8.1	4.9	6.4 [c]
GDP per capita (current US$)	8 662.8	10 965.8	15 445.8 [c]
Employment in agriculture (% of employed) [d]	33.1	26.0	22.2 [c]
Employment in industry (% of employed) [d]	28.1	28.5	27.6 [c]
Employment in services & other sectors (% employed) [d]	38.7	45.5	50.2 [c]
Unemployment rate (% of labour force) [d]	4.5	4.5	4.4
Labour force participation rate (female/male pop. %) [d]	61.7 / 77.2	61.1 / 75.2	59.7 / 72.0
Agricultural production index (2014-2016=100)	89	101	108 [c]
International trade: exports (million current US$)	3 219 271	3 942 643	5 648 849 [b]
International trade: imports (million current US$)	2 967 424	3 317 929	5 041 360 [b]
International trade: balance (million current US$)	251 847	624 714	607 489 [b]

Social indicators	2010	2015	2023
Population growth rate (average annual %)	0.6	0.5	---0.0 [a,b]
Urban population (% of total population)	54.4	59.8	63.9 [e]
Urban population growth rate (average annual %) [f]	2.9	2.4	...
Fertility rate, total (live births per woman)	1.7	1.6	1.2 [a,b]
Life expectancy at birth (females/males, years)	79.6 / 73.8	80.9 / 75.2	82.4 / 76.7 [a,b]
Population age distribution (0-14/60+ years old, %)	18.0 / 14.4	17.7 / 17.1	16.6 / 20.1 [a,b]
International migrant stock (000/% of total pop.)	7 062.5 / 0.4	7 866.7 / 0.5	8 975.7 / 0.5 [g]
Infant mortality rate (per 1 000 live births)	12.3	8.5	5.7 [a,b]
Education: Primary gross enrol. ratio (f/m per 100 pop.)	98.3 / 99.8	96.6 / 96.4	103.0 / 102.2 [g]
Education: Lowr. sec. gross enrol. ratio (f/m per 100 pop.)	100.6 / 99.7	89.9 / 89.7	97.6 / 96.8 [g]
Education: Upr. sec. gross enrol. ratio (f/m per 100 pop.)	78.5 / 79.6	83.3 / 79.8	84.3 / 82.2 [g]
Intentional homicide rate (per 100 000 pop.) [d]	1.0	0.7	0.5 [c]
Seats held by women in the National Parliament (%)	18.7	20.4	21.8 [h]

Environment and infrastructure indicators	2010	2015	2023
Individuals using the Internet (per 100 inhabitants)	39.5	54.5	75.2 [c]
Research & Development expenditure (% of GDP)	2.2	2.4	2.7 [g]
Forested area (% of land area) [d]	21.8	22.6	23.5 [g]
Important sites for terrestrial biodiversity protected (%)	21.6	25.5	26.6 [b]
Pop. using safely managed drinking water (urban/rural, %)	91.4 / ...	94.6 / ...	97.6 / ... [b]
Pop. using safely managed sanitation (urban/rural %)	54.6 / 17.6	66.9 / 26.1	77.8 / 38.3 [b]

a Projected estimate (medium fertility variant). **b** 2022. **c** 2021. **d** Estimate. **e** 2019. **f** Data refers to a 5-year period preceding the reference year. **g** 2020. **h** Data are as at 1 January of reporting year.

South-eastern Asia

Region	Asia	Population (000, 2023)	681 125[a,b]
Surface area (km2)	4 340 700[c]	Pop. density (per km2, 2023)	153.1[a,b]
Sex ratio (m per 100 f)	100.3[a,b]		

Economic indicators	2010	2015	2023
GDP: Gross domestic product (million current US$)	2 024 587	2 528 008	3 342 329[c]
GDP growth rate (annual %, const. 2015 prices)	8.2	4.8	3.3[c]
GDP per capita (current US$)	3 375.6	3 970.4	4 945.8[c]
Employment in agriculture (% of employed)[d]	40.3	35.2	29.2[c]
Employment in industry (% of employed)[d]	19.2	21.3	23.4[c]
Employment in services & other sectors (% employed)[d]	40.5	43.5	47.4[c]
Unemployment rate (% of labour force)[d]	3.3	2.9	2.4
Labour force participation rate (female/male pop. %)	55.6 / 79.9	55.6 / 79.8	54.9 / 77.3
Agricultural production index (2014-2016=100)	90	100	106[c]
International trade: exports (million current US$)	1 054 178	1 172 850	1 957 818[b]
International trade: imports (million current US$)	953 410	1 100 730	1 903 794[b]
International trade: balance (million current US$)	100 767	72 119	54 024[b]

Social indicators	2010	2015	2023
Population growth rate (average annual %)	1.2	1.1	0.8[a,b]
Urban population (% of total population)	44.3	47.2	49.4[e]
Urban population growth rate (average annual %)[f]	2.7	2.5	...
Fertility rate, total (live births per woman)	2.4	2.3	2.1[a,b]
Life expectancy at birth (females/males, years)	72.9 / 67.7	74.1 / 68.7	74.3 / 68.7[a,b]
Population age distribution (0-14/60+ years old, %)	27.5 / 8.8	26.2 / 9.9	24.5 / 12.1[a,b]
International migrant stock (000/% of total pop.)	8 697.9 / 1.5	10 161.1 / 1.6	10 615.4 / 1.6[g]
Infant mortality rate (per 1 000 live births)	26.4	22.6	18.6[a,b]
Education: Primary gross enrol. ratio (f/m per 100 pop.)	107.1 / 106.8	106.1 / 108.9	104.6 / 107.0[d,g]
Education: Lowr. sec. gross enrol. ratio (f/m per 100 pop.)	84.9 / 82.6	93.2 / 90.9	97.3 / 95.3[d,g]
Education: Upr. sec. gross enrol. ratio (f/m per 100 pop.)	54.4 / 55.3	65.9 / 67.8	69.5 / 66.3[d,g]
Intentional homicide rate (per 100 000 pop.)[d]	2.8	2.7	3.7[c]
Seats held by women in the National Parliament (%)	19.3	17.8	23.0[h]

Environment and infrastructure indicators	2010	2015	2023
Individuals using the Internet (per 100 inhabitants)	18.9	31.6	65.2[c]
Research & Development expenditure (% of GDP)	0.7	0.9	1.0[g]
Forested area (% of land area)[d]	49.7	48.2	47.1[g]
Important sites for terrestrial biodiversity protected (%)	28.4	31.4	36.5[b]
Pop. using safely managed drinking water (urban/rural, %)	48.1 / 30.5	48.7 / 32.1	49.5 / 34.3[b]
Pop. using safely managed sanitation (urban/rural %)	42.7 / 38.0	44.1 / 43.5	46.4 / 51.8[b]

a Projected estimate (medium fertility variant). **b** 2022. **c** 2021. **d** Estimate. **e** 2019. **f** Data refers to a 5-year period preceding the reference year. **g** 2020. **h** Data are as at 1 January of reporting year.

Southern Asia

		Population (000, 2023)	2 007 550[a,b]
Region	Asia	Pop. density (per km2, 2023)	313.6[a,b]
Surface area (km2)	6 688 000[c,d]		
Sex ratio (m per 100 f)	104.6[a,b]		

Economic indicators	2010	2015	2023
GDP: Gross domestic product (million current US$)	2 593 394	3 218 870	4 698 012[e]
GDP growth rate (annual %, const. 2015 prices)	7.6	6.4	7.6[e]
GDP per capita (current US$)	1 494.0	1 733.1	2 361.5[e]
Employment in agriculture (% of employed)[f]	49.3	43.8	41.8[e]
Employment in industry (% of employed)[f]	21.6	24.2	25.0[e]
Employment in services & other sectors (% employed)[f]	29.1	32.0	33.2[e]
Unemployment rate (% of labour force)[f]	7.3	7.3	7.2
Labour force participation rate (female/male pop. %)[f]	27.4 / 78.6	24.2 / 75.9	24.9 / 74.6
Agricultural production index (2014-2016=100)	86	99	119[e]
International trade: exports (million current US$)	354 892	390 610	564 666[b]
International trade: imports (million current US$)	497 340	559 091	956 312[b]
International trade: balance (million current US$)	- 142 448	- 168 481	- 391 646[b]

Social indicators	2010	2015	2023
Population growth rate (average annual %)	1.5	1.2	0.9[a,b]
Urban population (% of total population)	32.5	34.5	36.2[g]
Urban population growth rate (average annual %)[h]	2.6	2.5	...
Fertility rate, total (live births per woman)	2.7	2.5	2.2[a,b]
Life expectancy at birth (females/males, years)	68.8 / 65.1	71.0 / 67.6	70.1 / 66.4[a,b]
Population age distribution (0-14/60+ years old, %)	32.0 / 7.4	30.0 / 8.4	27.0 / 9.9[a,b]
International migrant stock (000/% of total pop.)	14 411.8 / 0.8	13 873.5 / 0.8	13 863.5 / 0.7[i]
Infant mortality rate (per 1 000 live births)	47.8	38.4	30.1[a,b]
Education: Primary gross enrol. ratio (f/m per 100 pop.)	105.8 / 105.9[f]	109.8 / 103.4[f]	101.7 / 102.3[i]
Education: Lowr. sec. gross enrol. ratio (f/m per 100 pop.)	73.2 / 75.9	84.8 / 81.2	83.3 / 80.8[i]
Education: Upr. sec. gross enrol. ratio (f/m per 100 pop.)	44.6 / 49.6	56.7 / 59.6	62.5 / 65.5[i]
Intentional homicide rate (per 100 000 pop.)[f]	3.9	3.5	3.0[e]
Seats held by women in the National Parliament (%)	18.2	17.6	16.5[j]

Environment and infrastructure indicators	2010	2015	2023
Individuals using the Internet (per 100 inhabitants)	7.5	15.5	45.2[e]
Research & Development expenditure (% of GDP)	0.7	0.6	0.6[i]
Forested area (% of land area)[f]	15.3	15.5	15.7[i]
Important sites for terrestrial biodiversity protected (%)	14.6	18.0	18.8[b]
Pop. using safely managed drinking water (urban/rural, %)	61.5 / 50.2	63.5 / 57.3	65.8 / 67.7[b]
Pop. using safely managed sanitation (urban/rural %)	34.2 / 23.4	38.3 / 35.8	44.5 / 53.0[b]

a Projected estimate (medium fertility variant). **b** 2022. **c** Calculated by the UN Statistics Division. **d** 2017. **e** 2021. **f** Estimate. **g** 2019. **h** Data refers to a 5-year period preceding the reference year. **i** 2020. **j** Data are as at 1 January of reporting year.

Western Asia

Region	Asia	Population (000, 2023)	293 720 [a,b]
Surface area (km2)	4 805 058 [c]	Pop. density (per km2, 2023)	61.3 [a,b]
Sex ratio (m per 100 f)	109.2 [a,b]		

Economic indicators	2010	2015	2023
GDP: Gross domestic product (million current US$)	2 566 809	2 975 416	3 433 391 [c]
GDP growth rate (annual %, const. 2015 prices)	5.7	3.8	6.2 [c]
GDP per capita (current US$)	10 772.0	11 252.8	11 865.1 [c]
Employment in agriculture (% of employed) [d,e]	11.4	10.9	9.2 [c]
Employment in industry (% of employed) [d,e]	26.1	25.2	23.7 [c]
Employment in services & other sectors (% employed) [d,e]	62.5	64.0	67.1 [c]
Unemployment rate (% of labour force) [d,f]	7.2	7.7	9.4
Labour force participation rate (female/male pop. %) [d,f]	16.9 / 75.0	18.6 / 76.5	19.5 / 76.3
Agricultural production index (2014-2016=100)	92	101	119 [c]
International trade: exports (million current US$)	919 156	976 785	1 831 491 [b]
International trade: imports (million current US$)	749 249	953 680	1 362 937 [b]
International trade: balance (million current US$)	169 907	23 105	468 555 [b]

Social indicators	2010	2015	2023
Population growth rate (average annual %)	2.2	1.9	1.5 [a,b]
Urban population (% of total population)	68.2	70.4	72.0 [g]
Urban population growth rate (average annual %) [h]	3.2	2.7	...
Fertility rate, total (live births per woman)	3.0	2.9	2.6 [a,b]
Life expectancy at birth (females/males, years)	75.9 / 70.5	76.4 / 70.9	77.4 / 72.0 [a,b]
Population age distribution (0-14/60+ years old, %)	31.2 / 6.7	30.3 / 7.4	28.7 / 8.6 [a,b]
International migrant stock (000/% of total pop.)	30 686.4 / 13.2	39 897.2 / 15.5	46 599.8 / 16.7 [i]
Infant mortality rate (per 1 000 live births)	21.9	20.3	17.6 [a,b]
Education: Primary gross enrol. ratio (f/m per 100 pop.)	98.1 / 105.5	96.9 / 103.0 [d]	94.1 / 100.0 [d,i]
Education: Lowr. sec. gross enrol. ratio (f/m per 100 pop.)	83.1 / 91.4	83.3 / 88.2 [d]	85.9 / 90.6 [i]
Education: Upr. sec. gross enrol. ratio (f/m per 100 pop.)	60.3 / 66.7	76.7 / 82.1 [d]	75.0 / 82.1 [i]
Intentional homicide rate (per 100 000 pop.) [d]	3.6	4.6	5.0 [c]
Seats held by women in the National Parliament (%)	9.3	12.8	16.6 [j]

Environment and infrastructure indicators	2010	2015	2023
Individuals using the Internet (per 100 inhabitants)	32.4	50.0	71.9 [c]
Research & Development expenditure (% of GDP)	0.7	0.8	0.9 [i]
Forested area (% of land area) [d]	6.1	6.2	6.3 [i]
Important sites for terrestrial biodiversity protected (%)	16.0	17.8	18.5 [b]
Pop. using safely managed drinking water (urban/rural, %)	75.5 / ... [k]	75.7 / ...	76.1 / ... [b]
Pop. using safely managed sanitation (urban/rural %)	53.3 / 47.6	58.0 / 50.5	65.3 / 56.3 [b]

a Projected estimate (medium fertility variant). b 2022. c 2021. d Estimate. e Data excludes Armenia, Azerbaijan, Cyprus, Georgia, Israel and Turkey. f Data excludes Armenia, Azerbaijan, Cyprus, Georgia and Turkey g 2019. h Data refers to a 5-year period preceding the reference year. i 2020. j Data are as at 1 January of reporting year. k 2007.

Europe

Region	World	Population (000, 2023)	743 556 [a,b]
Surface area (km2)	22 134 900 [c]	Pop. density (per km2, 2023)	33.7 [a,b]
Sex ratio (m per 100 f)	93.3 [a,b]		

Economic indicators	2010	2015	2023
GDP: Gross domestic product (million current US$)	19 903 672	19 191 354	23 816 167 [c]
GDP growth rate (annual %, const. 2015 prices)	2.4	1.9	5.6 [c]
GDP per capita (current US$)	26 966.8	25 795.1	31 874.9 [c]
Agricultural production index (2014-2016=100)	91	100	105 [c]
International trade: exports (million current US$)	5 904 975	6 090 837	8 731 155 [b]
International trade: imports (million current US$)	5 868 691	5 730 577	8 853 085 [b]
International trade: balance (million current US$)	36 284	360 260	- 121 929 [b]

Social indicators	2010	2015	2023
Population growth rate (average annual %)	0.2	0.2	- 0.3 [a,b]
Urban population (% of total population)	72.9	73.9	74.7 [d]
Urban population growth rate (average annual %) [e]	0.5	0.3	...
Fertility rate, total (live births per woman)	1.6	1.6	1.5 [a,b]
Life expectancy at birth (females/males, years)	80.2 / 72.8	81.3 / 74.6	80.8 / 74.0 [a,b]
Population age distribution (0-14/60+ years old, %)	15.5 / 22.0	15.8 / 23.8	15.7 / 26.3 [a,b]
International migrant stock (000/% of total pop.)	70 627.2 / 9.6	74 759.1 / 10.1	86 706.1 / 11.6 [f]
Refugees and others of concern to the UNHCR (000)	...	4 673.8	16 562.4 [b]
Infant mortality rate (per 1 000 live births)	5.3	4.5	3.5 [a,b]
Education: Primary gross enrol. ratio (f/m per 100 pop.)	101.5 / 102.1	100.7 / 100.6	100.2 / 100.4 [f]
Education: Lowr. sec. gross enrol. ratio (f/m per 100 pop.)	100.4 / 101.2	101.5 / 102.3	101.6 / 102.1 [f]
Education: Upr. sec. gross enrol. ratio (f/m per 100 pop.)	100.2 / 101.0	112.2 / 112.0	110.7 / 110.7 [f]
Intentional homicide rate (per 100 000 pop.) [g]	3.5	3.5	2.2 [c]
Seats held by women in the National Parliament (%)	23.2	26.7	32.4 [h]

Environment and infrastructure indicators	2010	2015	2023
Individuals using the Internet (per 100 inhabitants)	62.5	74.1	87.6 [c]
Research & Development expenditure (% of GDP)	1.7	1.8	2.0 [f]
Forested area (% of land area) [g]	45.8	45.9	46.0 [f]
Energy production, primary (Petajoules)	102 690	101 380	101 441 [f]
Energy supply per capita (Gigajoules)	152	140	135 [f]
Important sites for terrestrial biodiversity protected (%)	60.5	64.9	67.0 [b]
Pop. using safely managed drinking water (urban/rural, %)	95.2 / 84.2	95.2 / 86.7	95.3 / 86.6 [b]
Pop. using safely managed sanitation (urban/rural %)	75.3 / 44.8	77.8 / 46.4	80.1 / 49.1 [b]

a Projected estimate (medium fertility variant). b 2022. c 2021. d 2019. e Data refers to a 5-year period preceding the reference year. f 2020. g Estimate. h Data are as at 1 January of reporting year.

Eastern Europe

Region	Europe	Population (000, 2023)	289 626[a,b]
Surface area (km2)	18 052 768[c]	Pop. density (per km2, 2023)	16.0[a,b]
Sex ratio (m per 100 f)	88.8[a,b]		

Economic indicators	2010	2015	2023
GDP: Gross domestic product (million current US$)	2 868 792	2 626 563	3 688 492[c]
GDP growth rate (annual %, const. 2015 prices)	3.2	0.2	5.1[c]
GDP per capita (current US$)	9 734.4	8 928.1	12 655.0[c]
Employment in agriculture (% of employed)[d]	11.2	9.8	8.3[c]
Employment in industry (% of employed)[d]	28.8	28.1	28.2[c]
Employment in services & other sectors (% employed)[d]	60.0	62.0	63.5[c]
Unemployment rate (% of labour force)[d]	8.0	6.6	5.1
Labour force participation rate (female/male pop. %)[d]	52.6 / 66.7	52.5 / 67.7	51.7 / 67.0
Agricultural production index (2014-2016=100)	81	98	110[c]
International trade: exports (million current US$)	994 605	1 023 967	1 644 470[b]
International trade: imports (million current US$)	868 649	847 926	1 369 756[b]
International trade: balance (million current US$)	125 955	176 042	274 714[b]

Social indicators	2010	2015	2023
Population growth rate (average annual %)	- 0.1	~0.0	- 0.7[a,b]
Urban population (% of total population)	68.9	69.3	69.8[e]
Urban population growth rate (average annual %)[f]	- 0.1	~0.0	...
Fertility rate, total (live births per woman)	1.5	1.7	1.5[a,b]
Life expectancy at birth (females/males, years)	76.5 / 66.3	78.3 / 68.8	76.5 / 66.7[a,b]
Population age distribution (0-14/60+ years old, %)	15.0 / 19.4	16.0 / 21.4	16.6 / 24.1[a,b]
International migrant stock (000/% of total pop.)	19 110.7 / 6.5	19 834.0 / 6.7	20 835.4 / 7.1[g]
Infant mortality rate (per 1 000 live births)	7.5	5.8	4.4[a,b]
Intentional homicide rate (per 100 000 pop.)[d]	6.9	7.2	4.3[c]
Seats held by women in the National Parliament (%)	15.2	16.9	22.7[h]

Environment and infrastructure indicators	2010	2015	2023
Forested area (% of land area)[d]	47.6	47.7	47.7[g]
Pop. using safely managed drinking water (urban/rural, %)	... / 68.8	... / 73.8	... / 73.6[b]
Pop. using safely managed sanitation (urban/rural %)	54.2 / ...	58.0 / ...	61.5 / ...[b]

a Projected estimate (medium fertility variant). b 2022. c 2021. d Estimate. e 2019. f Data refers to a 5-year period preceding the reference year. g 2020. h Data are as at 1 January of reporting year.

Northern Europe

Region	Europe	Population (000, 2023)	106 550 [a,b]
Surface area (km2)	1 702 418 [c]	Pop. density (per km2, 2023)	65.0 [a,b]
Sex ratio (m per 100 f)	97.9 [a,d,b]		

Economic indicators	2010	2015	2023
GDP: Gross domestic product (million current US$)	4 303 230	4 763 604	5 618 097 [c]
GDP growth rate (annual %, const. 2015 prices)	2.5	3.6	7.0 [c]
GDP per capita (current US$)	43 309.2	46 388.9	53 057.2 [c]
Employment in agriculture (% of employed) [e]	2.2	2.1	1.8 [c]
Employment in industry (% of employed) [e]	19.9	19.3	18.7 [c]
Employment in services & other sectors (% employed) [e]	78.0	78.7	79.4 [c]
Unemployment rate (% of labour force) [e]	8.6	6.1	4.6
Labour force participation rate (female/male pop. %) [e]	56.6 / 68.3	57.4 / 67.9	59.1 / 66.8
Agricultural production index (2014-2016=100)	92	102	101 [c]
International trade: exports (million current US$)	1 045 978	1 045 828	1 539 902 [b]
International trade: imports (million current US$)	1 122 240	1 132 508	1 623 809 [b]
International trade: balance (million current US$)	- 76 262	- 86 680	- 83 908 [b]

Social indicators	2010	2015	2023
Population growth rate (average annual %) [d]	0.7	0.6	0.3 [a,b]
Urban population (% of total population)	80.1	81.4	82.4 [f]
Urban population growth rate (average annual %) [g]	1.1	0.9	...
Fertility rate, total (live births per woman) [d]	1.9	1.8	1.6 [a,b]
Life expectancy at birth (females/males, years) [d]	82.2 / 77.6	82.8 / 78.6	83.8 / 80.0 [a,b]
Population age distribution (0-14/60+ years old, %) [d]	17.5 / 22.5	17.6 / 23.5	17.2 / 25.4 [a,b]
International migrant stock (000/% of total pop.)	11 294.9 / 11.3	13 191.1 / 12.7	14 973.9 / 14.1 [h]
Infant mortality rate (per 1 000 live births) [d]	4.0	3.5	2.8 [a,b]
Intentional homicide rate (per 100 000 pop.) [e]	1.5	1.2	1.2 [c]
Seats held by women in the National Parliament (%)	29.6	30.4	37.8 [i]

Environment and infrastructure indicators	2010	2015	2023
Forested area (% of land area) [e]	44.0	44.2	44.4 [h]
Pop. using safely managed sanitation (urban/rural %)	95.9 / 75.9	96.7 / 76.8	97.0 / 77.0 [b]

a Projected estimate (medium fertility variant). b 2022. c 2021. d Including the Faroe Islands and the Isle of Man. e Estimate. f 2019. g Data refers to a 5-year period preceding the reference year. h 2020. i Data are as at 1 January of reporting year.

Southern Europe

Region	Europe	Population (000, 2023)	151 760[a,b]
Surface area (km2)	1 294 920[c]	Pop. density (per km2, 2023)	116.5[a,b]
Sex ratio (m per 100 f)	95.3[a,d,b]		

Economic indicators	2010	2015	2023
GDP: Gross domestic product (million current US$)	4 302 710	3 622 787	4 290 867[c]
GDP growth rate (annual %, const. 2015 prices)	0.7	1.9	6.5[c]
GDP per capita (current US$)	27 964.9	23 653.4	28 211.3[c]
Employment in agriculture (% of employed)[e]	7.5	6.9	6.1[c]
Employment in industry (% of employed)[e]	25.7	23.5	23.9[c]
Employment in services & other sectors (% employed)[e]	66.7	69.7	70.0[c]
Unemployment rate (% of labour force)[e]	14.2	17.2	10.7
Labour force participation rate (female/male pop. %)[e]	44.7 / 62.7	45.7 / 61.4	46.8 / 60.9
Agricultural production index (2014-2016=100)	101	101	107[c]
International trade: exports (million current US$)	830 354	886 303	1 401 951[b]
International trade: imports (million current US$)	1 039 442	925 163	1 664 058[b]
International trade: balance (million current US$)	- 209 088	- 38 860	- 262 107[b]

Social indicators	2010	2015	2023
Population growth rate (average annual %)[d]	0.2	- 0.2	- 0.3[a,b]
Urban population (% of total population)	69.2	70.6	71.8[f]
Urban population growth rate (average annual %)[g]	0.9	0.2	...
Fertility rate, total (live births per woman)[d]	1.5	1.4	1.3[a,b]
Life expectancy at birth (females/males, years)[d]	83.5 / 78.0	83.9 / 78.8	84.6 / 79.8[a,b]
Population age distribution (0-14/60+ years old, %)[d]	14.9 / 24.0	14.6 / 25.8	13.5 / 28.6[a,b]
International migrant stock (000/% of total pop.)	16 206.3 / 10.6	15 815.5 / 10.3	17 665.7 / 11.6[h]
Infant mortality rate (per 1 000 live births)[d]	3.8	3.3	2.7[a,b]
Intentional homicide rate (per 100 000 pop.)[e]	1.2	0.9	0.7[c]
Seats held by women in the National Parliament (%)	23.0	30.0	33.5[i]

Environment and infrastructure indicators	2010	2015	2023
Forested area (% of land area)[e]	34.9	35.3	35.5[h]
Pop. using safely managed drinking water (urban/rural, %)	96.8 / 93.3	96.3 / 92.6	95.8 / 91.8[b]
Pop. using safely managed sanitation (urban/rural %)	68.7 / 48.6	71.8 / 52.2	74.7 / 59.6[b]

a Projected estimate (medium fertility variant). b 2022. c 2021. d Including Andorra, Gibraltar, Holy See, and San Marino. e Estimate. f 2019. g Data refers to a 5-year period preceding the reference year. h 2020. i Data are as at 1 January of reporting year.

Western Europe

Region	Europe	Population (000, 2023)	195 620 [a,b]
Surface area (km2)	1 084 794 [c]	Pop. density (per km2, 2023)	179.6 [a,b]
Sex ratio (m per 100 f)	96.3 [a,d,b]		

Economic indicators	2010	2015	2023
GDP: Gross domestic product (million current US$)	8 428 940	8 178 400	10 218 711 [c]
GDP growth rate (annual %, const. 2015 prices)	3.0	1.5	4.5 [c]
GDP per capita (current US$)	44 327.4	42 167.2	51 681.1 [c]
Employment in agriculture (% of employed) [e]	2.4	2.1	1.9 [c]
Employment in industry (% of employed) [e]	24.7	23.6	22.9 [c]
Employment in services & other sectors (% employed) [e]	72.9	74.3	75.2 [c]
Unemployment rate (% of labour force) [e]	7.2	6.9	4.9
Labour force participation rate (female/male pop. %) [e]	53.0 / 65.3	54.0 / 64.6	55.2 / 64.9
Agricultural production index (2014-2016=100)	96	101	97 [c]
International trade: exports (million current US$)	3 034 038	3 134 738	4 144 833 [b]
International trade: imports (million current US$)	2 838 360	2 824 980	4 195 461 [b]
International trade: balance (million current US$)	195 679	309 758	- 50 628 [b]

Social indicators	2010	2015	2023
Population growth rate (average annual %) [d]	0.4	0.4	0.1 [a,b]
Urban population (% of total population)	78.5	79.4	80.0 [f]
Urban population growth rate (average annual %) [g]	0.6	0.6	...
Fertility rate, total (live births per woman) [d]	1.7	1.7	1.6 [a,b]
Life expectancy at birth (females/males, years) [d]	83.3 / 77.8	83.8 / 78.7	84.5 / 79.6 [a,b]
Population age distribution (0-14/60+ years old, %) [d]	15.8 / 24.2	15.5 / 25.8	15.4 / 28.3 [a,b]
International migrant stock (000/% of total pop.)	24 015.3 / 12.8	25 918.6 / 13.5	33 231.1 / 16.9 [h]
Infant mortality rate (per 1 000 live births) [d]	3.6	3.4	3.1 [a,b]
Intentional homicide rate (per 100 000 pop.) [e]	1.0	1.0	0.9 [c]
Seats held by women in the National Parliament (%)	28.4	32.0	37.8 [i]

Environment and infrastructure indicators	2010	2015	2023
Forested area (% of land area) [e]	31.4	31.8	32.2 [h]
Pop. using safely managed drinking water (urban/rural, %)	99.1 / 99.2	99.5 / 99.2	100.0 / 99.2 [b]
Pop. using safely managed sanitation (urban/rural %)	97.9 / 83.7	98.1 / 84.0	98.3 / 84.2 [b]

a Projected estimate (medium fertility variant). **b** 2022. **c** 2021. **d** Including Liechtenstein and Monaco. **e** Estimate. **f** 2019. **g** Data refers to a 5-year period preceding the reference year. **h** 2020. **i** Data are as at 1 January of reporting year.

Oceania

Region	World	Population (000, 2023)	45 039 [a,b]
Surface area (km2)	8 486 460 [c]	Pop. density (per km2, 2023)	5.3 [a,b]
Sex ratio (m per 100 f)	100.6 [a,b]		

Economic indicators	2010	2015	2023
GDP: Gross domestic product (million current US$)	1 484 238	1 468 468	2 037 591 [c]
GDP growth rate (annual %, const. 2015 prices)	2.3	3.0	3.5 [c]
GDP per capita (current US$)	40 318.7	36 604.7	46 087.6 [c]
Employment in agriculture (% of employed) [d]	8.4	7.2	6.5 [c]
Employment in industry (% of employed) [d]	18.9	18.4	17.4 [c]
Employment in services & other sectors (% employed) [d]	72.8	74.3	76.1 [c]
Unemployment rate (% of labour force) [d]	5.0	5.4	3.4
Labour force participation rate (female/male pop. %) [d]	57.0 / 68.6	57.2 / 67.4	58.5 / 66.4
Agricultural production index (2014-2016=100)	86	101	105 [c]
International trade: exports (million current US$)	253 360	235 133	472 560 [b]
International trade: imports (million current US$)	247 608	251 607	407 276 [b]
International trade: balance (million current US$)	5 752	- 16 475	65 284 [b]

Social indicators	2010	2015	2023
Population growth rate (average annual %)	1.7	1.7	1.2 [a,b]
Urban population (% of total population)	68.1	68.1	68.2 [e]
Urban population growth rate (average annual %) [f]	1.8	1.5	...
Fertility rate, total (live births per woman)	2.5	2.4	2.1 [a,b]
Life expectancy at birth (females/males, years)	79.8 / 75.0	80.7 / 75.7	81.6 / 76.8 [a,b]
Population age distribution (0-14/60+ years old, %)	24.3 / 14.9	23.9 / 15.9	22.9 / 17.7 [a,b]
International migrant stock (000/% of total pop.)	7 128.6 / 19.3	8 072.3 / 20.3	9 380.7 / 22.0 [g]
Refugees and others of concern to the UNHCR (000)	...	71.3	187.6 [b]
Infant mortality rate (per 1 000 live births)	20.0	18.1	15.7 [a,b]
Education: Primary gross enrol. ratio (f/m per 100 pop.)	96.4 / 99.4 [d]	101.8 / 104.8 [d]	103.7 / 106.3 [g]
Education: Lowr. sec. gross enrol. ratio (f/m per 100 pop.)	103.6 / 109.5 [d]	101.6 / 112.8	89.0 / 94.7 [g]
Education: Upr. sec. gross enrol. ratio (f/m per 100 pop.)	111.3 / 121.0 [d]	106.5 / 120.9	117.2 / 118.7 [g]
Intentional homicide rate (per 100 000 pop.) [d]	2.9	2.9	2.9 [c]
Seats held by women in the National Parliament (%)	13.2	13.2	19.5 [h]

Environment and infrastructure indicators	2010	2015	2023
Individuals using the Internet (per 100 inhabitants)	56.9	64.3	79.7 [c]
Research & Development expenditure (% of GDP)	2.2	1.8	1.7 [g]
Forested area (% of land area) [d]	21.3	21.7	21.8 [g]
Energy production, primary (Petajoules)	14 528	17 383	20 290 [g]
Energy supply per capita (Gigajoules)	175	164	154 [g]
Important sites for terrestrial biodiversity protected (%)	30.1	33.0	35.4 [b]
Pop. using safely managed drinking water (urban/rural, %)	96.8 / ...	97.8 / ...	97.5 / ... [b]
Pop. using safely managed sanitation (urban/rural %)	82.9 / 29.3	83.8 / 28.5	85.1 / 28.2 [b,i]

a Projected estimate (medium fertility variant). b 2022. c 2021. d Estimate. e 2019. f Data refers to a 5-year period preceding the reference year. g 2020. h Data are as at 1 January of reporting year. i 2018.

Australia and New Zealand

Region	Oceania	Population (000, 2023)	31 363[a,b]
Surface area (km2)	7 945 610[c]	Pop. density (per km2, 2023)	3.9[a,b]
Sex ratio (m per 100 f)	98.6[a,b]		

Economic indicators	2010	2015	2023
GDP: Gross domestic product (million current US$)	1 447 614	1 423 313	1 984 983[c]
GDP growth rate (annual %, const. 2015 prices)	2.2	2.9	3.6[c]
GDP per capita (current US$)	54 905.6	50 097.6	63 926.9[c]
Agricultural production index (2014-2016=100)	86	101	105[c]
International trade: exports (million current US$)	243 502	222 149	455 868[b]
International trade: imports (million current US$)	232 319	236 642	364 150[b]
International trade: balance (million current US$)	11 183	- 14 493	91 718[b]

Social indicators	2010	2015	2023
Population growth rate (average annual %)	1.4	1.5	1.0[a,b]
Urban population (% of total population)	85.3	85.8	86.2[d]
Urban population growth rate (average annual %)[e]	1.8	1.5	...
Fertility rate, total (live births per woman)	2.0	1.8	1.6[a,b]
Life expectancy at birth (females/males, years)	84.0 / 79.7	84.5 / 80.5	85.3 / 81.6[a,b]
Population age distribution (0-14/60+ years old, %)	19.4 / 18.9	19.1 / 20.3	18.3 / 22.5[a,b]
International migrant stock (000/% of total pop.)	6 830.4 / 25.8	7 769.5 / 27.2	9 067.6 / 29.9[f]
Infant mortality rate (per 1 000 live births)	4.3	3.3	2.9[a,b]
Education: Primary gross enrol. ratio (f/m per 100 pop.)	104.9 / 105.0	101.1 / 101.0	99.4 / 99.5[f]
Education: Lowr. sec. gross enrol. ratio (f/m per 100 pop.)	115.8 / 120.1[g]	114.0 / 126.0	106.3 / 110.4[f]
Education: Upr. sec. gross enrol. ratio (f/m per 100 pop.)	195.8 / 208.8[g]	187.2 / 211.3	176.4 / 177.8[f]
Intentional homicide rate (per 100 000 pop.)[g]	1.0	1.0	0.9[c]
Seats held by women in the National Parliament (%)	30.1	28.8	43.5[h]

Environment and infrastructure indicators	2010	2015	2023
Individuals using the Internet (per 100 inhabitants)	76.7	84.7	96.2[c]
Research & Development expenditure (% of GDP)	2.2	1.8	1.8[f]
Forested area (% of land area)[g]	17.5	18.0	18.1[f]
Important sites for terrestrial biodiversity protected (%)	45.9	50.4	54.2[b]
Pop. using safely managed drinking water (urban/rural, %)	99.5 / ...	99.7 / ...	99.5 / ...[b]

a Projected estimate (medium fertility variant). b 2022. c 2021. d 2019. e Data refers to a 5-year period preceding the reference year. f 2020. g Estimate. h Data are as at 1 January of reporting year.

Melanesia

Region	Oceania	Population (000, 2023)	12 413 [a,b]
Surface area (km2)	529 590 [c]	Pop. density (per km2, 2023)	23.4 [a,b]
Sex ratio (m per 100 f)	105.6 [a,b]		

Economic indicators	2010	2015	2023
GDP: Gross domestic product (million current US$)	28 345	37 208	43 575 [c]
GDP growth rate (annual %, const. 2015 prices)	8.1	4.6	- 0.3 [c]
GDP per capita (current US$)	2 972.6	3 454.3	3 575.0 [c]
Agricultural production index (2014-2016=100)	88	101	104 [c]
International trade: exports (million current US$)	8 112	10 998	12 854 [b]
International trade: imports (million current US$)	9 665	7 968	14 488 [b]
International trade: balance (million current US$)	- 1 553	3 030	- 1 634 [b]

Social indicators	2010	2015	2023
Population growth rate (average annual %)	2.7	2.2	1.8 [a,b]
Urban population (% of total population)	19.0	19.2	19.5 [d]
Urban population growth rate (average annual %) [e]	2.3	2.2	...
Fertility rate, total (live births per woman)	3.8	3.5	3.1 [a,b]
Life expectancy at birth (females/males, years)	66.6 / 62.5	68.6 / 63.2	70.0 / 64.4 [a,b]
Population age distribution (0-14/60+ years old, %)	37.1 / 4.8	36.0 / 5.1	34.0 / 6.1 [a,b]
International migrant stock (000/% of total pop.)	110.7 / 1.2	119.3 / 1.2	124.1 / 1.1 [f]
Infant mortality rate (per 1 000 live births)	40.5	36.4	30.9 [a,b]
Intentional homicide rate (per 100 000 pop.) [g]	8.0	7.9	8.0 [c]
Seats held by women in the National Parliament (%)	1.4	4.2	4.8 [h]

Environment and infrastructure indicators	2010	2015	2023
Forested area (% of land area) [g]	77.5	77.3	77.0 [f]
Pop. using safely managed drinking water (urban/rural, %)	48.8 / ...	48.8 / ...	48.6 / ... [b]
Pop. using safely managed sanitation (urban/rural %)	35.5 / ...	35.2 / ...	33.5 / ... [b]

a Projected estimate (medium fertility variant). b 2022. c 2021. d 2019. e Data refers to a 5-year period preceding the reference year. f 2020. g Estimate. h Data are as at 1 January of reporting year.

Micronesia

Region	Oceania	Population (000, 2023)	539 [a,b]
Surface area (km2)	3 170 [c]	Pop. density (per km2, 2023)	174.8 [a,b]
Sex ratio (m per 100 f)	101.4 [a,d,b]		

Economic indicators	2010	2015	2023
GDP: Gross domestic product (million current US$)	855	1 056	1 261 [c]
GDP growth rate (annual %, const. 2015 prices)	2.5	8.5	- 2.3 [c]
GDP per capita (current US$)	2 872.0	3 466.7	4 009.8 [c]
Agricultural production index (2014-2016=100)	83	94	98 [c]
International trade: exports (million current US$)	1 508	1 766	3 606 [b]
International trade: imports (million current US$)	3 292	4 721	25 528 [b]
International trade: balance (million current US$)	- 1 783	- 2 955	- 21 922 [b]

Social indicators	2010	2015	2023
Population growth rate (average annual %) [d]	- 0.1	0.3	1.0 [a,b]
Urban population (% of total population)	66.6	67.9	69.0 [e]
Urban population growth rate (average annual %) [f]	0.2	1.0	...
Fertility rate, total (live births per woman) [d]	3.2	3.0	2.8 [a,b]
Life expectancy at birth (females/males, years) [d]	73.7 / 68.6	74.2 / 68.7	75.7 / 69.8 [a,b]
Population age distribution (0-14/60+ years old, %) [d]	32.1 / 7.1	30.9 / 8.9	29.6 / 12.0 [a,b]
International migrant stock (000/% of total pop.)	114.7 / 22.8	113.5 / 21.7	118.9 / 21.7 [g]
Infant mortality rate (per 1 000 live births) [d]	27.1	25.9	22.0 [a,b]
Intentional homicide rate (per 100 000 pop.) [h]	2.8	3.7	3.7 [c]
Seats held by women in the National Parliament (%)	2.4	4.7	7.1 [i]

Environment and infrastructure indicators	2010	2015	2023
Individuals using the Internet (per 100 inhabitants)	20.0	31.5	40.4 [c]
Forested area (% of land area) [h]	53.5	53.7	53.2 [g]
Pop. using safely managed drinking water (urban/rural, %)	73.2 / 34.7	72.4 / 32.7	69.6 / 26.8 [b]
Pop. using safely managed sanitation (urban/rural %)	... / 31.7	... / 36.6	... / 36.9 [b]

a Projected estimate (medium fertility variant). b 2022. c 2021. d Including Marshall Islands, Nauru, Northern Mariana Islands and Palau. e 2019. f Data refers to a 5-year period preceding the reference year. g 2020. h Estimate. i Data are as at 1 January of reporting year.

Polynesia

Region	Oceania	Population (000, 2023)	724[a,b,c]
Surface area (km2)	8 090[d]	Pop. density (per km2, 2023)	89.9[a,c]
Sex ratio (m per 100 f)	101.4[a,b,c]		

Economic indicators	2010	2015	2023
GDP: Gross domestic product (million current US$)	7 423	6 891	7 771[d]
GDP growth rate (annual %, const. 2015 prices)	- 2.0	2.5	1.0[d]
GDP per capita (current US$)	12 097.2	10 937.0	11 828.4[d]
Agricultural production index (2014-2016=100)	116	98	92[d]
International trade: exports (million current US$)	238	219	233[c]
International trade: imports (million current US$)	2 333	2 277	3 110[c]
International trade: balance (million current US$)	- 2 095	- 2 058	- 2 877[c]

Social indicators	2010	2015	2023
Population growth rate (average annual %)[b]	0.5	0.3	0.9[a,c]
Urban population (% of total population)	44.3	44.5	44.4[e]
Urban population growth rate (average annual %)[f]	0.9	0.6	...
Fertility rate, total (live births per woman)[b]	3.2	2.9	2.6[a,c]
Life expectancy at birth (females/males, years)[b]	77.9 / 72.9	78.7 / 73.9	79.7 / 74.8[a,c]
Population age distribution (0-14/60+ years old, %)[b]	32.3 / 8.5	31.0 / 9.6	28.8 / 12.0[a,c]
International migrant stock (000/% of total pop.)[b]	72.7 / 11.1	70.0 / 10.5	70.1 / 10.3[g]
Infant mortality rate (per 1 000 live births)[b]	11.9	11.3	10.7[a,c]
Intentional homicide rate (per 100 000 pop.)[h]	3.7	2.8	3.3[d]
Seats held by women in the National Parliament (%)	5.2	4.4	10.2[i]

Environment and infrastructure indicators	2010	2015	2023
Forested area (% of land area)[h]	48.7	48.4	48.4[g]
Pop. using safely managed drinking water (urban/rural, %)	87.0 / 59.8	84.8 / 58.7	78.4 / 56.8[c]
Pop. using safely managed sanitation (urban/rural %)	37.4 / 46.2	34.5 / 44.3	32.1 / 41.2[c]

a Projected estimate (medium fertility variant). b Including Pitcairn. c 2022. d 2021. e 2019. f Data refers to a 5-year period preceding the reference year. g 2020. h Estimate. i Data are as at 1 January of reporting year.

Afghanistan

Region	Southern Asia
Population (000, 2023)	41 129[a,b]
Pop. density (per km2, 2023)	63.3[a,b]
Capital city	Kabul
Capital city pop. (000, 2023)	4 114.0[d]

UN membership date	19 November 1946
Surface area (km2)	652 864[c]
Sex ratio (m per 100 f)	102.0[a,b]
National currency	Afghani (AFN)
Exchange rate (per US$)	77.1[e]

Economic indicators

	2010	2015	2023
GDP: Gross domestic product (million current US$)	14 699	18 713	14 939[c]
GDP growth rate (annual %, const. 2015 prices)	5.2	- 1.4	- 20.7[c]
GDP per capita (current US$)	521.4	554.4	372.5[c]
Economy: Agriculture (% of Gross Value Added)[f]	33.2	27.3	35.0[g,c]
Economy: Industry (% of Gross Value Added)[f]	13.0	10.8	16.3[h,c]
Economy: Services and other activity (% of GVA)[f]	53.8	61.9	48.7[i,c]
Employment in agriculture (% of employed)[j]	53.8	44.7	46.9[c]
Employment in industry (% of employed)[j]	15.3	20.7	18.8[c]
Employment in services & other sectors (% employed)[j]	31.0	34.7	34.3[c]
Unemployment rate (% of labour force)	8.1[j]	9.0[j]	11.7[e]
Labour force participation rate (female/male pop. %)	15.5 / 78.6[j]	19.1 / 75.3[j]	16.5 / 66.7[e]
CPI: Consumer Price Index (2010=100)	100	133	150[d]
Agricultural production index (2014-2016=100)	93	96	114[c]
International trade: exports (million current US$)	388	571	632[j,b]
International trade: imports (million current US$)	5 154	7 723	4 957[j,b]
International trade: balance (million current US$)	- 4 766	- 7 151	- 4 324[j,b]
Balance of payments, current account (million current US$)	- 578	- 4 193	- 3 137[e]

Major trading partners

						2022
Export partners (% of exports)[j]	Pakistan	34.6	United Arab Emirates	30.3	India	22.1
Import partners (% of imports)[j]	United Arab Emirates	26.2	Kazakhstan	15.9	Pakistan	14.2

Social indicators

	2010	2015	2023
Population growth rate (average annual %)	2.7	2.3	2.7[a,b]
Urban population (% of total population)	23.7	24.8	25.8[d]
Urban population growth rate (average annual %)[k]	3.7	4.0	...
Fertility rate, total (live births per woman)	6.1	5.4	4.5[a,b]
Life expectancy at birth (females/males, years)	62.4 / 59.3	64.6 / 60.8	66.2 / 59.8[a,b]
Population age distribution (0-14/60+ years old, %)	49.0 / 3.8	45.8 / 3.8	43.1 / 3.8[a,b]
International migrant stock (000/% of total pop.)[l]	102.3 / 0.4	339.4 / 1.0	144.1 / 0.4[e]
Refugees and others of concern to the UNHCR (000)	1 200.0	1 421.4	3 612.3[b]
Infant mortality rate (per 1 000 live births)	64.8	54.5	40.8[a,b]
Health: Current expenditure (% of GDP)[m]	8.6	10.1	15.5[n,e]
Health: Physicians (per 1 000 pop.)	0.2	0.3	0.3[e]
Education: Government expenditure (% of GDP)	3.5	3.3	2.9[e]
Education: Primary gross enrol. ratio (f/m per 100 pop.)	80.6 / 118.6	83.5 / 122.7	85.4 / 127.1[d]
Education: Lowr. sec. gross enrol. ratio (f/m per 100 pop.)	46.4 / 87.4	45.5 / 77.9	52.2 / 87.6[d]
Education: Upr. sec. gross enrol. ratio (f/m per 100 pop.)	17.8 / 42.7	27.1 / 52.6	28.5 / 52.4[o]
Intentional homicide rate (per 100 000 pop.)	3.5	10.0	4.0[c]
Seats held by women in the National Parliament (%)	27.3	27.7	27.0[p,q,b]

Environment and infrastructure indicators

	2010	2015	2023
Individuals using the Internet (per 100 inhabitants)[j]	4.0	8.3	18.4[e]
Threatened species (number)	34	38	55[b]
Forested area (% of land area)	1.9	1.9	1.9[b]
Energy production, primary (Petajoules)[r]	41	61	71[j,e]
Energy supply per capita (Gigajoules)[r]	5[j]	5	5[e]
Important sites for terrestrial biodiversity protected (%)	5.8	5.8	46.4[b]
Pop. using safely managed drinking water (urban/rural, %)	28.1 / 16.6	31.8 / 21.2	36.4 / 27.7[b]
Net Official Development Assist. received (% of GNI)	39.26	22.14	20.73[e]

a Projected estimate (medium fertility variant). **b** 2022. **c** 2021. **d** 2019. **e** 2020. **f** Data classified according to ISIC Rev. 4. **g** Excludes irrigation canals and landscaping care. **h** Excludes publishing activities, recycling. Includes irrigation canals. **i** Includes publishing activities and landscape care. Excludes repair of personal and household goods. **j** Estimate. **k** Data refers to a 5-year period preceding the reference year. **l** Including refugees. **m** Data based on calendar year (January 1 to December 31). **n** Data are based on SHA2011. **o** 2018. **p** Data corresponds to the composition of the House of the People elected in 2018. **q** Data are as at 1 January of reporting year. **r** Data refer to fiscal years beginning 21 March.

Albania

Region	Southern Europe	
Population (000, 2023)	2 842 [a,b]	
Pop. density (per km2, 2023)	103.7 [a,b]	
Capital city	Tirana	
Capital city pop. (000, 2023)	484.6 [d]	

UN membership date	14 December 1955
Surface area (km2)	28 748 [c]
Sex ratio (m per 100 f)	99.5 [a,b]
National currency	Lek (ALL)
Exchange rate (per US$)	107.0 [b]

Economic indicators

	2010	2015	2023
GDP: Gross domestic product (million current US$)	11 927	11 387	18 260 [c]
GDP growth rate (annual %, const. 2015 prices)	3.7	2.2	8.5 [c]
GDP per capita (current US$)	4 093.8	3 950.4	6 396.5 [c]
Economy: Agriculture (% of Gross Value Added) [e,f]	20.7	22.5	20.3 [c]
Economy: Industry (% of Gross Value Added) [e,g]	28.7	24.8	25.0 [c]
Economy: Services and other activity (% of GVA) [e,h]	50.7	52.7	54.7 [c]
Employment in agriculture (% of employed)	42.1	41.3	34.6 [i,c]
Employment in industry (% of employed)	20.6	18.6	21.6 [i,c]
Employment in services & other sectors (% employed)	37.3	40.1	43.9 [i,c]
Unemployment rate (% of labour force)	14.1	17.2	12.5 [i]
Labour force participation rate (female/male pop. %)	46.7 / 63.8	47.0 / 64.1	52.3 / 66.6 [i]
CPI: Consumer Price Index (2010=100) [j]	100	111	132 [b]
Agricultural production index (2014-2016=100)	86	100	103 [c]
International trade: exports (million current US$) [k]	1 550	1 930	4 306 [b]
International trade: imports (million current US$) [k]	4 603	4 320	8 407 [b]
International trade: balance (million current US$) [k]	- 3 053	- 2 391	- 4 101 [b]
Balance of payments, current account (million US$)	- 1 356	- 980	- 1 135 [b]

Major trading partners

						2022
Export partners (% of exports)	Italy	49.5	Serbia	10.2	Montenegro	7.9
Import partners (% of imports)	Italy	23.4	Türkiye	12.0	Greece	10.1

Social indicators

	2010	2015	2023
Population growth rate (average annual %)	- 0.5	~0.0	- 0.4 [a,b]
Urban population (% of total population)	52.2	57.4	61.2 [d]
Urban population growth rate (average annual %) [l]	1.3	1.8	...
Fertility rate, total (live births per woman)	1.7	1.6	1.4 [a,b]
Life expectancy at birth (females/males, years)	80.7 / 75.5	81.2 / 76.4	79.5 / 74.5 [a,b]
Population age distribution (0-14/60+ years old, %)	21.0 / 16.2	18.2 / 19.0	16.1 / 23.5 [a,b]
International migrant stock (000/% of total pop.)	52.8 / 1.8	52.0 / 1.8	48.8 / 1.7 [m]
Refugees and others of concern to the UNHCR (000)	0.1 [n]	8.1	6.3 [o,b]
Infant mortality rate (per 1 000 live births)	11.9	9.6	8.2 [a,b]
Health: Current expenditure (% of GDP)	6.2	6.4 [p]	...
Health: Physicians (per 1 000 pop.)	1.2	1.3 [q]	1.9 [m]
Education: Government expenditure (% of GDP)	3.4	3.4	3.3 [m]
Education: Primary gross enrol. ratio (f/m per 100 pop.)	93.8 / 93.2	107.3 / 104.0	96.8 / 95.1 [c]
Education: Lowr. sec. gross enrol. ratio (f/m per 100 pop.)	95.5 / 93.1	99.9 / 99.4	100.3 / 96.6 [c]
Education: Upr. sec. gross enrol. ratio (f/m per 100 pop.)	79.0 / 81.1	89.6 / 99.6	94.8 / 92.6 [c]
Intentional homicide rate (per 100 000 pop.)	4.1	2.2	2.3 [c]
Seats held by women in the National Parliament (%)	16.4	20.7	35.7 [r]

Environment and infrastructure indicators

	2010	2015	2023
Individuals using the Internet (per 100 inhabitants)	45.0	56.9 [i]	79.3 [s,c]
Research & Development expenditure (% of GDP)	0.2 [t,u]	...	...
Threatened species (number)	100	112	157 [b]
Forested area (% of land area)	28.5	28.8	28.8 [m]
CO2 emission estimates (million tons/tons per capita)	4.1 / 1.4	4.0 / 1.3	4.2 / 1.2 [c,m]
Energy production, primary (Petajoules)	69	87	63 [m]
Energy supply per capita (Gigajoules)	31	31	30 [m]
Tourist/visitor arrivals at national borders (000) [v]	2 191	3 784	5 515 [c]
Important sites for terrestrial biodiversity protected (%)	39.3	47.7	48.6 [b]
Pop. using safely managed sanitation (urban/rural %)	27.0 / ...	34.0 / ...	49.6 / ... [b]
Net Official Development Assist. received (% of GNI)	3.09	2.91	3.52 [c]

a Projected estimate (medium fertility variant). b 2022. c 2021. d 2019. e Data classified according to ISIC Rev. 4. f Excludes irrigation canals and landscaping care. g Excludes publishing activities, recycling. Includes irrigation canals. h Includes publishing activities and landscape care. Excludes repair of personal and household goods. i Estimate. j Calculated by the UN Statistics Division from national indices. k In 2020, the reported share of non-standard HS codes was relatively high. l Data refers to a 5-year period preceding the reference year. m 2020. n Data as at the end of December. o UNHCR estimates the number of people with undetermined nationality (at risk of statelessness) from various sources. p 2014. q 2013. r Data are as at 1 January of reporting year. s Users in the last 3 months. t Partial data. u 2008. v Excluding nationals residing abroad.

Algeria

Region	Northern Africa	UN membership date	08 October 1962
Population (000, 2023)	44 903 [a,b]	Surface area (km2)	2 381 741 [c]
Pop. density (per km2, 2023)	18.9 [a,b]	Sex ratio (m per 100 f)	103.7 [a,b]
Capital city	Algiers	National currency	Algerian Dinar (DZD)
Capital city pop. (000, 2023)	2 729.3 [d,e]	Exchange rate (per US$)	137.2 [b]

Economic indicators

	2010	2015	2023
GDP: Gross domestic product (million current US$)	161 207	165 979	163 473 [c]
GDP growth rate (annual %, const. 2015 prices)	3.6	3.7	3.4 [c]
GDP per capita (current US$)	4 495.9	4 197.4	3 700.3 [c]
Economy: Agriculture (% of Gross Value Added)	8.6	12.1	12.6 [c]
Economy: Industry (% of Gross Value Added)	51.4	37.3	41.0 [c]
Economy: Services and other activity (% of GVA)	40.0	50.6	46.3 [c]
Employment in agriculture (% of employed) [f]	12.0	9.6	10.3 [c]
Employment in industry (% of employed) [f]	30.3	31.8	31.1 [c]
Employment in services & other sectors (% employed) [f]	57.6	58.6	58.6 [c]
Unemployment rate (% of labour force)	10.0	11.2	11.6 [f]
Labour force participation rate (female/male pop. %)	14.1 / 68.4	16.2 / 66.3	16.6 / 64.2 [f]
CPI: Consumer Price Index (2010=100) [g]	100	127	182 [h,b]
Agricultural production index (2014-2016=100)	76	100	104 [c]
International trade: exports (million current US$)	57 051	34 796	65 102 [f,b]
International trade: imports (million current US$)	41 000	51 803	40 905 [f,b]
International trade: balance (million current US$)	16 051	- 17 007	24 197 [f,b]
Balance of payments, current account (million US$)	12 220	- 27 038	18 279 [b]

Major trading partners

						2022
Export partners (% of exports) [f]	Italy	33.0	Spain	12.2	France	10.7
Import partners (% of imports) [f]	China	15.9	France	12.0	Russian Federation	8.8

Social indicators

	2010	2015	2023
Population growth rate (average annual %)	1.9	2.0	1.6 [a,b]
Urban population (% of total population)	67.5	70.8	73.2 [e]
Urban population growth rate (average annual %) [i]	2.8	2.9	...
Fertility rate, total (live births per woman)	2.8	3.0	2.8 [a,b]
Life expectancy at birth (females/males, years)	74.9 / 72.8	76.8 / 74.5	78.5 / 75.9 [a,b]
Population age distribution (0-14/60+ years old, %)	27.6 / 7.1	29.0 / 8.1	30.6 / 9.7 [a,b]
International migrant stock (000/% of total pop.) [j]	217.3 / 0.6	239.5 / 0.6	250.4 / 0.6 [k]
Refugees and others of concern to the UNHCR (000)	94.4 [l]	100.0	101.8 [m,b]
Infant mortality rate (per 1 000 live births)	23.0	21.2	16.6 [a,b]
Health: Current expenditure (% of GDP) [n,o]	5.1	7.0	6.3 [k]
Health: Physicians (per 1 000 pop.)	1.2 [p]	...	1.7 [q]
Education: Government expenditure (% of GDP)	4.3 [r]	...	...
Education: Primary gross enrol. ratio (f/m per 100 pop.)	111.5 / 119.0	113.0 / 118.7	107.5 / 110.5 [b]
Education: Lowr. sec. gross enrol. ratio (f/m per 100 pop.)	123.7 / 134.8	126.5 / 136.8 [s]	... / ...
Education: Upr. sec. gross enrol. ratio (f/m per 100 pop.)	69.7 / 49.2	72.8 / 52.6 [s]	... / ...
Intentional homicide rate (per 100 000 pop.)	0.7	1.4	1.6 [c]
Seats held by women in the National Parliament (%)	7.7	31.6	7.9 [t]

Environment and infrastructure indicators

	2010	2015	2023
Individuals using the Internet (per 100 inhabitants)	12.5	38.2 [f]	70.8 [f,c]
Research & Development expenditure (% of GDP)	0.1 [u,v]	...	0.5 [w,x]
Threatened species (number)	105	114	186 [b]
Forested area (% of land area)	0.8	0.8	0.8 [k]
CO2 emission estimates (million tons/tons per capita)	96.5 / 2.7	131.7 / 3.3	135.6 / 3.1 [k]
Energy production, primary (Petajoules)	6 200	5 883	5 506 [k]
Energy supply per capita (Gigajoules)	46	56	55 [k]
Tourist/visitor arrivals at national borders (000) [y]	2 070	1 710	125 [c]
Important sites for terrestrial biodiversity protected (%)	41.6	42.4	43.5 [b]
Pop. using safely managed drinking water (urban/rural, %)	81.7 / 61.1	81.5 / 65.9	73.1 / 63.1 [b]
Pop. using safely managed sanitation (urban/rural %)	66.6 / 52.4	65.8 / 54.1	64.6 / 56.0 [b]
Net Official Development Assist. received (% of GNI)	0.13	0.04	0.13 [c]

a Projected estimate (medium fertility variant). b 2022. c 2021. d Refers to the Governorate of Grand Algiers. e 2019. f Estimate. g Algiers h Calculated by the UN Statistics Division from national indices. i Data refers to a 5-year period preceding the reference year. j Including refugees. k 2020. l Data as at the end of December. m The Government estimates 165,000 Sahrawi refugees. Persons in need of humanitarian assistance services is estimated to be higher. n Data based on calendar year (January 1 to December 31). o Estimates should be viewed with caution as these are derived from scarce data. p 2007. q 2018. r 2008. s 2011. t Data are as at 1 January of reporting year. u Partial data. v 2005. w Break in the time series. x 2017. y Including nationals residing abroad.

American Samoa

Region	Polynesia	Population (000, 2023)	44 a,b,c	
Surface area (km2)	199 d	Pop. density (per km2, 2023)	221.4 a,b,c	
Sex ratio (m per 100 f)	97.6 a,b,c	Capital city	Pago Pago	
National currency	US Dollar (USD)	Capital city pop. (000, 2023)	48.5 e	

Economic indicators	2010	2015	2023
Employment in agriculture (% of employed)	3.0 f,g,h	...	...
Employment in industry (% of employed)	23.2 f,g,h	...	...
Employment in services & other sectors (% employed)	73.8 f,g,h	...	...
Unemployment rate (% of labour force)	9.2 g,h	...	...

Social indicators	2010	2015	2023
Population growth rate (average annual %) b	- 0.9	- 1.7	- 0.8 a,c
Urban population (% of total population)	87.6	87.2	87.1 i
Urban population growth rate (average annual %) j	- 1.3	- 0.1	
Fertility rate, total (live births per woman) b	3.3	2.7	2.3 a,c
Life expectancy at birth (females/males, years) b	74.3 / 70.0	74.8 / 70.3	75.5 / 70.0 a,c
Population age distribution (0-14/60+ years old, %) b	34.6 / 6.7	31.5 / 8.3	27.1 / 12.1 a,c
International migrant stock (000/% of total pop.)	23.6 / 42.0	23.5 / 42.1	23.6 / 42.8 k
Infant mortality rate (per 1 000 live births) b	8.0	7.4	7.0 a,c
Education: Government expenditure (% of GDP)	14.7 l	...	...
Intentional homicide rate (per 100 000 pop.)	9.1	7.8	0.0 i

Environment and infrastructure indicators	2010	2015	2023
Research & Development expenditure (% of GDP)	0.4 m,l	...	...
Threatened species (number)	79	90	105 c
Forested area (% of land area)	87.2	86.4	85.6 k
Energy production, primary (Petajoules)	...	0	0 n,k
Energy supply per capita (Gigajoules) n	131	83	92 k
Tourist/visitor arrivals at national borders (000)	23	20	1 k
Important sites for terrestrial biodiversity protected (%)	71.1	71.1	71.1 c

a Projected estimate (medium fertility variant). b For statistical purposes, the data for United States of America do not include this area. c 2022. d 2021. e 2018. f Data classified according to ISIC Rev. 3. g Break in the time series. h Population aged 16 years and over. i 2019. j Data refers to a 5-year period preceding the reference year. k 2020. l 2006. m Partial data. n Estimate.

Andorra

Region	Southern Europe
Population (000, 2023)	80[a,b]
Pop. density (per km2, 2023)	169.8[a,b]
Capital city	Andorra la Vella
Capital city pop. (000, 2023)	22.6[d]

UN membership date	28 July 1993
Surface area (km2)	468[c]
Sex ratio (m per 100 f)	104.5[a,b]
National currency	Euro (EUR)
Exchange rate (per US$)	0.9[b]

Economic indicators	2010	2015	2023
GDP: Gross domestic product (million current US$)	3 447	2 789	3 325[c]
GDP growth rate (annual %, const. 2015 prices)	- 2.0	1.4	8.3[c]
GDP per capita (current US$)	48 190.9	38 869.9	42 066.0[c]
Economy: Agriculture (% of Gross Value Added)[e,f]	0.5	0.6	0.6[c]
Economy: Industry (% of Gross Value Added)[e,g]	14.5	11.2	13.4[c]
Economy: Services and other activity (% of GVA)[e]	85.0	88.2	86.0[c]
CPI: Consumer Price Index (2010=100)[h]	92	95	106[b]
International trade: exports (million current US$)	92	90	386[b]
International trade: imports (million current US$)	1 541	1 294	1 864[b]
International trade: balance (million current US$)	- 1 448	- 1 204	- 1 478[b]
Balance of payments, current account (million US$)	...	...	467[c]

Major trading partners						2022
Export partners (% of exports)	Spain	78.3	France	6.2	United Kingdom	3.2
Import partners (% of imports)	Spain	66.1	France	11.5	Germany	5.0

Social indicators	2010	2015	2023
Population growth rate (average annual %)	- 3.3	0.1	0.3[a,b]
Urban population (% of total population)	88.8	88.3	88.0[i]
Urban population growth rate (average annual %)[j]	1.0	- 1.7	...
Fertility rate, total (live births per woman)	1.4	1.4	1.1[a,b]
Life expectancy at birth (females/males, years)	85.4 / 80.5	85.4 / 80.6	85.8 / 81.4[a,b]
Population age distribution (0-14/60+ years old, %)	16.3 / 15.3	15.5 / 17.6	12.8 / 21.6[a,b]
International migrant stock (000/% of total pop.)[k]	52.1 / 61.6	42.3 / 54.2	45.6 / 59.0[i]
Infant mortality rate (per 1 000 live births)	6.0	6.0	5.4[a,b]
Health: Current expenditure (% of GDP)	7.9	7.0	9.1[l]
Health: Physicians (per 1 000 pop.)	3.6[m]	3.6	...
Education: Government expenditure (% of GDP)	3.0	3.3	3.2[i]
Intentional homicide rate (per 100 000 pop.)	0.0	0.0	2.6[l]
Seats held by women in the National Parliament (%)	35.7	50.0	46.4[n]

Environment and infrastructure indicators	2010	2015	2023
Individuals using the Internet (per 100 inhabitants)	81.0	87.9[o]	93.9[o,c]
Threatened species (number)	8	11	15[b]
Forested area (% of land area)	34.0	34.0	34.0[l]
Energy production, primary (Petajoules)	1	1	1[l]
Energy supply per capita (Gigajoules)	134	123	96[l]
Tourist/visitor arrivals at national borders (000)	1 808[p]	2 663	1 949[c]
Important sites for terrestrial biodiversity protected (%)	26.2	26.2	26.2[b]
Pop. using safely managed sanitation (urban/rural %)	75.2 / 75.2	98.2 / 98.2	100.0 / 100.0[b]

a Projected estimate (medium fertility variant). b 2022. c 2021. d 2018. e Data classified according to ISIC Rev. 4. f Excludes irrigation canals and landscaping care. g Excludes publishing activities, recycling. Includes irrigation canals. h Base 2021 = 100. i 2019. j Data refers to a 5-year period preceding the reference year. k Refers to foreign citizens. l 2020. m 2009. n Data are as at 1 January of reporting year. o Estimate. p Break in the time series.

Angola

Region	Middle Africa	UN membership date	01 December 1976
Population (000, 2023)	35 589[a,b]	Surface area (km2)	1 246 700[c]
Pop. density (per km2, 2023)	28.5[a,b]	Sex ratio (m per 100 f)	97.7[a,b]
Capital city	Luanda	National currency	Kwanza (AOA)
Capital city pop. (000, 2023)	8 044.7[d,e]	Exchange rate (per US$)	503.7[b]

Economic indicators

	2010	2015	2023
GDP: Gross domestic product (million current US$)	83 799	116 194	70 533[c]
GDP growth rate (annual %, const. 2015 prices)	4.9	0.9	1.1[c]
GDP per capita (current US$)	3 586.7	4 130.9	2 044.2[c]
Economy: Agriculture (% of Gross Value Added)	6.2	9.1	9.0[c]
Economy: Industry (% of Gross Value Added)	52.1	42.1	43.4[c]
Economy: Services and other activity (% of GVA)	41.7	48.8	47.5[c]
Employment in agriculture (% of employed)	48.4	58.0[f]	58.7[f,c]
Employment in industry (% of employed)[f]	8.4	8.0	7.8[c]
Employment in services & other sectors (% employed)[f]	43.3	34.1	33.6[c]
Unemployment rate (% of labour force)	9.4	9.6[f]	10.1[f]
Labour force participation rate (female/male pop. %)	75.6 / 79.0	74.9 / 79.9[f]	75.1 / 79.1[f]
CPI: Consumer Price Index (2010=100)[f,g]	100	159	379[e]
Agricultural production index (2014-2016=100)	90	100	114[c]
International trade: exports (million current US$)	52 612	33 925	51 275[b]
International trade: imports (million current US$)	18 143	21 549	17 803[b]
International trade: balance (million current US$)	34 469	12 376	33 472[b]
Balance of payments, current account (million US$)	7 506	- 10 273	11 763[b]

Major trading partners

						2022
Export partners (% of exports)	China	43.2[f]	India	10.0	France	7.1[f]
Import partners (% of imports)	China	16.0	Portugal	10.7	Republic of Korea	9.2

Social indicators

	2010	2015	2023
Population growth rate (average annual %)	3.8	3.6	3.0[a,b]
Urban population (% of total population)	59.8	63.4	66.2[e]
Urban population growth rate (average annual %)[h]	4.9	4.7	...
Fertility rate, total (live births per woman)	6.2	5.8	5.2[a,b]
Life expectancy at birth (females/males, years)	59.0 / 54.4	63.1 / 58.2	64.5 / 59.4[a,b]
Population age distribution (0-14/60+ years old, %)	45.7 / 4.1	45.8 / 4.1	45.0 / 4.3[a,b]
International migrant stock (000/% of total pop.)[i]	336.4 / 1.4	632.2 / 2.3	656.4 / 2.0[i]
Refugees and others of concern to the UNHCR (000)	19.4[k]	45.7[k]	56.6[b]
Infant mortality rate (per 1 000 live births)	77.2	59.4	48.2[a,b]
Health: Current expenditure (% of GDP)[l,m]	2.7	2.6	2.9[j]
Health: Physicians (per 1 000 pop.)	0.1[n]	...	0.2[o]
Education: Government expenditure (% of GDP)	3.4	3.1	2.1[c]
Education: Primary gross enrol. ratio (f/m per 100 pop.)	94.1 / 117.7	105.9 / 121.1	82.2 / 87.8[o]
Education: Lowr. sec. gross enrol. ratio (f/m per 100 pop.)	28.6 / 38.3	27.0 / 39.3[p]	53.6 / 90.0[q]
Education: Upr. sec. gross enrol. ratio (f/m per 100 pop.)	13.2 / 23.7	13.7 / 24.6[p]	24.1 / 29.9[q]
Intentional homicide rate (per 100 000 pop.)	...	4.5	4.1[q]
Seats held by women in the National Parliament (%)	38.6	36.8	33.6[r]

Environment and infrastructure indicators

	2010	2015	2023
Individuals using the Internet (per 100 inhabitants)[f]	2.8	22.0	32.6[c]
Research & Development expenditure (% of GDP)	...	...	~0.0[s,t,u,q]
Threatened species (number)	117	130	229[b]
Forested area (% of land area)	57.9	55.7	53.4[j]
CO2 emission estimates (million tons/tons per capita)	15.9 / 0.6	23.3 / 0.8	16.9 / 0.5[j]
Energy production, primary (Petajoules)	4 016	4 030	3 253[j]
Energy supply per capita (Gigajoules)	20	18	15[j]
Tourist/visitor arrivals at national borders (000)	425	592	64[c]
Important sites for terrestrial biodiversity protected (%)	28.1	28.1	28.1[b]
Net Official Development Assist. received (% of GNI)	0.32	0.46	0.37[c]

a Projected estimate (medium fertility variant). **b** 2022. **c** 2021. **d** Refers to the urban population of the province of Luanda. **e** 2019. **f** Estimate. **g** Luanda **h** Data refers to a 5-year period preceding the reference year. **i** Including refugees. **j** 2020. **k** Data as at the end of December. **l** Data based on calendar year (January 1 to December 31). **m** Estimates should be viewed with caution as these are derived from scarce data. **n** 2009. **o** 2018. **p** 2011. **q** 2016. **r** Data are as at 1 January of reporting year. **s** Partial data. **t** Excluding private non-profit. **u** Excluding business enterprise.

Anguilla

Region	Caribbean	Population (000, 2023)	16 [a,b,c]
Surface area (km2)	91 [d]	Pop. density (per km2, 2023)	180.2 [a,b,c]
Sex ratio (m per 100 f)	95.8 [a,b,c]	Capital city	The Valley
National currency	E. Caribbean Dollar (XCD) [e]	Capital city pop. (000, 2023)	1.4 [f]
Exchange rate (per US$)	2.7 [c]		

Economic indicators

	2010	2015	2023
GDP: Gross domestic product (million current US$)	270	331	303 [d]
GDP growth rate (annual %, const. 2015 prices)	- 4.6	3.7	14.5 [d]
GDP per capita (current US$)	20 461.5	22 756.2	19 216.3 [d]
Economy: Agriculture (% of Gross Value Added)	2.0	2.3	1.0 [d]
Economy: Industry (% of Gross Value Added)	15.8	15.3	16.5 [d]
Economy: Services and other activity (% of GVA)	82.2	82.4	82.4 [d]
CPI: Consumer Price Index (2010=100)	100 [g]	105	109 [d]
International trade: exports (million current US$) [h]	12	11	37 [c]
International trade: imports (million current US$) [h]	149	204	853 [c]
International trade: balance (million current US$) [h]	- 137	- 193	- 817 [c]
Balance of payments, current account (million US$)	- 51	- 100	- 142 [d]

Major trading partners

						2022
Export partners (% of exports) [h]	Chile	61.0	United States	18.5	Hungary	5.5
Import partners (% of imports) [h]	Chile	44.1	United States	29.0	Botswana	16.6

Social indicators

	2010	2015	2023
Population growth rate (average annual %) [a]	1.8	2.3	0.3 [b,c]
Urban population (% of total population)	100.0	100.0	100.0 [i]
Urban population growth rate (average annual %) [j]	1.7	1.2	...
Fertility rate, total (live births per woman) [a]	1.7	1.4	1.3 [b,c]
Life expectancy at birth (females/males, years) [a]	81.2 / 74.5	80.8 / 73.7	81.2 / 74.1 [b,c]
Population age distribution (0-14/60+ years old, %) [a]	23.6 / 10.3	20.3 / 12.2	17.3 / 16.0 [b,c]
International migrant stock (000/% of total pop.) [k]	5.1 / 38.0	5.5 / 38.3	5.7 / 38.1 [l]
Refugees and others of concern to the UNHCR (000)	...	...	~0.0 [c]
Infant mortality rate (per 1 000 live births) [a]	7.6	7.3	6.1 [b,c]
Education: Government expenditure (% of GDP)	2.8 [m]	3.0	4.0 [l]
Education: Primary gross enrol. ratio (f/m per 100 pop.)	118.9 / 124.4	108.9 / 108.4	105.8 / 106.8 [i]
Education: Lowr. sec. gross enrol. ratio (f/m per 100 pop.)	108.9 / 118.2	121.2 / 109.9 [n]	102.0 / 104.2 [i]
Education: Upr. sec. gross enrol. ratio (f/m per 100 pop.)	113.9 / 103.2	104.2 / 120.5 [n]	94.9 / 99.5 [i]
Intentional homicide rate (per 100 000 pop.)	0.0	28.3 [o]	...

Environment and infrastructure indicators

	2010	2015	2023
Individuals using the Internet (per 100 inhabitants) [h]	49.6	76.0	81.6 [p]
Threatened species (number)	33	51	85 [c]
Forested area (% of land area)	61.1	61.1	61.1 [l]
Energy production, primary (Petajoules)	0 [h]	0	0 [h,l]
Energy supply per capita (Gigajoules)	140 [h]	136	126 [l]
Tourist/visitor arrivals at national borders (000) [q]	62	73	28 [d]
Important sites for terrestrial biodiversity protected (%)	18.6	18.6	18.6 [c]

a For statistical purposes, the data for United Kingdom do not include this area. b Projected estimate (medium fertility variant). c 2022. d 2021. e East Caribbean Dollar. f 2018. g Break in the time series. h Estimate. i 2019. j Data refers to a 5-year period preceding the reference year. k Including refugees. l 2020. m 2008. n 2011. o 2014. p 2016. q Excluding nationals residing abroad.

Antigua and Barbuda

Region	Caribbean	UN membership date	11 November 1981
Population (000, 2023)	94 a,b	Surface area (km2)	442 c
Pop. density (per km2, 2023)	213.1 a,b	Sex ratio (m per 100 f)	91.4 a,b
Capital city	Saint John's	National currency	E. Caribbean Dollar (XCD) d
Capital city pop. (000, 2023)	20.8 e	Exchange rate (per US$)	2.7 b

Economic indicators

	2010	2015	2023
GDP: Gross domestic product (million current US$)	1 149	1 337	1 421 c
GDP growth rate (annual %, const. 2015 prices)	- 7.8	3.8	1.8 c
GDP per capita (current US$)	13 404.5	14 861.9	15 245.8 c
Economy: Agriculture (% of Gross Value Added)	1.8	1.8	2.6 c
Economy: Industry (% of Gross Value Added)	18.3	18.7	24.5 c
Economy: Services and other activity (% of GVA)	79.9	79.5	72.9 c
Employment in agriculture (% of employed)	2.8 f,g	...	...
Employment in industry (% of employed)	15.6 f,g	...	...
Employment in services & other sectors (% employed)	81.6 f,g	...	...
CPI: Consumer Price Index (2010=100)	100	110	127 b
Agricultural production index (2014-2016=100)	102	100	85 c
International trade: exports (million current US$)	35	26	2 085 h,b
International trade: imports (million current US$)	501	465	1 105 h,b
International trade: balance (million current US$)	- 466	- 439	980 h,b
Balance of payments, current account (million US$)	- 167	30	- 244 c

Major trading partners

					2022
Export partners (% of exports) h	Suriname	25.8	Poland	18.8	Germany	12.0
Import partners (% of imports) h	United States	60.1	China	6.1	Singapore	5.6

Social indicators

	2010	2015	2023
Population growth rate (average annual %)	1.2	0.8	0.6 a,b
Urban population (% of total population)	26.2	25.0	24.5 i
Urban population growth rate (average annual %) j	- 1.0	0.1	...
Fertility rate, total (live births per woman)	1.8	1.6	1.6 a,b
Life expectancy at birth (females/males, years)	79.4 / 74.0	80.4 / 75.1	81.6 / 76.5 a,b
Population age distribution (0-14/60+ years old, %)	23.8 / 10.4	21.2 / 12.2	18.5 / 16.1 a,b
International migrant stock (000/% of total pop.) k	26.4 / 30.0	28.1 / 30.0	29.4 / 30.0 l
Refugees and others of concern to the UNHCR (000)	...	~0.0	0.1 b
Infant mortality rate (per 1 000 live births)	8.2	6.3	5.0 a,b
Health: Current expenditure (% of GDP) h,m,n	5.4	5.3	5.6 l
Health: Physicians (per 1 000 pop.)	0.5 o	...	2.9 o
Education: Government expenditure (% of GDP)	2.5 p	2.8	4.3 b
Education: Primary gross enrol. ratio (f/m per 100 pop.)	107.3 / 117.2	103.2 / 106.8	101.0 / 103.4 i
Education: Lowr. sec. gross enrol. ratio (f/m per 100 pop.)	123.1 / 137.0	122.4 / 126.9	108.3 / 124.2 e
Education: Upr. sec. gross enrol. ratio (f/m per 100 pop.)	104.2 / 68.1	90.7 / 79.0	110.2 / 97.5 e
Intentional homicide rate (per 100 000 pop.)	7.0	11.4 q	17.2 c
Seats held by women in the National Parliament (%)	10.5	11.1	11.1 r

Environment and infrastructure indicators

	2010	2015	2023
Individuals using the Internet (per 100 inhabitants) h	47.0	70.0	95.7 c
Threatened species (number)	38	53	88 b
Forested area (% of land area)	20.0	19.2	18.5 l
Energy production, primary (Petajoules)	...	0	0 h,l
Energy supply per capita (Gigajoules) h	89	91	94 l
Tourist/visitor arrivals at national borders (000) s,t	230	250	169 c
Important sites for terrestrial biodiversity protected (%)	8.7	9.1	14.0 b
Net Official Development Assist. received (% of GNI)	1.76	0.12	0.42 c

a Projected estimate (medium fertility variant). b 2022. c 2021. d East Caribbean Dollar. e 2018. f Data classified according to ISIC Rev. 3. g 2008. h Estimate. i 2019. j Data refers to a 5-year period preceding the reference year. k Including refugees. l 2020. m Estimates should be viewed with caution as these are derived from scarce data. n Data based on calendar year (January 1 to December 31). o 2017. p 2009. q 2012. r Data are as at 1 January of reporting year. s Arrivals by air. t Excluding nationals residing abroad.

Argentina

Region	South America	
Population (000, 2023)	45 510[a,b]	
Pop. density (per km2, 2023)	16.3[a,b]	
Capital city	Buenos Aires	
Capital city pop. (000, 2023)	15 057.3[e,f]	

UN membership date	24 October 1945
Surface area (km2)	2 796 427[c,d]
Sex ratio (m per 100 f)	98.0[a,b]
National currency	Argentine Peso (ARS)
Exchange rate (per US$)	177.1[b]

Economic indicators

	2010	2015	2023
GDP: Gross domestic product (million current US$)	426 487	644 903	487 227[d]
GDP growth rate (annual %, const. 2015 prices)	10.1	2.7	10.4[d]
GDP per capita (current US$)	10 376.8	14 908.6	10 761.1[d]
Economy: Agriculture (% of Gross Value Added)	8.5	6.1	7.2[d]
Economy: Industry (% of Gross Value Added)	30.1	27.5	27.4[d]
Economy: Services and other activity (% of GVA)	61.4	66.3	65.4[d]
Employment in agriculture (% of employed)[g]	9.5	8.3	7.7[d]
Employment in industry (% of employed)	13.7[g]	22.2	19.9[d]
Employment in services & other sectors (% employed)	69.1	69.5	72.4[d]
Unemployment rate (% of labour force)	7.7	7.5[g]	6.6[g]
Labour force participation rate (female/male pop. %)	47.7 / 73.3	47.5 / 71.5[g]	50.0 / 69.3[g]
CPI: Consumer Price Index (2010=100)	...	...	846[h,b]
Agricultural production index (2014-2016=100)	89	104	108[d]
International trade: exports (million current US$)	68 174	56 784	88 446[b]
International trade: imports (million current US$)	56 792	60 203	81 523[b]
International trade: balance (million current US$)	11 382	- 3 419	6 923[b]
Balance of payments, current account (million US$)	- 1 623	- 17 622	- 3 788[b]

Major trading partners

					2022	
Export partners (% of exports)	Brazil	14.3	China	9.0	United States	7.6
Import partners (% of imports)	China	21.5	Brazil	19.6	United States	13.1

Social indicators

	2010	2015	2023
Population growth rate (average annual %)	1.0	1.0	0.5[a,b]
Urban population (% of total population)	90.8	91.5	92.0[f]
Urban population growth rate (average annual %)[i]	1.2	1.2	...
Fertility rate, total (live births per woman)	2.3	2.3	1.9[a,b]
Life expectancy at birth (females/males, years)	78.8 / 72.5	80.2 / 73.3	79.3 / 72.9[a,b]
Population age distribution (0-14/60+ years old, %)	25.6 / 14.6	24.7 / 15.3	23.1 / 16.2[a,b]
International migrant stock (000/% of total pop.)[j]	1 806.0 / 4.4	2 086.3 / 4.8	2 281.7 / 5.0[k]
Refugees and others of concern to the UNHCR (000)	4.2[l]	4.4	180.9[b]
Infant mortality rate (per 1 000 live births)	13.1	11.1	8.8[a,b]
Health: Current expenditure (% of GDP)[g,m]	9.4	10.2	10.0[k]
Health: Physicians (per 1 000 pop.)	...	4.0	3.9[k]
Education: Government expenditure (% of GDP)	5.0	5.8	5.1[k]
Education: Primary gross enrol. ratio (f/m per 100 pop.)	116.2 / 117.7	111.2 / 111.4	109.2 / 108.6[k]
Education: Lowr. sec. gross enrol. ratio (f/m per 100 pop.)	131.1 / 125.9	128.9 / 128.0	127.1 / 126.6[k]
Education: Upr. sec. gross enrol. ratio (f/m per 100 pop.)	77.8 / 64.7	91.1 / 79.4	97.9 / 88.9[k]
Intentional homicide rate (per 100 000 pop.)	5.8	6.6	4.6[d]
Seats held by women in the National Parliament (%)	38.5	36.2	44.8[n]

Environment and infrastructure indicators

	2010	2015	2023
Individuals using the Internet (per 100 inhabitants)	45.0[g]	68.0[o]	87.2[d]
Research & Development expenditure (% of GDP)	0.6	0.6	0.5[k]
Threatened species (number)	213	243	375[b]
Forested area (% of land area)	11.0	10.6	10.4[k]
CO2 emission estimates (million tons/tons per capita)	164.2 / 4.0	181.8 / 4.2	167.7 / 3.6[d]
Energy production, primary (Petajoules)	3 331	3 059	3 108[k]
Energy supply per capita (Gigajoules)	80	79	69[k]
Tourist/visitor arrivals at national borders (000)	6 800[p]	6 816	297[d]
Important sites for terrestrial biodiversity protected (%)	30.0	31.2	32.3[b]
Pop. using safely managed sanitation (urban/rural %)	45.4 / ...	46.0 / ...	46.2 / ...[b]
Net Official Development Assist. received (% of GNI)	0.03	0.00	0.03[d]

a Projected estimate (medium fertility variant). b 2022. c The total area includes continental areas and islands, and excludes Antarctic area. d 2021. e Refers to Gran Buenos Aires. f 2019. g Estimate. h Index base: December 2016=100. i Data refers to a 5-year period preceding the reference year. j Including refugees. k 2020. l Data as at the end of December. m Data based on calendar year (January 1 to December 31). n Data are as at 1 January of reporting year. o Population aged 10 years and over. p Break in the time series.

Armenia

Region	Western Asia	UN membership date	02 March 1992	
Population (000, 2023)	2 780[a,b]	Surface area (km2)	29 743[a]	
Pop. density (per km2, 2023)	97.7[a,b]	Sex ratio (m per 100 f)	81.7[a,b]	
Capital city	Yerevan	National currency	Armenian Dram (AMD)	
Capital city pop. (000, 2023)	1 083.3[d]	Exchange rate (per US$)	393.6[b]	

Economic indicators

	2010	2015	2023
GDP: Gross domestic product (million current US$)	9 875	10 553	13 861[c]
GDP growth rate (annual %, const. 2015 prices)	2.2	3.2	5.7[c]
GDP per capita (current US$)	3 351.8	3 666.1	4 966.5[c]
Economy: Agriculture (% of Gross Value Added)[e,f]	17.8	18.9	12.5[c]
Economy: Industry (% of Gross Value Added)[e,g]	34.7	28.2	29.3[c]
Economy: Services and other activity (% of GVA)[e]	47.4	52.9	58.2[c]
Employment in agriculture (% of employed)	38.6	35.3	30.3[h,c]
Employment in industry (% of employed)	17.3	15.8	17.6[h,c]
Employment in services & other sectors (% employed)	44.0	48.8	52.2[h,c]
Unemployment rate (% of labour force)[h]	10.5	12.2	13.0
Labour force participation rate (female/male pop. %)[h]	55.4 / 68.8	55.7 / 69.3	57.6 / 68.5
CPI: Consumer Price Index (2010=100)	100	125	152[b]
Agricultural production index (2014-2016=100)	73	107	85[c]
International trade: exports (million current US$)	1 011	1 483	5 307[b]
International trade: imports (million current US$)	3 782	3 257	8 633[b]
International trade: balance (million current US$)	- 2 770	- 1 774	- 3 326[b]
Balance of payments, current account (million US$)	- 1 261	- 281	- 167[b]

Major trading partners

					2022
Export partners (% of exports)	Russian Federation	44.6	United Arab Emirates	10.1	China 7.0
Import partners (% of imports)	Russian Federation	30.4[h]	China	15.4	Iran 6.9[h]

Social indicators

	2010	2015	2023
Population growth rate (average annual %)	- 0.6	- 0.4	- 0.2[a,b]
Urban population (% of total population)	63.4	63.1	63.2[d]
Urban population growth rate (average annual %)[i]	- 0.9	0.2	...
Fertility rate, total (live births per woman)	1.5	1.6	1.6[a,b]
Life expectancy at birth (females/males, years)	77.4 / 68.6	78.8 / 69.6	78.4 / 67.9[a,b]
Population age distribution (0-14/60+ years old, %)	19.3 / 14.0	19.6 / 15.8	20.5 / 20.3[a,b]
International migrant stock (000/% of total pop.)[j]	211.1 / 7.3	191.2 / 6.5	190.3 / 6.4[k]
Refugees and others of concern to the UNHCR (000)	85.8[l]	16.0	35.5[b]
Infant mortality rate (per 1 000 live births)	16.3	12.6	8.1[a,b]
Health: Current expenditure (% of GDP)	9.2	10.1	12.2[k]
Health: Physicians (per 1 000 pop.)	2.8	3.0	4.5[m]
Education: Government expenditure (% of GDP)	3.2	2.8	2.8[c]
Education: Primary gross enrol. ratio (f/m per 100 pop.)	100.7 / 97.7	95.8 / 94.3	91.4 / 90.9[c]
Education: Lowr. sec. gross enrol. ratio (f/m per 100 pop.)	106.9 / 107.5	... / ...	91.9 / 90.4[c]
Education: Upr. sec. gross enrol. ratio (f/m per 100 pop.)	97.7 / 101.7	95.0 / 85.3	87.2 / 82.4[c]
Intentional homicide rate (per 100 000 pop.)	1.9	2.6	2.2[c]
Seats held by women in the National Parliament (%)	9.2	10.7	35.5[n]

Environment and infrastructure indicators

	2010	2015	2023
Individuals using the Internet (per 100 inhabitants)	25.0[h]	59.1	78.6[c]
Research & Development expenditure (% of GDP)	0.2[o]	0.2[p,q]	0.2[p,q,c]
Threatened species (number)	36	111	116[b]
Forested area (% of land area)	11.6	11.6	11.5[b]
CO2 emission estimates (million tons/tons per capita)	4.1 / 1.4	5.2 / 1.7	7.0 / 2.1[c,k]
Energy production, primary (Petajoules)	39	45	42[k]
Energy supply per capita (Gigajoules)	36[h]	47	54[k]
Tourist/visitor arrivals at national borders (000)	684	1 192	870[c]
Important sites for terrestrial biodiversity protected (%)	21.6	22.6	22.6[b]
Pop. using safely managed sanitation (urban/rural %)	3.0 / ...	1.1 / ...	0.0 / ...[b]
Net Official Development Assist. received (% of GNI)	3.30	3.16	1.21[c]

a Projected estimate (medium fertility variant). b 2022. c 2021. d 2019. e Data classified according to ISIC Rev. 4. f Excludes irrigation canals and landscaping care. g Excludes publishing activities, recycling. Includes irrigation canals. h Estimate. i Data refers to a 5-year period preceding the reference year. j Including refugees. k 2020. l Data as at the end of December. m 2017. n Data are as at 1 January of reporting year. o Partial data. p Excluding business enterprise. q Excluding private non-profit.

Aruba

Region	Caribbean	Population (000, 2023)	106[a,b]
Surface area (km2)	180[c]	Pop. density (per km2, 2023)	591.4[a,b]
Sex ratio (m per 100 f)	89.2[a,b]	Capital city	Oranjestad
National currency	Aruban Florin (AWG)	Capital city pop. (000, 2023)	29.9[d]
Exchange rate (per US$)	1.8[b]		

Economic indicators

	2010	2015	2023
GDP: Gross domestic product (million current US$)	2 454	2 963	3 126[c]
GDP growth rate (annual %, const. 2015 prices)	- 2.8	3.6	17.2[c]
GDP per capita (current US$)	24 452.6	28 419.2	29 342.1[c]
Economy: Agriculture (% of Gross Value Added)[e,f,g]	~0.0	~0.0	~0.0[c]
Economy: Industry (% of Gross Value Added)[e,h]	12.8	10.5	10.5[c]
Economy: Services and other activity (% of GVA)[e]	87.2	89.5	89.5[c]
Employment in agriculture (% of employed)[i,k]	0.6[j]	0.6[l]	...
Employment in industry (% of employed)[i,k]	14.5[j]	14.0[l]	...
Employment in services & other sectors (% employed)[i,k]	84.4[j]	85.1[l]	...
Unemployment rate (% of labour force)	10.6[j,k]	...	...
Labour force participation rate (female/male pop. %)	59.5 / 68.9[j,k,m]	58.8 / 69.6[k,l]	... / ...
CPI: Consumer Price Index (2010=100)[n]	100	103	115[b]
International trade: exports (million current US$)	125	80	105[o,b]
International trade: imports (million current US$)	1 071	1 165	1 475[o,b]
International trade: balance (million current US$)	- 947	- 1 085	- 1 370[o,b]
Balance of payments, current account (million US$)	- 460	111	389[b]

Major trading partners

						2022
Export partners (% of exports)[o]	Colombia	49.3	United States	22.9	Curaçao	9.6
Import partners (% of imports)[o]	United States	50.6	Netherlands	15.5	Areas nes[p]	10.9

Social indicators

	2010	2015	2023
Population growth rate (average annual %)	1.0	0.6	- 0.2[a,b]
Urban population (% of total population)	43.1	43.1	43.5[q]
Urban population growth rate (average annual %)[r]	- 0.5	0.5	...
Fertility rate, total (live births per woman)	1.9	2.0	1.2[a,b]
Life expectancy at birth (females/males, years)	78.6 / 72.1	78.6 / 72.6	77.7 / 72.1[a,b]
Population age distribution (0-14/60+ years old, %)	20.7 / 14.7	18.8 / 18.2	16.2 / 23.9[a,b]
International migrant stock (000/% of total pop.)[s]	34.3 / 33.8	36.1 / 34.6	53.6 / 50.2[t]
Refugees and others of concern to the UNHCR (000)	~0.0[u]	~0.0	17.0[b]
Infant mortality rate (per 1 000 live births)	15.5	14.2	12.6[a,b]
Education: Government expenditure (% of GDP)	6.8	5.9	5.5[v]
Education: Primary gross enrol. ratio (f/m per 100 pop.)	113.0 / 114.5	112.9 / 117.0	... / ...
Education: Lowr. sec. gross enrol. ratio (f/m per 100 pop.)	109.0 / 116.5	119.9 / 117.3[w]	... / ...
Education: Upr. sec. gross enrol. ratio (f/m per 100 pop.)	91.2 / 78.5	107.0 / 105.6[w]	... / ...
Intentional homicide rate (per 100 000 pop.)	4.0	1.9[x]	...

Environment and infrastructure indicators

	2010	2015	2023
Individuals using the Internet (per 100 inhabitants)[o]	62.0	88.7	97.2[y]
Threatened species (number)	22	29	86[b]
Forested area (% of land area)	2.3	2.3	2.3[t]
Energy production, primary (Petajoules)[o]	5	1	1[t]
Energy supply per capita (Gigajoules)[o]	558	122	120[t]
Tourist/visitor arrivals at national borders (000)[z]	824	1 225	807[c]
Important sites for terrestrial biodiversity protected (%)	37.1	37.1	37.1[b]

a Projected estimate (medium fertility variant). b 2022. c 2021. d 2018. e Data classified according to ISIC Rev. 4. f Excludes irrigation canals and landscaping care. g Includes mining and quarrying. h Excludes publishing activities, recycling. Includes irrigation canals. i Data classified according to ISIC Rev. 3. j Population aged 14 years and over. k Break in the time series. l 2011. m Resident population (de jure). n Calculated by the UN Statistics Division from national indices. o Estimate. p Areas not elsewhere specified. q 2019. r Data refers to a 5-year period preceding the reference year. s Including refugees. t 2020. u Data as at the end of December. v 2016. w 2012. x 2014. y 2017. z Arrivals by air.

Australia

Region	Oceania	UN membership date	01 November 1945
Population (000, 2023)	26 177 [a,b,c]	Surface area (km2)	7 692 024 [d,e]
Pop. density (per km2, 2023)	3.4 [a,b,c]	Sex ratio (m per 100 f)	98.6 [a,b,c]
Capital city	Canberra	National currency	Australian Dollar (AUD)
Capital city pop. (000, 2023)	452.5 [f,g]	Exchange rate (per US$)	1.5 [c]

Economic indicators

	2010	2015	2023
GDP: Gross domestic product (million current US$)	1 301 097	1 245 248	1 734 532 [e]
GDP growth rate (annual %, const. 2015 prices)	2.4	2.7	3.6 [e]
GDP per capita (current US$)	59 089.3	52 276.9	66 915.9 [e]
Economy: Agriculture (% of Gross Value Added) [h,i]	2.5	2.6	3.4 [e]
Economy: Industry (% of Gross Value Added) [i,j]	28.4	24.0	29.8 [e]
Economy: Services and other activity (% of GVA) [i]	69.2	73.4	66.8 [e]
Employment in agriculture (% of employed)	3.2	2.6	2.4 [e]
Employment in industry (% of employed)	18.1 [k]	20.0	18.7 [e]
Employment in services & other sectors (% employed)	75.8	77.3	78.8 [e]
Unemployment rate (% of labour force)	5.2	6.0	3.5 [k]
Labour force participation rate (female/male pop. %)	58.6 / 72.3	59.1 / 71.1	61.2 / 70.2 [k]
CPI: Consumer Price Index (2010=100) [m,n]	100 [l]	112	132 [c]
Agricultural production index (2014-2016=100)	86	100	105 [e]
International trade: exports (million current US$)	212 109	187 792	410 253 [c]
International trade: imports (million current US$)	201 703	200 114	309 300 [c]
International trade: balance (million current US$)	10 405	- 12 322	100 953 [c]
Balance of payments, current account (million US$)	- 44 714	- 56 959	19 548 [c]

Major trading partners   2022

Export partners (% of exports) [k]	China	30.0	Japan	20.9	Republic of Korea	8.5
Import partners (% of imports) [k]	China	27.2	United States	10.6	Republic of Korea	6.3

Social indicators

	2010	2015	2023
Population growth rate (average annual %) [a]	1.5	1.5	1.0 [b,c]
Urban population (% of total population) [a]	85.2	85.7	86.1 [g]
Urban population growth rate (average annual %) [a,o]	1.9	1.6	...
Fertility rate, total (live births per woman) [a]	2.0	1.8	1.6 [b,c]
Life expectancy at birth (females/males, years) [a]	84.2 / 79.8	84.7 / 80.6	85.5 / 81.7 [b,c]
Population age distribution (0-14/60+ years old, %) [a]	19.1 / 19.0	18.9 / 20.3	18.2 / 22.6 [b,c]
International migrant stock (000/% of total pop.) [a]	5 883.0 / 26.6	6 729.7 / 28.1	7 685.9 / 30.1 [p]
Refugees and others of concern to the UNHCR (000)	25.6 [q]	58.4	148.1 [r,c]
Infant mortality rate (per 1 000 live births) [a]	4.1	3.1	2.8 [b,c]
Health: Current expenditure (% of GDP)	8.4	10.2	10.6 [p]
Health: Physicians (per 1 000 pop.)	3.4	3.5	4.1 [p]
Education: Government expenditure (% of GDP)	5.5	5.3	5.1 [g]
Education: Primary gross enrol. ratio (f/m per 100 pop.)	105.5 / 105.7	101.6 / 101.6	98.9 / 99.1 [p]
Education: Lowr. sec. gross enrol. ratio (f/m per 100 pop.)	... / ...	116.5 / 130.9	106.6 / 111.4 [p]
Education: Upr. sec. gross enrol. ratio (f/m per 100 000 pop.)	... / ...	202.7 / 239.8	184.6 / 190.6 [p]
Intentional homicide rate (per 100 000 pop.)	1.0	1.0	0.7 [e]
Seats held by women in the National Parliament (%)	27.3	26.7	38.4 [s]

Environment and infrastructure indicators

	2010	2015	2023
Individuals using the Internet (per 100 inhabitants)	76.0 [k]	84.6 [t]	96.2 [k,e]
Research & Development expenditure (% of GDP) [k]	2.4	1.9	1.8 [g]
Threatened species (number) [u]	853	909	1 871 [c]
Forested area (% of land area)	16.9	17.3	17.4 [p]
CO2 emission estimates (million tons/tons per capita) [u,v]	396.2 / 17.8	384.9 / 16.0	382.7 / 14.7 [e]
Energy production, primary (Petajoules) [u]	13 646	16 033	18 950 [p]
Energy supply per capita (Gigajoules) [u]	245	224	215 [p]
Tourist/visitor arrivals at national borders (000) [w]	5 790	7 449	246 [e]
Important sites for terrestrial biodiversity protected (%)	45.5	51.8	57.3 [c]
Pop. using safely managed drinking water (urban/rural, %)	99.3 / ...	99.7 / ...	99.5 / ... [c]
Net Official Development Assist. disbursed (% of GNI) [x]	1.23	1.15	0.22 [e]

a Including Christmas Island, Cocos (Keeling) Islands and Norfolk Island. **b** Projected estimate (medium fertility variant). **c** 2022. **d** Including Norfolk Island. **e** 2021. **f** Refers to Significant Urban Areas as of 2001. **g** 2019. **h** Excludes irrigation canals and landscaping care. **i** Data classified according to ISIC Rev. 4. **j** Excludes publishing activities, recycling. Includes irrigation canals. **k** Estimate. **l** Break in the time series. **m** Weighted average of index values computed for the 8 capital cities. **n** Calculated by the UN Statistics Division from national indices. **o** Data refers to a 5-year period preceding the reference year. **p** 2020. **q** Data as at the end of December. **r** Refugee estimate methodology under review. **s** Data as at 1 January of reporting year. **t** Population aged 15 years and over. Accessed the internet for personal use in a typical week. **u** Excluding overseas territories. **v** Data refer to fiscal years beginning 1 July. **w** Excluding nationals residing abroad and crew members. **x** Development Assistance Committee member (OECD).

Austria

Region	Western Europe	UN membership date	14 December 1955
Population (000, 2023)	8 940[a,b]	Surface area (km2)	83 878[c]
Pop. density (per km2, 2023)	108.3[a,b]	Sex ratio (m per 100 f)	97.0[a,b]
Capital city	Vienna	National currency	Euro (EUR)
Capital city pop. (000, 2023)	1 915.3[d]	Exchange rate (per US$)	0.9[b]

Economic indicators

	2010	2015	2023
GDP: Gross domestic product (million current US$)	391 893	381 818	480 368[c]
GDP growth rate (annual %, const. 2015 prices)	1.8	1.0	4.6[c]
GDP per capita (current US$)	46 861.3	44 179.5	53 840.4[c]
Economy: Agriculture (% of Gross Value Added)[e,f]	1.4	1.3	1.4[c]
Economy: Industry (% of Gross Value Added)[e,g]	28.7	28.2	28.9[c]
Economy: Services and other activity (% of GVA)[e]	69.9	70.5	69.8[c]
Employment in agriculture (% of employed)	5.2	4.5	3.7[c]
Employment in industry (% of employed)	24.8	25.8	25.6[c]
Employment in services & other sectors (% employed)	69.9	69.7	70.6[c]
Unemployment rate (% of labour force)	4.8	5.7	4.8[h]
Labour force participation rate (female/male pop. %)	54.2 / 67.1	55.4 / 66.4	55.9 / 66.8[h]
CPI: Consumer Price Index (2010=100)	100	111	134[b]
Agricultural production index (2014-2016=100)	95	97	100[c]
International trade: exports (million current US$)	144 882	145 276	210 279[b]
International trade: imports (million current US$)	150 593	147 928	231 947[b]
International trade: balance (million current US$)	- 5 711	- 2 652	- 21 667[b]
Balance of payments, current account (million US$)	11 472	6 634	1 627[c]

Major trading partners   2022

Export partners (% of exports)	Germany	29.3	Italy	6.6	United States	6.3
Import partners (% of imports)	Germany	40.2	Italy	6.6	Czechia	4.9

Social indicators

	2010	2015	2023
Population growth rate (average annual %)	0.3	1.3	0.2[a,b]
Urban population (% of total population)	57.4	57.7	58.5[d]
Urban population growth rate (average annual %)[i]	- 0.1	0.7	...
Fertility rate, total (live births per woman)	1.4	1.5	1.5[a,b]
Life expectancy at birth (females/males, years)	83.1 / 77.7	83.6 / 78.6	84.6 / 80.2[a,b]
Population age distribution (0-14/60+ years old, %)	14.8 / 23.2	14.3 / 24.0	14.4 / 26.7[a,b]
International migrant stock (000/% of total pop.)	1 274.9 / 15.2	1 483.1 / 17.1	1 738.2 / 19.3[j]
Refugees and others of concern to the UNHCR (000)	68.7[k]	92.2[l]	269.2[b]
Infant mortality rate (per 1 000 live births)	4.0	3.1	2.5[a,b]
Health: Current expenditure (% of GDP)[h]	10.2	10.4	12.2[c]
Health: Physicians (per 1 000 pop.)	4.8	5.1	5.5[c]
Education: Government expenditure (% of GDP)	5.7	5.5	5.2[d]
Education: Primary gross enrol. ratio (f/m per 100 pop.)	99.1 / 100.4	101.5 / 102.4	102.2 / 102.8[j]
Education: Lowr. sec. gross enrol. ratio (f/m per 100 pop.)	101.8 / 102.0	99.7 / 100.5	101.5 / 101.3[j]
Education: Upr. sec. gross enrol. ratio (f/m per 100 pop.)	92.3 / 99.6	97.3 / 103.6	97.4 / 101.3[j]
Intentional homicide rate (per 100 000 pop.)	0.7	0.5	0.7[c]
Seats held by women in the National Parliament (%)	27.9	30.6	40.4[m]

Environment and infrastructure indicators

	2010	2015	2023
Individuals using the Internet (per 100 inhabitants)[n]	75.2	83.9[o]	92.5[c]
Research & Development expenditure (% of GDP)	2.7[h]	3.0	3.2[h,p,j]
Threatened species (number)	82	106	227[b]
Forested area (% of land area)	46.8	47.0	47.3[j]
CO2 emission estimates (million tons/tons per capita)	70.1 / 8.2	63.3 / 7.1	61.9 / 6.7[c]
Energy production, primary (Petajoules)	500	501	501[j]
Energy supply per capita (Gigajoules)	171	159	148[j]
Tourist/visitor arrivals at national borders (000)[q]	22 004	26 728	12 728[c]
Important sites for terrestrial biodiversity protected (%)	65.5	67.4	67.9[b]
Pop. using safely managed sanitation (urban/rural %)	100.0 / 99.3	100.0 / 99.3	100.0 / 99.3[b]
Net Official Development Assist. disbursed (% of GNI)[r]	1.70	1.25	0.45[c]

a Projected estimate (medium fertility variant). **b** 2022. **c** 2021. **d** 2019. **e** Data classified according to ISIC Rev. 4. **f** Excludes irrigation canals and landscaping care. **g** Excludes publishing activities, recycling. Includes irrigation canals. **h** Estimate. **i** Data refers to a 5-year period preceding the reference year. **j** 2020. **k** Data as at the end of December. **l** Data relates to the end of 2014. **m** Data are as at 1 January of reporting year. **n** Population aged 16 to 74 years. **o** Users in the last 3 months. **p** Provisional data. **q** Only paid accommodation; excluding stays at friends and relatives and second homes. **r** Development Assistance Committee member (OECD).

Azerbaijan

Region	Western Asia	UN membership date	02 March 1992
Population (000, 2023)	10 358[a,b,c]	Surface area (km2)	86 600[d]
Pop. density (per km2, 2023)	125.3[a,b,c]	Sex ratio (m per 100 f)	97.4[a,b,c]
Capital city	Baku	National currency	Azerbaijan manat (AZN)
Capital city pop. (000, 2023)	2 313.1[e,f]	Exchange rate (per US$)	1.7[c]

Economic indicators

	2010	2015	2023
GDP: Gross domestic product (million current US$)	52 906	53 076	54 622[d]
GDP growth rate (annual %, const. 2015 prices)	5.0	1.1	5.6[d]
GDP per capita (current US$)	5 727.5	5 381.1	5 296.4[d]
Economy: Agriculture (% of Gross Value Added)[g,h]	5.9	6.8	6.4[d]
Economy: Industry (% of Gross Value Added)[h,i]	64.1	49.3	52.9[d]
Economy: Services and other activity (% of GVA)[h]	30.0	43.9	40.7[d]
Employment in agriculture (% of employed)	38.2	36.4	34.2[j,d]
Employment in industry (% of employed)	13.6	14.0	15.5[j,d]
Employment in services & other sectors (% employed)	48.1	49.6	50.4[j,d]
Unemployment rate (% of labour force)	5.6	5.0	5.4[j]
Labour force participation rate (female/male pop. %)	59.7 / 62.2[j]	61.0 / 66.1	63.0 / 68.5[j]
CPI: Consumer Price Index (2010=100)	100	118	196[c]
Agricultural production index (2014-2016=100)	86	101	131[d]
International trade: exports (million current US$)	21 278	12 646	38 146[c]
International trade: imports (million current US$)	6 597	9 214	14 536[c]
International trade: balance (million current US$)	14 682	3 432	23 611[c]
Balance of payments, current account (million US$)	15 040	- 222	23 478[c]

Major trading partners

						2022
Export partners (% of exports)	Italy	46.6	Türkiye	9.3[j]	Israel	4.4
Import partners (% of imports)	Russian Federation	18.8	Türkiye	15.8	China	14.4

Social indicators

	2010	2015	2023
Population growth rate (average annual %)[a]	1.3	1.2	0.6[b,c]
Urban population (% of total population)[a]	53.4	54.7	56.0[f]
Urban population growth rate (average annual %)[a,k]	1.5	1.7	...
Fertility rate, total (live births per woman)[a]	2.1	2.1	1.7[b,c]
Life expectancy at birth (females/males, years)[a]	72.8 / 66.3	74.8 / 68.1	76.2 / 70.6[b,c]
Population age distribution (0-14/60+ years old, %)[a]	23.9 / 7.9	24.4 / 8.8	23.5 / 12.5[b,c]
International migrant stock (000/% of total pop.)[a,l]	276.9 / 3.1	264.4 / 2.7	252.2 / 2.5[m]
Refugees and others of concern to the UNHCR (000)	596.9[n]	628.1	665.0[c]
Infant mortality rate (per 1 000 live births)[a]	32.3	23.1	16.4[b,c]
Health: Current expenditure (% of GDP)	2.5	4.1	4.6[m]
Health: Physicians (per 1 000 pop.)	3.6	3.3	3.1[f]
Education: Government expenditure (% of GDP)	2.8	3.0	3.5[d]
Education: Primary gross enrol. ratio (f/m per 100 pop.)[j]	93.2 / 94.2	105.6 / 107.4	94.8 / 93.9[d]
Education: Lowr. sec. gross enrol. ratio (f/m per 100 pop.)[j]	90.5 / 92.9	89.2 / 91.7	102.5 / 103.0[d]
Education: Upr. sec. gross enrol. ratio (f/m per 100 pop.)	... / ...	... / ...	74.7 / 78.0[j,d]
Intentional homicide rate (per 100 000 pop.)	2.2	2.1	1.9[d]
Seats held by women in the National Parliament (%)	11.4	15.6	18.6[o]

Environment and infrastructure indicators

	2010	2015	2023
Individuals using the Internet (per 100 inhabitants)	46.0[p]	77.0	86.0[d]
Research & Development expenditure (% of GDP)	0.2	0.2	0.2[d]
Threatened species (number)	45	92	102[c]
Forested area (% of land area)	12.5	13.0	13.7[m]
CO2 emission estimates (million tons/tons per capita)	23.6 / 2.6	30.8 / 3.2	36.5 / 3.3[d,m]
Energy production, primary (Petajoules)	2 759	2 474	2 412[m]
Energy supply per capita (Gigajoules)	53	61	63[m]
Tourist/visitor arrivals at national borders (000)	1 280	1 922	587[m]
Important sites for terrestrial biodiversity protected (%)	36.1	36.1	36.6[c]
Pop. using safely managed drinking water (urban/rural, %)	90.7 / 58.0	91.5 / 72.6	92.3 / 81.1[c]
Pop. using safely managed sanitation (urban/rural %)	48.7 / ...	56.5 / ...	63.0 / ...[c]
Net Official Development Assist. disbursed (% of GNI)	...	...	0.10[m]
Net Official Development Assist. received (% of GNI)	0.32	0.14	0.02[d]

a Including Nagorno-Karabakh. b Projected estimate (medium fertility variant). c 2022. d 2021. e Including communities under the authority of the Town Council. f 2019. g Excludes irrigation canals and landscaping care. h Data classified according to ISIC Rev. 4. i Excludes publishing activities, recycling. Includes irrigation canals. j Estimate. k Data refers to a 5-year period preceding the reference year. l Including refugees. m 2020. n Data as at the end of December. o Data are as at 1 January of reporting year. p Population aged 7 years and over.

Bahamas

Region	Caribbean	UN membership date	18 September 1973	
Population (000, 2023)	410 a,b	Surface area (km2)	13 940 c	
Pop. density (per km2, 2023)	76.5 a,b	Sex ratio (m per 100 f)	91.4 a,b	
Capital city	Nassau	National currency	Bahamian Dollar (BSD)	
Capital city pop. (000, 2023)	279.7 d	Exchange rate (per US$)	1.0 b	

Economic indicators	2010	2015	2023
GDP: Gross domestic product (million current US$)	10 096	11 862	11 209 c
GDP growth rate (annual %, const. 2015 prices)	1.5	1.0	13.7 c
GDP per capita (current US$)	27 046.8	30 206.2	27 478.4 c
Economy: Agriculture (% of Gross Value Added) e	1.2	0.9	0.5 c
Economy: Industry (% of Gross Value Added) f,g	12.3	12.5	12.5 c
Economy: Services and other activity (% of GVA) g	86.6	86.6	87.0 c
Employment in agriculture (% of employed) h	3.3	3.6	3.2 c
Employment in industry (% of employed) h	14.5	11.6	11.7 c
Employment in services & other sectors (% employed) h	82.2	84.9	85.1 c
Unemployment rate (% of labour force)	14.3 h	12.0	9.6 h
Labour force participation rate (female/male pop. %) h	67.4 / 81.7	66.7 / 81.3	66.3 / 79.3
CPI: Consumer Price Index (2010=100) h	100	110	126 b
Agricultural production index (2014-2016=100)	93	100	100 c
International trade: exports (million current US$)	620	443	1 958 h,b
International trade: imports (million current US$)	2 862	3 161	5 102 h,b
International trade: balance (million current US$)	- 2 242	- 2 719	- 3 144 h,b
Balance of payments, current account (million US$)	- 814	- 1 203	- 2 592 c

Major trading partners						2022
Export partners (% of exports) h	United States	81.7	France	6.2	Areas nes	5.2
Import partners (% of imports) h	United States	79.8	Areas nes i	2.8	Canada	2.3

Social indicators	2010	2015	2023
Population growth rate (average annual %)	1.4	0.9	0.7 a,b
Urban population (% of total population)	82.4	82.7	83.1 j
Urban population growth rate (average annual %) k	1.9	1.5	...
Fertility rate, total (live births per woman)	1.8	1.6	1.4 a,b
Life expectancy at birth (females/males, years)	76.1 / 69.3	76.4 / 69.8	77.8 / 70.8 a,b
Population age distribution (0-14/60+ years old, %)	26.4 / 9.1	23.3 / 10.5	19.1 / 13.9 a,b
International migrant stock (000/% of total pop.) l	54.7 / 15.4	59.2 / 15.8	63.6 / 16.2 m
Refugees and others of concern to the UNHCR (000)	-0.0 n	0.1	-0.0 b
Infant mortality rate (per 1 000 live births)	13.4	12.4	10.1 a,b
Health: Current expenditure (% of GDP) h,o,p	5.3	5.1	7.6 m
Health: Physicians (per 1 000 pop.)	2.6 q	2.2 r	1.9 s
Education: Government expenditure (% of GDP)	...	2.2	2.8 b
Education: Primary gross enrol. ratio (f/m per 100 pop.)	94.5 / 97.6 t	... / ...	... / ...
Education: Lowr. sec. gross enrol. ratio (f/m per 100 pop.)	92.5 / 91.1	79.3 / 77.2 u	... / ...
Education: Upr. sec. gross enrol. ratio (f/m per 100 pop.)	89.8 / 84.0	78.5 / 72.6 u	... / ...
Intentional homicide rate (per 100 000 pop.)	25.2	37.2	29.2 c
Seats held by women in the National Parliament (%)	12.2	13.2	18.0 v

Environment and infrastructure indicators	2010	2015	2023
Individuals using the Internet (per 100 inhabitants) h	43.0	78.0	94.3 c
Threatened species (number)	62	81	143 b
Forested area (% of land area)	50.9	50.9	50.9 m
Energy production, primary (Petajoules)	0	0	0 m
Energy supply per capita (Gigajoules)	87	83	77 m
Tourist/visitor arrivals at national borders (000)	1 378	1 496	891 c
Important sites for terrestrial biodiversity protected (%)	11.2	29.8	29.8 b

a Projected estimate (medium fertility variant). b 2022. c 2021. d 2018. e Excludes irrigation canals and landscaping care. Data classified according to ISIC Rev. 4. f Excludes publishing activities, recycling. Includes irrigation canals. g Data classified according to ISIC Rev. 4. h Estimate. i Areas not elsewhere specified. j 2019. k Data refers to a 5-year period preceding the reference year. l Including refugees. m 2020. n Data as at the end of December. o Data refer to fiscal years beginning 1 July. p Estimates should be viewed with caution as these are derived from scarce data. q 2008. r 2011. s 2017. t 2006. u 2013. v Data are as at 1 January of reporting year.

Bahrain

Region	Western Asia	UN membership date	21 September 1971
Population (000, 2023)	1 472[a,b]	Surface area (km2)	778[c]
Pop. density (per km2, 2023)	1 880.2[a,b]	Sex ratio (m per 100 f)	162.9[a,b]
Capital city	Manama	National currency	Bahraini Dinar (BHD)
Capital city pop. (000, 2023)	600.4[d,e]	Exchange rate (per US$)	0.4[b]

Economic indicators

	2010	2015	2023
GDP: Gross domestic product (million current US$)	25 713	31 051	38 869[c]
GDP growth rate (annual %, const. 2015 prices)	4.3	2.5	2.2[c]
GDP per capita (current US$)	21 186.8	22 795.4	26 563.0[c]
Economy: Agriculture (% of Gross Value Added)[f]	0.3	0.3	0.3[c]
Economy: Industry (% of Gross Value Added)[f]	45.5	40.7	42.7[c]
Economy: Services and other activity (% of GVA)	54.2	59.0	57.0[c]
Employment in agriculture (% of employed)	1.1	1.1	1.0[g,c]
Employment in industry (% of employed)	35.8	35.1	34.9[g,c]
Employment in services & other sectors (% employed)	63.2	63.8	64.1[g,c]
Unemployment rate (% of labour force)	1.1	1.2[g]	1.4[g]
Labour force participation rate (female/male pop. %)	43.6 / 87.0	43.0 / 86.2	44.7 / 86.8[g]
CPI: Consumer Price Index (2010=100)[h]	100	111	120[b]
Agricultural production index (2014-2016=100)	37	99	128[c]
International trade: exports (million current US$)	16 059	13 882	22 252[b]
International trade: imports (million current US$)	16 002	16 390	15 535[b]
International trade: balance (million current US$)	58	- 2 508	6 718[b]
Balance of payments, current account (million US$)	770	- 752	- 2 435[i]

Major trading partners

2022

Export partners (% of exports)	Areas nes[j]	32.0[g]	Saudi Arabia	13.7[g]	United States	8.6
Import partners (% of imports)	China	14.5	Brazil	10.6[g]	Australia	8.7

Social indicators

	2010	2015	2023
Population growth rate (average annual %)	0.0	3.5	0.9[a,b]
Urban population (% of total population)	88.6	89.0	89.4[e]
Urban population growth rate (average annual %)[k]	6.7	2.1	...
Fertility rate, total (live births per woman)	2.1	2.1	1.8[a,b]
Life expectancy at birth (females/males, years)	80.0 / 77.7	80.8 / 78.3	80.5 / 78.2[a,b]
Population age distribution (0-14/60+ years old, %)	20.5 / 3.5	20.4 / 5.0	20.2 / 6.9[a,b]
International migrant stock (000/% of total pop.)[l,m]	666.4 / 53.7	722.5 / 52.7	936.1 / 55.0[n]
Refugees and others of concern to the UNHCR (000)	0.2[o]	0.4	0.4[b]
Infant mortality rate (per 1 000 live births)	7.3	6.5	5.4[a,b]
Health: Current expenditure (% of GDP)[p]	4.1	5.0[q]	4.2[q,n]
Health: Physicians (per 1 000 pop.)	1.0	0.9	0.8[r]
Education: Government expenditure (% of GDP)	2.5[s]	2.7	2.3[t]
Education: Primary gross enrol. ratio (f/m per 100 pop.)	101.0 / 96.1[u]	101.7 / 100.7	97.7 / 98.3[e]
Education: Lower. sec. gross enrol. ratio (f/m per 100 pop.)	94.1 / 95.7	99.5 / 103.4	101.2 / 95.5[e]
Education: Upr. sec. gross enrol. ratio (f/m per 100 pop.)	92.9 / 88.5	104.2 / 101.5	101.9 / 90.9[e]
Intentional homicide rate (per 100 000 pop.)	0.2	0.2	0.1[c]
Seats held by women in the National Parliament (%)	2.5	7.5	20.0[v]

Environment and infrastructure indicators

	2010	2015	2023
Individuals using the Internet (per 100 inhabitants)	55.0	93.5	100.0[g,c]
Research & Development expenditure (% of GDP)	...	0.1[w]	...
Threatened species (number)	32	32	63[b]
Forested area (% of land area)	0.7	0.8	0.9[n]
CO2 emission estimates (million tons/tons per capita)	25.6 / 20.6	30.2 / 21.9	32.2 / 18.9[n]
Energy production, primary (Petajoules)	849	957	1 045[n]
Energy supply per capita (Gigajoules)	423	424	451[n]
Tourist/visitor arrivals at national borders (000)[x]	11 952	9 670[y]	3 612[c]
Important sites for terrestrial biodiversity protected (%)	0.0	0.0	0.0[b]

a Projected estimate (medium fertility variant). b 2022. c 2021. d Refers to the urban area of the municipality of Al-Manamah. e 2019. f At producers' prices. g Estimate. h Calculated by the UN Statistics Division from national indices. i 2018. j Areas not elsewhere specified. k Data refers to a 5-year period preceding the reference year. l Including refugees. m Refers to foreign citizens. n 2020. o Data as at the end of December. p Data based on calendar year (January 1 to December 31). q Data are based on SHA2011. r 2016. s 2008. t 2017. u 2006. v Data are as at 1 January of reporting year. w 2014. x Excluding nationals residing abroad. y Break in the time series.

Bangladesh

Region	Southern Asia	UN membership date	17 September 1974
Population (000, 2023)	171 186 [a,b]	Surface area (km2)	148 460 [c]
Pop. density (per km2, 2023)	1 315.1 [a,b]	Sex ratio (m per 100 f)	98.3 [a,b]
Capital city	Dhaka	National currency	Taka (BDT)
Capital city pop. (000, 2023)	20 283.6 [d,e]	Exchange rate (per US$)	99.0 [b]

Economic indicators	2010	2015	2023
GDP: Gross domestic product (million current US$)	123 085	228 785	414 907 [c]
GDP growth rate (annual %, const. 2015 prices)	7.5	8.5	6.9 [c]
GDP per capita (current US$)	829.5	1 449.6	2 449.9 [c]
Economy: Agriculture (% of Gross Value Added) [f]	17.6	14.7	12.1 [g,c]
Economy: Industry (% of Gross Value Added) [f]	27.6	31.1	34.6 [h,c]
Economy: Services and other activity (% of GVA) [f]	54.8	54.3	53.3 [c]
Employment in agriculture (% of employed)	47.3	43.5 [i]	37.1 [i,c]
Employment in industry (% of employed)	17.6	20.5 [i]	21.7 [i,c]
Employment in services & other sectors (% employed)	35.1	36.0 [i]	41.2 [i,c]
Unemployment rate (% of labour force)	3.4	4.4 [i]	4.7 [i]
Labour force participation rate (female/male pop. %) [i]	30.8 / 84.2	32.8 / 80.4	37.7 / 80.5
CPI: Consumer Price Index (2010=100) [j]	100	145	216 [b]
Agricultural production index (2014-2016=100)	90	101	117 [c]
International trade: exports (million current US$)	19 231	31 734	46 851 [i,b]
International trade: imports (million current US$)	30 504	48 059	80 162 [i,b]
International trade: balance (million current US$)	- 11 273	- 16 325	- 33 311 [i,b]
Balance of payments, current account (million US$)	2 108	2 580	- 14 370 [b]

Major trading partners						2022
Export partners (% of exports) [i]	United States	17.8	Germany	15.8	United Kingdom	7.3
Import partners (% of imports) [i]	China	30.7	India	15.8	Singapore	5.5

Social indicators	2010	2015	2023
Population growth rate (average annual %)	1.2	1.2	1.0 [a,b]
Urban population (% of total population)	30.5	34.3	37.4 [e]
Urban population growth rate (average annual %) [k]	3.7	3.5	...
Fertility rate, total (live births per woman)	2.3	2.1	2.0 [a,b]
Life expectancy at birth (females/males, years)	70.3 / 67.2	72.7 / 68.5	76.0 / 71.5 [a,b]
Population age distribution (0-14/60+ years old, %)	33.4 / 6.7	30.2 / 7.5	26.0 / 9.3 [a,b]
International migrant stock (000/% of total pop.) [i]	1 345.5 / 0.9	1 422.2 / 0.9	2 115.4 / 1.3 [m]
Refugees and others of concern to the UNHCR (000)	229.3 [n]	233.0	929.7 [b]
Infant mortality rate (per 1 000 live births)	39.0	30.9	20.4 [a,m]
Health: Current expenditure (% of GDP) [o]	2.7	2.7	2.6 [m]
Health: Physicians (per 1 000 pop.)	0.4	0.5	0.7 [c]
Education: Government expenditure (% of GDP)	1.9 [p]	1.9	1.8 [c]
Education: Primary gross enrol. ratio (f/m per 100 pop.)	109.3 / 102.8	107.2 / 105.5 [q]	117.1 / 114.9 [c]
Education: Lowr. sec. gross enrol. ratio (f/m per 100 pop.)	73.6 / 59.8	95.9 / 77.0	101.2 / 74.8 [c]
Education: Upr. sec. gross enrol. ratio (f/m per 100 pop.)	40.0 / 40.2	49.8 / 50.3	75.4 / 58.2 [c]
Intentional homicide rate (per 100 000 pop.)	2.7	2.6	2.3 [r]
Seats held by women in the National Parliament (%)	18.6	20.0	20.9 [s]

Environment and infrastructure indicators	2010	2015	2023
Individuals using the Internet (per 100 inhabitants)	3.7 [i]	12.9 [i]	38.9 [c]
Threatened species (number)	122	137	224 [b]
Forested area (% of land area)	14.5	14.5	14.5 [m]
CO2 emission estimates (million tons/tons per capita) [o]	53.2 / 0.3	75.5 / 0.5	87.5 / 0.5 [m]
Energy production, primary (Petajoules)	1 294	1 475	1 457 [m]
Energy supply per capita (Gigajoules)	10	11	12 [m]
Tourist/visitor arrivals at national borders (000)	139	126	135 [c]
Important sites for terrestrial biodiversity protected (%)	41.5	41.5	41.5 [b]
Pop. using safely managed drinking water (urban/rural, %)	42.4 / 60.6	47.1 / 61.3	54.2 / 62.4 [b]
Pop. using safely managed sanitation (urban/rural, %)	26.2 / 14.7	27.3 / 20.3	28.8 / 32.4 [b]
Net Official Development Assist. received (% of GNI)	1.06	1.25	1.16 [c]

a Projected estimate (medium fertility variant). b 2022. c 2021. d Mega city. e 2019. f Data classified according to ISIC Rev. 4. g Excludes irrigation canals and landscaping care. h Excludes publishing activities, recycling. Includes irrigation canals. i Estimate. j Calculated by the UN Statistics Division from national indices. k Data refers to a 5-year period preceding the reference year. l Including refugees. m 2020. n Data as at the end of December. o Data refer to fiscal years beginning 1 July. p 2009. q 2011. r 2018. s Data are as at 1 January of reporting year.

Barbados

Region	Caribbean
Population (000, 2023)	282[a,b]
Pop. density (per km2, 2023)	655.0[a,b]
Capital city	Bridgetown
Capital city pop. (000, 2023)	89.2[d]

UN membership date	09 December 1966
Surface area (km2)	431[c]
Sex ratio (m per 100 f)	92.2[a,b]
National currency	Barbados Dollar (BBD)
Exchange rate (per US$)	2.0[b]

Economic indicators

	2010	2015	2023
GDP: Gross domestic product (million current US$)	4 530	4 725	4 844[c]
GDP growth rate (annual %, const. 2015 prices)	- 2.3	2.5	- 0.2[c]
GDP per capita (current US$)	16 489.8	16 990.2	17 225.5[c]
Economy: Agriculture (% of Gross Value Added)[e,f]	1.5	1.5	1.7[c]
Economy: Industry (% of Gross Value Added)[e,g]	15.8	15.4	15.6[c]
Economy: Services and other activity (% of GVA)[e]	82.7	83.1	82.7[c]
Employment in agriculture (% of employed)	2.9	2.9	2.8[h,c]
Employment in industry (% of employed)	19.2[h]	19.4	16.6[h,c]
Employment in services & other sectors (% employed)	77.9[h]	77.8	80.6[h,c]
Unemployment rate (% of labour force)	10.7	9.8	7.6[h]
Labour force participation rate (female/male pop. %)	62.9 / 72.9[h]	60.8 / 67.5	57.9 / 63.9[h]
CPI: Consumer Price Index (2010=100)[j]	100[i]	168[k]	222[k,b]
Agricultural production index (2014-2016=100)	107	103	89[c]
International trade: exports (million current US$)	314	483	498[b]
International trade: imports (million current US$)	1 196	1 618	2 147[b]
International trade: balance (million current US$)	- 883	- 1 135	- 1 650[b]
Balance of payments, current account (million US$)	- 272	- 99	- 296[l]

Major trading partners

						2022
Export partners (% of exports)	Areas nes[m]	35.3	United States	17.1	Jamaica	7.3
Import partners (% of imports)	United States	40.2	Trinidad and Tobago	19.1	Netherlands	4.6

Social indicators

	2010	2015	2023
Population growth rate (average annual %)	0.3	0.2	0.1[a,b]
Urban population (% of total population)	31.9	31.2	31.2[n]
Urban population growth rate (average annual %)[o]	- 0.2	- 0.1	...
Fertility rate, total (live births per woman)	1.7	1.6	1.6[a,b]
Life expectancy at birth (females/males, years)	77.7 / 73.6	78.6 / 74.5	79.6 / 75.7[a,b]
Population age distribution (0-14/60+ years old, %)	20.1 / 16.6	18.8 / 18.7	16.9 / 23.1[a,b]
International migrant stock (000/% of total pop.)[p]	32.8 / 11.6	34.5 / 12.1	34.9 / 12.1[q]
Refugees and others of concern to the UNHCR (000)	...	~0.0	~0.0[c]
Infant mortality rate (per 1 000 live births)	13.5	12.7	10.4[a,b]
Health: Current expenditure (% of GDP)[h,r,s]	6.8	6.8	7.2[q]
Health: Physicians (per 1 000 pop.)	1.8[t]	...	2.6[l]
Education: Government expenditure (% of GDP)	6.1	5.4	5.9[b]
Education: Primary gross enrol. ratio (f/m per 100 pop.)	100.4 / 98.8[h]	95.6 / 96.2	96.9 / 99.7[c]
Education: Lowr. sec. gross enrol. ratio (f/m per 100 pop.)	97.2 / 101.7[h]	106.8 / 104.3	101.1 / 102.9[c]
Education: Upr. sec. gross enrol. ratio (f/m per 100 pop.)	109.4 / 101.7[h]	113.5 / 107.8	115.2 / 106.0[c]
Intentional homicide rate (per 100 000 pop.)	11.3	11.1	11.4[c]
Seats held by women in the National Parliament (%)	10.0	16.7	26.7[u]

Environment and infrastructure indicators

	2010	2015	2023
Individuals using the Internet (per 100 inhabitants)[h]	65.1	76.1	85.8[c]
Threatened species (number)	36	51	90[b]
Forested area (% of land area)	14.7	14.7	14.7[q]
Energy production, primary (Petajoules)	4	3	2[q]
Energy supply per capita (Gigajoules)	93	81	60[q]
Tourist/visitor arrivals at national borders (000)	532	592	144[c]
Important sites for terrestrial biodiversity protected (%)	1.8	1.8	1.8[b]
Net Official Development Assist. received (% of GNI)	0.35	...	...

a Projected estimate (medium fertility variant). b 2022. c 2021. d 2018. e Data classified according to ISIC Rev. 4. f Excludes irrigation canals and landscaping care. g Excludes publishing activities, recycling. Includes irrigation canals. h Estimate. i Calculated by the UN Statistics Division from national indices. j Data refer to the Retail Price Index. k Index base: July 2001=100. l 2017. m Areas not elsewhere specified. n 2019. o Data refers to a 5-year period preceding the reference year. p Including refugees. q 2020. r Data refer to fiscal years beginning 1 April. s Estimates should be viewed with caution as these are derived from scarce data. t 2005. u Data are as at 1 January of reporting year.

Belarus

Region	Eastern Europe	UN membership date	24 October 1945
Population (000, 2023)	9 535 a,b	Surface area (km2)	207 600 c
Pop. density (per km2, 2023)	47.0 a,b	Sex ratio (m per 100 f)	85.3 a,b
Capital city	Minsk	National currency	Belarusian Ruble (BYN)
Capital city pop. (000, 2023)	2 016.7 d,e	Exchange rate (per US$)	2.7 b

Economic indicators

	2010	2015	2023
GDP: Gross domestic product (million current US$)	57 232	56 455	68 206 c
GDP growth rate (annual %, const. 2015 prices)	7.8	- 3.8	2.3 c
GDP per capita (current US$)	5 881.1	5 819.7	7 121.0 c
Economy: Agriculture (% of Gross Value Added) f,g	10.1	7.2	7.8 c
Economy: Industry (% of Gross Value Added) g,h	40.3	37.7	36.8 c
Economy: Services and other activity (% of GVA) g	49.5	55.1	55.4 c
Employment in agriculture (% of employed)	12.5 i	9.7	8.1 i,c
Employment in industry (% of employed)	32.2 i	31.1	32.5 i,c
Employment in services & other sectors (% employed)	55.3 i	59.3	59.3 i,c
Unemployment rate (% of labour force) i	6.3	5.8	4.4
Labour force participation rate (female/male pop. %) i	57.0 / 68.9	58.2 / 70.3	57.1 / 69.5
CPI: Consumer Price Index (2010=100)	100 i	387	676 b
Agricultural production index (2014-2016=100)	97	100	103 c
International trade: exports (million current US$)	25 283	26 660	34 261 i,b
International trade: imports (million current US$)	34 884	30 291	45 463 i,b
International trade: balance (million current US$)	- 9 601	- 3 631	- 11 203 i,b
Balance of payments, current account (million US$)	- 8 280	- 1 831	2 677 b

Major trading partners

					2022
Export partners (% of exports) i	Areas nes j	40.3	Russian Federation	35.0	Poland 4.0
Import partners (% of imports) i	Areas nes j	37.0	Russian Federation	28.6	China 8.1

Social indicators

	2010	2015	2023
Population growth rate (average annual %)	- 0.3	0.1	- 0.3 a,b
Urban population (% of total population)	74.7	77.2	79.0 e
Urban population growth rate (average annual %) k	0.3	0.7	...
Fertility rate, total (live births per woman)	1.5	1.7	1.5 a,b
Life expectancy at birth (females/males, years)	77.0 / 65.5	78.8 / 68.9	78.4 / 68.1 a,b
Population age distribution (0-14/60+ years old, %)	14.9 / 19.7	16.3 / 21.4	16.8 / 24.5 a,b
International migrant stock (000/% of total pop.)	1 090.4 / 11.6	1 082.9 / 11.5	1 067.1 / 11.3 l
Refugees and others of concern to the UNHCR (000)	8.4 m	7.9	19.0 b
Infant mortality rate (per 1 000 live births)	4.4	3.1	1.9 a,b
Health: Current expenditure (% of GDP)	5.7	6.1	6.4 l
Health: Physicians (per 1 000 pop.)	...	5.1	4.4 e
Education: Government expenditure (% of GDP)	5.2	4.8	4.7 c
Education: Primary gross enrol. ratio (f/m per 100 pop.)	104.3 / 104.5	99.2 / 99.1	94.4 / 94.0 c
Education: Lowr. sec. gross enrol. ratio (f/m per 100 pop.)	98.4 / 99.1	102.4 / 102.3	104.5 / 104.7 c
Education: Upr. sec. gross enrol. ratio (f/m per 100 pop.)	123.0 / 132.3	110.1 / 115.9	102.2 / 107.3 c
Intentional homicide rate (per 100 000 pop.)	4.1	3.4	2.3 e
Seats held by women in the National Parliament (%)	31.8	27.3	40.0 n

Environment and infrastructure indicators

	2010	2015	2023
Individuals using the Internet (per 100 inhabitants)	31.8 o	62.2 p	86.9 p,q,c
Research & Development expenditure (% of GDP)	0.7 r	0.5 r	0.5 c
Threatened species (number)	16	21	36 b
Forested area (% of land area)	42.5	42.5	43.2 l
CO2 emission estimates (million tons/tons per capita)	60.3 / 6.3	53.3 / 5.6	53.2 / 5.6 l
Energy production, primary (Petajoules)	167	163	187 l
Energy supply per capita (Gigajoules)	118	110	109 l
Tourist/visitor arrivals at national borders (000)	5 674 s	4 386 s	3 361 t,c
Important sites for terrestrial biodiversity protected (%)	77.4	87.9	87.9 b
Pop. using safely managed sanitation (urban/rural %)	85.1 / 62.8	81.5 / 55.5	81.5 / 48.7 b
Net Official Development Assist. received (% of GNI)	0.24	0.19	- 0.40 c

a Projected estimate (medium fertility variant). **b** 2022. **c** 2021. **d** Including communities under the authority of the Town Council. **e** 2019. **f** Excludes irrigation canals and landscaping care. **g** Data classified according to ISIC Rev. 4. **h** Excludes publishing activities, recycling. Includes irrigation canals. **i** Estimate. **j** Areas not elsewhere specified. **k** Data refers to a 5-year period preceding the reference year. **l** 2020. **m** Data as at the end of December. **n** Data are as at 1 January of reporting year. **o** Population aged 16 years and over. **p** Users in the last 12 months. **q** Population aged 6 to 72 years. **r** Data have been converted from the former national currency using the appropriate conversion rate. **s** Excludes the Belarusian-Russian border segment. **t** Includes estimation of the Belarusian-Russian border segment.

Belgium

Region	Western Europe	UN membership date	27 December 1945
Population (000, 2023)	11 656[a,b]	Surface area (km2)	30 528[c]
Pop. density (per km2, 2023)	385.0[a,b]	Sex ratio (m per 100 f)	97.7[a,b]
Capital city	Brussels	National currency	Euro (EUR)
Capital city pop. (000, 2023)	2 065.3[d,e]	Exchange rate (per US$)	0.9[b]

Economic indicators

	2010	2015	2023
GDP: Gross domestic product (million current US$)	480 952	462 150	594 104[c]
GDP growth rate (annual %, const. 2015 prices)	2.9	2.0	6.1[c]
GDP per capita (current US$)	44 213.5	41 086.2	51 165.5[c]
Economy: Agriculture (% of Gross Value Added)[f,g]	0.9	0.8	0.7[c]
Economy: Industry (% of Gross Value Added)[g,h]	23.4	22.0	22.0[c]
Economy: Services and other activity (% of GVA)[g]	75.7	77.3	77.2[c]
Employment in agriculture (% of employed)	1.4	1.2	0.9[c]
Employment in industry (% of employed)	23.3	21.4	19.4[c]
Employment in services & other sectors (% employed)	75.3	77.4	79.7[c]
Unemployment rate (% of labour force)	8.3	8.5	5.9[i]
Labour force participation rate (female/male pop. %)	47.7 / 60.8	48.0 / 58.9	50.3 / 59.2[i]
CPI: Consumer Price Index (2010=100)	100[j]	109[j]	132[b]
Agricultural production index (2014-2016=100)	96	101	103[c]
International trade: exports (million current US$)	407 596	397 739	463 446[b]
International trade: imports (million current US$)	391 256	371 025	471 448[b]
International trade: balance (million current US$)	16 340	26 714	- 8 003[b]
Balance of payments, current account (million US$)	7 338	6 363	- 20 252[b]

Major trading partners
						2022
Export partners (% of exports)	Germany	20.2	Netherlands	14.1	France	12.4
Import partners (% of imports)	Netherlands	20.5	Germany	12.5	France	10.4

Social indicators

	2010	2015	2023
Population growth rate (average annual %)	0.7	0.6	0.3[a,b]
Urban population (% of total population)	97.7	97.9	98.0[e]
Urban population growth rate (average annual %)[k]	0.8	0.7	...
Fertility rate, total (live births per woman)	1.9	1.7	1.6[a,b]
Life expectancy at birth (females/males, years)	82.6 / 77.4	83.1 / 78.6	84.4 / 80.2[a,b]
Population age distribution (0-14/60+ years old, %)	16.9 / 23.1	17.0 / 24.1	16.5 / 26.2[a,b]
International migrant stock (000/% of total pop.)	1 503.8 / 13.7	1 783.5 / 15.8	2 005.5 / 17.3[l]
Refugees and others of concern to the UNHCR (000)	36.9[m]	45.8	149.1[b]
Infant mortality rate (per 1 000 live births)	3.6	3.2	2.9[a,b]
Health: Current expenditure (% of GDP)	10.2	10.8	11.1[l]
Health: Physicians (per 1 000 pop.)	2.9	3.0	6.3[c]
Education: Government expenditure (% of GDP)	6.4	6.5	6.3[e]
Education: Primary gross enrol. ratio (f/m per 100 pop.)	101.8 / 102.0	103.1 / 103.2	102.9 / 101.5[l]
Education: Lowr. sec. gross enrol. ratio (f/m per 100 pop.)	139.5 / 134.7	186.7 / 175.6	171.4 / 162.1[l]
Education: Upr. sec. gross enrol. ratio (f/m per 100 pop.)	180.6 / 152.6	168.7 / 142.8	155.8 / 132.4[l]
Intentional homicide rate (per 100 000 pop.)	...	...	1.1[c]
Seats held by women in the National Parliament (%)	38.0	39.3	42.7[n]

Environment and infrastructure indicators

	2010	2015	2023
Individuals using the Internet (per 100 inhabitants)	75.0	85.1[o]	92.8[c]
Research & Development expenditure (% of GDP)	2.1	2.4	3.5[l]
Threatened species (number)	27	30	80[b]
Forested area (% of land area)	22.8	22.8	22.8[l]
CO2 emission estimates (million tons/tons per capita)	105.6 / 9.6	94.0 / 8.2	88.0 / 7.5[c]
Energy production, primary (Petajoules)	658	446	571[l]
Energy supply per capita (Gigajoules)	230	194	181[l]
Tourist/visitor arrivals at national borders (000)	7 186	8 355[p]	3 243[c]
Important sites for terrestrial biodiversity protected (%)	65.3	67.0	75.9[b]
Net Official Development Assist. disbursed (% of GNI)[q]	1.68	0.79	0.92[c]

a Projected estimate (medium fertility variant). b 2022. c 2021. d Refers to the population of Brussels-Capital Region and "communes" of the agglomeration and suburbs. e 2019. f Excludes irrigation canals and landscaping care. g Data classified according to ISIC Rev. 4. h Excludes publishing activities, recycling. Includes irrigation canals. i Estimate. j Calculated by the UN Statistics Division from national indices. k Data refers to a 5-year period preceding the reference year. l 2020. m Data as at the end of December. n Data are as at 1 January of reporting year. o Users in the last 3 months. p Break in the time series. q Development Assistance Committee member (OECD).

Belize

Region	Central America	UN membership date	25 September 1981
Population (000, 2023)	405 [a,b]	Surface area (km2)	22 965 [c]
Pop. density (per km2, 2023)	17.8 [a,b]	Sex ratio (m per 100 f)	101.1 [a,b]
Capital city	Belmopan	National currency	Belize Dollar (BZD)
Capital city pop. (000, 2023)	23.0 [d]	Exchange rate (per US$)	2.0 [b]

Economic indicators

	2010	2015	2023
GDP: Gross domestic product (million current US$)	1 739	2 210	2 492 [c]
GDP growth rate (annual %, const. 2015 prices)	1.3	3.4	15.2 [c]
GDP per capita (current US$)	5 397.8	6 142.3	6 228.7 [c]
Economy: Agriculture (% of Gross Value Added) [e,f]	9.9	11.0	8.9 [c]
Economy: Industry (% of Gross Value Added) [e,g]	20.4	17.1	19.4 [c]
Economy: Services and other activity (% of GVA) [e]	69.7	71.9	71.6 [c]
Employment in agriculture (% of employed)	18.1 [h]	18.1	21.2 [h,c]
Employment in industry (% of employed)	15.8 [h]	15.4	18.9 [h,c]
Employment in services & other sectors (% employed)	66.0 [h]	66.4	59.8 [h,c]
Unemployment rate (% of labour force)	8.2 [h]	7.6	10.2 [h]
Labour force participation rate (female/male pop. %) [h]	44.9 / 79.4	48.6 / 80.0	50.2 / 79.9
CPI: Consumer Price Index (2010=100) [i]	100	104	117 [b]
Agricultural production index (2014-2016=100)	97	102	101 [c]
International trade: exports (million current US$)	282	314	286 [b]
International trade: imports (million current US$)	700	996	1 378 [b]
International trade: balance (million current US$)	- 418	- 682	- 1 092 [b]
Balance of payments, current account (million US$)	- 46	- 175	- 258 [b]

Major trading partners

						2022
Export partners (% of exports)	United States	24.9	United Kingdom	20.2	Guatemala	11.0
Import partners (% of imports)	United States	41.6	China	17.6	Mexico	10.2

Social indicators

	2010	2015	2023
Population growth rate (average annual %)	2.3	2.1	1.3 [a,b]
Urban population (% of total population)	45.2	45.4	45.9 [j]
Urban population growth rate (average annual %) [k]	2.5	2.3	...
Fertility rate, total (live births per woman)	2.6	2.4	2.0 [a,b]
Life expectancy at birth (females/males, years)	75.4 / 69.6	76.5 / 70.4	74.7 / 67.7 [a,b]
Population age distribution (0-14/60+ years old, %)	35.5 / 5.9	31.8 / 6.6	27.7 / 8.0 [a,b]
International migrant stock (000/% of total pop.) [l]	46.4 / 14.2	54.6 / 15.1	62.0 / 15.6 [m]
Refugees and others of concern to the UNHCR (000)	0.2 [n]	0.1	5.6 [b]
Infant mortality rate (per 1 000 live births)	16.0	13.0	10.1 [a,b]
Health: Current expenditure (% of GDP) [h,o,p]	5.6	5.9	6.9 [m]
Health: Physicians (per 1 000 pop.)	0.8 [q]	1.1 [r]	1.1 [d]
Education: Government expenditure (% of GDP)	5.3	5.4	7.7 [m]
Education: Primary gross enrol. ratio (f/m per 100 pop.)	110.3 / 114.8	110.2 / 115.5	100.2 / 104.9 [c]
Education: Lowr. sec. gross enrol. ratio (f/m per 100 pop.)	88.4 / 84.3	90.8 / 91.0	98.5 / 100.0 [c]
Education: Upr. sec. gross enrol. ratio (f/m per 100 pop.)	56.6 / 47.3	63.3 / 56.1	72.4 / 61.7 [c]
Intentional homicide rate (per 100 000 pop.)	40.0	33.1	31.2 [c]
Seats held by women in the National Parliament (%)	0.0	3.1	15.6 [s]

Environment and infrastructure indicators

	2010	2015	2023
Individuals using the Internet (per 100 inhabitants)	28.2 [t]	41.6 [h]	62.0 [h,c]
Threatened species (number)	92	117	212 [b]
Forested area (% of land area)	61.0	58.4	56.0 [m]
Energy production, primary (Petajoules)	14	9	7 [m]
Energy supply per capita (Gigajoules)	40	43	39 [m]
Tourist/visitor arrivals at national borders (000)	242	341	219 [c]
Important sites for terrestrial biodiversity protected (%)	41.1	43.3	43.3 [b]
Net Official Development Assist. received (% of GNI)	1.94	1.73	4.53 [c]

a Projected estimate (medium fertility variant). b 2022. c 2021. d 2018. e Data classified according to ISIC Rev. 4. f Excludes irrigation canals and landscaping care. g Excludes publishing activities, recycling. Includes irrigation canals. h Estimate. i Calculated by the UN Statistics Division from national indices. j 2019. k Data refers to a 5-year period preceding the reference year. l Including refugees. m 2020. n Data as at the end of December. o Country is still reporting data based on SHA 1.0. p Data refer to fiscal years beginning 1 April. q 2009. r 2012. s Data are as at 1 January of reporting year. t Population aged 5 years and over.

Benin

Region	Western Africa	UN membership date	20 September 1960
Population (000, 2023)	13 353[a,b]	Surface area (km2)	114 763[c]
Pop. density (per km2, 2023)	118.4[a,b]	Sex ratio (m per 100 f)	100.4[a,b]
Capital city	Porto-Novo[d]	National currency	CFA Franc, BCEAO (XOF)[e]
Capital city pop. (000, 2023)	285.3[f]	Exchange rate (per US$)	615.0[b]

Economic indicators

	2010	2015	2023
GDP: Gross domestic product (million current US$)	9 526	11 380	17 688[c]
GDP growth rate (annual %, const. 2015 prices)	2.1	1.8	7.2[c]
GDP per capita (current US$)	1 008.5	1 040.9	1 360.9[c]
Economy: Agriculture (% of Gross Value Added)[g,h]	29.2	28.7	31.4[c]
Economy: Industry (% of Gross Value Added)[g,i]	20.4	17.8	18.1[c]
Economy: Services and other activity (% of GVA)[g]	50.4	53.5	50.5[c]
Employment in agriculture (% of employed)	45.1	36.0[j]	28.1[j,c]
Employment in industry (% of employed)[j]	18.3	20.0	22.5[c]
Employment in services & other sectors (% employed)[j]	36.7	44.0	49.3[c]
Unemployment rate (% of labour force)	1.0	2.0[j]	1.6[j]
Labour force participation rate (female/male pop. %)[j]	69.1 / 74.7	62.2 / 71.5	56.2 / 68.9
CPI: Consumer Price Index (2010=100)[j,k]	100	110	116[c]
Agricultural production index (2014-2016=100)	76	93	127[c]
International trade: exports (million current US$)	534	626	895[b]
International trade: imports (million current US$)	2 134	2 475	3 646[b]
International trade: balance (million current US$)	- 1 600	- 1 849	- 2 752[b]
Balance of payments, current account (million US$)	- 531	- 679	- 735[c]

Major trading partners

						2022
Export partners (% of exports)	Bangladesh	45.3	India	11.9	China	6.1
Import partners (% of imports)	India	15.7	China	13.1	France	8.1

Social indicators

	2010	2015	2023
Population growth rate (average annual %)	2.9	2.9	2.7[a,b]
Urban population (% of total population)	43.1	45.7	47.9[l]
Urban population growth rate (average annual %)[m]	4.1	4.0	...
Fertility rate, total (live births per woman)	5.4	5.3	4.9[a,b]
Life expectancy at birth (females/males, years)	59.7 / 57.0	60.7 / 58.1	61.7 / 58.3[a,b]
Population age distribution (0-14/60+ years old, %)	43.7 / 4.8	43.2 / 4.8	42.4 / 4.9[a,b]
International migrant stock (000/% of total pop.)[n,o]	309.2 / 3.4	366.3 / 3.5	394.3 / 3.3[p]
Refugees and others of concern to the UNHCR (000)	7.3[q]	0.6	2.3[b]
Infant mortality rate (per 1 000 live births)	69.6	63.1	54.4[a,b]
Health: Current expenditure (% of GDP)[r]	3.0	2.7	2.6[p]
Health: Physicians (per 1 000 pop.)	0.1	0.1[s]	0.1[l]
Education: Government expenditure (% of GDP)	3.7	3.2	3.2[c]
Education: Primary gross enrol. ratio (f/m per 100 pop.)	113.2 / 126.9	127.6 / 137.2	112.1 / 121.2[c]
Education: Lowr. sec. gross enrol. ratio (f/m per 100 pop.)	31.9 / 55.5[j,t]	64.6 / 80.0	54.4 / 60.7[c]
Education: Upr. sec. gross enrol. ratio (f/m per 100 pop.)	15.2 / 29.6[j,t]	25.8 / 51.5	27.4 / 39.7[c]
Seats held by women in the National Parliament (%)	10.8	8.4	7.4[u]

Environment and infrastructure indicators

	2010	2015	2023
Individuals using the Internet (per 100 inhabitants)	3.1	11.3[j]	34.0[j,c]
Threatened species (number)	62	74	135[b]
Forested area (% of land area)	32.2	30.0	27.8[p]
CO2 emission estimates (million tons/tons per capita)	5.1 / 0.5	6.0 / 0.5	8.5 / 0.6[p]
Energy production, primary (Petajoules)	82	104	124[p]
Energy supply per capita (Gigajoules)	16	16	18[p]
Tourist/visitor arrivals at national borders (000)	200	255	325[p]
Important sites for terrestrial biodiversity protected (%)	66.7	66.7	66.7[b]
Pop. using safely managed sanitation (urban/rural %)	2.9 / 1.1	3.3 / 1.4	3.6 / 1.8[b]
Net Official Development Assist. received (% of GNI)	7.27	3.87	4.83[c]

a Projected estimate (medium fertility variant). b 2022. c 2021. d Porto-Novo is the constitutional capital and Cotonou is the economic capital. e African Financial Community (CFA) Franc, Central Bank of West African States (BCEAO). f 2018. g Data classified according to ISIC Rev. 4. h Excludes irrigation canals and landscaping care. i Excludes publishing activities, recycling. Includes irrigation canals. j Estimate. k For Cotonou only. l 2019. m Data refers to a 5-year period preceding the reference year. n Refers to foreign citizens. o Including refugees. p 2020. q Data as at the end of December. r Data based on calendar year (January 1 to December 31). s 2011. t 2005. u Data are as at 1 January of reporting year.

Bermuda

Region	Northern America	Population (000, 2023)	64 [a,b]
Surface area (km2)	54 [c]	Pop. density (per km2, 2023)	1 188.6 [a,b]
Sex ratio (m per 100 f)	93.0 [a,b]	Capital city	Hamilton
National currency	Bermudian Dollar (BMD)	Capital city pop. (000, 2023)	10.1 [d]
Exchange rate (per US$)	1.0 [b]		

Economic indicators

	2010	2015	2023
GDP: Gross domestic product (million current US$)	6 635	6 655	7 231 [c]
GDP growth rate (annual %, const. 2015 prices)	0.6	0.8	4.0 [c]
GDP per capita (current US$)	104 568.0	105 386.8	112 652.6 [c]
Economy: Agriculture (% of Gross Value Added) [e,f]	0.3	0.2	0.2 [c]
Economy: Industry (% of Gross Value Added) [f,g,h]	6.9	5.4	6.2 [c]
Economy: Services and other activity (% of GVA) [f]	92.8	94.4	93.6 [c]
Employment in agriculture (% of employed) [i,j,k]	1.4	1.6 [l,m]	...
Employment in industry (% of employed) [i,j,k]	12.9	10.3 [l,m]	...
Employment in services & other sectors (% employed) [i,j,k]	85.7	87.6 [l,m]	...
Unemployment rate (% of labour force) [k]	4.5 [j,n]	6.7 [l,m]	...
Labour force participation rate (female/male pop. %)	81.0 / 87.0 [k]	72.6 / 80.0 [k,l,o]	... / ...
CPI: Consumer Price Index (2010=100)	...	148 [p,q]	...
International trade: exports (million current US$)	15 [r]	9	34 [b]
International trade: imports (million current US$)	970	929	1 192 [b]
International trade: balance (million current US$)	- 955	- 920	- 1 159 [b]
Balance of payments, current account (million US$)	696	943	962 [c]

Major trading partners

						2022
Export partners (% of exports)	United States	84.6	United Kingdom	9.6	Canada	2.9
Import partners (% of imports)	United States	71.5	Canada	8.5	United Kingdom	5.4

Social indicators

	2010	2015	2023
Population growth rate (average annual %)	0.2	- 0.4	- 0.2 [a,b]
Urban population (% of total population)	100.0	100.0	100.0 [s]
Urban population growth rate (average annual %) [t]	- 0.4	- 0.6	...
Fertility rate, total (live births per woman)	1.7	1.4	1.4 [a,b]
Life expectancy at birth (females/males, years)	85.3 / 75.9	85.8 / 76.4	84.5 / 78.4 [a,b]
Population age distribution (0-14/60+ years old, %)	16.2 / 19.0	15.1 / 22.6	14.7 / 28.6 [a,b]
International migrant stock (000/% of total pop.)	18.5 / 28.4	19.2 / 30.2	19.7 / 31.7 [u]
Infant mortality rate (per 1 000 live births)	1.9	3.1	2.1 [a,b]
Education: Government expenditure (% of GDP)	2.3	1.5	1.9 [b]
Education: Primary gross enrol. ratio (f/m per 100 pop.)	101.2 / 93.8 [v]	100.2 / 102.1	100.5 / 96.5 [u]
Education: Lowr. sec. gross enrol. ratio (f/m per 100 pop.)	93.6 / 81.1	86.0 / 84.4	... / ...
Education: Upr. sec. gross enrol. ratio (f/m per 100 pop.)	76.6 / 63.9	78.2 / 64.1	... / ...
Intentional homicide rate (per 100 000 pop.)	11.0	6.3	10.9 [c]

Environment and infrastructure indicators

	2010	2015	2023
Individuals using the Internet (per 100 inhabitants) [r]	84.2	98.3	98.4 [w]
Research & Development expenditure (% of GDP) [y]	0.2 [x]	0.2	0.2 [u]
Threatened species (number)	50	64	91 [b]
Forested area (% of land area)	18.5	18.5	18.5 [u]
Energy production, primary (Petajoules) [r]	1	1	1 [u]
Energy supply per capita (Gigajoules)	139 [r]	128	107 [u]
Tourist/visitor arrivals at national borders (000) [z]	232	220	72 [c]
Important sites for terrestrial biodiversity protected (%)	52.0	52.0	52.0 [b]

a Projected estimate (medium fertility variant). b 2022. c 2021. d 2018. e Excludes irrigation canals and landscaping care. f Data classified according to ISIC Rev. 4. g Excludes publishing activities, recycling. Includes irrigation canals. h Excludes mining and quarrying. i Data classified according to ISIC Rev. 3. j Break in the time series. k Population aged 16 years and over. l Excluding the institutional population. m 2013. n 2009. o 2012. p Index base: 2000=100. q 2014. r Estimate. s 2019. t Data refers to a 5-year period preceding the reference year. u 2020. v 2006. w 2017. x Excluding most or all capital expenditures. y Overestimated or based on overestimated data. z Arrivals by air. Excluding nationals residing abroad.

Bhutan

Region	Southern Asia
Population (000, 2023)	782[a,b]
Pop. density (per km2, 2023)	20.4[a,b]
Capital city	Thimphu
Capital city pop. (000, 2023)	203.3[d]

UN membership date	21 September 1971
Surface area (km2)	38 394[c]
Sex ratio (m per 100 f)	112.3[a,b]
National currency	Ngultrum (BTN)
Exchange rate (per US$)	82.9[b]

Economic indicators

	2010	2015	2023
GDP: Gross domestic product (million current US$)	1 548	2 004	2 381[c]
GDP growth rate (annual %, const. 2015 prices)	11.9	6.6	- 3.3[c]
GDP per capita (current US$)	2 194.1	2 695.6	3 062.9[c]
Economy: Agriculture (% of Gross Value Added)	15.4	15.1	17.8[c]
Economy: Industry (% of Gross Value Added)	45.7	44.5	37.9[c]
Economy: Services and other activity (% of GVA)	38.9	40.4	44.3[c]
Employment in agriculture (% of employed)	54.7	58.0	56.0[e,c]
Employment in industry (% of employed)	6.2	9.7	10.1[e,c]
Employment in services & other sectors (% employed)	39.2[e]	32.4	33.8[e,c]
Unemployment rate (% of labour force)	3.3	2.4	3.5[e]
Labour force participation rate (female/male pop. %)	63.4 / 72.2	55.1 / 70.1	54.1 / 69.2[e]
CPI: Consumer Price Index (2010=100)	100	88[f]	120[f,b]
Agricultural production index (2014-2016=100)	84	96	99[c]
International trade: exports (million current US$)	413	549[e]	766[e,b]
International trade: imports (million current US$)	854	1 062[e]	4 163[e,b]
International trade: balance (million current US$)	- 440	- 512[e]	- 3 397[e,b]
Balance of payments, current account (million US$)	- 323	- 548	- 853[b]

Major trading partners

					2022
Export partners (% of exports)[e]	India	87.5	Italy	6.0	Nepal	2.8
Import partners (% of imports)[e]	India	75.5	China	12.3	Thailand	5.2

Social indicators

	2010	2015	2023
Population growth rate (average annual %)	1.1	0.9	0.6[a,b]
Urban population (% of total population)	34.8	38.7	41.6[g]
Urban population growth rate (average annual %)[h]	4.4	3.7	...
Fertility rate, total (live births per woman)	2.3	2.0	1.4[a,b]
Life expectancy at birth (females/males, years)	70.1 / 67.0	72.1 / 68.9	74.2 / 70.6[a,b]
Population age distribution (0-14/60+ years old, %)	29.6 / 7.5	27.0 / 8.3	22.1 / 9.3[a,b]
International migrant stock (000/% of total pop.)	48.4 / 7.1	51.1 / 7.0	53.6 / 6.9[i]
Infant mortality rate (per 1 000 live births)	34.2	27.3	20.7[a,b]
Health: Current expenditure (% of GDP)[j]	3.6	3.8	4.4[i]
Health: Physicians (per 1 000 pop.)	0.2[k]	0.3	0.6[c]
Education: Government expenditure (% of GDP)	4.1	6.3	7.0[c]
Education: Primary gross enrol. ratio (f/m per 100 pop.)	109.4 / 107.0	104.8 / 103.7	107.7 / 103.8[c]
Education: Lowr. sec. gross enrol. ratio (f/m per 100 pop.)	77.3 / 72.1	96.9 / 87.6	103.6 / 88.0[c]
Education: Upr. sec. gross enrol. ratio (f/m per 100 pop.)	39.8 / 43.7	67.4 / 69.1	75.0 / 71.0[e,d]
Intentional homicide rate (per 100 000 pop.)	2.3	1.6	2.5[l]
Seats held by women in the National Parliament (%)	8.5	8.5	17.4[l]

Environment and infrastructure indicators

	2010	2015	2023
Individuals using the Internet (per 100 inhabitants)	13.6[e]	39.8[e]	85.6[c]
Threatened species (number)	59	71	123[b]
Forested area (% of land area)	71.0	71.2	71.4[i]
Energy production, primary (Petajoules)	73	77	91[i]
Energy supply per capita (Gigajoules)	80	86	87[i]
Tourist/visitor arrivals at national borders (000)[m]	41[n]	155	~0[o,c]
Important sites for terrestrial biodiversity protected (%)	45.4	47.0	47.0[b]
Pop. using safely managed drinking water (urban/rural, %)	40.9 / 18.6	44.9 / 49.1	58.9 / 84.6[b]
Pop. using safely managed sanitation (urban/rural, %)	47.3 / 45.6	43.5 / 51.2	41.0 / 57.9[b]
Net Official Development Assist. received (% of GNI)	6.66	5.23	9.33[i]

a Projected estimate (medium fertility variant). b 2022. c 2021. d 2018. e Estimate. f Base: April 2019 = 100 g 2019. h Data refers to a 5-year period preceding the reference year. i 2020. j Data refer to fiscal years beginning 1 July. k 2008. l Data are as at 1 January of reporting year. m Including regional high end tourists. n Break in the time series. o Due to covid mandatory quarantine only 1 tourist staying 113 nights was received.

Bolivia (Plurin. State of)

Region	South America	UN membership date	14 November 1945
Population (000, 2023)	12 224[a,b]	Surface area (km2)	1 098 581[c,d]
Pop. density (per km2, 2023)	11.3[a,b]	Sex ratio (m per 100 f)	100.5[a,b]
Capital city	Sucre[e]	National currency	Boliviano (BOB)
Capital city pop. (000, 2023)	277.9[f]	Exchange rate (per US$)	6.9[b]

Economic indicators

	2010	2015	2023
GDP: Gross domestic product (million current US$)	19 650	33 000	40 408[d]
GDP growth rate (annual %, const. 2015 prices)	4.1	4.9	6.1[d]
GDP per capita (current US$)	1 922.1	2 975.6	3 345.2[d]
Economy: Agriculture (% of Gross Value Added)	12.4	12.6	14.4[d]
Economy: Industry (% of Gross Value Added)	35.8	31.0	29.3[d]
Economy: Services and other activity (% of GVA)	51.8	56.5	56.3[d]
Employment in agriculture (% of employed)	31.7[g]	29.7	29.2[g,d]
Employment in industry (% of employed)	19.0[g]	20.9	18.6[g,d]
Employment in services & other sectors (% employed)	49.3[g]	49.3	52.2[g,d]
Unemployment rate (% of labour force)	2.6[g]	3.1	4.6[g]
Labour force participation rate (female/male pop. %)	62.2 / 81.8[g]	54.6 / 79.5	59.8 / 80.1[g]
CPI: Consumer Price Index (2010=100)[h]	100	134	153[b]
Agricultural production index (2014-2016=100)	79	102	116[d]
International trade: exports (million current US$)	7 051	8 923	13 653[b]
International trade: imports (million current US$)	5 604	9 843	13 049[b]
International trade: balance (million current US$)	1 448	- 920	603[b]
Balance of payments, current account (million US$)	874	- 1 936	- 152[b]

Major trading partners

						2022
Export partners (% of exports)	India	16.5	Brazil	13.9	Argentina	12.8
Import partners (% of imports)	China	19.4	Brazil	15.1	Argentina	12.5

Social indicators

	2010	2015	2023
Population growth rate (average annual %)	1.7	1.6	1.2[a,b]
Urban population (% of total population)	66.4	68.4	69.8[i]
Urban population growth rate (average annual %)[j]	2.4	2.1	...
Fertility rate, total (live births per woman)	3.2	2.9	2.6[a,b]
Life expectancy at birth (females/males, years)	68.7 / 63.8	69.9 / 64.9	67.9 / 62.3[a,b]
Population age distribution (0-14/60+ years old, %)	34.8 / 7.2	33.1 / 7.3	30.8 / 7.6[a,b]
International migrant stock (000/% of total pop.)[k]	122.8 / 1.2	143.0 / 1.3	164.1 / 1.4[l]
Refugees and others of concern to the UNHCR (000)	0.7[m]	0.8	14.7[n,b]
Infant mortality rate (per 1 000 live births)	36.7	30.6	24.9[a,b]
Health: Current expenditure (% of GDP)[o]	5.2[p]	6.6[p]	7.9[g,l]
Health: Physicians (per 1 000 pop.)	0.4	0.5[q]	1.0[r]
Education: Government expenditure (% of GDP)	7.0	8.1	8.4[l]
Education: Primary gross enrol. ratio (f/m per 100 pop.)	104.2 / 104.8	94.9 / 96.9	98.9 / 98.8[d]
Education: Lowr. sec. gross enrol. ratio (f/m per 100 pop.)	97.7 / 100.3	95.9 / 100.4	96.2 / 98.5[d]
Education: Upr. sec. gross enrol. ratio (f/m per 100 pop.)	83.7 / 82.9	88.0 / 87.7	89.6 / 89.0[d]
Intentional homicide rate (per 100 000 pop.)	...	4.9	3.5[d]
Seats held by women in the National Parliament (%)	22.3	53.1	46.2[s]

Environment and infrastructure indicators

	2010	2015	2023
Individuals using the Internet (per 100 inhabitants)	22.4[g]	37.5[t,u]	66.0[d]
Research & Development expenditure (% of GDP)	0.2[v,w]	...	...
Threatened species (number)	163	216	452[b]
Forested area (% of land area)	49.0	48.0	46.9[l]
CO2 emission estimates (million tons/tons per capita)	13.9 / 1.4	18.9 / 1.7	17.4 / 1.5[l]
Energy production, primary (Petajoules)	664	951	716[l]
Energy supply per capita (Gigajoules)	26	31	27[l]
Tourist/visitor arrivals at national borders (000)	679	882	180[d]
Important sites for terrestrial biodiversity protected (%)	45.4	45.4	45.4[b]
Net Official Development Assist. received (% of GNI)	2.99	2.48	1.29[d]

a Projected estimate (medium fertility variant). b 2022. c Data updated according to "Superintendencia Agraria". Interior waters correspond to natural or artificial bodies of water or snow. d 2021. e La Paz is the seat of government and Sucre is the constitutional capital. f 2018. g Estimate. h Calculated by the UN Statistics Division from national indices. i 2019. j Data refers to a 5-year period preceding the reference year. k Including refugees. l 2020. m Data as at the end of December. n Data is as of end-2021. o Data based on calendar year (January 1 to December 31). p Data are based on SHA2011. q 2011. r 2017. s Data are as at 1 January of reporting year. t Population aged 5 years and over. u Users in the last 3 months. v Break in the time series. w 2009.

Bonaire, St. Eustatius & Saba

Region	Caribbean	Population (000, 2023)	27 [a,b,c]
Pop. density (per km2, 2023)	82.4 [a,b,c]	Sex ratio (m per 100 f)	104.8 [a,b,c]
Capital city	Kralendijk	National currency	US Dollar (USD)
Capital city pop. (000, 2023)	11.3 [d,e]		

Social indicators	2010	2015	2023
Population growth rate (average annual %) [b]	3.5	2.6	0.4 [a,c]
Urban population (% of total population)	74.7	74.8	75.0 [f]
Urban population growth rate (average annual %) [g]	7.5	3.2	...
Fertility rate, total (live births per woman) [b]	1.7	1.7	1.6 [a,c]
Life expectancy at birth (females/males, years) [b]	78.3 / 72.8	79.8 / 75.5	78.2 / 73.2 [a,c]
Population age distribution (0-14/60+ years old, %) [b]	18.9 / 13.9	17.5 / 16.4	16.8 / 21.1 [a,c]
International migrant stock (000/% of total pop.)	20.9 / 100.0	24.6 / 100.0	26.2 / 100.0 [h]
Refugees and others of concern to the UNHCR (000)	~0.0 [i,j]	...	...
Infant mortality rate (per 1 000 live births) [b]	14.5	10.9	12.8 [a,c]

Environment and infrastructure indicators	2010	2015	2023
Threatened species (number)	...	55	95 [c]
Forested area (% of land area)	...	~0.0	5.9 [h]
Energy production, primary (Petajoules)	...	0	0 [h]
Energy supply per capita (Gigajoules) [k]	...	65	66 [h]
Important sites for terrestrial biodiversity protected (%)	39.3	62.5	62.5 [c]

a Projected estimate (medium fertility variant). b For statistical purposes, the data for Netherlands do not include this area. c 2022. d Refers to the island of Bonaire. e 2018. f 2019. g Data refers to a 5-year period preceding the reference year. h 2020. i Bonaire only. j Data as at the end of December. k Estimate.

Bosnia and Herzegovina

Region	Southern Europe	UN membership date	22 May 1992
Population (000, 2023)	3 234 [a,b]	Surface area (km2)	51 209 [c]
Pop. density (per km2, 2023)	63.2 [a,b]	Sex ratio (m per 100 f)	97.0 [a,b]
Capital city	Sarajevo	National currency	Convertible Mark (BAM)
Capital city pop. (000, 2023)	342.7 [d,e]	Exchange rate (per US$)	1.8 [b]

Economic indicators

	2010	2015	2023
GDP: Gross domestic product (million current US$)	17 176	16 212	23 365 [c]
GDP growth rate (annual %, const. 2015 prices)	0.9	3.1	7.5 [c]
GDP per capita (current US$)	4 506.9	4 599.9	7 143.3 [c]
Economy: Agriculture (% of Gross Value Added) [f,g]	8.0	7.3	6.0 [c]
Economy: Industry (% of Gross Value Added) [f,h]	26.5	26.6	29.8 [c]
Economy: Services and other activity (% of GVA) [f]	65.5	66.1	64.1 [c]
Employment in agriculture (% of employed)	19.7	17.9	11.3 [i,c]
Employment in industry (% of employed) [i]	17.4	23.8	34.3 [c]
Employment in services & other sectors (% employed)	49.5	52.7	54.4 [i,c]
Unemployment rate (% of labour force)	27.3	27.7	14.6 [i]
Labour force participation rate (female/male pop. %)	34.0 / 58.2	35.4 / 57.8	39.0 / 59.9 [i]
CPI: Consumer Price Index (2010=100)	100	104	121 [b]
Agricultural production index (2014-2016=100)	100	99	95 [c]
International trade: exports (million current US$)	4 803	5 099	9 678 [b]
International trade: imports (million current US$)	9 223	8 994	15 380 [b]
International trade: balance (million current US$)	- 4 420	- 3 895	- 5 701 [b]
Balance of payments, current account (million US$)	- 1 031	- 826	- 1 101 [b]

Major trading partners

						2022
Export partners (% of exports)	Croatia	14.9	Germany	14.8	Serbia	13.9
Import partners (% of imports)	Italy	12.3	Serbia	10.8	Germany	10.5

Social indicators

	2010	2015	2023
Population growth rate (average annual %)	- 1.8	- 1.3	- 0.8 [a,b]
Urban population (% of total population)	45.6	47.2	48.6 [e]
Urban population growth rate (average annual %) [j]	0.4	- 0.3	...
Fertility rate, total (live births per woman)	1.3	1.3	1.3 [a,b]
Life expectancy at birth (females/males, years)	79.7 / 74.3	78.1 / 74.2	77.5 / 73.1 [a,b]
Population age distribution (0-14/60+ years old, %)	15.9 / 19.5	15.1 / 21.9	14.9 / 25.8 [a,b]
International migrant stock (000/% of total pop.) [i,k]	38.9 / 1.1	38.6 / 1.1	36.0 / 1.1 [l]
Refugees and others of concern to the UNHCR (000)	179.0 [m]	143.9	98.5 [b]
Infant mortality rate (per 1 000 live births)	6.3	5.5	4.9 [a,b]
Health: Current expenditure (% of GDP)	9.0	9.4	9.8 [l]
Health: Physicians (per 1 000 pop.)	1.7	2.1	...
Education: Upr. sec. gross enrol. ratio (f/m per 100 pop.)	... / ...	... / ...	87.8 / 84.3 [c]
Intentional homicide rate (per 100 000 pop.)	1.5	1.6	1.0 [c]
Seats held by women in the National Parliament (%)	19.0	21.4	19.0 [n]

Environment and infrastructure indicators

	2010	2015	2023
Individuals using the Internet (per 100 inhabitants)	42.8 [i]	52.6 [i]	75.7 [c]
Research & Development expenditure (% of GDP)	~0.0 [o,p]	0.2	0.2 [c]
Threatened species (number)	67	85	133 [b]
Forested area (% of land area)	41.1	42.2	42.7 [l]
CO2 emission estimates (million tons/tons per capita)	20.7 / 5.5	19.6 / 5.6	23.7 / 6.2 [c,l]
Energy production, primary (Petajoules)	182	173	219 [l]
Energy supply per capita (Gigajoules)	71	71	90 [l]
Tourist/visitor arrivals at national borders (000)	365	678	502 [c]
Important sites for terrestrial biodiversity protected (%)	28.9	29.0	37.1 [b]
Pop. using safely managed sanitation (urban/rural %)	8.0 / ...	28.2 / ...	58.1 / ... [b]
Net Official Development Assist. received (% of GNI)	2.93	2.18	2.52 [c]

a Projected estimate (medium fertility variant). b 2022. c 2021. d Refers to the municipalities of Stari Grad Sarajevo, Centar Sarajevo, Novo Sarajevo, Novi Grad Sarajevo and Ilidza. e 2019. f Data classified according to ISIC Rev. 4. g Excludes irrigation canals and landscaping care. h Excludes publishing activities, recycling. Includes irrigation canals. i Estimate. j Data refers to a 5-year period preceding the reference year. k Including refugees. l 2020. m Data as at the end of December. n Data are as at 1 January of reporting year. o Partial data. p 2009.

Botswana

Region	Southern Africa	UN membership date	17 October 1966
Population (000, 2023)	2 630 a,b	Surface area (km2)	582 000 c
Pop. density (per km2, 2023)	4.6 a,b	Sex ratio (m per 100 f)	97.5 a,b
Capital city	Gaborone	National currency	Pula (BWP)
Capital city pop. (000, 2023)	269.3 d	Exchange rate (per US$)	12.8 b

Economic indicators	2010	2015	2023
GDP: Gross domestic product (million current US$)	12 637	13 531	17 615 c
GDP growth rate (annual %, const. 2015 prices)	10.1	- 4.9	11.4 c
GDP per capita (current US$)	6 041.7	5 869.7	6 805.2 c
Economy: Agriculture (% of Gross Value Added) e,f	2.2	2.0	1.8 c
Economy: Industry (% of Gross Value Added) e,g	39.6	39.0	31.2 c
Economy: Services and other activity (% of GVA) e	58.2	59.0	67.0 c
Employment in agriculture (% of employed)	26.1	22.2 h	23.1 h,c
Employment in industry (% of employed)	17.3	15.2 h	14.7 h,c
Employment in services & other sectors (% employed) h	56.6	62.5	62.3 c
Unemployment rate (% of labour force)	17.9	19.3 h	20.8 h
Labour force participation rate (female/male pop. %)	52.7 / 66.1	56.0 / 68.0 h	60.0 / 70.0 h
CPI: Consumer Price Index (2010=100) i	100	133	183 b
Agricultural production index (2014-2016=100)	126	105	106 c
International trade: exports (million current US$)	4 693	6 330	8 277 b
International trade: imports (million current US$)	5 657	8 048	8 005 b
International trade: balance (million current US$)	- 964	- 1 718	272 b
Balance of payments, current account (million US$)	- 744	301	- 123 c

Major trading partners						2022
Export partners (% of exports)	United Arab Emirates	27.2	Belgium	18.8	India	15.2
Import partners (% of imports)	South Africa	62.8	Namibia	7.2	Belgium	5.6

Social indicators	2010	2015	2023
Population growth rate (average annual %)	2.1	2.0	1.7 a,b
Urban population (% of total population)	62.4	67.2	70.2 j
Urban population growth rate (average annual %) k	3.8	3.3	...
Fertility rate, total (live births per woman)	3.0	2.9	2.8 a,b
Life expectancy at birth (females/males, years)	61.8 / 58.1	66.3 / 61.3	68.4 / 63.3 a,b
Population age distribution (0-14/60+ years old, %)	34.8 / 4.8	34.2 / 5.1	32.6 / 5.9 a,b
International migrant stock (000/% of total pop.) l	94.9 / 4.8	103.1 / 4.9	110.3 / 4.7 m
Refugees and others of concern to the UNHCR (000)	3.3 n	2.4	0.9 b
Infant mortality rate (per 1 000 live births)	38.6	37.4	33.1 a,b
Health: Current expenditure (% of GDP)	6.3	6.1	6.2 m
Health: Physicians (per 1 000 pop.)	0.4	0.4 p	0.3 d
Education: Government expenditure (% of GDP)	9.8 q	8.3	8.1 m
Education: Primary gross enrol. ratio (f/m per 100 pop.)	105.2 / 108.4	102.1 / 104.4	98.1 / 99.9 c
Education: Lowr. sec. gross enrol. ratio (f/m per 100 pop.)	97.3 / 92.5 q	97.8 / 94.8	84.5 / 81.5 c
Education: Upr. sec. gross enrol. ratio (f/m per 100 pop.)	62.9 / 54.5 r	... / ...	66.8 / 51.2 c
Intentional homicide rate (per 100 000 pop.)	14.5	...	10.5 c
Seats held by women in the National Parliament (%)	7.9	9.5	11.1 s

Environment and infrastructure indicators	2010	2015	2023
Individuals using the Internet (per 100 inhabitants)	6.0	37.3 h	73.5 h,c
Research & Development expenditure (% of GDP)	0.5 t	0.6 u	...
Threatened species (number)	18	24	35 b
Forested area (% of land area)	29.0	28.0	26.9 m
CO2 emission estimates (million tons/tons per capita)	3.5 / 1.6	7.2 / 3.3	6.0 / 2.4 m
Energy production, primary (Petajoules)	30	56	51 m
Energy supply per capita (Gigajoules)	36	35	33 m
Tourist/visitor arrivals at national borders (000)	1 973	1 528	328 m
Important sites for terrestrial biodiversity protected (%)	51.1	51.1	51.1 b
Pop. using safely managed drinking water (urban/rural, %)	80.2 / ...	76.2 / ...	72.9 / ... b
Net Official Development Assist. received (% of GNI)	1.27	0.50	0.58 c

a Projected estimate (medium fertility variant). b 2022. c 2021. d 2018. e Data classified according to ISIC Rev. 4. f Excludes irrigation canals and landscaping care. g Excludes publishing activities, recycling. Includes irrigation canals. h Estimate. i Calculated by the UN Statistics Division from national indices. j 2019. k Data refers to a 5-year period preceding the reference year. l Including refugees. m 2020. n Data as at the end of December. o Data refer to fiscal years beginning 1 April. p 2012. q 2009. r 2008. s Data are as at 1 January of reporting year. t 2005. u 2013.

Brazil

Region	South America	UN membership date	24 October 1945
Population (000, 2023)	215 314 [a,b]	Surface area (km2)	8 515 767 [c]
Pop. density (per km2, 2023)	25.8 [a,b]	Sex ratio (m per 100 f)	96.5 [a,b]
Capital city	Brasilia	National currency	Brazilian Real (BRL)
Capital city pop. (000, 2023)	4 559.0 [d,e]	Exchange rate (per US$)	5.2 [b]

Economic indicators	2010	2015	2023
GDP: Gross domestic product (million current US$)	2 208 838	1 802 212	1 608 981 [c]
GDP growth rate (annual %, const. 2015 prices)	7.5	- 3.5	4.6 [c]
GDP per capita (current US$)	11 249.3	8 783.2	7 507.2 [c]
Economy: Agriculture (% of Gross Value Added) [f,g]	4.8	5.0	8.1 [c]
Economy: Industry (% of Gross Value Added) [f,h]	27.4	22.5	22.2 [c]
Economy: Services and other activity (% of GVA) [f]	67.8	72.5	69.8 [c]
Employment in agriculture (% of employed)	12.4 [i]	0.4 [i]	9.7 [c]
Employment in industry (% of employed)	23.0 [i]	22.6	20.6 [c]
Employment in services & other sectors (% of employed)	64.6 [i]	67.4	69.6 [c]
Unemployment rate (% of labour force)	8.0 [i]	8.6	9.1 [i]
Labour force participation rate (female/male pop. %)	53.7 / 76.0 [i]	52.9 / 75.1	53.3 / 72.7 [i]
CPI: Consumer Price Index (2010=100) [j]	100	138	204 [b]
Agricultural production index (2014-2016=100)	89	102	112 [c]
International trade: exports (million current US$)	201 915	191 127	334 463 [b]
International trade: imports (million current US$)	181 768	171 446	292 344 [b]
International trade: balance (million current US$)	20 147	19 681	42 119 [b]
Balance of payments, current account (million US$)	- 86 718	- 63 409	- 56 997 [b]

Major trading partners						2022
Export partners (% of exports)	China	26.8	United States	11.4	Argentina	4.6
Import partners (% of imports)	China	23.2	United States	18.6	Argentina	4.7

Social indicators	2010	2015	2023
Population growth rate (average annual %)	0.9	0.8	0.5 [a,b]
Urban population (% of total population)	84.3	85.8	86.8 [e]
Urban population growth rate (average annual %) [k]	1.4	1.2	...
Fertility rate, total (live births per woman)	1.8	1.8	1.6 [a,b]
Life expectancy at birth (females/males, years)	76.6 / 69.8	77.6 / 71.1	76.6 / 70.3 [a,b]
Population age distribution (0-14/60+ years old, %)	24.8 / 10.3	22.5 / 11.9	20.3 / 14.6 [a,b]
International migrant stock (000/% of total pop.) [i]	592.6 / 0.3	710.3 / 0.3	1 079.7 / 0.5 [m]
Refugees and others of concern to the UNHCR (000)	5.2 [n]	66.0	562.6 [b]
Infant mortality rate (per 1 000 live births)	16.5	14.1	12.3 [a,b]
Health: Current expenditure (% of GDP) [o]	7.9 [p]	8.9 [p]	10.3 [i,m]
Health: Physicians (per 1 000 pop.)	...	1.9 [q]	2.1 [c]
Education: Government expenditure (% of GDP)	5.6	6.2	6.0 [e]
Education: Primary gross enrol. ratio (f/m per 100 pop.) [i]	128.2 / 133.9 [r]	106.7 / 111.5	102.9 / 108.1 [m]
Education: Lowr. sec. gross enrol. ratio (f/m per 100 pop.) [i]	104.0 / 100.1 [r]	107.0 / 108.6	110.2 / 110.0 [m]
Education: Upr. sec. gross enrol. ratio (f/m per 100 pop.) [i]	99.5 / 79.5 [r]	99.8 / 85.5	101.9 / 91.5 [m]
Intentional homicide rate (per 100 000 pop.)	26.6	28.4	22.4 [m]
Seats held by women in the National Parliament (%)	8.8	9.0	17.7 [s]

Environment and infrastructure indicators	2010	2015	2023
Individuals using the Internet (per 100 inhabitants)	40.6 [t,u]	58.3	80.7 [c]
Research & Development expenditure (% of GDP)	1.2	1.4	1.2 [m]
Threatened species (number)	773	966	2 229 [b]
Forested area (% of land area)	61.2	60.3	59.4 [m]
CO2 emission estimates (million tons/tons per capita)	389.6 / 1.9	474.0 / 2.2	456.7 / 2.0 [c]
Energy production, primary (Petajoules)	10 116	11 567	13 393 [m]
Energy supply per capita (Gigajoules)	56	60	56 [m]
Tourist/visitor arrivals at national borders (000) [v]	5 161	6 306	746 [c]
Important sites for terrestrial biodiversity protected (%)	42.1	42.9	43.7 [b]
Pop. using safely managed drinking water (urban/rural, %)	83.4 / 55.8	85.2 / 62.8	88.9 / 76.0 [b]
Pop. using safely managed sanitation (urban/rural %)	42.2 / ...	46.1 / ...	51.4 / ... [b]
Net Official Development Assist. received (% of GNI)	0.02	0.06	0.07 [c]

a Projected estimate (medium fertility variant). b 2022. c 2021. d Refers to the "Região Integrada de Desenvolvimento do Distrito Federal e Entorno". e 2019. f Data classified according to ISIC Rev. 4. g Excludes irrigation canals and landscaping care. h Excludes publishing activities, recycling. Includes irrigation canals. i Estimate. j Calculated by the UN Statistics Division from national indices. k Data refers to a 5-year period preceding the reference year. l Including refugees. m 2020. n Data as at the end of December. o Data based on calendar year (January 1 to preceding December 31). p Health expenditure data 2000-2019 based on health satellite accounts and converted to SHA 2011 HC, HF, and HK series by the country. q 2013. r 2009. s Data are as at 1 January of reporting year. t Users in the last 3 months. u Population aged 10 years and over. v Including nationals residing abroad.

British Virgin Islands

Region	Caribbean	Population (000, 2023)	31 [a,b,c]
Surface area (km2)	151 [d]	Pop. density (per km2, 2023)	203.3 [a,b,c]
Sex ratio (m per 100 f)	92.7 [a,b,c]	Capital city	Road Town
National currency	US Dollar (USD)	Capital city pop. (000, 2023)	15.1 [e]

Economic indicators

	2010	2015	2023
GDP: Gross domestic product (million current US$)	1 114	1 279	1 539 [d]
GDP growth rate (annual %, const. 2015 prices)	1.7	0.8	1.9 [d]
GDP per capita (current US$)	40 431.5	43 558.5	49 443.9 [d]
Economy: Agriculture (% of Gross Value Added) [f,g]	0.1	0.1	0.1 [d]
Economy: Industry (% of Gross Value Added) [h]	4.4	6.2	6.8 [d]
Economy: Services and other activity (% of GVA) [g]	95.4	93.7	93.1 [d]
Employment in agriculture (% of employed)	0.5 [i]	...	...
Employment in industry (% of employed)	11.1 [i]	...	...
Employment in services & other sectors (% employed)	87.4 [i]	...	...
International trade: exports (million current US$) [j]	~0	~0	0 [c]
International trade: imports (million current US$) [j]	313	430	669 [c]
International trade: balance (million current US$) [j]	- 313	- 430	- 669 [c]

Major trading partners   2022

Export partners (% of exports) [j]	Malta	28.9	Guyana	25.7	Cyprus	...
Import partners (% of imports) [j]	United States	41.0	Italy	11.3	Switzerland	10.3

Social indicators

	2010	2015	2023
Population growth rate (average annual %) [b]	0.4	1.4	0.8 [a,c]
Urban population (% of total population)	44.8	46.6	48.1 [k]
Urban population growth rate (average annual %) [l]	4.0	2.8	...
Fertility rate, total (live births per woman) [b]	1.2	1.2	1.0 [a,c]
Life expectancy at birth (females/males, years) [b]	78.2 / 72.9	78.6 / 73.0	79.3 / 73.6 [a,c]
Population age distribution (0-14/60+ years old, %) [b]	22.1 / 9.5	19.1 / 11.6	14.5 / 16.1 [a,c]
International migrant stock (000/% of total pop.) [m]	17.1 / 61.4	19.5 / 67.0	22.2 / 73.3 [n]
Refugees and others of concern to the UNHCR (000)	~0.0 [o]	...	~0.0 [d]
Infant mortality rate (per 1 000 live births) [b]	17.9	16.4	13.7 [a,c]
Education: Government expenditure (% of GDP)	3.5	4.7	2.6 [n]
Education: Primary gross enrol. ratio (f/m per 100 pop.)	107.2 / 110.0	114.5 / 122.3	130.2 / 131.5 [d]
Education: Lowr. sec. gross enrol. ratio (f/m per 100 pop.)	114.9 / 121.8	105.7 / 102.2	104.8 / 111.6 [d]
Education: Upr. sec. gross enrol. ratio (f/m per 100 pop.)	99.7 / 83.1	83.4 / 69.1	61.5 / 47.4 [e]
Intentional homicide rate (per 100 000 pop.)	8.2 [p]	...	...

Environment and infrastructure indicators

	2010	2015	2023
Individuals using the Internet (per 100 inhabitants)	37.0	37.6 [j,q]	77.7 [j,r]
Threatened species (number)	43	61	117 [c]
Forested area (% of land area)	24.3	24.1	24.1 [n]
Energy production, primary (Petajoules)	0	0	0 [n]
Energy supply per capita (Gigajoules) [j]	108	109	74 [n]
Tourist/visitor arrivals at national borders (000)	330	393	56 [d]
Important sites for terrestrial biodiversity protected (%)	7.4	7.4	7.4 [c]

a Projected estimate (medium fertility variant). b For statistical purposes, the data for United Kingdom do not include this area. c 2022. d 2021. e 2018. f Excludes irrigation canals and landscaping care. g Data classified according to ISIC Rev. 4. h Data classified according to ISIC Rev. 4. Excludes publishing activities. Includes irrigation canals. i Data classified according to ISIC Rev. 3. j Estimate. k 2019. l Data refers to a 5-year period preceding the reference year. m Including refugees. n 2020. o Data as at the end of December. p 2006. q 2012. r 2017.

Brunei Darussalam

Region	South-eastern Asia	
Population (000, 2023)	449[a,b]	
Pop. density (per km2, 2023)	77.9[a,b]	
Capital city	Bandar Seri Begawan	
Capital city pop. (000, 2023)	40.8[d]	
UN membership date	21 September 1984	
Surface area (km2)	5 765[c]	
Sex ratio (m per 100 f)	107.1[a,b]	
National currency	Brunei Dollar (BND)	
Exchange rate (per US$)	1.4[b]	

Economic indicators

	2010	2015	2023
GDP: Gross domestic product (million current US$)	13 707	12 930	14 006[c]
GDP growth rate (annual %, const. 2015 prices)	2.6	- 0.4	- 1.6[c]
GDP per capita (current US$)	34 609.3	30 681.5	31 448.9[c]
Economy: Agriculture (% of Gross Value Added)[e,f]	0.7	1.1	1.2[c]
Economy: Industry (% of Gross Value Added)[f,g]	67.4	60.2	61.7[c]
Economy: Services and other activity (% of GVA)[f]	31.9	38.7	37.0[c]
Employment in agriculture (% of employed)[h]	1.3	1.3	1.3[c]
Employment in industry (% of employed)[h]	18.0	16.6	24.3[c]
Employment in services & other sectors (% employed)[h]	80.7	82.0	74.3[c]
Unemployment rate (% of labour force)[h]	6.6	7.7	7.0
Labour force participation rate (female/male pop. %)[h]	56.3 / 76.0	56.3 / 71.1	55.8 / 72.1
CPI: Consumer Price Index (2010=100)	100	100	106[b]
Agricultural production index (2014-2016=100)	89	97	117[c]
International trade: exports (million current US$)	8 908	6 353	14 230[b]
International trade: imports (million current US$)	2 539	3 229	9 184[b]
International trade: balance (million current US$)	6 369	3 124	5 046[b]
Balance of payments, current account (million US$)	5 016	2 157	1 570[c]

Major trading partners

						2022
Export partners (% of exports)	Australia	20.6	Japan	17.4	China	15.6
Import partners (% of imports)	Malaysia	24.0	United Arab Emirates	12.2	China	8.8

Social indicators

	2010	2015	2023
Population growth rate (average annual %)	1.5	1.1	0.8[a,b]
Urban population (% of total population)	75.0	76.7	77.9[i]
Urban population growth rate (average annual %)[j]	1.7	1.9	...
Fertility rate, total (live births per woman)	1.9	1.9	1.8[a,b]
Life expectancy at birth (females/males, years)	77.1 / 72.8	77.0 / 72.7	76.8 / 72.5[a,b]
Population age distribution (0-14/60+ years old, %)	26.0 / 5.5	24.2 / 7.0	22.1 / 10.4[a,b]
International migrant stock (000/% of total pop.)	100.6 / 25.9	102.7 / 24.8	112.0 / 25.6[k]
Refugees and others of concern to the UNHCR (000)	21.0[l]	20.5	20.9[b]
Infant mortality rate (per 1 000 live births)	7.8	8.5	9.3[a,b]
Health: Current expenditure (% of GDP)[m]	2.3	2.4[n]	2.4[n,k]
Health: Physicians (per 1 000 pop.)	1.4	1.8	1.9[c]
Education: Government expenditure (% of GDP)	2.0	3.4[o]	4.4[p]
Education: Primary gross enrol. ratio (f/m per 100 pop.)	106.3 / 106.8	105.3 / 105.7	98.5 / 98.1[k]
Education: Lowr. sec. gross enrol. ratio (f/m per 100 pop.)	103.9 / 104.3	103.5 / 105.5	106.8 / 106.5[k]
Education: Upr. sec. gross enrol. ratio (f/m per 100 pop.)	97.7 / 96.6	109.3 / 108.4	87.8 / 83.7[k]
Intentional homicide rate (per 100 000 pop.)	0.3	0.5[q]	...
Seats held by women in the National Parliament (%)	...	...	9.1[r]

Environment and infrastructure indicators

	2010	2015	2023
Individuals using the Internet (per 100 inhabitants)[h]	53.0	71.2	98.1[c]
Research & Development expenditure (% of GDP)	...	...	0.3[n,s,d]
Threatened species (number)	170	189	359[b]
Forested area (% of land area)	72.1	72.1	72.1[k]
CO2 emission estimates (million tons/tons per capita)	6.9 / 17.6	6.0 / 14.4	9.3 / 21.0[k]
Energy production, primary (Petajoules)	775	673	603[k]
Energy supply per capita (Gigajoules)	343	270	370[k]
Tourist/visitor arrivals at national borders (000)[t]	214	218	4[c]
Important sites for terrestrial biodiversity protected (%)	41.7	41.7	41.7[b]

a Projected estimate (medium fertility variant). **b** 2022. **c** 2021. **d** 2018. **e** Excludes irrigation canals and landscaping care. **f** Data classified according to ISIC Rev. 4. **g** Excludes publishing activities, recycling. Includes irrigation canals. **h** Estimate. **i** 2019. **j** Data refers to a 5-year period preceding the reference year. **k** 2020. **l** Data as at the end of December. **m** Data refer to fiscal years beginning 1 April. **n** Break in the time series. **o** 2014. **p** 2016. **q** 2013. **r** Data are as at 1 January of reporting year. **s** Higher Education only. **t** Arrivals by air.

Bulgaria

Region	Eastern Europe	UN membership date	14 December 1955
Population (000, 2023)	6 782 a,b	Surface area (km2)	110 372 c
Pop. density (per km2, 2023)	62.6 a,b	Sex ratio (m per 100 f)	94.1 a,b
Capital city	Sofia	National currency	Bulgarian Lev (BGN)
Capital city pop. (000, 2023)	1 276.9 d	Exchange rate (per US$)	1.8 b

Economic indicators

	2010	2015	2023
GDP: Gross domestic product (million current US$)	50 682	50 782	84 058 c
GDP growth rate (annual %, const. 2015 prices)	1.5	3.4	7.6 c
GDP per capita (current US$)	6 675.5	6 947.6	12 207.3 c
Economy: Agriculture (% of Gross Value Added) e,f	4.6	4.7	5.0 c
Economy: Industry (% of Gross Value Added) e,g	27.2	27.8	23.8 c
Economy: Services and other activity (% of GVA) e	68.2	67.5	71.2 c
Employment in agriculture (% of employed)	6.8	6.9	6.3 c
Employment in industry (% of employed)	32.9	29.9	30.8 c
Employment in services & other sectors (% employed)	60.2	63.3	62.9 c
Unemployment rate (% of labour force)	10.3	9.1	4.2 h
Labour force participation rate (female/male pop. %)	47.8 / 59.5	48.6 / 60.0	51.1 / 63.7 h
CPI: Consumer Price Index (2010=100) i	100	107	139 b
Agricultural production index (2014-2016=100)	92	98	108 c
International trade: exports (million current US$)	20 608	25 779	50 250 b
International trade: imports (million current US$)	25 360	29 265	58 092 b
International trade: balance (million current US$)	- 4 752	- 3 486	- 7 841 b
Balance of payments, current account (million US$)	- 965	- 123	- 592 b

Major trading partners

						2022
Export partners (% of exports)	Germany	14.0	Romania	10.1	Italy	7.5
Import partners (% of imports)	Russian Federation	10.8	Germany	10.8	Türkiye	8.4

Social indicators

	2010	2015	2023
Population growth rate (average annual %)	- 0.6	- 0.9	- 1.5 a,b
Urban population (% of total population)	72.3	74.0	75.3 d
Urban population growth rate (average annual %) j	- 0.3	- 0.2	...
Fertility rate, total (live births per woman)	1.6	1.5	1.6 a,b
Life expectancy at birth (females/males, years)	77.4 / 70.4	78.1 / 71.2	75.1 / 68.3 a,b
Population age distribution (0-14/60+ years old, %)	13.7 / 25.4	14.1 / 27.4	14.0 / 29.2 a,b
International migrant stock (000/% of total pop.)	76.3 / 1.0	123.8 / 1.7	184.4 / 2.7 c
Refugees and others of concern to the UNHCR (000)	6.9 l	19.0	155.1 m,b
Infant mortality rate (per 1 000 live births)	9.1	6.5	5.3 a,b
Health: Current expenditure (% of GDP)	7.1	7.4	8.5 k
Health: Physicians (per 1 000 pop.)	3.7	4.0	4.2 n
Education: Government expenditure (% of GDP)	3.9	3.9	4.2 d
Education: Primary gross enrol. ratio (f/m per 100 pop.)	108.2 / 108.5	93.7 / 94.7	85.0 / 85.4 k
Education: Lowr. sec. gross enrol. ratio (f/m per 100 pop.)	83.8 / 89.1	89.3 / 93.6	68.4 / 68.8 k
Education: Upr. sec. gross enrol. ratio (f/m per 100 pop.)	91.7 / 94.5	111.8 / 114.1	108.8 / 112.3 k
Intentional homicide rate (per 100 000 pop.)	1.9	1.7	1.3 c
Seats held by women in the National Parliament (%)	20.8	20.4	24.2 o

Environment and infrastructure indicators

	2010	2015	2023
Individuals using the Internet (per 100 inhabitants)	46.2 p	56.7	75.3 c
Research & Development expenditure (% of GDP)	0.6	0.9	0.8 k
Threatened species (number)	66	85	146 b
Forested area (% of land area)	34.4	35.3	35.9 k
CO2 emission estimates (million tons/tons per capita)	44.6 / 5.9	44.2 / 6.0	41.5 / 4.8 c,k
Energy production, primary (Petajoules)	441	505	453 k
Energy supply per capita (Gigajoules)	98	106	105 k
Tourist/visitor arrivals at national borders (000)	6 047	7 099	2 300 c
Important sites for terrestrial biodiversity protected (%)	98.3	98.3	99.3 b
Pop. using safely managed sanitation (urban/rural %)	64.6 / 50.1	69.6 / 55.7	77.2 / 61.4 b
Net Official Development Assist. disbursed (% of GNI)	...	0.09 q	0.12 c

a Projected estimate (medium fertility variant). b 2022. c 2021. d 2019. e Data classified according to ISIC Rev. 4. f Excludes irrigation canals and landscaping care. g Excludes publishing activities, recycling. Includes irrigation canals. h Estimate. i Calculated by the UN Statistics Division from national indices. j Data refers to a 5-year period preceding the reference year. k 2020. l Data as at the end of December. m No official data on the actual number of refugees residing in Bulgaria is available. According to estimates, between 1,000 and 2,000 refugees and humanitarian status holders remain in the country. It is expected that the 2021 National Census, which will include the first-time refugee and stateless populations, will provide more accurate data. n 2018. o Data are as at 1 January of reporting year. p Population aged 16 to 74 years. q 2014.

Burkina Faso

Region	Western Africa	UN membership date	20 September 1960
Population (000, 2023)	22 674 [a,b]	Surface area (km2)	274 200 [c]
Pop. density (per km2, 2023)	82.9 [a,b]	Sex ratio (m per 100 f)	99.3 [a,b]
Capital city	Ouagadougou	National currency	CFA Franc, BCEAO (XOF) [d]
Capital city pop. (000, 2023)	2 652.7 [e]	Exchange rate (per US$)	615.0 [b]

Economic indicators

	2010	2015	2023
GDP: Gross domestic product (million current US$)	10 100	11 823	19 738 [c]
GDP growth rate (annual %, const. 2015 prices)	8.4	3.9	6.9 [c]
GDP per capita (current US$)	626.7	631.6	893.1 [c]
Economy: Agriculture (% of Gross Value Added) [f,g]	26.2	24.9	19.1 [c]
Economy: Industry (% of Gross Value Added) [f,h]	28.2	26.8	35.0 [c]
Economy: Services and other activity (% of GVA) [f]	45.6	48.3	46.0 [c]
Employment in agriculture (% of employed) [i]	79.2	76.8	73.3 [c]
Employment in industry (% of employed) [i]	5.9	6.2	7.1 [c]
Employment in services & other sectors (% employed) [i]	15.0	17.0	19.6 [c]
Unemployment rate (% of labour force) [i]	3.6	4.3	5.2
Labour force participation rate (female/male pop. %) [i]	58.9 / 80.2	57.7 / 73.8	58.0 / 72.9
CPI: Consumer Price Index (2010=100) [j]	100	108	131 [b]
Agricultural production index (2014-2016=100)	80	98	113 [c]
International trade: exports (million current US$)	1 288	2 177	4 525 [i,b]
International trade: imports (million current US$)	2 048	2 980	5 531 [i,b]
International trade: balance (million current US$)	- 760	- 802	- 1 006 [i,b]
Balance of payments, current account (million US$)	- 182	- 895	77 [c]

Major trading partners

					2022
Export partners (% of exports) [i]	Switzerland	72.7	India	9.6	Singapore 3.8
Import partners (% of imports) [i]	China	13.9	Côte d'Ivoire	8.5	France 7.8

Social indicators

	2010	2015	2023
Population growth rate (average annual %)	2.9	2.9	2.5 [a,b]
Urban population (% of total population)	24.6	27.5	30.0 [e]
Urban population growth rate (average annual %) [k]	5.7	5.2	...
Fertility rate, total (live births per woman)	5.9	5.5	4.7 [a,b]
Life expectancy at birth (females/males, years)	57.9 / 55.0	60.4 / 57.2	61.5 / 58.0 [a,b]
Population age distribution (0-14/60+ years old, %)	45.6 / 4.2	45.6 / 4.1	43.7 / 4.1 [a,b]
International migrant stock (000/% of total pop.) [l]	674.4 / 4.3	704.7 / 3.9	724.0 / 3.5 [m]
Refugees and others of concern to the UNHCR (000)	1.1 [n]	34.2	1 936.7 [b]
Infant mortality rate (per 1 000 live births)	67.8	58.3	47.4 [a,b]
Health: Current expenditure (% of GDP) [o]	5.2	5.1	6.7 [m]
Health: Physicians (per 1 000 pop.)	~0.0	0.1	0.1 [e]
Education: Government expenditure (% of GDP)	3.5	3.7	5.2 [c]
Education: Primary gross enrol. ratio (f/m per 100 pop.)	74.3 / 81.6	87.2 / 89.5	93.0 / 91.4 [c]
Education: Lowr. sec. gross enrol. ratio (f/m per 100 pop.)	26.5 / 33.0	46.8 / 47.6	54.6 / 45.6 [c]
Education: Upr. sec. gross enrol. ratio (f/m per 100 pop.)	7.6 / 12.4	10.6 / 16.1	22.5 / 25.0 [c]
Seats held by women in the National Parliament (%)	15.3	13.3	16.9 [p]

Environment and infrastructure indicators

	2010	2015	2023
Individuals using the Internet (per 100 inhabitants) [i]	2.4	6.6	21.6 [c]
Research & Development expenditure (% of GDP)	0.2 [q]	0.2 [r,s,t]	0.3 [r,u,c]
Threatened species (number)	24	29	40 [b]
Forested area (% of land area)	24.5	23.6	22.7 [m]
Energy production, primary (Petajoules)	118	126	133 [i,m]
Energy supply per capita (Gigajoules)	9	9	9 [i,m]
Tourist/visitor arrivals at national borders (000)	274	163	106 [c]
Important sites for terrestrial biodiversity protected (%)	78.8	78.8	78.8 [b]
Pop. using safely managed sanitation (urban/rural %)	13.2 / 4.4	12.6 / 6.2	12.1 / 8.6 [b]
Net Official Development Assist. received (% of GNI)	10.65	8.84	8.61 [c]

a Projected estimate (medium fertility variant). b 2022. c 2021. d African Financial Community (CFA) Franc, Central Bank of West African States (BCEAO). e 2019. f Data classified according to ISIC Rev. 4. g Excludes irrigation canals and landscaping care. h Excludes publishing activities, recycling. Includes irrigation canals. i Estimate. j Ouagadougou k Data refers to a 5-year period preceding the reference year. l Including refugees. m 2020. n Data as at the end of December. o Data based on calendar year (January 1 to December 31). p Data are as at 1 January of reporting year. q 2009. r Excluding business enterprise. s Break in the time series. t 2014. u Excluding private non-profit.

Burundi

Region	Eastern Africa	UN membership date	18 September 1962
Population (000, 2023)	12 890 a,b	Surface area (km2)	27 834 c
Pop. density (per km2, 2023)	496.7 a,b	Sex ratio (m per 100 f)	98.6 a,b
Capital city	Gitega	National currency	Burundi Franc (BIF)
Capital city pop. (000, 2023)	899.0 d	Exchange rate (per US$)	2 063.4 b

Economic indicators

	2010	2015	2023
GDP: Gross domestic product (million current US$)	2 032	2 811	3 900 c
GDP growth rate (annual %, const. 2015 prices)	5.1	- 0.4	1.8 c
GDP per capita (current US$)	222.7	262.0	310.7 c
Economy: Agriculture (% of Gross Value Added)	40.7	37.5	37.5 c
Economy: Industry (% of Gross Value Added)	16.3	16.4	18.7 c
Economy: Services and other activity (% of GVA)	43.0	46.2	43.8 c
Employment in agriculture (% of employed) e	88.4	86.3	85.8 c
Employment in industry (% of employed) e	3.0	3.5	3.6 c
Employment in services & other sectors (% of employed) e	8.7	10.2	10.5 c
Unemployment rate (% of labour force) e	1.6	1.5	1.0
Labour force participation rate (female/male pop. %) e	81.0 / 78.0	80.7 / 77.8	81.5 / 78.0
CPI: Consumer Price Index (2010=100) f	100	154	252 b
Agricultural production index (2014-2016=100)	99	96	122 c
International trade: exports (million current US$)	118	114	125 e,b
International trade: imports (million current US$)	404	561	981 e,b
International trade: balance (million current US$)	- 286	- 447	- 855 e,b
Balance of payments, current account (million US$)	- 301	- 373	- 363 d

Major trading partners

							2022
Export partners (% of exports) e	Dem. Rep. of Congo	23.9	Belgium	12.2	Pakistan	8.6
Import partners (% of imports) e	China	18.0	Saudi Arabia	13.4	United Rep. Tanzania	9.2

Social indicators

	2010	2015	2023
Population growth rate (average annual %)	3.7	1.1	2.7 a,b
Urban population (% of total population)	10.6	12.1	13.4 g
Urban population growth rate (average annual %) h	5.9	5.6	...
Fertility rate, total (live births per woman)	6.3	5.7	5.0 a,b
Life expectancy at birth (females/males, years)	58.4 / 55.7	62.2 / 58.2	63.9 / 60.1 a,b
Population age distribution (0-14/60+ years old, %)	44.9 / 3.7	46.8 / 3.8	45.8 / 3.8 a,b
International migrant stock (000/% of total pop.) i	247.3 / 2.9	298.3 / 2.9	344.8 / 2.9 i
Refugees and others of concern to the UNHCR (000)	200.8 k	137.7	108.1 b
Infant mortality rate (per 1 000 live births)	59.4	46.3	36.3 a,b
Health: Current expenditure (% of GDP) l	11.3	6.3	6.5 j
Health: Physicians (per 1 000 pop.)	~0.0	~0.0	0.1 c
Education: Government expenditure (% of GDP)	6.8	6.4 e	5.1 j
Education: Primary gross enrol. ratio (f/m per 100 pop.)	136.4 / 138.0	132.8 / 129.0	115.9 / 114.4 j
Education: Lowr. sec. gross enrol. ratio (f/m per 100 pop.)	26.9 / 35.5	57.3 / 56.7	52.8 / 41.7 j
Education: Upr. sec. gross enrol. ratio (f/m per 100 pop.)	9.2 / 15.5	22.6 / 30.4	51.6 / 44.5 j
Intentional homicide rate (per 100 000 pop.)	...	4.3	5.8 m
Seats held by women in the National Parliament (%)	31.4	30.5	38.2 n

Environment and infrastructure indicators

	2010	2015	2023
Individuals using the Internet (per 100 inhabitants) e	1.0	2.0	5.8 c
Research & Development expenditure (% of GDP) o	0.1	0.1 p	0.2 q,d
Threatened species (number)	52	60	218 b
Forested area (% of land area)	7.6	10.9	10.9 j
Energy production, primary (Petajoules)	54 e	56	56 j
Energy supply per capita (Gigajoules)	6 e	6	6 j
Tourist/visitor arrivals at national borders (000) r	142 q	131	299 s
Important sites for terrestrial biodiversity protected (%)	47.4	47.4	47.4 b
Net Official Development Assist. received (% of GNI)	31.05	11.82	20.90 c

a Projected estimate (medium fertility variant). b 2022. c 2021. d 2018. e Estimate. f Bujumbura g 2019. h Data refers to a 5-year period preceding the reference year. i Including refugees. j 2020. k Data as at the end of December. l Data based on calendar year (January 1 to December 31). m 2016. n Data are as at 1 January of reporting year. o Partial data. p 2012. q Break in the time series. r Including nationals residing abroad. s 2017.

Cabo Verde

Region	Western Africa	UN membership date	16 September 1975	
Population (000, 2023)	593[a,b]	Surface area (km2)	4 033[c]	
Pop. density (per km2, 2023)	147.2[a,b]	Sex ratio (m per 100 f)	98.9[a,b]	
Capital city	Praia	National currency	Cabo Verde Escudo (CVE)	
Capital city pop. (000, 2023)	167.5[d]	Exchange rate (per US$)	106.4[b]	

Economic indicators	2010	2015	2023
GDP: Gross domestic product (million current US$)	1 664	1 596	1 936[c]
GDP growth rate (annual %, const. 2015 prices)	1.5	1.0	7.0[c]
GDP per capita (current US$)	3 193.2	2 890.7	3 293.2[c]
Economy: Agriculture (% of Gross Value Added)[e,f]	9.2	10.0	5.1[c]
Economy: Industry (% of Gross Value Added)[e,g]	20.8	20.7	28.9[c]
Economy: Services and other activity (% of GVA)[e]	70.1	69.3	66.0[c]
Employment in agriculture (% of employed)	17.7[h]	15.7	11.0[h,c]
Employment in industry (% of employed)	17.9[h]	18.8	22.2[h,c]
Employment in services & other sectors (% employed)	64.4[h]	65.5	66.9[h,c]
Unemployment rate (% of labour force)	10.7	11.8[h]	13.5[h]
Labour force participation rate (female/male pop. %)[h]	48.1 / 70.4	50.9 / 67.6	50.3 / 62.7
CPI: Consumer Price Index (2010=100)[i]	100	109	122[b]
Agricultural production index (2014-2016=100)	93	101	82[c]
International trade: exports (million current US$)	220	67	59[h,b]
International trade: imports (million current US$)	731	603	1 276[h,b]
International trade: balance (million current US$)	- 511	- 537	- 1 217[h,b]
Balance of payments, current account (million US$)	- 223	- 51	- 77[b]

Major trading partners						2022
Export partners (% of exports)[h]	Spain	63.0	Portugal	15.2	Italy	11.6
Import partners (% of imports)[h]	Portugal	41.9	Netherlands	16.2	Spain	8.4

Social indicators	2010	2015	2023
Population growth rate (average annual %)	1.2	1.1	0.9[a,b]
Urban population (% of total population)	61.8	64.3	66.2[i]
Urban population growth rate (average annual %)[k]	2.5	2.0	...
Fertility rate, total (live births per woman)	2.5	2.1	1.9[a,b]
Life expectancy at birth (females/males, years)	78.1 / 69.0	79.0 / 70.1	79.0 / 70.3[a,b]
Population age distribution (0-14/60+ years old, %)	32.0 / 7.6	29.1 / 7.4	26.2 / 8.7[a,b]
International migrant stock (000/% of total pop.)[l]	14.4 / 2.9	14.9 / 2.8	15.8 / 2.8[m]
Refugees and others of concern to the UNHCR (000)	~0.0[n,o]	0.1	0.1[b]
Infant mortality rate (per 1 000 live births)	21.7	16.4	11.4[a,b]
Health: Current expenditure (% of GDP)[p]	4.5	4.8	6.0[m]
Health: Physicians (per 1 000 pop.)	0.6	0.7	0.8[d]
Education: Government expenditure (% of GDP)	5.6	5.3	6.5[c]
Education: Primary gross enrol. ratio (f/m per 100 pop.)	107.0 / 115.2	101.7 / 109.2	97.9 / 103.9[i]
Education: Lowr. sec. gross enrol. ratio (f/m per 100 pop.)	115.0 / 103.9	113.2 / 111.4	105.2 / 105.6[i]
Education: Upr. sec. gross enrol. ratio (f/m per 100 pop.)	74.8 / 56.5	86.5 / 67.7	79.9 / 64.7[i]
Intentional homicide rate (per 100 000 pop.)	7.0[q]	8.3	6.2[m]
Seats held by women in the National Parliament (%)	18.1	20.8	41.7[r]

Environment and infrastructure indicators	2010	2015	2023
Individuals using the Internet (per 100 inhabitants)	30.0[h]	42.7	69.8[h,c]
Research & Development expenditure (% of GDP)	...	0.1[s,t,u]	...
Threatened species (number)	31	51	129[b]
Forested area (% of land area)	10.6	11.0	11.3[m]
Energy production, primary (Petajoules)	1	2[h]	2[h,m]
Energy supply per capita (Gigajoules)	18	16[h]	15[h,m]
Tourist/visitor arrivals at national borders (000)[v]	336	520	135[c]
Important sites for terrestrial biodiversity protected (%)	12.0	12.0	12.0[b]
Net Official Development Assist. received (% of GNI)	20.55	9.97	7.65[c]

a Projected estimate (medium fertility variant). b 2022. c 2021. d 2018. e Data classified according to ISIC Rev. 4. f Excludes irrigation canals and landscaping care. g Excludes publishing activities, recycling. Includes irrigation canals. h Estimate. i Calculated by the UN Statistics Division from national indices. j 2019. k Data refers to a 5-year period preceding the reference year. l Including refugees. m 2020. n Data as at the end of December. o 2005. p Data based on calendar year (January 1 to December 31). q 2006. r Data are as at 1 January of reporting year. s Partial data. t Higher Education only. u 2011. v Non-resident tourists staying in hotels and similar establishments.

Cambodia

Region	South-eastern Asia	UN membership date	14 December 1955
Population (000, 2023)	16 768 [a,b]	Surface area (km2)	181 035 [c]
Pop. density (per km2, 2023)	92.6 [a,b]	Sex ratio (m per 100 f)	98.0 [a,b]
Capital city	Phnom Penh	National currency	Riel (KHR)
Capital city pop. (000, 2023)	2 014.0 [d,e]	Exchange rate (per US$)	4 118.0 [b]

Economic indicators

	2010	2015	2023
GDP: Gross domestic product (million current US$)	11 242	18 050	26 669 [c]
GDP growth rate (annual %, const. 2015 prices)	6.0	7.0	3.0 [c]
GDP per capita (current US$)	782.7	1 170.7	1 607.7 [c]
Economy: Agriculture (% of Gross Value Added)	36.0	28.2	24.5 [c]
Economy: Industry (% of Gross Value Added)	23.3	29.4	39.4 [c]
Economy: Services and other activity (% of GVA)	40.7	42.3	36.1 [c]
Employment in agriculture (% of employed)	54.8	42.5	38.9 [f,c]
Employment in industry (% of employed)	16.0	24.9	25.4 [f,c]
Employment in services & other sectors (% employed)	29.2	32.6	35.7 [f,c]
Unemployment rate (% of labour force)	1.0	0.4	0.3 [f]
Labour force participation rate (female/male pop. %) [f]	63.5 / 76.0	65.0 / 78.4	69.4 / 81.9
CPI: Consumer Price Index (2010=100) [g]	100	117	145 [b]
Agricultural production index (2014-2016=100)	82	98	120 [c]
International trade: exports (million current US$)	5 590	8 542	23 049 [f,b]
International trade: imports (million current US$)	4 903	10 669	30 695 [f,b]
International trade: balance (million current US$)	688	- 2 126	- 7 646 [f,b]
Balance of payments, current account (million US$)	- 981	- 1 598	- 7 582 [b]

Major trading partners

						2022
Export partners (% of exports) [f]	United States	42.6	China	8.6	Japan	6.2
Import partners (% of imports) [f]	China	33.7	Singapore	17.8	Thailand	12.1

Social indicators

	2010	2015	2023
Population growth rate (average annual %)	1.5	1.3	1.0 [a,b]
Urban population (% of total population)	20.3	22.2	23.8 [e]
Urban population growth rate (average annual %) [h]	2.6	3.4	...
Fertility rate, total (live births per woman)	2.8	2.6	2.3 [a,b]
Life expectancy at birth (females/males, years)	69.8 / 65.4	72.0 / 67.6	72.6 / 67.1 [a,b]
Population age distribution (0-14/60+ years old, %)	32.1 / 5.7	30.9 / 7.0	28.9 / 9.7 [a,b]
International migrant stock (000/% of total pop.) [i]	82.0 / 0.6	74.0 / 0.5	79.3 / 0.5 [j]
Refugees and others of concern to the UNHCR (000)	0.2 [k]	0.2	75.0 [b]
Infant mortality rate (per 1 000 live births)	35.7	26.4	20.6 [a,b]
Health: Current expenditure (% of GDP) [l]	6.9	6.2	7.5 [j]
Health: Physicians (per 1 000 pop.)	0.2	0.2 [m]	0.2 [e]
Education: Government expenditure (% of GDP)	1.5	1.7	1.7 [c]
Education: Primary gross enrol. ratio (f/m per 100 pop.)	120.2 / 127.4	106.0 / 110.2	101.9 / 103.9 [c]
Education: Lowr. sec. gross enrol. ratio (f/m per 100 pop.)	58.5 / 60.5	61.9 / 59.9	75.4 / 64.0 [c]
Education: Upr. sec. gross enrol. ratio (f/m per 100 pop.)	24.3 / 33.0 [f,n]	... / ...	48.2 / 40.9 [c]
Intentional homicide rate (per 100 000 pop.)	2.3	1.8 [o]	...
Seats held by women in the National Parliament (%)	21.1	20.3	20.8 [p]

Environment and infrastructure indicators

	2010	2015	2023
Individuals using the Internet (per 100 inhabitants)	1.3	18.0 [f]	60.2 [f,c]
Research & Development expenditure (% of GDP)	...	0.1 [q]	...
Threatened species (number)	204	243	339 [b]
Forested area (% of land area)	60.0	50.1	45.7 [j]
CO2 emission estimates (million tons/tons per capita)	5.6 / 0.3	8.7 / 0.5	14.4 / 0.8 [j]
Energy production, primary (Petajoules)	124	143	161 [j]
Energy supply per capita (Gigajoules)	14	16	22 [j]
Tourist/visitor arrivals at national borders (000) [r]	2 508	4 775	196 [c]
Important sites for terrestrial biodiversity protected (%)	24.7	25.8	54.5 [b]
Pop. using safely managed drinking water (urban/rural, %)	51.1 / 14.6	53.8 / 16.7	57.5 / 19.6 [b]
Pop. using safely managed sanitation (urban/rural %)	35.5 / 15.4	39.0 / 22.4	44.7 / 34.1 [b]
Net Official Development Assist. received (% of GNI)	6.35	4.01	5.35 [c]

a Projected estimate (medium fertility variant). b 2022. c 2021. d Refers to the municipality of Phnom Penh including suburban areas. e 2019. f Estimate. g Phnom Penh h Data refers to a 5-year period preceding the reference year. i Including refugees. j 2020. k Data as at the end of December. l Data refer to fiscal years beginning 1 July. m 2014. n 2008. o 2011. p Data are as at 1 January of reporting year. q Break in the time series. r Arrivals by all means of transport.

Cameroon

Region	Middle Africa	UN membership date	20 September 1960
Population (000, 2023)	27 914[a,b]	Surface area (km2)	475 650[c]
Pop. density (per km2, 2023)	59.9[a,b]	Sex ratio (m per 100 f)	99.5[a,b]
Capital city	Yaoundé	National currency	CFA Franc, BEAC (XAF)[d]
Capital city pop. (000, 2023)	3 822.4[e]	Exchange rate (per US$)	615.0[b]

Economic indicators	2010	2015	2023
GDP: Gross domestic product (million current US$)	27 481	32 186	45 368[c]
GDP growth rate (annual %, const. 2015 prices)	2.9	5.7	3.6[c]
GDP per capita (current US$)	1 382.5	1 398.6	1 668.0[c]
Economy: Agriculture (% of Gross Value Added)[f,g]	18.4	18.7	18.6[c]
Economy: Industry (% of Gross Value Added)[f,h]	27.6	27.3	26.0[c]
Economy: Services and other activity (% of GVA)[f]	54.0	54.0	55.4[c]
Employment in agriculture (% of employed)[i]	55.0	46.7	42.6[c]
Employment in industry (% of employed)[i]	12.2	14.3	15.5[c]
Employment in services & other sectors (% employed)[i]	32.8	39.0	41.9[c]
Unemployment rate (% of labour force)	4.1	3.5[i]	4.0[i]
Labour force participation rate (female/male pop. %)	70.5 / 82.1	67.0 / 77.2[i]	67.4 / 76.1[i]
CPI: Consumer Price Index (2010=100)[i]	100	113	132[b]
Agricultural production index (2014-2016=100)	82	101	104[c]
International trade: exports (million current US$)	3 878	4 053	6 172[i,b]
International trade: imports (million current US$)	5 133	6 037	8 474[i,b]
International trade: balance (million current US$)	- 1 255	- 1 984	- 2 303[i,b]
Balance of payments, current account (million US$)	- 857	- 1 174	- 1 795[c]

Major trading partners						2022
Export partners (% of exports)[i]	Netherlands	19.3	France	13.4	India	12.7
Import partners (% of imports)[i]	China	35.1	France	7.3	Nigeria	6.8

Social indicators	2010	2015	2023
Population growth rate (average annual %)	2.9	3.0	2.6[a,b]
Urban population (% of total population)	51.6	54.6	57.0[e]
Urban population growth rate (average annual %)[j]	3.9	3.8	...
Fertility rate, total (live births per woman)	5.2	4.8	4.4[a,b]
Life expectancy at birth (females/males, years)	58.0 / 55.2	61.2 / 58.1	62.6 / 59.4[a,b]
Population age distribution (0-14/60+ years old, %)	43.8 / 4.5	43.3 / 4.3	42.2 / 4.2[a,b]
International migrant stock (000/% of total pop.)[k]	291.5 / 1.4	508.3 / 2.2	579.2 / 2.2[i]
Refugees and others of concern to the UNHCR (000)	106.7[m]	391.8	1 420.0[b]
Infant mortality rate (per 1 000 live births)	71.4	59.1	45.8[a,b]
Health: Current expenditure (% of GDP)[n]	3.6	3.6	3.8[i]
Health: Physicians (per 1 000 pop.)	0.1	0.1[o]	0.1[c]
Education: Government expenditure (% of GDP)	2.8	2.7[i]	2.8[c]
Education: Primary gross enrol. ratio (f/m per 100 pop.)	100.2 / 116.0	109.9 / 122.4	103.8 / 114.5[c]
Education: Lowr. sec. gross enrol. ratio (f/m per 100 pop.)	46.0 / 56.9	64.3 / 73.5	43.8 / 49.6[c]
Education: Upr. sec. gross enrol. ratio (f/m per 100 pop.)	28.7 / 35.2	39.7 / 49.0	40.2 / 44.9[c]
Intentional homicide rate (per 100 000 pop.)	5.0	3.7	4.5[i]
Seats held by women in the National Parliament (%)	13.9	31.1	33.9[p]

Environment and infrastructure indicators	2010	2015	2023
Individuals using the Internet (per 100 inhabitants)[i]	4.3	18.3	45.6[c]
Threatened species (number)	624	697	1 250[b]
Forested area (% of land area)	44.2	43.6	43.0[i]
CO2 emission estimates (million tons/tons per capita)	6.7 / 0.2	8.0 / 0.3	9.1 / 0.3[i]
Energy production, primary (Petajoules)	353	494	556[i]
Energy supply per capita (Gigajoules)	15	17	16[i]
Tourist/visitor arrivals at national borders (000)	569	812[q]	...
Important sites for terrestrial biodiversity protected (%)	35.0	35.5	35.5[b]
Net Official Development Assist. received (% of GNI)	1.98	2.09	2.57[c]

a Projected estimate (medium fertility variant). b 2022. c 2021. d African Financial Community (CFA) Franc, Bank of Central African States (BEAC). e 2019. f Data classified according to ISIC Rev. 4. g Excludes irrigation canals and landscaping care. h Excludes publishing activities, recycling. Includes irrigation canals. i Estimate. j Data refers to a 5-year period preceding the reference year. k Including refugees. l 2020. m Data as at the end of December. n Data based on calendar year (January 1 to December 31). o 2011. p Data are as at 1 January of reporting year. q 2012.

Canada

Region	Northern America	UN membership date	09 November 1945
Population (000, 2023)	38 454 a,b	Surface area (km2)	9 984 670 c
Pop. density (per km2, 2023)	4.2 a,b	Sex ratio (m per 100 f)	98.8 a,b
Capital city	Ottawa	National currency	Canadian Dollar (CAD)
Capital city pop. (000, 2023)	1 378.2 d,e	Exchange rate (per US$)	1.4 b

Economic indicators

	2010	2015	2023
GDP: Gross domestic product (million current US$)	1 617 267	1 556 129	1 988 336 c
GDP growth rate (annual %, const. 2015 prices)	3.1	0.7	4.5 c
GDP per capita (current US$)	47 617.9	43 549.9	52 112.1 c
Economy: Agriculture (% of Gross Value Added) f,g	1.6	2.0	1.9 c
Economy: Industry (% of Gross Value Added) g,h	27.9	25.8	25.7 c
Economy: Services and other activity (% of GVA) g	70.5	72.1	72.4 c
Employment in agriculture (% of employed)	1.8	1.6	1.3 c
Employment in industry (% of employed)	20.1	19.8	19.3 c
Employment in services & other sectors (% employed)	78.0	78.5	79.4 c
Unemployment rate (% of labour force)	8.1	6.9	5.6 i
Labour force participation rate (female/male pop. %)	62.4 / 71.6	61.2 / 70.6	60.2 / 68.5 i
CPI: Consumer Price Index (2010=100) j	100	109	130 b
Agricultural production index (2014-2016=100)	86	99	96 c
International trade: exports (million current US$)	386 580	408 697	596 657 b
International trade: imports (million current US$)	392 109	419 375	568 203 b
International trade: balance (million current US$)	- 5 529	- 10 677	28 454 b
Balance of payments, current account (million US$)	- 58 163	- 54 696	- 7 955 b

Major trading partners

							2022
Export partners (% of exports)	United States	76.9	China	3.7	United Kingdom	2.4
Import partners (% of imports)	United States	49.1	China	13.5	Mexico	5.5

Social indicators

	2010	2015	2023
Population growth rate (average annual %)	1.1	1.0	0.8 a,b
Urban population (% of total population)	80.9	81.3	81.5 e
Urban population growth rate (average annual %) k	1.3	1.1	...
Fertility rate, total (live births per woman)	1.6	1.6	1.5 a,b
Life expectancy at birth (females/males, years)	83.5 / 79.1	83.9 / 79.9	84.8 / 80.9 a,b
Population age distribution (0-14/60+ years old, %)	16.6 / 19.9	16.2 / 22.3	15.6 / 25.9 a,b
International migrant stock (000/% of total pop.)	6 761.2 / 19.8	7 428.7 / 20.6	8 049.3 / 21.3 l
Refugees and others of concern to the UNHCR (000)	216.6 m	155.8 m	130.3 n,b
Infant mortality rate (per 1 000 live births)	5.0	4.5	3.9 a,b
Health: Current expenditure (% of GDP) o,p	10.7	10.7	11.7 c
Health: Physicians (per 1 000 pop.)	...	...	2.5 c
Education: Government expenditure (% of GDP)	5.4	4.7	4.8 e
Education: Primary gross enrol. ratio (f/m per 100 pop.)	98.9 / 98.4	102.9 / 102.1	101.5 / 102.2 l
Education: Lowr. sec. gross enrol. ratio (f/m per 100 pop.)	99.2 / 100.5	101.0 / 100.8	109.8 / 109.1 l
Education: Upr. sec. gross enrol. ratio (f/m per 100 pop.)	102.0 / 105.0	119.9 / 118.2	121.3 / 119.4 l
Intentional homicide rate (per 100 000 pop.)	1.6	1.7	2.1 c
Seats held by women in the National Parliament (%)	22.1	25.2	30.6 q

Environment and infrastructure indicators

	2010	2015	2023
Individuals using the Internet (per 100 inhabitants)	80.3 r,s	90.0 i	92.8 i,c
Research & Development expenditure (% of GDP)	1.8	1.7	1.7 t,l
Threatened species (number)	77	97	195 b
Forested area (% of land area)	38.7	38.7	38.7 l
CO2 emission estimates (million tons/tons per capita)	534.0 / 15.5	557.0 / 15.4	536.2 / 13.8 c
Energy production, primary (Petajoules)	16 597	19 687	21 671 l
Energy supply per capita (Gigajoules)	319	325	314 l
Tourist/visitor arrivals at national borders (000) u	16 219	17 977	3 062 c
Important sites for terrestrial biodiversity protected (%)	26.5	27.1	30.9 b
Pop. using safely managed sanitation (urban/rural %)	80.8 / 80.1	82.7 / 82.0	84.0 / 83.5 b
Net Official Development Assist. disbursed (% of GNI) v	1.46	0.24	0.51 c

a Projected estimate (medium fertility variant). b 2022. c 2021. d Refers to the Census Metropolitan Area. e 2019. f Excludes irrigation canals and landscaping care. g Data classified according to ISIC Rev. 4. h Excludes publishing activities, recycling. Includes irrigation canals. i Estimate. j Calculated by the UN Statistics Division from national indices. k Data refers to a 5-year period preceding the reference year. l 2020. m Data as at the end of December. n The statistics on asylum-seekers and refugees individually recognized in Canada include persons who had their claim assessed before National Immigration Agencies through a Pre-Removal Risk Assessment. o Data based on calendar year (January 1 to December 31). p Data are based on SHA2011. q Data are as at 1 January of reporting year. r Population aged 16 years and over. s Break in the time series. t Provisional data. u Data based on customs counts and adjusted using questionnaire surveys. v Development Assistance Committee member (OECD).

Cayman Islands

Region	Caribbean	Population (000, 2023)	69[a,b,c]
Surface area (km2)	264[d]	Pop. density (per km2, 2023)	285.1[a,b,c]
Sex ratio (m per 100 f)	101.9[a,b,c]	Capital city	George Town
National currency	Cayman Islands Dollar (KYD)	Capital city pop. (000, 2023)	34.9[e]
Exchange rate (per US$)	0.8[c]		

Economic indicators

	2010	2015	2023
GDP: Gross domestic product (million current US$)	4 157	4 708	5 809[d]
GDP growth rate (annual %, const. 2015 prices)	- 2.7	2.8	1.7[d]
GDP per capita (current US$)	76 872.2	77 295.9	85 250.3[d]
Economy: Agriculture (% of Gross Value Added)[f,g]	0.3	0.4	0.4[d]
Economy: Industry (% of Gross Value Added)[f,h]	7.4	7.4	8.1[d]
Economy: Services and other activity (% of GVA)[f]	92.2	92.2	91.4[d]
Employment in agriculture (% of employed)[i]	0.6	0.8[j]	...
Employment in industry (% of employed)[i]	14.9	15.5[j]	...
Employment in services & other sectors (% employed)[i]	84.2	83.6[j]	...
Unemployment rate (% of labour force)	6.7	6.3[j]	...
Labour force participation rate (female/male pop. %)	80.6 / 88.0[i,k,l]	80.6 / 85.6[j]	... / ...
CPI: Consumer Price Index (2010=100)[m]	100	104	120[d]
International trade: exports (million current US$)[n]	24	65	8[c]
International trade: imports (million current US$)	828[n]	915	1 538[d]
International trade: balance (million current US$)	- 804[n]	- 851	- 1 521[d]
Balance of payments, current account (million US$)	...	...	- 764[o]

Major trading partners

						2022
Export partners (% of exports)[n]	United States	77.8	Jamaica	13.1	United Kingdom	9.1
Import partners (% of imports)	United States	...	Jamaica	...	United Kingdom	...

Social indicators

	2010	2015	2023
Population growth rate (average annual %)[b]	2.7	2.2	0.9[a,c]
Urban population (% of total population)	100.0	100.0	100.0[p]
Urban population growth rate (average annual %)[q]	2.6	1.5	...
Fertility rate, total (live births per woman)[b]	1.8	1.2	1.2[a,c]
Life expectancy at birth (females/males, years)[b]	78.8 / 73.0	77.3 / 72.5	78.1 / 73.2[a,c]
Population age distribution (0-14/60+ years old, %)[b]	18.3 / 8.5	17.5 / 10.0	16.8 / 13.1[a,c]
International migrant stock (000/% of total pop.)[r,s]	24.1 / 42.5	26.2 / 42.4	29.2 / 44.5[o]
Refugees and others of concern to the UNHCR (000)	~0.0[t]	0.1	0.4[c]
Infant mortality rate (per 1 000 live births)[b]	7.2	8.7	7.3[a,c]
Education: Government expenditure (% of GDP)	...	...	2.1[p]
Education: Primary gross enrol. ratio (f/m per 100 pop.)	92.8 / 98.9[u]	89.1 / 91.9	94.3 / 93.7[d]
Education: Lowr. sec. gross enrol. ratio (f/m per 100 pop.)	86.9 / 81.8[u]	94.6 / 91.7[j]	83.7 / 80.2[e]
Education: Upr. sec. gross enrol. ratio (f/m per 100 pop.)	81.4 / 71.2[u]	74.3 / 73.9[j]	71.2 / 66.1[o]
Intentional homicide rate (per 100 000 pop.)	16.6	8.4[v]	4.5[o]

Environment and infrastructure indicators

	2010	2015	2023
Individuals using the Internet (per 100 inhabitants)[n]	66.0	77.0	81.1[w]
Threatened species (number)	34	71	109[c]
Forested area (% of land area)	53.0	53.0	53.0[o]
Energy supply per capita (Gigajoules)	148	131	136[o]
Tourist/visitor arrivals at national borders (000)[x]	288	385	17[d]
Important sites for terrestrial biodiversity protected (%)	31.7	32.5	32.5[o]

a Projected estimate (medium fertility variant). b For statistical purposes, the data for United Kingdom do not include this area. c 2022. d 2021. e 2018. f Data classified according to ISIC Rev. 4. g Excludes irrigation canals and landscaping care. h Excludes publishing activities, recycling. Includes irrigation canals. i Break in the time series. j 2013. k Resident population (de jure). l 2009. m Calculated by the UN Statistics Division from national indices. n Estimate. o 2020. p 2019. q Data refers to a 5-year period preceding the reference year. r Refers to foreign citizens. s Including refugees. t Data as at the end of December. u 2008. v 2014. w 2017. x Arrivals by air.

Central African Republic

Region	Middle Africa	UN membership date	20 September 1960
Population (000, 2023)	5 579[a,b]	Surface area (km2)	622 984[c]
Pop. density (per km2, 2023)	9.0[a,b]	Sex ratio (m per 100 f)	99.9[a,b]
Capital city	Bangui	National currency	CFA Franc, BEAC (XAF)[d]
Capital city pop. (000, 2023)	869.6[e]	Exchange rate (per US$)	615.0[b]

Economic indicators

	2010	2015	2023
GDP: Gross domestic product (million current US$)	2 141	1 695	2 518[c]
GDP growth rate (annual %, const. 2015 prices)	4.6	4.3	1.0[c]
GDP per capita (current US$)	459.3	351.6	461.4[c]
Economy: Agriculture (% of Gross Value Added)	39.8	32.5	33.3[c]
Economy: Industry (% of Gross Value Added)	26.1	22.8	21.8[c]
Economy: Services and other activity (% of GVA)	34.1	44.6	45.0[c]
Employment in agriculture (% of employed)[f]	71.7	71.6	68.5[c]
Employment in industry (% of employed)[f]	6.8	6.5	6.7[c]
Employment in services & other sectors (% employed)[f]	21.4	21.9	24.8[c]
Unemployment rate (% of labour force)[f]	5.5	5.7	6.3
Labour force participation rate (female/male pop. %)[f]	63.2 / 77.9	63.0 / 78.8	63.7 / 77.7
CPI: Consumer Price Index (2010=100)[f,g]	100	133	161[c]
Agricultural production index (2014-2016=100)	94	99	111[c]
International trade: exports (million current US$)	90	97	51[f,b]
International trade: imports (million current US$)	210	457	873[f,b]
International trade: balance (million current US$)	- 120	- 360	- 822[f,b]

Major trading partners

						2022
Export partners (% of exports)[f]	United Arab Emirates	24.6	Sweden	15.4	France	10.4
Import partners (% of imports)[f]	Cameroon	26.2	China	17.1	France	14.0

Social indicators

	2010	2015	2023
Population growth rate (average annual %)	2.0	1.6	2.8[a,b]
Urban population (% of total population)	38.9	40.3	41.8[e]
Urban population growth rate (average annual %)[h]	1.9	1.1	...
Fertility rate, total (live births per woman)	5.9	6.0	5.9[a,b]
Life expectancy at birth (females/males, years)	50.5 / 48.1	54.5 / 51.2	56.8 / 52.3[a,b]
Population age distribution (0-14/60+ years old, %)	46.0 / 3.5	48.8 / 3.9	48.1 / 4.1[a,b]
International migrant stock (000/% of total pop.)[i,j]	94.7 / 2.2	81.6 / 1.8	88.5 / 1.8[k]
Refugees and others of concern to the UNHCR (000)	215.3[l]	517.2	899.2[b]
Infant mortality rate (per 1 000 live births)	97.3	84.7	67.7[a,b]
Health: Current expenditure (% of GDP)[m]	3.6	5.0	9.4[k]
Health: Physicians (per 1 000 pop.)	~0.0[n]	0.1	0.1[o]
Education: Government expenditure (% of GDP)	1.1	1.9	1.9[c]
Education: Primary gross enrol. ratio (f/m per 100 pop.)	73.4 / 101.2	75.7 / 99.8[p]	111.0 / 145.0[q]
Education: Lowr. sec. gross enrol. ratio (f/m per 100 pop.)	12.7 / 22.4[n]	15.3 / 30.3[p]	18.3 / 26.3[q]
Education: Upr. sec. gross enrol. ratio (f/m per 100 pop.)	5.6 / 10.0[n]	6.9 / 11.7[p]	7.0 / 11.8[q]
Seats held by women in the National Parliament (%)	9.6	12.5[r]	12.9[s]

Environment and infrastructure indicators

	2010	2015	2023
Individuals using the Internet (per 100 inhabitants)[f]	2.0	2.9	10.6[c]
Threatened species (number)	36	54	101[b]
Forested area (% of land area)	36.3	36.0	35.8[k]
Energy production, primary (Petajoules)	33	33	35[f,k]
Energy supply per capita (Gigajoules)	8	7	7[f,k]
Tourist/visitor arrivals at national borders (000)[t]	54	120	35[k]
Important sites for terrestrial biodiversity protected (%)	74.2	74.2	74.2[b]
Pop. using safely managed drinking water (urban/rural, %)	14.2 / 2.8	12.8 / 2.6	11.3 / 2.2[b]
Pop. using safely managed sanitation (urban/rural %)	31.5 / 8.0	27.7 / 7.0	23.4 / 5.7[b]
Net Official Development Assist. received (% of GNI)	12.13	28.38	24.53[c]

a Projected estimate (medium fertility variant). **b** 2022. **c** 2021. **d** African Financial Community (CFA) Franc, Bank of Central African States (BEAC). **e** 2019. **f** Estimate. **g** Bangui. **h** Data refers to a 5-year period preceding the reference year. **i** Including refugees. **j** Refers to foreign citizens. **k** 2020. **l** Data as at the end of December. **m** Data based on calendar year (January 1 to December 31). **n** 2009. **o** 2018. **p** 2012. **q** 2017. **r** 2013. **s** Data are as at 1 January of reporting year. **t** Arrivals by air at Bangui only.

Region	Middle Africa	UN membership date	20 September 1960
Population (000, 2023)	17 723[a,b]	Surface area (km2)	1 284 000[c]
Pop. density (per km2, 2023)	14.1[a,b]	Sex ratio (m per 100 f)	100.8[a,b]
Capital city	N'Djamena	National currency	CFA Franc, BEAC (XAF)[d]
Capital city pop. (000, 2023)	1 371.5[e]	Exchange rate (per US$)	615.0[b]

Economic indicators

	2010	2015	2023
GDP: Gross domestic product (million current US$)	12 176	14 401	16 410[c]
GDP growth rate (annual %, const. 2015 prices)	17.4	3.9	- 1.1[c]
GDP per capita (current US$)	1 023.7	1 018.4	955.2[c]
Economy: Agriculture (% of Gross Value Added)[f]	35.1	29.8	46.5[g,c]
Economy: Industry (% of Gross Value Added)[f]	42.5	43.1	22.9[h,c]
Economy: Services and other activity (% of GVA)[f]	22.4	27.0	30.6[c]
Employment in agriculture (% of employed)[i]	74.5	70.5	68.9[c]
Employment in industry (% of employed)[i]	5.9	7.6	9.7[c]
Employment in services & other sectors (% employed)[i]	19.6	21.9	21.3[c]
Unemployment rate (% of labour force)[i]	1.0	1.1	1.3
Labour force participation rate (female/male pop. %)[i]	53.7 / 74.8	50.5 / 72.8	48.3 / 70.8
CPI: Consumer Price Index (2010=100)	100[i,j]	117[i,j]	129[k,b]
Agricultural production index (2014-2016=100)	88	97	122[c]
International trade: exports (million current US$)[i]	3 410	2 900	4 194[b]
International trade: imports (million current US$)[i]	2 507	2 200	1 219[b]
International trade: balance (million current US$)[i]	904	700	2 975[b]

Major trading partners

2022

Export partners (% of exports)[i]	Germany	26.3	China	22.5	United Arab Emirates	19.3
Import partners (% of imports)[i]	United Arab Emirates	28.3	China	22.4	France	6.6

Social indicators

	2010	2015	2023
Population growth rate (average annual %)	3.4	2.9	3.1[a,b]
Urban population (% of total population)	22.0	22.5	23.3[e]
Urban population growth rate (average annual %)[l]	3.5	3.8	...
Fertility rate, total (live births per woman)	7.0	6.7	6.2[a,b]
Life expectancy at birth (females/males, years)	50.8 / 48.4	53.1 / 50.1	54.8 / 51.3[a,b]
Population age distribution (0-14/60+ years old, %)	48.6 / 3.4	48.4 / 3.3	47.5 / 3.4[a,b]
International migrant stock (000/% of total pop.)[m]	417.0 / 3.5	467.0 / 3.3	547.5 / 3.3[n]
Refugees and others of concern to the UNHCR (000)	533.0[o]	473.5	1 093.2[b]
Infant mortality rate (per 1 000 live births)	91.1	80.6	65.5[a,b]
Health: Current expenditure (% of GDP)[p]	4.1	4.5	5.4[n]
Health: Physicians (per 1 000 pop.)	~0.0[q]	~0.0	0.1[c]
Education: Government expenditure (% of GDP)	2.0	2.3	2.9[c]
Education: Primary gross enrol. ratio (f/m per 100 pop.)	69.1 / 94.6	79.4 / 103.7	83.3 / 104.1[c]
Education: Lowr. sec. gross enrol. ratio (f/m per 100 pop.)	16.4 / 36.6	17.1 / 34.6	20.6 / 32.5[c]
Education: Upr. sec. gross enrol. ratio (f/m per 100 pop.)	8.7 / 24.2	9.0 / 25.3	13.0 / 26.6[c]
Seats held by women in the National Parliament (%)	5.2	14.9	25.9[r]

Environment and infrastructure indicators

	2010	2015	2023
Individuals using the Internet (per 100 inhabitants)[i]	1.7	3.5	17.9[c]
Research & Development expenditure (% of GDP)	...	...	0.3[s,t,u]
Threatened species (number)	30	38	55[b]
Forested area (% of land area)	4.4	3.9	3.4[n]
Energy production, primary (Petajoules)	328	377	372[n]
Energy supply per capita (Gigajoules)	7	7	6[n]
Tourist/visitor arrivals at national borders (000)	71[v]	120[v]	40[w,c]
Important sites for terrestrial biodiversity protected (%)	67.3	67.3	67.3[b]
Pop. using safely managed drinking water (urban/rural, %)	16.2 / 2.9	16.8 / 2.8	17.6 / 2.7[b]
Pop. using safely managed sanitation (urban/rural %)	23.0 / 5.2	26.9 / 4.8	32.0 / 4.2[b]
Net Official Development Assist. received (% of GNI)	4.75	5.71	6.42[c]

a Projected estimate (medium fertility variant). **b** 2022. **c** 2021. **d** African Financial Community (CFA) Franc, Bank of Central African States (BEAC). **e** 2019. **f** Data classified according to ISIC Rev. 4. **g** Excludes irrigation canals and landscaping care. **h** Excludes publishing activities, recycling. Includes irrigation canals. **i** Estimate. **j** N'Djamena **k** Calculated by the UN Statistics Division from national indices. **l** Data refers to a 5-year period preceding the reference year. **m** Including refugees. **n** 2020. **o** Data as at the end of December. **p** Data based on calendar year (January 1 to December 31). **q** 2006. **r** Data are as at 1 January of reporting year. **s** Excluding private non-profit. **t** Excluding business enterprise. **u** 2016. **v** Arrivals by air. **w** Non-resident tourists staying in hotels and similar establishments.

Channel Islands

Region	Northern Europe	Surface area (km2)	180 [a,b]
Capital city	Saint Helier [c]	National currency	Pound Sterling (GBP)
Capital city pop. (000, 2023)	34.4 [d]	Exchange rate (per US$)	0.8 [e]

Economic indicators	2010	2015	2023
Employment in agriculture (% of employed) [f]	3.1	2.6	2.3 [g]
Employment in industry (% of employed) [f]	28.8	27.1	25.2 [g]
Employment in services & other sectors (% employed) [f]	67.9	70.2	72.4 [g]
Unemployment rate (% of labour force) [f]	7.6	8.6	7.4
Labour force participation rate (female/male pop. %) [f]	52.7 / 67.9	51.6 / 67.4	51.9 / 65.6

Social indicators	2010	2015	2023
Urban population (% of total population) [a]	31.1	31.0	30.9 [h]
Urban population growth rate (average annual %) [a,i]	0.9	0.5	...
International migrant stock (000/% of total pop.) [j]	77.6 / 48.6	82.3 / 49.8	84.1 / 48.4 [k]

Environment and infrastructure indicators	2010	2015	2023
Forested area (% of land area)	5.2	5.2 [f]	5.2 [f,k]

a Refers to Guernsey and Jersey. b 2017. c The capital of the Bailiwick of Jersey. d 2018. e 2022. f Estimate. g 2021. h 2019. i Data refers to a 5-year period preceding the reference year. j Refers to Guernsey, and Jersey. For statistical purposes, the data for United Kingdom do not include this area. k 2020.

Chile

Region	South America
Population (000, 2023)	19 604 [a,b]
Pop. density (per km2, 2023)	26.0 [a,b]
Capital city	Santiago
Capital city pop. (000, 2023)	6 723.5 [d,e]

UN membership date	24 October 1945
Surface area (km2)	756 102 [c]
Sex ratio (m per 100 f)	98.5 [a,b]
National currency	Chilean Peso (CLP)
Exchange rate (per US$)	867.0 [b]

Economic indicators	2010	2015	2023
GDP: Gross domestic product (million current US$)	218 538	243 919	317 059 [c]
GDP growth rate (annual %, const. 2015 prices)	5.8	2.3	11.7 [c]
GDP per capita (current US$)	12 852.0	13 649.5	16 265.1 [c]
Economy: Agriculture (% of Gross Value Added) [f,g]	3.9	4.0	3.7 [c]
Economy: Industry (% of Gross Value Added) [g,h]	38.8	32.6	35.4 [c]
Economy: Services and other activity (% of GVA) [g]	57.3	63.4	60.9 [c]
Employment in agriculture (% of employed)	10.7	9.2	6.6 [c]
Employment in industry (% of employed)	15.3 [i]	23.7	1.0 [i,c]
Employment in services & other sectors (% employed)	66.4	67.1	70.4 [c]
Unemployment rate (% of labour force)	8.4	6.5	8.5 [i]
Labour force participation rate (female/male pop. %)	45.5 / 72.3	48.4 / 71.7	47.9 / 68.4 [i]
CPI: Consumer Price Index (2010=100)	100	118	159 [b]
Agricultural production index (2014-2016=100)	93	101	107 [c]
International trade: exports (million current US$)	71 106	62 033	97 491 [b]
International trade: imports (million current US$)	59 007	62 387	104 402 [b]
International trade: balance (million current US$)	12 099	- 354	- 6 911 [b]
Balance of payments, current account (million US$)	3 069	- 6 631	- 27 102 [b]

Major trading partners						2022
Export partners (% of exports)	China	39.4	United States	13.9	Japan	7.6
Import partners (% of imports) [i]	China	25.3	United States	20.9	Brazil	9.8

Social indicators	2010	2015	2023
Population growth rate (average annual %)	1.0	1.0	0.1 [a,b]
Urban population (% of total population)	87.1	87.4	87.6 [e]
Urban population growth rate (average annual %) [j]	1.1	1.0	...
Fertility rate, total (live births per woman)	1.8	1.7	1.5 [a,b]
Life expectancy at birth (females/males, years)	81.2 / 75.7	82.4 / 77.0	81.9 / 77.2 [a,b]
Population age distribution (0-14/60+ years old, %)	21.5 / 13.9	20.0 / 15.8	18.3 / 18.3 [a,b]
International migrant stock (000/% of total pop.)	375.4 / 2.2	639.7 / 3.6	1 645.0 / 8.6 [k]
Refugees and others of concern to the UNHCR (000)	1.9 [l]	2.5	513.2 [m,b]
Infant mortality rate (per 1 000 live births)	7.3	6.8	4.9 [a,b]
Health: Current expenditure (% of GDP) [n]	6.8 [o]	8.3 [p]	9.1 [p,c]
Health: Physicians (per 1 000 pop.)	1.4	2.2	3.0 [c]
Education: Government expenditure (% of GDP)	4.2	4.9	5.6 [e]
Education: Primary gross enrol. ratio (f/m per 100 pop.)	102.2 / 105.2	99.1 / 102.2	99.8 / 103.1 [k]
Education: Lowr. sec. gross enrol. ratio (f/m per 100 pop.)	98.1 / 98.4	104.4 / 106.4	103.2 / 106.9 [k]
Education: Upr. sec. gross enrol. ratio (f/m per 100 pop.)	88.3 / 84.1	101.0 / 99.1	103.1 / 102.7 [k]
Intentional homicide rate (per 100 000 pop.)	3.2	2.3	3.6 [c]
Seats held by women in the National Parliament (%)	14.2	15.8	35.5 [q]

Environment and infrastructure indicators	2010	2015	2023
Individuals using the Internet (per 100 inhabitants)	45.0 [i,r]	76.6	90.2 [i,c]
Research & Development expenditure (% of GDP)	0.3	0.4	0.3 [i,e]
Threatened species (number)	145	182	283 [b]
Forested area (% of land area)	22.5	23.7	24.5 [k]
CO2 emission estimates (million tons/tons per capita)	70.5 / 4.0	83.0 / 4.5	88.6 / 4.4 [c]
Energy production, primary (Petajoules)	386	541	535 [i,k]
Energy supply per capita (Gigajoules)	76	85	82 [k]
Tourist/visitor arrivals at national borders (000) [s]	2 801	4 478	190 [c]
Important sites for terrestrial biodiversity protected (%)	26.9	28.9	33.3 [b]
Pop. using safely managed drinking water (urban/rural, %)	99.0 / ...	99.3 / ...	99.4 / ... [b]
Pop. using safely managed sanitation (urban/rural %)	85.9 / ...	97.2 / ...	99.2 / ... [b]
Net Official Development Assist. received (% of GNI)	0.09	0.02	0.03 [t]

a Projected estimate (medium fertility variant). b 2022. c 2021. d Refers to the urban population of Santiago Metropolitan Area Region. e 2019. f Excludes irrigation canals and landscaping care. g Data classified according to ISIC Rev. 4. h Excludes publishing activities, recycling. Includes irrigation canals. i Estimate. j Data refers to a 5-year period preceding the reference year. k 2020. l Data as at the end of December. m The number of other people in need of international protection is estimated from the Refugee and Migrant Response Plan. n Data based on calendar year (January 1 to December 31). o Country is still reporting data based on SHA 1.0. p Data are based on SHA2011. q Data are as at 1 January of reporting year. r Population aged 5 years and over. s Including nationals residing abroad. t 2017.

China

Region	Eastern Asia	UN membership date	24 October 1945
Population (000, 2023)	1 425 887 [a,b,c]	Surface area (km2)	9 600 000 [d]
Pop. density (per km2, 2023)	148.5 [a,b,c]	Sex ratio (m per 100 f)	104.2 [a,b,c]
Capital city	Beijing	National currency	Yuan Renminbi (CNY)
Capital city pop. (000, 2023)	20 035.5 [e,f]	Exchange rate (per US$)	7.0 [b,c]

Economic indicators

	2010	2015	2023
GDP: Gross domestic product (million current US$) [b]	6 087 188	11 061 570	17 734 131 [d]
GDP growth rate (annual %, const. 2015 prices) [b]	10.6	7.0	8.1 [d]
GDP per capita (current US$) [b]	4 515.1	7 936.7	12 437.2 [d]
Economy: Agriculture (% of Gross Value Added) [g,h]	9.9	8.7 [i]	7.6 [i,d]
Economy: Industry (% of Gross Value Added) [h]	46.4	41.0 [g,j]	39.6 [g,j,d]
Economy: Services and other activity (% of GVA) [g,h]	43.7 [k]	50.3 [l]	52.8 [l,d]
Employment in agriculture (% of employed) [b,m]	36.7	28.6	24.4 [d]
Employment in industry (% of employed) [b,m]	28.7	29.2	28.2 [d]
Employment in services & other sectors (% employed) [b,m]	34.6	42.2	47.3 [d]
Unemployment rate (% of labour force) [b,m]	4.5	4.6	4.6
Labour force participation rate (female/male pop. %) [b]	63.7 / 78.1	62.7 / 75.8 [m]	60.4 / 72.0 [m]
CPI: Consumer Price Index (2010=100)	100	115	115 [n,c]
Agricultural production index (2014-2016=100) [b]	88	101	109 [d]
International trade: exports (million current US$) [b]	1 577 764	2 273 468	3 593 601 [c]
International trade: imports (million current US$) [b]	1 396 002	1 679 564	2 715 998 [c]
International trade: balance (million current US$) [b]	181 762	593 904	877 604 [c]
Balance of payments, current account (million US$) [b]	237 810	293 022	401 855 [c]

Major trading partners

						2022
Export partners (% of exports)	United States	16.2	China, Hong Kong SAR	8.3	Japan	4.8
Import partners (% of imports)	Other Asia, nes	8.8	Republic of Korea	7.4	Japan	6.8

Social indicators

	2010	2015	2023
Population growth rate (average annual %) [b]	0.7	0.6	-–0.0 [a,c]
Urban population (% of total population) [b]	49.2	55.5	60.3 [f]
Urban population growth rate (average annual %) [b,o]	3.5	2.9	...
Fertility rate, total (live births per woman) [b]	1.7	1.7	1.2 [a,c]
Life expectancy at birth (females/males, years) [b]	78.3 / 73.1	79.8 / 74.4	81.3 / 76.0 [a,c]
Population age distribution (0-14/60+ years old, %) [b]	18.5 / 12.8	18.4 / 15.6	17.2 / 18.6 [a,c]
International migrant stock (000/% of total pop.) [b,p]	849.9 / 0.1	978.0 / 0.1	1 039.7 / 0.1 [q]
Refugees and others of concern to the UNHCR (000)	301.1 [b,p]	301.6 [b]	1.1 [r,c]
Infant mortality rate (per 1 000 live births) [b]	13.0	8.9	5.9 [a,c]
Health: Current expenditure (% of GDP)	4.2	4.9	5.6 [q]
Health: Physicians (per 1 000 pop.)	1.5	1.8	2.4 [q]
Education: Government expenditure (% of GDP)	3.8	3.8	3.5 [s]
Education: Primary gross enrol. ratio (f/m per 100 pop.)	98.0 / 99.8	96.4 / 96.2	104.6 / 103.7 [d]
Education: Lowr. sec. gross enrol. ratio (f/m per 100 pop.)	100.8 / 99.8	... / ...	... / ...
Education: Upr. sec. gross enrol. ratio (f/m per 100 pop.)	76.1 / 77.5	81.1 / 77.4	85.5 / 83.8 [d]
Intentional homicide rate (per 100 000 pop.)	1.0	0.7	0.5 [q]
Seats held by women in the National Parliament (%)	21.3	23.6	24.9 [t]

Environment and infrastructure indicators

	2010	2015	2023
Individuals using the Internet (per 100 inhabitants) [b]	34.3	50.3 [m,u,v,w]	73.0 [d]
Research & Development expenditure (% of GDP) [b]	1.7	2.1	2.4 [q]
Threatened species (number) [b]	859	1 040	1 419 [c]
Forested area (% of land area) [b]	21.4	22.4	23.4 [q]
CO2 emission estimates (million tons/tons per capita) [b]	7 943.8 / 5.8	9 248.0 / 6.6	10 190.6 / 7.2 [q]
Energy production, primary (Petajoules) [b]	88 642	100 963	111 744 [q]
Energy supply per capita (Gigajoules) [b]	75	86	98 [q]
Tourist/visitor arrivals at national borders (000) [b]	55 664	56 886	7 967 [q]
Important sites for terrestrial biodiversity protected (%)	8.6	9.5	10.1 [c]
Pop. using safely managed drinking water (urban/rural, %)	89.7 / ...	93.8 / ...	97.9 / ... [c]
Pop. using safely managed sanitation (urban/rural %) [b]	53.4 / 15.3	69.8 / 24.0	84.7 / 36.7 [c]
Net Official Development Assist. received (% of GNI) [b]	0.01	0.00	0.00 [d]

a Projected estimate (medium fertility variant). b For statistical purposes, the data for China do not include those for the Hong Kong Special Administrative Region (Hong Kong SAR), Macao Special Administrative Region (Macao SAR) and Taiwan Province of China. c 2022. d 2021. e Refers to all city districts (excluding Yanqing District) meeting the criteria such as contiguous built-up areas, being the location of the local government, being a Street or Having a Resident Committee. f 2019. g Includes taxes less subsidies on production and imports. h Data classified according to ISIC Rev. 4. i Excludes irrigation canals and landscaping care. j Excludes publishing activities, recycling. Includes irrigation canals. k Excludes repair of motor vehicles and motorcycles, personal and household goods. l Excludes repair of personal and household goods. m Estimate. n Index base: 2015=100. o Data refers to a 5-year period preceding the reference year. p Refers to foreign citizens. q 2020. r Indo-Chinese population is no longer considered as refugees since June 2022. s 2018. t Data are as at 1 January of reporting year. u Population aged 6 years and over. v Users in the last 6 months. w Data refer to permanent residents.

China, Hong Kong SAR

Region	Eastern Asia	Population (000, 2023)	7 489[a,b]
Surface area (km2)	1 107[c]	Pop. density (per km2, 2023)	6 814.3[a,b]
Sex ratio (m per 100 f)	85.4[a,b]	Capital city	Hong Kong
National currency	Hong Kong Dollar (HKD)	Capital city pop. (000, 2023)	7 490.8[d,e]
Exchange rate (per US$)	7.8[b]		

Economic indicators	2010	2015	2023
GDP: Gross domestic product (million current US$)	228 639	309 386	369 174[c]
GDP growth rate (annual %, const. 2015 prices)	6.8	2.4	6.3[c]
GDP per capita (current US$)	32 056.2	41 809.8	49 258.8[c]
Economy: Agriculture (% of Gross Value Added)[f,g,h]	0.1	0.1	0.1[c]
Economy: Industry (% of Gross Value Added)[g,i,j]	7.0	7.3	6.2[c]
Economy: Services and other activity (% of GVA)[g]	93.0	92.7	93.7[c]
Employment in agriculture (% of employed)[k]	0.3	0.2	0.2[c]
Employment in industry (% of employed)	13.7	13.7	13.5[k,c]
Employment in services & other sectors (% of employed)	86.1	86.1	86.3[k,c]
Unemployment rate (% of labour force)	4.3	3.3	4.8[k]
Labour force participation rate (female/male pop. %)	51.9 / 68.5	54.7 / 68.8	53.4 / 64.8[k]
CPI: Consumer Price Index (2010=100)	100	123	140[b]
Agricultural production index (2014-2016=100)	101	97	220[c]
International trade: exports (million current US$)	400 692	510 553	610 138[b]
International trade: imports (million current US$)	441 369	559 306	668 483[b]
International trade: balance (million current US$)	- 40 677	- 48 753	- 58 345[b]
Balance of payments, current account (million US$)	16 012	10 264	38 603[b]

Major trading partners						2022
Export partners (% of exports)	China	57.4	United States	6.2	India	3.7
Import partners (% of imports)	China	40.1	Other Asia, nes	11.3	Singapore	7.7

Social indicators	2010	2015	2023
Population growth rate (average annual %)	0.5	0.6	--0.0[a,b]
Urban population (% of total population)	100.0	100.0	100.0[e]
Urban population growth rate (average annual %)[l]	0.6	0.6	...
Fertility rate, total (live births per woman)	1.1	1.2	0.8[a,b]
Life expectancy at birth (females/males, years)	85.9 / 80.2	87.2 / 81.5	86.9 / 81.8[a,b]
Population age distribution (0-14/60+ years old, %)	12.3 / 18.5	11.6 / 21.9	12.0 / 28.7[a,b]
International migrant stock (000/% of total pop.)[m]	2 780.0 / 39.9	2 841.1 / 39.5	2 962.5 / 39.5[n]
Refugees and others of concern to the UNHCR (000)	0.6[o]	10.1	0.3[b]
Infant mortality rate (per 1 000 live births)	1.7	1.4	1.4[a,b]
Education: Government expenditure (% of GDP)	3.5	3.3	4.0[c]
Education: Primary gross enrol. ratio (f/m per 100 pop.)	... / ...	111.2 / 109.3	106.0 / 101.6[c]
Education: Lowr. sec. gross enrol. ratio (f/m per 100 pop.)	104.1 / 105.1	105.6 / 107.9	107.4 / 105.7[c]
Education: Upr. sec. gross enrol. ratio (f/m per 100 pop.)	77.7 / 76.4	97.9 / 99.2	104.7 / 107.9[c]
Intentional homicide rate (per 100 000 pop.)	0.5	0.3	0.3[c]

Environment and infrastructure indicators	2010	2015	2023
Individuals using the Internet (per 100 inhabitants)[p]	72.0	84.9[q]	93.1[q,c]
Research & Development expenditure (% of GDP)	0.7	0.8	1.0[c]
Threatened species (number)	49	60	100[b]
CO2 emission estimates (million tons/tons per capita)	41.7 / 5.9	43.5 / 5.9	34.6 / 4.6[n]
Energy supply per capita (Gigajoules)	76	78	68[n]
Tourist/visitor arrivals at national borders (000)	20 085	26 686	89[c]
Important sites for terrestrial biodiversity protected (%)	48.9	48.9	48.9[b]
Pop. using safely managed drinking water (urban/rural, %)	99.4 / ...	100.0 / ...	100.0 / ...[b]
Pop. using safely managed sanitation (urban/rural %)	75.1 / ...	80.2 / ...	96.5 / ...[b]

a Projected estimate (medium fertility variant). b 2022. c 2021. d Consists of the population of Hong Kong Island, New Kowloon the new towns in New Territories and the marine areas. e 2019. f Excluding hunting and forestry. g Data classified according to ISIC Rev. 4. h Includes mining and quarrying. i Excludes publishing activities, recycling. Includes irrigation canals. j Excludes mining and quarrying. k Estimate. l Data refers to a 5-year period preceding the reference year. m Including refugees. n 2020. o Data as at the end of December. p Population aged 10 years and over. q Users in the last 12 months.

China, Macao SAR

Region	Eastern Asia
Surface area (km2)	33 [c,d]
Sex ratio (m per 100 f)	88.4 [a,b]
National currency	Pataca (MOP)
Exchange rate (per US$)	8.0 [b]

Population (000, 2023)	695 [a,b]
Pop. density (per km2, 2023)	21 724.0 [a,b]
Capital city	Macao
Capital city pop. (000, 2023)	642.1 [e]

Economic indicators

	2010	2015	2023
GDP: Gross domestic product (million current US$)	28 242	45 048	29 905 [d]
GDP growth rate (annual %, const. 2015 prices)	25.1	- 21.5	18.0 [d]
GDP per capita (current US$)	50 676.4	73 220.6	43 554.9 [d]
Economy: Industry (% of Gross Value Added)	7.4	10.4	7.4 [d]
Economy: Services and other activity (% of GVA)	92.6	89.6	92.6 [d]
Employment in agriculture (% of employed) [f]	0.4	0.7	1.3 [d]
Employment in industry (% of employed)	17.6 [f]	15.7	2.1 [f,d]
Employment in services & other sectors (% employed)	82.0	83.6	88.0 [f,d]
Unemployment rate (% of labour force)	2.8	1.8	1.9 [f]
Labour force participation rate (female/male pop. %)	64.3 / 75.9	65.9 / 76.0	63.8 / 74.4 [f]
CPI: Consumer Price Index (2010=100)	100	131 [g]	147 [g,b]
Agricultural production index (2014-2016=100)	107	87	72 [d]
International trade: exports (million current US$)	870	1 339	1 367 [b]
International trade: imports (million current US$)	5 629	10 603	17 431 [b]
International trade: balance (million current US$)	- 4 760	- 9 264	- 16 064 [b]
Balance of payments, current account (million US$)	10 992	10 515	1 760 [d]

Major trading partners

							2022
Export partners (% of exports)	China, Hong Kong SAR	84.4	China	9.3	United States	3.8
Import partners (% of imports)	China	30.6	France	18.6	Italy	10.9

Social indicators

	2010	2015	2023
Population growth rate (average annual %)	2.6	1.8	1.3 [a,b]
Urban population (% of total population)	100.0	100.0	100.0 [e]
Urban population growth rate (average annual %) [h]	2.1	2.3	...
Fertility rate, total (live births per woman)	1.0	1.2	1.1 [a,b]
Life expectancy at birth (females/males, years)	86.2 / 80.0	86.8 / 81.1	88.0 / 82.8 [a,b]
Population age distribution (0-14/60+ years old, %)	12.9 / 11.3	12.9 / 14.5	14.8 / 19.5 [a,b]
International migrant stock (000/% of total pop.)	318.5 / 59.2	376.1 / 62.5	403.5 / 62.1 [i]
Refugees and others of concern to the UNHCR (000)	~0.0 [j]	~0.0	~0.0 [i]
Infant mortality rate (per 1 000 live births)	3.4	2.8	2.2 [a,b]
Education: Government expenditure (% of GDP)	2.6	3.0	6.4 [i]
Education: Primary gross enrol. ratio (f/m per 100 pop.)	94.0 / 95.8	98.5 / 100.1	96.4 / 98.5 [d]
Education: Lowr. sec. gross enrol. ratio (f/m per 100 pop.)	100.6 / 108.7	102.7 / 106.9	108.7 / 109.4 [d]
Education: Upr. sec. gross enrol. ratio (f/m per 100 pop.)	75.3 / 73.3	87.4 / 86.7	100.4 / 100.4 [d]
Intentional homicide rate (per 100 000 pop.)	0.4	0.2	0.4 [d]

Environment and infrastructure indicators

	2010	2015	2023
Individuals using the Internet (per 100 inhabitants)	55.2 [k]	77.6 [l]	88.5 [k,d]
Research & Development expenditure (% of GDP) [m]	0.1	0.1	0.4 [d]
Threatened species (number)	9	11	27 [b]
Energy production, primary (Petajoules)	4 [f]	3	3 [i]
Energy supply per capita (Gigajoules)	58	69	54 [i]
Tourist/visitor arrivals at national borders (000) [n]	11 926	14 308	3 697 [d]
Important sites for terrestrial biodiversity protected (%)	0.0	0.0	0.0 [b]
Pop. using safely managed drinking water (urban/rural, %)	100.0 / ...	100.0 / ...	100.0 / ... [b]
Pop. using safely managed sanitation (urban/rural %)	56.0 / ...	61.1 / ...	68.1 / ... [b]

a Projected estimate (medium fertility variant). b 2022. c Inland waters include the reservoirs. d 2021. e 2019. f Estimate. g Calculated by the UN Statistics Division from national indices. h Data refers to a 5-year period preceding the reference year. i 2020. j Data as at the end of December. k Population aged 3 years and over. l Users in the last 3 months. m Partial data. n Does not include other non-residents namely workers, students, etc.

Colombia

Region	South America	UN membership date	05 November 1945
Population (000, 2023)	51 874 [a,b]	Surface area (km2)	1 141 748 [c]
Pop. density (per km2, 2023)	46.2 [a,b]	Sex ratio (m per 100 f)	97.3 [a,b]
Capital city	Bogota	National currency	Colombian Peso (COP)
Capital city pop. (000, 2023)	10 779.4 [d,e]	Exchange rate (per US$)	4 810.2 [b]

Economic indicators	2010	2015	2023
GDP: Gross domestic product (million current US$)	286 563	293 482	314 464 [c]
GDP growth rate (annual %, const. 2015 prices)	4.5	3.0	10.7 [c]
GDP per capita (current US$)	6 394.2	6 228.4	6 104.1 [c]
Economy: Agriculture (% of Gross Value Added) [f,g]	6.9	6.6	8.2 [c]
Economy: Industry (% of Gross Value Added) [g,h]	34.4	31.5	27.7 [c]
Economy: Services and other activity (% of GVA) [g]	58.6	61.9	64.1 [c]
Employment in agriculture (% of employed)	18.4	16.0	15.9 [c]
Employment in industry (% of employed)	20.0	19.8	20.1 [c]
Employment in services & other sectors (% employed)	61.6	64.2	63.9 [c]
Unemployment (% of labour force)	11.0	8.3	10.6 [i]
Labour force participation rate (female/male pop. %)	55.3 / 80.8	58.1 / 81.4	51.9 / 76.2 [i]
CPI: Consumer Price Index (2010=100) [j]	100	118	165 [b]
Agricultural production index (2014-2016=100)	81	101	104 [c]
International trade: exports (million current US$)	39 820	35 691	57 451 [i,b]
International trade: imports (million current US$)	40 683	54 036	76 300 [i,b]
International trade: balance (million current US$)	- 863	- 18 345	- 18 849 [i,b]
Balance of payments, current account (million US$)	- 8 583	- 18 702	- 21 446 [b]

Major trading partners						2022
Export partners (% of exports) [i]	United States	28.1	China	8.8	Panama	5.8
Import partners (% of imports) [i]	China	24.2	United States	23.2	Mexico	6.2

Social indicators	2010	2015	2023
Population growth rate (average annual %)	1.1	1.0	0.3 [a,b]
Urban population (% of total population)	78.0	79.8	81.1 [e]
Urban population growth rate (average annual %) [k]	1.7	1.4	...
Fertility rate, total (live births per woman)	2.0	1.9	1.7 [a,b]
Life expectancy at birth (females/males, years)	78.3 / 71.8	79.3 / 73.3	77.1 / 70.3 [a,b]
Population age distribution (0-14/60+ years old, %)	27.1 / 9.0	24.4 / 10.8	21.3 / 13.5 [a,b]
International migrant stock (000/% of total pop.)	130.3 / 0.3	159.4 / 0.3	1 905.4 / 3.7 [l]
Refugees and others of concern to the UNHCR (000)	3 672.4 [m]	6 520.6	9 752.9 [n,b]
Infant mortality rate (per 1 000 live births)	15.5	13.2	10.9 [a,b]
Health: Current expenditure (% of GDP) [o]	7.1	7.5 [p]	9.0 [p,l]
Health: Physicians (per 1 000 pop.)	1.7	2.0	2.4 [c]
Education: Government expenditure (% of GDP)	4.8	4.5	5.2 [l]
Education: Primary gross enrol. ratio (f/m per 100 pop.)	119.3 / 121.3	113.4 / 117.0	111.4 / 114.9 [c]
Education: Lowr. sec. gross enrol. ratio (f/m per 100 pop.)	110.0 / 103.4	104.7 / 101.3	114.3 / 113.0 [c]
Education: Upr. sec. gross enrol. ratio (f/m per 100 pop.)	87.0 / 72.6	85.2 / 72.0	94.4 / 83.6 [c]
Intentional homicide rate (per 100 000 pop.)	34.5	27.1	27.5 [c]
Seats held by women in the National Parliament (%)	8.4	19.9	28.9 [q]

Environment and infrastructure indicators	2010	2015	2023
Individuals using the Internet (per 100 inhabitants)	36.5 [r]	55.9	73.0 [r,c]
Research & Development expenditure (% of GDP)	0.2	0.4	0.3 [i,l]
Threatened species (number)	681	751	1 711 [b]
Forested area (% of land area)	54.8	54.2	53.3 [l]
CO2 emission estimates (million tons/tons per capita)	60.9 / 1.3	76.5 / 1.6	64.8 / 1.2 [c]
Energy production, primary (Petajoules)	4 486	5 456	4 025 [l]
Energy supply per capita (Gigajoules)	31	36	33 [l]
Tourist/visitor arrivals at national borders (000) [s]	1 405	3 099 [t,u]	2 155 [t,u,c]
Important sites for terrestrial biodiversity protected (%)	38.9	49.5	58.6 [b]
Pop. using safely managed drinking water (urban/rural, %)	81.1 / 36.9	81.2 / 38.3	81.2 / 40.2 [b]
Pop. using safely managed sanitation (urban/rural %)	15.4 / ...	16.0 / ...	16.8 / ... [b]
Net Official Development Assist. received (% of GNI)	0.24	0.47	0.63 [c]

a Projected estimate (medium fertility variant). b 2022. c 2021. d Refers to the nuclei of Santa Fe de Bogotá, Soacha, Chia and Funza. e 2019. f Excludes irrigation canals and landscaping care. g Data classified according to ISIC Rev. 4. h Excludes publishing activities, recycling. Includes irrigation canals. i Estimate. j Calculated by the UN Statistics Division from national indices. k Data refers to a 5-year period preceding the reference year. l 2020. m Data as at the end of December. n The National Victims Registry contains the historical accumulated figure of the number of victims of displacement (exceeding 8.2 million) which includes the number of IDPs who are subject to attention and/or reparation established in Colombian Law 1448 (6.7 million). o Data based on calendar year (January 1 to December 31). p Data are based on SHA2011. q Data are as at 1 January of reporting year. r Population aged 5 years and over. s Arrivals of non-resident travellers by immigration checkpoints. t The nationals residing abroad are calculated with the country of residence reported at the exit. u Including nationals residing abroad.

Comoros

Region	Eastern Africa	UN membership date	12 November 1975
Population (000, 2023)	837[a,b]	Surface area (km2)	2 235[c]
Pop. density (per km2, 2023)	449.6[a,b]	Sex ratio (m per 100 f)	100.9[a,b]
Capital city	Moroni	National currency	Comorian Franc (KMF)
Capital city pop. (000, 2023)	62.4[d]	Exchange rate (per US$)	461.2[b]

Economic indicators	2010	2015	2023
GDP: Gross domestic product (million current US$)	907	966	1 340[c]
GDP growth rate (annual %, const. 2015 prices)	4.8	2.0	2.3[c]
GDP per capita (current US$)	1 382.7	1 322.4	1 631.5[c]
Economy: Agriculture (% of Gross Value Added)	31.6	31.7	38.7[c]
Economy: Industry (% of Gross Value Added)	12.2	10.8	8.7[c]
Economy: Services and other activity (% of GVA)	56.1	57.5	52.5[c]
Employment in agriculture (% of employed)[e]	45.3	37.5	35.0[c]
Employment in industry (% of employed)[e]	17.1	19.1	20.2[c]
Employment in services & other sectors (% employed)[e]	37.7	43.3	44.9[c]
Unemployment rate (% of labour force)[e]	6.7	8.1	8.9
Labour force participation rate (female/male pop. %)[e]	32.6 / 54.2	32.8 / 56.2	33.3 / 55.1
CPI: Consumer Price Index (2010=100)	100	104[f]	...
Agricultural production index (2014-2016=100)	98	99	106[c]
International trade: exports (million current US$)	14	15	39[e,b]
International trade: imports (million current US$)	181	173	537[e,b]
International trade: balance (million current US$)	- 167	- 158	- 498[e,b]
Balance of payments, current account (million US$)	- 39	- 2	6[c]

Major trading partners						2022
Export partners (% of exports)[e]	India	24.7	United Rep. Tanzania	21.3	France	19.9
Import partners (% of imports)[e]	United Arab Emirates	43.4	France	10.5	Pakistan	7.2

Social indicators	2010	2015	2023
Population growth rate (average annual %)	2.1	2.2	1.8[a,b]
Urban population (% of total population)	28.0	28.5	29.2[g]
Urban population growth rate (average annual %)[h]	2.5	2.7	...
Fertility rate, total (live births per woman)	4.8	4.4	3.9[a,b]
Life expectancy at birth (females/males, years)	63.1 / 59.3	65.2 / 60.8	66.1 / 61.5[a,b]
Population age distribution (0-14/60+ years old, %)	42.0 / 6.0	39.8 / 6.2	38.0 / 6.5[a,b]
International migrant stock (000/% of total pop.)	12.6 / 1.8	12.6 / 1.6	12.5 / 1.4[i]
Refugees and others of concern to the UNHCR (000)	~0.0[j,k]	...	~0.0[b]
Infant mortality rate (per 1 000 live births)	62.4	54.4	45.5[a,b]
Health: Current expenditure (% of GDP)[l]	5.0	4.6	5.3[i]
Health: Physicians (per 1 000 pop.)	0.2[m]	0.2[n]	0.3[d]
Education: Government expenditure (% of GDP)	4.4[o]	2.5	...
Education: Primary gross enrol. ratio (f/m per 100 pop.)	104.1 / 113.0[o]	101.2 / 108.6[p]	99.4 / 99.6[d]
Education: Lowr. sec. gross enrol. ratio (f/m per 100 pop.)	... / ...	68.7 / 65.4[p]	70.8 / 67.7[d]
Education: Upr. sec. gross enrol. ratio (f/m per 100 pop.)	... / ...	55.1 / 50.0[p]	47.8 / 42.9[d]
Seats held by women in the National Parliament (%)	3.0	3.0[p]	16.7[q]

Environment and infrastructure indicators	2010	2015	2023
Individuals using the Internet (per 100 inhabitants)[e]	5.1	7.5	27.3[c]
Threatened species (number)	89	106	149[b]
Forested area (% of land area)	20.0	18.9	17.7[i]
Energy production, primary (Petajoules)[e]	3	4	4[i]
Energy supply per capita (Gigajoules)[e]	8	8	11[i]
Tourist/visitor arrivals at national borders (000)[r]	15	24	29[c]
Important sites for terrestrial biodiversity protected (%)	57.4	57.4	57.4[b]
Net Official Development Assist. received (% of GNI)	7.71	6.79	11.65[c]

a Projected estimate (medium fertility variant). b 2022. c 2021. d 2018. e Estimate. f 2013. g 2019. h Data refers to a 5-year period preceding the reference year. i 2020. j Data as at the end of December. k 2005. l Data based on calendar year (January 1 to December 31). m 2009. n 2012. o 2008. p 2014. q Data are as at 1 January of reporting year. r Arrivals by air.

Congo

Region	Middle Africa	UN membership date	20 September 1960
Population (000, 2023)	5 970[a,b]	Surface area (km2)	342 000[c]
Pop. density (per km2, 2023)	17.5[a,b]	Sex ratio (m per 100 f)	99.8[a,b]
Capital city	Brazzaville	National currency	CFA Franc, BEAC (XAF)[d]
Capital city pop. (000, 2023)	2 308.1[e]	Exchange rate (per US$)	615.0[d]

Economic indicators

	2010	2015	2023
GDP: Gross domestic product (million current US$)	13 136	11 881	12 841[c]
GDP growth rate (annual %, const. 2015 prices)	9.9	- 3.6	- 0.6[c]
GDP per capita (current US$)	2 959.9	2 346.0	2 200.3[c]
Economy: Agriculture (% of Gross Value Added)	4.2	6.3	8.7[c]
Economy: Industry (% of Gross Value Added)	68.0	50.4	43.8[c]
Economy: Services and other activity (% of GVA)	27.8	43.3	47.5[c]
Employment in agriculture (% of employed)[f]	36.4	34.5	36.3[c]
Employment in industry (% of employed)[f]	24.6	24.4	21.1[c]
Employment in services & other sectors (% employed)[f]	39.0	41.2	42.6[c]
Unemployment rate (% of labour force)[f]	20.0	20.5	21.6
Labour force participation rate (female/male pop. %)[f]	66.9 / 68.8	66.7 / 69.3	67.0 / 68.4
CPI: Consumer Price Index (2010=100)[f,g]	100	116	133[b]
Agricultural production index (2014-2016=100)	85	102	108[c]
International trade: exports (million current US$)	6 918	8 623	3 714[f,b]
International trade: imports (million current US$)	4 369	10 550	3 048[f,b]
International trade: balance (million current US$)	2 548	- 1 927	666[f,b]
Balance of payments, current account (million US$)	901	- 4 631	1 441[h]

Major trading partners

					2022
Export partners (% of exports)[f]	China	45.8	Côte d'Ivoire	8.6	Togo 7.5
Import partners (% of imports)[f]	China	19.6	France	12.5	Belgium 9.0

Social indicators

	2010	2015	2023
Population growth rate (average annual %)	3.3	2.4	2.3[a,b]
Urban population (% of total population)	63.3	65.5	67.4[e]
Urban population growth rate (average annual %)[i]	4.0	3.3	...
Fertility rate, total (live births per woman)	4.8	4.6	4.1[a,b]
Life expectancy at birth (females/males, years)	62.8 / 60.6	64.3 / 62.1	64.6 / 61.5[a,b]
Population age distribution (0-14/60+ years old, %)	40.6 / 4.1	42.0 / 4.1	41.1 / 4.6[a,b]
International migrant stock (000/% of total pop.)[j]	425.2 / 9.9	390.1 / 8.0	387.6 / 7.0[h]
Refugees and others of concern to the UNHCR (000)	138.7[k]	65.8	199.4[b]
Infant mortality rate (per 1 000 live births)	43.6	37.6	36.7[a,b]
Health: Current expenditure (% of GDP)[l]	1.9	2.5	4.5[h]
Health: Physicians (per 1 000 pop.)	0.1	0.2[m]	0.1[n]
Education: Government expenditure (% of GDP)	5.7	3.3[f]	3.9[c]
Education: Primary gross enrol. ratio (f/m per 100 pop.)	106.1 / 112.2	111.2 / 109.9	92.4 / 95.0[n]
Education: Lowr. sec. gross enrol. ratio (f/m per 100 pop.)	58.0 / 66.1[f,o]	63.6 / 62.7[p]	72.4 / 75.4[n]
Education: Upr. sec. gross enrol. ratio (f/m per 100 pop.)	25.1 / 42.6	36.8 / 47.6[q]	50.8 / 59.5[n]
Seats held by women in the National Parliament (%)	7.3	7.4	14.6[r]

Environment and infrastructure indicators

	2010	2015	2023
Individuals using the Internet (per 100 inhabitants)[f]	5.0	7.6	8.6[s]
Threatened species (number)	103	119	235[b]
Forested area (% of land area)	64.6	64.5	64.3[h]
CO2 emission estimates (million tons/tons per capita)	2.1 / 0.4	3.6 / 0.6	4.0 / 0.6[h]
Energy production, primary (Petajoules)	724	607	776[h]
Energy supply per capita (Gigajoules)	16	23	24[h]
Tourist/visitor arrivals at national borders (000)	194	220	156[n]
Important sites for terrestrial biodiversity protected (%)	58.3	61.6	72.0[b]
Pop. using safely managed drinking water (urban/rural, %)	55.4 / 12.4	58.5 / 17.0	58.6 / 19.1[c]
Net Official Development Assist. received (% of GNI)	10.76	0.75	2.06[c]

a Projected estimate (medium fertility variant). **b** 2022. **c** 2021. **d** African Financial Community (CFA) Franc, Bank of Central African States (BEAC). **e** 2019. **f** Estimate. **g** Brazzaville **h** 2020. **i** Data refers to a 5-year period preceding the reference year. **j** Including refugees. **k** Data as at the end of December. **l** Data based on calendar year (January 1 to December 31). **m** 2011. **n** 2018. **o** 2005. **p** 2012. **q** 2014. **r** Data are as at 1 January of reporting year. **s** 2017.

Cook Islands

Region	Polynesia	Population (000, 2023)	17 [a,b]
Surface area (km2)	236 [c,d]	Pop. density (per km2, 2023)	70.9 [a,b]
Sex ratio (m per 100 f)	90.8 [a,b]	Capital city	Avarua
National currency	New Zealand Dollar (NZD)	Capital city pop. (000, 2023)	13.1 [e,f]
Exchange rate (per US$)	1.6 [b]		

Economic indicators	2010	2015	2023
GDP: Gross domestic product (million current US$)	241	302	328 [d]
GDP growth rate (annual %, const. 2015 prices)	- 4.9	5.7	- 10.4 [d]
GDP per capita (current US$)	13 989.6	17 076.8	19 263.9 [d]
Economy: Agriculture (% of Gross Value Added) [g,h]	3.4	3.2	3.0 [d]
Economy: Industry (% of Gross Value Added) [g,i,j]	7.9	11.3	11.5 [d]
Economy: Services and other activity (% of GVA) [g]	88.7	85.4	85.5 [d]
Employment in agriculture (% of employed)	...	4.3 [k,l]	...
Employment in industry (% of employed)	...	11.7 [k,l]	...
Employment in services & other sectors (% employed)	...	84.0 [k,l]	...
Unemployment rate (% of labour force) [k]	6.9 [m,n]	8.2 [l]	...
Labour force participation rate (female/male pop. %)	64.2 / 76.1 [k,m,n]	65.4 / 76.6 [k,l]	... / ...
CPI: Consumer Price Index (2010=100) [e,o]	100	109	124 [b]
Agricultural production index (2014-2016=100)	107	100	87 [d]
International trade: exports (million current US$)	5	14 [p]	1 [p,b]
International trade: imports (million current US$)	91	109 [p]	42 [p,b]
International trade: balance (million current US$)	- 85	- 95 [p]	- 42 [p,b]

Major trading partners						2022
Export partners (% of exports) [p]	Japan	30.2	Italy	22.6	France	18.4
Import partners (% of imports) [p]	New Zealand	47.1	Italy	16.4	Fiji	10.0

Social indicators	2010	2015	2023
Population growth rate (average annual %)	3.4	- 0.8	0.3 [a,b]
Urban population (% of total population)	73.3	74.4	75.3 [q]
Urban population growth rate (average annual %) [r]	- 0.6	- 0.9	...
Fertility rate, total (live births per woman)	2.6	2.4	2.2 [a,b]
Life expectancy at birth (females/males, years)	77.8 / 69.9	78.3 / 70.6	79.0 / 71.4 [a,b]
Population age distribution (0-14/60+ years old, %)	28.1 / 12.1	26.2 / 14.0	23.6 / 17.5 [a,b]
International migrant stock (000/% of total pop.) [s]	3.8 / 20.5	4.2 / 23.7	4.6 / 26.1 [t]
Infant mortality rate (per 1 000 live births)	9.2	7.5	5.7 [a,b]
Health: Current expenditure (% of GDP) [u]	3.7	2.7	3.2 [t]
Health: Physicians (per 1 000 pop.)	1.4 [v]	1.4 [w]	1.3 [q]
Education: Government expenditure (% of GDP)	...	3.9	4.6 [d]
Education: Primary gross enrol. ratio (f/m per 100 pop.)	85.4 / 89.8	99.8 / 104.2	106.9 / 113.5 [d]
Education: Lowr. sec. gross enrol. ratio (f/m per 100 pop.)	92.5 / 90.5	95.8 / 95.5	116.0 / 120.3 [d]
Education: Upr. sec. gross enrol. ratio (f/m per 100 pop.)	77.8 / 61.7	82.7 / 71.5	90.5 / 75.4 [d]
Intentional homicide rate (per 100 000 pop.)	...	3.5 [x]	...

Environment and infrastructure indicators	2010	2015	2023
Individuals using the Internet (per 100 inhabitants)	35.7	51.0 [p]	54.0 [p,y]
Threatened species (number)	53	73	82 [b]
Forested area (% of land area)	65.0	65.0	65.0 [t]
Energy production, primary (Petajoules) [p]	0	0	0 [t]
Energy supply per capita (Gigajoules) [p]	62	64	60 [t]
Tourist/visitor arrivals at national borders (000) [z]	104	125	26 [d]
Important sites for terrestrial biodiversity protected (%)	24.4	24.4	30.9 [b]

a Projected estimate (medium fertility variant). b 2022. c Excluding Niue, shown separately, which is part of Cook Islands, but because of remoteness is administered separately. d 2021. e Refers to the island of Rarotonga. f 2018. g Data classified according to ISIC Rev. 4. h Excludes irrigation canals and landscaping care. i Includes mining and quarrying. j Excludes publishing activities, recycling. Includes irrigation canals. k Resident population (de jure). l 2011. m Break in the time series. n 2006. o Calculated by the UN Statistics Division from national indices. p Estimate. q 2019. r Data refers to a 5-year period preceding the reference year. s Including refugees. t 2020. u Data refer to fiscal years beginning 1 July. v 2009. w 2014. x 2012. y 2016. z Air and sea arrivals.

Costa Rica

Region	Central America	UN membership date	02 November 1945
Population (000, 2023)	5 181 [a,b]	Surface area (km2)	51 100 [c]
Pop. density (per km2, 2023)	101.5 [a,b]	Sex ratio (m per 100 f)	100.0 [a,b]
Capital city	San José	National currency	Costa Rican Colon (CRC)
Capital city pop. (000, 2023)	1 378.5 [d,e]	Exchange rate (per US$)	598.1 [b]

Economic indicators	2010	2015	2023
GDP: Gross domestic product (million current US$)	37 659	56 442	64 282 [c]
GDP growth rate (annual %, const. 2015 prices)	5.4	3.7	7.6 [c]
GDP per capita (current US$)	8 147.2	11 530.0	12 472.4 [c]
Economy: Agriculture (% of Gross Value Added) [f,g]	7.1	5.2	4.8 [c]
Economy: Industry (% of Gross Value Added) [g,h]	25.4	21.7	22.4 [c]
Economy: Services and other activity (% of GVA) [g]	67.5	73.1	72.8 [c]
Employment in agriculture (% of employed)	12.4	15.3 [i]	17.1 [c]
Employment in industry (% of employed)	17.7 [i]	19.0	17.2 [c]
Employment in services & other sectors (% employed)	68.0	65.8 [i]	65.7 [c]
Unemployment rate (% of labour force)	7.2	8.4	11.2 [i]
Labour force participation rate (female/male pop. %)	43.9 / 74.6	49.9 / 75.8	50.4 / 73.2 [i]
CPI: Consumer Price Index (2010=100) [j,k]	100	122	143 [b]
Agricultural production index (2014-2016=100)	88	98	103 [c]
International trade: exports (million current US$)	9 045	9 578	17 458 [i,b]
International trade: imports (million current US$)	13 920	15 504	24 764 [i,b]
International trade: balance (million current US$)	- 4 875	- 5 926	- 7 306 [i,b]
Balance of payments, current account (million US$)	- 1 214	- 1 921	- 2 706 [b]

Major trading partners					2022
Export partners (% of exports) [i]	United States	43.7	Netherlands	7.2	Belgium 5.2
Import partners (% of imports) [i]	United States	37.8	China	15.9	Mexico 6.4

Social indicators	2010	2015	2023
Population growth rate (average annual %)	1.3	1.0	0.5 [a,b]
Urban population (% of total population)	71.7	76.9	80.1 [e]
Urban population growth rate (average annual %) [l]	3.1	2.5	...
Fertility rate, total (live births per woman)	1.9	1.8	1.5 [a,b]
Life expectancy at birth (females/males, years)	81.1 / 76.3	81.6 / 76.7	80.0 / 74.8 [a,b]
Population age distribution (0-14/60+ years old, %)	24.7 / 10.9	22.6 / 12.7	20.2 / 15.8 [a,b]
International migrant stock (000/% of total pop.) [m]	405.8 / 8.9	411.7 / 8.5	520.7 / 10.2 [n]
Refugees and others of concern to the UNHCR (000)	19.9 [o]	7.9	236.4 [p,b]
Infant mortality rate (per 1 000 live births)	9.1	7.8	6.8 [a,b]
Health: Current expenditure (% of GDP) [q]	8.0	7.6 [r]	7.9 [r,n]
Health: Physicians (per 1 000 pop.)	2.3	2.7	2.8 [c]
Education: Government expenditure (% of GDP)	6.6	6.9	6.7 [n]
Education: Primary gross enrol. ratio (f/m per 100 pop.)	115.7 / 118.0	111.0 / 111.6	106.2 / 107.1 [c]
Education: Lowr. sec. gross enrol. ratio (f/m per 100 pop.)	117.7 / 118.6	130.2 / 134.9	138.6 / 135.7 [n]
Education: Upr. sec. gross enrol. ratio (f/m per 100 pop.)	82.2 / 70.6	118.2 / 99.9	162.2 / 137.1 [n]
Intentional homicide rate (per 100 000 pop.)	11.4	11.4	11.4 [c]
Seats held by women in the National Parliament (%)	36.8	33.3	47.4 [s]

Environment and infrastructure indicators	2010	2015	2023
Individuals using the Internet (per 100 inhabitants)	36.5 [t,u]	59.8 [t]	82.8 [c]
Research & Development expenditure (% of GDP)	0.5	0.4	0.4 [v]
Threatened species (number)	285	323	655 [b]
Forested area (% of land area)	56.2	57.8	59.4 [n]
CO2 emission estimates (million tons/tons per capita)	6.9 / 1.4	7.2 / 1.4	7.6 / 1.4 [c]
Energy production, primary (Petajoules)	104	110	116 [n]
Energy supply per capita (Gigajoules)	44	42	40 [n]
Tourist/visitor arrivals at national borders (000)	2 100	2 660	1 347 [c]
Important sites for terrestrial biodiversity protected (%)	43.8	43.8	43.9 [b]
Pop. using safely managed drinking water (urban/rural, %)	80.2 / 76.9	80.3 / 79.6	80.4 / 81.1 [b]
Pop. using safely managed sanitation (urban/rural %)	19.3 / 34.6	21.0 / 35.0	23.1 / 35.6 [b]
Net Official Development Assist. received (% of GNI)	0.28	0.21	0.13 [c]

a Projected estimate (medium fertility variant). b 2022. c 2021. d Refers to the urban population of cantons. e 2019. f Excludes irrigation canals and landscaping care. g Data classified according to ISIC Rev. 4. h Excludes publishing activities, recycling. Includes irrigation canals. i Estimate. j Central area. k Calculated by the UN Statistics Division from national indices. l Data refers to a 5-year period preceding the reference year. m Including refugees. n 2020. o Data as at the end of December. p Includes 65,200 applications by Nicaraguans during the first half of the year to formalize their asylum claim. Of these, 38,800 claims were formalized, 12,700 remained to be formalized and 13,700 were closed. q Data based on calendar year (January 1 to December 31). r Data are based on SHA2011. s Data are as at 1 January of reporting year. t Population aged 5 years and over. u Users in the last 3 months. v 2018.

Côte d'Ivoire

Region	Western Africa	UN membership date	20 September 1960
Population (000, 2023)	28 160[a,b]	Surface area (km2)	322 462[c]
Pop. density (per km2, 2023)	88.6[a,b]	Sex ratio (m per 100 f)	101.9[a,b]
Capital city	Yamoussoukro[d]	National currency	CFA Franc, BCEAO (XOF)[e]
Capital city pop. (000, 2023)	231.1[f]	Exchange rate (per US$)	615.0[b]

Economic indicators

	2010	2015	2023
GDP: Gross domestic product (million current US$)	26 264	45 780	69 765[c]
GDP growth rate (annual %, const. 2015 prices)	7.7	14.9	7.0[c]
GDP per capita (current US$)	1 243.6	1 940.1	2 538.9[c]
Economy: Agriculture (% of Gross Value Added)	25.2	19.8	21.9[c]
Economy: Industry (% of Gross Value Added)	22.6	21.1	22.5[c]
Economy: Services and other activity (% of GVA)	52.2	59.1	55.6[c]
Employment in agriculture (% of employed)[g]	47.6	43.5	45.0[c]
Employment in industry (% of employed)[g]	11.3	12.2	10.8[c]
Employment in services & other sectors (% employed)[g]	41.1	44.4	44.2[c]
Unemployment rate (% of labour force)[g]	6.8	2.7	2.6
Labour force participation rate (female/male pop. %)[g]	52.7 / 76.7	54.7 / 74.6	57.5 / 73.1
CPI: Consumer Price Index (2010=100)[g,h]	100	111	125[b]
Agricultural production index (2014-2016=100)	75	104	125[c]
International trade: exports (million current US$)	10 284	12 560	16 669[g,b]
International trade: imports (million current US$)	7 849	10 406	17 608[g,b]
International trade: balance (million current US$)	2 434	2 154	- 939[g,b]
Balance of payments, current account (million US$)	465	- 201	- 2 874[c]

Major trading partners

						2022
Export partners (% of exports)[g]	Netherlands	10.0	United States	6.7	Switzerland	6.5
Import partners (% of imports)[g]	China	15.0	Nigeria	13.1	France	10.8

Social indicators

	2010	2015	2023
Population growth rate (average annual %)	2.1	2.6	2.5[a,b]
Urban population (% of total population)	47.3	49.4	51.2[i]
Urban population growth rate (average annual %)[j]	3.0	3.4	...
Fertility rate, total (live births per woman)	5.1	4.8	4.3[a,b]
Life expectancy at birth (females/males, years)	56.2 / 53.9	58.9 / 56.7	60.3 / 57.7[a,b]
Population age distribution (0-14/60+ years old, %)	44.0 / 3.8	43.6 / 3.8	41.5 / 3.8[a,b]
International migrant stock (000/% of total pop.)[k,l]	2 366.5 / 11.5	2 470.6 / 10.6	2 564.9 / 9.7[m]
Refugees and others of concern to the UNHCR (000)	564.5[n]	726.8	952.0[o,b]
Infant mortality rate (per 1 000 live births)	76.6	66.6	56.8[a,b]
Health: Current expenditure (% of GDP)[p]	4.4	3.2	3.3[m]
Health: Physicians (per 1 000 pop.)	0.1[q]	0.2[r]	0.2[i]
Education: Government expenditure (% of GDP)	3.2	3.5[g]	3.5[c]
Education: Primary gross enrol. ratio (f/m per 100 pop.)	64.1 / 79.5[s]	84.9 / 96.4	97.1 / 101.6[b]
Education: Lowr. sec. gross enrol. ratio (f/m per 100 pop.)	... / ...	44.3 / 61.7	72.3 / 81.4[c]
Education: Upr. sec. gross enrol. ratio (f/m per 100 pop.)	... / ...	21.6 / 32.4	32.9 / 42.1[c]
Seats held by women in the National Parliament (%)	8.9	9.2	13.7[t]

Environment and infrastructure indicators

	2010	2015	2023
Individuals using the Internet (per 100 inhabitants)[g]	2.7	16.7	45.4[c]
Research & Development expenditure (% of GDP)	...	...	0.1[u,v,w]
Threatened species (number)	210	226	333[b]
Forested area (% of land area)	12.5	10.7	8.9[m]
CO2 emission estimates (million tons/tons per capita)	7.7 / 0.3	11.1 / 0.4	12.5 / 0.4[m]
Energy production, primary (Petajoules)	389	395	432[m]
Energy supply per capita (Gigajoules)	16	17	17[m]
Tourist/visitor arrivals at national borders (000)	252[x]	1 441[y,z]	576[c]
Important sites for terrestrial biodiversity protected (%)	73.8	73.8	73.8[b]
Pop. using safely managed drinking water (urban/rural, %)	35.5 / 14.8	46.0 / 24.3	58.8 / 27.3[b]
Pop. using safely managed sanitation (urban/rural, %)	18.1 / 8.4	19.0 / 10.8	20.1 / 14.1[b]
Net Official Development Assist. received (% of GNI)	3.52	1.46	2.33[c]

a Projected estimate (medium fertility variant). b 2022. c 2021. d Yamoussoukro is the capital and Abidjan is the administrative capital. e African Financial Community (CFA) Franc, Central Bank of West African States (BCEAO). f 2018. g Estimate. h Abidjan i 2019. j Data refers to a 5-year period preceding the reference year. k Refers to foreign citizens. l Including refugees. m 2020. n Data as at the end of December. o On 30 June 2022, the cessation clause for Ivorian refugees recommended by UNHCR came into effect. p Data based on calendar year (January 1 to December 31). q 2008. r 2014. s 2009. t Data are as at 1 January of reporting year. u Excluding business enterprise. v Partial data. w 2016. x Arrivals to Félix Houphouët Boigny Airport only. y Break in the time series. z Figures include arrivals by land (road and railway).

Croatia

		UN membership date	22 May 1992
Region	Southern Europe		
Population (000, 2023)	4 030[a,b]	Surface area (km2)	56 594[c]
Pop. density (per km2, 2023)	72.1[a,b]	Sex ratio (m per 100 f)	95.0[a,b]
Capital city	Zagreb	National currency	Euro (EUR)
Capital city pop. (000, 2023)	685.2[d,e]	Exchange rate (per US$)	7.1[b]

Economic indicators

	2010	2015	2023
GDP: Gross domestic product (million current US$)	60 672	50 243	68 955[c]
GDP growth rate (annual %, const. 2015 prices)	- 1.2	2.5	13.1[c]
GDP per capita (current US$)	13 888.0	11 808.5	16 983.4[c]
Economy: Agriculture (% of Gross Value Added)[f,g]	4.3	3.6	3.5[c]
Economy: Industry (% of Gross Value Added)[g,h]	25.1	24.8	23.8[c]
Economy: Services and other activity (% of GVA)[g]	70.6	71.6	72.7[c]
Employment in agriculture (% of employed)	14.3	9.2	6.8[c]
Employment in industry (% of employed)	27.4	26.7	28.7[c]
Employment in services & other sectors (% employed)	58.3	64.0	64.4[c]
Unemployment rate (% of labour force)	11.6	16.2	6.5[i]
Labour force participation rate (female/male pop. %)	46.1 / 59.7	46.9 / 59.1	46.0 / 58.1[i]
CPI: Consumer Price Index (2010=100)	100	107	125[b]
Agricultural production index (2014-2016=100)	94	97	82[c]
International trade: exports (million current US$)	11 811	12 844	25 383[b]
International trade: imports (million current US$)	20 067	20 580	44 115[b]
International trade: balance (million current US$)	- 8 256	- 7 737	- 18 732[b]
Balance of payments, current account (million US$)	- 1 485	1 644	- 1 464[b]

Major trading partners

						2022
Export partners (% of exports)	Italy	12.2	Slovenia	11.6	Germany	11.4
Import partners (% of imports)	Italy	13.8	Germany	12.5	Slovenia	10.8

Social indicators

	2010	2015	2023
Population growth rate (average annual %)	- 0.3	- 0.8	- 0.5[a,b]
Urban population (% of total population)	55.2	56.2	57.2[e]
Urban population growth rate (average annual %)[j]	0.1	- 0.1	...
Fertility rate, total (live births per woman)	1.5	1.4	1.4[a,b]
Life expectancy at birth (females/males, years)	80.0 / 73.6	80.5 / 74.5	82.0 / 76.4[a,b]
Population age distribution (0-14/60+ years old, %)	15.3 / 23.8	14.4 / 26.3	14.1 / 29.6[a,b]
International migrant stock (000/% of total pop.)	573.2 / 13.2	561.1 / 13.3	528.1 / 12.9[k]
Refugees and others of concern to the UNHCR (000)	25.5[l]	17.5	21.4[b]
Infant mortality rate (per 1 000 live births)	3.9	3.8	3.0[a,b]
Health: Current expenditure (% of GDP)	8.0	6.7	7.8[k]
Health: Physicians (per 1 000 pop.)	2.8	3.2	3.5[e]
Education: Government expenditure (% of GDP)	4.2	4.9	3.9[e]
Education: Primary gross enrol. ratio (f/m per 100 pop.)	92.0 / 91.9	100.6 / 100.6	93.0 / 92.8[k]
Education: Lower sec. gross enrol. ratio (f/m per 100 pop.)	107.9 / 104.7	108.6 / 104.3	109.6 / 103.6[k]
Education: Upr. sec. gross enrol. ratio (f/m per 100 pop.)	98.9 / 88.3	94.4 / 89.8	96.7 / 91.4[k]
Intentional homicide rate (per 100 000 pop.)	1.4	0.9	0.8[c]
Seats held by women in the National Parliament (%)	23.5	25.8	31.8[m]

Environment and infrastructure indicators

	2010	2015	2023
Individuals using the Internet (per 100 inhabitants)	56.6[n]	69.8[n,o]	81.3[c]
Research & Development expenditure (% of GDP)	0.7	0.8	1.2[k]
Threatened species (number)	101	159	244[b]
Forested area (% of land area)	34.3	34.3	34.7[k]
CO2 emission estimates (million tons/tons per capita)	18.9 / 4.2	16.0 / 3.7	17.8 / 3.6[c,k]
Energy production, primary (Petajoules)	215	184	157[k]
Energy supply per capita (Gigajoules)	89	82	85[k]
Tourist/visitor arrivals at national borders (000)[p]	9 111	12 683	10 641[c]
Important sites for terrestrial biodiversity protected (%)	24.8	80.8	80.8[b]
Pop. using safely managed drinking water (urban/rural, %)	96.6 / 72.0[q]	96.6 / ...	96.6 / ...[b]
Pop. using safely managed sanitation (urban/rural, %)	88.4 / ...	88.1 / ...	88.1 / ...[c]
Net Official Development Assist. disbursed (% of GNI)	...	0.08[r]	0.13[c]
Net Official Development Assist. received (% of GNI)	0.23	...	...

a Projected estimate (medium fertility variant). b 2022. c 2021. d Refers to the settlement of Zagreb. e 2019. f Excludes irrigation canals and landscaping care. g Data classified according to ISIC Rev. 4. h Excludes publishing activities, recycling. Includes irrigation canals. i Estimate. j Data refers to a 5-year period preceding the reference year. k 2020. l Data as at the end of December. m Data are as at 1 January of reporting year. n Population aged 16 to 74 years. o Users in the last 3 months. p Excluding arrivals in ports of nautical tourism. q 2007. r 2013.

Cuba

Region	Caribbean	UN membership date	24 October 1945
Population (000, 2023)	11 212[a,b]	Surface area (km2)	109 884[c]
Pop. density (per km2, 2023)	105.0[a,b]	Sex ratio (m per 100 f)	98.5[a,b]
Capital city	Havana	National currency	Cuban Peso (CUP)[d]
Capital city pop. (000, 2023)	2 138.4[e]	Exchange rate (per US$)	24.0[f,b]

Economic indicators

	2010	2015	2023
GDP: Gross domestic product (million current US$)	64 328	87 206	126 694[c]
GDP growth rate (annual %, const. 2015 prices)	2.4	4.4	1.3[c]
GDP per capita (current US$)	5 697.6	7 690.2	11 255.3[c]
Economy: Agriculture (% of Gross Value Added)	3.7	3.9	2.0[c]
Economy: Industry (% of Gross Value Added)	23.1	22.6	17.8[c]
Economy: Services and other activity (% of GVA)	73.2	73.5	80.2[c]
Employment in agriculture (% of employed)	18.6	18.6[g]	17.7[g,c]
Employment in industry (% of employed)	17.0	17.0[g]	17.1[g,c]
Employment in services & other sectors (% employed)	64.3	64.4[g]	65.2[g,c]
Unemployment rate (% of labour force)	2.5	2.4	1.4[g]
Labour force participation rate (female/male pop. %)	41.9 / 68.4	42.4 / 70.0[g]	41.9 / 68.9[g]
Agricultural production index (2014-2016=100)	86	100	69[c]
International trade: exports (million current US$)[g]	4 914	3 618	1 318[b]
International trade: imports (million current US$)[g]	11 488	12 638	5 293[b]
International trade: balance (million current US$)[g]	- 6 574	- 9 020	- 3 976[b]

Major trading partners

					2022
Export partners (% of exports)[g]	Canada	38.6	China	23.9	Spain	7.5
Import partners (% of imports)[g]	Spain	19.4	China	9.8	United States	8.8

Social indicators

	2010	2015	2023
Population growth rate (average annual %)	0.1	0.1	- 0.2[a,b]
Urban population (% of total population)	76.6	76.9	77.1[e]
Urban population growth rate (average annual %)[h]	0.2	0.3	...
Fertility rate, total (live births per woman)	1.7	1.7	1.4[a,b]
Life expectancy at birth (females/males, years)	80.0 / 75.5	80.1 / 75.5	80.6 / 75.8[a,b]
Population age distribution (0-14/60+ years old, %)	17.7 / 17.6	16.7 / 19.3	15.7 / 22.0[a,b]
International migrant stock (000/% of total pop.)	7.4 / 0.1	4.6 / ~0.0	3.0 / ~0.0[i]
Refugees and others of concern to the UNHCR (000)	0.4[j]	0.3	0.1[b]
Infant mortality rate (per 1 000 live births)	5.2	4.6	4.0[a,b]
Health: Current expenditure (% of GDP)[g,k]	10.7	12.8	12.5[i]
Health: Physicians (per 1 000 pop.)	6.8	7.8	8.4[l]
Education: Government expenditure (% of GDP)	12.8	...	0.0[i]
Education: Primary gross enrol. ratio (f/m per 100 pop.)	100.2 / 102.6	96.5 / 102.3	100.5 / 102.4[c]
Education: Lowr. sec. gross enrol. ratio (f/m per 100 pop.)	93.6 / 95.5	96.9 / 102.4	89.5 / 89.3[c]
Education: Upr. sec. gross enrol. ratio (f/m per 100 pop.)	91.1 / 88.8	101.2 / 91.4	105.1 / 104.1[c]
Intentional homicide rate (per 100 000 pop.)	4.5	5.5	4.4[e]
Seats held by women in the National Parliament (%)	43.2	48.9	53.4[m]

Environment and infrastructure indicators

	2010	2015	2023
Individuals using the Internet (per 100 inhabitants)	15.9[n]	37.3	71.1[g,o,c]
Research & Development expenditure (% of GDP)	0.6	0.4	0.5[i]
Threatened species (number)	304	337	420[b]
Forested area (% of land area)	27.5	30.6	31.2[i]
CO2 emission estimates (million tons/tons per capita)	27.3 / 2.4	28.6 / 2.5	24.1 / 2.1[i]
Energy production, primary (Petajoules)	200	212	170[i]
Energy supply per capita (Gigajoules)	45	40	30[i]
Tourist/visitor arrivals at national borders (000)[p]	2 507	3 506	356[c]
Important sites for terrestrial biodiversity protected (%)	51.2	54.5	54.5[b]
Pop. using safely managed sanitation (urban/rural %)	38.7 / 54.5	37.9 / 54.9	37.1 / 56.0[b]
Net Official Development Assist. received (% of GNI)	0.23	0.65	0.76[i]

a Projected estimate (medium fertility variant). b 2022. c 2021. d The national currency of Cuba is the Cuban Peso (CUP). The convertible peso (CUC) is used by foreigners and tourists in Cuba. e 2019. f UN operational exchange rate. g Estimate. h Data refers to a 5-year period preceding the reference year. i 2020. j Data as at the end of December. k Data based on calendar year (January 1 to December 31). l 2018. m Data are as at 1 January of reporting year. n Including users of the international network and also those having access only to the Cuban network. o Surveys collecting the releavant information were not carried out in 2021. p Arrivals by air.

Curaçao

		Population (000, 2023)	191 [a,b,c]
Region	Caribbean	Pop. density (per km2, 2023)	450.9 [a,b,c]
Surface area (km2)	444 [d]	Capital city	Willemstad
Sex ratio (m per 100 f)	92.1 [a,b,c]	Capital city pop. (000, 2023)	144.0 [f,g]
National currency	Neth. Ant. Guilder (ANG) [e]		
Exchange rate (per US$)	1.8 [c]		

Economic indicators	2010	2015	2023
GDP: Gross domestic product (million current US$)	2 951	3 043	2 700 [d]
GDP growth rate (annual %, const. 2015 prices)	0.1	0.3	4.2 [d]
GDP per capita (current US$)	18 517.6	17 943.6	14 183.3 [d]
Economy: Agriculture (% of Gross Value Added) [h,i,j]	0.4	0.2	0.2 [d]
Economy: Industry (% of Gross Value Added) [h,k]	16.3	19.3	16.1 [d]
Economy: Services and other activity (% of GVA) [h]	83.3	80.4	83.7 [d]
Employment in agriculture (% of employed)	1.1 [l,m]	...	...
Employment in industry (% of employed)	17.6 [l,m]	...	...
Employment in services & other sectors (% employed)	81.3 [l,m]	...	...
Unemployment rate (% of labour force) [o]	9.6 [n,p]	13.0 [q]	...
Labour force participation rate (female/male pop. %)	53.2 / 66.5 [m]	... / ...	... / ...
CPI: Consumer Price Index (2010=100) [r]	100	108	132 [c]
Balance of payments, current account (million US$)	...	- 519	- 596 [d]

Social indicators	2010	2015	2023
Population growth rate (average annual %) [a]	1.5	0.8	0.5 [b,c]
Urban population (% of total population)	89.9	89.4	89.1 [s]
Urban population growth rate (average annual %) [t]	2.5	1.2	...
Fertility rate, total (live births per woman) [a]	2.2	1.9	1.6 [b,c]
Life expectancy at birth (females/males, years) [a]	78.0 / 71.4	79.8 / 72.1	80.3 / 72.7 [b,c]
Population age distribution (0-14/60+ years old, %) [a]	22.1 / 17.3	20.8 / 19.5	17.2 / 21.4 [b,c]
International migrant stock (000/% of total pop.) [u]	34.6 / 23.2	37.6 / 23.5	57.2 / 34.9 [v]
Refugees and others of concern to the UNHCR (000)	–0.0 [w]	0.1	17.0 [c]
Infant mortality rate (per 1 000 live births) [a]	11.6	9.5	7.8 [b,c]
Education: Government expenditure (% of GDP)	...	7.4	7.7 [v]
Education: Primary gross enrol. ratio (f/m per 100 pop.)	... / ...	157.7 / 164.2 [q]	100.9 / 106.6 [v]
Education: Lowr. sec. gross enrol. ratio (f/m per 100 pop.)	... / ...	100.2 / 97.6 [q]	99.7 / 97.1 [v]
Education: Upr. sec. gross enrol. ratio (f/m per 100 pop.)	... / ...	86.1 / 76.8 [q]	167.2 / 107.6 [v]
Intentional homicide rate (per 100 000 pop.)	17.1 [x]	...	...

Environment and infrastructure indicators	2010	2015	2023
Individuals using the Internet (per 100 inhabitants)	...	...	68.1 [y]
Threatened species (number)	...	49	85 [c]
Forested area (% of land area)	...	–0.0	0.2 [v]
CO2 emission estimates (million tons/tons per capita)	4.3 / 18.5	5.7 / 36.0	2.0 / 13.0 [v]
Energy production, primary (Petajoules)	...	1	1 [v]
Energy supply per capita (Gigajoules)	...	634	158 [v]
Tourist/visitor arrivals at national borders (000) [z]	342	468	265 [d]
Important sites for terrestrial biodiversity protected (%)	6.1	40.4	44.8 [c]

a For statistical purposes, the data for Netherlands do not include this area. **b** Projected estimate (medium fertility variant). **c** 2022. **d** 2021. **e** Netherlands Antillean Guilder. **f** Total population of Curaçao excluding some neighborhoods (see source). **g** 2018. **h** Data classified according to ISIC Rev. 4. **i** Includes mining and quarrying. **j** Excludes irrigation canals and landscaping care. **k** Excludes publishing activities, recycling. Includes irrigation canals. **l** Data classified according to ISIC Rev. 3. **m** 2008. **n** Break in the time series. **o** Excluding the institutional population. **p** 2009. **q** 2013. **r** Calculated by the UN Statistics Division from national indices. **s** 2019. **t** Data refers to a 5-year period preceding the reference year. **u** Including refugees. **v** 2020. **w** Data as at the end of December. **x** 2007. **y** 2017. **z** Arrivals by air.

Cyprus

Region	Western Asia	UN membership date	20 September 1960
Population (000, 2023)	1 252 [a,b,c]	Surface area (km2)	9 251 [d]
Pop. density (per km2, 2023)	135.4 [a,b,c]	Sex ratio (m per 100 f)	100.3 [a,b,c]
Capital city	Nicosia	National currency	Euro (EUR)
Capital city pop. (000, 2023)	269.5 [e]	Exchange rate (per US$)	0.9 [c]

Economic indicators	2010	2015	2023
GDP: Gross domestic product (million current US$) [f]	25 775	19 901	28 408 [d]
GDP growth rate (annual %, const. 2015 prices) [f]	2.3	3.4	6.6 [d]
GDP per capita (current US$) [f]	31 074.7	23 476.8	32 280.9 [d]
Economy: Agriculture (% of Gross Value Added) [g,h]	2.3	2.1	1.9 [d]
Economy: Industry (% of Gross Value Added) [h,i]	16.4	11.6	14.9 [d]
Economy: Services and other activity (% of GVA) [h]	81.2	86.2	83.2 [d]
Employment in agriculture (% of employed)	3.8	0.2 [j]	2.8 [d]
Employment in industry (% of employed)	9.9 [j]	16.3	17.9 [d]
Employment in services & other sectors (% employed)	75.8	79.8	79.2 [d]
Unemployment rate (% of labour force)	6.3	14.9	6.9 [d]
Labour force participation rate (female/male pop. %)	57.5 / 71.0	57.5 / 67.1	57.3 / 69.2 [i]
CPI: Consumer Price Index (2010=100) [k,l]	100	102	113 [c]
Agricultural production index (2014-2016=100)	107	103	110 [d]
International trade: exports (million current US$)	1 506	3 367	4 411 [c]
International trade: imports (million current US$)	8 645	7 133	11 889 [c]
International trade: balance (million current US$)	- 7 138	- 3 766	- 7 477 [c]
Balance of payments, current account (million US$)	- 2 799	- 84	- 2 625 [c]

Major trading partners						2022
Export partners (% of exports)	China, Hong Kong SAR	10.7	Bunkers	8.9	Lebanon	7.5 [j]
Import partners (% of imports)	Greece	23.4	Italy	10.5	China	8.0

Social indicators	2010	2015	2023
Population growth rate (average annual %) [b]	1.7	0.9	0.7 [a,c]
Urban population (% of total population) [b]	67.6	66.9	66.8 [m]
Urban population growth rate (average annual %) [b,n]	1.4	0.7	...
Fertility rate, total (live births per woman) [b]	1.4	1.3	1.3 [a,c]
Life expectancy at birth (females/males, years) [b]	82.0 / 77.4	82.9 / 79.1	83.7 / 80.1 [a,c]
Population age distribution (0-14/60+ years old, %) [b]	17.0 / 15.9	16.1 / 17.6	15.9 / 20.4 [a,c]
International migrant stock (000/% of total pop.) [b]	188.5 / 16.9	176.7 / 15.2	190.4 / 15.8 [o]
Refugees and others of concern to the UNHCR (000)	8.8 [p]	14.1	63.7 [c]
Infant mortality rate (per 1 000 live births) [b]	2.9	2.5	2.1 [a,c]
Health: Current expenditure (% of GDP) [q]	6.5	6.8	8.1 [o]
Health: Physicians (per 1 000 pop.)	2.1	2.6	5.4 [d]
Education: Government expenditure (% of GDP)	6.5	6.3	5.2 [m]
Education: Primary gross enrol. ratio (f/m per 100 pop.) [j]	101.6 / 101.6	99.3 / 99.3	100.4 / 101.0 [o]
Education: Lowr. sec. gross enrol. ratio (f/m per 100 pop.) [j]	96.6 / 96.6	99.2 / 100.0	103.5 / 106.1 [o]
Education: Upr. sec. gross enrol. ratio (f/m per 100 pop.) [j]	88.1 / 86.0	99.6 / 100.3	96.4 / 100.0 [o]
Intentional homicide rate (per 100 000 pop.)	0.7	1.3	1.3 [d]
Seats held by women in the National Parliament (%)	12.5	12.5	14.3 [r]

Environment and infrastructure indicators	2010	2015	2023
Individuals using the Internet (per 100 inhabitants)	53.0 [s]	71.7	90.8 [d]
Research & Development expenditure (% of GDP)	0.4	0.5	0.8 [t,o]
Threatened species (number)	43	60	108 [c]
Forested area (% of land area)	18.7	18.7	18.7 [o]
CO2 emission estimates (million tons/tons per capita) [f]	7.4 / 9.0	6.0 / 7.0	6.2 / 6.7 [d,o]
Energy production, primary (Petajoules)	4	5	7 [o]
Energy supply per capita (Gigajoules)	92	72	72 [o]
Tourist/visitor arrivals at national borders (000)	2 173	2 659	1 937 [d]
Important sites for terrestrial biodiversity protected (%)	58.1	69.2	74.3 [c]
Pop. using safely managed sanitation (urban/rural %)	86.2 / ...	86.2 / ...	86.2 / ... [c]
Net Official Development Assist. disbursed (% of GNI)	...	...	0.07 [l,d]

a Projected estimate (medium fertility variant). b Refers to the whole country. c 2022. d 2021. e 2018. f Excluding northern Cyprus. g Excludes irrigation canals and landscaping care. h Data classified according to ISIC Rev. 4. i Excludes publishing activities, recycling. Includes irrigation canals. j Estimate. k Calculated by the UN Statistics Division from national indices. l Data refer to government controlled areas. m 2019. n Data refers to a 5-year period preceding the reference year. o 2020. p Data as at the end of December. q Since 2016 health expenditure data do not include foreign health insurance provided insurance to the country's residents is missing. r Data are as at 1 January of reporting year. s Population aged 16 to 74 years. t Provisional data.

Region	Eastern Europe	UN membership date	19 January 1993
Population (000, 2023)	10 494 [a,b]	Surface area (km2)	78 871 [c]
Pop. density (per km2, 2023)	135.9 [a,b]	Sex ratio (m per 100 f)	97.1 [a,b]
Capital city	Prague	National currency	Czech Koruna (CZK)
Capital city pop. (000, 2023)	1 298.8 [d]	Exchange rate (per US$)	22.6 [b]

Economic indicators	2010	2015	2023
GDP: Gross domestic product (million current US$)	209 070	188 033	281 778 [c]
GDP growth rate (annual %, const. 2015 prices)	2.4	5.4	3.5 [c]
GDP per capita (current US$)	19 978.5	17 867.4	26 808.5 [c]
Economy: Agriculture (% of Gross Value Added) [e,f]	1.7	2.5	2.0 [c]
Economy: Industry (% of Gross Value Added) [f,g]	36.7	37.5	33.3 [c]
Economy: Services and other activity (% of GVA) [f]	61.6	60.0	64.7 [c]
Employment in agriculture (% of employed)	3.1	2.9	2.5 [c]
Employment in industry (% of employed)	38.0	38.1	36.9 [c]
Employment in services & other sectors (% employed)	58.9	59.0	60.6 [c]
Unemployment rate (% of labour force)	7.3	5.0	2.3 [h]
Labour force participation rate (female/male pop. %)	49.3 / 68.0	51.2 / 68.0	52.7 / 68.6 [h]
CPI: Consumer Price Index (2010=100)	100	108	144 [b]
Agricultural production index (2014-2016=100)	89	97	98 [c]
International trade: exports (million current US$)	132 141	157 194	241 132 [b]
International trade: imports (million current US$)	125 691	140 716	235 919 [b]
International trade: balance (million current US$)	6 450	16 478	5 214 [b]
Balance of payments, current account (million US$)	- 7 351	845	- 17 366 [b]

Major trading partners						2022
Export partners (% of exports)	Germany	32.8	Slovakia	8.4	Poland	7.1
Import partners (% of imports)	Germany	19.8	China	18.8	Poland	8.0

Social indicators	2010	2015	2023
Population growth rate (average annual %)	0.4	−0.0	- 0.1 [a,b]
Urban population (% of total population)	73.3	73.5	73.9 [d]
Urban population growth rate (average annual %) [i]	0.4	0.2	...
Fertility rate, total (live births per woman)	1.5	1.6	1.7 [a,b]
Life expectancy at birth (females/males, years)	80.6 / 74.4	81.5 / 75.6	81.2 / 75.1 [a,b]
Population age distribution (0-14/60+ years old, %)	14.4 / 22.5	15.3 / 25.0	16.0 / 26.3 [a,b]
International migrant stock (000/% of total pop.) [j]	398.5 / 3.8	416.5 / 3.9	540.9 / 5.1 [k]
Refugees and others of concern to the UNHCR (000)	3.5 [l]	5.0	390.7 [b]
Infant mortality rate (per 1 000 live births)	2.6	2.5	2.4 [a,b]
Health: Current expenditure (% of GDP)	6.9 [m]	7.2	9.2 [k]
Health: Physicians (per 1 000 pop.)	3.6	3.7 [n]	5.5 [c]
Education: Government expenditure (% of GDP)	4.0	5.8	4.5 [d]
Education: Primary gross enrol. ratio (f/m per 100 pop.)	103.6 / 104.0	99.7 / 99.3	100.1 / 99.8 [k]
Education: Lower. sec. gross enrol. ratio (f/m per 100 pop.)	97.5 / 98.0	101.0 / 101.2	99.3 / 98.6 [k]
Education: Upr. sec. gross enrol. ratio (f/m per 100 pop.)	92.9 / 91.6	110.2 / 108.0	104.0 / 102.6 [k]
Intentional homicide rate (per 100 000 pop.)	1.0	0.8	0.4 [c]
Seats held by women in the National Parliament (%)	15.5	19.0	26.0 [o]

Environment and infrastructure indicators	2010	2015	2023
Individuals using the Internet (per 100 inhabitants)	68.8 [p]	75.7	82.7 [c]
Research & Development expenditure (% of GDP)	1.3	1.9	2.0 [q,k]
Threatened species (number)	33	45	127 [b]
Forested area (% of land area)	34.4	34.6	34.7 [k]
CO2 emission estimates (million tons/tons per capita) [r]	114.5 / 10.7	101.4 / 9.4	93.2 / 8.5 [c]
Energy production, primary (Petajoules)	1 340	1 207	987 [k]
Energy supply per capita (Gigajoules)	181	167	160 [k]
Tourist/visitor arrivals at national borders (000)	8 629	11 619	3 919 [k]
Important sites for terrestrial biodiversity protected (%)	94.1	94.1	94.7 [b]
Pop. using safely managed drinking water (urban/rural, %)	97.7 / 96.4	98.0 / 97.7	98.0 / 97.7 [b]
Net Official Development Assist. disbursed (% of GNI) [s]	0.13	0.16	0.16 [c]

a Projected estimate (medium fertility variant). b 2022. c 2021. d 2019. e Excludes irrigation canals and landscaping care. f Data classified according to ISIC Rev. 4. g Excludes publishing activities, recycling. Includes irrigation canals. h Estimate. i Data refers to a 5-year period preceding the reference year. j Refers to foreign citizens. k 2020. l Data as at the end of December. m Country is still reporting data based on SHA 1.0. n 2013. o Data are as at 1 January of reporting year. p Population aged 16 to 74 years. q Provisional data. r Refers to Czechia and Slovakia. s Development Assistance Committee member (OECD).

Dem. People's Rep. Korea

Region	Eastern Asia	UN membership date	17 September 1991
Population (000, 2023)	26 069[a,b]	Surface area (km2)	120 538[c]
Pop. density (per km2, 2023)	216.5[a,b]	Sex ratio (m per 100 f)	98.0[a,b]
Capital city	Pyongyang	National currency	North Korean Won (KPW)
Capital city pop. (000, 2023)	3 060.9[d]	Exchange rate (per US$)	110.0[e,b]

Economic indicators	2010	2015	2023
GDP: Gross domestic product (million current US$)[f]	13 945	16 283	16 750[c]
GDP growth rate (annual %, const. 2015 prices)[f]	- 0.5	- 1.1	- 0.1[c]
GDP per capita (current US$)[f]	573.0	653.8	654.1[c]
Economy: Agriculture (% of Gross Value Added)[f]	20.8	21.6	23.8[c]
Economy: Industry (% of Gross Value Added)[f]	48.2	46.2	43.8[g]
Economy: Services and other activity (% of GVA)[f]	31.0	32.2	33.8[g]
Employment in agriculture (% of employed)[h]	47.8	45.8	43.5[c]
Employment in industry (% of employed)[h]	14.4	14.0	14.2[c]
Employment in services & other sectors (% employed)[h]	37.7	40.2	42.3[c]
Unemployment rate (% of labour force)[h]	2.8	2.9	2.9
Labour force participation rate (female/male pop. %)[h]	69.4 / 80.2	69.3 / 80.2	69.8 / 79.9
Agricultural production index (2014-2016=100)	99	99	93[c]
International trade: exports (million current US$)[h]	882	987	249[b]
International trade: imports (million current US$)[h]	1 957	2 604	982[b]
International trade: balance (million current US$)[h]	- 1 075	- 1 617	- 733[b]

Major trading partners						2022
Export partners (% of exports)[h]	China	43.9	Senegal	16.9	Ethiopia	3.7
Import partners (% of imports)[h]	China	95.6	Dem. Rep. of Congo	2.4	United Arab Emirates	0.3

Social indicators	2010	2015	2023
Population growth rate (average annual %)	0.4	0.5	0.4[a,b]
Urban population (% of total population)	60.4	61.3	62.1[d]
Urban population growth rate (average annual %)[i]	0.8	0.8	...
Fertility rate, total (live births per woman)	1.8	1.9	1.8[a,b]
Life expectancy at birth (females/males, years)	73.5 / 66.5	75.5 / 69.7	76.1 / 71.0[a,b]
Population age distribution (0-14/60+ years old, %)	21.7 / 13.9	19.8 / 14.2	18.9 / 17.3[a,b]
International migrant stock (000/% of total pop.)[h]	44.0 / 0.2	48.5 / 0.2	49.5 / 0.2[g]
Infant mortality rate (per 1 000 live births)	23.1	16.8	13.6[a,b]
Health: Physicians (per 1 000 pop.)	3.3[j]	3.5[k]	3.7[l]
Education: Primary gross enrol. ratio (f/m per 100 pop.)	99.4 / 99.4[m]	... / ...	89.3 / 89.3[n]
Education: Lowr. sec. gross enrol. ratio (f/m per 100 pop.)	... / ...	90.8 / 90.3	... / ...
Education: Upr. sec. gross enrol. ratio (f/m per 100 pop.)	... / ...	94.9 / 93.1	95.4 / 93.4[n]
Seats held by women in the National Parliament (%)	15.6	16.3	17.6[o]

Environment and infrastructure indicators	2010	2015	2023
Individuals using the Internet (per 100 inhabitants)[h]	0.0	0.0[p]	...
Threatened species (number)	52	64	120[b]
Forested area (% of land area)	51.8	51.0	50.1[g]
CO2 emission estimates (million tons/tons per capita)	49.9 / 2.0	22.9 / 0.9	51.2 / 2.0[g]
Energy production, primary (Petajoules)	699	788	582[g]
Energy supply per capita (Gigajoules)	25	13	24[g]
Important sites for terrestrial biodiversity protected (%)	0.0	0.0	0.0[b]
Pop. using safely managed drinking water (urban/rural, %)	78.0 / 52.4	77.4 / 50.4	77.0 / 48.8[b]
Pop. using safely managed sanitation (urban/rural %)	... / 18.4	... / 9.0	... / 1.2[b]

a Projected estimate (medium fertility variant). b 2022. c 2021. d 2019. e UN operational exchange rate. f Data compiled in accordance with the System of National Accounts 1968 (1968 SNA). g 2020. h Estimate. i Data refers to a 5-year period preceding the reference year. j 2008. k 2014. l 2017. m 2009. n 2018. o Data are as at 1 January of reporting year. p 2012.

Dem. Rep. of the Congo

Region	Middle Africa	UN membership date	20 September 1960
Population (000, 2023)	99 010[a,b]	Surface area (km2)	2 345 410[c]
Pop. density (per km2, 2023)	43.7[a,b]	Sex ratio (m per 100 f)	98.4[a,b]
Capital city	Kinshasa	National currency	Congolese Franc (CDF)
Capital city pop. (000, 2023)	13 743.3[d]	Exchange rate (per US$)	2 000.0[c]

Economic indicators	2010	2015	2023
GDP: Gross domestic product (million current US$)	21 566	37 918	52 850[c]
GDP growth rate (annual %, const. 2015 prices)	7.1	6.9	5.7[c]
GDP per capita (current US$)	324.8	482.1	551.1[c]
Economy: Agriculture (% of Gross Value Added)	22.4	19.7	20.4[c]
Economy: Industry (% of Gross Value Added)	40.5	44.8	45.1[c]
Economy: Services and other activity (% of GVA)	37.0	35.5	34.5[c]
Employment in agriculture (% of employed)[e]	66.2	58.3	55.3[c]
Employment in industry (% of employed)[e]	8.2	9.3	10.1[c]
Employment in services & other sectors (% employed)[e]	25.7	32.4	34.7[c]
Unemployment rate (% of labour force)[e]	4.0	4.5	5.0
Labour force participation rate (female/male pop. %)[e]	65.1 / 70.9	62.5 / 69.7	63.1 / 69.5
CPI: Consumer Price Index (2010=100)	100	130	134[f]
Agricultural production index (2014-2016=100)	82	100	120[c]
International trade: exports (million current US$)[e]	5 300	5 800	35 619[b]
International trade: imports (million current US$)[e]	4 500	6 200	9 511[b]
International trade: balance (million current US$)[e]	800	- 400	26 108[b]
Balance of payments, current account (million US$)	- 2 174	- 1 484	- 587[c]

Major trading partners						2022
Export partners (% of exports)[e]	China	47.4	United Rep. Tanzania	8.9	South Africa	8.8
Import partners (% of imports)[e]	China	26.9	South Africa	13.4	United States	9.5

Social indicators	2010	2015	2023
Population growth rate (average annual %)	3.3	3.4	3.2[a,b]
Urban population (% of total population)	40.0	42.7	45.0[d]
Urban population growth rate (average annual %)[g]	4.6	4.6	...
Fertility rate, total (live births per woman)	6.6	6.4	6.1[a,b]
Life expectancy at birth (females/males, years)	58.0 / 54.8	60.3 / 56.7	62.0 / 57.5[a,b]
Population age distribution (0-14/60+ years old, %)	46.2 / 4.9	46.3 / 4.7	46.5 / 4.6[a,b]
International migrant stock (000/% of total pop.)[h]	589.9 / 0.9	810.0 / 1.1	952.9 / 1.1[i]
Refugees and others of concern to the UNHCR (000)	2 363.9[j]	2 001.0	6 382.6[k,b]
Infant mortality rate (per 1 000 live births)	72.2	62.2	50.0[a,b]
Health: Current expenditure (% of GDP)[l]	3.9	4.0	4.1[i]
Health: Physicians (per 1 000 pop.)	0.1[m]	0.1[n]	0.4[o]
Education: Government expenditure (% of GDP)	1.5	2.2	2.7[c]
Education: Primary gross enrol. ratio (f/m per 100 pop.)	93.0 / 106.9	107.6 / 108.4	120.5 / 127.2[i]
Education: Lowr. sec. gross enrol. ratio (f/m per 100 pop.)	40.9 / 62.7	47.6 / 71.7	... / ...
Education: Upr. sec. gross enrol. ratio (f/m per 100 pop.)	24.2 / 46.4	29.5 / 47.6	... / ...
Seats held by women in the National Parliament (%)	8.4	8.9	12.8[p]

Environment and infrastructure indicators	2010	2015	2023
Individuals using the Internet (per 100 inhabitants)[e]	0.7	3.8	22.9[c]
Research & Development expenditure (% of GDP)	0.1[q,r,m]	0.4[s,t,u]	...
Threatened species (number)	296	333	746[b]
Forested area (% of land area)	60.5	58.1	55.6[b]
CO2 emission estimates (million tons/tons per capita)	7.3 / ~0.0	8.8 / ~0.0	8.6 / ~0.0[i]
Energy production, primary (Petajoules)	857	1 218	1 316[i]
Energy supply per capita (Gigajoules)	13	15	14[i]
Tourist/visitor arrivals at national borders (000)	81[v]	354[w]	351[w,f]
Important sites for terrestrial biodiversity protected (%)	48.2	48.2	50.5[b]
Pop. using safely managed drinking water (urban/rural, %)	29.1 / 0.6	26.6 / 0.6	24.2 / 0.5[b]
Pop. using safely managed sanitation (urban/rural, %)	17.7 / 17.4	16.6 / 14.2	15.2 / 11.2[b]
Net Official Development Assist. received (% of GNI)	16.87	7.40	6.94[c]

a Projected estimate (medium fertility variant). b 2022. c 2021. d 2019. e Estimate. f 2016. g Data refers to a 5-year period preceding the reference year. h Including refugees. i 2020. j Data as at the end of December. k All refugees are assessed on an individual basis by the National Commission for Refugees. l Data based on calendar year (January 1 to December 31). m 2009. n 2013. o 2018. p Data are as at 1 January of reporting year. q Government only. r S&T budget instead of R&D expenditure. s Overestimated or based on overestimated data. t Excluding business enterprise. u Break in the time series. v Arrivals by air. w The arrivals data relate only to three border posts (N'Djili airport in Kinshasa, the Luano airport in Lubumbashi, and the land border-crossing of Kasumbalesa in Katanga province).

Denmark

Region	Northern Europe	UN membership date	24 October 1945
Population (000, 2023)	5 882[a,b,c]	Surface area (km2)	42 938[d,e]
Pop. density (per km2, 2023)	138.8[a,b,c]	Sex ratio (m per 100 f)	99.0[a,b,c]
Capital city	Copenhagen	National currency	Danish Krone (DKK)
Capital city pop. (000, 2023)	1 333.9[f,g]	Exchange rate (per US$)	7.0[c]

Economic indicators

	2010	2015	2023
GDP: Gross domestic product (million current US$)	321 995	302 673	398 303[e]
GDP growth rate (annual %, const. 2015 prices)	1.9	2.3	4.9[e]
GDP per capita (current US$)	58 008.3	53 308.2	68 036.7[e]
Economy: Agriculture (% of Gross Value Added)[h,i]	1.4	1.1	1.0[e]
Economy: Industry (% of Gross Value Added)[h,j]	22.8	23.0	22.2[e]
Economy: Services and other activity (% of GVA)[h]	75.8	75.9	76.8[e]
Employment in agriculture (% of employed)	2.5	2.5	0.1[k,e]
Employment in industry (% of employed)	14.2[k]	7.4[k]	19.3[e]
Employment in services & other sectors (% employed)	77.6	78.1	78.6[e]
Unemployment rate (% of labour force)	7.8	6.3	4.2[e]
Labour force participation rate (female/male pop. %)	58.8 / 68.3	56.7 / 66.0	58.3 / 67.1[k]
CPI: Consumer Price Index (2010=100)[l]	100	107	122[c]
Agricultural production index (2014-2016=100)	97	101	103[e]
International trade: exports (million current US$)	96 217	94 619	129 059[c]
International trade: imports (million current US$)	82 724	85 327	125 732[c]
International trade: balance (million current US$)	13 492	9 291	3 328[c]
Balance of payments, current account (million US$)	21 051	24 953	51 461[c]

Major trading partners

							2022
Export partners (% of exports)[k]	Germany	15.5	Sweden	9.7	United States	9.6
Import partners (% of imports)	Germany	20.5	Sweden	12.4	Netherlands	8.7

Social indicators

	2010	2015	2023
Population growth rate (average annual %)[a]	0.5	0.5	0.5[b,c]
Urban population (% of total population)	86.8	87.5	88.0[g]
Urban population growth rate (average annual %)[m]	0.7	0.6	...
Fertility rate, total (live births per woman)[a]	1.9	1.7	1.7[b,c]
Life expectancy at birth (females/males, years)[a]	81.3 / 77.1	82.7 / 78.8	83.8 / 80.0[b,c]
Population age distribution (0-14/60+ years old, %)[a]	18.0 / 23.2	16.9 / 24.7	16.1 / 26.5[b,c]
International migrant stock (000/% of total pop.)[a]	500.8 / 9.0	595.9 / 10.5	717.6 / 12.4[n]
Refugees and others of concern to the UNHCR (000)	24.5[o]	27.3	74.8[c]
Infant mortality rate (per 1 000 live births)[a]	3.4	3.7	2.9[b,c]
Health: Current expenditure (% of GDP)	10.6	10.3	10.8[e]
Health: Physicians (per 1 000 pop.)	3.7	3.9	4.3[g]
Education: Government expenditure (% of GDP)	8.6	7.0	6.9[g]
Education: Primary gross enrol. ratio (f/m per 100 pop.)	99.7 / 99.5	100.8 / 102.1	100.1 / 100.1[n]
Education: Lowr. sec. gross enrol. ratio (f/m per 100 pop.)	118.3 / 116.5	117.8 / 116.4	120.0 / 121.4[n]
Education: Upr. sec. gross enrol. ratio (f/m per 100 pop.)	121.8 / 121.5	148.1 / 137.6	140.6 / 141.2[n]
Intentional homicide rate (per 100 000 pop.)	0.8	1.1	0.8[e]
Seats held by women in the National Parliament (%)	38.0	38.0	43.6[p]

Environment and infrastructure indicators

	2010	2015	2023
Individuals using the Internet (per 100 inhabitants)	88.7[q]	96.3[r]	98.9[e]
Research & Development expenditure (% of GDP)	2.9	3.1	3.0[n]
Threatened species (number)	33	36	91[c]
Forested area (% of land area)	14.7	15.6	15.7[n]
CO2 emission estimates (million tons/tons per capita)[s]	48.3 / 8.5	33.5 / 5.7	29.6 / 4.9[e]
Energy production, primary (Petajoules)[s]	972	668	385[n]
Energy supply per capita (Gigajoules)[s]	147	119	111[n]
Tourist/visitor arrivals at national borders (000)	26 730	28 209	18 405[e]
Important sites for terrestrial biodiversity protected (%)	87.9	88.6	88.6[c]
Net Official Development Assist. disbursed (% of GNI)[t]	1.52	0.97	0.94[e]

a For statistical purposes, the data for Denmark do not include Faroe Islands, and Greenland. b Projected estimate (medium fertility variant). c 2022. d Excluding Faeroe Islands and Greenland shown separately, if available. e 2021. f Refers to the Greater Copenhagen Region, consisting of (parts of) 16 municipalities. g 2019. h Data classified according to ISIC Rev. 4. i Excludes irrigation canals and landscaping care. j Excludes publishing activities, recycling. Includes irrigation canals. k Estimate. l Calculated by the UN Statistics Division from national indices. m Data refers to a 5-year period preceding the reference year. n 2020. o Data as at the end of December. p Data are as at 1 January of reporting year. q Population aged 16 to 74 years. r Users in the last 3 months. s Excluding the Faroe Islands and Greenland. t Development Assistance Committee member (OECD).

Djibouti

Region	Eastern Africa	UN membership date	20 September 1977
Population (000, 2023)	1 121 [a,b]	Surface area (km2)	23 200 [c]
Pop. density (per km2, 2023)	48.4 [a,b]	Sex ratio (m per 100 f)	98.5 [a,b]
Capital city	Djibouti	National currency	Djibouti Franc (DJF)
Capital city pop. (000, 2023)	568.8 [d,e]	Exchange rate (per US$)	177.7 [b]

Economic indicators

	2010	2015	2023
GDP: Gross domestic product (million current US$)	1 244	2 445	3 701 [c]
GDP growth rate (annual %, const. 2015 prices)	11.7	7.7	5.6 [c]
GDP per capita (current US$)	1 353.0	2 430.3	3 348.0 [c]
Economy: Agriculture (% of Gross Value Added)	2.8	1.3	1.4 [c]
Economy: Industry (% of Gross Value Added)	16.1	12.1	11.8 [c]
Economy: Services and other activity (% of GVA)	81.1	86.6	86.8 [c]
Employment in agriculture (% of employed) [f]	1.8	1.5	1.2 [c]
Employment in industry (% of employed) [f]	5.1	5.5	6.0 [c]
Employment in services & other sectors (% employed) [f]	93.0	93.1	92.7 [c]
Unemployment rate (% of labour force) [f]	27.2	26.3	28.0
Labour force participation rate (female/male pop. %) [f]	17.4 / 49.1	18.0 / 47.3	18.3 / 45.0
CPI: Consumer Price Index (2010=100)	100	112	122 [g]
Agricultural production index (2014-2016=100)	118	84	144 [c]
International trade: exports (million current US$) [f]	470	132	825 [b]
International trade: imports (million current US$) [f]	603	890	1 689 [b]
International trade: balance (million current US$) [f]	- 133	- 758	- 864 [b]
Balance of payments, current account (million US$)	50	714	- 225 [c]

Major trading partners
2022

Export partners (% of exports) [f]	Ethiopia	81.5	China	6.3	United States	2.8
Import partners (% of imports) [f]	China	29.2	Saudi Arabia	23.6	United Arab Emirates	12.7

Social indicators

	2010	2015	2023
Population growth rate (average annual %)	1.9	1.7	1.4 [a,b]
Urban population (% of total population)	77.0	77.4	77.9 [e]
Urban population growth rate (average annual %) [h]	1.7	1.8	...
Fertility rate, total (live births per woman)	3.4	3.1	2.8 [a,b]
Life expectancy at birth (females/males, years)	62.3 / 58.3	64.3 / 59.7	65.5 / 60.3 [a,b]
Population age distribution (0-14/60+ years old, %)	36.1 / 5.9	33.9 / 6.3	30.4 / 7.1 [a,b]
International migrant stock (000/% of total pop.) [i]	102.3 / 12.2	112.4 / 12.3	119.7 / 12.1 [g]
Refugees and others of concern to the UNHCR (000)	15.8 [j]	17.4	35.5 [b]
Infant mortality rate (per 1 000 live births)	51.3	45.2	36.5 [a,b]
Health: Current expenditure (% of GDP) [f,k]	3.1	3.1 [l]	2.0 [l,g]
Health: Physicians (per 1 000 pop.)	0.2 [m]	0.2 [n]	...
Education: Government expenditure (% of GDP)	4.5	3.6 [f]	3.8 [f,o]
Education: Primary gross enrol. ratio (f/m per 100 pop.)	58.5 / 58.9 [p]	72.8 / 67.9	69.4 / 77.4 [b]
Education: Lowr. sec. gross enrol. ratio (f/m per 100 pop.)	39.5 / 47.0 [p]	51.4 / 52.4	67.4 / 65.9 [b]
Education: Upr. sec. gross enrol. ratio (f/m per 100 pop.)	19.8 / 26.8 [p]	37.2 / 41.9	44.8 / 43.4 [b]
Seats held by women in the National Parliament (%)	13.8	12.7	26.2 [q]

Environment and infrastructure indicators

	2010	2015	2023
Individuals using the Internet (per 100 inhabitants) [f]	6.5	22.9	68.9 [c]
Threatened species (number)	81	94	129 [b]
Forested area (% of land area)	0.2	0.2	0.3 [g]
Energy production, primary (Petajoules)	3	4	4 [g]
Energy supply per capita (Gigajoules)	12	10	9 [g]
Tourist/visitor arrivals at national borders (000)	51	63 [r]	114 [c]
Important sites for terrestrial biodiversity protected (%)	0.0	0.8	0.8 [b]
Pop. using safely managed sanitation (urban/rural %)	36.8 / 14.9	41.2 / 18.2	44.8 / 20.9 [b]
Net Official Development Assist. received (% of GNI)	11.53	7.23	5.39 [c]

a Projected estimate (medium fertility variant). **b** 2022. **c** 2021. **d** Refers to the population of the "cercle". **e** 2019. **f** Estimate. **g** 2020. **h** Data refers to a 5-year period preceding the reference year. **i** Including refugees. **j** Data as at the end of December. **k** Data based on calendar year (January 1 to December 31). **l** Estimates should be viewed with caution as these are derived from scarce data. **m** 2006. **n** 2014. **o** 2018. **p** 2009. **q** Data are as at 1 January of reporting year. **r** 2013.

Dominica

Region	Caribbean	UN membership date	18 December 1978
Population (000, 2023)	73[a,b]	Surface area (km2)	750[c]
Pop. density (per km2, 2023)	97.0[a,b]	Sex ratio (m per 100 f)	98.9[a,b]
Capital city	Roseau	National currency	E. Caribbean Dollar (XCD)[d]
Capital city pop. (000, 2023)	14.9[e]	Exchange rate (per US$)	2.7[b]

Economic indicators

	2010	2015	2023
GDP: Gross domestic product (million current US$)	494	541	548[c]
GDP growth rate (annual %, const. 2015 prices)	0.7	- 2.4	6.5[c]
GDP per capita (current US$)	7 182.4	7 724.0	7 570.8[c]
Economy: Agriculture (% of Gross Value Added)	13.7	16.5	20.3[c]
Economy: Industry (% of Gross Value Added)	14.0	14.7	13.9[c]
Economy: Services and other activity (% of GVA)	72.2	68.8	65.8[c]
CPI: Consumer Price Index (2010=100)	100	102	105[c]
Agricultural production index (2014-2016=100)	98	99	100[c]
International trade: exports (million current US$)	34	30[f]	28[f,b]
International trade: imports (million current US$)	225	214[f]	393[f,b]
International trade: balance (million current US$)	- 190	- 184[f]	- 365[f,b]
Balance of payments, current account (million US$)	- 80	- 25	- 153[c]

Major trading partners

2022

Export partners (% of exports)[f]	Saudi Arabia	23.9	Bahamas	18.6	Saint Lucia	5.4
Import partners (% of imports)[f]	United States	48.9	Trinidad and Tobago	10.7	China	8.5

Social indicators

	2010	2015	2023
Population growth rate (average annual %)	- 0.1	- 0.3	0.4[a,b]
Urban population (% of total population)	68.1	69.6	70.8[g]
Urban population growth rate (average annual %)[h]	0.7	0.9	...
Fertility rate, total (live births per woman)	1.9	1.7	1.6[a,b]
Life expectancy at birth (females/males, years)	74.9 / 68.7	71.1 / 66.6	76.5 / 69.9[a,b]
Population age distribution (0-14/60+ years old, %)	23.6 / 14.8	21.7 / 13.4	19.6 / 14.5[a,b]
International migrant stock (000/% of total pop.)	8.1 / 11.4	8.1 / 11.4	8.3 / 11.5[i]
Refugees and others of concern to the UNHCR (000)	...	...	~0.0[i]
Infant mortality rate (per 1 000 live births)	21.2	33.9	11.4[a,b]
Health: Current expenditure (% of GDP)[f,j]	5.2	5.2	5.6[i]
Health: Physicians (per 1 000 pop.)	...	...	1.1[e]
Education: Government expenditure (% of GDP)	...	3.4	5.2[b]
Education: Primary gross enrol. ratio (f/m per 100 pop.)	101.8 / 103.6	115.2 / 117.1	100.1 / 104.8[c]
Education: Lowr. sec. gross enrol. ratio (f/m per 100 pop.)	96.2 / 100.9	104.3 / 112.2	102.9 / 115.0[c]
Education: Upr. sec. gross enrol. ratio (f/m per 100 pop.)	88.5 / 63.9	80.1 / 71.7	100.8 / 85.6[c]
Intentional homicide rate (per 100 000 pop.)	21.8	12.9	13.8[c]
Seats held by women in the National Parliament (%)	14.3	21.9	37.5[k]

Environment and infrastructure indicators

	2010	2015	2023
Individuals using the Internet (per 100 inhabitants)	47.4	65.0[f]	80.9[f,c]
Threatened species (number)	48	62	108[b]
Forested area (% of land area)	63.8	63.8	63.8[i]
Energy production, primary (Petajoules)	0	0	0[i]
Energy supply per capita (Gigajoules)	37	38[f]	33[f,i]
Tourist/visitor arrivals at national borders (000)	77	75	15[c]
Important sites for terrestrial biodiversity protected (%)	33.3	33.3	33.3[b]
Net Official Development Assist. received (% of GNI)	6.71	2.25	14.46[c]

a Projected estimate (medium fertility variant). b 2022. c 2021. d East Caribbean Dollar. e 2018. f Estimate. g 2019. h Data refers to a 5-year period preceding the reference year. i 2020. j Data refer to fiscal years beginning 1 July. k Data are as at 1 January of reporting year.

Dominican Republic

Region	Caribbean	
Population (000, 2023)	11 229[a,b]	
Pop. density (per km2, 2023)	232.4[a,b]	
Capital city	Santo Domingo	
Capital city pop. (000, 2023)	3 245.0[d,e]	

UN membership date	24 October 1945
Surface area (km2)	48 671[c]
Sex ratio (m per 100 f)	100.7[a,b]
National currency	Dominican Peso (DOP)
Exchange rate (per US$)	56.4[b]

Economic indicators

	2010	2015	2023
GDP: Gross domestic product (million current US$)	53 160	71 155	94 243[c]
GDP growth rate (annual %, const. 2015 prices)	8.3	6.9	12.3[c]
GDP per capita (current US$)	5 437.9	6 838.0	8 476.7[c]
Economy: Agriculture (% of Gross Value Added)[f,g]	6.5	5.9	6.1[c]
Economy: Industry (% of Gross Value Added)[g,h]	29.9	30.6	35.1[c]
Economy: Services and other activity (% of GVA)[g]	63.6	63.5	58.8[c]
Employment in agriculture (% of employed)	12.4	9.7	8.3[c]
Employment in industry (% of employed)	18.5	18.4	20.3[c]
Employment in services & other sectors (% employed)	69.1	71.9	71.4[c]
Unemployment rate (% of labour force)	5.2	7.6	7.7[i]
Labour force participation rate (female/male pop. %)	41.5 / 71.7	48.0 / 75.9	53.0 / 76.6[i]
CPI: Consumer Price Index (2010=100)[j]	100	122	166[b]
Agricultural production index (2014-2016=100)	79	100	116[c]
International trade: exports (million current US$)	4 767	8 384	9 836[b]
International trade: imports (million current US$)	15 138	17 348	29 955[b]
International trade: balance (million current US$)	- 10 371	- 8 964	- 20 119[b]
Balance of payments, current account (million US$)	- 4 024	- 1 280	- 6 327[b]

Major trading partners

						2022
Export partners (% of exports)	United States	51.8	Switzerland	10.5	Haiti	10.4
Import partners (% of imports)	United States	41.0	China	15.9	Brazil	4.3

Social indicators

	2010	2015	2023
Population growth rate (average annual %)	1.3	1.2	0.9[a,b]
Urban population (% of total population)	73.8	78.6	81.8[e]
Urban population growth rate (average annual %)[k]	3.2	2.5	...
Fertility rate, total (live births per woman)	2.5	2.4	2.2[a,b]
Life expectancy at birth (females/males, years)	75.7 / 68.9	76.4 / 69.8	77.5 / 71.0[a,b]
Population age distribution (0-14/60+ years old, %)	30.7 / 8.1	29.0 / 9.1	27.1 / 11.2[a,b]
International migrant stock (000/% of total pop.)[l]	395.5 / 4.1	549.3 / 5.3	603.8 / 5.6[m]
Refugees and others of concern to the UNHCR (000)	2.4[n]	135.1[o]	116.5[b]
Infant mortality rate (per 1 000 live births)	28.5	28.3	24.4[a,b]
Health: Current expenditure (% of GDP)[i,q]	4.9[p]	4.7[p]	4.9[m]
Health: Physicians (per 1 000 pop.)	1.1[r]	1.5[s]	1.4[e]
Education: Government expenditure (% of GDP)	2.0[t]	3.6	3.7[c]
Education: Primary gross enrol. ratio (f/m per 100 pop.)[i]	103.4 / 117.3	106.2 / 116.4	95.2 / 98.1[c]
Education: Lowr. sec. gross enrol. ratio (f/m per 100 pop.)[i]	92.3 / 89.7	90.3 / 88.2	86.1 / 83.8[c]
Education: Upr. sec. gross enrol. ratio (f/m per 100 pop.)[i]	78.0 / 65.4	80.5 / 70.0	71.9 / 60.4[c]
Intentional homicide rate (per 100 000 pop.)	25.3	17.6[d]	10.5[c]
Seats held by women in the National Parliament (%)	19.7	20.8	27.9[v]

Environment and infrastructure indicators

	2010	2015	2023
Individuals using the Internet (per 100 inhabitants)	31.4[i]	54.2[w]	85.2[c]
Threatened species (number)	126	153	304[b]
Forested area (% of land area)	42.9	43.5	44.4[m]
CO2 emission estimates (million tons/tons per capita)	19.5 / 2.0	22.0 / 2.1	21.3 / 1.9[m]
Energy production, primary (Petajoules)	38	33	44[m]
Energy supply per capita (Gigajoules)	32	32	31[m]
Tourist/visitor arrivals at national borders (000)[x]	4 125	5 600	4 994[c]
Important sites for terrestrial biodiversity protected (%)	74.1	76.9	76.9[b]
Pop. using safely managed drinking water (urban/rural, %)	47.0 / 34.3	46.9 / 34.5	46.9 / 34.9[b]
Pop. using safely managed sanitation (urban/rural, %)	46.5 / 53.9	44.8 / 51.3	42.3 / 47.6[b]
Net Official Development Assist. received (% of GNI)	0.37	0.41	0.50[c]

a Projected estimate (medium fertility variant). b 2022. c 2021. d Refers to the urban population of the Municipalities of Santo Domingo de Guzmán, Santo Domingo Este, Santo Domingo Oeste, and Santo Domingo Norte. e 2019. f Excludes irrigation canals and landscaping care. g Data classified according to ISIC Rev. 4. h Excludes publishing activities, recycling. Includes irrigation canals. i Estimate. j Calculated by the UN Statistics Division from national indices. k Data refers to a 5-year period preceding the reference year. l Including refugees. m 2020. n Data as at the end of December. o Revised estimate includes only individuals born in the country where both parents were born abroad. This estimate does not include subsequent generations of individuals of foreign descent as such it does not include all persons without nationality. p Data are based on SHA2011. q Data based on calendar year (January 1 to December 31). r 2008. s 2011. t 2007. u 2014. v Data are as at 1 January of reporting year. w Users in the last 3 months. x Arrivals by air only.

Ecuador

Region	South America
Population (000, 2023)	18 001 [a,b]
Pop. density (per km2, 2023)	72.5 [a,b]
Capital city	Quito
Capital city pop. (000, 2023)	1 847.7 [d]

UN membership date	21 December 1945
Surface area (km2)	257 217 [c]
Sex ratio (m per 100 f)	99.6 [a,b]
National currency	US Dollar (USD)

Economic indicators	2010	2015	2023
GDP: Gross domestic product (million current US$)	69 555	99 290	106 166 [c]
GDP growth rate (annual %, const. 2015 prices)	3.5	0.1	4.2 [c]
GDP per capita (current US$)	4 640.2	6 130.6	5 965.1 [c]
Economy: Agriculture (% of Gross Value Added) [e,f]	10.2	10.2	10.0 [c]
Economy: Industry (% of Gross Value Added) [f,g]	36.3	34.4	33.2 [c]
Economy: Services and other activity (% of GVA) [f]	53.5	55.4	56.8 [c]
Employment in agriculture (% of employed)	27.9	26.2	32.2 [c]
Employment in industry (% of employed)	17.5 [h]	9.2 [h]	16.9 [c]
Employment in services & other sectors (% employed)	53.6	54.1	51.0 [c]
Unemployment rate (% of labour force)	4.1	3.6	3.8 [h]
Labour force participation rate (female/male pop. %)	48.0 / 77.6	51.9 / 79.7	55.2 / 79.0 [h]
CPI: Consumer Price Index (2010=100)	100	121	128 [b]
Agricultural production index (2014-2016=100)	101	104	103 [c]
International trade: exports (million current US$)	17 490	18 331	38 485 [h,b]
International trade: imports (million current US$)	20 591	21 387	37 046 [h,b]
International trade: balance (million current US$)	- 3 101	- 3 057	1 440 [h,b]
Balance of payments, current account (million US$)	- 1 582	- 2 221	2 711 [b]

Major trading partners						2022
Export partners (% of exports) [h]	United States	24.0	China	15.3	Panama	14.9
Import partners (% of imports) [h]	China	23.5	United States	22.1	Colombia	7.0

Social indicators	2010	2015	2023
Population growth rate (average annual %)	1.6	1.5	1.1 [a,b]
Urban population (% of total population)	62.7	63.4	64.0 [d]
Urban population growth rate (average annual %) [i]	2.0	1.8	...
Fertility rate, total (live births per woman)	2.6	2.3	2.0 [a,b]
Life expectancy at birth (females/males, years)	78.5 / 72.5	79.2 / 74.4	80.5 / 75.3 [a,b]
Population age distribution (0-14/60+ years old, %)	31.2 / 8.6	29.0 / 9.8	25.7 / 11.3 [a,b]
International migrant stock (000/% of total pop.) [j]	375.3 / 2.5	387.5 / 2.4	784.8 / 4.4 [k]
Refugees and others of concern to the UNHCR (000)	171.1 [l]	133.1 [l]	564.9 [b]
Infant mortality rate (per 1 000 live births)	16.0	13.0	10.7 [a,b]
Health: Current expenditure (% of GDP) [m,n]	6.1	7.5	8.5 [k]
Health: Physicians (per 1 000 pop.)	2.1	2.1	2.2 [o]
Education: Government expenditure (% of GDP)	4.5	5.0	3.7 [c]
Education: Primary gross enrol. ratio (f/m per 100 pop.)	113.2 / 112.9	107.9 / 107.4	97.1 / 95.1 [c]
Education: Lowr. sec. gross enrol. ratio (f/m per 100 pop.)	105.6 / 103.4	113.8 / 110.6	104.3 / 103.9 [c]
Education: Upr. sec. gross enrol. ratio (f/m per 100 pop.)	82.9 / 76.5	98.5 / 93.3	99.6 / 95.7 [c]
Intentional homicide rate (per 100 000 pop.)	17.5	6.5	14.0 [c]
Seats held by women in the National Parliament (%)	32.3	41.6	38.7 [p]

Environment and infrastructure indicators	2010	2015	2023
Individuals using the Internet (per 100 inhabitants)	29.0 [q]	48.9 [q]	76.2 [h,c]
Research & Development expenditure (% of GDP)	0.4	0.4 [r]	...
Threatened species (number)	2 255	2 308	2 692 [b]
Forested area (% of land area)	52.5	51.6	50.3 [k]
CO2 emission estimates (million tons/tons per capita)	32.1 / 2.1	37.8 / 2.3	31.1 / 1.7 [k]
Energy production, primary (Petajoules)	1 110	1 260	1 167 [k]
Energy supply per capita (Gigajoules)	35	37	30 [k]
Tourist/visitor arrivals at national borders (000) [s]	1 047	1 676	669 [c]
Important sites for terrestrial biodiversity protected (%)	23.0	24.7	28.1 [b]
Pop. using safely managed drinking water (urban/rural, %)	72.1 / 47.9	74.0 / 50.3	74.7 / 53.3 [b]
Pop. using safely managed sanitation (urban/rural %)	35.3 / 50.7	34.0 / 55.0	30.9 / 61.0 [b]
Net Official Development Assist. received (% of GNI)	0.25	0.33	0.29 [c]

a Projected estimate (medium fertility variant). b 2022. c 2021. d 2019. e Excludes irrigation canals and landscaping care. f Data classified according to ISIC Rev. 4. g Excludes publishing activities, recycling. Includes irrigation canals. h Estimate. i Data refers to a 5-year period preceding the reference year. j Including refugees. k 2020. l Data as at the end of December. m Data based on calendar year (January 1 to December 31). n Data are based on SHA2011. o 2017. p Data are as at 1 January of reporting year. q Population aged 5 years and over. r 2014. s Including nationals residing abroad.

Egypt

Region	Northern Africa	
Population (000, 2023)	110 990 [a,b]	
Pop. density (per km2, 2023)	111.5 [a,b]	
Capital city	Cairo	
Capital city pop. (000, 2023)	20 485.0 [d,e]	

UN membership date	24 October 1945
Surface area (km2)	1 002 000 [c]
Sex ratio (m per 100 f)	102.3 [a,b]
National currency	Egyptian Pound (EGP)
Exchange rate (per US$)	24.7 [b]

Economic indicators

	2010	2015	2023
GDP: Gross domestic product (million current US$)	214 630	317 745	425 906 [c]
GDP growth rate (annual %, const. 2015 prices)	5.1	4.4	8.8 [c]
GDP per capita (current US$)	2 459.9	3 251.5	3 898.0 [c]
Economy: Agriculture (% of Gross Value Added) [f]	14.0	11.3	12.0 [c]
Economy: Industry (% of Gross Value Added) [f]	37.5	36.2	32.8 [c]
Economy: Services and other activity (% of GVA)	48.5	52.5	55.2 [c]
Employment in agriculture (% of employed)	28.3	25.8	19.8 [g,c]
Employment in industry (% of employed)	25.3	25.0	29.1 [g,c]
Employment in services & other sectors (% employed)	46.4	49.1	51.1 [g,c]
Unemployment rate (% of labour force)	8.8	13.1	7.0 [g]
Labour force participation rate (female/male pop. %)	23.2 / 75.2	22.8 / 70.8	15.2 / 68.2 [g]
CPI: Consumer Price Index (2010=100) [h]	100	157	365 [i,b]
Agricultural production index (2014-2016=100)	91	101	103 [c]
International trade: exports (million current US$)	26 332	21 852	48 149 [b]
International trade: imports (million current US$)	53 003	73 975	79 712 [b]
International trade: balance (million current US$)	- 26 672	- 52 123	- 31 563 [b]
Balance of payments, current account (million US$)	- 4 504	- 17 243	- 18 611 [c]

Major trading partners

							2022
Export partners (% of exports)	Türkiye	7.9	Spain	7.3	Italy	6.9	
Import partners (% of imports)	China	14.3	Saudi Arabia	8.9	United States	7.2	

Social indicators

	2010	2015	2023
Population growth rate (average annual %)	2.1	2.1	1.5 [a,b]
Urban population (% of total population)	43.0	42.8	42.7 [e]
Urban population growth rate (average annual %) [j]	1.8	2.1	...
Fertility rate, total (live births per woman)	3.2	3.4	2.9 [a,b]
Life expectancy at birth (females/males, years)	72.3 / 67.1	73.1 / 68.0	72.6 / 67.9 [a,b]
Population age distribution (0-14/60+ years old, %)	33.3 / 6.6	33.5 / 6.9	32.9 / 7.7 [a,b]
International migrant stock (000/% of total pop.) [k]	310.0 / 0.4	353.6 / 0.4	543.9 / 0.5 [l]
Refugees and others of concern to the UNHCR (000)	109.9 [m]	256.4	359.5 [b]
Infant mortality rate (per 1 000 live births)	23.8	19.6	16.0 [a,b]
Health: Current expenditure (% of GDP) [n]	4.2	5.3	4.4 [g,o,p,l]
Health: Physicians (per 1 000 pop.)	...	0.8	0.7 [e]
Education: Government expenditure (% of GDP)	3.5	3.9	...
Education: Primary gross enrol. ratio (f/m per 100 pop.)	100.7 / 103.7	103.7 / 104.0 [q]	106.9 / 106.0 [e]
Education: Lowr. sec. gross enrol. ratio (f/m per 100 pop.)	88.9 / 89.5	94.6 / 93.7 [q]	100.7 / 101.2 [e]
Education: Upr. sec. gross enrol. ratio (f/m per 100 pop.)	46.6 / 49.7	66.5 / 68.0 [q]	76.9 / 78.2 [e]
Intentional homicide rate (per 100 000 pop.)	2.1	1.8	1.3 [r]
Seats held by women in the National Parliament (%)	...	...	27.5 [s]

Environment and infrastructure indicators

	2010	2015	2023
Individuals using the Internet (per 100 inhabitants)	21.6 [t]	37.8	72.1 [g,c]
Research & Development expenditure (% of GDP)	0.4 [u,v]	0.7	1.0 [c]
Threatened species (number)	121	141	209 [b]
Forested area (% of land area)	0.1	-0.0	-0.0 [l]
CO2 emission estimates (million tons/tons per capita) [n]	178.7 / 2.1	201.6 / 2.2	190.3 / 1.8 [l]
Energy production, primary (Petajoules)	3 632	2 991	3 656 [l]
Energy supply per capita (Gigajoules)	36	35	34 [l]
Tourist/visitor arrivals at national borders (000)	14 731	9 328	3 677 [l]
Important sites for terrestrial biodiversity protected (%)	39.6	39.6	39.6 [b]
Pop. using safely managed sanitation (urban/rural %)	67.6 / 52.9	69.9 / 57.9	72.6 / 63.1 [b]
Net Official Development Assist. received (% of GNI)	0.28	0.78	2.03 [c]

a Projected estimate (medium fertility variant). b 2022. c 2021. d Refers to Greater Cairo as the sum of the Governorate of Al-Qahirah (Cairo) and the surrounding districts of the Governorates of Al-Jizah (Giza) and Al-Qalyūbyah (Qalyubia). e 2019. f At factor cost. g Estimate. h For urban population only. i Calculated by the UN Statistics Division from national indices. j Data refers to a 5-year period preceding the reference year. k Including refugees. l 2020. m Data as at the end of December. n Data refer to scal years beginning 1 July. o Break in the time series. p Data are based on SHA2011. q 2014. r 2017. s Data are as at 1 January of reporting year. t Population aged 6 years and over. u Excluding private non-profit. v Excluding business enterprise.

El Salvador

Region	Central America	UN membership date	24 October 1945
Population (000, 2023)	6 336 [a,b]	Surface area (km2)	21 041 [c]
Pop. density (per km2, 2023)	305.8 [a,b]	Sex ratio (m per 100 f)	90.9 [a,b]
Capital city	San Salvador	National currency	US Dollar (USD)
Capital city pop. (000, 2023)	1 105.7 [d,e]		

Economic indicators	2010	2015	2023
GDP: Gross domestic product (million current US$)	18 448	23 438	28 737 [c]
GDP growth rate (annual %, const. 2015 prices)	2.1	2.4	10.3 [c]
GDP per capita (current US$)	3 017.3	3 761.5	4 551.2 [c]
Economy: Agriculture (% of Gross Value Added) [f,g]	7.6	6.1	5.5 [c]
Economy: Industry (% of Gross Value Added) [h]	27.5	27.8	27.1 [c]
Economy: Services and other activity (% of GVA)	64.8	66.1	67.4 [c]
Employment in agriculture (% of employed)	20.8	18.1	15.2 [i,c]
Employment in industry (% of employed)	21.4	22.1	23.8 [i,c]
Employment in services & other sectors (% employed)	57.9	59.7	61.0 [i,c]
Unemployment rate (% of labour force)	4.9	4.0	4.2 [i]
Labour force participation (female/male pop. %)	45.9 / 76.2	45.0 / 74.5	45.8 / 74.7 [i]
CPI: Consumer Price Index (2010=100) [j]	100	108	123 [b]
Agricultural production index (2014-2016=100)	102	97	98 [c]
International trade: exports (million current US$)	4 499	5 509	7 115 [b]
International trade: imports (million current US$)	8 416	10 293	17 108 [b]
International trade: balance (million current US$)	- 3 917	- 4 784	- 9 993 [b]
Balance of payments, current account (million US$)	- 533	- 754	- 2 146 [b]

Major trading partners						2022
Export partners (% of exports)	United States	39.2	Guatemala	17.1	Honduras	16.7
Import partners (% of imports)	United States	29.8	China	16.6	Guatemala	9.9

Social indicators	2010	2015	2023
Population growth rate (average annual %)	0.4	0.3	0.4 [a,b]
Urban population (% of total population)	65.5	69.7	72.7 [e]
Urban population growth rate (average annual %) [k]	1.6	1.7	...
Fertility rate, total (live births per woman)	2.2	2.1	1.8 [a,b]
Life expectancy at birth (females/males, years)	76.2 / 67.2	76.6 / 66.8	75.8 / 66.8 [a,b]
Population age distribution (0-14/60+ years old, %)	31.8 / 9.7	28.4 / 10.4	25.4 / 11.6 [a,b]
International migrant stock (000/% of total pop.) [l]	40.3 / 0.7	42.1 / 0.7	42.8 / 0.7 [m]
Refugees and others of concern to the UNHCR (000)	0.1 [n]	~0.0	76.0 [b]
Infant mortality rate (per 1 000 live births)	16.3	13.1	9.9 [a,b]
Health: Current expenditure (% of GDP) [o]	8.9	8.8	9.9 [p,q,m]
Health: Physicians (per 1 000 pop.)	1.9 [r]	...	2.9 [c]
Education: Government expenditure (% of GDP)	4.0	3.9	4.6 [c]
Education: Primary gross enrol. ratio (f/m per 100 pop.)	112.3 / 117.6	103.9 / 108.5 [s]	... / ...
Education: Lowr. sec. gross enrol. ratio (f/m per 100 pop.)	89.7 / 90.6	95.9 / 97.0 [s]	... / ...
Education: Upr. sec. gross enrol. ratio (f/m per 100 pop.)	47.3 / 46.6	58.6 / 55.9	56.6 / 51.9 [c]
Intentional homicide rate (per 100 000 pop.)	65.2	106.8	18.2 [c]
Seats held by women in the National Parliament (%)	19.0	27.4	27.4 [t]

Environment and infrastructure indicators	2010	2015	2023
Individuals using the Internet (per 100 inhabitants)	15.9 [u]	26.8	62.9 [i,c]
Research & Development expenditure (% of GDP)	0.1	0.1 [v]	0.2 [m]
Threatened species (number)	72	83	177 [b]
Forested area (% of land area)	30.4	29.3	28.2 [m]
CO2 emission estimates (million tons/tons per capita)	6.3 / 1.0	6.8 / 1.0	6.2 / 0.9 [m]
Energy production, primary (Petajoules)	92	79	87 [m]
Energy supply per capita (Gigajoules)	29	28	28 [m]
Tourist/visitor arrivals at national borders (000)	1 150	1 402	1 219 [c]
Important sites for terrestrial biodiversity protected (%)	22.8	28.0	28.0 [b]
Pop. using safely managed drinking water (urban/rural, %)	82.0 / ...	80.6 / ...	78.6 / ... [b]
Pop. using safely managed sanitation (urban/rural, %)	18.1 / ...	17.8 / ...	17.4 / ... [b]
Net Official Development Assist. received (% of GNI)	1.69	0.40	0.79 [c]

a Projected estimate (medium fertility variant). b 2022. c 2021. d Refers to the urban parts of the municipalities San Salvador, Mejicanos, Soyapango, Delgado, Ilopango, Cuscatancingo, Ayutuxtepeque and San Marcos. e 2019. f Data classified according to ISIC Rev. 4. g Excludes irrigation canals and landscaping care. h Excludes publishing activities, recycling. Includes irrigation canals. i Estimate. j Urban areas. k Data refers to a 5-year period preceding the reference year. l Including refugees. m 2020. n Data as at the end of December. o Data based on calendar year (January 1 to December 31). p Last available data reported by the country using Government reports and national accounts data. q Data are based on SHA2011. r 2008. s 2014. t Data are as at 1 January of reporting year. u Population aged 10 years and over. v Break in the time series.

Equatorial Guinea

Region	Middle Africa	UN membership date	12 November 1968
Population (000, 2023)	1 675[a,b]	Surface area (km2)	28 052[c]
Pop. density (per km2, 2023)	59.7[a,b]	Sex ratio (m per 100 f)	111.8[a,b]
Capital city	Malabo	National currency	CFA Franc, BEAC (XAF)[d]
Capital city pop. (000, 2023)	296.8[e]	Exchange rate (per US$)	615.0[b]

Economic indicators

	2010	2015	2023
GDP: Gross domestic product (million current US$)	16 299	13 176	12 431[c]
GDP growth rate (annual %, const. 2015 prices)	- 8.9	- 9.1	2.6[c]
GDP per capita (current US$)	14 891.0	9 781.6	7 605.5[c]
Economy: Agriculture (% of Gross Value Added)	1.1	1.9	2.6[c]
Economy: Industry (% of Gross Value Added)	74.3	59.0	53.1[c]
Economy: Services and other activity (% of GVA)	24.6	39.1	44.3[c]
Employment in agriculture (% of employed)[f]	54.1	54.7	55.5[c]
Employment in industry (% of employed)[f]	16.0	14.9	13.8[c]
Employment in services & other sectors (% employed)[f]	29.9	30.5	30.7[c]
Unemployment rate (% of labour force)[f]	8.4	8.2	8.6
Labour force participation rate (female/male pop. %)[f]	50.9 / 60.9	51.2 / 59.8	51.3 / 58.7
CPI: Consumer Price Index (2010=100)	100[g]	119	130[h]
Agricultural production index (2014-2016=100)	93	103	102[c]
International trade: exports (million current US$)[f]	9 964	9 570	7 673[b]
International trade: imports (million current US$)[f]	5 679	6 010	1 018[b]
International trade: balance (million current US$)[f]	4 285	3 560	6 655[b]

Major trading partners

						2022
Export partners (% of exports)[f]	China	18.9	Spain	18.8	India	10.6
Import partners (% of imports)[f]	China	20.9	Spain	15.3	Nigeria	11.7

Social indicators

	2010	2015	2023
Population growth rate (average annual %)	4.7	3.9	2.4[a,b]
Urban population (% of total population)	65.9	70.6	72.6[i]
Urban population growth rate (average annual %)[j]	7.2	5.6	...
Fertility rate, total (live births per woman)	5.2	4.8	4.2[a,b]
Life expectancy at birth (females/males, years)	59.6 / 56.3	62.1 / 58.3	63.3 / 59.4[a,b]
Population age distribution (0-14/60+ years old, %)	38.9 / 5.0	38.7 / 5.0	38.5 / 5.1[a,b]
International migrant stock (000/% of total pop.)[k]	8.7 / 0.9	209.6 / 17.9	230.6 / 16.4[h]
Infant mortality rate (per 1 000 live births)	79.6	68.1	53.8[a,b]
Health: Current expenditure (% of GDP)[l,m]	1.8	2.9	3.8[h]
Health: Physicians (per 1 000 pop.)	...	...	0.4[n]
Education: Government expenditure (% of GDP)	...	...	0.3[c]
Education: Primary gross enrol. ratio (f/m per 100 pop.)	68.9 / 69.8	61.6 / 62.0	66.2 / 66.9[i]
Education: Lowr. sec. gross enrol. ratio (f/m per 100 pop.)	33.8 / 42.2[o]	34.0 / 33.0	... / ...
Education: Upr. sec. gross enrol. ratio (f/m per 100 pop.)	5.6 / 13.3[o]	... / ...	... / ...
Seats held by women in the National Parliament (%)	10.0	24.0	31.0[p]

Environment and infrastructure indicators

	2010	2015	2023
Individuals using the Internet (per 100 inhabitants)	6.0	21.3[f]	53.9[f,c]
Threatened species (number)	130	155	297[b]
Forested area (% of land area)	90.3	88.8	87.3[h]
CO2 emission estimates (million tons/tons per capita)	4.0 / 4.3	4.5 / 3.8	3.8 / 2.7[h]
Energy production, primary (Petajoules)	884	821	552[h]
Energy supply per capita (Gigajoules)	71	81	55[h]
Important sites for terrestrial biodiversity protected (%)	100.0	100.0	100.0[b]
Net Official Development Assist. received (% of GNI)	0.89	0.08	0.14[c]

a Projected estimate (medium fertility variant). **b** 2022. **c** 2021. **d** African Financial Community (CFA) Franc, Bank of Central African States (BEAC). **e** 2018. **f** Estimate. **g** Break in the time series. **h** 2020. **i** 2019. **j** Data refers to a 5-year period preceding the reference year. **k** Refers to foreign citizens. **l** Estimates should be viewed with caution as these are derived from scarce data. **m** Data based on calendar year (January 1 to December 31). **n** 2017. **o** 2005. **p** Data are as at 1 January of reporting year.

Eritrea

Region	Eastern Africa	UN membership date	28 May 1993
Population (000, 2023)	3 684[a,b]	Surface area (km2)	121 144[c]
Pop. density (per km2, 2023)	30.4[a,b]	Sex ratio (m per 100 f)	97.4[a,b]
Capital city	Asmara	National currency	Nakfa (ERN)
Capital city pop. (000, 2023)	928.8[d]	Exchange rate (per US$)	15.1[b]

Economic indicators	2010	2015	2023
GDP: Gross domestic product (million current US$)[e]	1 590	2 013	2 255[c]
GDP growth rate (annual %, const. 2015 prices)[e]	10.9	- 20.6	2.2[c]
GDP per capita (current US$)[e]	505.0	602.8	623.0[c]
Economy: Agriculture (% of Gross Value Added)[e]	19.1	17.2	17.3[c]
Economy: Industry (% of Gross Value Added)[e]	30.9	31.2	31.3[c]
Economy: Services and other activity (% of GVA)[e]	50.0	51.6	51.4[c]
Employment in agriculture (% of employed)[f]	65.3	64.5	62.4[c]
Employment in industry (% of employed)[f]	8.5	8.4	8.6[c]
Employment in services & other sectors (% employed)[f]	26.2	27.1	29.0[c]
Unemployment rate (% of labour force)[f]	5.9	5.8	6.7
Labour force participation rate (female/male pop. %)[f]	71.9 / 84.2	71.4 / 86.2	71.1 / 84.8
Agricultural production index (2014-2016=100)	95	99	105[c]
International trade: exports (million current US$)[f]	13	15	578[b]
International trade: imports (million current US$)[f]	1 187	2 801	509[b]
International trade: balance (million current US$)[f]	- 1 175	- 2 786	69[b]

Major trading partners						2022
Export partners (% of exports)[f]	China	56.5	United Arab Emirates	25.2	Republic of Korea	14.8
Import partners (% of imports)[f]	China	29.5	United Arab Emirates	28.9	Türkiye	10.7

Social indicators	2010	2015	2023
Population growth rate (average annual %)	2.2	0.8	1.7[a,b]
Urban population (% of total population)	35.2	38.2	40.7[d]
Urban population growth rate (average annual %)[g]	4.5	3.6	...
Fertility rate, total (live births per woman)	4.6	4.2	3.8[a,b]
Life expectancy at birth (females/males, years)	65.5 / 62.0	68.0 / 64.0	68.7 / 64.5[a,b]
Population age distribution (0-14/60+ years old, %)	42.7 / 5.5	42.2 / 5.7	39.2 / 6.1[a,b]
International migrant stock (000/% of total pop.)[f,h]	15.8 / 0.5	15.9 / 0.5	13.9 / 0.4[i]
Refugees and others of concern to the UNHCR (000)	5.0[j]	3.0	0.1[b]
Infant mortality rate (per 1 000 live births)	39.0	33.9	28.6[a,b]
Health: Current expenditure (% of GDP)[k,l]	4.9	4.5	4.1[i]
Health: Physicians (per 1 000 pop.)	-0.0	0.1	0.1[i]
Education: Government expenditure (% of GDP)	2.1[m]	...	...
Education: Primary gross enrol. ratio (f/m per 100 pop.)	76.9 / 90.2	70.4 / 81.7	63.4 / 73.6[d]
Education: Lowr. sec. gross enrol. ratio (f/m per 100 pop.)	70.3 / 87.3	59.7 / 70.4	60.3 / 67.4[d]
Education: Upr. sec. gross enrol. ratio (f/m per 100 pop.)	28.1 / 39.5	36.5 / 42.8	29.6 / 30.6[d]
Intentional homicide rate (per 100 000 pop.)	...	14.6[n]	...
Seats held by women in the National Parliament (%)	22.0	22.0	22.0[d]

Environment and infrastructure indicators	2010	2015	2023
Individuals using the Internet (per 100 inhabitants)[f]	0.6	1.1	21.7[c]
Threatened species (number)	97	113	161[b]
Forested area (% of land area)	9.0	8.8	8.7[i]
CO2 emission estimates (million tons/tons per capita)	0.6 / 0.2	0.6 / 0.2	0.8 / 0.2[i]
Energy production, primary (Petajoules)	24	29	31[i]
Energy supply per capita (Gigajoules)	10	11	11[i]
Tourist/visitor arrivals at national borders (000)[o]	84	114	142[p]
Important sites for terrestrial biodiversity protected (%)	0.0	0.0	0.0[b]
Net Official Development Assist. received (% of GNI)	10.35	6.54[q]	...

a Projected estimate (medium fertility variant). b 2022. c 2021. d 2019. e Data compiled in accordance with the System of National Accounts 1968 (1968 SNA). f Estimate. g Data refers to a 5-year period preceding the reference year. h Including refugees. i 2020. j Data as at the end of December. k Data based on calendar year (January 1 to December 31). l Estimates should be viewed with caution as these are derived from scarce data. m 2006. n 2012. o Including nationals residing abroad. p 2016. q 2011.

Estonia

Region	Northern Europe	UN membership date	17 September 1991
Population (000, 2023)	1 326 [a,b]	Surface area (km2)	45 261 [c]
Pop. density (per km2, 2023)	30.5 [a,b]	Sex ratio (m per 100 f)	90.4 [a,b]
Capital city	Tallinn	National currency	Euro (EUR)
Capital city pop. (000, 2023)	441.3 [d]	Exchange rate (per US$)	0.9 [b]

Economic indicators

	2010	2015	2023
GDP: Gross domestic product (million current US$)	19 535	22 882	37 191 [c]
GDP growth rate (annual %, const. 2015 prices)	2.4	1.9	8.0 [c]
GDP per capita (current US$)	14 671.1	17 405.0	27 990.6 [c]
Economy: Agriculture (% of Gross Value Added) [e,f]	3.6	3.3	2.3 [c]
Economy: Industry (% of Gross Value Added) [e,g]	27.9	27.5	26.4 [c]
Economy: Services and other activity (% of GVA) [e]	68.5	69.2	71.3 [c]
Employment in agriculture (% of employed)	4.2	3.9	2.7 [c]
Employment in industry (% of employed)	30.3	30.7	29.1 [c]
Employment in services & other sectors (% employed)	65.4	65.4	68.3 [c]
Unemployment rate (% of labour force)	16.7	6.4	6.0 [h]
Labour force participation rate (female/male pop. %)	55.1 / 67.0	55.7 / 69.0	59.8 / 70.8 [h]
CPI: Consumer Price Index (2010=100)	100	111	152 [b]
Agricultural production index (2014-2016=100)	79	111	98 [c]
International trade: exports (million current US$) [i]	12 811	13 908	23 146 [b]
International trade: imports (million current US$) [i]	13 197	15 732	27 003 [b]
International trade: balance (million current US$) [i]	- 385	- 1 824	- 3 857 [b]
Balance of payments, current account (million US$)	340	403	- 847 [b]

Major trading partners

						2022
Export partners (% of exports)	Finland	14.1	Latvia	13.6	Sweden	8.9
Import partners (% of imports)	Germany	9.4	Finland	9.1	China	8.8

Social indicators

	2010	2015	2023
Population growth rate (average annual %)	- 0.3	0.2	- 0.2 [a,b]
Urban population (% of total population)	68.1	68.4	69.1 [d]
Urban population growth rate (average annual %) [j]	- 0.5	- 0.2	...
Fertility rate, total (live births per woman)	1.7	1.6	1.7 [a,b]
Life expectancy at birth (females/males, years)	80.4 / 70.7	81.7 / 73.1	83.0 / 75.0 [a,b]
Population age distribution (0-14/60+ years old, %)	15.2 / 23.3	16.0 / 25.2	16.4 / 27.0 [a,b]
International migrant stock (000/% of total pop.)	217.9 / 16.4	194.7 / 14.8	199.3 / 15.0 [k]
Refugees and others of concern to the UNHCR (000)	101.0 [l]	86.8	99.4 [m,b]
Infant mortality rate (per 1 000 live births)	4.1	2.8	1.8 [a,b]
Health: Current expenditure (% of GDP)	6.3	6.6	7.5 [c]
Health: Physicians (per 1 000 pop.)	3.2	3.4	3.9 [k]
Education: Government expenditure (% of GDP)	5.5	5.1	5.3 [d]
Education: Primary gross enrol. ratio (f/m per 100 pop.)	102.2 / 103.8	97.1 / 97.1	97.7 / 97.5 [k]
Education: Lowr. sec. gross enrol. ratio (f/m per 100 pop.)	100.8 / 104.8	105.3 / 109.4	103.5 / 105.1 [k]
Education: Upr. sec. gross enrol. ratio (f/m per 100 pop.)	109.1 / 105.6	116.1 / 113.1	133.6 / 120.7 [k]
Intentional homicide rate (per 100 000 pop.)	5.3	3.4	2.0 [c]
Seats held by women in the National Parliament (%)	22.8	19.8	27.7 [n]

Environment and infrastructure indicators

	2010	2015	2023
Individuals using the Internet (per 100 inhabitants)	74.1 [o,p]	88.4	91.0 [c]
Research & Development expenditure (% of GDP)	1.6	1.5	1.8 [k]
Threatened species (number)	11	17	56 [b]
Forested area (% of land area)	55.1	55.7	57.0 [k]
CO2 emission estimates (million tons/tons per capita)	18.5 / 13.6	14.5 / 10.8	8.7 / 6.2 [c]
Energy production, primary (Petajoules)	206	234	183 [k]
Energy supply per capita (Gigajoules)	182	176	141 [k]
Tourist/visitor arrivals at national borders (000) [q]	2 511	2 961	808 [c]
Important sites for terrestrial biodiversity protected (%)	94.7	94.8	94.9 [b]
Pop. using safely managed sanitation (urban/rural %)	95.7 / ...	96.4 / ...	97.7 / ... [b]
Net Official Development Assist. disbursed (% of GNI)	...	...	0.16 [c]

a Projected estimate (medium fertility variant). **b** 2022. **c** 2021. **d** 2019. **e** Data classified according to ISIC Rev. 4. **f** Excludes irrigation canals and landscaping care. **g** Excludes publishing activities, recycling. Includes irrigation canals. **h** Estimate. **i** General Extra-EU/Special Intra-EU **j** Data refers to a 5-year period preceding the reference year. **k** 2020. **l** Data as at the end of December. **m** Most stateless people have permanent residence and enjoy more rights than foreseen in the 1954 Convention. **n** Data are as at 1 January of reporting year. **o** Users in the last 3 months. **p** Population aged 16 to 74 years. **q** Based on mobile positioning data by the Bank of Estonia and Positium LBS.

Eswatini

Region	Southern Africa	UN membership date	24 September 1968
Population (000, 2023)	1 202[a,b]	Surface area (km2)	17 363[c]
Pop. density (per km2, 2023)	69.2[a,b]	Sex ratio (m per 100 f)	98.5[a,b]
Capital city	Mbabane[d]	National currency	Lilangeni (SZL)
Capital city pop. (000, 2023)	68.0[d,e]	Exchange rate (per US$)	17.1[b]

Economic indicators	2010	2015	2023
GDP: Gross domestic product (million current US$)	4 439	4 059	4 732[c]
GDP growth rate (annual %, const. 2015 prices)	3.8	2.2	7.9[c]
GDP per capita (current US$)	4 035.5	3 579.2	3 968.9[c]
Economy: Agriculture (% of Gross Value Added)[f,g]	10.4	9.8	9.0[c]
Economy: Industry (% of Gross Value Added)[f,h]	38.7	37.6	35.0[c]
Economy: Services and other activity (% of GVA)[f]	50.9	52.6	56.0[c]
Employment in agriculture (% of employed)[i]	15.3	13.5	12.4[c]
Employment in industry (% of employed)[i]	24.9	24.6	24.4[c]
Employment in services & other sectors (% employed)[i]	59.8	61.8	63.1[c]
Unemployment rate (% of labour force)[i]	26.4	23.3	24.7
Labour force participation rate (female/male pop. %)[i]	46.5 / 57.4	46.8 / 56.1	47.2 / 54.0
CPI: Consumer Price Index (2010=100)	100	135	167[j]
Agricultural production index (2014-2016=100)	95	100	105[c]
International trade: exports (million current US$)	1 557[i]	1 820	2 011[i,b]
International trade: imports (million current US$)	1 710[i]	1 508	2 407[i,b]
International trade: balance (million current US$)	- 153[i]	312	- 396[i,b]
Balance of payments, current account (million US$)	- 388	533	124[c]

Major trading partners						2022
Export partners (% of exports)[i]	South Africa	67.9	Kenya	5.6	Nigeria	3.9
Import partners (% of imports)[i]	South Africa	72.4	China	9.7	India	2.7

Social indicators	2010	2015	2023
Population growth rate (average annual %)	0.5	0.7	0.7[a,b]
Urban population (% of total population)	22.5	23.3	24.0[i]
Urban population growth rate (average annual %)[k]	2.1	2.6	...
Fertility rate, total (live births per woman)	3.4	3.1	2.8[a,b]
Life expectancy at birth (females/males, years)	48.3 / 44.9	58.1 / 52.1	60.6 / 52.6[a,b]
Population age distribution (0-14/60+ years old, %)	38.8 / 4.7	37.5 / 5.3	34.7 / 6.2[a,b]
International migrant stock (000/% of total pop.)[l]	32.6 / 3.1	32.4 / 2.9	32.9 / 2.8[m]
Refugees and others of concern to the UNHCR (000)	0.8[n]	0.9	1.8[b]
Infant mortality rate (per 1 000 live births)	61.3	43.0	39.2[a,b]
Health: Current expenditure (% of GDP)[o]	8.6	7.1	6.5[m]
Health: Physicians (per 1 000 pop.)	0.2[p]	0.1[q]	0.1[m]
Education: Government expenditure (% of GDP)	6.1	5.4	5.5[b]
Education: Primary gross enrol. ratio (f/m per 100 pop.)	118.8 / 131.0	113.5 / 124.9	109.8 / 119.0[j]
Education: Lowr. sec. gross enrol. ratio (f/m per 100 pop.)	73.1 / 76.0	85.2 / 85.1	89.1 / 88.9[r]
Education: Upr. sec. gross enrol. ratio (f/m per 100 pop.)	49.5 / 53.9	61.7 / 62.1	71.4 / 73.0[r]
Intentional homicide rate (per 100 000 pop.)	18.9	9.9	12.7[c]
Seats held by women in the National Parliament (%)	13.6	6.2	14.9[s]

Environment and infrastructure indicators	2010	2015	2023
Individuals using the Internet (per 100 inhabitants)	11.0	25.6[i]	58.9[i,c]
Research & Development expenditure (% of GDP)	...	0.3	...
Threatened species (number)	29	34	47[b]
Forested area (% of land area)	28.2	28.6	28.9[m]
CO2 emission estimates (million tons/tons per capita)	1.0 / 0.8	1.2 / 0.9	1.3 / 1.0[m]
Energy production, primary (Petajoules)	29	33	30[i,m]
Energy supply per capita (Gigajoules)	38	40	39[i,m]
Tourist/visitor arrivals at national borders (000)	868	873	170[c]
Important sites for terrestrial biodiversity protected (%)	20.9	21.2	22.7[b]
Pop. using safely managed drinking water (urban/rural, %)	80.3 / ...	79.1 / ...	77.5 / ...[b]
Net Official Development Assist. received (% of GNI)	2.16	2.37	2.80[c]

a Projected estimate (medium fertility variant). b 2022. c 2021. d Mbabane is the administrative capital and Lobamba is the legislative capital. e 2018. f Data classified according to ISIC Rev. 4. g Excludes irrigation canals and landscaping care. h Excludes publishing activities, recycling. Includes irrigation canals. i Estimate. j 2019. k Data refers to a 5-year period preceding the reference year. l Including refugees. m 2020. n Data as at the end of December. o Data refer to fiscal years beginning 1 April. p 2009. q 2011. r 2016. s Data are as at 1 January of reporting year.

Ethiopia

Region	Eastern Africa	UN membership date	13 November 1945
Population (000, 2023)	123 380[a,b]	Surface area (km2)	1 104 300[c]
Pop. density (per km2, 2023)	123.4[a,b]	Sex ratio (m per 100 f)	100.9[a,b]
Capital city	Addis Ababa	National currency	Ethiopian Birr (ETB)
Capital city pop. (000, 2023)	4 592.0[d]	Exchange rate (per US$)	53.3[b]

Economic indicators

	2010	2015	2023
GDP: Gross domestic product (million current US$)	26 311	63 079	99 269[c]
GDP growth rate (annual %, const. 2015 prices)	12.6	10.4	5.6[c]
GDP per capita (current US$)	294.8	615.6	825.3[c]
Economy: Agriculture (% of Gross Value Added)	45.3	38.8	39.2[c]
Economy: Industry (% of Gross Value Added)	10.4	17.5	22.8[c]
Economy: Services and other activity (% of GVA)	44.3	43.7	38.1[c]
Employment in agriculture (% of employed)[e]	73.6	68.3	63.7[c]
Employment in industry (% of employed)[e]	7.9	8.9	10.1[c]
Employment in services & other sectors (% employed)[e]	18.4	22.8	26.2[c]
Unemployment rate (% of labour force)[e]	2.3	2.6	4.0
Labour force participation rate (female/male pop. %)[e]	74.3 / 88.8	74.4 / 87.6	75.1 / 86.1
CPI: Consumer Price Index (2010=100)[f]	100	205	652[b]
Agricultural production index (2014-2016=100)	82	101	116[c]
International trade: exports (million current US$)	2 330	2 024	7 128[e,b]
International trade: imports (million current US$)	8 602	17 686	101 088[e,b]
International trade: balance (million current US$)	- 6 272	- 15 662	- 93 960[e,b]
Balance of payments, current account (million US$)	- 635	- 7 567	- 4 507[c]

Major trading partners

							2022
Export partners (% of exports)[e]	Somalia	11.8	United States	10.8	Germany		8.0
Import partners (% of imports)[e]	China	26.4	India	15.7	United States		7.6

Social indicators

	2010	2015	2023
Population growth rate (average annual %)	2.8	2.7	2.5[a,b]
Urban population (% of total population)	17.3	19.4	21.2[d]
Urban population growth rate (average annual %)[g]	4.6	4.9	
Fertility rate, total (live births per woman)	5.2	4.5	4.1[a,b]
Life expectancy at birth (females/males, years)	61.8 / 57.7	66.3 / 61.1	68.9 / 62.6[a,b]
Population age distribution (0-14/60+ years old, %)	45.1 / 4.4	42.5 / 4.6	39.6 / 4.9[a,b]
International migrant stock (000/% of total pop.)[h]	568.7 / 0.6	1 161.6 / 1.2	1 085.5 / 0.9[i]
Refugees and others of concern to the UNHCR (000)	155.4[j]	705.7	5 370.5[b]
Infant mortality rate (per 1 000 live births)	54.4	43.2	31.9[a,b]
Health: Current expenditure (% of GDP)[k]	5.5	3.8	3.5[i]
Health: Physicians (per 1 000 pop.)	~0.0[l]	...	0.1[i]
Education: Government expenditure (% of GDP)	4.5	4.7	3.7[b]
Education: Primary gross enrol. ratio (f/m per 100 pop.)	88.0 / 95.2	96.1 / 105.8	101.1 / 110.8[c]
Education: Lowr. sec. gross enrol. ratio (f/m per 100 pop.)	39.5 / 46.2	42.0 / 43.9	40.9 / 45.8[m]
Education: Upr. sec. gross enrol. ratio (f/m per 100 pop.)	13.4 / 19.1	17.4 / 17.7	10.5 / 11.7[n]
Intentional homicide rate (per 100 000 pop.)	...	8.6[o]	...
Seats held by women in the National Parliament (%)	21.9	27.8	41.3[p]

Environment and infrastructure indicators

	2010	2015	2023
Individuals using the Internet (per 100 inhabitants)	0.8[e]	13.9	16.7[q,c]
Research & Development expenditure (% of GDP)	0.2[r]	0.6[s]	0.3[r,m]
Threatened species (number)	120	145	237[b]
Forested area (% of land area)	15.8	15.4	15.1[i]
CO2 emission estimates (million tons/tons per capita)[t,u]	16.4 / 0.1	22.2 / 0.1	27.9 / 0.1[i]
Energy production, primary (Petajoules)[t]	1 212	1 327	1 441[i]
Energy supply per capita (Gigajoules)[t]	14	14	14[i]
Tourist/visitor arrivals at national borders (000)[v,w]	468	864	518[c]
Important sites for terrestrial biodiversity protected (%)	13.1	15.0	16.4[b]
Pop. using safely managed drinking water (urban/rural, %)	36.9 / 1.6	37.6 / 3.1	38.6 / 5.8[b]
Pop. using safely managed sanitation (urban/rural %)	14.3 / 2.5	15.7 / 3.4	17.4 / 4.2[b]
Net Official Development Assist. received (% of GNI)	11.58	5.04	3.68[c]

a Projected estimate (medium fertility variant). **b** 2022. **c** 2021. **d** 2019. **e** Estimate. **f** Calculated by the UN Statistics Division from national indices. **g** Data refers to a 5-year period preceding the reference year. **h** Including refugees. **i** 2020. **j** Data as at the end of December. **k** Data refer to fiscal years beginning 8 July. **l** 2009. **m** 2017. **n** 2018. **o** 2012. **p** Data are as at 1 January of reporting year. **q** Population aged 10 years and over. **r** Break in the time series. **s** 2013. **t** Excluding Eritrea. **u** Data refer to fiscal years beginning 1 July. **v** Arrivals through all ports of entry. **w** Including nationals residing abroad.

Falkland Islands (Malvinas)

Region	South America	Population (000, 2023)	4 [a,b,c]
Surface area (km2)	12 173 [d,e]	Pop. density (per km2, 2023)	0.3 [a,b,c]
Sex ratio (m per 100 f)	100.7 [a,b,c]	Capital city	Stanley
National currency	Falkland Islands Pound (FKP)	Capital city pop. (000, 2023)	2.3 [d,f]
Exchange rate (per US$)	0.8 [c]		

Economic indicators	2010	2015	2023
Unemployment rate (% of labour force)	...	1.2 [g,h]	...
Labour force participation rate (female/male pop. %)	... / ...	77.2 / 86.0 [g,i,h]	... / ...
International trade: exports (million current US$) [i]	9	4	366 [c]
International trade: imports (million current US$) [i]	50	21	117 [c]
International trade: balance (million current US$) [i]	- 41	- 17	249 [c]

Major trading partners							2022
Export partners (% of exports) [i]	Spain	69.8	Morocco	8.8	United States	8.0
Import partners (% of imports) [i]	United Kingdom	72.9	Spain	23.7	Netherlands	1.4

Social indicators	2010	2015	2023
Population growth rate (average annual %) [b]	- 0.3	2.3	0.4 [a,c]
Urban population (% of total population) [d]	73.7	76.3	78.1 [k]
Urban population growth rate (average annual %) [d,l]	0.2	1.0	...
Fertility rate, total (live births per woman) [b]	1.5	1.6	1.6 [a,c]
Life expectancy at birth (females/males, years) [b]	79.8 / 75.9	80.1 / 76.6	81.2 / 77.4 [a,c]
Population age distribution (0-14/60+ years old, %) [b]	17.6 / 15.9	17.9 / 14.8	17.7 / 17.4 [a,c]
International migrant stock (000/% of total pop.) [b]	1.4 / 49.5	1.6 / 55.4	2.0 / 56.2 [m]
Infant mortality rate (per 1 000 live births) [b]	10.7	10.1	9.0 [a,c]

Environment and infrastructure indicators	2010	2015	2023
Individuals using the Internet (per 100 inhabitants)	95.8	98.3 [j]	99.0 [j,n]
Threatened species (number)	23	23	30 [c]
Forested area (% of land area)	0.0	0.0	0.0 [m]
Energy production, primary (Petajoules)	0 [j]	0 [j]	0 [m]
Energy supply per capita (Gigajoules)	176	165	159 [m]
Important sites for terrestrial biodiversity protected (%)	20.8	20.8	20.8 [c]

a Projected estimate (medium fertility variant). b A dispute exists between the Governments of Argentina and the United Kingdom of Great Britain and Northern Ireland concerning sovereignty over the Falkland Islands (Malvinas). For statistical purposes, the data for United Kingdom do not include this area. c 2022. d A dispute exists between the Governments of Argentina and the United Kingdom of Great Britain and Northern Ireland concerning sovereignty over the Falkland Islands (Malvinas). e 2021. f 2018. g Population aged 16 to 65 years. h 2013. i Break in the time series. j Estimate. k 2019. l Data refers to a 5-year period preceding the reference year. m 2020. n 2016.

Faroe Islands

Region	Northern Europe	Population (000, 2023)	53 [a,b,c]
Surface area (km2)	1 393 [d]	Pop. density (per km2, 2023)	38.3 [a,b,c]
Sex ratio (m per 100 f)	107.3 [a,b,c]	Capital city	Tórshavn
National currency	Danish Krone (DKK)	Capital city pop. (000, 2023)	20.8 [e]
Exchange rate (per US$)	7.0 [c]		

Economic indicators

	2010	2015	2023
Employment in agriculture (% of employed)	11.1 [f,g,h]	...	...
Employment in industry (% of employed)	22.2 [f,g,h]	...	...
Employment in services & other sectors (% employed)	66.7 [f,g,h]	...	...
Unemployment rate (% of labour force)	6.4 [i]	4.0 [l]	...
Labour force participation rate (female/male pop. %)	77.5 / 85.3 [j,k]	79.4 / 86.0 [j,k,l]	... / ...
Agricultural production index (2014-2016=100)	93	98	92 [d]
International trade: exports (million current US$) [m]	839	1 024	2 264 [c]
International trade: imports (million current US$) [m]	780	911	1 901 [c]
International trade: balance (million current US$) [m]	59	113	362 [c]
Balance of payments, current account (million US$)	144	194 [n]	...

Major trading partners

						2022
Export partners (% of exports) [m]	United Kingdom	21.3	Denmark	16.6	United States	15.9
Import partners (% of imports) [m]	Denmark	45.6	Norway	13.2	Netherlands	12.1

Social indicators

	2010	2015	2023
Population growth rate (average annual %) [b]	- 0.1	1.3	0.4 [a,c]
Urban population (% of total population)	40.9	41.6	42.2 [o]
Urban population growth rate (average annual %) [p]	0.7	0.5	...
Fertility rate, total (live births per woman) [b]	2.5	2.4	2.7 [a,c]
Life expectancy at birth (females/males, years) [b]	78.9 / 75.7	82.0 / 77.7	80.7 / 77.3 [a,c]
Population age distribution (0-14/60+ years old, %) [b]	21.8 / 20.5	21.0 / 22.8	20.7 / 23.6 [a,c]
International migrant stock (000/% of total pop.)	5.1 / 10.7	5.5 / 11.4	6.8 / 13.9 [q]
Infant mortality rate (per 1 000 live births) [b]	6.1	5.3	5.3 [a,c]
Education: Government expenditure (% of GDP)	...	7.6	8.0 [q]

Environment and infrastructure indicators

	2010	2015	2023
Individuals using the Internet (per 100 inhabitants)	75.2	94.2 [m]	97.6 [m,r]
Threatened species (number)	13	14	35 [c]
Forested area (% of land area)	0.1	0.1	0.1 [m,q]
Energy production, primary (Petajoules)	0	1	1 [q]
Energy supply per capita (Gigajoules) [m]	185	186	210 [q]
Important sites for terrestrial biodiversity protected (%)	0.0	15.8	15.8 [c]

a Projected estimate (medium fertility variant). b For statistical purposes, the data for Denmark do not include this area. c 2022. d 2021. e 2018. f Data classified according to ISIC Rev. 2. g Population aged 16 years and over. h 2005. i Break in the time series. j Excluding the institutional population. k Population aged 15 to 74 years. l 2013. m Estimate. n 2011. o 2019. p Data refers to a 5-year period preceding the reference year. q 2020. r 2017.

Fiji

Region	Melanesia	UN membership date	13 October 1970
Population (000, 2023)	930[a,b]	Surface area (km2)	18 272[a]
Pop. density (per km2, 2023)	50.9[a,b]	Sex ratio (m per 100 f)	100.5[a,b]
Capital city	Suva	National currency	Fiji Dollar (FJD)
Capital city pop. (000, 2023)	178.3[d]	Exchange rate (per US$)	2.2[b]

Economic indicators

	2010	2015	2023
GDP: Gross domestic product (million current US$)	3 140	4 682	4 296[c]
GDP growth rate (annual %, const. 2015 prices)	3.0	4.7	- 5.1[c]
GDP per capita (current US$)	3 469.5	5 105.1	4 646.5[c]
Economy: Agriculture (% of Gross Value Added)[e,f]	10.2	10.0	17.0[c]
Economy: Industry (% of Gross Value Added)[e,g]	19.9	19.3	19.8[c]
Economy: Services and other activity (% of GVA)[e]	69.9	70.6	63.1[c]
Employment in agriculture (% of employed)[h]	29.8	30.4	28.9[c]
Employment in industry (% of employed)[h]	16.7	14.6	14.7[c]
Employment in services & other sectors (% employed)[h]	53.6	55.0	56.4[c]
Unemployment rate (% of labour force)[h]	4.3	4.3	4.2
Labour force participation rate (female/male pop. %)[h]	43.8 / 79.8	39.9 / 76.4	38.2 / 75.5
CPI: Consumer Price Index (2010=100)[i]	100	116	135[b]
Agricultural production index (2014-2016=100)	89	109	115[c]
International trade: exports (million current US$)	841	895	1 055[b]
International trade: imports (million current US$)	1 808	2 081	2 997[b]
International trade: balance (million current US$)	- 967	- 1 186	- 1 942[b]
Balance of payments, current account (million US$)	- 149	- 163	- 868[b]

Major trading partners

							2022
Export partners (% of exports)	United States	20.9	Tonga	14.7[h]	Australia	10.6[h]
Import partners (% of imports)	Singapore	25.9	China	15.7	Australia	15.6

Social indicators

	2010	2015	2023
Population growth rate (average annual %)	0.4	0.1	0.7[a,b]
Urban population (% of total population)	52.2	54.7	56.8[i]
Urban population growth rate (average annual %)[k]	1.8	1.7	...
Fertility rate, total (live births per woman)	2.7	2.6	2.5[a,b]
Life expectancy at birth (females/males, years)	69.3 / 65.5	68.9 / 64.9	70.2 / 66.5[a,b]
Population age distribution (0-14/60+ years old, %)	31.1 / 6.9	30.2 / 7.8	28.6 / 9.7[a,b]
International migrant stock (000/% of total pop.)[l]	13.4 / 1.6	13.8 / 1.6	14.1 / 1.6[m]
Refugees and others of concern to the UNHCR (000)	~0.0[n]	~0.0	~0.0[b]
Infant mortality rate (per 1 000 live births)	19.8	20.3	17.9[a,b]
Health: Current expenditure (% of GDP)	3.4	3.3	3.7[o,m]
Health: Physicians (per 1 000 pop.)	0.4[p]	0.8	...
Education: Government expenditure (% of GDP)	4.5[p]	4.8	5.6[c]
Education: Primary gross enrol. ratio (f/m per 100 pop.)	104.0 / 105.6[p]	105.8 / 107.9	111.7 / 115.7[c]
Education: Lowr. sec. gross enrol. ratio (f/m per 100 pop.)	100.4 / 96.6	107.4 / 106.4	103.3 / 105.0[c]
Education: Upr. sec. gross enrol. ratio (f/m per 100 pop.)	75.3 / 63.8[p]	91.4 / 77.9	95.6 / 75.5[c]
Intentional homicide rate (per 100 000 pop.)	2.2	2.2[q]	2.2[m]
Seats held by women in the National Parliament (%)	8.5[r]	14.0	10.9[s]

Environment and infrastructure indicators

	2010	2015	2023
Individuals using the Internet (per 100 inhabitants)[h]	20.0	42.5	87.7[c]
Threatened species (number)	192	278	357[b]
Forested area (% of land area)	58.7	60.6	62.4[m]
Energy production, primary (Petajoules)	5	7	6[m]
Energy supply per capita (Gigajoules)	22	27	22[h,m]
Tourist/visitor arrivals at national borders (000)[t]	632	755	32[c]
Important sites for terrestrial biodiversity protected (%)	11.2	11.2	11.2[b]
Pop. using safely managed drinking water (urban/rural, %)	52.4 / 27.1	52.5 / 27.1	52.5 / 27.0[b]
Pop. using safely managed sanitation (urban/rural, %)	42.6 / 50.7	42.9 / 54.5	42.7 / 57.3[b]
Net Official Development Assist. received (% of GNI)	2.49	2.33	13.98[c]

a Projected estimate (medium fertility variant). b 2022. c 2021. d 2018. e Data classified according to ISIC Rev. 4. f Excludes irrigation canals and landscaping care. g Excludes publishing activities, recycling. Includes irrigation canals. h Estimate. i Calculated by the UN Statistics Division from national indices. j 2019. k Data refers to a 5-year period preceding the reference year. l Including refugees. m 2020. n Data as at the end of December. o Data refer to fiscal years beginning 1 April. p 2009. q 2014. r 2006. s Data are as at 1 January of reporting year. t Excluding nationals residing abroad.

Finland

Region	Northern Europe	UN membership date	14 December 1955
Population (000, 2023)	5 541 [a,b,c]	Surface area (km2)	336 884 [d,e]
Pop. density (per km2, 2023)	18.3 [a,b,c]	Sex ratio (m per 100 f)	97.7 [a,b,c]
Capital city	Helsinki	National currency	Euro (EUR)
Capital city pop. (000, 2023)	1 292.2 [f]	Exchange rate (per US$)	0.9 [c]

Economic indicators

	2010	2015	2023
GDP: Gross domestic product (million current US$)	249 181	234 440	297 302 [e]
GDP growth rate (annual %, const. 2015 prices)	3.2	0.5	3.0 [e]
GDP per capita (current US$)	46 460.7	42 785.2	53 703.5 [e]
Economy: Agriculture (% of Gross Value Added) [g,h]	2.8	2.6	2.6 [e]
Economy: Industry (% of Gross Value Added) [g,i]	29.9	27.0	28.4 [e]
Economy: Services and other activity (% of GVA) [g]	67.3	70.4	69.0 [e]
Employment in agriculture (% of employed)	4.4	4.2	4.1 [e]
Employment in industry (% of employed)	23.4	21.7	21.4 [e]
Employment in services & other sectors (% employed)	72.3	74.0	74.5 [e]
Unemployment rate (% of labour force)	8.4	9.4	7.1 [j]
Labour force participation rate (female/male pop. %)	55.9 / 64.0	55.6 / 62.4	57.0 / 62.9 [j]
CPI: Consumer Price Index (2010=100)	100 [k]	109 [k]	123 [c]
Agricultural production index (2014-2016=100)	94	100	94 [e]
International trade: exports (million current US$)	70 117	59 682	86 062 [c]
International trade: imports (million current US$)	68 767	60 174	97 265 [c]
International trade: balance (million current US$)	1 349	- 492	- 11 203 [c]
Balance of payments, current account (million US$)	2 792	- 2 209	- 11 059 [c]

Major trading partners

						2022
Export partners (% of exports)	Germany	11.6	Sweden	10.6	United States	9.3
Import partners (% of imports)	Sweden	12.5	Germany	12.3	China	9.1

Social indicators

	2010	2015	2023
Population growth rate (average annual %) [b]	0.4	0.3	0.1 [a,c]
Urban population (% of total population) [b]	83.8	85.2	85.4 [f]
Urban population growth rate (average annual %) [b,l]	0.6	0.8	...
Fertility rate, total (live births per woman) [b]	1.9	1.6	1.4 [a,c]
Life expectancy at birth (females/males, years) [b]	83.2 / 76.7	84.2 / 78.6	84.9 / 79.8 [a,c]
Population age distribution (0-14/60+ years old, %) [b]	16.6 / 24.7	16.4 / 27.0	15.2 / 29.7 [a,c]
International migrant stock (000/% of total pop.) [b]	228.5 / 4.3	314.9 / 5.7	386.1 / 7.0 [m]
Refugees and others of concern to the UNHCR (000)	14.0 [n]	16.3	61.8 [c]
Infant mortality rate (per 1 000 live births) [b]	2.3	1.7	1.6 [a,c]
Health: Current expenditure (% of GDP)	9.1	9.6 [o]	9.6 [m]
Health: Physicians (per 1 000 pop.)	3.4	3.4	4.3 [m]
Education: Government expenditure (% of GDP)	6.5	7.0	6.4 [f]
Education: Primary gross enrol. ratio (f/m per 100 pop.)	99.1 / 99.8	100.3 / 100.8	99.9 / 100.2 [m]
Education: Lowr. sec. gross enrol. ratio (f/m per 100 pop.)	99.2 / 99.9	101.7 / 102.0	103.4 / 104.3 [m]
Education: Upr. sec. gross enrol. ratio (f/m per 100 pop.)	120.5 / 110.2	210.2 / 181.8	200.1 / 171.3 [m]
Intentional homicide rate (per 100 000 pop.)	2.2	1.5	1.6 [m]
Seats held by women in the National Parliament (%)	40.0	42.5	45.5 [p]

Environment and infrastructure indicators

	2010	2015	2023
Individuals using the Internet (per 100 inhabitants)	86.9 [q]	86.4	92.8 [e]
Research & Development expenditure (% of GDP)	3.7	2.9	2.9 [m]
Threatened species (number)	18	25	68 [c]
Forested area (% of land area)	73.2	73.7	73.7 [m]
CO2 emission estimates (million tons/tons per capita)	63.6 / 11.6	43.9 / 7.7	37.6 / 6.5 [e]
Energy production, primary (Petajoules)	725	732	761 [m]
Energy supply per capita (Gigajoules)	285	247	239 [m]
Tourist/visitor arrivals at national borders (000)	3 670	2 622 [r]	807 [e]
Important sites for terrestrial biodiversity protected (%)	68.7	71.7	71.8 [c]
Net Official Development Assist. disbursed (% of GNI) [s]	1.78	- 0.02	1.10 [e]

a Projected estimate (medium fertility variant). b Including Åland Islands. c 2022. d Excluding Åland Islands. e 2021. f 2019. g Data classified according to ISIC Rev. 4. h Excludes irrigation canals and landscaping care. i Excludes publishing activities, recycling. Includes irrigation canals. j Estimate. k Calculated by the UN Statistics Division from national indices. l Data refers to a 5-year period preceding the reference year. m 2020. n Data as at the end of December. o Break in the time series. p Data are as at 1 January of reporting year. q Population aged 16 to 74 years. r Non-resident tourists staying in all types of accommodation establishments. s Development Assistance Committee member (OECD).

France

Region	Western Europe	UN membership date	24 October 1945
Population (000, 2023)	64 627 [a,b,c]	Surface area (km2)	551 500 [d]
Pop. density (per km2, 2023)	117.2 [a,b,c]	Sex ratio (m per 100 f)	93.5 [a,b,c,d]
Capital city	Paris	National currency	Euro (EUR)
Capital city pop. (000, 2023)	10 958.2 [e]	Exchange rate (per US$)	0.9 [c]

Economic indicators	2010	2015	2023
GDP: Gross domestic product (million current US$) [f]	2 642 610	2 438 208	2 957 880 [d]
GDP growth rate (annual %, const. 2015 prices) [f]	1.9	1.1	6.8 [d]
GDP per capita (current US$) [f]	40 926.2	36 930.5	44 229.4 [d]
Economy: Agriculture (% of Gross Value Added) [g,h]	1.8	1.8	1.9 [d]
Economy: Industry (% of Gross Value Added) [h,i]	19.8	19.8	18.8 [d]
Economy: Services and other activity (% of GVA) [h]	78.4	78.5	79.4 [d]
Employment in agriculture (% of employed)	2.9	2.7	2.5 [d]
Employment in industry (% of employed)	22.3	20.3	19.5 [d]
Employment in services & other sectors (% employed)	74.9	77.0	78.0 [d]
Unemployment rate (% of labour force)	8.9	10.4	7.6 [j]
Labour force participation rate (female/male pop. %)	51.5 / 62.0	51.6 / 60.8	52.0 / 59.9 [j]
CPI: Consumer Price Index (2010=100) [k,l]	100	106	118 [c]
Agricultural production index (2014-2016=100)	98	102	97 [d]
International trade: exports (million current US$)	511 651	493 941	618 299 [c]
International trade: imports (million current US$)	599 172	563 398	819 398 [c]
International trade: balance (million current US$)	- 87 520	- 69 457	- 201 099 [c]
Balance of payments, current account (million US$)	- 22 031	- 9 130	- 59 499 [c]

Major trading partners						2022
Export partners (% of exports)	Germany	13.7	Italy	9.2	United States	7.9
Import partners (% of imports)	Germany	14.6	Belgium	11.3	Netherlands	8.2

Social indicators	2010	2015	2023
Population growth rate (average annual %) [a]	0.6	0.3	0.2 [b,c]
Urban population (% of total population)	78.4	79.7	80.7 [e]
Urban population growth rate (average annual %) [m]	0.9	0.8	...
Fertility rate, total (live births per woman) [a]	2.0	1.9	1.8 [b,c]
Life expectancy at birth (females/males, years) [a]	84.7 / 78.0	85.2 / 79.0	86.0 / 80.4 [b,c]
Population age distribution (0-14/60+ years old, %) [a]	18.3 / 23.2	18.2 / 25.3	17.2 / 27.8 [b,c]
International migrant stock (000/% of total pop.)	7 310.0 / 11.6	7 878.3 / 12.2	8 524.9 / 13.1 [n]
Refugees and others of concern to the UNHCR (000)	250.4 [o]	320.1	679.1 [c]
Infant mortality rate (per 1 000 live births) [a]	3.6	3.6	3.3 [b,c]
Health: Current expenditure (% of GDP) [p]	11.2 [q]	11.4	12.2 [n]
Health: Physicians (per 1 000 pop.)	3.4	3.2	3.3 [n]
Education: Government expenditure (% of GDP)	5.6	5.4	5.4 [e]
Education: Primary gross enrol. ratio (f/m per 100 pop.) [j]	102.1 / 103.4	101.7 / 102.3	102.4 / 103.2 [n]
Education: Lowr. sec. gross enrol. ratio (f/m per 100 pop.) [j]	102.7 / 103.1	100.5 / 101.0	101.6 / 102.2 [n]
Education: Upr. sec. gross enrol. ratio (f/m per 100 pop.) [j]	112.7 / 109.6	108.6 / 105.4	108.8 / 107.9 [n]
Intentional homicide rate (per 100 000 pop.)	1.3	1.6	1.1 [d]
Seats held by women in the National Parliament (%)	18.9	26.2	37.8 [r]

Environment and infrastructure indicators	2010	2015	2023
Individuals using the Internet (per 100 inhabitants)	77.3 [s]	78.0 [q,t,u]	86.1 [d]
Research & Development expenditure (% of GDP)	2.2 [q]	2.2	2.3 [j,v,n]
Threatened species (number)	168	236	466 [c]
Forested area (% of land area)	30.0	30.7	31.5 [n]
CO2 emission estimates (million tons/tons per capita)	347.1 / 5.2	311.3 / 4.6 [w]	293.3 / 4.2 [w,d]
Energy production, primary (Petajoules) [w]	5 632	5 770	4 976 [n]
Energy supply per capita (Gigajoules) [w]	176	159	136 [n]
Tourist/visitor arrivals at national borders (000)	76 647 [x]	84 452 [x]	48 395 [j,d]
Important sites for terrestrial biodiversity protected (%)	49.5	64.5	81.1 [c]
Pop. using safely managed drinking water (urban/rural, %)	98.2 / 98.4	99.0 / 98.4	100.0 / 98.4 [c]
Net Official Development Assist. disbursed (% of GNI) [y]	1.35	0.05	0.63 [d]

a For statistical purposes, the data for France do not include French Guiana, French Polynesia, Guadeloupe, Martinique, Mayotte, New Caledonia, Réunion, Saint Pierre and Miquelon, Saint Barthélemy, Saint Martin (French part), Wallis and Futuna Islands. b Projected estimate (medium fertility variant). c 2022. d 2021. e 2019. f Including French Guiana, Guadeloupe, Martinique and Réunion. g Excludes irrigation canals and landscaping care. h Data classified according to ISIC Rev. 4. i Excludes publishing activities, recycling. Includes irrigation canals. j Estimate. k Calculated by the UN Statistics Division from national indices. l All households. Metropolitan France and overseas departments. m Data refers to a 5-year period preceding the reference year. n 2020. o Data as at the end of December. p Data are based on SHA2011. q Break in the time series. r Data are as at 1 January of reporting year. s Population aged 16 to 74 years. t Population aged 15 years and over. u Users in the last 3 months. v Provisional data. w From 2011 onwards, data include Monaco and the overseas departments (Guadeloupe, French Guiana, Martinique, Mayotte and Réunion), excluding the overseas collectivities: New Caledonia, French Polynesia, Saint Barthélemy, Saint Martin, St. Pierre and Miquelon, and Wallis and Futuna. x Arrivals of non-resident visitors. y Development Assistance Committee member (OECD).

French Guiana

Region	South America	
Surface area (km2)	83 534[d]	
Sex ratio (m per 100 f)	98.8[a,b,c]	
National currency	Euro (EUR)	
Exchange rate (per US$)	0.9[c]	

Population (000, 2023)	305[a,b,c]	
Pop. density (per km2, 2023)	3.7[a,b,c]	
Capital city	Cavenne	
Capital city pop. (000, 2023)	57.5[e]	

Economic indicators	2010	2015	2023
Employment in industry (% of employed)[f,g]	14.1	14.9[h]	...
Employment in services & other sectors (% employed)[f,g]	51.5	58.3[h]	...
Unemployment rate (% of labour force)[f]	21.0	21.3[i,j]	...
Labour force participation rate (female/male pop. %)	43.2 / 54.9[f]	48.4 / 58.8[f,i,j]	... / ...
CPI: Consumer Price Index (2010=100)[k]	100	105	114[c]

Social indicators	2010	2015	2023
Population growth rate (average annual %)[b]	2.2	2.2	2.5[a,c]
Urban population (% of total population)	82.9	84.5	85.6[l]
Urban population growth rate (average annual %)[m]	3.2	3.1	...
Fertility rate, total (live births per woman)[b]	3.5	3.5	3.5[a,c]
Life expectancy at birth (females/males, years)[b]	79.1 / 72.8	79.6 / 74.1	80.3 / 74.8[a,c]
Population age distribution (0-14/60+ years old, %)[b]	35.2 / 6.2	33.7 / 7.6	32.1 / 9.4[a,c]
International migrant stock (000/% of total pop.)[n]	96.3 / 41.3	106.1 / 40.7	119.2 / 39.9[o]
Infant mortality rate (per 1 000 live births)[b]	9.7	8.9	7.6[a,c]
Intentional homicide rate (per 100 000 pop.)	13.4[p]	...	13.3[o]

Environment and infrastructure indicators	2010	2015	2023
Individuals using the Internet (per 100 inhabitants)	25.7[q,p]	...	...
Threatened species (number)	56	67	130[c]
Forested area (% of land area)	97.1	96.8	96.6[o]
Energy production, primary (Petajoules)	3[r]	...	...
Energy supply per capita (Gigajoules)	52[q,r]	...	...
Tourist/visitor arrivals at national borders (000)[s]	83[p]	87	111[t]
Important sites for terrestrial biodiversity protected (%)	81.0	81.3	83.2[c]

a Projected estimate (medium fertility variant). b For statistical purposes, the data for France do not include this area. c 2022. d 2021. e 2018. f Excluding the institutional population. g Population aged 15 to 64 years. h 2012. i Break in the time series. j 2013. k Calculated by the UN Statistics Division from national indices. l 2019. m Data refers to a 5-year period preceding the reference year. n Including refugees. o 2020. p 2009. q Estimate. r Data after 2010 are included in France. s Survey at Cayenne-Rochambeau airport on departure. t 2017.

French Polynesia

Region	Polynesia	Population (000, 2023)	306 [a,b,c]
Surface area (km2)	3 687 [d,e]	Pop. density (per km2, 2023)	83.1 [a,b,c]
Sex ratio (m per 100 f)	102.2 [a,b,c]	Capital city	Papeete
National currency	CFP Franc (XPF) [f]	Capital city pop. (000, 2023)	136.0 [g,h]
Exchange rate (per US$)	111.9 [c]		

Economic indicators	2010	2015	2023
GDP: Gross domestic product (million current US$)	6 081	5 324	6 055 [e]
GDP growth rate (annual %, const. 2015 prices)	- 2.5	1.8	2.4 [e]
GDP per capita (current US$)	21 427.0	18 245.2	19 914.6 [e]
Economy: Agriculture (% of Gross Value Added)	2.5	3.6	3.3 [e]
Economy: Industry (% of Gross Value Added)	12.3	12.0	11.6 [e]
Economy: Services and other activity (% of GVA)	85.2	84.4	85.1 [e]
Employment in agriculture (% of employed)	2.8	2.4 [i]	2.1 [i,e]
Employment in industry (% of employed)	15.9	15.2 [i]	14.9 [i,e]
Employment in services & other sectors (% employed)	81.4	82.4 [i]	83.1 [i,e]
Unemployment rate (% of labour force) [i]	12.2	12.1	13.1
Labour force participation rate (female/male pop. %) [i]	48.3 / 63.9	49.2 / 63.3	49.1 / 62.0
CPI: Consumer Price Index (2010=100)	...	122 [j,k]	...
Agricultural production index (2014-2016=100)	97	102	104 [e]
International trade: exports (million current US$)	153	130	146 [c]
International trade: imports (million current US$)	1 726	1 527	2 220 [c]
International trade: balance (million current US$)	- 1 573	- 1 397	- 2 074 [c]
Balance of payments, current account (million US$)	- 18	291	412 [i]

Major trading partners					2022
Export partners (% of exports)	France	24.4 [i]	China, Hong Kong SAR 21.0	United States	18.1 [i]
Import partners (% of imports)	France	20.8	China 14.4	Republic of Korea	10.1

Social indicators	2010	2015	2023
Population growth rate (average annual %) [b]	0.5	0.6	0.9 [a,c]
Urban population (% of total population)	60.3	61.7	61.9 [m]
Urban population growth rate (average annual %) [n]	2.0	1.2	...
Fertility rate, total (live births per woman) [b]	2.2	1.9	1.7 [a,c]
Life expectancy at birth (females/males, years) [b]	83.8 / 78.6	85.1 / 80.0	86.0 / 81.3 [a,c]
Population age distribution (0-14/60+ years old, %) [b]	25.7 / 9.5	24.1 / 11.3	21.3 / 15.2 [a,c]
International migrant stock (000/% of total pop.) [o]	31.6 / 11.9	30.1 / 11.0	30.1 / 10.7 [p]
Infant mortality rate (per 1 000 live births) [b]	7.4	6.3	5.4 [a,c]
Intentional homicide rate (per 100 000 pop.)	0.4 [q]	...	...

Environment and infrastructure indicators	2010	2015	2023
Individuals using the Internet (per 100 inhabitants)	49.0	64.6 [i]	72.7 [i,r]
Threatened species (number)	160	175	199 [c]
Forested area (% of land area)	43.1	43.1	43.1 [p]
Energy production, primary (Petajoules)	1	1	1 [p]
Energy supply per capita (Gigajoules)	49	44	42 [p]
Tourist/visitor arrivals at national borders (000) [s,t]	154	184	83 [e]
Important sites for terrestrial biodiversity protected (%)	0.0	0.0	~0.0 [c]

a Projected estimate (medium fertility variant). b For statistical purposes, the data for France do not include this area. c 2022. d Including water bodies of lake Vaihiria, lake Temae and the Maiao lagoons, but not lake Maeva and the lagoons of Raiatea and Tahaa from the upper islands. No lagoons from lower islands are included. e 2021. f Communauté financière du Pacifique (CFP) Franc. g Refers to the total population in the communes of Arue, Faaa, Mahina, Papara, Papeete, Pirae and Punaauia. h 2018. i Estimate. j Index base: 2000=100. k 2014. l 2016. m 2019. n Data refers to a 5-year period preceding the reference year. o Including refugees. p 2020. q 2009. r 2017. s Arrivals by air. t Excluding nationals residing abroad.

Gabon

Region	Middle Africa	
Population (000, 2023)	2 389[a,b]	
Pop. density (per km2, 2023)	9.3[a,b]	
Capital city	Libreville	
Capital city pop. (000, 2023)	823.9[e]	

UN membership date	20 September 1960
Surface area (km2)	267 668[a]
Sex ratio (m per 100 f)	103.6[a,b]
National currency	CFA Franc, BEAC (XAF)[d]
Exchange rate (per US$)	615.0[b]

Economic indicators	2010	2015	2023
GDP: Gross domestic product (million current US$)	14 359	14 372	18 521[c]
GDP growth rate (annual %, const. 2015 prices)	7.1	3.9	1.5[c]
GDP per capita (current US$)	8 391.4	7 085.1	7 910.8[c]
Economy: Agriculture (% of Gross Value Added)	4.2	4.7	6.5[c]
Economy: Industry (% of Gross Value Added)	59.6	51.9	49.8[c]
Economy: Services and other activity (% of GVA)	36.2	43.4	43.7[c]
Employment in agriculture (% of employed)[f]	35.9	32.1	29.0[c]
Employment in industry (% of employed)[f]	11.1	13.3	16.1[c]
Employment in services & other sectors (% employed)[f]	52.9	54.6	54.9[c]
Unemployment rate (% of labour force)	20.4	20.6[f]	21.4[f]
Labour force participation rate (female/male pop. %)	39.5 / 57.6	39.8 / 56.4[f]	39.4 / 56.2[f]
CPI: Consumer Price Index (2010=100)[f,g]	100	109	131[b]
Agricultural production index (2014-2016=100)	88	100	105[c]
International trade: exports (million current US$)[f]	8 539	5 677	7 381[b]
International trade: imports (million current US$)[f]	2 969	2 938	2 894[b]
International trade: balance (million current US$)[f]	5 570	2 739	4 487[b]
Balance of payments, current account (million US$)	2 453	141	...

Major trading partners						2022
Export partners (% of exports)[f]	China	44.8	Italy	8.6	Republic of Korea	8.1
Import partners (% of imports)[f]	China	20.2	France	19.3	United Arab Emirates	5.5

Social indicators	2010	2015	2023
Population growth rate (average annual %)	3.5	2.9	2.0[a,b]
Urban population (% of total population)	85.5	88.1	89.7[e]
Urban population growth rate (average annual %)[h]	3.9	3.9	...
Fertility rate, total (live births per woman)	4.2	3.9	3.5[a,b]
Life expectancy at birth (females/males, years)	65.8 / 62.1	67.8 / 63.4	68.4 / 63.4[a,b]
Population age distribution (0-14/60+ years old, %)	37.4 / 6.1	36.7 / 5.9	36.3 / 6.0[a,b]
International migrant stock (000/% of total pop.)[i,j]	270.8 / 16.7	378.7 / 19.4	416.7 / 18.7[k]
Refugees and others of concern to the UNHCR (000)	13.2[l]	2.9	0.3[b]
Infant mortality rate (per 1 000 live births)	42.4	35.6	29.5[a,b]
Health: Current expenditure (% of GDP)[m]	2.5	2.7	3.4[c]
Health: Physicians (per 1 000 pop.)	...	...	0.6[k]
Education: Government expenditure (% of GDP)	3.1	2.8	3.0[c]
Education: Primary gross enrol. ratio (f/m per 100 pop.)	... / ...	137.7 / 142.1[n]	106.0 / 109.6[e]
Education: Lowr. sec. gross enrol. ratio (f/m per 100 pop.)	... / ...	... / ...	91.1 / 83.4[e]
Education: Upr. sec. gross enrol. ratio (f/m per 100 pop.)	... / ...	... / ...	53.8 / 50.3[e]
Seats held by women in the National Parliament (%)	14.7	14.2	14.7[o]

Environment and infrastructure indicators	2010	2015	2023
Individuals using the Internet (per 100 inhabitants)[f]	13.0	45.8	71.7[c]
Research & Development expenditure (% of GDP)	0.6[p]	...	...
Threatened species (number)	204	231	610[b]
Forested area (% of land area)	91.8	91.6	91.3[k]
CO2 emission estimates (million tons/tons per capita)	3.3 / 1.6	3.9 / 1.7	3.1 / 1.1[k]
Energy production, primary (Petajoules)	589	561	516[k]
Energy supply per capita (Gigajoules)	54	55	47[k]
Tourist/visitor arrivals at national borders (000)	269[q,r]	...	...
Important sites for terrestrial biodiversity protected (%)	61.2	61.2	61.7[b]
Net Official Development Assist. received (% of GNI)	0.85	0.75	0.58[c]

a Projected estimate (medium fertility variant). b 2022. c 2021. d African Financial Community (CFA) Franc, Bank of Central African States (BEAC). e 2019. f Estimate. g Libreville and Owendo. h Data refers to a 5-year period preceding the reference year. i Including refugees. j Refers to foreign citizens. k 2020. l Data as at the end of December. m Data based on calendar year (January 1 to December 31). n 2011. o Data are as at 1 January of reporting year. p 2009. q Arrivals by air only. r 2005.

Gambia

Region	Western Africa	UN membership date	21 September 1965
Population (000, 2023)	2 706[a,b]	Surface area (km2)	11 295[c]
Pop. density (per km2, 2023)	267.4[a,b]	Sex ratio (m per 100 f)	99.0[a,b]
Capital city	Banjul	National currency	Dalasi (GMD)
Capital city pop. (000, 2023)	443.4[d,e]	Exchange rate (per US$)	60.8[b]

Economic indicators

	2010	2015	2023
GDP: Gross domestic product (million current US$)	1 543	1 378	2 038[c]
GDP growth rate (annual %, const. 2015 prices)	5.9	4.1	4.3[c]
GDP per capita (current US$)	796.6	611.7	772.2[c]
Economy: Agriculture (% of Gross Value Added)[f,g]	37.4	24.3	24.1[c]
Economy: Industry (% of Gross Value Added)[f,h]	10.4	18.8	18.4[c]
Economy: Services and other activity (% of GVA)[f]	52.2	56.9	57.5[c]
Employment in agriculture (% of employed)[i]	52.1	51.8	48.5[c]
Employment in industry (% of employed)[i]	6.4	6.6	7.3[c]
Employment in services & other sectors (% employed)[i]	41.5	41.6	44.1[c]
Unemployment rate (% of labour force)[i]	9.2	6.8	4.7
Labour force participation rate (female/male pop. %)[i]	49.6 / 68.5	53.1 / 67.1	57.4 / 65.9
CPI: Consumer Price Index (2010=100)[j]	100	131	219[b]
Agricultural production index (2014-2016=100)	147	108	73[c]
International trade: exports (million current US$)	68	83	35[i,b]
International trade: imports (million current US$)	284	391	660[i,b]
International trade: balance (million current US$)	- 215	- 308	- 625[i,b]
Balance of payments, current account (million US$)	18	- 54	- 94[c]

Major trading partners

						2022
Export partners (% of exports)[i]	Mali	44.7	China	29.1	Senegal	10.9
Import partners (% of imports)[i]	Togo	25.5	Côte d'Ivoire	12.4	China	7.6

Social indicators

	2010	2015	2023
Population growth rate (average annual %)	3.1	2.8	2.4[a,b]
Urban population (% of total population)	55.7	59.2	61.9[e]
Urban population growth rate (average annual %)[k]	4.5	4.4	...
Fertility rate, total (live births per woman)	5.7	5.3	4.6[a,b]
Life expectancy at birth (females/males, years)	61.6 / 59.8	63.6 / 61.4	64.3 / 61.5[a,b]
Population age distribution (0-14/60+ years old, %)	45.7 / 4.2	45.4 / 3.8	43.1 / 4.0[a,b]
International migrant stock (000/% of total pop.)[l]	185.8 / 10.4	192.5 / 9.2	215.7 / 8.9[m]
Refugees and others of concern to the UNHCR (000)	8.5[n]	11.8	5.5[b]
Infant mortality rate (per 1 000 live births)	43.9	36.9	28.0[a,b]
Health: Current expenditure (% of GDP)	4.1	3.2	2.6[m]
Health: Physicians (per 1 000 pop.)	0.1[o]	0.1	0.1[m]
Education: Government expenditure (% of GDP)	2.6	2.2	2.9[c]
Education: Primary gross enrol. ratio (f/m per 100 pop.)	80.8 / 78.8	93.0 / 87.1	109.7 / 96.3[b]
Education: Lowr. sec. gross enrol. ratio (f/m per 100 pop.)	59.2 / 57.7	64.0 / 62.0	78.7 / 63.0[b]
Education: Upr. sec. gross enrol. ratio (f/m per 100 pop.)	38.2 / 44.1[i]	... / ...	175.2 / 150.4[c]
Seats held by women in the National Parliament (%)	7.5	9.4	8.6[p]

Environment and infrastructure indicators

	2010	2015	2023
Individuals using the Internet (per 100 inhabitants)	9.2	17.6[i]	33.0[i,c]
Research & Development expenditure (% of GDP)	−0.0[q,r]	0.1[s,t]	0.1[q,u,v,w,x]
Threatened species (number)	43	55	124[b]
Forested area (% of land area)	29.6	26.8	24.0[m]
Energy production, primary (Petajoules)	6	7	7[m]
Energy supply per capita (Gigajoules)	6	7	7[i,m]
Tourist/visitor arrivals at national borders (000)[y]	91[z]	449	332[c]
Important sites for terrestrial biodiversity protected (%)	41.7	41.7	41.7[b]
Pop. using safely managed drinking water (urban/rural, %)	57.5 / 6.9	65.3 / 9.0	67.8 / 12.2[b]
Pop. using safely managed sanitation (urban/rural %)	30.2 / 41.5	31.3 / 33.7	31.0 / 22.6[b]
Net Official Development Assist. received (% of GNI)	8.00	8.47	12.24[c]

a Projected estimate (medium fertility variant). **b** 2022. **c** 2021. **d** Refers to the local government areas of Banjul and Kanifing. **e** 2019. **f** Data classified according to ISIC Rev. 4. **g** Excludes irrigation canals and landscaping care. **h** Excludes publishing activities, recycling. Includes irrigation canals. **i** Estimate. **j** Banjul, Kombo St. Mary **k** Data refers to a 5-year period preceding the reference year. **l** Including refugees. **m** 2020. **n** Data as at the end of December. **o** 2008. **p** Data are as at 1 January of reporting year. **q** Partial data. **r** 2009. **s** Overestimated or based on overestimated data. **t** 2011. **u** Excluding Higher Education. **v** Excluding private non-profit. **w** Break in the time series. **x** 2018. **y** Including nationals residing abroad. **z** Arrivals by air only.

Georgia

Region	Western Asia	UN membership date	31 July 1992
Population (000, 2023)	3 744 [a,b,c]	Surface area (km2)	69 700 [d]
Pop. density (per km2, 2023)	53.9 [a,b,c]	Sex ratio (m per 100 f)	88.7 [a,b,c]
Capital city	Tbilisi	National currency	Lari (GEL)
Capital city pop. (000, 2023)	1 077.3 [e]	Exchange rate (per US$)	2.7 [c]

Economic indicators

	2010	2015	2023
GDP: Gross domestic product (million current US$)	12 243	14 954	18 696 [d]
GDP growth rate (annual %, const. 2015 prices)	6.2	3.0	10.4 [d]
GDP per capita (current US$)	3 191.0	3 965.3	4 975.1 [d]
Economy: Agriculture (% of Gross Value Added) [f,g]	9.6	8.8	7.0 [d]
Economy: Industry (% of Gross Value Added) [f,h,i]	19.1	21.5	25.0 [d]
Economy: Services and other activity (% of GVA) [f]	71.4	69.7	68.0 [d]
Employment in agriculture (% of employed)	48.1	44.0	40.4 [j,d]
Employment in industry (% of employed)	10.6	11.0	13.7 [j,d]
Employment in services & other sectors (% employed)	41.4	45.0	45.9 [j,d]
Unemployment rate (% of labour force)	20.2	16.5	11.7 [j]
Labour force participation rate (female/male pop. %)	55.8 / 77.0	59.0 / 80.3	55.3 / 73.0 [j]
CPI: Consumer Price Index (2010=100) [k]	100	115	172 [c]
Agricultural production index (2014-2016=100)	89	102	117 [d]
International trade: exports (million current US$)	1 677	2 205	5 593 [c]
International trade: imports (million current US$)	5 236	7 281	13 592 [c]
International trade: balance (million current US$)	- 3 558	- 5 077	- 7 999 [c]
Balance of payments, current account (million US$)	- 1 199	- 1 767	- 1 937 [d]

Major trading partners

							2022
Export partners (% of exports)	China	13.2	Azerbaijan	12.0	Russian Federation	11.7
Import partners (% of imports)	Türkiye	17.5	Russian Federation	13.5	China	8.3

Social indicators

	2010	2015	2023
Population growth rate (average annual %) [b]	- 0.4	-–0.0	- 0.5 [a,c]
Urban population (% of total population) [b]	55.5	57.4	59.0 [e]
Urban population growth rate (average annual %) [b,l]	- 0.5	- 0.7	...
Fertility rate, total (live births per woman) [b]	1.9	2.2	2.1 [a,c]
Life expectancy at birth (females/males, years) [b]	76.6 / 67.6	78.1 / 68.5	76.5 / 66.8 [a,c]
Population age distribution (0-14/60+ years old, %) [b]	18.7 / 17.8	19.4 / 19.5	21.3 / 21.0 [a,c]
International migrant stock (000/% of total pop.) [b,m]	73.1 / 1.8	76.7 / 1.9	79.4 / 2.0 [n]
Refugees and others of concern to the UNHCR (000)	362.2 [o]	268.3	317.1 [c]
Infant mortality rate (per 1 000 live births) [b]	12.7	9.5	8.2 [a,c]
Health: Current expenditure (% of GDP)	9.1	7.4	7.6 [j,n]
Health: Physicians (per 1 000 pop.)	4.8	5.3	5.4 [d]
Education: Government expenditure (% of GDP)	2.8	3.2	3.6 [d]
Education: Primary gross enrol. ratio (f/m per 100 pop.)	104.1 / 102.7	102.8 / 102.7	101.1 / 100.4 [d]
Education: Lowr. sec. gross enrol. ratio (f/m per 100 pop.)	103.6 / 101.8	104.3 / 103.7	94.5 / 93.4 [d]
Education: Upr. sec. gross enrol. ratio (f/m per 100 pop.)	104.6 / 100.4 [p]	97.6 / 92.9	109.5 / 109.8 [d]
Intentional homicide rate (per 100 000 pop.)	4.9	...	2.0 [e]
Seats held by women in the National Parliament (%)	5.1	11.3	18.4 [q]

Environment and infrastructure indicators

	2010	2015	2023
Individuals using the Internet (per 100 inhabitants)	26.9	47.6 [r]	76.4 [d]
Research & Development expenditure (% of GDP)	0.2 [s]	0.3 [t,u,v]	0.3 [t,u,v,d]
Threatened species (number)	46	114	132 [c]
Forested area (% of land area)	40.6	40.6	40.6 [n]
CO2 emission estimates (million tons/tons per capita)	5.2 / 1.3	9.0 / 2.3	9.5 / 2.5 [d,n]
Energy production, primary (Petajoules)	58	55	44 [n]
Energy supply per capita (Gigajoules)	36	52	55 [n]
Tourist/visitor arrivals at national borders (000)	1 067	3 012	1 577 [d]
Important sites for terrestrial biodiversity protected (%)	34.4	40.3	42.4 [c]
Pop. using safely managed drinking water (urban/rural, %)	87.6 / 39.4	87.7 / 39.9	88.0 / 40.5 [c]
Pop. using safely managed sanitation (urban/rural %)	22.9 / 48.3	18.8 / 44.5	14.1 / 39.2 [c]
Net Official Development Assist. received (% of GNI)	4.90	3.07	4.35 [d]

a Projected estimate (medium fertility variant). b Including Abkhazia and South Ossetia. c 2022. d 2021. e 2019. f Data classified according to ISIC Rev. 4. g Excludes irrigation canals and landscaping care. h Includes mining and quarrying. i Excludes publishing activities, recycling. Includes irrigation canals. j Estimate. k Data refer to 5 cities only. l Data refers to a 5-year period preceding the reference year. m Including refugees. n 2020. o Data as at the end of December. p 2008. q Data are as at 1 January of reporting year. r Population aged 6 years and over. s 2005. t Excluding private non-profit. u Excluding business enterprise. v Partial data.

Germany

Region	Western Europe	UN membership date	18 September 1973
Population (000, 2023)	83 370 [a,b]	Surface area (km2)	357 581 [c]
Pop. density (per km2, 2023)	239.2 [a,b]	Sex ratio (m per 100 f)	97.4 [a,b]
Capital city	Berlin	National currency	Euro (EUR)
Capital city pop. (000, 2023)	3 556.8 [d]	Exchange rate (per US$)	0.9 [b]

Economic indicators

	2010	2015	2023
GDP: Gross domestic product (million current US$)	3 396 354	3 356 236	4 259 935 [c]
GDP growth rate (annual %, const. 2015 prices)	4.2	1.5	2.6 [c]
GDP per capita (current US$)	41 762.7	40 893.2	51 073.1 [c]
Economy: Agriculture (% of Gross Value Added) [e,f]	0.9	0.8	0.9 [c]
Economy: Industry (% of Gross Value Added) [f,g]	29.9	30.1	29.6 [c]
Economy: Services and other activity (% of GVA) [f]	69.2	69.1	69.5 [c]
Employment in agriculture (% of employed)	1.6	1.4	1.3 [c]
Employment in industry (% of employed)	28.4	27.7	27.6 [c]
Employment in services & other sectors (% employed)	70.0	70.9	71.1 [c]
Unemployment rate (% of labour force)	7.0	4.6	3.3 [h]
Labour force participation rate (female/male pop. %)	53.1 / 66.1	54.7 / 65.9	56.5 / 67.1 [h]
CPI: Consumer Price Index (2010=100)	100	107	118 [i,b]
Agricultural production index (2014-2016=100)	95	99	94 [c]
International trade: exports (million current US$)	1 267 743	1 328 500	1 665 636 [b]
International trade: imports (million current US$)	1 060 672	1 057 536	1 577 564 [b]
International trade: balance (million current US$)	207 071	270 964	88 072 [b]
Balance of payments, current account (million US$)	196 172	288 065	172 724 [b]

Major trading partners

							2022
Export partners (% of exports) [h]	United States	9.9	France	7.4	Netherlands	6.8	
Import partners (% of imports)	China	13.0	Netherlands	7.6	United States	6.2 [h]	

Social indicators

	2010	2015	2023
Population growth rate (average annual %)	0.1	0.3	- 0.1 [a,b]
Urban population (% of total population)	77.0	77.2	77.4 [d]
Urban population growth rate (average annual %) [j]	0.1	0.3	...
Fertility rate, total (live births per woman)	1.4	1.5	1.5 [a,b]
Life expectancy at birth (females/males, years)	82.6 / 77.4	83.0 / 78.1	83.5 / 78.5 [a,b]
Population age distribution (0-14/60+ years old, %)	13.6 / 25.9	13.2 / 27.3	14.0 / 29.7 [a,b]
International migrant stock (000/% of total pop.)	9 812.3 / 12.1	10 220.4 / 12.5	15 762.5 / 18.8 [a,b]
Refugees and others of concern to the UNHCR (000)	670.6 [l]	573.8	2 487.8 [b]
Infant mortality rate (per 1 000 live births)	3.5	3.3	3.0 [a,b]
Health: Current expenditure (% of GDP)	11.1 [m]	11.2	12.8 [c]
Health: Physicians (per 1 000 pop.)	3.7	4.1	4.5 [c]
Education: Government expenditure (% of GDP)	5.1	4.9	5.1 [d]
Education: Primary gross enrol. ratio (f/m per 100 pop.)	102.7 / 103.3	101.6 / 101.7	101.5 / 100.7 [k]
Education: Lowr. sec. gross enrol. ratio (f/m per 100 pop.)	101.3 / 102.8	96.6 / 98.1	97.4 / 97.6 [k]
Education: Upr. sec. gross enrol. ratio (f/m per 100 pop.)	100.8 / 113.9	96.0 / 106.7	89.8 / 102.5 [k]
Intentional homicide rate (per 100 000 pop.)	1.0	0.8	0.8 [c]
Seats held by women in the National Parliament (%)	32.8	36.5	35.0 [n]

Environment and infrastructure indicators

	2010	2015	2023
Individuals using the Internet (per 100 inhabitants)	82.0 [o]	87.6 [o]	91.4 [p,c]
Research & Development expenditure (% of GDP)	2.7	2.9	3.1 [q,k]
Threatened species (number)	79	107	256 [b]
Forested area (% of land area)	32.7	32.7	32.7 [k]
CO2 emission estimates (million tons/tons per capita)	769.6 / 9.4	739.9 / 8.9	631.6 / 7.5 [c]
Energy production, primary (Petajoules)	5 490	5 016	4 034 [k]
Energy supply per capita (Gigajoules)	170	158	140 [k]
Tourist/visitor arrivals at national borders (000) [r]	26 875	34 970	11 688 [c]
Important sites for terrestrial biodiversity protected (%)	76.2	77.0	79.1 [b]
Pop. using safely managed drinking water (urban/rural, %)	99.9 / 99.8	99.9 / 99.7	100.0 / 99.6 [b]
Pop. using safely managed sanitation (urban/rural, %)	98.0 / 91.0	98.3 / 91.2	98.5 / 91.4 [b]
Net Official Development Assist. disbursed (% of GNI) [s]	1.24	0.60	1.58 [c]

a Projected estimate (medium fertility variant). b 2022. c 2021. d 2019. e Excludes irrigation canals and landscaping care. f Data classified according to ISIC Rev. 4. g Excludes publishing activities, recycling. Includes irrigation canals. h Estimate. i Index base: 2015=100. j Data refers to a 5-year period preceding the reference year. k 2020. l Data as at the end of December. m Break in the time series. n Data are as at 1 January of reporting year. o Population aged 16 to 74 years. p Users in the last 3 months. q Provisional data. r Non-resident tourists staying in all types of accommodation establishments. s Development Assistance Committee member (OECD).

Ghana

Region	Western Africa	UN membership date	08 March 1957
Population (000, 2023)	33 476 [a,b]	Surface area (km2)	238 537 [c]
Pop. density (per km2, 2023)	147.1 [a,b]	Sex ratio (m per 100 f)	99.5 [a,b]
Capital city	Accra	National currency	Ghana Cedi (GHS)
Capital city pop. (000, 2023)	2 475.2 [d]	Exchange rate (per US$)	8.6 [b]

Economic indicators

	2010	2015	2023
GDP: Gross domestic product (million current US$)	42 587	50 034	79 083 [c]
GDP growth rate (annual %, const. 2015 prices)	7.9	2.1	5.4 [c]
GDP per capita (current US$)	1 665.2	1 733.0	2 408.6 [c]
Economy: Agriculture (% of Gross Value Added) [e,f]	28.9	21.8	21.0 [c]
Economy: Industry (% of Gross Value Added) [f,g]	28.2	34.0	30.1 [c]
Economy: Services and other activity (% of GVA) [f]	43.0	44.2	48.9 [c]
Employment in agriculture (% of employed)	42.0	35.2	39.5 [h,c]
Employment in industry (% of employed)	12.3 [h]	18.7	19.1 [h,c]
Employment in services & other sectors (% employed)	42.8	46.1	41.4 [h,c]
Unemployment rate (% of labour force)	5.4	6.8	3.9 [h]
Labour force participation rate (female/male pop. %)	67.7 / 74.6 [h]	65.1 / 73.5	65.1 / 72.2 [h]
CPI: Consumer Price Index (2010=100)	100	183	336 [c]
Agricultural production index (2014-2016=100)	84	100	118 [c]
International trade: exports (million current US$) [i]	5 233	13 756	18 564 [h,b]
International trade: imports (million current US$) [i]	8 057	14 687	13 796 [h,b]
International trade: balance (million current US$) [i]	- 2 824	- 932	4 769 [h,b]
Balance of payments, current account (million US$)	- 2 747	- 2 824	- 2 541 [c]

Major trading partners   2022

Export partners (% of exports) [h]	Switzerland	17.6	United States	14.8	China	12.2
Import partners (% of imports) [h]	China	37.2	Netherlands	6.0	United Arab Emirates	5.3

Social indicators

	2010	2015	2023
Population growth rate (average annual %)	2.4	2.3	1.9 [a,b]
Urban population (% of total population)	50.7	54.1	56.7 [d]
Urban population growth rate (average annual %) [j]	4.0	3.6	...
Fertility rate, total (live births per woman)	4.2	4.4	3.5 [a,b]
Life expectancy at birth (females/males, years)	62.5 / 59.8	65.0 / 61.4	66.1 / 61.8 [a,b]
Population age distribution (0-14/60+ years old, %)	39.2 / 4.8	38.9 / 5.0	36.9 / 5.9 [a,b]
International migrant stock (000/% of total pop.) [k]	337.8 / 1.4	414.7 / 1.5	476.4 / 1.5 [l]
Refugees and others of concern to the UNHCR (000)	14.8 [m]	21.3	8.5 [b]
Infant mortality rate (per 1 000 live births)	47.0	38.7	31.6 [a,b]
Health: Current expenditure (% of GDP) [n]	4.2	4.5	4.0 [l]
Health: Physicians (per 1 000 pop.)	0.1	0.1	0.2 [l]
Education: Government expenditure (% of GDP)	5.5	4.4 [h]	3.9 [h,o]
Education: Primary gross enrol. ratio (f/m per 100 pop.)	99.5 / 101.1 [p]	108.3 / 108.4	105.5 / 103.8 [c]
Education: Lowr. sec. gross enrol. ratio (f/m per 100 pop.)	73.1 / 79.9 [p]	85.4 / 87.5	90.5 / 87.9 [c]
Education: Upr. sec. gross enrol. ratio (f/m per 100 pop.)	23.6 / 29.0 [p]	45.8 / 50.9	69.5 / 70.7 [c]
Intentional homicide rate (per 100 000 pop.)	1.7	1.8	1.8 [c]
Seats held by women in the National Parliament (%)	8.3	10.9	14.6 [q]

Environment and infrastructure indicators

	2010	2015	2023
Individuals using the Internet (per 100 inhabitants)	7.8 [r,s]	23.0 [h]	68.2 [c]
Research & Development expenditure (% of GDP)	0.4 [s]	...	...
Threatened species (number)	202	223	292 [b]
Forested area (% of land area)	34.9	34.6	35.1 [l]
CO2 emission estimates (million tons/tons per capita)	11.1 / 0.4	15.0 / 0.5	20.1 / 0.6 [l]
Energy production, primary (Petajoules)	168	424	704 [l]
Energy supply per capita (Gigajoules)	11	13	15 [l]
Tourist/visitor arrivals at national borders (000) [t]	931	897	624 [c]
Important sites for terrestrial biodiversity protected (%)	68.8	68.8	68.8 [b]
Pop. using safely managed drinking water (urban/rural, %)	43.1 / 6.1	52.1 / 11.0	62.6 / 18.8 [b]
Pop. using safely managed sanitation (urban/rural %)	9.7 / 7.9	11.6 / 11.9	14.0 / 18.4 [b]
Net Official Development Assist. received (% of GNI)	5.36	3.69	1.64 [c]

a Projected estimate (medium fertility variant). **b** 2022. **c** 2021. **d** 2019. **e** Excludes irrigation canals and landscaping care. **f** Data classified according to ISIC Rev. 4. **g** Excludes publishing activities, recycling. Includes irrigation canals. **h** Estimate. **i** Since 2011, Ghana have been exporting crude petroleum & natural gas in relatively larger quantities. **j** Data refers to a 5-year period preceding the reference year. **k** Including refugees. **l** 2020. **m** Data as at the end of December. **n** Data based on calendar year (January 1 to December 31). **o** 2018. **p** 2009. **q** Data are as at 1 January of reporting year. **r** Population aged 12 years and over. **s** Break in the time series. **t** Including nationals residing abroad.

Gibraltar

Region	Southern Europe	Population (000, 2023)	33 a,b,c
Surface area (km2)	6 d	Pop. density (per km2, 2023)	3 264.9 a,b,c
Sex ratio (m per 100 f)	99.8 a,b,c	Capital city	Gibraltar
National currency	Gibraltar Pound (GIP)	Capital city pop. (000, 2023)	34.7 e
Exchange rate (per US$)	0.8 c		

Economic indicators

	2010	2015	2023
CPI: Consumer Price Index (2010=100)	...	142 f,g	...
International trade: exports (million current US$) h	259	295	414 c
International trade: imports (million current US$) h	627	815	13 300 c
International trade: balance (million current US$) h	- 368	- 520	- 12 886 c

Major trading partners

						2022
Export partners (% of exports) h	Ireland	23.8	India	18.7	Brazil	14.1
Import partners (% of imports) h	Spain	17.6	Italy	17.2	Greece	10.2

Social indicators

	2010	2015	2023
Population growth rate (average annual %) b	1.4	0.2	0.1 a,c
Urban population (% of total population)	100.0	100.0	100.0 i
Urban population growth rate (average annual %) j	0.7	0.6	...
Fertility rate, total (live births per woman) b	1.8	2.2	1.8 a,c
Life expectancy at birth (females/males, years) b	84.1 / 77.8	84.2 / 76.9	84.7 / 80.9 a,c
Population age distribution (0-14/60+ years old, %) b	18.1 / 22.0	17.8 / 23.7	17.0 / 27.2 a,c
International migrant stock (000/% of total pop.)	10.4 / 30.9	11.1 / 32.8	11.2 / 33.2 k
Infant mortality rate (per 1 000 live births) b	10.9	11.4	8.9 a,c
Education: Primary gross enrol. ratio (f/m per 100 pop.)	112.8 / 110.9 l	... / ...	116.5 / 109.2 d
Education: Lowr. sec. gross enrol. ratio (f/m per 100 pop.)	86.5 / 86.8 l	... / ...	97.0 / 107.2 d
Education: Upr. sec. gross enrol. ratio (f/m per 100 pop.)	79.8 / 83.7 l	... / ...	91.0 / 96.8 d
Intentional homicide rate (per 100 000 pop.)	3.2	...	...

Environment and infrastructure indicators

	2010	2015	2023
Individuals using the Internet (per 100 inhabitants)	65.0	65.0 h,m	94.4 h,n
Threatened species (number)	22	26	59 c
Forested area (% of land area)	0.0	0.0	0.0 k
CO2 emission estimates (million tons/tons per capita)	0.5 / 14.0	0.6 / 17.2	0.7 / 19.0 k
Energy production, primary (Petajoules)	...	...	0 h,k
Energy supply per capita (Gigajoules)	234	274	321 k
Important sites for terrestrial biodiversity protected (%)	0.0	0.0	0.0 c
Pop. using safely managed drinking water (urban/rural, %)	100.0 / ...	100.0 / ...	100.0 / ... c

a Projected estimate (medium fertility variant). b For statistical purposes, the data for United Kingdom do not include this area. c 2022. d 2021. e 2018. f Index base: 2000=100. g 2014. h Estimate. i 2019. j Data refers to a 5-year period preceding the reference year. k 2020. l 2009. m 2012. n 2016.

Greece

Region	Southern Europe	UN membership date	25 October 1945
Population (000, 2023)	10 385 a,b	Surface area (km2)	131 957 c
Pop. density (per km2, 2023)	79.4 a,b	Sex ratio (m per 100 f)	95.8 a,b
Capital city	Athens	National currency	Euro (EUR)
Capital city pop. (000, 2023)	3 154.2 d,e	Exchange rate (per US$)	0.9 b

Economic indicators

	2010	2015	2023
GDP: Gross domestic product (million current US$)	296 835	195 605	214 874 c
GDP growth rate (annual %, const. 2015 prices)	- 5.5	- 0.2	8.4 c
GDP per capita (current US$)	26 902.4	18 100.4	20 571.2 c
Economy: Agriculture (% of Gross Value Added) f,g	3.4	4.4	4.4 c
Economy: Industry (% of Gross Value Added) g,h	16.9	16.4	17.5 c
Economy: Services and other activity (% of GVA) g	79.7	79.2	78.0 c
Employment in agriculture (% of employed)	12.4	12.9	11.4 c
Employment in industry (% of employed)	19.6	11.2 i	15.2 c
Employment in services & other sectors (% employed)	68.0	72.2	73.3 c
Unemployment rate (% of labour force)	12.7	24.9	11.7 i
Labour force participation rate (female/male pop. %)	44.1 / 63.1	44.9 / 59.0	43.9 / 57.9 i
CPI: Consumer Price Index (2010=100) j	100	101	112 b
Agricultural production index (2014-2016=100)	102	104	96 c
International trade: exports (million current US$)	27 586	28 289	57 568 b
International trade: imports (million current US$)	66 453	47 264	97 970 b
International trade: balance (million current US$)	- 38 867	- 18 975	- 40 402 b
Balance of payments, current account (million US$)	- 30 263	- 1 611	- 21 424 b

Major trading partners

							2022
Export partners (% of exports)	Italy	10.4	Bulgaria	7.7	Germany	6.3	
Import partners (% of imports)	Russian Federation	10.8	Germany	9.1	China	8.5	

Social indicators

	2010	2015	2023
Population growth rate (average annual %)	- 0.2	- 0.6	- 0.5 a,b
Urban population (% of total population)	76.3	78.0	79.4 e
Urban population growth rate (average annual %) k	0.7	0.1	...
Fertility rate, total (live births per woman)	1.4	1.3	1.4 a,b
Life expectancy at birth (females/males, years)	83.4 / 77.7	83.6 / 77.9	83.3 / 78.0 a,b
Population age distribution (0-14/60+ years old, %)	14.6 / 25.0	14.6 / 26.7	13.9 / 29.4 a,b
International migrant stock (000/% of total pop.)	1 321.1 / 12.1	1 242.9 / 11.7	1 340.5 / 12.9 l
Refugees and others of concern to the UNHCR (000)	57.4 m	37.6	173.2 b
Infant mortality rate (per 1 000 live births)	3.4	3.8	3.4 a,b
Health: Current expenditure (% of GDP)	9.6	8.2 n	9.5 l
Health: Physicians (per 1 000 pop.)	5.8	5.9	6.3 l
Education: Government expenditure (% of GDP)	4.1	3.7	3.6 e
Education: Primary gross enrol. ratio (f/m per 100 pop.)	97.4 / 99.6	99.1 / 100.0	101.5 / 100.7 l
Education: Lowr. sec. gross enrol. ratio (f/m per 100 pop.)	102.6 / 108.6	97.4 / 102.5	100.2 / 103.7 l
Education: Upr. sec. gross enrol. ratio (f/m per 100 pop.)	106.2 / 107.6	99.4 / 109.1	106.0 / 112.3 l
Intentional homicide rate (per 100 000 pop.)	1.6	0.9	0.9 c
Seats held by women in the National Parliament (%)	17.3	23.0	21.0 o

Environment and infrastructure indicators

	2010	2015	2023
Individuals using the Internet (per 100 inhabitants)	44.4 p	66.8	78.5 c
Research & Development expenditure (% of GDP)	0.6 i	1.0	1.5 l
Threatened species (number)	156	291	601 b
Forested area (% of land area)	30.3	30.3	30.3 l
CO2 emission estimates (million tons/tons per capita)	84.5 / 7.5	65.5 / 6.0	49.2 / 4.5 c
Energy production, primary (Petajoules)	397	357	191 l
Energy supply per capita (Gigajoules)	105	90	78 l
Tourist/visitor arrivals at national borders (000) q	15 007	23 599	14 705 c
Important sites for terrestrial biodiversity protected (%)	80.4	86.5	86.5 b
Pop. using safely managed sanitation (urban/rural %)	90.9 / ...	93.7 / ...	97.4 / ... b
Net Official Development Assist. disbursed (% of GNI) r	0.26	- 0.04	0.08 c

a Projected estimate (medium fertility variant). b 2022. c 2021. d Refers to the localities of Calithèa, Peristérion and Piraeus, among others. e 2019. f Excludes irrigation canals and landscaping care. g Data classified according to ISIC Rev. 4. h Excludes publishing activities, recycling. Includes irrigation canals. i Estimate. j Calculated by the UN Statistics Division from national indices. k Data refers to a 5-year period preceding the reference year. l 2020. m Data as at the end of December. n Break in the time series. o Data are as at 1 January of reporting year. p Population aged 16 to 74 years. q Information is based on the border survey conducted by the Bank of Greece. r Development Assistance Committee member (OECD).

Greenland

Region	Northern America	Population (000, 2023)	56[a,b,c]
Surface area (km2)	2 166 086[d]	Pop. density (per km2, 2023)	0.1[a,b,c]
Sex ratio (m per 100 f)	110.6[a,b,c]	Capital city	Nuuk
National currency	Danish Krone (DKK)	Capital city pop. (000, 2023)	18.4[e]
Exchange rate (per US$)	7.0[c]		

Economic indicators		2010	2015	2023
GDP: Gross domestic product (million current US$)		2 503	2 499	3 273[d]
GDP growth rate (annual %, const. 2015 prices)		1.7	- 2.5	1.1[d]
GDP per capita (current US$)		44 421.0	44 710.9	58 185.2[d]
Economy: Agriculture (% of Gross Value Added)[f]		13.8	17.6	18.7[d]
Economy: Industry (% of Gross Value Added)[g]		18.6	17.6	18.6[d]
Economy: Services and other activity (% of GVA)		67.6	64.9	62.7[d]
Employment in agriculture (% of employed)		...	4.6[h,i,j]	...
Employment in industry (% of employed)		...	12.6[h,i,j]	...
Employment in services & other sectors (% employed)		...	82.5[h,i,j]	...
Unemployment rate (% of labour force)		8.4[k]	9.7[h,l,m,n,o]	...
International trade: exports (million current US$)		389	406	998[p,c]
International trade: imports (million current US$)		847	667	1 086[p,c]
International trade: balance (million current US$)		- 458	- 261	- 88[p,c]

Major trading partners						2022
Export partners (% of exports)[p]	Denmark	46.9	China	23.1	United Kingdom	5.5
Import partners (% of imports)[p]	Denmark	56.7	Sweden	21.7	France	9.4

Social indicators	2010	2015	2023
Population growth rate (average annual %)[b]	- 0.1	0.1	0.4[a,c]
Urban population (% of total population)	84.4	86.1	87.1[q]
Urban population growth rate (average annual %)[r]	0.3	0.3	...
Fertility rate, total (live births per woman)[b]	2.2	2.1	2.0[a,c]
Life expectancy at birth (females/males, years)[b]	73.8 / 67.8	75.7 / 69.5	76.0 / 70.1[a,c]
Population age distribution (0-14/60+ years old, %)[b]	22.4 / 10.9	21.1 / 12.8	20.9 / 16.9[a,c]
International migrant stock (000/% of total pop.)	6.1 / 10.8	6.0 / 10.7	5.9 / 10.4[s]
Infant mortality rate (per 1 000 live births)[b]	9.3	9.6	8.6[a,c]
Education: Government expenditure (% of GDP)	...	12.0	10.2[s]
Intentional homicide rate (per 100 000 pop.)	19.5	7.2	5.4[t]

Environment and infrastructure indicators	2010	2015	2023
Individuals using the Internet (per 100 inhabitants)	63.0	67.6[p]	69.5[p,u]
Threatened species (number)	14	17	31[c]
Forested area (% of land area)	~0.0	~0.0	~0.0[s]
Energy production, primary (Petajoules)	1	2	2[s]
Energy supply per capita (Gigajoules)	187	156	167[s]
Important sites for terrestrial biodiversity protected (%)	26.3	29.7	29.7[c]

a Projected estimate (medium fertility variant). b For statistical purposes, the data for Denmark do not include this area. c 2022. d 2021. e 2018. f Excludes irrigation canals and landscaping care. g Excludes publishing activities, recycling. Includes irrigation canals. h Nationals, residents. i Population aged 15 to 64 years. j 2011. k 2006. l Excluding the institutional population. m Population aged 18 to 64 years. n Break in the time series. o 2013. p Estimate. q 2019. r Data refers to a 5-year period preceding the reference year. s 2020. t 2016. u 2017.

Grenada

Region	Caribbean
Population (000, 2023)	125[a,b]
Pop. density (per km2, 2023)	368.9[a,b]
Capital city	Saint George's
Capital city pop. (000, 2023)	39.3[e,f]

UN membership date	17 September 1974
Surface area (km2)	345[c]
Sex ratio (m per 100 f)	100.0[a,b]
National currency	E. Caribbean Dollar (XCD)[d]
Exchange rate (per US$)	2.7[b]

Economic indicators

	2010	2015	2023
GDP: Gross domestic product (million current US$)	771	997	1 115[c]
GDP growth rate (annual %, const. 2015 prices)	- 0.5	6.4	5.6[c]
GDP per capita (current US$)	6 761.0	8 379.6	8 950.2[c]
Economy: Agriculture (% of Gross Value Added)	5.2	8.6	6.0[c]
Economy: Industry (% of Gross Value Added)	16.8	14.2	17.2[c]
Economy: Services and other activity (% of GVA)	78.1	77.2	76.8[c]
CPI: Consumer Price Index (2010=100)	100	104	109[c]
Agricultural production index (2014-2016=100)	78	103	94[c]
International trade: exports (million current US$)	25[g]	33[g]	37[b]
International trade: imports (million current US$)	306[g]	372[g]	589[b]
International trade: balance (million current US$)	- 281[g]	- 339[g]	- 552[b]
Balance of payments, current account (million US$)	- 204	- 125	- 294[c]

Major trading partners

						2022
Export partners (% of exports)	Saint Lucia	27.7[g]	United States	19.7[g]	Areas nes	9.2
Import partners (% of imports)	United States	34.0	Trinidad and Tobago	17.3[g]	Îles Caïmanes	11.8

Social indicators

	2010	2015	2023
Population growth rate (average annual %)	0.7	0.8	0.6[a,b]
Urban population (% of total population)	35.9	36.0	36.4[h]
Urban population growth rate (average annual %)[i]	0.3	0.5	...
Fertility rate, total (live births per woman)	2.2	2.1	2.0[a,b]
Life expectancy at birth (females/males, years)	77.6 / 72.5	78.1 / 72.2	78.3 / 72.6[a,b]
Population age distribution (0-14/60+ years old, %)	24.7 / 12.1	24.0 / 12.9	24.0 / 14.9[a,b]
International migrant stock (000/% of total pop.)	7.0 / 6.6	7.1 / 6.4	7.2 / 6.4[j]
Refugees and others of concern to the UNHCR (000)	~0.0[k]	...	0.2[b]
Infant mortality rate (per 1 000 live births)	12.4	13.3	12.3[a,b]
Health: Current expenditure (% of GDP)[g,l]	5.4	4.6	5.8[j]
Health: Physicians (per 1 000 pop.)	0.6[m]	...	1.3[f]
Education: Government expenditure (% of GDP)	...	4.2	4.1[c]
Education: Primary gross enrol. ratio (f/m per 100 pop.)	113.9 / 119.1	116.3 / 120.6	106.0 / 107.7[f]
Education: Lowr. sec. gross enrol. ratio (f/m per 100 pop.)	126.7 / 135.7	108.7 / 119.8	114.1 / 117.9[j]
Education: Upr. sec. gross enrol. ratio (f/m per 100 pop.)	107.1 / 85.2	113.4 / 103.3	117.0 / 101.6[j]
Intentional homicide rate (per 100 000 pop.)	8.8	5.0	4.0[c]
Seats held by women in the National Parliament (%)	13.3	33.3	31.2[n]

Environment and infrastructure indicators

	2010	2015	2023
Individuals using the Internet (per 100 inhabitants)[g]	27.0	52.5	77.8[c]
Threatened species (number)	37	51	94[b]
Forested area (% of land area)	52.1	52.1	52.1[j]
Energy production, primary (Petajoules)	0	0	0[j]
Energy supply per capita (Gigajoules)	35	34	36[j]
Tourist/visitor arrivals at national borders (000)	110	155	47[c]
Important sites for terrestrial biodiversity protected (%)	34.5	34.5	34.5[b]
Net Official Development Assist. received (% of GNI)	4.63	2.74	6.37[c]

a Projected estimate (medium fertility variant). **b** 2022. **c** 2021. **d** East Caribbean Dollar. **e** Refers to Saint George Parish. **f** 2018. **g** Estimate. **h** 2019. **i** Data refers to a 5-year period preceding the reference year. **j** 2020. **k** Data as at the end of December. **l** Data based on calendar year (January 1 to December 31). **m** 2006. **n** Data are as at 1 January of reporting year.

Guadeloupe

Region	Caribbean	Population (000, 2023)	396[a,b,c]
Surface area (km2)	1 639[d]	Pop. density (per km2, 2023)	243.1[a,b,c]
Sex ratio (m per 100 f)	82.6[a,b,c]	Capital city	Basse-Terre
National currency	Euro (EUR)	Capital city pop. (000, 2023)	58.4[e]
Exchange rate (per US$)	0.9[c]		

Economic indicators	2010	2015	2023
Employment in agriculture (% of employed)	...	3.3[f,g,h]	...
Employment in industry (% of employed)[f,g]	13.8	13.5[h]	...
Employment in services & other sectors (% employed)[f,g]	64.4	65.5[h]	...
Unemployment rate (% of labour force)[g]	23.8	26.1[i,j]	...
Labour force participation rate (female/male pop. %)	39.5 / 44.2[g]	49.6 / 56.5[g,i,j]	... / ...
CPI: Consumer Price Index (2010=100)[k]	100	106	116[c]

Social indicators	2010	2015	2023
Population growth rate (average annual %)[b]	0.1	- 0.4	- 0.1[a,c]
Urban population (% of total population)[l]	98.4	98.4	98.5[m]
Urban population growth rate (average annual %)[l,n]	0.5	--0.0	...
Fertility rate, total (live births per woman)[b]	2.2	2.2	2.0[a,c]
Life expectancy at birth (females/males, years)[b]	83.9 / 76.9	85.3 / 78.1	83.9 / 77.3[a,c]
Population age distribution (0-14/60+ years old, %)[b]	22.0 / 18.8	20.5 / 22.2	18.1 / 27.0[a,c]
International migrant stock (000/% of total pop.)	94.9 / 23.4	91.0 / 22.7	90.2 / 22.5[o]
Infant mortality rate (per 1 000 live births)[b]	6.3	5.2	4.4[a,c]
Intentional homicide rate (per 100 000 pop.)	8.9[p]	9.8	5.8[q]

Environment and infrastructure indicators	2010	2015	2023
Individuals using the Internet (per 100 inhabitants)	23.4[r,p]	...	...
Threatened species (number)[s]	54	70	121[c]
Forested area (% of land area)	43.2	44.6	44.4[o]
Energy production, primary (Petajoules)	2[r,t]	...	...
Energy supply per capita (Gigajoules)	81[r,t]	...	...
Tourist/visitor arrivals at national borders (000)[s,u]	392	512	735[e]
Important sites for terrestrial biodiversity protected (%)	81.9	82.0	82.0[c]

a Projected estimate (medium fertility variant). **b** For statistical purposes, the data for France do not include this area. **c** 2022. **d** 2021. **e** 2018. **f** Population aged 15 to 64 years. **g** Excluding the institutional population. **h** 2012. **i** Break in the time series. **j** 2013. **k** Calculated by the UN Statistics Division from national indices. **l** Including Saint Barthélemy and Saint Martin (French part). **m** 2019. **n** Data refers to a 5-year period preceding the reference year. **o** 2020. **p** 2009. **q** 2016. **r** Estimate. **s** Excluding the north islands, Saint Barthélemy and Saint Martin (French part). **t** Data after 2010 are included in France. **u** Arrivals by air.

Guam

		Population (000, 2023)	172 [a,b,c]
Region	Micronesia	Pop. density (per km2, 2023)	317.5 [a,b,c]
Surface area (km2)	541 [d]	Capital city	Hagåtña
Sex ratio (m per 100 f)	101.3 [a,b,c]	Capital city pop. (000, 2023)	146.9 [e]
National currency	US Dollar (USD)		

Economic indicators	2010	2015	2023
Employment in agriculture (% of employed)	0.3	0.3 [f]	0.3 [f,d]
Employment in industry (% of employed) [f]	14.7	14.6	14.1 [d]
Employment in services & other sectors (% employed)	84.6	85.1 [f]	85.7 [f,d]
Unemployment rate (% of labour force)	8.2	6.9	6.1 [f]
Labour force participation rate (female/male pop. %)	56.5 / 66.2	56.5 / 68.6 [f]	55.7 / 67.8 [f]
CPI: Consumer Price Index (2010=100) [g]	100	106	137 [c]

Social indicators	2010	2015	2023
Population growth rate (average annual %) [a]	0.5	0.2	0.7 [b,c]
Urban population (% of total population)	94.1	94.5	94.9 [h]
Urban population growth rate (average annual %) [i]	0.2	0.4	...
Fertility rate, total (live births per woman) [a]	3.0	2.9	2.6 [b,c]
Life expectancy at birth (females/males, years) [a]	80.5 / 73.6	80.5 / 73.1	82.0 / 74.8 [b,c]
Population age distribution (0-14/60+ years old, %) [a]	27.1 / 10.6	26.9 / 13.2	26.1 / 17.0 [b,c]
International migrant stock (000/% of total pop.)	75.4 / 47.3	76.1 / 47.0	80.5 / 47.7 [j]
Infant mortality rate (per 1 000 live births) [a]	11.6	11.7	9.7 [b,c]
Intentional homicide rate (per 100 000 pop.)	1.8	2.4 [k]	4.2 [h]

Environment and infrastructure indicators	2010	2015	2023
Individuals using the Internet (per 100 inhabitants) [f]	54.0	73.1	80.5 [l]
Research & Development expenditure (% of GDP)	0.3 [m]	...	...
Threatened species (number)	34	95	111 [c]
Forested area (% of land area)	44.4	46.3	51.9 [j]
Energy production, primary (Petajoules)	...	0	0 [j]
Energy supply per capita (Gigajoules)	0 [f]	1	1 [j]
Tourist/visitor arrivals at national borders (000) [n]	1 197	1 409	79 [d]
Important sites for terrestrial biodiversity protected (%)	2.4	2.4	2.4 [c]

a For statistical purposes, the data for United States of America do not include this area. b Projected estimate (medium fertility variant). c 2022. d 2021. e 2018. f Estimate. g Calculated by the UN Statistics Division from national indices. h 2019. i Data refers to a 5-year period preceding the reference year. j 2020. k 2011. l 2017. m 2005. n Air and sea arrivals.

Guatemala

Region	Central America	UN membership date	21 November 1945
Population (000, 2023)	17 844[a,b]	Surface area (km2)	108 889[c]
Pop. density (per km2, 2023)	166.5[a,b]	Sex ratio (m per 100 f)	98.0[a,b]
Capital city	Guatemala City	National currency	Quetzal (GTQ)
Capital city pop. (000, 2023)	2 891.2[d]	Exchange rate (per US$)	7.9[b]

Economic indicators

	2010	2015	2023
GDP: Gross domestic product (million current US$)	40 682	62 186	85 986[c]
GDP growth rate (annual %, const. 2015 prices)	2.9	4.1	8.0[c]
GDP per capita (current US$)	2 797.3	3 886.4	4 883.2[c]
Economy: Agriculture (% of Gross Value Added)[e,f]	11.4	10.6	10.0[c]
Economy: Industry (% of Gross Value Added)[f,g]	24.2	24.1	23.7[c]
Economy: Services and other activity (% of GVA)[f]	64.4	65.3	66.3[c]
Employment in agriculture (% of employed)	33.5	31.9	29.2[c]
Employment in industry (% of employed)	22.0	18.9	14.3[h,c]
Employment in services & other sectors (% employed)	44.5	49.2	48.7[c]
Unemployment rate (% of labour force)	3.5	2.5	2.8[h]
Labour force participation rate (female/male pop. %)	41.6 / 80.1	38.5 / 83.7	37.2 / 81.3[h]
CPI: Consumer Price Index (2010=100)	100[i]	122	164[b]
Agricultural production index (2014-2016=100)	76	101	102[c]
International trade: exports (million current US$)	8 460	10 677	15 806[b]
International trade: imports (million current US$)	13 830	17 637	32 099[b]
International trade: balance (million current US$)	- 5 370	- 6 960	- 16 293[b]
Balance of payments, current account (million US$)	- 767	- 774	2 113[c]

Major trading partners

						2022
Export partners (% of exports)	United States	32.3	El Salvador	13.0	Honduras	10.0
Import partners (% of imports)	United States	32.0	China	18.2	Mexico	10.1

Social indicators

	2010	2015	2023
Population growth rate (average annual %)	2.0	1.8	1.4[a,b]
Urban population (% of total population)	48.4	50.0	51.4[d]
Urban population growth rate (average annual %)[j]	2.8	2.7	...
Fertility rate, total (live births per woman)	3.4	3.0	2.4[a,b]
Life expectancy at birth (females/males, years)	74.3 / 67.6	75.2 / 69.1	71.8 / 65.7[a,b]
Population age distribution (0-14/60+ years old, %)	39.1 / 6.0	36.2 / 6.5	32.4 / 7.1[a,b]
International migrant stock (000/% of total pop.)[k]	66.4 / 0.5	74.9 / 0.5	84.3 / 0.5[l]
Refugees and others of concern to the UNHCR (000)	0.1[m]	0.3	144.3[b]
Infant mortality rate (per 1 000 live births)	28.3	23.3	19.8[a,b]
Health: Current expenditure (% of GDP)[n]	6.1[o]	6.0	6.5[l]
Health: Physicians (per 1 000 pop.)	0.9[p]	...	1.3[l]
Education: Government expenditure (% of GDP)	2.8	3.0	3.1[c]
Education: Primary gross enrol. ratio (f/m per 100 pop.)	114.3 / 116.6	99.9 / 103.1	101.2 / 102.8[c]
Education: Lowr. sec. gross enrol. ratio (f/m per 100 pop.)	65.3 / 71.6	67.2 / 74.4	60.6 / 63.0[c]
Education: Upr. sec. gross enrol. ratio (f/m per 100 pop.)	35.3 / 34.9	37.2 / 36.1	34.7 / 30.7[c]
Intentional homicide rate (per 100 000 pop.)	41.0	33.4[q]	20.0[c]
Seats held by women in the National Parliament (%)	12.0	13.3	19.4[r]

Environment and infrastructure indicators

	2010	2015	2023
Individuals using the Internet (per 100 inhabitants)	10.5[h]	28.8[h]	50.8[s,c]
Research & Development expenditure (% of GDP)[t]	~0.0	~0.0	0.1[c]
Threatened species (number)	230	282	698[b]
Forested area (% of land area)	34.7	33.5	32.9[l]
CO2 emission estimates (million tons/tons per capita)	12.5 / 0.7	17.5 / 1.0	18.6 / 0.9[l]
Energy production, primary (Petajoules)	279	311	360[l]
Energy supply per capita (Gigajoules)	27	30	32[l]
Tourist/visitor arrivals at national borders (000)	1 119	1 473	602[c]
Important sites for terrestrial biodiversity protected (%)	26.1	29.8	31.1[b]
Pop. using safely managed drinking water (urban/rural, %)	61.5 / 42.5	64.5 / 43.9	65.5 / 46.0[b]
Net Official Development Assist. received (% of GNI)	1.01	0.68	0.61[c]

a Projected estimate (medium fertility variant). **b** 2022. **c** 2021. **d** 2019. **e** Excludes irrigation canals and landscaping care. **f** Data classified according to ISIC Rev. 4. **g** Excludes publishing activities, recycling. Includes irrigation canals. **h** Estimate. **i** Break in the time series. **j** Data refers to a 5-year period preceding the reference year. **k** Including refugees. **l** 2020. **m** Data as at the end of December. **n** Data based on calendar year (January 1 to December 31). **o** Country is still reporting data based on SHA 1.0. **p** 2009. **q** 2014. **r** Data are as at 1 January of reporting year. **s** Population aged 12 years and over. **t** Partial data.

Region	Western Africa	UN membership date	12 December 1958
Population (000, 2023)	13 859[a,b]	Surface area (km2)	245 836[c]
Pop. density (per km2, 2023)	56.4[a,b]	Sex ratio (m per 100 f)	97.8[a,b]
Capital city	Conakry	National currency	Guinean Franc (GNF)
Capital city pop. (000, 2023)	1 889.2[d]	Exchange rate (per US$)	9 990.0[e]

Economic indicators	2010	2015	2023
GDP: Gross domestic product (million current US$)	6 853	8 794	16 036[c]
GDP growth rate (annual %, const. 2015 prices)	4.8	3.8	3.8[c]
GDP per capita (current US$)	667.3	756.4	1 185.1[c]
Economy: Agriculture (% of Gross Value Added)	18.6	20.1	28.1[c]
Economy: Industry (% of Gross Value Added)	34.3	28.6	31.0[c]
Economy: Services and other activity (% of GVA)	47.1	51.3	40.9[c]
Employment in agriculture (% of employed)[f]	66.7	62.9	59.2[c]
Employment in industry (% of employed)[f]	5.7	6.0	7.1[c]
Employment in services & other sectors (% employed)[f]	27.6	31.1	33.8[c]
Unemployment rate (% of labour force)[f]	4.8	4.9	5.7
Labour force participation rate (female/male pop. %)[f]	53.3 / 65.5	47.2 / 64.9	41.6 / 63.6
CPI: Consumer Price Index (2010=100)[g]	100	186	362[b]
Agricultural production index (2014-2016=100)	82	100	129[c]
International trade: exports (million current US$)	1 471[f]	1 574	7 431[f,b]
International trade: imports (million current US$)	1 402[f]	2 139	4 876[f,b]
International trade: balance (million current US$)	69[f]	- 565	2 555[f,b]
Balance of payments, current account (million US$)	- 327	- 1 020	4 639[c]

Major trading partners						2022
Export partners (% of exports)[f]	China	38.4	United Arab Emirates	26.7	India	23.5
Import partners (% of imports)[f]	China	35.6	India	9.3	Netherlands	7.4

Social indicators	2010	2015	2023
Population growth rate (average annual %)	2.5	2.6	2.4[a,b]
Urban population (% of total population)	33.7	35.1	36.5[d]
Urban population growth rate (average annual %)[h]	3.0	3.1	...
Fertility rate, total (live births per woman)	5.4	5.0	4.3[a,b]
Life expectancy at birth (females/males, years)	57.8 / 55.5	59.3 / 56.9	60.2 / 57.6[a,b]
Population age distribution (0-14/60+ years old, %)	44.5 / 5.4	43.3 / 5.2	41.5 / 5.1[a,b]
International migrant stock (000/% of total pop.)[i,j]	178.8 / 1.8	126.7 / 1.1	121.4 / 0.9[e]
Refugees and others of concern to the UNHCR (000)	15.0[k]	9.0	4.4[b]
Infant mortality rate (per 1 000 live births)	78.8	72.7	63.9[a,b]
Health: Current expenditure (% of GDP)[l]	3.4	5.8	4.0[e]
Health: Physicians (per 1 000 pop.)	0.1[m]	0.1	0.2[n]
Education: Government expenditure (% of GDP)	2.6	2.5	2.1[c]
Education: Primary gross enrol. ratio (f/m per 100 pop.)	76.0 / 92.3	77.7 / 95.5	92.4 / 109.0[e]
Education: Lower. sec. gross enrol. ratio (f/m per 100 pop.)	30.3 / 49.9[o]	32.1 / 47.9	33.7 / 47.1[e]
Education: Upr. sec. gross enrol. ratio (f/m per 100 pop.)	16.0 / 32.5[o]	22.4 / 36.2	25.2 / 34.2[e]
Seats held by women in the National Parliament (%)	19.3[o]	21.9	29.6[p]

Environment and infrastructure indicators	2010	2015	2023
Individuals using the Internet (per 100 inhabitants)[f]	1.0	9.2	34.7[c]
Threatened species (number)	134	163	422[b]
Forested area (% of land area)	26.7	26.0	25.2[e]
Energy production, primary (Petajoules)	112	116	119[e]
Energy supply per capita (Gigajoules)	14	13	14[e]
Tourist/visitor arrivals at national borders (000)[q]	12	35	99[r]
Important sites for terrestrial biodiversity protected (%)	71.7	71.7	71.7[b]
Net Official Development Assist. received (% of GNI)	3.26	6.24	4.23[c]

a Projected estimate (medium fertility variant). b 2022. c 2021. d 2019. e 2020. f Estimate. g Conakry h Data refers to a 5-year period preceding the reference year. i Refers to foreign citizens. j Including refugees. k Data as at the end of December. l Data based on calendar year (January 1 to December 31). m 2005. n 2018. o 2008. p Data are as at 1 January of reporting year. q Arrivals by air at Conakry airport. r 2017.

Guinea-Bissau

Region	Western Africa	UN membership date	17 September 1974
Population (000, 2023)	2 106[a,b]	Surface area (km2)	36 125[c]
Pop. density (per km2, 2023)	74.9[a,b]	Sex ratio (m per 100 f)	97.6[a,b]
Capital city	Bissau	National currency	CFA Franc, BCEAO (XOF)[d]
Capital city pop. (000, 2023)	578.8[e]	Exchange rate (per US$)	615.0[b]

Economic indicators

	2010	2015	2023
GDP: Gross domestic product (million current US$)	849	1 047	1 563[c]
GDP growth rate (annual %, const. 2015 prices)	4.6	6.1	5.0[c]
GDP per capita (current US$)	541.8	585.5	758.6[c]
Economy: Agriculture (% of Gross Value Added)	46.2	49.0	32.4[c]
Economy: Industry (% of Gross Value Added)	13.5	12.8	13.9[c]
Economy: Services and other activity (% of GVA)	40.3	38.2	53.7[c]
Employment in agriculture (% of employed)[f]	58.3	56.5	50.3[c]
Employment in industry (% of employed)[f]	9.8	9.9	10.4[c]
Employment in services & other sectors (% employed)[f]	32.0	33.7	39.1[c]
Unemployment rate (% of labour force)[f]	3.1	3.1	3.6
Labour force participation rate (female/male pop. %)[f]	48.6 / 64.6	48.7 / 64.1	49.0 / 63.1
CPI: Consumer Price Index (2010=100)[g]	100	109	128[b]
Agricultural production index (2014-2016=100)	95	101	121[c]
International trade: exports (million current US$)[f]	120	548	264[b]
International trade: imports (million current US$)[f]	197	221	403[b]
International trade: balance (million current US$)[f]	- 77	327	- 139[b]
Balance of payments, current account (million US$)	- 71	21	- 14[c]

Major trading partners

						2022
Export partners (% of exports)[f]	India	74.4	Côte d'Ivoire	11.7	Pakistan	8.2
Import partners (% of imports)[f]	Portugal	31.9	Senegal	19.3	China	13.2

Social indicators

	2010	2015	2023
Population growth rate (average annual %)	2.6	2.6	2.1[a,b]
Urban population (% of total population)	40.1	42.1	43.8[e]
Urban population growth rate (average annual %)[h]	3.4	3.6	...
Fertility rate, total (live births per woman)	5.1	4.7	3.9[a,b]
Life expectancy at birth (females/males, years)	58.4 / 53.9	61.2 / 56.9	61.9 / 57.7[a,b]
Population age distribution (0-14/60+ years old, %)	43.6 / 4.2	42.8 / 4.3	40.1 / 4.5[a,b]
International migrant stock (000/% of total pop.)[i]	21.4 / 1.4	22.3 / 1.3	17.9 / 0.9[j]
Refugees and others of concern to the UNHCR (000)	8.0[k]	8.8	0.1[b]
Infant mortality rate (per 1 000 live births)	73.6	61.2	50.1[a,b]
Health: Current expenditure (% of GDP)[l]	6.3	8.1	8.4[j]
Health: Physicians (per 1 000 pop.)	0.1[m]	0.2	0.2[c]
Education: Government expenditure (% of GDP)	1.9	2.4	2.6[c]
Education: Primary gross enrol. ratio (f/m per 100 pop.)	114.5 / 122.9	... / ...	... / ...
Intentional homicide rate (per 100 000 pop.)	...	...	1.1[n]
Seats held by women in the National Parliament (%)	10.0	13.7	13.7[o]

Environment and infrastructure indicators

	2010	2015	2023
Individuals using the Internet (per 100 inhabitants)[f]	2.4	6.1	35.2[c]
Threatened species (number)	52	66	125[b]
Forested area (% of land area)	73.4	71.9	70.4[j]
Energy production, primary (Petajoules)	24	25	27[j]
Energy supply per capita (Gigajoules)	18	17	16[j]
Tourist/visitor arrivals at national borders (000)[p]	22	44	52[e]
Important sites for terrestrial biodiversity protected (%)	45.1	59.5	59.5[b]
Pop. using safely managed drinking water (urban/rural, %)	39.4 / 8.2	38.1 / 10.6	36.3 / 13.7[b]
Pop. using safely managed sanitation (urban/rural %)	12.0 / 3.8	16.1 / 6.9	21.3 / 10.7[b]
Net Official Development Assist. received (% of GNI)	15.25	8.86	10.31[c]

a Projected estimate (medium fertility variant). b 2022. c 2021. d African Financial Community (CFA) Franc, Central Bank of West African States (BCEAO). e 2019. f Estimate. g Bissau h Data refers to a 5-year period preceding the reference year. i Including refugees. j 2020. k Data as at the end of December. l Data based on calendar year (January 1 to December 31). m 2009. n 2017. o Data are as at 1 January of reporting year. p Arrivals at "Osvaldo Vieira" Airport.

Guyana

		UN membership date	20 September 1966
Region	South America	Surface area (km2)	214 969 c
Population (000, 2023)	809 a,b	Sex ratio (m per 100 f)	95.9 a,b
Pop. density (per km2, 2023)	4.1 a,b	National currency	Guyana Dollar (GYD)
Capital city	Georgetown	Exchange rate (per US$)	208.5 c
Capital city pop. (000, 2023)	109.9 d		

Economic indicators	2010	2015	2023
GDP: Gross domestic product (million current US$)	3 433	4 280	8 044 c
GDP growth rate (annual %, const. 2015 prices)	4.1	0.7	20.1 c
GDP per capita (current US$)	4 589.9	5 668.4	9 998.5 c
Economy: Agriculture (% of Gross Value Added) e,f	30.0	27.0	19.5 c
Economy: Industry (% of Gross Value Added) f,g	26.2	26.2	33.8 c
Economy: Services and other activity (% of GVA) f	43.8	46.8	46.7 c
Employment in agriculture (% of employed)	20.2 h	18.8 h	13.1 c
Employment in industry (% of employed)	23.8 h	23.1 h	25.4 c
Employment in services & other sectors (% employed)	56.1 h	58.2 h	61.6 c
Unemployment rate (% of labour force) h	11.8	13.3	11.8
Labour force participation rate (female/male pop. %) h	38.2 / 73.2	40.9 / 69.2	39.3 / 60.9
CPI: Consumer Price Index (2010=100) h,i	100	109	123 c
Agricultural production index (2014-2016=100)	77	111	106 c
International trade: exports (million current US$)	901	1 169	7 893 b
International trade: imports (million current US$)	1 452	1 484	8 586 b
International trade: balance (million current US$)	- 551	- 315	- 693 b
Balance of payments, current account (million US$)	- 246	- 39	- 2 087 c

Major trading partners						2022
Export partners (% of exports)	United States	34.4	Trinidad and Tobago	25.9	Singapore	10.2
Import partners (% of imports)	Bahamas	59.6	United States	14.3	Trinidad and Tobago	4.9

Social indicators	2010	2015	2023
Population growth rate (average annual %)	- 0.5	0.5	0.5 a,b
Urban population (% of total population)	26.6	26.4	26.7 j
Urban population growth rate (average annual %) k	- 1.0	0.4	...
Fertility rate, total (live births per woman)	2.7	2.5	2.4 a,b
Life expectancy at birth (females/males, years)	70.2 / 63.6	71.6 / 65.0	69.4 / 62.8 a,b
Population age distribution (0-14/60+ years old, %)	32.3 / 7.1	30.1 / 8.3	28.6 / 9.9 a,b
International migrant stock (000/% of total pop.) l	8.2 / 1.1	8.7 / 1.1	31.2 / 4.0 m
Refugees and others of concern to the UNHCR (000)	~0.0 n	~0.0	19.5 b
Infant mortality rate (per 1 000 live births)	30.1	26.9	23.6 a,b
Health: Current expenditure (% of GDP) h,o	4.2	4.0	5.5 m
Health: Physicians (per 1 000 pop.)	0.7	...	1.4 m
Education: Government expenditure (% of GDP)	2.4	3.9	4.5 h,d
Education: Primary gross enrol. ratio (f/m per 100 pop.)	95.0 / 97.9	96.0 / 99.6 p	... / ...
Education: Lower. sec. gross enrol. ratio (f/m per 100 pop.)	103.7 / 100.5	105.3 / 104.5 p	... / ...
Education: Upr. sec. gross enrol. ratio (f/m per 100 pop.)	74.0 / 69.6	90.0 / 83.8 p	... / ...
Intentional homicide rate (per 100 000 pop.)	18.7	19.7	16.3 c
Seats held by women in the National Parliament (%)	30.0	31.3	36.6 q

Environment and infrastructure indicators	2010	2015	2023
Individuals using the Internet (per 100 inhabitants)	29.9	34.0 h	84.8 h,c
Threatened species (number)	69	87	202 b
Forested area (% of land area)	94.1	93.8	93.6 m
CO2 emission estimates (million tons/tons per capita)	1.8 / 2.3	2.1 / 2.7	2.7 / 3.3 m
Energy production, primary (Petajoules)	8	7	4 m
Energy supply per capita (Gigajoules)	46	46	49 m
Tourist/visitor arrivals at national borders (000)	152	207	158 c
Important sites for terrestrial biodiversity protected (%)	100.0	100.0	100.0 b
Pop. using safely managed sanitation (urban/rural %)	39.1 / 54.7	37.0 / 51.9	34.1 / 48.0 b
Net Official Development Assist. received (% of GNI)	3.09	0.75	1.95 c

a Projected estimate (medium fertility variant). b 2022. c 2021. d 2018. e Excludes irrigation canals and landscaping care. f Data classified according to ISIC Rev. 4. g Excludes publishing activities, recycling. Includes irrigation canals. h Estimate. i Georgetown j 2019. k Data refers to a 5-year period preceding the reference year. l Including refugees. m 2020. n Data as at the end of December. o Data based on calendar year (January 1 to December 31). p 2012. q Data are as at 1 January of reporting year.

Haiti

Region	Caribbean	UN membership date	24 October 1945
Population (000, 2023)	11 585[a,b]	Surface area (km2)	27 750[c]
Pop. density (per km2, 2023)	420.2[a,b]	Sex ratio (m per 100 f)	98.2[a,b]
Capital city	Port-au-Prince	National currency	Gourde (HTG)
Capital city pop. (000, 2023)	2 704.2[d]	Exchange rate (per US$)	145.4[b]

Economic indicators

	2010	2015	2023
GDP: Gross domestic product (million current US$)	11 812	14 228	19 044[c]
GDP growth rate (annual %, const. 2015 prices)	- 3.8	1.6	- 1.8[c]
GDP per capita (current US$)	1 200.0	1 346.8	1 663.6[c]
Economy: Agriculture (% of Gross Value Added)[e,f]	21.0	18.0	21.1[c]
Economy: Industry (% of Gross Value Added)[f,g]	24.4	27.1	26.1[c]
Economy: Services and other activity (% of GVA)[f]	54.5	54.9	52.8[c]
Employment in agriculture (% of employed)[h]	49.7	47.7	45.6[c]
Employment in industry (% of employed)[h]	11.4	12.0	12.4[c]
Employment in services & other sectors (% employed)[h]	39.0	40.2	42.1[c]
Unemployment rate (% of labour force)[h]	15.4	13.9	15.6
Labour force participation rate (female/male pop. %)	60.6 / 70.8	62.0 / 70.0[h]	62.3 / 69.3[h]
CPI: Consumer Price Index (2010=100)	100	139	236[i,b]
Agricultural production index (2014-2016=100)	90	98	82[c]
International trade: exports (million current US$)[h]	579	1 018	1 205[b]
International trade: imports (million current US$)[h]	3 147	3 523	2 339[b]
International trade: balance (million current US$)[h]	- 2 568	- 2 505	- 1 135[b]
Balance of payments, current account (million US$)	- 102	- 271	141[c]

Major trading partners

							2022
Export partners (% of exports)[h]	United States	83.1	Canada	3.9	Mexico	3.2
Import partners (% of imports)[h]	United States	32.5	Dominican Rep.	23.1	China	14.4

Social indicators

	2010	2015	2023
Population growth rate (average annual %)	0.7	1.4	1.2[a,b]
Urban population (% of total population)	47.5	52.4	56.2[d]
Urban population growth rate (average annual %)[j]	3.7	3.3	...
Fertility rate, total (live births per woman)	3.5	3.1	2.8[a,b]
Life expectancy at birth (females/males, years)	46.3 / 45.8	66.0 / 60.6	66.7 / 60.9[a,b]
Population age distribution (0-14/60+ years old, %)	36.0 / 6.1	34.2 / 6.5	32.1 / 7.1[a,b]
International migrant stock (000/% of total pop.)[k]	17.2 / 0.2	18.0 / 0.2	18.9 / 0.2[l]
Refugees and others of concern to the UNHCR (000)	~0.0[m]	~0.0	~0.0[c]
Infant mortality rate (per 1 000 live births)	75.9	52.8	43.4[a,b]
Health: Current expenditure (% of GDP)[h,n]	4.5[o]	5.1[p]	3.3[l]
Health: Physicians (per 1 000 pop.)	...	0.1	0.2[q]
Education: Government expenditure (% of GDP)	...	1.9	1.8[c]
Intentional homicide rate (per 100 000 pop.)	6.9	10.1	13.0[c]
Seats held by women in the National Parliament (%)	4.1	4.2	2.5[r,s,l]

Environment and infrastructure indicators

	2010	2015	2023
Individuals using the Internet (per 100 inhabitants)[h]	8.4	14.2	38.9[c]
Threatened species (number)	137	169	450[b]
Forested area (% of land area)	13.7	13.2	12.6[l]
CO2 emission estimates (million tons/tons per capita)	3.1 / 0.2	4.0 / 0.3	3.9 / 0.3[l]
Energy production, primary (Petajoules)	131	139	142[l]
Energy supply per capita (Gigajoules)	16	17	16[l]
Tourist/visitor arrivals at national borders (000)[t,u]	255	516	148[c]
Important sites for terrestrial biodiversity protected (%)	12.2	24.3	29.2[b]
Net Official Development Assist. received (% of GNI)	24.32	7.03	4.54[c]

a Projected estimate (medium fertility variant). b 2022. c 2021. d 2019. e Excludes irrigation canals and landscaping care. f Data classified according to ISIC Rev. 4. g Excludes publishing activities, recycling. Includes irrigation canals. h Estimate. i Base: October 2017-September 2018=100. j Data refers to a 5-year period preceding the reference year. k Including refugees. l 2020. m Data as at the end of December. n Data refer to fiscal years beginning 1 October. o Estimates should be viewed with caution as these are derived from scarce data. p Data are based on SHA2011. q 2018. r The term of all members in the 119-member Chamber of Deputies and 20 of 30 senators expired on 13 January 2020. There are currently only 10 sitting senators. s Data are as at 1 January of reporting year. t Arrivals by air. u Including nationals residing abroad.

Holy See

Region	Southern Europe	Surface area (km2)	~0 [a,b]
Pop. density (per km2, 2023)	1 160.2 [c,d,e]	Capital city	Vatican City
National currency	Euro (EUR)	Capital city pop. (000, 2023)	0.8 [f]
Exchange rate (per US$)	0.9 [e]		

Social indicators	2010	2015	2023
Population growth rate (average annual %) [c]	- 0.5	- 1.1	1.0 [d,e]
Urban population (% of total population)	100.0	100.0	100.0 [g]
Urban population growth rate (average annual %) [h]	- 0.1	0.2	...
International migrant stock (000/% of total pop.) [c,i]	0.8 / 100.0	0.8 / 100.0	0.8 / 100.0 [i]
Intentional homicide rate (per 100 000 pop.)	0.0	0.0	0.0 [b]

Environment and infrastructure indicators	2010	2015	2023
Threatened species (number)	1	1	2 [e]
Forested area (% of land area)	0.0	0.0	0.0 [i]

a Surface area is 0.44 Km2. **b** 2021. **c** Data refer to the Vatican City State. **d** Projected estimate (medium fertility variant). **e** 2022. **f** 2018. **g** 2019. **h** Data refers to a 5-year period preceding the reference year. **i** Estimate. **j** 2020.

Honduras

Region	Central America	UN membership date	17 December 1945
Population (000, 2023)	10 433 a,b	Surface area (km2)	112 492 c
Pop. density (per km2, 2023)	95.6 a,b	Sex ratio (m per 100 f)	102.0 a,b
Capital city	Tegucigalpa	National currency	Lempira (HNL)
Capital city pop. (000, 2023)	1 403.2 d	Exchange rate (per US$)	24.6 b

Economic indicators

	2010	2015	2023
GDP: Gross domestic product (million current US$)	15 839	20 980	28 489 c
GDP growth rate (annual %, const. 2015 prices)	3.7	3.8	12.5 c
GDP per capita (current US$)	1 874.3	2 257.2	2 771.7 c
Economy: Agriculture (% of Gross Value Added)	11.9	12.6	11.7 c
Economy: Industry (% of Gross Value Added)	26.2	26.5	28.1 c
Economy: Services and other activity (% of GVA)	62.0	60.8	60.2 c
Employment in agriculture (% of employed)	36.5	28.7	24.8 e,c
Employment in industry (% of employed)	19.2	21.9	23.4 e,c
Employment in services & other sectors (% employed)	44.5	49.5	51.9 e,c
Unemployment rate (% of labour force)	4.1	6.2	7.5 e
Labour force participation rate (female/male pop. %)	42.6 / 81.1	46.5 / 81.5	49.8 / 77.3 e
CPI: Consumer Price Index (2010=100) e	100	129	177 b
Agricultural production index (2014-2016=100)	91	100	107 c
International trade: exports (million current US$)	3 104	4 201	5 845 e,b
International trade: imports (million current US$)	6 895	8 381	13 365 e,b
International trade: balance (million current US$)	- 3 791	- 4 179	- 7 520 e,b
Balance of payments, current account (million US$)	- 804	- 980	- 1 074 b

Major trading partners

						2022
Export partners (% of exports) e	United States	43.3	Germany	6.7	El Salvador	6.0
Import partners (% of imports) e	United States	34.3	China	17.9	Mexico	7.6

Social indicators

	2010	2015	2023
Population growth rate (average annual %)	2.0	1.8	1.5 a,b
Urban population (% of total population)	51.9	55.2	57.7 d
Urban population growth rate (average annual %) f	3.4	3.0	...
Fertility rate, total (live births per woman)	3.0	2.6	2.3 a,b
Life expectancy at birth (females/males, years)	73.3 / 69.0	75.0 / 70.2	73.2 / 68.5 a,b
Population age distribution (0-14/60+ years old, %)	37.7 / 5.0	34.2 / 5.7	30.1 / 6.6 a,b
International migrant stock (000/% of total pop.) g	27.3 / 0.3	38.3 / 0.4	39.2 / 0.4 h
Refugees and others of concern to the UNHCR (000)	~0.0 i	~0.0	304.1 b
Infant mortality rate (per 1 000 live births)	19.7	16.2	12.8 a,b
Health: Current expenditure (% of GDP) j	8.7 e	7.5 e	9.1 k,l,c
Health: Physicians (per 1 000 pop.)	0.3	...	0.5 h
Education: Government expenditure (% of GDP)	...	6.4	6.1 m
Education: Primary gross enrol. ratio (f/m per 100 pop.)	100.7 / 100.6	96.3 / 96.7 n	88.6 / 87.1 c
Education: Lowr. sec. gross enrol. ratio (f/m per 100 pop.)	70.3 / 61.7	68.7 / 60.5 n	... / ...
Education: Upr. sec. gross enrol. ratio (f/m per 100 pop.)	76.7 / 55.0	72.7 / 53.3 n	... / ...
Intentional homicide rate (per 100 000 pop.)	73.8	55.4	38.3 c
Seats held by women in the National Parliament (%)	18.0	25.8	27.3 o

Environment and infrastructure indicators

	2010	2015	2023
Individuals using the Internet (per 100 inhabitants)	11.1	27.1 p	48.1 e,c
Research & Development expenditure (% of GDP)	...	~0.0 k,q	0.1 d
Threatened species (number)	240	294	480 b
Forested area (% of land area)	58.8	57.8	56.8 b
CO2 emission estimates (million tons/tons per capita)	8.1 / 0.9	10.7 / 1.1	8.9 / 0.8 h
Energy production, primary (Petajoules)	97	103	101 h
Energy supply per capita (Gigajoules)	23	26	22 h
Tourist/visitor arrivals at national borders (000)	863	880	459 c
Important sites for terrestrial biodiversity protected (%)	72.1	72.1	72.3 b
Pop. using safely managed drinking water (urban/rural, %)	65.6 / 41.5	77.5 / 43.3	78.4 / 45.7 b
Pop. using safely managed sanitation (urban/rural %)	39.5 / 58.6	39.9 / 63.6	40.5 / 70.5 b
Net Official Development Assist. received (% of GNI)	3.11	2.77	2.36 c

a Projected estimate (medium fertility variant). b 2022. c 2021. d 2019. e Estimate. f Data refers to a 5-year period preceding the reference year. g Including refugees. h 2020. i Data as at the end of December. j Data based on calendar year (January 1 to December 31). k Break in the time series. l Data are based on SHA2011. m 2018. n 2012. o Data are as at 1 January of reporting year. p Users in the last 3 months. q Partial data.

Hungary

Region	Eastern Europe
Population (000, 2023)	9 967 [a,b]
Pop. density (per km2, 2023)	110.1 [a,b]
Capital city	Budapest
Capital city pop. (000, 2023)	1 763.9 [d]

UN membership date	14 December 1955
Surface area (km2)	93 023 [c]
Sex ratio (m per 100 f)	92.3 [a,b]
National currency	Forint (HUF)
Exchange rate (per US$)	375.7 [b]

Economic indicators	2010	2015	2023
GDP: Gross domestic product (million current US$)	132 175	125 174	181 848 [c]
GDP growth rate (annual %, const. 2015 prices)	1.1	3.7	7.1 [c]
GDP per capita (current US$)	13 235.0	12 715.5	18 728.3 [c]
Economy: Agriculture (% of Gross Value Added) [e,f]	3.6	4.5	4.0 [c]
Economy: Industry (% of Gross Value Added) [f,g]	29.7	31.3	28.7 [c]
Economy: Services and other activity (% of GVA) [f]	66.7	64.2	67.4 [c]
Employment in agriculture (% of employed)	4.5	4.9	4.4 [c]
Employment in industry (% of employed)	30.7	30.3	31.4 [c]
Employment in services & other sectors (% employed)	64.8	64.8	64.2 [c]
Unemployment rate (% of labour force)	11.2	6.8	3.5 [h]
Labour force participation rate (female/male pop. %)	43.6 / 58.1	47.0 / 63.0	51.8 / 67.3 [h]
CPI: Consumer Price Index (2010=100)	100	111	151 [b]
Agricultural production index (2014-2016=100)	79	95	92 [c]
International trade: exports (million current US$)	94 749	100 297	149 581 [b]
International trade: imports (million current US$)	87 432	90 761	158 414 [b]
International trade: balance (million current US$)	7 317	9 536	- 8 833 [b]
Balance of payments, current account (million US$)	342	2 926	- 14 243 [b]

Major trading partners						2022
Export partners (% of exports)	Germany	25.2	Italy	5.7	Romania	5.3
Import partners (% of imports)	Germany	21.2	Austria	7.2	China	6.8

Social indicators	2010	2015	2023
Population growth rate (average annual %)	- 0.3	- 0.3	5.6 [a,b]
Urban population (% of total population)	68.9	70.5	71.6 [d]
Urban population growth rate (average annual %) [i]	0.4	0.2	...
Fertility rate, total (live births per woman)	1.3	1.4	1.6 [a,b]
Life expectancy at birth (females/males, years)	78.3 / 70.6	78.9 / 72.2	78.3 / 71.6 [a,b]
Population age distribution (0-14/60+ years old, %)	14.7 / 22.6	14.5 / 25.4	14.4 / 25.8 [a,b]
International migrant stock (000/% of total pop.)	436.6 / 4.4	475.5 / 4.9	584.6 / 6.1 [i]
Refugees and others of concern to the UNHCR (000)	5.8 [k]	28.8	31.6 [b]
Infant mortality rate (per 1 000 live births)	5.2	4.1	3.3 [a,b]
Health: Current expenditure (% of GDP)	7.4 [l]	6.9 [l]	7.3 [j]
Health: Physicians (per 1 000 pop.)	2.9	3.1	3.3 [c]
Education: Government expenditure (% of GDP)	4.7	4.5	4.2 [d]
Education: Primary gross enrol. ratio (f/m per 100 pop.)	100.5 / 101.2	102.2 / 102.5	94.9 / 96.9 [j]
Education: Lowr. sec. gross enrol. ratio (f/m per 100 pop.)	96.1 / 98.7	98.8 / 99.9	100.9 / 101.3 [j]
Education: Upr. sec. gross enrol. ratio (f/m per 100 pop.)	96.7 / 96.8	107.6 / 105.4	104.6 / 105.3 [j]
Intentional homicide rate (per 100 000 pop.)	1.4	2.2	0.8 [c]
Seats held by women in the National Parliament (%)	11.1	10.1	13.1 [m]

Environment and infrastructure indicators	2010	2015	2023
Individuals using the Internet (per 100 inhabitants)	65.0 [n]	72.8 [o]	88.6 [c]
Research & Development expenditure (% of GDP)	1.1	1.3	1.6 [j]
Threatened species (number)	47	67	143 [b]
Forested area (% of land area)	22.6	22.6	22.5 [j]
CO2 emission estimates (million tons/tons per capita)	48.3 / 4.7	43.9 / 4.3	47.0 / 4.7 [c]
Energy production, primary (Petajoules)	495	471	449 [j]
Energy supply per capita (Gigajoules)	111	107	113 [j]
Tourist/visitor arrivals at national borders (000)	9 510	14 316	7 929 [c]
Important sites for terrestrial biodiversity protected (%)	84.3	84.3	84.3 [b]
Pop. using safely managed drinking water (urban/rural, %)	89.7 / 81.0	93.3 / 87.7	100.0 / 100.0 [b]
Pop. using safely managed sanitation (urban/rural %)	77.3 / 69.2	86.0 / 75.5	90.5 / 80.7 [b]
Net Official Development Assist. disbursed (% of GNI) [p]	0.09	0.13	4.09 [c]

a Projected estimate (medium fertility variant). b 2022. c 2021. d 2019. e Excludes irrigation canals and landscaping care. f Data classified according to ISIC Rev. 4. g Excludes publishing activities, recycling. Includes irrigation canals. h Estimate. i Data refers to a 5-year period preceding the reference year. j 2020. k Data as at the end of December. l Break in the time series. m Data are as at 1 January of reporting year. n Population aged 16 to 74 years. o Users in the last 3 months. p Development Assistance Committee member (OECD).

Iceland

Region	Northern Europe	UN membership date	19 November 1946
Population (000, 2023)	373 [a,b]	Surface area (km2)	103 000 [c]
Pop. density (per km2, 2023)	3.7 [a,b]	Sex ratio (m per 100 f)	105.2 [a,b]
Capital city	Reykjavik	National currency	Iceland Krona (ISK)
Capital city pop. (000, 2023)	216.4 [d]	Exchange rate (per US$)	142.0 [b]

Economic indicators

	2010	2015	2023
GDP: Gross domestic product (million current US$)	13 751	17 517	25 602 [c]
GDP growth rate (annual %, const. 2015 prices)	- 2.8	4.4	4.4 [c]
GDP per capita (current US$)	43 197.4	52 912.5	69 133.1 [c]
Economy: Agriculture (% of Gross Value Added) [e,f]	7.0	5.9	5.1 [c]
Economy: Industry (% of Gross Value Added) [e,g]	24.4	22.5	22.8 [c]
Economy: Services and other activity (% of GVA) [e]	68.6	71.6	72.2 [c]
Employment in agriculture (% of employed)	5.6	4.2	0.2 [h,c]
Employment in industry (% of employed)	18.5	17.9	11.2 [h,c]
Employment in services & other sectors (% employed)	75.9	77.9	77.2 [c]
Unemployment rate (% of labour force)	7.6	4.0	3.7 [h]
Labour force participation rate (female/male pop. %) [h]	70.6 / 79.2	73.2 / 81.1	72.5 / 80.5
CPI: Consumer Price Index (2010=100)	100	118	150 [b]
Agricultural production index (2014-2016=100)	89	100	103 [c]
International trade: exports (million current US$)	4 603	4 722	7 404 [b]
International trade: imports (million current US$)	3 914	5 285	9 644 [b]
International trade: balance (million current US$)	689	- 563	- 2 240 [b]
Balance of payments, current account (million US$)	- 845	986	- 448 [b]

Major trading partners
2022

Export partners (% of exports)	Netherlands	37.7	United Kingdom	9.0	United States	7.8
Import partners (% of imports)	Norway	12.3	China	9.4	Germany	8.3

Social indicators

	2010	2015	2023
Population growth rate (average annual %)	0.3	1.0	0.7 [a,b]
Urban population (% of total population)	93.6	93.7	93.9 [i]
Urban population growth rate (average annual %) [j]	1.8	0.6	...
Fertility rate, total (live births per woman)	2.2	1.8	1.7 [a,b]
Life expectancy at birth (females/males, years)	83.8 / 79.6	83.6 / 81.1	84.3 / 81.4 [a,b]
Population age distribution (0-14/60+ years old, %)	20.9 / 17.0	20.2 / 19.1	18.5 / 21.0 [a,b]
International migrant stock (000/% of total pop.)	35.1 / 11.0	39.1 / 11.8	65.4 / 19.2 [k]
Refugees and others of concern to the UNHCR (000)	0.2 [l]	0.4	4.0 [b]
Infant mortality rate (per 1 000 live births)	2.1	2.0	1.4 [a,b]
Health: Current expenditure (% of GDP)	8.4	8.1	9.7 [c]
Health: Physicians (per 1 000 pop.)	3.6	3.8	3.9 [i]
Education: Government expenditure (% of GDP)	6.9	7.5	7.6 [i]
Education: Primary gross enrol. ratio (f/m per 100 pop.)	99.6 / 99.0	98.6 / 98.7	101.4 / 100.6 [k]
Education: Lowr. sec. gross enrol. ratio (f/m per 100 pop.)	94.6 / 96.0	100.6 / 99.7	100.5 / 102.3 [k]
Education: Upr. sec. gross enrol. ratio (f/m per 100 pop.)	118.1 / 114.2	132.9 / 131.7	121.1 / 127.7 [k]
Intentional homicide rate (per 100 000 pop.)	0.6	0.9	0.5 [c]
Seats held by women in the National Parliament (%)	42.9	41.3	47.6 [m]

Environment and infrastructure indicators

	2010	2015	2023
Individuals using the Internet (per 100 inhabitants)	93.4 [n,o]	98.2 [h]	99.7 [c]
Research & Development expenditure (% of GDP)	2.6 [p]	2.2	2.5 [k]
Threatened species (number)	17	21	41 [b]
Forested area (% of land area)	0.4	0.5	0.5 [k]
CO2 emission estimates (million tons/tons per capita)	2.0 / 6.1	2.1 / 6.2	1.6 / 4.2 [c]
Energy production, primary (Petajoules)	260	299	335 [k]
Energy supply per capita (Gigajoules)	900	986	988 [k]
Tourist/visitor arrivals at national borders (000)	489	1 289	698 [c]
Important sites for terrestrial biodiversity protected (%)	16.1	18.3	19.6 [b]
Net Official Development Assist. disbursed (% of GNI) [q]	0.26	0.24	0.28 [c]

a Projected estimate (medium fertility variant). b 2022. c 2021. d 2018. e Data classified according to ISIC Rev. 4. f Excludes irrigation canals and landscaping care. g Excludes publishing activities, recycling. Includes irrigation canals. h Estimate. i 2019. j Data refers to a 5-year period preceding the reference year. k 2020. l Data as at the end of December. m Data are as at 1 January of reporting year. n Population aged 16 to 74 years. o Users in the last 3 months. p 2009. q Development Assistance Committee member (OECD).

India

Region	Southern Asia	UN membership date	30 October 1945
Population (000, 2023)	1 417 173[a,b]	Surface area (km2)	3 287 263[c]
Pop. density (per km2, 2023)	476.7[a,b]	Sex ratio (m per 100 f)	106.6[a,b]
Capital city	New Delhi	National currency	Indian Rupee (INR)
Capital city pop. (000, 2023)	29 399.1[d,e]	Exchange rate (per US$)	82.8[b]

Economic indicators	2010	2015	2023
GDP: Gross domestic product (million current US$)	1 669 620	2 146 759	3 201 471[c]
GDP growth rate (annual %, const. 2015 prices)	8.5	8.0	8.7[c]
GDP per capita (current US$)	1 345.8	1 622.8	2 274.5[c]
Economy: Agriculture (% of Gross Value Added)[f,g]	18.4	17.7	18.6[c]
Economy: Industry (% of Gross Value Added)[g,h]	33.1	30.0	28.7[c]
Economy: Services and other activity (% of GVA)[g]	48.5	52.3	52.7[c]
Employment in agriculture (% of employed)	51.5	45.2[i]	44.0[c]
Employment in industry (% of employed)	20.8[i]	24.6[i]	25.3[c]
Employment in services & other sectors (% employed)	26.7	30.3[i]	30.7[i,c]
Unemployment rate (% of labour force)[i]	8.3	7.9	7.3
Labour force participation rate (female/male pop. %)	28.8 / 79.3	23.7 / 75.9[i]	24.1 / 73.8[i]
CPI: Consumer Price Index (2010=100)[j]	100	149	212[b]
Agricultural production index (2014-2016=100)	86	98	122[c]
International trade: exports (million current US$)	220 408	264 381	452 684[b]
International trade: imports (million current US$)	350 029	390 745	732 566[b]
International trade: balance (million current US$)	- 129 621	- 126 364	- 279 882[b]
Balance of payments, current account (million US$)	- 54 516	- 22 457	- 80 433[b]

Major trading partners					2022
Export partners (% of exports)	United States	17.7	United Arab Emirates 6.9	Netherlands	4.1
Import partners (% of imports)	China	14.0	United Arab Emirates 7.4	United States	7.1

Social indicators	2010	2015	2023
Population growth rate (average annual %)	1.4	1.2	0.7[a,b]
Urban population (% of total population)	30.9	32.8	34.5[e]
Urban population growth rate (average annual %)[k]	2.6	2.4	...
Fertility rate, total (live births per woman)	2.6	2.3	2.0[a,b]
Life expectancy at birth (females/males, years)	68.6 / 65.3	71.1 / 68.3	69.4 / 66.3[a,b]
Population age distribution (0-14/60+ years old, %)	31.0 / 7.8	28.6 / 8.9	25.3 / 10.5[a,b]
International migrant stock (000/% of total pop.)[l]	5 574.0 / 0.5	5 210.8 / 0.4	4 878.7 / 0.4[m]
Refugees and others of concern to the UNHCR (000)	193.7[n]	205.8	249.5[b]
Infant mortality rate (per 1 000 live births)	45.2	34.7	26.3[a,b]
Health: Current expenditure (% of GDP)[o]	3.3	3.6[p]	3.0[i,m]
Health: Physicians (per 1 000 pop.)	...	...	0.7[m]
Education: Government expenditure (% of GDP)	3.4	4.1	4.6[c]
Education: Primary gross enrol. ratio (f/m per 100 pop.)	110.7 / 107.1[i]	102.2 / 98.3	112.0 / 111.0[b]
Education: Lowr. sec. gross enrol. ratio (f/m per 100 pop.)	78.9 / 81.0	90.5 / 84.9	90.7 / 87.7[b]
Education: Upr. sec. gross enrol. ratio (f/m per 100 pop.)	47.4 / 52.5	62.6 / 64.2	69.9 / 72.2[b]
Intentional homicide rate (per 100 000 pop.)	3.7	3.4	2.9[c]
Seats held by women in the National Parliament (%)	10.8	12.0	15.1[q]

Environment and infrastructure indicators	2010	2015	2023
Individuals using the Internet (per 100 inhabitants)	7.5[i]	14.9[i]	46.3[c]
Research & Development expenditure (% of GDP)	0.8	0.7	0.7[i,r]
Threatened species (number)	758	1 039	1 355[b]
Forested area (% of land area)	23.4	23.8	24.3[m]
CO2 emission estimates (million tons/tons per capita)[o]	1 625.1 / 1.3	2 094.1 / 1.6	2 135.2 / 1.5[m]
Energy production, primary (Petajoules)	21 105	21 875	23 600[m]
Energy supply per capita (Gigajoules)	22	27	27[m]
Tourist/visitor arrivals at national borders (000)	5 776	13 284[s]	7 010[s,c]
Important sites for terrestrial biodiversity protected (%)	1.5	6.2	6.3[b]
Pop. using safely managed drinking water (urban/rural, %)	... / 43.8	... / 52.6	... / 66.0[b]
Pop. using safely managed sanitation (urban/rural %)	29.7 / 23.8	34.8 / 38.0	42.7 / 57.4[b]
Net Official Development Assist. received (% of GNI)	0.17	0.15	0.10[c]

a Projected estimate (medium fertility variant). b 2022. c 2021. d Refers to the Delhi metropolitan area that is not restricted to state boundaries (National Capital Territory), includes contiguous suburban cities and towns, such as Faridabad, Gurgaon, and Ghaziabad. e 2019. f Excludes irrigation canals and landscaping care. g Data classified according to ISIC Rev. 4. h Excludes publishing activities, recycling. Includes irrigation canals. i Estimate. j Industrial workers. k Data refers to a 5-year period preceding the reference year. l Including refugees. m 2020. n Data as at the end of December. o Data refer to fiscal years beginning 1 April. p Break in the time series. q Data are as at 1 January of reporting year. r 2018. s Including nationals residing abroad.

Indonesia

Region	South-eastern Asia	UN membership date	28 September 1950
Population (000, 2023)	275 501 [a,b]	Surface area (km2)	1 910 931 [c]
Pop. density (per km2, 2023)	144.2 [a,b]	Sex ratio (m per 100 f)	101.4 [a,b]
Capital city	Jakarta	National currency	Rupiah (IDR)
Capital city pop. (000, 2023)	10 638.7 [d,e]	Exchange rate (per US$)	15 731.0 [b]

Economic indicators

	2010	2015	2023
GDP: Gross domestic product (million current US$)	755 094	860 854	1 186 093 [c]
GDP growth rate (annual %, const. 2015 prices)	6.2	4.9	3.7 [c]
GDP per capita (current US$)	3 094.4	3 322.6	4 332.7 [c]
Economy: Agriculture (% of Gross Value Added) [f,g]	14.3	13.9	13.8 [c]
Economy: Industry (% of Gross Value Added) [f,h]	43.9	41.4	41.5 [c]
Economy: Services and other activity (% of GVA) [f]	41.8	44.7	44.6 [c]
Employment in agriculture (% of employed)	39.1	33.0	29.0 [c]
Employment in industry (% of employed)	18.6	22.1	21.8 [c]
Employment in services & other sectors (% employed)	42.2	44.9	49.2 [c]
Unemployment rate (% of labour force)	5.6	4.5	3.3 [i]
Labour force participation rate (female/male pop. %)	50.9 / 82.3	50.7 / 82.4	53.1 / 81.0 [i]
CPI: Consumer Price Index (2010=100)	100	132	163 [b]
Agricultural production index (2014-2016=100)	91	101	118 [c]
International trade: exports (million current US$)	157 779	150 366	292 305 [i,b]
International trade: imports (million current US$)	135 663	142 695	237 171 [i,b]
International trade: balance (million current US$)	22 116	7 671	55 135 [i,b]
Balance of payments, current account (million US$)	5 144	- 17 519	13 216 [b]

Major trading partners
2022

Export partners (% of exports) [i]	China	23.2	United States	11.2	Japan	7.7
Import partners (% of imports) [i]	China	28.7	Singapore	7.9	Japan	7.5

Social indicators

	2010	2015	2023
Population growth rate (average annual %)	1.2	1.1	0.6 [a,b]
Urban population (% of total population)	49.9	53.3	56.0 [e]
Urban population growth rate (average annual %) [j]	3.0	2.6	...
Fertility rate, total (live births per woman)	2.5	2.3	2.2 [a,b]
Life expectancy at birth (females/males, years)	70.4 / 66.9	71.6 / 67.8	70.4 / 66.2 [a,b]
Population age distribution (0-14/60+ years old, %)	27.9 / 8.7	26.9 / 9.3	25.2 / 10.9 [a,b]
International migrant stock (000/% of total pop.) [k]	307.5 / 0.1	338.1 / 0.1	355.5 / 0.1 [i]
Refugees and others of concern to the UNHCR (000)	2.9 [m]	13.2	13.2 [n,b]
Infant mortality rate (per 1 000 live births)	27.6	22.8	17.7 [a,b]
Health: Current expenditure (% of GDP)	2.8 [o,p]	2.9 [o]	3.4 [p,l]
Health: Physicians (per 1 000 pop.)	0.1	0.3	0.7 [c]
Education: Government expenditure (% of GDP)	2.8	3.6	2.8 [e]
Education: Primary gross enrol. ratio (f/m per 100 pop.)	111.0 / 107.4	104.4 / 107.4	104.6 / 108.1 [q]
Education: Lowr. sec. gross enrol. ratio (f/m per 100 pop.)	89.8 / 87.4	97.8 / 93.9	98.1 / 96.9 [q]
Education: Upr. sec. gross enrol. ratio (f/m per 100 pop.)	63.1 / 64.5	74.4 / 77.8	81.9 / 78.7 [q]
Seats held by women in the National Parliament (%)	18.0	17.1	21.6 [r]

Environment and infrastructure indicators

	2010	2015	2023
Individuals using the Internet (per 100 inhabitants)	10.9 [s]	22.1	62.1 [t,c]
Research & Development expenditure (% of GDP)	0.1 [p,i,u,v]	0.1 [i,w]	0.3 [l]
Threatened species (number)	1 142	1 246	2 282 [b]
Forested area (% of land area)	53.1	50.6	49.1 [l]
CO2 emission estimates (million tons/tons per capita)	410.8 / 1.6	474.4 / 1.8	544.5 / 2.0 [l]
Energy production, primary (Petajoules) [x]	16 605	17 364	20 464 [l]
Energy supply per capita (Gigajoules) [x]	33	34	38 [l]
Tourist/visitor arrivals at national borders (000)	...	9 963	1 546 [c]
Important sites for terrestrial biodiversity protected (%)	19.7	23.0	25.9 [b]
Pop. using safely managed drinking water (urban/rural, %)	32.9 / 20.8	33.6 / 22.2	34.6 / 24.3 [b]
Net Official Development Assist. received (% of GNI)	0.18	0.04	0.05 [c]

a Projected estimate (medium fertility variant). b 2022. c 2021. d Refers to the functional urban area. e 2019. f Data classified according to ISIC Rev. 4. g Excludes irrigation canals and landscaping care. h Excludes publishing activities, recycling. Includes irrigation canals. i Estimate. j Data refers to a 5-year period preceding the reference year. k Including refugees. l 2020. m Data as at the end of December. n There are indications that a potentially sizable population of non-displaced stateless persons exists for whom no data is available. o Data revision. p Break in the time series. q 2018. r Data are as at 1 January of reporting year. s Refers to total population. t Population aged 5 years and over. u Partial data. v 2009. w 2013. x Data include Timor-Leste.

Iran (Islamic Republic of)

Region	Southern Asia	
Population (000, 2023)	88 551 [a,b]	
Pop. density (per km2, 2023)	54.4 [a,b]	
Capital city	Tehran	
Capital city pop. (000, 2023)	9 013.7 [d]	

UN membership date	24 October 1945	
Surface area (km2)	1 630 848 [c]	
Sex ratio (m per 100 f)	102.0 [a,b]	
National currency	Iranian Rial (IRR)	
Exchange rate (per US$)	42 000.0 [c]	

Economic indicators	2010	2015	2023
GDP: Gross domestic product (million current US$)	523 804	417 210	594 892 [c]
GDP growth rate (annual %, const. 2015 prices)	6.9	- 1.4	4.7 [c]
GDP per capita (current US$)	6 949.4	5 100.9	6 766.0 [c]
Economy: Agriculture (% of Gross Value Added) [e,f]	5.6	10.4	13.0 [c]
Economy: Industry (% of Gross Value Added) [e,g]	43.3	33.0	36.2 [c]
Economy: Services and other activity (% of GVA) [e]	51.1	56.6	50.8 [c]
Employment in agriculture (% of employed)	18.0	17.1	16.3 [h,c]
Employment in industry (% of employed)	33.3 [h]	32.9	34.3 [h,c]
Employment in services & other sectors (% employed)	48.7 [h]	50.0	49.4 [h,c]
Unemployment rate (% of labour force)	13.7	11.2	11.1 [h]
Labour force participation rate (female/male pop. %)	15.1 / 67.3	14.3 / 67.9	16.1 / 69.3 [h]
CPI: Consumer Price Index (2010=100) [i]	...	92	476 [b]
Agricultural production index (2014-2016=100)	90	99	84 [c]
International trade: exports (million current US$)	83 785	60 041	18 531 [h,b]
International trade: imports (million current US$)	54 697	40 037	25 291 [h,b]
International trade: balance (million current US$)	29 088	20 003	- 6 760 [h,b]

Major trading partners
2022

Export partners (% of exports) [h]	China	36.7	Türkiye	19.4	Pakistan	3.9
Import partners (% of imports) [h]	China	23.6	United Arab Emirates	22.7	Brazil	10.8

Social indicators	2010	2015	2023
Population growth rate (average annual %)	1.4	2.2	0.7 [a,b]
Urban population (% of total population)	70.6	73.4	75.4 [d]
Urban population growth rate (average annual %) [j]	2.0	2.0	...
Fertility rate, total (live births per woman)	1.8	2.1	1.7 [a,b]
Life expectancy at birth (females/males, years)	75.7 / 70.6	77.8 / 72.7	77.5 / 71.9 [a,b]
Population age distribution (0-14/60+ years old, %)	22.3 / 7.8	23.5 / 9.2	23.6 / 11.6 [a,b]
International migrant stock (000/% of total pop.) [k,l]	2 722.4 / 3.7	2 729.9 / 3.5	2 797.2 / 3.3 [m]
Refugees and others of concern to the UNHCR (000)	1 085.3 [n]	979.5	848.1 [o,b]
Infant mortality rate (per 1 000 live births)	16.3	13.1	10.3 [a,b]
Health: Current expenditure (% of GDP) [p,q]	6.3	7.3	5.3 [m]
Health: Physicians (per 1 000 pop.)	0.5 [r]	1.1	1.5 [s]
Education: Government expenditure (% of GDP)	3.7	2.6	3.2 [m]
Education: Primary gross enrol. ratio (f/m per 100 pop.)	99.6 / 101.7	112.3 / 105.7	113.0 / 106.6 [m]
Education: Lowr. sec. gross enrol. ratio (f/m per 100 pop.)	89.8 / 96.5	92.5 / 98.6 [t]	95.9 / 97.9 [m]
Education: Upr. sec. gross enrol. ratio (f/m per 100 pop.)	70.4 / 74.5	77.3 / 83.3 [t]	81.4 / 81.2 [m]
Intentional homicide rate (per 100 000 pop.)	3.0 [u]	2.4 [t]	...
Seats held by women in the National Parliament (%)	2.8	3.1	5.6 [v]

Environment and infrastructure indicators	2010	2015	2023
Individuals using the Internet (per 100 inhabitants) [w]	15.9	45.3	78.6 [c]
Research & Development expenditure (% of GDP)	0.3 [x,y]	0.4	0.8 [d]
Threatened species (number)	102	121	191 [b]
Forested area (% of land area)	6.6	6.6	6.6 [m]
CO2 emission estimates (million tons/tons per capita) [q]	503.0 / 6.8	560.8 / 7.1	572.9 / 6.8 [m]
Energy production, primary (Petajoules) [q]	14 283	13 637	13 893 [m]
Energy supply per capita (Gigajoules) [q]	114	123	127 [m]
Tourist/visitor arrivals at national borders (000)	2 938	5 237	989 [c]
Important sites for terrestrial biodiversity protected (%)	43.5	43.5	43.5 [b]
Pop. using safely managed drinking water (urban/rural, %)	95.9 / 84.1	96.0 / 85.6	96.2 / 87.1 [b]
Pop. using safely managed sanitation (urban/rural, %)	80.9 / ...	79.5 / ...	76.2 / ... [b]
Net Official Development Assist. received (% of GNI)	0.02	0.03	0.10 [m]

a Projected estimate (medium fertility variant). b 2022. c 2021. d 2019. e Data classified according to ISIC Rev. 4. f Excludes irrigation canals and landscaping care. g Excludes publishing activities, recycling. Includes irrigation canals. h Estimate. i Index base: fiscal (solar) year 2016 (21 March 2016 - 20 March 2017)=100. j Data refers to a 5-year period preceding the reference year. k Including refugees. l Refers to foreign citizens. m 2020. n Data as at the end of December. o This includes around 800,000 refugees and 40,700 UNHCR pre-registered new arrivals, reported as refugee-like. In October 2020, the country hosts 800,000 refugees, of which 780,000 are Afghan Amayesh cardholders and 20,000 are Iraqi Hoviat cardholders with refugee status. p Country is still reporting data based on SHA 1.0. q Data refer to fiscal years beginning 21 March. r 2006. s 2018. t 2014. u 2009. v Data are as at 1 January of reporting year. w Population aged 6 years and over. x Excluding private non-profit. y Excluding government.

Iraq

Region	Western Asia	UN membership date	21 December 1945
Population (000, 2023)	44 496 [a,b]	Surface area (km2)	435 052 [c]
Pop. density (per km2, 2023)	102.5 [a,b]	Sex ratio (m per 100 f)	100.4 [a,b]
Capital city	Baghdad	National currency	Iraqi Dinar (IQD)
Capital city pop. (000, 2023)	6 974.4 [d]	Exchange rate (per US$)	1 450.0 [b]

Economic indicators	2010	2015	2023
GDP: Gross domestic product (million current US$) [e]	138 517	166 774	204 004 [c]
GDP growth rate (annual %, const. 2015 prices) [e]	6.4	4.7	2.8 [c]
GDP per capita (current US$) [e]	4 430.4	4 416.9	4 686.1 [c]
Economy: Agriculture (% of Gross Value Added) [e]	5.1	4.2	4.0 [c]
Economy: Industry (% of Gross Value Added) [e]	55.4	45.0	52.0 [c]
Economy: Services and other activity (% of GVA) [e]	39.4	50.9	44.0 [c]
Employment in agriculture (% of employed) [f]	24.2	21.6	19.8 [c]
Employment in industry (% of employed) [f]	20.3	20.5	21.3 [c]
Employment in services & other sectors (% employed) [f]	55.6	57.9	58.9 [c]
Unemployment rate (% of labour force) [f]	8.3	10.7	15.7
Labour force participation rate (female/male pop. %) [f]	12.1 / 72.0	14.2 / 73.0	12.0 / 70.7
CPI: Consumer Price Index (2010=100)	100	119	134 [b]
Agricultural production index (2014-2016=100)	121	81	123 [c]
International trade: exports (million current US$)	52 483	49 403	124 428 [f,b]
International trade: imports (million current US$)	43 915	32 667	50 397 [f,b]
International trade: balance (million current US$)	8 568	16 736	74 031 [f,b]
Balance of payments, current account (million US$)	6 488	- 2 762	24 563 [c]

Major trading partners						2022
Export partners (% of exports) [f]	China	30.3	India	30.0	United States	7.9
Import partners (% of imports) [f]	United Arab Emirates	29.8	China	21.2	Türkiye	20.8

Social indicators	2010	2015	2023
Population growth rate (average annual %)	3.2	2.6	2.2 [a,b]
Urban population (% of total population)	69.1	69.9	70.7 [d]
Urban population growth rate (average annual %) [g]	2.7	3.4	...
Fertility rate, total (live births per woman)	4.4	4.1	3.4 [a,b]
Life expectancy at birth (females/males, years)	70.1 / 63.9	71.2 / 67.5	73.4 / 69.2 [a,b]
Population age distribution (0-14/60+ years old, %)	41.2 / 4.7	40.3 / 5.0	37.7 / 5.1 [a,b]
International migrant stock (000/% of total pop.) [h,i]	120.5 / 0.4	359.4 / 1.0	365.8 / 0.9 [i]
Refugees and others of concern to the UNHCR (000)	1 796.3 [k]	4 311.7	1 544.7 [b]
Infant mortality rate (per 1 000 live births)	28.6	24.5	17.6 [a,b]
Health: Current expenditure (% of GDP) [l]	3.2	3.1	5.1 [f,m,j]
Health: Physicians (per 1 000 pop.)	0.6	1.0 [n]	0.9 [i]
Education: Primary gross enrol. ratio (f/m per 100 pop.)	99.1 / 117.8 [o]	... / ...	... / ...
Education: Lowr. sec. gross enrol. ratio (f/m per 100 pop.)	55.9 / 76.7 [o]	... / ...	... / ...
Education: Upr. sec. gross enrol. ratio (f/m per 100 pop.)	35.3 / 44.8 [o]	... / ...	... / ...
Intentional homicide rate (per 100 000 pop.)	8.6	9.4 [p]	...
Seats held by women in the National Parliament (%)	25.5	26.5	28.9 [q]

Environment and infrastructure indicators	2010	2015	2023
Individuals using the Internet (per 100 inhabitants)	2.5	15.2 [f]	48.9 [f,c]
Research & Development expenditure (% of GDP)	~0.0 [r,s,t]	~0.0	~0.0 [c]
Threatened species (number)	60	69	98 [b]
Forested area (% of land area)	1.9	1.9	1.9 [i]
CO2 emission estimates (million tons/tons per capita)	90.1 / 3.0	100.8 / 2.8	122.8 / 3.0 [i]
Energy production, primary (Petajoules)	5 274	7 565	8 916 [i]
Energy supply per capita (Gigajoules)	46	43	45 [i]
Tourist/visitor arrivals at national borders (000)	1 518	892 [p]	...
Important sites for terrestrial biodiversity protected (%)	2.8	5.5	5.6 [b]
Pop. using safely managed drinking water (urban/rural, %)	62.7 / 37.8	63.7 / 42.8	64.6 / 47.6 [b]
Pop. using safely managed sanitation (urban/rural, %)	34.9 / 32.8	43.1 / 38.4	54.7 / 48.0 [b]
Net Official Development Assist. received (% of GNI)	1.55	0.90	0.88 [c]

a Projected estimate (medium fertility variant). b 2022. c 2021. d 2019. e Data compiled in accordance with the System of National Accounts 1968 (1968 SNA). f Estimate. g Data refers to a 5-year period preceding the reference year. h Including refugees. i Refers to foreign citizens. j 2020. k Data as at the end of December. l Data based on calendar year (January 1 to December 31). m Data are based on SHA2011. n 2014. o 2007. p 2013. q Data are as at 1 January of reporting year. r Excluding private non-profit. s Based on R&D budget instead of R&D expenditure. t Excluding business enterprise.

Ireland

Region	Northern Europe
Population (000, 2023)	5 023[a,b]
Pop. density (per km2, 2023)	73.5[a,b]
Capital city	Dublin
Capital city pop. (000, 2023)	1 214.7[d]
UN membership date	14 December 1955
Surface area (km2)	69 825[c]
Sex ratio (m per 100 f)	98.3[a,b]
National currency	Euro (EUR)
Exchange rate (per US$)	0.9[b]

Economic indicators

	2010	2015	2023
GDP: Gross domestic product (million current US$)	221 697	291 658	504 183[c]
GDP growth rate (annual %, const. 2015 prices)	1.7	24.4	13.6[c]
GDP per capita (current US$)	48 998.4	62 510.3	101 109.0[c]
Economy: Agriculture (% of Gross Value Added)[e,f]	1.0	1.0	1.1[c]
Economy: Industry (% of Gross Value Added)[f,g]	25.6	41.1	40.1[c]
Economy: Services and other activity (% of GVA)[f]	73.3	57.9	58.8[c]
Employment in agriculture (% of employed)	5.8	5.3	4.5[c]
Employment in industry (% of employed)	18.1	18.1	18.8[c]
Employment in services & other sectors (% of employed)	76.2	76.5	76.7[c]
Unemployment rate (% of labour force)	14.5	9.9	4.3[h]
Labour force participation rate (female/male pop. %)	55.3 / 70.2	54.9 / 69.1	59.3 / 70.3[h]
CPI: Consumer Price Index (2010=100)[i]	100	105	117[b]
Agricultural production index (2014-2016=100)	88	101	118[c]
International trade: exports (million current US$)	120 645	124 731	219 304[b]
International trade: imports (million current US$)	64 601	77 795	147 914[b]
International trade: balance (million current US$)	56 045	46 935	71 390[b]
Balance of payments, current account (million US$)	2 320	12 912	47 621[b]

Major trading partners

						2022
Export partners (% of exports)	United States	30.3	Germany	12.1	United Kingdom	10.6
Import partners (% of imports)	United Kingdom	20.9	United States	15.7	China	10.3

Social indicators

	2010	2015	2023
Population growth rate (average annual %)	0.5	1.0	0.7[a,b]
Urban population (% of total population)	61.5	62.5	63.4[d]
Urban population growth rate (average annual %)[j]	2.2	0.6	...
Fertility rate, total (live births per woman)	2.1	1.9	1.8[a,b]
Life expectancy at birth (females/males, years)	82.7 / 78.3	83.3 / 79.5	84.4 / 81.0[a,b]
Population age distribution (0-14/60+ years old, %)	21.1 / 16.1	21.4 / 18.1	19.6 / 20.5[a,b]
International migrant stock (000/% of total pop.)	730.5 / 16.0	759.3 / 16.3	871.3 / 17.6[k]
Refugees and others of concern to the UNHCR (000)	14.2[l]	10.5[l]	61.4[b]
Infant mortality rate (per 1 000 live births)	3.7	3.5	2.5[a,b]
Health: Current expenditure (% of GDP)	10.5	7.3[m]	6.7[m,c]
Health: Physicians (per 1 000 pop.)	4.2	3.1	4.1[c]
Education: Government expenditure (% of GDP)	6.1	3.8	3.3[d]
Education: Primary gross enrol. ratio (f/m per 100 pop.)[h]	103.3 / 103.2	101.0 / 101.4	101.2 / 101.5[k]
Education: Lowr. sec. gross enrol. ratio (f/m per 100 pop.)[h]	108.3 / 106.6	103.8 / 103.4	111.1 / 107.7[k]
Education: Upr. sec. gross enrol. ratio (f/m per 100 pop.)[h]	141.6 / 126.9	141.5 / 133.7	187.8 / 161.1[k]
Intentional homicide rate (per 100 000 pop.)	1.2	0.7	0.4[c]
Seats held by women in the National Parliament (%)	13.9	16.3	23.1[n]

Environment and infrastructure indicators

	2010	2015	2023
Individuals using the Internet (per 100 inhabitants)	69.8[o]	83.5	95.2[h,c]
Research & Development expenditure (% of GDP)	1.6[h]	1.2[h]	1.2[p,k]
Threatened species (number)	27	39	92[b]
Forested area (% of land area)	10.5	11.0	11.4[k]
CO2 emission estimates (million tons/tons per capita)	39.8 / 8.6	36.0 / 7.6	34.4 / 6.7[c]
Energy production, primary (Petajoules)	78	81	146[k]
Energy supply per capita (Gigajoules)	134	120	112[k]
Tourist/visitor arrivals at national borders (000)[q]	7 134	9 528	10 951[b]
Important sites for terrestrial biodiversity protected (%)	75.0	76.6	83.4[b]
Pop. using safely managed sanitation (urban/rural %)	70.1 / 68.5	81.8 / 70.7	84.8 / 70.7[b]
Net Official Development Assist. disbursed (% of GNI)[r]	1.57	0.54	0.30[c]

a Projected estimate (medium fertility variant). b 2022. c 2021. d 2019. e Excludes irrigation canals and landscaping care. f Data classified according to ISIC Rev. 4. g Excludes publishing activities, recycling. Includes irrigation canals. h Estimate. i Calculated by the UN Statistics Division from national indices. j Data refers to a 5-year period preceding the reference year. k 2020. l Data as at the end of December. m Data are based on SHA2011. n Data are as at 1 January of reporting year. o Population aged 16 to 74 years. p Provisional data. q Including tourists from Northern Ireland. r Development Assistance Committee member (OECD).

Isle of Man

Region	Northern Europe	Population (000, 2023)	84 [a,b,c]
Surface area (km2)	572 [d]	Pop. density (per km2, 2023)	147.8 [a,b,c]
Sex ratio (m per 100 f)	98.1 [a,b,c]	Capital city	Douglas
National currency	Pound Sterling (GBP)	Capital city pop. (000, 2023)	27.2 [e]
Exchange rate (per US$)	0.8 [c]		

Economic indicators	2010	2015	2023
Employment in agriculture (% of employed)	1.9 [f,g]	...	...
Employment in industry (% of employed)	14.8 [f,g]	...	...
Employment in services & other sectors (% employed)	83.3 [f,g]	...	...
Unemployment rate (% of labour force)	2.4 [g]	2.6 [h,i,j]	...
Labour force participation rate (female/male pop. %)	56.3 / 69.9 [g]	57.5 / 69.3 [h,k,l]	... / ...
CPI: Consumer Price Index (2010=100)	...	161 [m,n]	

Social indicators	2010	2015	2023
Population growth rate (average annual %) [b]	1.1	- 0.4	0.2 [a,c]
Urban population (% of total population)	52.0	52.2	52.7 [o]
Urban population growth rate (average annual %) [p]	1.0	0.9	...
Fertility rate, total (live births per woman) [b]	2.2	1.7	1.6 [a,c]
Life expectancy at birth (females/males, years) [b]	81.4 / 76.6	80.8 / 77.1	82.7 / 78.8 [a,c]
Population age distribution (0-14/60+ years old, %) [b]	16.7 / 24.4	16.1 / 26.5	14.7 / 29.4 [a,c]
International migrant stock (000/% of total pop.)	43.4 / 51.2	42.2 / 50.7	43.0 / 50.6 [q]
Infant mortality rate (per 1 000 live births) [b]	13.0	13.1	10.4 [a,c]
Intentional homicide rate (per 100 000 pop.)	...	1.2	0.0 [r]

Environment and infrastructure indicators	2010	2015	2023
Threatened species (number)	2	3	10 [c]
Forested area (% of land area)	6.1	6.1	6.1 [q]
Energy production, primary (Petajoules) [s]	0	0	1 [q]
Energy supply per capita (Gigajoules)	48	49	57 [q]
Important sites for terrestrial biodiversity protected (%)	18.2	19.1	26.5 [c]

a Projected estimate (medium fertility variant). b For statistical purposes, the data for United Kingdom do not include this area. c 2022. d 2021. e 2018. f Data classified according to ISIC Rev. 3. g 2006. h Break in the time series. i Population aged 15 to 64 years. j 2013. k Population aged 16 years and over. l 2011. m Index base: 2000=100. n 2014. o 2019. p Data refers to a 5-year period preceding the reference year. q 2020. r 2016. s Estimate.

Israel

Region	Western Asia
Population (000, 2023)	9 038[a,b]
Pop. density (per km2, 2023)	417.6[a,b]
Capital city	Jerusalem[d]
Capital city pop. (000, 2023)	919.4[e,f]

UN membership date	11 May 1949
Surface area (km2)	22 072[c]
Sex ratio (m per 100 f)	99.5[a,b]
National currency	New Israeli Sheqel (ILS)
Exchange rate (per US$)	3.5[b]

Economic indicators	2010	2015	2023
GDP: Gross domestic product (million current US$)	234 655	300 078	481 591[c]
GDP growth rate (annual %, const. 2015 prices)	5.7	2.3	8.2[c]
GDP per capita (current US$)	32 019.7	37 473.3	54 111.0[c]
Economy: Agriculture (% of Gross Value Added)[g,h]	1.8	1.4	1.2[c]
Economy: Industry (% of Gross Value Added)[h,i,j]	23.3	22.1	20.1[c]
Economy: Services and other activity (% of GVA)[h]	74.9	76.5	78.7[c]
Employment in agriculture (% of employed)	1.6	~0.0[k]	0.9[k,c]
Employment in industry (% of employed)	19.7	11.8[k]	17.0[k,c]
Employment in services & other sectors (% employed)	78.7[k]	81.4	82.1[k,c]
Unemployment rate (% of labour force)	8.5	5.2	3.3[k]
Labour force participation rate (female/male pop. %)	57.5 / 69.3	59.1 / 69.3	60.2 / 67.1[k]
CPI: Consumer Price Index (2010=100)	100	107	114[b]
Agricultural production index (2014-2016=100)	91	99	99[c]
International trade: exports (million current US$)	58 413	64 062	73 583[b]
International trade: imports (million current US$)	59 194	62 068	107 083[b]
International trade: balance (million current US$)	- 781	1 994	- 33 499[b]
Balance of payments, current account (million US$)	8 247	16 138	19 212[b]

Major trading partners						2022
Export partners (% of exports)	United States	28.3[k]	China	6.4	India	5.5[k]
Import partners (% of imports)[k]	China	18.2	United States	9.5	Türkiye	6.3

Social indicators	2010	2015	2023
Population growth rate (average annual %)	1.8	1.9	1.5[a,b]
Urban population (% of total population)	91.8	92.2	92.5[f]
Urban population growth rate (average annual %)[l]	2.4	1.7	...
Fertility rate, total (live births per woman)	3.0	3.2	2.9[a,b]
Life expectancy at birth (females/males, years)	83.6 / 79.8	84.0 / 80.1	84.5 / 80.6[a,b]
Population age distribution (0-14/60+ years old, %)	27.8 / 14.3	28.1 / 15.2	28.1 / 16.1[a,b]
International migrant stock (000/% of total pop.)[m]	1 956.2 / 26.6	2 011.7 / 25.2	1 953.6 / 22.6[n]
Refugees and others of concern to the UNHCR (000)	31.1[o]	45.2	73.7[b]
Infant mortality rate (per 1 000 live births)	3.8	3.3	2.9[a,b]
Health: Current expenditure (% of GDP)[p]	7.0	7.1	8.3[n]
Health: Physicians (per 1 000 pop.)	3.5	3.5	3.7[c]
Education: Government expenditure (% of GDP)	5.4	5.8	6.1[f]
Education: Primary gross enrol. ratio (f/m per 100 pop.)	105.7 / 105.2	106.0 / 105.3	105.1 / 103.9[n]
Education: Lowr. sec. gross enrol. ratio (f/m per 100 pop.)	105.1 / 102.5	105.7 / 105.2	104.3 / 103.4[n]
Education: Upr. sec. gross enrol. ratio (f/m per 100 pop.)	103.9 / 101.5	102.6 / 101.0	107.3 / 105.0[n]
Intentional homicide rate (per 100 000 pop.)	2.0	1.4	1.9[c]
Seats held by women in the National Parliament (%)	19.2	22.5	24.2[q]

Environment and infrastructure indicators	2010	2015	2023
Individuals using the Internet (per 100 inhabitants)	67.5[r]	77.4	90.3[c]
Research & Development expenditure (% of GDP)[s]	3.9	4.2	5.4[n]
Threatened species (number)	131	152	247[b]
Forested area (% of land area)	7.1	7.6	6.5[n]
CO2 emission estimates (million tons/tons per capita)	69.1 / 9.0	64.6 / 7.6	58.6 / 6.2[c]
Energy production, primary (Petajoules)	162	273	495[n]
Energy supply per capita (Gigajoules)	133	114	101[n]
Tourist/visitor arrivals at national borders (000)[t]	2 803	2 799	397[c]
Important sites for terrestrial biodiversity protected (%)	16.1	16.4	17.1[b]
Pop. using safely managed drinking water (urban/rural, %)	99.7 / 99.5	99.6 / 99.4	99.5 / 99.4[b]
Pop. using safely managed sanitation (urban/rural %)	87.5 / 85.7	91.2 / 89.1	96.4 / 93.8[b]
Net Official Development Assist. disbursed (% of GNI)	...	0.07[u]	0.09[c]

a Projected estimate (medium fertility variant). **b** 2022. **c** 2021. **d** Designation and data provided by Israel. The position of the UN on Jerusalem is stated in A/RES/181 (II) and subsequent General Assembly and Security Council resolutions. **e** Including East Jerusalem. **f** 2019. **g** Excludes irrigation canals and landscaping care. **h** Data classified according to ISIC Rev. 4. **i** Excludes publishing activities, recycling. Includes irrigation canals. **j** Includes mining and quarrying. **k** Estimate. **l** Data refers to a 5-year period preceding the reference year. **m** Including refugees. **n** 2020. **o** Data as at the end of December. **p** Data are based on SHA2011. **q** Data are as at 1 January of reporting year. **r** Population aged 20 years and over. **s** Do not correspond exactly to Frascati Manual recommendations. **t** Excluding nationals residing abroad. **u** 2014.

Italy

Region	Southern Europe	UN membership date	14 December 1955
Population (000, 2023)	59 038[a,b]	Surface area (km2)	302 068[c]
Pop. density (per km2, 2023)	199.5[a,b]	Sex ratio (m per 100 f)	95.2[a,b]
Capital city	Rome	National currency	Euro (EUR)
Capital city pop. (000, 2023)	4 234.0[d,e]	Exchange rate (per US$)	0.9[b]

Economic indicators

	2010	2015	2023
GDP: Gross domestic product (million current US$)	2 134 018	1 835 899	2 107 703[c]
GDP growth rate (annual %, const. 2015 prices)	1.7	0.8	6.7[c]
GDP per capita (current US$)	35 672.5	30 480.0	35 578.9[c]
Economy: Agriculture (% of Gross Value Added)[f,g]	2.0	2.3	2.2[c]
Economy: Industry (% of Gross Value Added)[f,h]	24.3	23.2	25.1[c]
Economy: Services and other activity (% of GVA)[f]	73.7	74.5	72.8[c]
Employment in agriculture (% of employed)	3.8	3.8	4.1[c]
Employment in industry (% of employed)	28.6	26.5	26.6[c]
Employment in services & other sectors (% employed)	67.7	69.6	69.3[c]
Unemployment rate (% of labour force)	8.4	11.9	8.5[i]
Labour force participation rate (female/male pop. %)	38.2 / 59.1	39.8 / 58.9	41.1 / 58.5[i]
CPI: Consumer Price Index (2010=100)	100	107	122[j,b]
Agricultural production index (2014-2016=100)	109	103	100[c]
International trade: exports (million current US$)	446 840	456 989	700 315[b]
International trade: imports (million current US$)	486 984	410 933	743 030[b]
International trade: balance (million current US$)	- 40 145	46 055	- 42 715[b]
Balance of payments, current account (million US$)	- 70 819	26 369	- 26 658[b]

Major trading partners

						2022
Export partners (% of exports)	Germany	12.4	United States	10.4	France	10.0
Import partners (% of imports)	Germany	13.7	China	8.9	France	7.3

Social indicators

	2010	2015	2023
Population growth rate (average annual %)	0.4	- 0.2	- 0.3[a,b]
Urban population (% of total population)	68.3	69.6	70.7[e]
Urban population growth rate (average annual %)[k]	0.5	0.3	...
Fertility rate, total (live births per woman)	1.4	1.3	1.3[a,b]
Life expectancy at birth (females/males, years)	84.5 / 79.5	84.7 / 80.2	86.0 / 82.0[a,b]
Population age distribution (0-14/60+ years old, %)	14.1 / 26.7	13.7 / 28.0	12.4 / 31.0[a,b]
International migrant stock (000/% of total pop.)	5 787.9 / 9.8	5 805.3 / 9.6	6 387.0 / 10.6[i]
Refugees and others of concern to the UNHCR (000)	61.3[m]	142.6	357.4[b]
Infant mortality rate (per 1 000 live births)	3.2	2.9	2.1[a,b]
Health: Current expenditure (% of GDP)	8.9	8.9	9.5[c]
Health: Physicians (per 1 000 pop.)	3.8	3.9	4.1[c]
Education: Government expenditure (% of GDP)	4.3	4.1	4.1[e]
Education: Primary gross enrol. ratio (f/m per 100 pop.)	102.5 / 103.5	100.2 / 100.6	99.8 / 99.8[i]
Education: Lowr. sec. gross enrol. ratio (f/m per 100 pop.)	106.6 / 109.6	104.2 / 106.0	101.8 / 104.2[i]
Education: Upr. sec. gross enrol. ratio (f/m per 100 pop.)	99.9 / 99.9	100.9 / 100.2	99.1 / 100.1[i]
Intentional homicide rate (per 100 000 pop.)	0.9	0.8	0.5[c]
Seats held by women in the National Parliament (%)	21.3	31.0	32.2[n]

Environment and infrastructure indicators

	2010	2015	2023
Individuals using the Internet (per 100 inhabitants)	53.7[o]	58.1	74.9[c]
Research & Development expenditure (% of GDP)	1.2	1.3	1.5[i]
Threatened species (number)	174	279	558[b]
Forested area (% of land area)	30.5	31.4	32.3[i]
CO2 emission estimates (million tons/tons per capita)[p]	398.4 / 6.6	335.5 / 5.5	302.2 / 5.0[c]
Energy production, primary (Petajoules)[p]	1 378	1 509	1 469[i]
Energy supply per capita (Gigajoules)[p]	122	106	96[i]
Tourist/visitor arrivals at national borders (000)[q]	43 626	50 732	26 888[c]
Important sites for terrestrial biodiversity protected (%)	72.9	73.8	76.6[b]
Pop. using safely managed sanitation (urban/rural %)	79.4 / 78.1	79.4 / 78.1	79.4 / 78.1[b]
Net Official Development Assist. disbursed (% of GNI)[r]	0.47	0.86	0.56[b]

a Projected estimate (medium fertility variant). b 2022. c 2021. d Refers to the official Metropolitan City. e 2019. f Data classified according to ISIC Rev. 4. g Excludes irrigation canals and landscaping care. h Excludes publishing activities, recycling. Includes irrigation canals. i Estimate. j Calculated by the UN Statistics Division from national indices. k Data refers to a 5-year period preceding the reference year. l 2020. m Data as at the end of December. n Data are as at 1 January of reporting year. o Population aged 16 to 74 years. p Data include San Marino and the Holy See. q Excluding seasonal and border workers. r Development Assistance Committee member (OECD).

Jamaica

		UN membership date	18 September 1962
Region	Caribbean	UN membership date	18 September 1962
Population (000, 2023)	2 827 [a,b]	Surface area (km2)	10 990 [c]
Pop. density (per km2, 2023)	261.1 [a,b]	Sex ratio (m per 100 f)	98.4 [a,b]
Capital city	Kingston	National currency	Jamaican Dollar (JMD)
Capital city pop. (000, 2023)	589.8 [d]	Exchange rate (per US$)	151.0 [b]

Economic indicators

	2010	2015	2023
GDP: Gross domestic product (million current US$)	13 221	14 198	14 658 [c]
GDP growth rate (annual %, const. 2015 prices)	- 1.5	0.9	4.6 [c]
GDP per capita (current US$)	4 835.8	5 080.7	5 183.6 [c]
Economy: Agriculture (% of Gross Value Added)	5.9	7.2	9.5 [c]
Economy: Industry (% of Gross Value Added)	20.0	22.0	23.9 [c]
Economy: Services and other activity (% of GVA)	74.1	70.7	66.5 [c]
Employment in agriculture (% of employed)	17.7 [e]	17.7	15.5 [e,c]
Employment in industry (% of employed)	15.0 [e]	14.9	16.2 [e,c]
Employment in services & other sectors (% employed)	66.3 [e]	67.3	68.2 [e,c]
Unemployment rate (% of labour force)	7.6	8.8 [e]	6.0
Labour force participation rate (female/male pop. %)	52.3 / 68.9	58.8 / 72.9	63.7 / 76.9 [e]
CPI: Consumer Price Index (2010=100) [f]	100	141	200 [b]
Agricultural production index (2014-2016=100)	92	98	106 [c]
International trade: exports (million current US$)	1 328	1 263	1 043 [e,b]
International trade: imports (million current US$)	5 225	4 993	8 297 [e,b]
International trade: balance (million current US$)	- 3 898	- 3 730	- 7 255 [e,b]
Balance of payments, current account (million US$)	- 934	- 430	- 130 [b]

Major trading partners

					2022
Export partners (% of exports) [e]	United States	50.7	Netherlands	10.2	Canada	6.8
Import partners (% of imports) [e]	United States	40.8	Brazil	8.6	China	7.8

Social indicators

	2010	2015	2023
Population growth rate (average annual %)	0.4	0.3	- 0.1 [a,b]
Urban population (% of total population)	53.7	54.8	56.0 [d]
Urban population growth rate (average annual %) [g]	0.9	0.8	...
Fertility rate, total (live births per woman)	1.7	1.6	1.3 [a,b]
Life expectancy at birth (females/males, years)	74.7 / 70.6	74.0 / 70.8	72.7 / 68.5 [a,b]
Population age distribution (0-14/60+ years old, %)	26.6 / 8.4	23.3 / 9.4	19.8 / 11.9 [a,b]
International migrant stock (000/% of total pop.) [h]	23.7 / 0.8	23.2 / 0.8	23.6 / 0.8 [i]
Refugees and others of concern to the UNHCR (000)	~0.0 [i]	~0.0	0.1 [b]
Infant mortality rate (per 1 000 live births)	15.2	13.2	11.3 [a,b]
Health: Current expenditure (% of GDP) [e,k]	5.3	5.6	6.6 [i]
Health: Physicians (per 1 000 pop.)	0.4 [i]	0.4	0.6 [m]
Education: Government expenditure (% of GDP)	6.4	5.5	5.2 [d]
Education: Primary gross enrol. ratio (f/m per 100 pop.)	90.8 / 90.4 [n]	... / ...	... / ...
Education: Lowr. sec. gross enrol. ratio (f/m per 100 pop.)	98.6 / 97.7 [n]	... / ...	... / ...
Education: Upr. sec. gross enrol. ratio (f/m per 100 pop.)	102.8 / 86.0	78.6 / 74.0	83.5 / 79.9 [c]
Intentional homicide rate (per 100 000 pop.)	52.9	43.3	52.1 [c]
Seats held by women in the National Parliament (%)	13.3	12.7	28.6 [o]

Environment and infrastructure indicators

	2010	2015	2023
Individuals using the Internet (per 100 inhabitants)	27.7 [p]	42.2	82.4 [c]
Threatened species (number)	282	298	359 [b]
Forested area (% of land area)	51.6	53.3	55.1 [i]
CO2 emission estimates (million tons/tons per capita)	7.3 / 2.6	6.8 / 2.3	5.5 / 1.8 [i]
Energy production, primary (Petajoules)	8	10	11 [i]
Energy supply per capita (Gigajoules)	41	42	36 [i]
Tourist/visitor arrivals at national borders (000) [q,r]	1 922	2 123	1 464 [c]
Important sites for terrestrial biodiversity protected (%)	18.9	19.2	20.1 [b]
Net Official Development Assist. received (% of GNI)	1.11	0.43	0.44 [c]

a Projected estimate (medium fertility variant). b 2022. c 2021. d 2019. e Estimate. f Calculated by the UN Statistics Division from national indices. g Data refers to a 5-year period preceding the reference year. h Including refugees. i 2020. j Data as at the end of December. k Data refer to fiscal years beginning 1 April. l 2008. m 2018. n 2007. o Data are as at 1 January of reporting year. p Population aged 14 years and over. q Including nationals residing abroad; E/D cards. r Arrivals of non-resident tourists by air.

Japan

Region	Eastern Asia	UN membership date	18 December 1956
Population (000, 2023)	123 952 a,b	Surface area (km2)	377 930 c,d
Pop. density (per km2, 2023)	328.9 a,b	Sex ratio (m per 100 f)	94.6 a,b
Capital city	Tokyo	National currency	Yen (JPY)
Capital city pop. (000, 2023)	37 435.2 e,f	Exchange rate (per US$)	132.6 b

Economic indicators

	2010	2015	2023
GDP: Gross domestic product (million current US$)	5 759 072	4 444 931	4 940 878 d
GDP growth rate (annual %, const. 2015 prices)	4.1	1.6	1.7 d
GDP per capita (current US$)	44 955.7	34 930.4	39 649.9 d
Economy: Agriculture (% of Gross Value Added) g,h,i	1.1	1.0	1.0 d
Economy: Industry (% of Gross Value Added) g,h,j	28.3	28.8	29.1 d
Economy: Services and other activity (% of GVA) g	70.6	70.2	69.9 d
Employment in agriculture (% of employed)	3.9	3.5	3.2 d
Employment in industry (% of employed)	25.8	24.1 k	23.7 d
Employment in services & other sectors (% employed)	70.3	71.4	73.2 d
Unemployment rate (% of labour force)	5.1	3.4	2.6 k
Labour force participation rate (female/male pop. %)	48.4 / 71.5	49.4 / 70.3	54.6 / 72.1 k
CPI: Consumer Price Index (2010=100) l	100	104	108 b
Agricultural production index (2014-2016=100)	96	100	101 d
International trade: exports (million current US$)	769 774	624 874	746 672 b
International trade: imports (million current US$)	694 059	625 568	898 600 b
International trade: balance (million current US$)	75 715	- 695	- 151 928 b
Balance of payments, current account (million US$)	220 888	136 472	90 963 b

Major trading partners 2022

Export partners (% of exports)	China	19.4	United States	18.7	Republic of Korea	7.2
Import partners (% of imports)	China	21.0	United States	10.1	Australia	9.8

Social indicators

	2010	2015	2023
Population growth rate (average annual %)	-~0.0	- 0.2	- 0.5 a,b
Urban population (% of total population)	90.8	91.4	91.7 f
Urban population growth rate (average annual %) m	1.1	-0.0	...
Fertility rate, total (live births per woman)	1.4	1.4	1.3 a,b
Life expectancy at birth (females/males, years)	86.2 / 79.5	87.0 / 80.7	87.8 / 81.8 a,b
Population age distribution (0-14/60+ years old, %)	13.2 / 31.5	12.7 / 33.9	11.6 / 35.8 a,b
International migrant stock (000/% of total pop.) n	2 134.2 / 1.7	2 232.2 / 1.7	2 771.0 / 2.2 o
Refugees and others of concern to the UNHCR (000)	7.0 p	13.8 k	18.7 q,r,b
Infant mortality rate (per 1 000 live births)	2.3	2.0	1.7 a,b
Health: Current expenditure (% of GDP)	9.1	10.7	10.9 o
Health: Physicians (per 1 000 pop.)	2.2	2.4 s	2.6 o
Education: Government expenditure (% of GDP)	3.6	3.3	3.2 f
Education: Primary gross enrol. ratio (f/m per 100 pop.)	... / ...	99.0 / 98.7	97.6 / 97.3 o
Education: Lowr. sec. gross enrol. ratio (f/m per 100 pop.)	... / ...	102.4 / 102.3	97.6 / 97.2 o
Education: Upr. sec. gross enrol. ratio (f/m per 100 pop.)	... / ...	102.5 / 101.5	103.0 / 102.6 o
Intentional homicide rate (per 100 000 pop.)	0.4	0.3	0.2 d
Seats held by women in the National Parliament (%)	11.2	9.5	10.0 t

Environment and infrastructure indicators

	2010	2015	2023
Individuals using the Internet (per 100 inhabitants)	78.2 u	91.1	82.9 k,v,d
Research & Development expenditure (% of GDP)	3.1	3.2	3.3 o
Threatened species (number)	330	364	612 b
Forested area (% of land area)	68.5	68.4	68.4 o
CO2 emission estimates (million tons/tons per capita) w	1 143.2 / 8.8	1 162.4 / 9.1	1 016.1 / 8.0 d
Energy production, primary (Petajoules) w	4 205	1 321	1 811 o
Energy supply per capita (Gigajoules) w	164	143	129 o
Tourist/visitor arrivals at national borders (000) x	8 611	19 737	246 d
Important sites for terrestrial biodiversity protected (%)	49.9	63.3	65.1 b
Net Official Development Assist. disbursed (% of GNI) y	0.86	0.83	0.73 d

a Projected estimate (medium fertility variant). b 2022. c Data refer to 1 October 2007. d 2021. e Major metropolitan areas. f 2019. g Data classified according to ISIC Rev. 4. h At producers' prices. i Excludes irrigation canals and landscaping care. j Excludes publishing activities, recycling. Includes irrigation canals. k Estimate. l Calculated by the UN Statistics Division from national indices. m Data refers to a 5-year period preceding the reference year. n Refers to foreign citizens. o 2020. p Data as at the end of December. q UNHCR estimates r Data is as of end-2021. s 2014. t Data are as at 1 January of reporting year. u Population aged 6 years and over. v Users in the last 12 months. w Data include Okinawa. x Excluding nationals residing abroad. y Development Assistance Committee member (OECD).

Jordan

Region	Western Asia	
Population (000, 2023)	11 286 [a,b]	
Pop. density (per km2, 2023)	127.1 [a,b]	
Capital city	Amman	
Capital city pop. (000, 2023)	2 108.5 [d]	

UN membership date	14 December 1955
Surface area (km2)	89 318 [c]
Sex ratio (m per 100 f)	107.5 [a,b]
National currency	Jordanian Dinar (JOD)
Exchange rate (per US$)	0.7 [b]

Economic indicators

	2010	2015	2023
GDP: Gross domestic product (million current US$)	27 134	38 587	45 244 [c]
GDP growth rate (annual %, const. 2015 prices)	2.3	2.5	2.2 [c]
GDP per capita (current US$)	3 914.7	4 064.3	4 058.4 [c]
Economy: Agriculture (% of Gross Value Added) [e,f]	4.0	4.9	5.8 [c]
Economy: Industry (% of Gross Value Added) [f,g]	29.5	28.1	26.7 [c]
Economy: Services and other activity (% of GVA) [f]	66.5	67.0	67.5 [c]
Employment in agriculture (% of employed) [h]	3.6	3.5	3.2 [c]
Employment in industry (% of employed) [h]	23.6	21.0	17.7 [c]
Employment in services & other sectors (% employed) [h]	72.8	75.5	79.1 [c]
Unemployment rate (% of labour force)	12.5	13.1	17.7 [h]
Labour force participation rate (female/male pop. %)	14.6 / 62.9	13.6 / 59.2 [h]	14.9 / 62.4 [h]
CPI: Consumer Price Index (2010=100)	100	116	107 [i,b]
Agricultural production index (2014-2016=100)	88	101	103 [c]
International trade: exports (million current US$)	7 023	7 833	8 790 [b]
International trade: imports (million current US$)	15 262	20 475	19 376 [b]
International trade: balance (million current US$)	- 8 239	- 12 642	- 10 586 [b]
Balance of payments, current account (million US$)	- 1 882	- 3 470	- 4 030 [c]

Major trading partners

						2022
Export partners (% of exports) [h]	United States	20.1	India	14.8	Saudi Arabia	10.2
Import partners (% of imports) [h]	China	15.3	Saudi Arabia	14.9	United Arab Emirates	7.8

Social indicators

	2010	2015	2023
Population growth rate (average annual %)	2.6	7.2	0.5 [a,b]
Urban population (% of total population)	86.1	90.3	91.2 [d]
Urban population growth rate (average annual %) [j]	6.2	5.8	...
Fertility rate, total (live births per woman)	3.8	3.2	2.8 [a,b]
Life expectancy at birth (females/males, years)	76.1 / 72.1	77.3 / 73.0	76.7 / 72.1 [a,b]
Population age distribution (0-14/60+ years old, %)	36.6 / 5.3	35.1 / 4.9	32.1 / 6.3 [a,b]
International migrant stock (000/% of total pop.) [k,l]	2 786.9 / 38.4	3 167.0 / 34.2	3 457.7 / 33.9 [m]
Refugees and others of concern to the UNHCR (000)	453.2 [n]	684.8	763.2 [o,b]
Infant mortality rate (per 1 000 live births)	17.0	14.9	12.4 [a,b]
Health: Current expenditure (% of GDP) [p]	8.2	7.5 [q]	7.5 [h,m]
Health: Physicians (per 1 000 pop.)	2.3	2.7	2.5 [d]
Education: Government expenditure (% of GDP)	...	...	3.2 [c]
Education: Primary gross enrol. ratio (f/m per 100 pop.)	81.1 / 82.7	79.1 / 79.9 [r]	79.5 / 80.5 [c]
Education: Lowr. sec. gross enrol. ratio (f/m per 100 pop.)	86.2 / 85.9	72.5 / 72.4 [r]	76.5 / 76.7 [c]
Education: Upr. sec. gross enrol. ratio (f/m per 100 pop.)	71.9 / 63.1	65.7 / 58.5 [r]	64.7 / 59.7 [c]
Intentional homicide rate (per 100 000 pop.)	1.7	1.6	1.0 [c]
Seats held by women in the National Parliament (%)	6.4	12.0	12.3 [s]

Environment and infrastructure indicators

	2010	2015	2023
Individuals using the Internet (per 100 inhabitants)	27.2 [t]	54.2 [h]	82.8 [h,c]
Research & Development expenditure (% of GDP)	0.4 [u]	...	0.7 [v,w,x]
Threatened species (number)	90	102	131 [b]
Forested area (% of land area)	1.1	1.1	1.1 [m]
CO2 emission estimates (million tons/tons per capita)	19.0 / 2.6	24.0 / 2.6	20.2 / 2.0 [m]
Energy production, primary (Petajoules)	14	14	33 [m]
Energy supply per capita (Gigajoules)	44	39	32 [m]
Tourist/visitor arrivals at national borders (000) [y]	4 207	3 761	2 012 [c]
Important sites for terrestrial biodiversity protected (%)	6.6	9.5	12.7 [b]
Pop. using safely managed sanitation (urban/rural %)	83.8 / ...	84.1 / ...	84.4 / ... [b]
Net Official Development Assist. received (% of GNI)	3.55	5.61	7.66 [c]

a Projected estimate (medium fertility variant). b 2022. c 2021. d 2019. e Excludes irrigation canals and landscaping care. f Data classified according to ISIC Rev. 4. g Excludes publishing activities, recycling. Includes irrigation canals. h Estimate. i Base: 2018=100. j Data refers to a 5-year period preceding the reference year. k Refers to foreign citizens. l Including refugees. m 2020. n Data as at the end of December. o The refugee population includes 34,000 Iraqis registered with UNHCR. Government estimated the number of Iraqis at 400,000 individuals at the end of March 2015 including refugees and other categories. p Data based on calendar year (January 1 to December 31). q Data are based on SHA2011. r 2014. s Data are as at 1 January of reporting year. t Population aged 5 years and over. u 2008. v Overestimated or based on overestimated data. w Break in the time series. x 2016. y Including nationals residing abroad.

Kazakhstan

Region	Central Asia	UN membership date	02 March 1992
Population (000, 2023)	19 398[a,b]	Surface area (km2)	2 724 902[c]
Pop. density (per km2, 2023)	7.2[a,b]	Sex ratio (m per 100 f)	92.8[a,b]
Capital city	Nur-Sultan	National currency	Tenge (KZT)
Capital city pop. (000, 2023)	1 117.6[d]	Exchange rate (per US$)	462.6[b]

Economic indicators

	2010	2015	2023
GDP: Gross domestic product (million current US$)	148 047	184 388	193 018[c]
GDP growth rate (annual %, const. 2015 prices)	7.3	1.2	4.1[c]
GDP per capita (current US$)	8 903.6	10 338.0	10 054.9[c]
Economy: Agriculture (% of Gross Value Added)[e,f]	4.7	5.0	5.4[c]
Economy: Industry (% of Gross Value Added)[f,g]	41.9	32.5	37.6[c]
Economy: Services and other activity (% of GVA)[f]	53.4	62.5	56.9[c]
Employment in agriculture (% of employed)	28.3	18.0	15.0[h,c]
Employment in industry (% of employed)[h]	5.3	12.9	21.2[c]
Employment in services & other sectors (% employed)	53.0	61.4	63.7[h,c]
Unemployment rate (% of labour force)	5.8	4.9	5.0[h]
Labour force participation rate (female/male pop. %)[h]	66.6 / 75.9	66.2 / 75.2	65.2 / 74.9
CPI: Consumer Price Index (2010=100)	100	137	217[c]
Agricultural production index (2014-2016=100)	77	99	115[c]
International trade: exports (million current US$)	57 244	45 954	84 392[b]
International trade: imports (million current US$)	24 024	30 567	50 044[b]
International trade: balance (million current US$)	33 220	15 387	34 348[b]
Balance of payments, current account (million US$)	2 678	- 9 980	8 528[b]

Major trading partners   2022

Export partners (% of exports)	Italy	16.4	China	15.6	Russian Federation	10.4
Import partners (% of imports)	Russian Federation	34.7	China	21.9	Germany	4.5

Social indicators

	2010	2015	2023
Population growth rate (average annual %)	1.4	1.3	1.1[a,b]
Urban population (% of total population)	56.8	57.2	57.5[d]
Urban population growth rate (average annual %)[i]	1.2	1.7	...
Fertility rate, total (live births per woman)	2.6	2.7	3.0[a,b]
Life expectancy at birth (females/males, years)	72.5 / 63.6	74.8 / 66.4	73.0 / 65.8[a,b]
Population age distribution (0-14/60+ years old, %)	24.6 / 10.1	27.0 / 11.0	29.7 / 12.8[a,b]
International migrant stock (000/% of total pop.)[j]	3 334.9 / 20.5	3 546.1 / 20.2	3 732.1 / 19.9[k]
Refugees and others of concern to the UNHCR (000)	12.7[l]	7.8	8.6[b]
Infant mortality rate (per 1 000 live births)	18.1	10.6	8.5[a,b]
Health: Current expenditure (% of GDP)	2.7	3.0	3.8[k]
Health: Physicians (per 1 000 pop.)	3.8	3.9	4.0[k]
Education: Government expenditure (% of GDP)	3.5	2.8	4.5[c]
Education: Primary gross enrol. ratio (f/m per 100 pop.)	109.1 / 108.5	111.7 / 111.5	100.2 / 100.4[k]
Education: Lowr. sec. gross enrol. ratio (f/m per 100 pop.)	100.5 / 101.2	113.6 / 112.1	101.3 / 101.0[k]
Education: Upr. sec. gross enrol. ratio (f/m per 100 pop.)	95.2 / 92.1	109.0 / 99.8	112.4 / 112.6[k]
Intentional homicide rate (per 100 000 pop.)	8.3	4.8	3.2[k]
Seats held by women in the National Parliament (%)	17.8	26.2	27.4[m]

Environment and infrastructure indicators

	2010	2015	2023
Individuals using the Internet (per 100 inhabitants)	31.6[n]	70.8	90.9[c]
Research & Development expenditure (% of GDP)	0.2	0.2	0.1[c]
Threatened species (number)	73	78	99[b]
Forested area (% of land area)	1.1	1.2	1.3[k]
CO2 emission estimates (million tons/tons per capita)	223.0 / 13.6	182.1 / 10.3	207.1 / 10.9[k]
Energy production, primary (Petajoules)	6 770	6 812	6 650[k]
Energy supply per capita (Gigajoules)	202	178	145[k]
Tourist/visitor arrivals at national borders (000)	4 097	6 430	1 330[c]
Important sites for terrestrial biodiversity protected (%)	26.2	26.9	28.5[b]
Pop. using safely managed sanitation (urban/rural %)	86.9 / ...	85.3 / ...	84.3 / ...[b]
Net Official Development Assist. disbursed (% of GNI)	...	...	0.03[c]
Net Official Development Assist. received (% of GNI)	0.17	0.05	0.03[c]

a Projected estimate (medium fertility variant). b 2022. c 2021. d 2019. e Excludes irrigation canals and landscaping care. f Data classified according to ISIC Rev. 4. g Excludes publishing activities, recycling. Includes irrigation canals. h Estimate. i Data refers to a 5-year period preceding the reference year. j Including refugees. k 2020. l Data as at the end of December. m Data are as at 1 January of reporting year. n Population aged 16 to 74 years.

Kenya

Region	Eastern Africa	UN membership date	16 December 1963	
Population (000, 2023)	54 028[a,b]	Surface area (km2)	591 958[c]	
Pop. density (per km2, 2023)	93.0[a,b]	Sex ratio (m per 100 f)	98.3[a,b]	
Capital city	Nairobi	National currency	Kenyan Shilling (KES)	
Capital city pop. (000, 2023)	4 556.4[d]	Exchange rate (per US$)	123.4[b]	

Economic indicators	2010	2015	2023
GDP: Gross domestic product (million current US$)	45 406	70 121	110 347[c]
GDP growth rate (annual %, const. 2015 prices)	8.1	5.0	7.5[c]
GDP per capita (current US$)	1 093.6	1 496.7	2 081.8[c]
Economy: Agriculture (% of Gross Value Added)[e,f]	17.0	20.6	23.6[c]
Economy: Industry (% of Gross Value Added)[f,g]	21.4	20.0	18.4[c]
Economy: Services and other activity (% of GVA)[f]	61.6	59.4	58.0[c]
Employment in agriculture (% of employed)[h]	40.1	36.6	33.0[c]
Employment in industry (% of employed)[h]	12.9	13.8	15.7[c]
Employment in services & other sectors (% of employed)[h]	46.9	49.6	51.3[c]
Unemployment rate (% of labour force)[h]	2.8	2.8	5.5
Labour force participation rate (female/male pop. %)[h]	71.1 / 76.4	71.4 / 77.3	72.8 / 76.1
CPI: Consumer Price Index (2010=100)	100	150	212[c]
Agricultural production index (2014-2016=100)	98	102	113[c]
International trade: exports (million current US$)	5 169	5 907	7 241[h,b]
International trade: imports (million current US$)	12 093	16 058	20 594[h,b]
International trade: balance (million current US$)	- 6 924	- 10 151	- 13 354[h,b]
Balance of payments, current account (million US$)	- 2 369	- 4 421	- 5 744[c]

Major trading partners						2022
Export partners (% of exports)[h]	Uganda	12.3	Netherlands	8.3	United States	8.0
Import partners (% of imports)[h]	China	20.5	India	10.8	United Arab Emirates	8.3

Social indicators	2010	2015	2023
Population growth rate (average annual %)	2.7	2.2	2.0[a,b]
Urban population (% of total population)	23.6	25.7	27.5[d]
Urban population growth rate (average annual %)[i]	4.4	4.4	...
Fertility rate, total (live births per woman)	4.4	3.8	3.3[a,b]
Life expectancy at birth (females/males, years)	62.4 / 58.9	64.1 / 59.7	64.7 / 59.6[a,b]
Population age distribution (0-14/60+ years old, %)	43.3 / 3.3	41.6 / 3.8	37.8 / 4.6[a,b]
International migrant stock (000/% of total pop.)[j]	954.9 / 2.3	1 126.9 / 2.4	1 050.1 / 2.0[k]
Refugees and others of concern to the UNHCR (000)	751.0[l]	613.8	571.9[b]
Infant mortality rate (per 1 000 live births)	40.2	34.9	28.0[a,b]
Health: Current expenditure (% of GDP)[m]	5.4	4.8	4.3[k]
Health: Physicians (per 1 000 pop.)	0.2	0.2[n]	0.2[c]
Education: Government expenditure (% of GDP)	4.8	4.7	5.1[h,o]
Education: Primary gross enrol. ratio (f/m per 100 pop.)	102.7 / 105.1[p]	103.6 / 103.7	76.2 / 78.4[d]
Education: Lowr. sec. gross enrol. ratio (f/m per 100 pop.)	79.8 / 86.2[p]	91.3 / 90.7	93.0 / 92.2[q]
Education: Upr. sec. gross enrol. ratio (f/m per 100 pop.)	39.1 / 45.1[p]	... / ...	... / ...
Intentional homicide rate (per 100 000 pop.)	4.6	4.8	5.3[c]
Seats held by women in the National Parliament (%)	9.8	19.7	23.3[r]

Environment and infrastructure indicators	2010	2015	2023
Individuals using the Internet (per 100 inhabitants)	7.2	16.6	28.8[h,c]
Research & Development expenditure (% of GDP)	0.7[s]	...	...
Threatened species (number)	338	463	697[b]
Forested area (% of land area)	6.4	6.2	6.3[k]
CO2 emission estimates (million tons/tons per capita)	14.9 / 0.3	18.8 / 0.3	20.1 / 0.3[k]
Energy production, primary (Petajoules)	650[h]	761	777[h,k]
Energy supply per capita (Gigajoules)	19[h]	20	20[h,k]
Tourist/visitor arrivals at national borders (000)[t,u]	1 470	1 114	1 364[v]
Important sites for terrestrial biodiversity protected (%)	33.4	33.6	33.6[b]
Pop. using safely managed sanitation (urban/rural %)	24.1 / 28.9	25.7 / 30.6	27.9 / 33.0[b]
Net Official Development Assist. received (% of GNI)	4.09	3.90	2.92[c]

a Projected estimate (medium fertility variant). b 2022. c 2021. d 2019. e Excludes irrigation canals and landscaping care. f Data classified according to ISIC Rev. 4. g Excludes publishing activities, recycling. Includes irrigation canals. h Estimate. i Data refers to a 5-year period preceding the reference year. j Including refugees. k 2020. l Data as at the end of December. m Data refer to fiscal years beginning 1 July. n 2014. o 2018. p 2009. q 2016. r Data are as at 1 January of reporting year. s Break in the time series. t Excluding nationals residing abroad. u Arrivals of non-resident visitors from all border entry points. v 2017.

Kiribati

Region	Micronesia	UN membership date	14 September 1999
Population (000, 2023)	131 [a,b]	Surface area (km2)	726 [c,d]
Pop. density (per km2, 2023)	180.8 [a,b]	Sex ratio (m per 100 f)	95.0 [a,b]
Capital city	Bairiki	National currency	Australian Dollar (AUD)
Capital city pop. (000)	3.2 [e]	Exchange rate (per US$)	1.5 [b]

Economic indicators

	2010	2015	2023
GDP: Gross domestic product (million current US$)	155	170	227 [d]
GDP growth rate (annual %, const. 2015 prices)	- 1.1	9.9	7.9 [d]
GDP per capita (current US$)	1 438.1	1 459.1	1 764.9 [d]
Economy: Agriculture (% of Gross Value Added) [f]	24.3	22.2	23.1 [d]
Economy: Industry (% of Gross Value Added) [f]	12.0	15.7	11.6 [d]
Economy: Services and other activity (% of GVA)	63.7	62.1	65.3 [d]
Employment in agriculture (% of employed)	22.1	...	...
Employment in industry (% of employed)	16.1	...	...
Employment in services & other sectors (% employed)	61.8	...	...
Unemployment rate (% of labour force)	30.6 [g]	...	...
Labour force participation rate (female/male pop. %)	52.3 / 66.8 [h]	... / ...	... / ...
CPI: Consumer Price Index (2010=100) [i]	100	100	101 [j]
Agricultural production index (2014-2016=100)	88	91	97 [d]
International trade: exports (million current US$)	4	10	73 [i,b]
International trade: imports (million current US$)	73	111	136 [i,b]
International trade: balance (million current US$)	- 69	- 101	- 63 [i,b]
Balance of payments, current account (million US$)	~0	56	20 [d]

Major trading partners

					2022
Export partners (% of exports) [i]	Japan	31.8	Malaysia	17.3	Australia	11.5
Import partners (% of imports) [i]	Fiji	18.0	Australia	15.6	China	14.1

Social indicators

	2010	2015	2023
Population growth rate (average annual %)	1.8	1.5	1.8 [a,b]
Urban population (% of total population)	47.4	51.6	54.8 [j]
Urban population growth rate (average annual %) [k]	3.8	3.5	...
Fertility rate, total (live births per woman)	3.9	3.5	3.3 [a,b]
Life expectancy at birth (females/males, years)	66.6 / 63.2	67.6 / 64.3	69.4 / 65.7 [a,b]
Population age distribution (0-14/60+ years old, %)	36.4 / 5.2	35.6 / 5.5	36.1 / 6.3 [a,b]
International migrant stock (000/% of total pop.)	2.9 / 2.8	2.9 / 2.6	3.1 / 2.6 [l]
Infant mortality rate (per 1 000 live births)	49.2	44.9	37.4 [a,b]
Health: Current expenditure (% of GDP) [m,n]	9.3	8.0	11.6 [l]
Health: Physicians (per 1 000 pop.)	0.4	0.2 [o]	...
Education: Government expenditure (% of GDP)	...	12.1	13.6 [p]
Education: Primary gross enrol. ratio (f/m per 100 pop.)	120.4 / 110.9	106.6 / 104.5	111.1 / 105.1 [l]
Education: Lowr. sec. gross enrol. ratio (f/m per 100 pop.)	92.1 / 92.9 [q]	114.7 / 98.7	102.2 / 96.6 [l]
Education: Upr. sec. gross enrol. ratio (f/m per 100 pop.)	81.4 / 67.5 [r]	... / ...	... / ...
Intentional homicide rate (per 100 000 pop.)	3.7	7.2 [s]	...
Seats held by women in the National Parliament (%)	4.3	8.7	6.7 [t]

Environment and infrastructure indicators

	2010	2015	2023
Individuals using the Internet (per 100 inhabitants)	9.1	14.9 [i]	53.6 [i,d]
Threatened species (number)	90	100	116 [b]
Forested area (% of land area)	1.5	1.5	1.5 [l]
Energy production, primary (Petajoules) [i]	1	1	1 [l]
Energy supply per capita (Gigajoules)	13	12	13 [i,j]
Tourist/visitor arrivals at national borders (000) [u]	5	4	~0 [d]
Important sites for terrestrial biodiversity protected (%)	40.0	40.0	40.0 [b]
Pop. using safely managed drinking water (urban/rural, %)	18.4 / 5.8	19.2 / 6.1	20.4 / 6.5 [b]
Pop. using safely managed sanitation (urban/rural %)	24.9 / 19.6	24.8 / 21.9	24.6 / 25.1 [b]
Net Official Development Assist. received (% of GNI)	10.47	18.51	17.22 [l]

a Projected estimate (medium fertility variant). b 2022. c Land area only. Excluding 84 square km of uninhabited islands. d 2021. e 2015. f At factor cost. g De facto population. h Persons present (de facto). i Estimate. j 2019. k Data refers to a 5-year period preceding the reference year. l 2020. m Data refer to fiscal years beginning 1 July. n General government expenditure (GGE) can be larger than the Gross domestic product (GDP) because government accounts for a very large part of domestic consumption and because a large part of domestic consumption in the country is accounted for by imports. o 2013. p 2017. q 2009. r 2008. s 2012. t Data are as at 1 January of reporting year. u Air arrivals. Tarawa and Christmas Island.

Kuwait

Region	Western Asia
Population (000, 2023)	4 269[a,b]
Pop. density (per km2, 2023)	239.6[a,b]
Capital city	Kuwait City
Capital city pop. (000, 2023)	3 052.5[d,e]

UN membership date	14 May 1963
Surface area (km2)	17 818[c]
Sex ratio (m per 100 f)	155.2[a,b]
National currency	Kuwaiti Dinar (KWD)
Exchange rate (per US$)	0.3[b]

Economic indicators

	2010	2015	2023
GDP: Gross domestic product (million current US$)	115 416	114 585	136 642[c]
GDP growth rate (annual %, const. 2015 prices)	- 2.4	0.6	1.3[c]
GDP per capita (current US$)	39 212.4	29 314.9	32 150.2[c]
Economy: Agriculture (% of Gross Value Added)	0.4	0.5	0.4[c]
Economy: Industry (% of Gross Value Added)	58.2	48.7	48.1[c]
Economy: Services and other activity (% of GVA)	41.4	50.9	51.5[c]
Employment in agriculture (% of employed)[f]	2.4	2.2	2.0[c]
Employment in industry (% of employed)[f]	24.3	24.9	25.3[c]
Employment in services & other sectors (% employed)[f]	73.2	72.8	72.8[c]
Unemployment rate (% of labour force)	1.8	2.2	2.5[f]
Labour force participation rate (female/male pop. %)[f]	47.3 / 83.9	49.6 / 87.3	48.1 / 85.9
CPI: Consumer Price Index (2010=100)[f]	100	118	134[c]
Agricultural production index (2014-2016=100)	64	95	123[c]
International trade: exports (million current US$)	62 698	54 121	93 990[f,b]
International trade: imports (million current US$)	22 691	30 957	31 880[f,b]
International trade: balance (million current US$)	40 007	23 164	62 110[f,b]
Balance of payments, current account (million US$)	36 989	8 584	63 082[b]

Major trading partners

					2022
Export partners (% of exports)[f]	China	27.6	India	13.6	Japan	10.4
Import partners (% of imports)[f]	China	18.0	United Arab Emirates	11.9	United States	8.0

Social indicators

	2010	2015	2023
Population growth rate (average annual %)	5.1	8.1	1.0[a,b]
Urban population (% of total population)	100.0	100.0	100.0[e]
Urban population growth rate (average annual %)[g]	5.5	5.4	...
Fertility rate, total (live births per woman)	2.3	2.2	2.1[a,b]
Life expectancy at birth (females/males, years)	80.1 / 76.4	82.0 / 77.9	82.8 / 78.9[a,b]
Population age distribution (0-14/60+ years old, %)	23.0 / 3.2	21.7 / 4.6	20.7 / 9.3[a,b]
International migrant stock (000/% of total pop.)[h,i]	1 874.8 / 62.7	2 866.1 / 74.7	3 110.2 / 72.8[j]
Refugees and others of concern to the UNHCR (000)	96.5[k]	94.6	93.8[b]
Infant mortality rate (per 1 000 live births)	8.9	7.5	6.7[a,b]
Health: Current expenditure (% of GDP)[f,l,m]	2.7	4.2	6.3[j]
Health: Physicians (per 1 000 pop.)	2.5	2.6	2.3[j]
Education: Government expenditure (% of GDP)	3.8[f,n]	...	...
Education: Primary gross enrol. ratio (f/m per 100 pop.)	101.2 / 103.2	104.3 / 101.0	89.0 / 77.1[c]
Education: Lowr. sec. gross enrol. ratio (f/m per 100 pop.)	102.8 / 104.6	98.3 / 98.8[o]	... / ...
Education: Upr. sec. gross enrol. ratio (f/m per 100 pop.)	92.9 / 86.4	100.8 / 86.5[o]	... / ...
Intentional homicide rate (per 100 000 pop.)	2.0	1.8[o]	0.3[j]
Seats held by women in the National Parliament (%)	7.7	1.5	6.2[p]

Environment and infrastructure indicators

	2010	2015	2023
Individuals using the Internet (per 100 inhabitants)	61.4[f]	82.0[f]	99.7[c]
Research & Development expenditure (% of GDP)	0.1[q,r]	0.1[r,s,t,u]	0.2[q,j]
Threatened species (number)	41	42	72[b]
Forested area (% of land area)	0.4	0.4	0.4[j]
CO2 emission estimates (million tons/tons per capita)	77.6 / 25.8	86.7 / 22.5	90.0 / 21.0[j]
Energy production, primary (Petajoules)	5 557	7 014	6 353[j]
Energy supply per capita (Gigajoules)	459	364	351[j]
Tourist/visitor arrivals at national borders (000)[v]	207	182	85[c]
Important sites for terrestrial biodiversity protected (%)	31.0	42.1	51.6[b]
Pop. using safely managed drinking water (urban/rural, %)	100.0 / ...	100.0 / ...	100.0 / ...[b]
Pop. using safely managed sanitation (urban/rural %)	100.0 / ...	100.0 / ...	100.0 / ...[b]
Net Official Development Assist. disbursed (% of GNI)	...	...	0.30[c]

a Projected estimate (medium fertility variant). **b** 2022. **c** 2021. **d** Data refers to the Governorates of Capital, Hawalli, Al-Farwaniya and Mubarak Al-Kabeer. **e** 2019. **f** Estimate. **g** Data refers to a 5-year period preceding the reference year. **h** Including refugees. **i** Refers to foreign citizens. **j** 2020. **k** Data as at the end of December. **l** Estimates should be viewed with caution as these are derived from scarce data. **m** Data refer to fiscal years beginning 1 April. **n** 2006. **o** 2012. **p** Data are as at 1 January of reporting year. **q** Government only. **r** Partial data. **s** Excluding private non-profit. **t** Break in the time series. **u** Excluding business enterprise. **v** Non-resident tourists staying in hotels and similar establishments.

Kyrgyzstan

Region	Central Asia	UN membership date	02 March 1992
Population (000, 2023)	6 631 a,b	Surface area (km2)	199 949 c
Pop. density (per km2, 2023)	34.6 a,b	Sex ratio (m per 100 f)	96.5 a,b
Capital city	Bishkek	National currency	Som (KGS)
Capital city pop. (000, 2023)	1 017.2 d	Exchange rate (per US$)	85.7 b

Economic indicators

	2010	2015	2023
GDP: Gross domestic product (million current US$)	4 794	6 678	8 741 c
GDP growth rate (annual %, const. 2015 prices)	- 0.5	3.9	6.2 c
GDP per capita (current US$)	874.3	1 129.0	1 339.0 c
Economy: Agriculture (% of Gross Value Added)e,f	18.8	15.4	15.3 c
Economy: Industry (% of Gross Value Added)e,g	28.2	27.5	28.6 c
Economy: Services and other activity (% of GVA)e	53.0	57.1	56.1 c
Employment in agriculture (% of employed)	32.1 h	29.3	16.6 h,c
Employment in industry (% of employed)	21.1 h	20.9	26.8 h,c
Employment in services & other sectors (% employed)	46.7 h	49.8	56.6 h,c
Unemployment rate (% of labour force)h	2.8	3.4	4.8
Labour force participation rate (female/male pop. %)	52.5 / 77.0	50.0 / 75.7	45.3 / 74.6 b
CPI: Consumer Price Index (2010=100)	100	146	211 b
Agricultural production index (2014-2016=100)	88	102	105 c
International trade: exports (million current US$)	1 488	1 441	2 187 b
International trade: imports (million current US$)	3 223	4 068	9 629 b
International trade: balance (million current US$)	- 1 734	- 2 627	- 7 442 b
Balance of payments, current account (million US$)	- 475	- 1 052	- 738 c

Major trading partners

						2022
Export partners (% of exports)	Russian Federation	44.5	Kazakhstan	20.0	Uzbekistan	10.8
Import partners (% of imports)	China	42.3	Russian Federation	23.6	Kazakhstan	7.8

Social indicators

	2010	2015	2023
Population growth rate (average annual %)	1.1	1.7	1.6 a,b
Urban population (% of total population)	35.3	35.8	36.6 d
Urban population growth rate (average annual %)i	1.3	1.8	...
Fertility rate, total (live births per woman)	3.1	3.2	2.9 a,b
Life expectancy at birth (females/males, years)	72.2 / 64.3	73.4 / 66.6	74.9 / 66.2 a,b
Population age distribution (0-14/60+ years old, %)	30.7 / 6.1	32.5 / 6.4	34.4 / 7.9 a,b
International migrant stock (000/% of total pop.)j	232.1 / 4.3	204.4 / 3.4	199.0 / 3.1 k
Refugees and others of concern to the UNHCR (000)	304.2 l	14.3	1.6 b
Infant mortality rate (per 1 000 live births)	25.8	19.7	13.1 a,b
Health: Current expenditure (% of GDP)	7.0	7.1	5.3 h,m,k
Health: Physicians (per 1 000 pop.)	2.3	2.2 n	2.2 d
Education: Government expenditure (% of GDP)	5.8	6.0	6.6 k
Education: Primary gross enrol. ratio (f/m per 100 pop.)	99.1 / 99.8	105.0 / 105.8	98.9 / 99.4 c
Education: Lowr. sec. gross enrol. ratio (f/m per 100 pop.)	93.5 / 94.3	94.8 / 95.2	103.4 / 103.5 c
Education: Upr. sec. gross enrol. ratio (f/m per 100 pop.)	73.7 / 72.8	84.4 / 79.2	92.4 / 90.1 c
Seats held by women in the National Parliament (%)	25.6	23.3	20.0 o

Environment and infrastructure indicators

	2010	2015	2023
Individuals using the Internet (per 100 inhabitants)h	16.3	30.2	77.9 c
Research & Development expenditure (% of GDP)	0.2	0.1 p	0.1 p,k
Threatened species (number)	40	41	61 b
Forested area (% of land area)	6.4	6.5	6.9 k
CO2 emission estimates (million tons/tons per capita)	6.1 / 1.1	9.8 / 1.6	8.4 / 1.2 k
Energy production, primary (Petajoules)	53	75	102 k
Energy supply per capita (Gigajoules)	21	28	23 k
Tourist/visitor arrivals at national borders (000)	1 224	4 000	3 169 c
Important sites for terrestrial biodiversity protected (%)	23.6	23.6	23.6 b
Pop. using safely managed drinking water (urban/rural, %)	87.6 / 41.2	90.6 / 53.7	91.8 / 67.3 b
Pop. using safely managed sanitation (urban/rural %)	81.5 / 93.5	83.6 / 95.8	86.3 / 96.5 b
Net Official Development Assist. received (% of GNI)	8.29	12.07	6.12 c

a Projected estimate (medium fertility variant). **b** 2022. **c** 2021. **d** 2019. **e** Data classified according to ISIC Rev. 4. **f** Excludes irrigation canals and landscaping care. **g** Excludes publishing activities, recycling. Includes irrigation canals. **h** Estimate. **i** Data refers to a 5-year period preceding the reference year. **j** Including refugees. **k** 2020. **l** Data as at the end of December. **m** Break in the time series. **n** 2014. **o** Data are as at 1 January of reporting year. **p** Excluding private non-profit.

Lao People's Dem. Rep.

Region	South-eastern Asia	UN membership date	14 December 1955	
Population (000, 2023)	7 530 a,b	Surface area (km2)	236 800 c	
Pop. density (per km2, 2023)	32.6 a,b	Sex ratio (m per 100 f)	101.6 a,b	
Capital city	Vientiane	National currency	Lao Kip (LAK)	
Capital city pop. (000, 2023)	673.1 d	Exchange rate (per US$)	16 600.0 b	

Economic indicators

	2010	2015	2023
GDP: Gross domestic product (million current US$)	7 313	14 390	19 074 c
GDP growth rate (annual %, const. 2015 prices)	8.1	7.3	3.5 c
GDP per capita (current US$)	1 156.6	2 120.2	2 568.9 c
Economy: Agriculture (% of Gross Value Added) e,f	23.6	19.7	18.1 c
Economy: Industry (% of Gross Value Added) f,g	30.9	31.0	38.6 c
Economy: Services and other activity (% of GVA) f	45.5	49.4	43.3 c
Employment in agriculture (% of employed)	71.5	64.0 h	58.1 h,c
Employment in industry (% of employed)	8.4	9.4 h	10.7 h,c
Employment in services & other sectors (% employed)	20.3	26.6 h	31.2 h,c
Unemployment rate (% of labour force)	0.7	2.5 h	2.9 h
Labour force participation rate (female/male pop. %) h	57.3 / 65.3	56.3 / 64.0	55.4 / 62.2
CPI: Consumer Price Index (2010=100) h	100 i	126	182 b
Agricultural production index (2014-2016=100)	61	104	118 c
International trade: exports (million current US$)	1 909	2 985	8 626 h,b
International trade: imports (million current US$)	1 837	3 778	6 992 h,b
International trade: balance (million current US$)	72	- 793	1 634 h,b
Balance of payments, current account (million US$)	29	- 2 268	447 c

Major trading partners

						2022
Export partners (% of exports) h	Thailand	32.2	China	31.4	Viet Nam	17.5
Import partners (% of imports) h	Thailand	46.7	China	22.6	Viet Nam	7.9

Social indicators

	2010	2015	2023
Population growth rate (average annual %)	1.5	1.5	1.4 a,b
Urban population (% of total population)	30.1	33.1	35.6 d
Urban population growth rate (average annual %) j	3.7	3.2	...
Fertility rate, total (live births per woman)	3.1	2.8	2.4 a,b
Life expectancy at birth (females/males, years)	66.2 / 61.9	68.7 / 64.7	71.2 / 66.9 a,b
Population age distribution (0-14/60+ years old, %)	35.9 / 5.8	33.1 / 6.4	30.6 / 7.2 a,b
International migrant stock (000/% of total pop.) k,l	33.0 / 0.5	45.5 / 0.7	48.7 / 0.7 m
Refugees and others of concern to the UNHCR (000)	...	...	~0.0 m
Infant mortality rate (per 1 000 live births)	51.8	42.3	30.6 a,b
Health: Current expenditure (% of GDP) n	2.9	2.5 o	2.7 o,m
Health: Physicians (per 1 000 pop.)	0.3	0.4	0.3 c
Education: Government expenditure (% of GDP)	1.7	2.7	1.9 c
Education: Primary gross enrol. ratio (f/m per 100 pop.)	117.9 / 128.9	111.3 / 116.6	97.0 / 99.8 c
Education: Lowr. sec. gross enrol. ratio (f/m per 100 pop.)	49.4 / 59.8	74.4 / 79.8	68.9 / 70.1 c
Education: Upr. sec. gross enrol. ratio (f/m per 100 pop.)	28.4 / 35.2	42.6 / 47.8	43.5 / 48.6 c
Seats held by women in the National Parliament (%)	25.2	25.0	22.0 p

Environment and infrastructure indicators

	2010	2015	2023
Individuals using the Internet (per 100 inhabitants)	7.0	18.2 h	62.0 c
Threatened species (number)	132	210	292 b
Forested area (% of land area)	73.4	72.7	71.9 m
CO2 emission estimates (million tons/tons per capita)	3.0 / 0.4	8.3 / 1.1	17.4 / 2.3 m
Energy production, primary (Petajoules)	98	162	297 m
Energy supply per capita (Gigajoules)	16	25	34 h,m
Tourist/visitor arrivals at national borders (000)	1 670	3 543	812 m
Important sites for terrestrial biodiversity protected (%)	35.4	37.3	48.6 b
Pop. using safely managed drinking water (urban/rural, %)	24.3 / 9.2	25.8 / 11.0	27.0 / 12.4 b
Pop. using safely managed sanitation (urban/rural, %)	55.5 / 39.1	60.4 / 50.7	63.3 / 59.8 b
Net Official Development Assist. received (% of GNI)	5.83	3.42	3.25 c

a Projected estimate (medium fertility variant). b 2022. c 2021. d 2019. e Excludes irrigation canals and landscaping care. f Data classified according to ISIC Rev. 4. g Excludes publishing activities, recycling. Includes irrigation canals. h Estimate. i Break in the time series. j Data refers to a 5-year period preceding the reference year. k Including refugees. l Refers to foreign citizens. m 2020. n Data refer to fiscal years beginning 1 October. o Data are based on SHA2011. p Data are as at 1 January of reporting year.

Latvia

Region	Northern Europe	UN membership date	17 September 1991
Population (000, 2023)	1 851[a,b]	Surface area (km2)	64 594[c]
Pop. density (per km2, 2023)	29.7[a,b]	Sex ratio (m per 100 f)	86.5[a,b]
Capital city	Riga	National currency	Euro (EUR)
Capital city pop. (000, 2023)	633.8[d]	Exchange rate (per US$)	0.9[b]

Economic indicators

	2010	2015	2023
GDP: Gross domestic product (million current US$)	23 964	27 252	39 854[c]
GDP growth rate (annual %, const. 2015 prices)	- 4.5	3.9	4.1[c]
GDP per capita (current US$)	11 403.1	13 681.1	21 267.5[c]
Economy: Agriculture (% of Gross Value Added)[e,f]	4.6	4.0	4.7[c]
Economy: Industry (% of Gross Value Added)[f,g]	23.0	21.7	22.7[c]
Economy: Services and other activity (% of GVA)[f]	72.5	74.3	72.6[c]
Employment in agriculture (% of employed)	8.6	7.9	6.8[c]
Employment in industry (% of employed)	23.1	15.9[h]	23.5[c]
Employment in services & other sectors (% employed)	68.3	68.4	69.6[c]
Unemployment rate (% of labour force)	19.5	9.9	6.3[h]
Labour force participation rate (female/male pop. %)	53.9 / 65.0	54.1 / 67.4	55.6 / 68.3[h]
CPI: Consumer Price Index (2010=100)	100	108	142[b]
Agricultural production index (2014-2016=100)	73	107	101[c]
International trade: exports (million current US$)	8 851	11 650	22 526[b]
International trade: imports (million current US$)	11 143	14 096	27 894[b]
International trade: balance (million current US$)	- 2 292	- 2 446	- 5 369[b]
Balance of payments, current account (million US$)	413	- 158	- 2 642[b]

Major trading partners

						2022
Export partners (% of exports)	Lithuania	18.2	Estonia	11.8	Germany	6.7
Import partners (% of imports)	Lithuania	24.4	Estonia	10.1	Germany	9.6

Social indicators

	2010	2015	2023
Population growth rate (average annual %)	- 1.2	- 0.9	- 1.1[a,b]
Urban population (% of total population)	67.8	68.0	68.2[d]
Urban population growth rate (average annual %)[i]	- 1.3	- 1.2	...
Fertility rate, total (live births per woman)	1.4	1.7	1.6[a,b]
Life expectancy at birth (females/males, years)	77.9 / 67.8	79.2 / 69.9	80.1 / 71.5[a,b]
Population age distribution (0-14/60+ years old, %)	14.2 / 24.3	15.0 / 26.2	15.6 / 29.1[a,b]
International migrant stock (000/% of total pop.)	313.8 / 14.8	265.4 / 13.3	239.4 / 12.7[j]
Refugees and others of concern to the UNHCR (000)	327.0[k]	263.2	230.6[b]
Infant mortality rate (per 1 000 live births)	5.2	4.0	2.8[a,b]
Health: Current expenditure (% of GDP)	6.1	5.7	7.4[l,j]
Health: Physicians (per 1 000 pop.)	3.1	3.2	3.3[j]
Education: Government expenditure (% of GDP)	5.0	5.3	4.4[d]
Education: Primary gross enrol. ratio (f/m per 100 pop.)[h]	101.9 / 103.9	99.4 / 99.4	99.9 / 99.8[j]
Education: Lowr. sec. gross enrol. ratio (f/m per 100 pop.)[h]	104.0 / 108.2	101.5 / 104.4	100.9 / 101.8[j]
Education: Upr. sec. gross enrol. ratio (f/m per 100 pop.)[h]	100.7 / 100.0	121.4 / 122.9	111.8 / 109.9[j]
Intentional homicide rate (per 100 000 pop.)	...	3.4	3.0[c]
Seats held by women in the National Parliament (%)	22.0	18.0	29.0[m]

Environment and infrastructure indicators

	2010	2015	2023
Individuals using the Internet (per 100 inhabitants)	68.4[n]	79.2[o]	91.2[o,c]
Research & Development expenditure (% of GDP)	0.6	0.6	0.7[j]
Threatened species (number)	18	25	47[b]
Forested area (% of land area)	54.2	54.5	54.8[j]
CO2 emission estimates (million tons/tons per capita)	8.5 / 3.9	7.2 / 3.5	7.0 / 3.5[c]
Energy production, primary (Petajoules)	83	98	113[j]
Energy supply per capita (Gigajoules)	90	90	95[j]
Tourist/visitor arrivals at national borders (000)[p]	1 373	2 024	478[c]
Important sites for terrestrial biodiversity protected (%)	97.3	97.3	97.3[b]
Net Official Development Assist. disbursed (% of GNI)	...	0.08[q]	0.12[c]

a Projected estimate (medium fertility variant). b 2022. c 2021. d 2019. e Excludes irrigation canals and landscaping care. f Data classified according to ISIC Rev. 4. g Excludes publishing activities, recycling. Includes irrigation canals. h Estimate. i Data refers to a 5-year period preceding the reference year. j 2020. k Data as at the end of December. l Break in the time series. m Data are as at 1 January of reporting year. n Population aged 16 to 74 years. o Users in the last 3 months. p Non-resident departures. Survey of persons crossing the state border. q 2014.

Lebanon

Region	Western Asia	
Population (000, 2023)	5 490 [a,b]	
Pop. density (per km2, 2023)	536.6 [a,b]	
Capital city	Beirut	
Capital city pop. (000, 2023)	2 406.9 [d,e,f]	

UN membership date	24 October 1945
Surface area (km2)	10 452 [c]
Sex ratio (m per 100 f)	94.2 [a,b]
National currency	Lebanese Pound (LBP)
Exchange rate (per US$)	1 507.5 [b]

Economic indicators

	2010	2015	2023
GDP: Gross domestic product (million current US$)	38 444	49 929	37 945 [c]
GDP growth rate (annual %, const. 2015 prices)	8.0	0.5	- 7.0 [c]
GDP per capita (current US$)	7 695.2	7 802.8	6 784.8 [c]
Economy: Agriculture (% of Gross Value Added) [g,h]	4.3	3.5	4.1 [c]
Economy: Industry (% of Gross Value Added) [h,i]	15.4	16.9	2.8 [c]
Economy: Services and other activity (% of GVA) [h]	80.3	79.5	95.8 [c]
Employment in agriculture (% of employed) [j]	3.9	3.9	3.8 [c]
Employment in industry (% of employed) [j]	23.6	22.2	20.8 [c]
Employment in services & other sectors (% employed) [j]	72.5	74.0	75.4 [c]
Unemployment rate (% of labour force) [j]	6.8	9.3	12.8
Labour force participation rate (female/male pop. %) [j]	22.9 / 67.4	26.1 / 68.7	29.3 / 67.6
CPI: Consumer Price Index (2010=100) [j]	100	115	612 [c]
Agricultural production index (2014-2016=100)	89	99	100 [c]
International trade: exports (million current US$)	4 254	2 953	3 862 [b]
International trade: imports (million current US$)	17 970	18 600	19 500 [b]
International trade: balance (million current US$)	- 13 716	- 15 646	- 15 638 [b]
Balance of payments, current account (million US$)	- 7 552	- 8 542	- 2 985 [c]

Major trading partners

							2022
Export partners (% of exports) [j]	United Arab Emirates	23.3	Syria	9.7	Türkiye	4.5
Import partners (% of imports)	China	13.8	Türkiye	12.4	Greece	9.8

Social indicators

	2010	2015	2023
Population growth rate (average annual %)	0.5	- 2.1	- 2.3 [a,b]
Urban population (% of total population)	87.3	88.1	88.8 [f]
Urban population growth rate (average annual %) [k]	1.8	6.2	...
Fertility rate, total (live births per woman)	2.1	2.2	2.1 [a,b]
Life expectancy at birth (females/males, years)	79.9 / 76.1	81.0 / 77.2	76.6 / 72.2 [a,b]
Population age distribution (0-14/60+ years old, %)	25.8 / 9.0	24.8 / 10.9	27.4 / 14.4 [a,b]
International migrant stock (000/% of total pop.) [l]	793.2 / 16.0	1 916.3 / 29.3	1 712.8 / 25.1 [m]
Refugees and others of concern to the UNHCR (000)	9.5 [n]	1 189.1	862.8 [b]
Infant mortality rate (per 1 000 live births)	8.7	7.2	6.2 [a,b]
Health: Current expenditure (% of GDP) [d,o]	7.4	7.4 [p]	8.0 [j,m]
Health: Physicians (per 1 000 pop.)	2.3	2.1	2.6 [f]
Education: Government expenditure (% of GDP)	1.6	2.4 [q]	...
Intentional homicide rate (per 100 000 pop.)	3.3	3.6	2.3 [m]
Seats held by women in the National Parliament (%)	3.1	3.1	6.2 [r]

Environment and infrastructure indicators

	2010	2015	2023
Individuals using the Internet (per 100 inhabitants) [j]	43.7 [s]	74.0	86.6 [c]
Threatened species (number)	50	69	193 [b]
Forested area (% of land area)	13.4	13.7	14.0 [m]
CO2 emission estimates (million tons/tons per capita)	18.6 / 3.7	25.0 / 3.8	20.8 / 3.0 [m]
Energy production, primary (Petajoules)	9	8	10 [m]
Energy supply per capita (Gigajoules)	52	53	55 [j,m]
Tourist/visitor arrivals at national borders (000) [t]	2 168	1 518	890 [c]
Important sites for terrestrial biodiversity protected (%)	4.4	4.4	4.7 [b]
Net Official Development Assist. received (% of GNI)	1.17	1.95	7.99 [c]

a Projected estimate (medium fertility variant). b 2022. c 2021. d Estimates should be viewed with caution as these are derived from scarce data. e Excluding Syrian refugees. f 2019. g Excludes irrigation canals and landscaping care. h Data classified according to ISIC Rev. 4. i Excludes publishing activities, recycling. Includes irrigation canals. j Estimate. k Data refers to a 5-year period preceding the reference year. l Including refugees. m 2020. n Data as at the end of December. o Data based on calendar year (January 1 to December 31). p Data are based on SHA2011. q 2013. r Data are as at 1 January of reporting year. s Population aged 15 years and over. t Excluding the Lebanon, Syria and Palestine nationalities.

Lesotho

Region	Southern Africa	UN membership date	17 October 1966
Population (000, 2023)	2 306 a,b	Surface area (km2)	30 355 a
Pop. density (per km2, 2023)	75.9 a,b	Sex ratio (m per 100 f)	97.4 a,b
Capital city	Maseru	National currency	Loti (LSL)
Capital city pop. (000, 2023)	201.9 d	Exchange rate (per US$)	17.0 b

Economic indicators

	2010	2015	2023
GDP: Gross domestic product (million current US$)	2 234	2 360	2 373 c
GDP growth rate (annual %, const. 2015 prices)	5.3	3.1	1.6 c
GDP per capita (current US$)	1 104.6	1 113.8	1 040.3 c
Economy: Agriculture (% of Gross Value Added) e,f	5.4	4.2	4.8 c
Economy: Industry (% of Gross Value Added) e,g	34.9	37.9	32.4 c
Economy: Services and other activity (% of GVA) e	59.7	57.9	62.8 c
Employment in agriculture (% of employed) h	31.7	30.2	30.0 c
Employment in industry (% of employed) h	32.9	34.2	35.0 c
Employment in services & other sectors (% employed) h	35.4	35.6	35.1 c
Unemployment rate (% of labour force) h	16.9	16.9	17.9
Labour force participation rate (female/male pop. %) h	59.4 / 75.0	57.3 / 73.1	57.4 / 71.6
CPI: Consumer Price Index (2010=100)	100	127	188 b
Agricultural production index (2014-2016=100)	104	101	100 c
International trade: exports (million current US$)	503	604	1 632 h,b
International trade: imports (million current US$)	1 277	1 410	1 544 h,b
International trade: balance (million current US$)	- 773	- 806	88 h,b
Balance of payments, current account (million US$)	- 158	- 78	- 150 b

Major trading partners

2022

Export partners (% of exports) h	South Africa	44.9	United States	30.2	Belgium	18.5
Import partners (% of imports) h	South Africa	74.9	China	8.6	Other Asia, nes	5.7

Social indicators

	2010	2015	2023
Population growth rate (average annual %)	0.7	1.2	1.0 a,b
Urban population (% of total population)	24.8	26.9	28.6 i
Urban population growth rate (average annual %) j	3.1	2.9	...
Fertility rate, total (live births per woman)	3.2	3.3	3.0 a,b
Life expectancy at birth (females/males, years)	48.2 / 43.2	53.9 / 48.5	55.9 / 50.3 a,b
Population age distribution (0-14/60+ years old, %)	36.1 / 6.3	35.1 / 6.3	34.0 / 6.6 a,b
International migrant stock (000/% of total pop.) k,l	6.4 / 0.3	9.2 / 0.4	12.1 / 0.6 m
Refugees and others of concern to the UNHCR (000)	...	~0.0	0.5 b
Infant mortality rate (per 1 000 live births)	73.9	72.6	69.0 a,b
Health: Current expenditure (% of GDP) h,n	8.4	9.0	11.8 m
Health: Physicians (per 1 000 pop.)	0.1	...	0.5 d
Education: Government expenditure (% of GDP)	12.3 o	7.1	6.1 b
Education: Primary gross enrol. ratio (f/m per 100 pop.)	122.1 / 127.4	113.7 / 119.6	105.7 / 111.1 i
Education: Lowr. sec. gross enrol. ratio (f/m per 100 pop.)	83.1 / 59.4	80.0 / 59.6	84.3 / 63.9 p
Education: Upr. sec. gross enrol. ratio (f/m per 100 pop.)	39.5 / 29.2	53.6 / 39.9	51.1 / 35.7 p
Intentional homicide rate (per 100 000 pop.)	37.7 o	...	...
Seats held by women in the National Parliament (%)	24.2	26.7	26.4 q

Environment and infrastructure indicators

	2010	2015	2023
Individuals using the Internet (per 100 inhabitants) h	3.9	25.0	48.0 c
Research & Development expenditure (% of GDP)	~0.0 r,s	0.1 t,u	...
Threatened species (number)	16	17	20 b
Forested area (% of land area)	1.1	1.1	1.1 m
Energy production, primary (Petajoules)	27	20 h	16 h,m
Energy supply per capita (Gigajoules)	26	22 h	19 h,m
Tourist/visitor arrivals at national borders (000)	414	320 v	...
Important sites for terrestrial biodiversity protected (%)	16.5	16.5	16.5 b
Pop. using safely managed drinking water (urban/rural, %)	59.1 / 5.0	66.2 / 7.0	72.6 / 9.2 b
Pop. using safely managed sanitation (urban/rural, %)	28.4 / 28.6	34.0 / 40.0	39.4 / 51.0 b
Net Official Development Assist. received (% of GNI)	8.92	3.28	6.30 c

a Projected estimate (medium fertility variant). b 2022. c 2021. d 2018. e Data classified according to ISIC Rev. 4. f Excludes irrigation canals and landscaping care. g Excludes publishing activities, recycling. Includes irrigation canals. h Estimate. i 2019. j Data refers to a 5-year period preceding the reference year. k Refers to foreign citizens. l Including refugees. m 2020. n Data refer to fiscal years beginning 1 April. o 2008. p 2017. q Data are as at 1 January of reporting year. r Partial data. s 2009. t Excluding private non-profit. u Excluding business enterprise. v 2013.

Liberia

Region	Western Africa	UN membership date	02 November 1945
Population (000, 2023)	5 303 [a,b]	Surface area (km2)	111 369 [a]
Pop. density (per km2, 2023)	55.1 [a,b]	Sex ratio (m per 100 f)	99.2 [a,b]
Capital city	Monrovia	National currency	Liberian Dollar (LRD)
Capital city pop. (000, 2023)	1 467.0 [d]	Exchange rate (per US$)	164.2 [e]

Economic indicators

	2010	2015	2023
GDP: Gross domestic product (million current US$)	1 292	2 669	2 445 [c]
GDP growth rate (annual %, const. 2015 prices)	7.3	9.3	- 0.4 [c]
GDP per capita (current US$)	321.4	578.7	470.8 [c]
Economy: Agriculture (% of Gross Value Added)	64.5	69.5	73.9 [c]
Economy: Industry (% of Gross Value Added)	12.5	10.5	8.5 [c]
Economy: Services and other activity (% of GVA)	17.9	20.0	17.6 [c]
Employment in agriculture (% of employed)	47.3	41.3 [f]	40.6 [f,c]
Employment in industry (% of employed)	10.9	8.9 [f]	8.1 [f,c]
Employment in services & other sectors (% employed)	41.9	49.7 [f]	51.3 [f,c]
Unemployment rate (% of labour force)	2.3	2.6 [f]	3.6 [f]
Labour force participation rate (female/male pop. %) [f]	71.8 / 83.0	71.9 / 82.3	72.6 / 81.1
CPI: Consumer Price Index (2010=100)	100	148	223 [g]
Agricultural production index (2014-2016=100)	92	98	107 [c]
International trade: exports (million current US$) [f]	222	627	822 [b]
International trade: imports (million current US$) [f]	710	901	1 720 [b]
International trade: balance (million current US$) [f]	- 488	- 273	- 898 [b]
Balance of payments, current account (million US$)	- 853	171	- 653 [d]

Major trading partners 2022

Export partners (% of exports) [f]	Switzerland	25.1	Germany	8.3	United Kingdom	7.4
Import partners (% of imports) [f]	China	35.0	Singapore	25.9	Japan	12.3

Social indicators

	2010	2015	2023
Population growth rate (average annual %)	2.9	2.1	2.1 [a,b]
Urban population (% of total population)	47.8	49.8	51.6 [d]
Urban population growth rate (average annual %) [h]	4.6	3.4	...
Fertility rate, total (live births per woman)	5.1	4.5	4.0 [a,b]
Life expectancy at birth (females/males, years)	60.6 / 58.2	60.4 / 57.9	62.4 / 59.8 [a,b]
Population age distribution (0-14/60+ years old, %)	43.3 / 5.4	42.6 / 5.2	40.5 / 5.1 [a,b]
International migrant stock (000/% of total pop.) [i]	99.2 / 2.5	112.1 / 2.5	87.9 / 1.7 [e]
Refugees and others of concern to the UNHCR (000)	26.6 [j]	40.4	4.6 [b]
Infant mortality rate (per 1 000 live births)	74.0	67.7	57.3 [a,b]
Health: Current expenditure (% of GDP) [k]	9.0	10.6	9.5 [e]
Health: Physicians (per 1 000 pop.)	~0.0	~0.0	~0.0 [g]
Education: Government expenditure (% of GDP)	1.7 [l]	2.1	2.6 [b]
Education: Primary gross enrol. ratio (f/m per 100 pop.)	96.5 / 108.0 [m]	90.2 / 100.3	77.3 / 77.6 [e]
Education: Lowr. sec. gross enrol. ratio (f/m per 100 pop.)	41.9 / 53.4 [m]	39.7 / 50.2	46.4 / 47.4 [e]
Education: Upr. sec. gross enrol. ratio (f/m per 100 pop.)	... / ...	25.3 / 34.5	31.5 / 32.3 [e]
Intentional homicide rate (per 100 000 pop.)	3.2	3.1 [n]	...
Seats held by women in the National Parliament (%)	12.5	11.0	11.0 [o]

Environment and infrastructure indicators

	2010	2015	2023
Individuals using the Internet (per 100 inhabitants)	2.3	10.0 [f]	33.6 [f,c]
Threatened species (number)	147	158	294 [b]
Forested area (% of land area)	82.2	80.7	79.1 [e]
Energy production, primary (Petajoules)	64	76	90 [e]
Energy supply per capita (Gigajoules)	19	18	19 [e]
Important sites for terrestrial biodiversity protected (%)	15.8	15.8	15.8 [b]
Net Official Development Assist. received (% of GNI)	77.89	37.14	18.52 [c]

a Projected estimate (medium fertility variant). b 2022. c 2021. d 2019. e 2020. f Estimate. g 2018. h Data refers to a 5-year period preceding the reference year. i Including refugees. j Data as at the end of December. k Data refer to fiscal years beginning 1 July. l 2008. m 2009. n 2012. o Data are as at 1 January of reporting year.

Libya

Region	Northern Africa	UN membership date	14 December 1955
Population (000, 2023)	6 812[a,b]	Surface area (km2)	1 676 198[a]
Pop. density (per km2, 2023)	4.1[a,b]	Sex ratio (m per 100 f)	102.4[a,b]
Capital city	Tripoli	National currency	Libyan Dinar (LYD)
Capital city pop. (000, 2023)	1 160.9[d]	Exchange rate (per US$)	4.8[b]

Economic indicators	2010	2015	2023
GDP: Gross domestic product (million current US$)	75 381	48 718	39 006[c]
GDP growth rate (annual %, const. 2015 prices)	5.0	- 0.8	28.3[c]
GDP per capita (current US$)	11 611.4	7 867.5	5 791.3[c]
Economy: Agriculture (% of Gross Value Added)	1.6	3.9	3.6[c]
Economy: Industry (% of Gross Value Added)	69.0	31.2	44.4[c]
Economy: Services and other activity (% of GVA)	29.3	64.9	52.0[c]
Employment in agriculture (% of employed)[e]	17.3	19.3	16.3[c]
Employment in industry (% of employed)[e]	22.0	17.5	19.3[c]
Employment in services & other sectors (% employed)[e]	60.7	63.2	64.4[c]
Unemployment rate (% of labour force)[e]	19.3	19.5	20.5
Labour force participation rate (female/male pop. %)[e]	33.9 / 61.4	33.9 / 61.1	34.8 / 60.8
CPI: Consumer Price Index (2010=100)	100	126[f]	...
Agricultural production index (2014-2016=100)	106	101	106[c]
International trade: exports (million current US$)	36 440	10 200[e]	46 483[e,b]
International trade: imports (million current US$)	17 674	13 000[e]	20 936[e,b]
International trade: balance (million current US$)	18 766	- 2 800[e]	25 547[e,b]
Balance of payments, current account (million US$)	16 801	- 9 346	- 4 780[9]

Major trading partners						2022
Export partners (% of exports)[e]	Italy	29.3	Spain	9.9	Germany	9.4
Import partners (% of imports)[e]	Türkiye	13.5	Italy	11.7	China	11.3

Social indicators	2010	2015	2023
Population growth rate (average annual %)	2.1	1.5	1.1[a,b]
Urban population (% of total population)	78.1	79.3	80.4[d]
Urban population growth rate (average annual %)[h]	1.5	0.5	...
Fertility rate, total (live births per woman)	2.6	2.7	2.4[a,b]
Life expectancy at birth (females/males, years)	74.9 / 70.2	75.4 / 68.5	74.8 / 69.7[a,b]
Population age distribution (0-14/60+ years old, %)	29.9 / 5.9	31.6 / 6.7	28.3 / 7.7[a,b]
International migrant stock (000/% of total pop.)[i,j]	687.2 / 11.1	771.1 / 12.0	826.5 / 12.0[9]
Refugees and others of concern to the UNHCR (000)	11.2[k]	471.7	218.9[b]
Infant mortality rate (per 1 000 live births)	14.2	11.9	9.1[a,b]
Health: Current expenditure (% of GDP)[l,m]	3.6	6.1[n]	...
Health: Physicians (per 1 000 pop.)	1.9[o]	2.0	2.2[p]
Education: Primary gross enrol. ratio (f/m per 100 pop.)	106.6 / 111.3[q]	... / ...	... / ...
Education: Lowr. sec. gross enrol. ratio (f/m per 100 pop.)	103.0 / 103.6[q]	... / ...	... / ...
Education: Upr. sec. gross enrol. ratio (f/m per 100 pop.)	108.8 / 77.3[q]	... / ...	... / ...
Seats held by women in the National Parliament (%)	7.7	16.0	16.5[r]

Environment and infrastructure indicators	2010	2015	2023
Individuals using the Internet (per 100 inhabitants)[e]	14.0	17.8[s]	...
Threatened species (number)	44	54	92[b]
Forested area (% of land area)	0.1	0.1	0.1[9]
CO2 emission estimates (million tons/tons per capita)	51.2 / 8.2	45.7 / 7.0	39.8 / 5.7[9]
Energy production, primary (Petajoules)	4 310	1 453	1 334[9]
Energy supply per capita (Gigajoules)	134	123	102[9]
Tourist/visitor arrivals at national borders (000)	34[t,u]	...	...
Important sites for terrestrial biodiversity protected (%)	0.0	0.0	0.0[b]
Net Official Development Assist. received (% of GNI)	0.01	0.32	0.81[c]

a Projected estimate (medium fertility variant). b 2022. c 2021. d 2019. e Estimate. f 2013. g 2020. h Data refers to a 5-year period preceding the reference year. i Including refugees. j Refers to foreign citizens. k Data as at the end of December. l Estimates should be viewed with caution as these are derived from scarce data. m Data based on calendar year (January 1 to December 31). n 2011. o 2009. p 2017. q 2006. r Data are as at 1 January of reporting year. s 2014. t Non-resident tourists staying in hotels and similar establishments. u 2008.

Liechtenstein

Region	Western Europe	UN membership date	18 September 1990	
Population (000, 2023)	39[a,b]	Surface area (km2)	160[c]	
Pop. density (per km2, 2023)	245.8[a,b]	Sex ratio (m per 100 f)	98.4[a,b]	
Capital city	Vaduz	National currency	Swiss Franc (CHF)	
Capital city pop. (000, 2023)	5.5[d]	Exchange rate (per US$)	0.9[b]	

Economic indicators	2010	2015	2023
GDP: Gross domestic product (million current US$)	5 621	6 269	6 608[c]
GDP growth rate (annual %, const. 2015 prices)	7.4	–0.0	4.6[c]
GDP per capita (current US$)	156 462.1	167 809.2	169 260.2[c]
Economy: Agriculture (% of Gross Value Added)[e,f]	0.1	0.1	0.1[c]
Economy: Industry (% of Gross Value Added)[e,g]	44.6	43.1	44.8[c]
Economy: Services and other activity (% of GVA)[e]	55.3	56.8	55.1[c]
Unemployment rate (% of labour force)[h]	2.6	2.6[i]	...
Labour force participation rate (female/male pop. %)	52.6 / 70.9	53.5 / 70.6[i]	... / ...

Social indicators	2010	2015	2023
Population growth rate (average annual %)	0.6	0.6	0.7[a,b]
Urban population (% of total population)	14.5	14.3	14.4[j]
Urban population growth rate (average annual %)[k]	0.3	0.5	...
Fertility rate, total (live births per woman)	1.4	1.4	1.5[a,b]
Life expectancy at birth (females/males, years)	84.3 / 79.5	84.5 / 80.9	86.1 / 83.0[a,b]
Population age distribution (0-14/60+ years old, %)	16.3 / 19.7	15.0 / 22.5	14.5 / 26.6[a,b]
International migrant stock (000/% of total pop.)	22.3 / 62.1	23.8 / 63.5	25.9 / 67.9[i]
Refugees and others of concern to the UNHCR (000)	0.1[m]	0.2	0.6[b]
Infant mortality rate (per 1 000 live births)	6.8	6.2	5.0[a,b]
Education: Government expenditure (% of GDP)	2.0[n]	2.6[o]	...
Education: Primary gross enrol. ratio (f/m per 100 pop.)[p]	102.3 / 108.6	104.8 / 106.5	100.8 / 103.3[c]
Education: Lowr. sec. gross enrol. ratio (f/m per 100 pop.)[p]	103.0 / 103.1	94.1 / 101.9	99.7 / 103.1[c]
Education: Upr. sec. gross enrol. ratio (f/m per 100 pop.)[p]	96.2 / 137.6	110.9 / 167.5	121.0 / 160.7[c]
Intentional homicide rate (per 100 000 pop.)	2.8	0.0	5.1[c]
Seats held by women in the National Parliament (%)	24.0	20.0	28.0[q]

Environment and infrastructure indicators	2010	2015	2023
Individuals using the Internet (per 100 inhabitants)[p]	80.0	96.6	95.6[c]
Threatened species (number)	2	4	15[b]
Forested area (% of land area)	41.9	41.9	41.9[l]
Energy production, primary (Petajoules)[p]	1	1	1[l]
Energy supply per capita (Gigajoules)	92	88	87[l]
Tourist/visitor arrivals at national borders (000)[r]	64	57	70[c]
Important sites for terrestrial biodiversity protected (%)	80.8	80.8	80.8[b]
Net Official Development Assist. disbursed (% of GNI)	...	0.64[i]	...

a Projected estimate (medium fertility variant). b 2022. c 2021. d 2018. e Data classified according to ISIC Rev. 4. f Excludes irrigation canals and landscaping care. g Excludes publishing activities, recycling. Includes irrigation canals. h Population aged 15 to 64 years. i 2013. j 2019. k Data refers to a 5-year period preceding the reference year. l 2020. m Data as at the end of December. n 2008. o 2011. p Estimate. q Data are as at 1 January of reporting year. r Excluding long term tourists on campgrounds and in holiday flats.

Lithuania

Region	Northern Europe	UN membership date	17 September 1991
Population (000, 2023)	2 750 [a,b]	Surface area (km2)	65 286 [c]
Pop. density (per km2, 2023)	43.9 [a,b]	Sex ratio (m per 100 f)	88.6 [a,b]
Capital city	Vilnius	National currency	Euro (EUR)
Capital city pop. (000, 2023)	537.6 [d]	Exchange rate (per US$)	0.9 [b]

Economic indicators

	2010	2015	2023
GDP: Gross domestic product (million current US$)	37 138	41 419	66 445 [c]
GDP growth rate (annual %, const. 2015 prices)	1.7	2.0	6.0 [c]
GDP per capita (current US$)	11 831.2	13 975.1	23 844.1 [c]
Economy: Agriculture (% of Gross Value Added) [e,f]	3.4	3.8	3.7 [c]
Economy: Industry (% of Gross Value Added) [e,g]	29.1	29.7	28.3 [c]
Economy: Services and other activity (% of GVA) [e]	67.5	66.5	68.0 [c]
Employment in agriculture (% of employed)	8.8	9.1	5.3 [c]
Employment in industry (% of employed)	17.9 [h]	23.2 [h]	26.3 [c]
Employment in services & other sectors (% employed)	66.6	65.9	68.4 [c]
Unemployment rate (% of labour force)	17.8	9.1	5.5 [h]
Labour force participation rate (female/male pop. %)	52.5 / 62.0	54.4 / 64.8	58.4 / 68.2 [h]
CPI: Consumer Price Index (2010=100) [i]	100	108	150 [b]
Agricultural production index (2014-2016=100)	73	106	96 [c]
International trade: exports (million current US$)	20 814	25 411	46 502 [b]
International trade: imports (million current US$)	23 378	28 176	55 110 [b]
International trade: balance (million current US$)	- 2 564	- 2 765	- 8 608 [b]
Balance of payments, current account (million US$)	73	- 1 014	- 3 583 [b]

Major trading partners   2022

Export partners (% of exports)	Latvia	12.8	Poland	9.1	Germany	7.9
Import partners (% of imports)	Poland	11.7	Germany	11.6	Latvia	7.9

Social indicators

	2010	2015	2023
Population growth rate (average annual %)	- 1.3	- 1.0	- 1.4 [a,b]
Urban population (% of total population)	66.8	67.2	67.9 [d]
Urban population growth rate (average annual %) [j]	- 1.3	- 1.1	...
Fertility rate, total (live births per woman)	1.5	1.7	1.6 [a,b]
Life expectancy at birth (females/males, years)	78.8 / 67.9	79.5 / 69.6	79.1 / 69.5 [a,b]
Population age distribution (0-14/60+ years old, %)	14.9 / 23.3	14.5 / 25.1	15.3 / 28.5 [a,b]
International migrant stock (000/% of total pop.)	160.8 / 5.1	136.0 / 4.6	145.2 / 5.3 [k]
Refugees and others of concern to the UNHCR (000)	4.6 [l]	4.7	52.6 [b]
Infant mortality rate (per 1 000 live births)	4.9	4.0	2.8 [a,b]
Health: Current expenditure (% of GDP)	6.8	6.5	7.9 [c]
Health: Physicians (per 1 000 pop.)	3.9	4.3	5.0 [c]
Education: Government expenditure (% of GDP)	5.3	4.2	4.0 [d]
Education: Primary gross enrol. ratio (f/m per 100 pop.) [h]	99.8 / 101.0	101.9 / 102.2	102.8 / 102.7 [k]
Education: Lowr. sec. gross enrol. ratio (f/m per 100 pop.) [h]	102.3 / 105.6	102.0 / 106.0	105.5 / 107.5 [k]
Education: Upr. sec. gross enrol. ratio (f/m per 100 pop.) [h]	108.3 / 106.8	114.0 / 119.6	112.6 / 117.8 [k]
Intentional homicide rate (per 100 000 pop.)	7.0	5.8	2.6 [c]
Seats held by women in the National Parliament (%)	19.1	23.4	28.4 [m]

Environment and infrastructure indicators

	2010	2015	2023
Individuals using the Internet (per 100 inhabitants)	62.1 [n,o]	71.4 [o]	86.9 [c]
Research & Development expenditure (% of GDP)	0.8	1.0	1.1 [p,k]
Threatened species (number)	17	22	44 [b]
Forested area (% of land area)	34.6	34.9	35.1 [k]
CO2 emission estimates (million tons/tons per capita)	12.7 / 4.0	11.0 / 3.6	11.7 / 4.0 [c]
Energy production, primary (Petajoules)	64	76	82 [k]
Energy supply per capita (Gigajoules)	93	99	110 [k]
Tourist/visitor arrivals at national borders (000)	1 507	2 071	948 [c]
Important sites for terrestrial biodiversity protected (%)	91.4	91.7	91.7 [b]
Pop. using safely managed drinking water (urban/rural, %)	96.9 / ...	98.8 / ...	99.3 / ... [b]
Pop. using safely managed sanitation (urban/rural %)	90.3 / 72.8	94.4 / 80.9	97.5 / 90.5 [b]
Net Official Development Assist. disbursed (% of GNI)	...	0.11 [q]	0.14 [c]

a Projected estimate (medium fertility variant). b 2022. c 2021. d 2019. e Data classified according to ISIC Rev. 4. f Excludes irrigation canals and landscaping care. g Excludes publishing activities, recycling. Includes irrigation canals. h Estimate. i Calculated by the UN Statistics Division from national indices. j Data refers to a 5-year period preceding the reference year. k 2020. l Data as at the end of December. m Data are as at 1 January of reporting year. n Users in the last 12 months. o Population aged 16 to 74 years. p Provisional data. q 2013.

Luxembourg

Region	Western Europe	
Population (000, 2023)	648 [a,b]	
Pop. density (per km2, 2023)	250.0 [a,b]	
Capital city	Luxembourg	
Capital city pop. (000, 2023)	119.8 [d]	

UN membership date	24 October 1945
Surface area (km2)	2 586 [c]
Sex ratio (m per 100 f)	101.3 [a,b]
National currency	Euro (EUR)
Exchange rate (per US$)	0.9 [b]

Economic indicators

	2010	2015	2023
GDP: Gross domestic product (million current US$)	56 159	60 047	85 506 [c]
GDP growth rate (annual %, const. 2015 prices)	3.8	2.3	5.1 [c]
GDP per capita (current US$)	110 752.3	105 455.9	133 745.4 [c]
Economy: Agriculture (% of Gross Value Added) [e,f]	0.3	0.2	0.2 [c]
Economy: Industry (% of Gross Value Added) [e,g]	12.2	12.6	12.4 [c]
Economy: Services and other activity (% of GVA) [e]	87.5	87.1	87.4 [c]
Employment in agriculture (% of employed)	1.1	1.1	1.1 [c]
Employment in industry (% of employed)	13.3	12.6	9.3 [c]
Employment in services & other sectors (% employed)	85.5	86.5	89.4 [c]
Unemployment rate (% of labour force)	4.4	6.7	5.0 [h]
Labour force participation rate (female/male pop. %)	49.8 / 65.8	54.6 / 65.4	57.3 / 64.8 [h]
CPI: Consumer Price Index (2010=100) [i]	100	109	126 [b]
Agricultural production index (2014-2016=100)	91	102	113 [c]
International trade: exports (million current US$)	13 911	12 626	16 810 [b]
International trade: imports (million current US$)	20 400	19 296	26 068 [b]
International trade: balance (million current US$)	- 6 489	- 6 671	- 9 258 [b]
Balance of payments, current account (million US$)	3 268	2 921	4 246 [b]

Major trading partners

						2022
Export partners (% of exports)	Germany	25.5	France	15.3	Belgium	12.4
Import partners (% of imports)	Belgium	24.3	Germany	22.1	France	10.7

Social indicators

	2010	2015	2023
Population growth rate (average annual %)	1.9	2.3	1.1 [a,b]
Urban population (% of total population)	88.5	90.2	91.2 [j]
Urban population growth rate (average annual %) [k]	2.5	2.6	...
Fertility rate, total (live births per woman)	1.6	1.5	1.4 [a,b]
Life expectancy at birth (females/males, years)	83.2 / 77.9	83.9 / 79.7	84.8 / 80.4 [a,b]
Population age distribution (0-14/60+ years old, %)	17.7 / 18.9	16.6 / 19.3	15.8 / 20.8 [a,b]
International migrant stock (000/% of total pop.)	163.1 / 32.1	248.9 / 43.9	298.1 / 47.6 [l]
Refugees and others of concern to the UNHCR (000)	4.1 [m]	2.1	11.7 [b]
Infant mortality rate (per 1 000 live births)	3.8	2.5	3.1 [a,b]
Health: Current expenditure (% of GDP)	6.7	5.1	5.4 [c]
Health: Physicians (per 1 000 pop.)	2.8	2.9	3.0 [n]
Education: Government expenditure (% of GDP)	5.3	3.8	3.7 [j]
Education: Primary gross enrol. ratio (f/m per 100 pop.)	98.1 / 97.1	98.9 / 99.0	104.9 / 106.4 [l]
Education: Lowr. sec. gross enrol. ratio (f/m per 100 pop.)	116.6 / 114.7	114.0 / 112.4	117.7 / 125.9 [l]
Education: Upr. sec. gross enrol. ratio (f/m per 100 pop.)	92.3 / 88.5	97.3 / 92.0	99.6 / 94.5 [l]
Intentional homicide rate (per 100 000 pop.)	2.0	0.9	0.6 [c]
Seats held by women in the National Parliament (%)	20.0	28.3	35.0 [o]

Environment and infrastructure indicators

	2010	2015	2023
Individuals using the Internet (per 100 inhabitants)	90.6 [p]	96.4	98.7 [c]
Research & Development expenditure (% of GDP)	1.4	1.3	1.1 [l]
Threatened species (number)	5	9	17 [b]
Forested area (% of land area)	34.5	34.5	34.5 [l]
CO2 emission estimates (million tons/tons per capita)	10.8 / 21.0	9.0 / 15.5	8.0 / 12.3 [c]
Energy production, primary (Petajoules)	5	6	13 [l]
Energy supply per capita (Gigajoules)	352	277	230 [l]
Tourist/visitor arrivals at national borders (000) [q,r]	805	1 090	756 [c]
Important sites for terrestrial biodiversity protected (%)	78.6	79.7	84.3 [b]
Pop. using safely managed drinking water (urban/rural, %)	99.8 / 100.0	99.8 / 98.0	99.8 / 96.5 [b]
Pop. using safely managed sanitation (urban/rural %)	93.3 / 85.9	94.3 / 86.6	96.4 / 88.5 [b]
Net Official Development Assist. disbursed (% of GNI) [s]	1.07	0.95	1.02 [c]

a Projected estimate (medium fertility variant). b 2022. c 2021. d 2018. e Data classified according to ISIC Rev. 4. f Excludes irrigation canals and landscaping care. g Excludes publishing activities, recycling. Includes irrigation canals. h Estimate. i Calculated by the UN Statistics Division from national indices. j 2019. k Data refers to a 5-year period preceding the reference year. l 2020. m Data as at the end of December. n 2017. o Data are as at 1 January of reporting year. p Population aged 16 to 74 years. q Non-resident tourists staying in all types of accommodation establishments. r Including youth hostels, tourist private accommodation and others. s Development Assistance Committee member (OECD).

Madagascar

Region	Eastern Africa	UN membership date	20 September 1960
Population (000, 2023)	29 612[a,b]	Surface area (km2)	587 041[c]
Pop. density (per km2, 2023)	50.9[a,b]	Sex ratio (m per 100 f)	100.4[a,b]
Capital city	Antananarivo	National currency	Malagasy Ariary (MGA)
Capital city pop. (000, 2023)	3 210.4[d]	Exchange rate (per US$)	4 462.0[b]

Economic indicators

	2010	2015	2023
GDP: Gross domestic product (million current US$)	9 983	11 323	14 450[c]
GDP growth rate (annual %, const. 2015 prices)	0.6	3.1	5.7[c]
GDP per capita (current US$)	459.4	455.6	499.7[c]
Economy: Agriculture (% of Gross Value Added)	30.3	27.0	25.4[c]
Economy: Industry (% of Gross Value Added)	18.8	19.9	22.3[c]
Economy: Services and other activity (% of GVA)	50.9	53.2	52.2[c]
Employment in agriculture (% of employed)	73.3[e]	74.6	73.9[e,c]
Employment in industry (% of employed)	5.9[e]	9.3	10.4[e,c]
Employment in services & other sectors (% employed)	20.7[e]	16.2	15.7[e,c]
Unemployment rate (% of labour force)	4.3	1.8	2.1[e]
Labour force participation rate (female/male pop. %)	83.9 / 89.1[e]	83.3 / 89.0	83.7 / 88.1[e]
CPI: Consumer Price Index (2010=100)	100	140	149[f,g,b]
Agricultural production index (2014-2016=100)	105	99	103[c]
International trade: exports (million current US$)	1 082	2 164	3 658[e,b]
International trade: imports (million current US$)	2 546	2 961	5 524[e,b]
International trade: balance (million current US$)	- 1 464	- 796	- 1 866[e,b]
Balance of payments, current account (million US$)	- 893	- 256	- 732[c]

Major trading partners

						2022
Export partners (% of exports)[e]	France	19.2	United States	18.2	China	13.3
Import partners (% of imports)[e]	China	19.4	France	10.2	Oman	10.2

Social indicators

	2010	2015	2023
Population growth rate (average annual %)	2.8	2.6	2.4[a,b]
Urban population (% of total population)	31.9	35.2	37.9[d]
Urban population growth rate (average annual %)[h]	4.9	4.7	...
Fertility rate, total (live births per woman)	4.6	4.2	3.8[a,b]
Life expectancy at birth (females/males, years)	64.6 / 61.2	66.3 / 62.4	67.6 / 63.0[a,b]
Population age distribution (0-14/60+ years old, %)	43.2 / 4.3	41.3 / 4.7	39.1 / 5.3[a,b]
International migrant stock (000/% of total pop.)[i,j]	28.9 / 0.1	32.1 / 0.1	35.6 / 0.1[k]
Refugees and others of concern to the UNHCR (000)	~0.0[l]	~0.0	0.3[b]
Infant mortality rate (per 1 000 live births)	47.1	41.3	32.6[a,b]
Health: Current expenditure (% of GDP)[m]	4.7	5.0	3.9[k]
Health: Physicians (per 1 000 pop.)	0.2	0.2[n]	0.2[o]
Education: Government expenditure (% of GDP)	2.6	2.2[e]	3.2[c]
Education: Primary gross enrol. ratio (f/m per 100 pop.)	142.4 / 145.0	147.3 / 147.3	135.2 / 132.9[d]
Education: Lowr. sec. gross enrol. ratio (f/m per 100 pop.)	40.2 / 42.1[p]	49.6 / 49.0[e]	44.5 / 42.1[d]
Education: Upr. sec. gross enrol. ratio (f/m per 100 pop.)	13.6 / 15.6[p,e]	22.1 / 23.8[e]	22.1 / 22.2[d]
Seats held by women in the National Parliament (%)	7.9[p]	20.5	18.5[q]

Environment and infrastructure indicators

	2010	2015	2023
Individuals using the Internet (per 100 inhabitants)[e]	1.7	4.2	19.7[c]
Research & Development expenditure (% of GDP)[r]	0.1	~0.0[s,t,n]	~0.0[s,u]
Threatened species (number)	663	965	3 747[b]
Forested area (% of land area)	21.6	21.5	21.4[k]
CO2 emission estimates (million tons/tons per capita)	2.9 / 0.1	4.5 / 0.1	4.5 / 0.1[k]
Energy production, primary (Petajoules)[e]	174	236	331[k]
Energy supply per capita (Gigajoules)[e]	9	11	14[k]
Tourist/visitor arrivals at national borders (000)[v]	196	244	68[k]
Important sites for terrestrial biodiversity protected (%)	23.8	24.6	26.6[b]
Pop. using safely managed drinking water (urban/rural, %)	28.4 / 6.7	33.6 / 8.6	41.3 / 9.6[b]
Pop. using safely managed sanitation (urban/rural, %)	11.2 / 5.4	13.3 / 7.2	16.3 / 9.7[b]
Net Official Development Assist. received (% of GNI)	4.85	6.19	7.46[c]

a Projected estimate (medium fertility variant). **b** 2022. **c** 2021. **d** 2019. **e** Estimate. **f** Base: 2016 = 100 **g** Data refer to 7 cities only. **h** Data refers to a 5-year period preceding the reference year. **i** Refers to foreign citizens. **j** Including refugees. **k** 2020. **l** Data as at the end of December. **m** Data based on calendar year (January 1 to December 31). **n** 2014. **o** 2018. **p** 2009. **q** Data are as at 1 January of reporting year. **r** Partial data. **s** Government only. **t** Break in the time series. **u** 2017. **v** Arrivals of non-resident tourists by air.

Malawi

Region	Eastern Africa	UN membership date	01 December 1964
Population (000, 2023)	20 405 [a,b]	Surface area (km2)	117 726 [c]
Pop. density (per km2, 2023)	215.8 [a,b]	Sex ratio (m per 100 f)	94.7 [a,b]
Capital city	Lilongwe	National currency	Malawi Kwacha (MWK)
Capital city pop. (000, 2023)	1 074.7 [d]	Exchange rate (per US$)	773.1 [e]

Economic indicators	2010	2015	2023
GDP: Gross domestic product (million current US$)	6 960	8 216	12 199 [c]
GDP growth rate (annual %, const. 2015 prices)	6.9	8.5	2.8 [c]
GDP per capita (current US$)	472.9	485.0	613.3 [c]
Economy: Agriculture (% of Gross Value Added) [f,g]	31.9	26.5	28.3 [c]
Economy: Industry (% of Gross Value Added) [f,h,i]	16.4	18.4	20.1 [c]
Economy: Services and other activity (% of GVA) [f]	51.7	55.1	51.6 [c]
Employment in agriculture (% of employed) [j]	67.8	64.7	61.9 [c]
Employment in industry (% of employed) [j]	7.2	7.6	8.1 [c]
Employment in services & other sectors (% employed) [j]	25.0	27.7	29.9 [c]
Unemployment rate (% of labour force) [j]	4.9	5.0	5.6
Labour force participation rate (female/male pop. %) [j]	70.5 / 79.4	65.2 / 74.4	63.2 / 72.1
CPI: Consumer Price Index (2010=100) [j]	100	251	454 [e]
Agricultural production index (2014-2016=100)	70	99	138 [c]
International trade: exports (million current US$)	1 066	1 080	994 [j,b]
International trade: imports (million current US$)	2 173	2 312	2 843 [j,b]
International trade: balance (million current US$)	- 1 107	- 1 232	- 1 848 [j,b]
Balance of payments, current account (million current US$)	- 969	- 1 064	- 1 543 [c]

Major trading partners						2022
Export partners (% of exports) [j]	Belgium	13.8	India	7.6	United Rep. Tanzania	7.0
Import partners (% of imports) [j]	China	18.2	South Africa	17.8	United Arab Emirates	9.3

Social indicators	2010	2015	2023
Population growth rate (average annual %)	2.9	2.7	2.5 [a,b]
Urban population (% of total population)	15.5	16.3	17.2 [d]
Urban population growth rate (average annual %) [k]	3.7	3.9	...
Fertility rate, total (live births per woman)	5.3	4.5	3.8 [a,b]
Life expectancy at birth (females/males, years)	58.4 / 54.3	64.7 / 58.2	66.3 / 59.6 [a,b]
Population age distribution (0-14/60+ years old, %)	46.5 / 5.4	46.0 / 4.4	42.6 / 3.8 [a,b]
International migrant stock (000/% of total pop.) [l]	217.7 / 1.5	197.3 / 1.2	191.4 / 1.0 [e]
Refugees and others of concern to the UNHCR (000)	15.2 [m]	22.6	55.0 [b]
Infant mortality rate (per 1 000 live births)	56.9	38.5	27.5 [a,b]
Health: Current expenditure (% of GDP) [n]	5.1	6.6	5.4 [e]
Health: Physicians (per 1 000 pop.)	~0.0 [o]	~0.0 [p]	~0.0 [e]
Education: Government expenditure (% of GDP)	3.5	5.6	3.3 [j,q]
Education: Primary gross enrol. ratio (f/m per 100 pop.)	140.2 / 137.3	147.9 / 144.9	133.6 / 126.5 [b]
Education: Lowr. sec. gross enrol. ratio (f/m per 100 pop.)	40.3 / 43.9	47.3 / 50.8 [i]	44.6 / 41.6 [b]
Education: Upr. sec. gross enrol. ratio (f/m per 100 pop.)	13.5 / 18.8	20.6 / 24.7	20.6 / 22.2 [b]
Intentional homicide rate (per 100 000 pop.)	3.5	1.8 [r]	...
Seats held by women in the National Parliament (%)	20.8	16.7	20.7 [s]

Environment and infrastructure indicators	2010	2015	2023
Individuals using the Internet (per 100 inhabitants)	2.3	6.0 [j]	24.4 [j,c]
Threatened species (number)	158	171	152 [b]
Forested area (% of land area)	28.2	26.0	23.8 [e]
Energy production, primary (Petajoules)	64	69	70 [e]
Energy supply per capita (Gigajoules)	5	5	5 [e]
Tourist/visitor arrivals at national borders (000) [t]	746	805	432 [c]
Important sites for terrestrial biodiversity protected (%)	63.2	63.2	63.2 [b]
Pop. using safely managed drinking water (urban/rural, %)	43.7 / 5.1	47.3 / 7.0	52.4 / 10.2 [b]
Pop. using safely managed sanitation (urban/rural, %)	26.0 / 20.0	32.4 / 31.5	41.2 / 47.3 [b]
Net Official Development Assist. received (% of GNI)	14.84	17.06	9.50 [c]

a Projected estimate (medium fertility variant). b 2022. c 2021. d 2019. e 2020. f Data classified according to ISIC Rev. 4. g Excludes irrigation canals and landscaping care. h Excludes publishing activities, recycling. Includes irrigation canals. i Includes mining and quarrying. j Estimate. k Data refers to a 5-year period preceding the reference year. l Including refugees. m Data as at the end of December. n Data refer to fiscal years beginning 1 July. o 2009. p 2013. q 2018. r 2012. s Data are as at 1 January of reporting year. t Departures.

Malaysia

Region	South-eastern Asia	UN membership date	17 September 1957
Population (000, 2023)	33 938 a,b,c	Surface area (km2)	330 621 d
Pop. density (per km2, 2023)	103.3 a,b,c	Sex ratio (m per 100 f)	104.5 a,b,c
Capital city	Kuala Lumpur e	National currency	Malaysian Ringgit (MYR)
Capital city pop. (000, 2023)	7 780.3 f,g	Exchange rate (per US$)	4.4 c

Economic indicators

	2010	2015	2023
GDP: Gross domestic product (million current US$)	255 018	301 355	372 702 d
GDP growth rate (annual %, const. 2015 prices)	7.4	5.1	3.1 d
GDP per capita (current US$)	8 880.1	9 699.6	11 100.9 d
Economy: Agriculture (% of Gross Value Added) h,i,j	10.2	8.4	9.7 d
Economy: Industry (% of Gross Value Added) h,i,k	40.9	38.9	38.2 d
Economy: Services and other activity (% of GVA) h	48.9	52.7	52.1 d
Employment in agriculture (% of employed)	13.3	12.5	9.6 l,d
Employment in industry (% of employed)	27.6	27.5	28.2 l,d
Employment in services & other sectors (% employed)	59.1	60.1	62.1 l,d
Unemployment rate (% of labour force)	3.4	3.1	3.8 l
Labour force participation rate (female/male pop. %)	43.5 / 76.3	50.7 / 78.1	52.7 / 78.6 l
CPI: Consumer Price Index (2010=100)	100	113	127 c
Agricultural production index (2014-2016=100)	89	104	97 d
International trade: exports (million current US$)	198 791	200 211	352 565 l,c
International trade: imports (million current US$)	164 586	176 175	294 093 l,c
International trade: balance (million current US$)	34 204	24 036	58 472 l,c
Balance of payments, current account (million US$)	25 644	9 068	10 487 c

Major trading partners

						2022
Export partners (% of exports) l	China	15.5	Singapore	14.0	United States	11.5
Import partners (% of imports) l	China	23.2	Singapore	9.5	Other Asia, nes	7.6

Social indicators

	2010	2015	2023
Population growth rate (average annual %) b	1.6	1.5	1.1 a,c
Urban population (% of total population) b	70.9	74.2	76.6 g
Urban population growth rate (average annual %) b,m	3.1	2.7	...
Fertility rate, total (live births per woman) b	2.1	2.0	1.8 a,c
Life expectancy at birth (females/males, years) b	77.1 / 72.1	77.7 / 72.8	78.8 / 74.0 a,c
Population age distribution (0-14/60+ years old, %) b	27.8 / 7.9	25.2 / 9.2	22.7 / 11.4 a,c
International migrant stock (000/% of total pop.) b,n,o	2 417.4 / 8.6	3 280.7 / 10.8	3 476.6 / 10.7 p
Refugees and others of concern to the UNHCR (000)	212.9 q	272.0	247.7 c
Infant mortality rate (per 1 000 live births) b	6.9	6.9	5.9 a,c
Health: Current expenditure (% of GDP)	3.2 r	3.8 r	4.1 p
Health: Physicians (per 1 000 pop.)	1.1	1.5	2.2 p
Education: Government expenditure (% of GDP)	5.0	4.9	4.3 d
Education: Primary gross enrol. ratio (f/m per 100 pop.)	100.2 / 99.3	104.1 / 103.5	103.7 / 102.3 d
Education: Lowr. sec. gross enrol. ratio (f/m per 100 pop.)	90.5 / 88.8	90.6 / 86.8	93.1 / 92.0 d
Education: Upr. sec. gross enrol. ratio (f/m per 100 pop.)	70.0 / 60.2	86.9 / 76.2	81.1 / 72.6 d
Intentional homicide rate (per 100 000 pop.)	1.9	1.6	0.7 d
Seats held by women in the National Parliament (%)	9.9	10.4	13.5 s

Environment and infrastructure indicators

	2010	2015	2023
Individuals using the Internet (per 100 inhabitants)	56.3 t	71.1	96.8 d
Research & Development expenditure (% of GDP)	1.0	1.3	1.0 p
Threatened species (number)	1 180	1 252	2 090 c
Forested area (% of land area)	57.7	59.2	58.2 p
CO2 emission estimates (million tons/tons per capita)	191.6 / 6.7	222.5 / 7.3	231.6 / 7.1 p
Energy production, primary (Petajoules) u	3 450	3 749	3 837 p
Energy supply per capita (Gigajoules) u	103	110	117 p
Tourist/visitor arrivals at national borders (000) v	24 577	25 721	135 d
Important sites for terrestrial biodiversity protected (%)	31.6	37.0	37.0 c
Net Official Development Assist. received (% of GNI)	0.00	0.00	0.00 d

a Projected estimate (medium fertility variant). b Including Sabah and Sarawak. c 2022. d 2021. e Kuala Lumpur is the capital and Putrajaya is the administrative capital. f Refers to the Greater Kuala Lumpur. g 2019. h Data classified according to ISIC Rev. 4. i At producers' prices. j Excludes irrigation canals and landscaping care. k Excludes publishing activities, recycling. Includes irrigation canals. l Estimate. m Data refers to a 5-year period preceding the reference year. n Including refugees. o Refers to foreign citizens. p 2020. q Data as at the end of December. r Provisional data. s Data are as at 1 January of reporting year. t Refers to total population. u Data comprises of Peninsular Malaysia, Sabah and Sarawak. v Including Singapore residents crossing the frontier by road through Johore Causeway.

Maldives

Region	Southern Asia	UN membership date	21 September 1965
Population (000, 2023)	524[a,b]	Surface area (km2)	300[c]
Pop. density (per km2, 2023)	1 746.0[a,b]	Sex ratio (m per 100 f)	135.4[a,b]
Capital city	Male	National currency	Rufiyaa (MVR)
Capital city pop. (000, 2023)	176.9[d]	Exchange rate (per US$)	15.4[b]

Economic indicators

	2010	2015	2023
GDP: Gross domestic product (million current US$)	2 588	4 109	5 406[c]
GDP growth rate (annual %, const. 2015 prices)	7.3	2.9	41.7[c]
GDP per capita (current US$)	7 158.1	9 434.3	10 366.3[c]
Economy: Agriculture (% of Gross Value Added)[e,f]	6.1	6.3	6.1[c]
Economy: Industry (% of Gross Value Added)[e,g]	10.2	12.1	10.4[c]
Economy: Services and other activity (% of GVA)[e]	83.8	81.7	83.5[c]
Employment in agriculture (% of employed)[h]	12.6	8.3	10.5[c]
Employment in industry (% of employed)[h]	17.3	23.3	26.5[c]
Employment in services & other sectors (% employed)[h]	70.0	68.5	63.1[c]
Unemployment rate (% of labour force)[h]	11.0	6.6	4.9
Labour force participation rate (female/male pop. %)[h]	37.0 / 65.7	40.0 / 69.9	43.1 / 78.1
CPI: Consumer Price Index (2010=100)	100[h]	132[h]	139[i,b]
Agricultural production index (2014-2016=100)	114	100	94[c]
International trade: exports (million current US$)[j]	74	144	159[h,b]
International trade: imports (million current US$)[j]	1 095	1 897	3 515[h,b]
International trade: balance (million current US$)[j]	- 1 021	- 1 753	- 3 356[h,b]
Balance of payments, current account (million US$)	- 196	- 302	- 1 033[b]

Major trading partners

						2022
Export partners (% of exports)[h]	Thailand	46.4	Germany	11.4	United Kingdom	6.8
Import partners (% of imports)[h]	Oman	13.1	United Arab Emirates	13.0	China	12.6

Social indicators

	2010	2015	2023
Population growth rate (average annual %)	3.5	4.3	- 0.4[a,b]
Urban population (% of total population)	36.4	38.5	40.2[k]
Urban population growth rate (average annual %)[l]	4.2	3.9	...
Fertility rate, total (live births per woman)	2.3	2.0	1.7[a,b]
Life expectancy at birth (females/males, years)	78.8 / 76.8	80.7 / 78.9	81.8 / 80.1[a,b]
Population age distribution (0-14/60+ years old, %)	25.7 / 6.1	22.9 / 5.9	21.7 / 7.8[a,b]
International migrant stock (000/% of total pop.)[m]	54.7 / 14.9	64.3 / 14.1	70.1 / 13.0[n]
Infant mortality rate (per 1 000 live births)	11.8	8.3	6.0[a,b]
Health: Current expenditure (% of GDP)	8.5[o,p]	8.7	11.3[n]
Health: Physicians (per 1 000 pop.)	1.5	1.8[q]	2.2[k]
Education: Government expenditure (% of GDP)	3.6	4.6	5.0[c]
Education: Primary gross enrol. ratio (f/m per 100 pop.)	104.6 / 108.2	100.0 / 103.0	100.6 / 101.0[n]
Education: Lowr. sec. gross enrol. ratio (f/m per 100 pop.)	125.3 / 111.4	114.0 / 110.9	94.8 / 102.3[n]
Education: Upr. sec. gross enrol. ratio (f/m per 100 pop.)	... / ...	... / ...	43.5 / 34.5[k]
Intentional homicide rate (per 100 000 pop.)	1.7	0.9	0.6[k]
Seats held by women in the National Parliament (%)	6.5	5.9	4.6[r]

Environment and infrastructure indicators

	2010	2015	2023
Individuals using the Internet (per 100 inhabitants)	26.5[s]	54.5[h]	85.8[h,c]
Threatened species (number)	59	69	91[b]
Forested area (% of land area)	2.7	2.7	2.7[n]
Energy production, primary (Petajoules)	0	0	0[n]
Energy supply per capita (Gigajoules)	37	42	46[n]
Tourist/visitor arrivals at national borders (000)[t]	792	1 234	1 322[c]
Important sites for terrestrial biodiversity protected (%)	0.0	0.0	0.0[b]
Net Official Development Assist. received (% of GNI)	3.88	0.64	2.54[c]

a Projected estimate (medium fertility variant). **b** 2022. **c** 2021. **d** 2018. **e** Data classified according to ISIC Rev. 4. **f** Excludes irrigation canals and landscaping care. **g** Excludes publishing activities, recycling. Includes irrigation canals. **h** Estimate. **i** Calculated by the UN Statistics Division from national indices. **j** As of 2011, trade in services data reflect the improvement of the coverage of balance of payments statistics that was implemented in September 2012. **k** 2019. **l** Data refers to a 5-year period preceding the reference year. **m** Refers to foreign citizens. **n** 2020. **o** Data revision. **p** Break in the time series. **q** 2014. **r** Data are as at 1 January of reporting year. **s** Population aged 15 years and over. **t** Arrivals by air.

Mali

Region	Western Africa	UN membership date	28 September 1960
Population (000, 2023)	22 594[a,b]	Surface area (km2)	1 240 192[c]
Pop. density (per km2, 2023)	18.5[a,b]	Sex ratio (m per 100 f)	102.0[a,b]
Capital city	Bamako	National currency	CFA Franc, BCEAO (XOF)[d]
Capital city pop. (000, 2023)	2 529.3[e]	Exchange rate (per US$)	615.0[b]

Economic indicators	2010	2015	2023
GDP: Gross domestic product (million current US$)	10 679	13 095	19 157[c]
GDP growth rate (annual %, const. 2015 prices)	10.9	7.5	3.7[c]
GDP per capita (current US$)	687.7	723.0	874.6[c]
Economy: Agriculture (% of Gross Value Added)	34.9	39.8	38.2[c]
Economy: Industry (% of Gross Value Added)	25.3	19.3	22.7[c]
Economy: Services and other activity (% of GVA)	39.7	40.9	39.0[c]
Employment in agriculture (% of employed)	69.0[f]	62.3	67.7[f,c]
Employment in industry (% of employed)	7.2[f]	8.3	10.0[f,c]
Employment in services & other sectors (% employed)	23.9[f]	29.5	22.3[f,c]
Unemployment rate (% of labour force)[f]	1.3	1.4	2.9
Labour force participation rate (female/male pop. %)	60.2 / 80.5[f]	61.2 / 79.7	55.2 / 80.6[f]
CPI: Consumer Price Index (2010=100)[g]	100	110	113[c]
Agricultural production index (2014-2016=100)	77	97	126[c]
International trade: exports (million current US$)	1 996	2 530[f]	5 177[f,b]
International trade: imports (million current US$)	4 704	3 169[f]	6 680[f,b]
International trade: balance (million current US$)	- 2 707	- 639[f]	- 1 503[f,b]
Balance of payments, current account (million US$)	- 1 191	- 698	- 1 469[c]

Major trading partners						2022
Export partners (% of exports)[f]	United Arab Emirates	80.9	Switzerland	11.4	Australia	3.7
Import partners (% of imports)[f]	Senegal	21.0	Côte d'Ivoire	15.9	China	10.4

Social indicators	2010	2015	2023
Population growth rate (average annual %)	3.3	3.1	3.1[a,b]
Urban population (% of total population)	36.0	40.0	43.1[e]
Urban population growth rate (average annual %)[h]	5.6	5.0	...
Fertility rate, total (live births per woman)	6.6	6.4	5.9[a,b]
Life expectancy at birth (females/males, years)	57.3 / 55.5	59.5 / 57.3	60.8 / 58.1[a,b]
Population age distribution (0-14/60+ years old, %)	47.2 / 4.4	48.1 / 4.1	47.2 / 3.7[a,b]
International migrant stock (000/% of total pop.)[i]	341.1 / 2.3	420.5 / 2.4	485.8 / 2.4[i]
Refugees and others of concern to the UNHCR (000)	15.3[k]	148.3	453.6[b]
Infant mortality rate (per 1 000 live births)	76.5	65.8	53.3[a,b]
Health: Current expenditure (% of GDP)[l]	4.7	4.1	4.3[j]
Health: Physicians (per 1 000 pop.)	0.1	0.1	0.1[m]
Education: Government expenditure (% of GDP)	3.3	3.8	4.4[c]
Education: Primary gross enrol. ratio (f/m per 100 pop.)	77.0 / 89.7	71.5 / 79.7	74.8 / 82.4[j]
Education: Lowr. sec. gross enrol. ratio (f/m per 100 pop.)	42.2 / 58.2	48.0 / 56.6	46.3 / 50.9[j]
Education: Upr. sec. gross enrol. ratio (f/m per 100 pop.)	20.5 / 33.4	24.1 / 35.0	21.7 / 26.9[j]
Seats held by women in the National Parliament (%)	10.2	9.5	28.6[n]

Environment and infrastructure indicators	2010	2015	2023
Individuals using the Internet (per 100 inhabitants)[f]	2.0	10.3	34.5[c]
Research & Development expenditure (% of GDP)	0.6[o]	0.3[o]	0.2[c]
Threatened species (number)	29	39	72[b]
Forested area (% of land area)	10.9	10.9	10.9[j]
Energy production, primary (Petajoules)[f]	125	154	165[j]
Energy supply per capita (Gigajoules)[f]	10	11	12[j]
Tourist/visitor arrivals at national borders (000)	169	159	168[c]
Important sites for terrestrial biodiversity protected (%)	61.6	61.6	61.6[b]
Pop. using safely managed sanitation (urban/rural %)	6.5 / 11.5	6.9 / 15.9	7.5 / 22.9[b]
Net Official Development Assist. received (% of GNI)	10.63	9.38	7.73[c]

a Projected estimate (medium fertility variant). b 2022. c 2021. d African Financial Community (CFA) Franc, Central Bank of West African States (BCEAO). e 2019. f Estimate. g Bamako h Data refers to a 5-year period preceding the reference year. i Including refugees. j 2020. k Data as at the end of December. l Data based on calendar year (January 1 to December 31). m 2018. n Data are as at 1 January of reporting year. o Excluding business enterprise.

Malta

Region	Southern Europe	UN membership date	01 December 1964
Population (000, 2023)	533[a,b]	Surface area (km2)	315[c]
Pop. density (per km2, 2023)	1 693.0[a,b]	Sex ratio (m per 100 f)	108.9[a,b]
Capital city	Valletta	National currency	Euro (EUR)
Capital city pop. (000, 2023)	212.8[d,e]	Exchange rate (per US$)	0.9[b]

Economic indicators

	2010	2015	2023
GDP: Gross domestic product (million current US$)	9 027	11 087	17 721[c]
GDP growth rate (annual %, const. 2015 prices)	5.5	9.6	11.7[c]
GDP per capita (current US$)	21 556.8	24 282.8	33 641.6[c]
Economy: Agriculture (% of Gross Value Added)[f,g]	1.5	1.0	1.0[c]
Economy: Industry (% of Gross Value Added)[f,h]	18.9	13.0	12.8[c]
Economy: Services and other activity (% of GVA)[f]	79.7	86.0	86.2[c]
Employment in agriculture (% of employed)	1.3	1.5	0.9[c]
Employment in industry (% of employed)	25.5	20.0	17.9[c]
Employment in services & other sectors (% employed)	73.1	78.5	81.3[c]
Unemployment rate (% of labour force)	6.8	5.4	2.8[i]
Labour force participation rate (female/male pop. %)	33.7 / 66.1	42.8 / 67.8	53.8 / 71.9[i]
CPI: Consumer Price Index (2010=100)	100	108	116[c]
Agricultural production index (2014-2016=100)	109	99	76[c]
International trade: exports (million current US$)	3 717	3 915	3 257[b]
International trade: imports (million current US$)	5 732	6 788	8 563[b]
International trade: balance (million current US$)	- 2 015	- 2 873	- 5 305[b]
Balance of payments, current account (million US$)	- 420	301	- 1 020[b]

Major trading partners

					2022
Export partners (% of exports)[i]	Germany	17.2	Japan	7.7	France	7.6
Import partners (% of imports)	Italy	22.3	Canada	9.4	France	6.6

Social indicators

	2010	2015	2023
Population growth rate (average annual %)	0.9	2.3	0.3[a,b]
Urban population (% of total population)	94.1	94.4	94.7[j]
Urban population growth rate (average annual %)[k]	0.5	0.6	...
Fertility rate, total (live births per woman)	1.4	1.4	1.2[a,b]
Life expectancy at birth (females/males, years)	83.7 / 79.6	85.3 / 80.4	85.7 / 81.6[a,b]
Population age distribution (0-14/60+ years old, %)	14.8 / 23.5	13.7 / 24.7	13.1 / 25.0[a,b]
International migrant stock (000/% of total pop.)	33.0 / 8.0	52.6 / 12.1	114.8 / 26.0[l]
Refugees and others of concern to the UNHCR (000)	7.4[m]	6.5	13.8[b]
Infant mortality rate (per 1 000 live births)	6.0	6.1	5.3[a,b]
Health: Current expenditure (% of GDP)	8.0	8.9	10.8[l]
Health: Physicians (per 1 000 pop.)	2.1	2.7	5.5[c]
Education: Government expenditure (% of GDP)	6.3	5.0	5.0[j]
Education: Primary gross enrol. ratio (f/m per 100 pop.)	101.9 / 101.6	104.3 / 102.8	106.4 / 106.8[l]
Education: Lowr. sec. gross enrol. ratio (f/m per 100 pop.)	103.2 / 108.6	102.2 / 103.1	107.2 / 112.5[l]
Education: Upr. sec. gross enrol. ratio (f/m per 100 pop.)	86.6 / 113.2	95.0 / 85.1	112.6 / 106.5[l]
Intentional homicide rate (per 100 000 pop.)	1.0	0.9	0.4[c]
Seats held by women in the National Parliament (%)	8.7	12.9	27.8[n]

Environment and infrastructure indicators

	2010	2015	2023
Individuals using the Internet (per 100 inhabitants)	63.0[o]	76.0[p]	87.5[c]
Research & Development expenditure (% of GDP)	0.6	0.7	0.7[q,l]
Threatened species (number)	26	31	69[b]
Forested area (% of land area)	1.1	1.1	1.4[l]
CO2 emission estimates (million tons/tons per capita)	2.6 / 6.2	1.7 / 3.7	1.6 / 3.1[c,l]
Energy production, primary (Petajoules)	0	1	1[l]
Energy supply per capita (Gigajoules)	84	59	56[l]
Tourist/visitor arrivals at national borders (000)[r]	1 339	1 783	968[c]
Important sites for terrestrial biodiversity protected (%)	89.3	90.6	90.9[b]
Net Official Development Assist. disbursed (% of GNI)	...	0.20[s]	...

a Projected estimate (medium fertility variant). b 2022. c 2021. d Refers to the localities of the Northern Harbour and Southern Harbour. e 2018. f Data classified according to ISIC Rev. 4. g Excludes irrigation canals and landscaping care. h Excludes publishing activities, recycling. Includes irrigation canals. i Estimate. j 2019. k Data refers to a 5-year period preceding the reference year. l 2020. m Data as at the end of December. n Data are as at 1 January of reporting year. o Population aged 16 to 74 years. p Users in the last 3 months. q Provisional data. r Departures by air and by sea. s 2014.

Marshall Islands

Region	Micronesia	UN membership date	17 September 1991
Population (000, 2023)	42 a,b	Surface area (km2)	181 c
Pop. density (per km2, 2023)	230.9 a,b	Sex ratio (m per 100 f)	104.3 a,b
Capital city	Majuro	National currency	US Dollar (USD)
Capital city pop. (000, 2023)	30.7 d		

Economic indicators

	2010	2015	2023
GDP: Gross domestic product (million current US$)	160	184	257 c
GDP growth rate (annual %, const. 2015 prices)	6.4	1.7	2.1 c
GDP per capita (current US$)	3 004.2	3 729.0	6 111.3 c
Economy: Agriculture (% of Gross Value Added) e,f	12.0	12.1	23.2 c
Economy: Industry (% of Gross Value Added) e,g,h	14.1	12.1	11.0 c
Economy: Services and other activity (% of GVA) e	73.9	75.8	65.8 c
Employment in agriculture (% of employed)	11.0 i,j	...	...
Employment in industry (% of employed)	9.4 i,j	...	...
Employment in services & other sectors (% employed)	79.6 i,j	...	...
Unemployment rate (% of labour force)	...	4.7 j,k	...
Agricultural production index (2014-2016=100)	113	90	95 c
International trade: exports (million current US$) l	17	25	1 233 b
International trade: imports (million current US$) l	76	84	17 144 b
International trade: balance (million current US$) l	- 60	- 59	- 15 912 b
Balance of payments, current account (million US$)	- 14	- 7	76 c

Major trading partners

						2022
Export partners (% of exports) l	Netherlands	21.2	Republic of Korea	19.1	Germany	18.8
Import partners (% of imports) l	Singapore	32.6	Republic of Korea	22.0	China	20.8

Social indicators

	2010	2015	2023
Population growth rate (average annual %)	- 0.3	- 2.1	1.0 a,b
Urban population (% of total population)	73.6	75.8	77.4 m
Urban population growth rate (average annual %) n	0.8	0.8	...
Fertility rate, total (live births per woman)	3.6	3.1	2.7 a,b
Life expectancy at birth (females/males, years)	65.1 / 61.7	65.7 / 62.3	67.1 / 63.5 a,b
Population age distribution (0-14/60+ years old, %)	39.6 / 3.9	37.4 / 5.1	32.5 / 7.6 a,b
International migrant stock (000/% of total pop.)	3.1 / 5.5	3.3 / 5.7	3.3 / 5.6 o
Infant mortality rate (per 1 000 live births)	31.4	28.7	24.5 a,b
Health: Current expenditure (% of GDP) p,q	13.9	15.3	13.0 o
Health: Physicians (per 1 000 pop.)	0.6	0.5 r	...
Education: Government expenditure (% of GDP)	...	...	15.7 c
Education: Primary gross enrol. ratio (f/m per 100 pop.)	97.4 / 98.8 s	86.5 / 88.5	70.7 / 74.9 c
Education: Lowr. sec. gross enrol. ratio (f/m per 100 pop.)	94.3 / 92.0 s	73.0 / 69.4	86.6 / 83.9 c
Education: Upr. sec. gross enrol. ratio (f/m per 100 pop.)	71.4 / 66.8 s	59.1 / 51.9	55.4 / 48.2 c
Seats held by women in the National Parliament (%)	3.0	3.0	6.1 t

Environment and infrastructure indicators

	2010	2015	2023
Individuals using the Internet (per 100 inhabitants) l	7.0	19.3	38.7 u
Threatened species (number)	84	95	111 b
Forested area (% of land area)	52.2	52.2	52.2 o
Energy production, primary (Petajoules) l	0	0	0 o
Energy supply per capita (Gigajoules) l	40	45	52 o
Tourist/visitor arrivals at national borders (000)	5 v	6 v	~0 c
Important sites for terrestrial biodiversity protected (%)	8.4	10.1	10.1 b
Net Official Development Assist. received (% of GNI)	12.79	23.01	35.24 c

a Projected estimate (medium fertility variant). b 2022. c 2021. d 2018. e Data classified according to ISIC Rev. 4. f Excludes irrigation canals and landscaping care. g Excludes publishing activities, recycling. Includes irrigation canals. h Includes mining and quarrying. i Data classified according to ISIC Rev. 3. j Break in the time series. k 2011. l Estimate. m 2019. n Data refers to a 5-year period preceding the reference year. o 2020. p Data refer to fiscal years beginning 1 October. q Health expenditure indicators are high as they spend a lot on health using direct funding from the United States and also from their domestic funds. Current health expenditure is mostly government. r 2012. s 2009. t Data are as at 1 January of reporting year. u 2017. v Arrivals by air.

Martinique

Region	Caribbean
Surface area (km2)	1 090 [d]
Sex ratio (m per 100 f)	85.3 [a,b,c]
National currency	Euro (EUR)
Exchange rate (per US$)	0.9 [c]

Population (000, 2023)	368 [a,b,c]
Pop. density (per km2, 2023)	346.7 [a,b,c]
Capital city	Fort-de-France
Capital city pop. (000, 2023)	79.4 [e]

Economic indicators	2010	2015	2023
Employment in agriculture (% of employed) [f,g]	4.1	3.9 [h]	...
Employment in industry (% of employed) [f,g]	11.9	11.8 [h]	...
Employment in services & other sectors (% employed) [f,g]	65.3	69.0 [h]	...
Unemployment rate (% of labour force) [f]	21.0	22.8 [i,j]	...
Labour force participation rate (female/male pop. %)	43.3 / 49.1 [f]	52.6 / 53.8 [f,i,j]	... / ...
CPI: Consumer Price Index (2010=100) [k]	100	106	116 [c]

Social indicators	2010	2015	2023
Population growth rate (average annual %) [b]	- 0.6	- 0.8	- 0.1 [a,c]
Urban population (% of total population)	89.0	89.0	89.1 [l]
Urban population growth rate (average annual %) [m]	- 0.2	- 0.5	...
Fertility rate, total (live births per woman) [b]	2.0	2.0	1.9 [a,c]
Life expectancy at birth (females/males, years) [b]	84.7 / 78.1	84.9 / 79.2	86.0 / 80.3 [a,c]
Population age distribution (0-14/60+ years old, %) [b]	19.7 / 20.3	18.1 / 24.3	15.9 / 30.6 [a,c]
International migrant stock (000/% of total pop.) [n]	59.6 / 15.1	69.2 / 18.3	68.6 / 18.3 [o]
Infant mortality rate (per 1 000 live births) [b]	7.3	7.1	6.2 [a,c]
Intentional homicide rate (per 100 000 pop.)	2.8 [p]	...	...

Environment and infrastructure indicators	2010	2015	2023
Individuals using the Internet (per 100 inhabitants)	42.0 [q,p]	...	...
Threatened species (number)	31	45	107 [c]
Forested area (% of land area)	47.4	48.4	49.3 [o]
Energy production, primary (Petajoules)	1 [q,r]	...	...
Energy supply per capita (Gigajoules)	75 [r]	...	...
Tourist/visitor arrivals at national borders (000)	478	487	291 [d]
Important sites for terrestrial biodiversity protected (%)	97.2	97.2	97.2 [c]

a Projected estimate (medium fertility variant). b For statistical purposes, the data for France do not include this area. c 2022. d 2021. e 2018. f Excluding the institutional population. g Population aged 15 to 64 years. h 2012. i Break in the time series. j 2013. k Calculated by the UN Statistics Division from national indices. l 2019. m Data refers to a 5-year period preceding the reference year. n Including refugees. o 2020. p 2009. q Estimate. r Data after 2010 are included in France.

Mauritania

Region	Western Africa	
Population (000, 2023)	4 736[a,b]	
Pop. density (per km2, 2023)	4.6[a,b]	
Capital city	Nouakchott	
Capital city pop. (000, 2023)	1 259.0[d]	

UN membership date	27 October 1961
Surface area (km2)	1 030 700[c]
Sex ratio (m per 100 f)	96.1[a,b]
National currency	Ouguiya (MRU)
Exchange rate (per US$)	36.2[c]

Economic indicators

	2010	2015	2023
GDP: Gross domestic product (million current US$)	5 629	6 167	9 996[c]
GDP growth rate (annual %, const. 2015 prices)	2.6	5.4	2.4[c]
GDP per capita (current US$)	1 646.1	1 562.7	2 166.0[c]
Economy: Agriculture (% of Gross Value Added)[e,f]	17.6	23.0	20.2[c]
Economy: Industry (% of Gross Value Added)[f,g]	40.3	25.3	35.8[c]
Economy: Services and other activity (% of GVA)[f]	42.1	51.7	44.0[c]
Employment in agriculture (% of employed)[h]	36.0	33.0	29.5[c]
Employment in industry (% of employed)[h]	17.1	17.8	18.8[c]
Employment in services & other sectors (% employed)[h]	46.9	49.3	51.7[c]
Unemployment rate (% of labour force)[h]	9.9	10.2	11.2
Labour force participation rate (female/male pop. %)[h]	27.5 / 61.6	26.7 / 59.0	26.4 / 56.5
CPI: Consumer Price Index (2010=100)	...	...	132[i,b]
Agricultural production index (2014-2016=100)	86	100	112[c]
International trade: exports (million current US$)	1 819	1 832	3 312[h,b]
International trade: imports (million current US$)	1 708	3 703	5 021[h,b]
International trade: balance (million current US$)	111	- 1 872	- 1 709[h,b]
Balance of payments, current account (million US$)	...	- 956	- 808[c]

Major trading partners

						2022
Export partners (% of exports)[h]	China	41.5	Italy	10.7	Canada	9.9
Import partners (% of imports)[h]	Spain	14.9	United Arab Emirates	14.0	France	11.4

Social indicators

	2010	2015	2023
Population growth rate (average annual %)	2.9	2.6	2.6[a,b]
Urban population (% of total population)	46.6	51.1	54.5[d]
Urban population growth rate (average annual %)[j]	4.9	4.8	...
Fertility rate, total (live births per woman)	5.0	4.8	4.3[a,b]
Life expectancy at birth (females/males, years)	64.7 / 61.5	66.3 / 62.8	66.4 / 63.0[a,b]
Population age distribution (0-14/60+ years old, %)	43.3 / 5.3	43.7 / 5.3	41.6 / 5.1[a,b]
International migrant stock (000/% of total pop.)[k,l]	84.9 / 2.4	166.6 / 4.1	182.3 / 3.9[m]
Refugees and others of concern to the UNHCR (000)	27.0[n]	77.3	118.7[b]
Infant mortality rate (per 1 000 live births)	59.8	53.0	43.6[a,b]
Health: Current expenditure (% of GDP)[o]	2.6	3.7	3.4[m]
Health: Physicians (per 1 000 pop.)	0.2	0.2	0.2[p]
Education: Government expenditure (% of GDP)	2.0[q]	2.3[r]	1.7[c]
Education: Primary gross enrol. ratio (f/m per 100 pop.)	102.0 / 97.5	107.0 / 102.0	97.6 / 91.1[m]
Education: Lowr. sec. gross enrol. ratio (f/m per 100 pop.)	23.4 / 26.5	37.3 / 39.1	44.2 / 41.4[m]
Education: Upr. sec. gross enrol. ratio (f/m per 100 pop.)	12.8 / 16.5[h]	20.0 / 23.0	32.4 / 30.6[m]
Intentional homicide rate (per 100 000 pop.)	...	...	1.0[m]
Seats held by women in the National Parliament (%)	22.1	25.2	20.3[s]

Environment and infrastructure indicators

	2010	2015	2023
Individuals using the Internet (per 100 inhabitants)[h]	4.0	17.6	58.8[c]
Research & Development expenditure (% of GDP)	...	...	~0.0[t,u,p]
Threatened species (number)	58	69	131[b]
Forested area (% of land area)	0.4	0.3	0.3[m]
Energy production, primary (Petajoules)	34	30	22[m]
Energy supply per capita (Gigajoules)	13	15[h]	18[m]
Important sites for terrestrial biodiversity protected (%)	11.2	11.2	11.2[b]
Net Official Development Assist. received (% of GNI)	6.72	5.50	5.27[c]

a Projected estimate (medium fertility variant). b 2022. c 2021. d 2019. e Excludes irrigation canals and landscaping care. f Data classified according to ISIC Rev. 4. g Excludes publishing activities, recycling. Includes irrigation canals. h Estimate. i Index base: 2014=100. j Data refers to a 5-year period preceding the reference year. k Including refugees. l Refers to foreign citizens. m 2020. n Data as at the end of December. o Data based on calendar year (January 1 to December 31). p 2018. q 2006. r 2013. s Data are as at 1 January of reporting year. t Higher Education only. u Partial data.

Mauritius

Region	Eastern Africa	UN membership date	24 April 1968
Population (000, 2023)	1 300 a,b,c	Surface area (km2)	1 979 d,e
Pop. density (per km2, 2023)	640.1 a,b,c	Sex ratio (m per 100 f)	97.3 a,b,c
Capital city	Port Louis	National currency	Mauritius Rupee (MUR)
Capital city pop. (000, 2023)	149.4 f	Exchange rate (per US$)	43.9 c

Economic indicators	2010	2015	2023
GDP: Gross domestic product (million current US$)	10 004	12 007	11 525 e
GDP growth rate (annual %, const. 2015 prices)	4.4	3.7	3.6 e
GDP per capita (current US$)	7 795.1	9 285.3	8 873.0 e
Economy: Agriculture (% of Gross Value Added) g,h	4.1	3.5	3.7 e
Economy: Industry (% of Gross Value Added) h,i	25.3	21.9	20.7 e
Economy: Services and other activity (% of GVA) h	70.7	74.6	75.6 e
Employment in agriculture (% of employed)	8.6	7.5	5.1 j,e
Employment in industry (% of employed)	28.7	25.3	23.6 j,e
Employment in services & other sectors (% employed)	62.6	67.1	71.2 j,e
Unemployment rate (% of labour force)	7.6	7.4	7.1 j
Labour force participation rate (female/male pop. %)	43.0 / 74.4	45.8 / 73.9	45.7 / 71.5 j
CPI: Consumer Price Index (2010=100) k	100	120	154 c
Agricultural production index (2014-2016=100)	106	100	83 e
International trade: exports (million current US$)	1 850	2 481	1 881 c
International trade: imports (million current US$)	4 402	4 458	6 617 c
International trade: balance (million current US$)	- 2 553	- 1 977	- 4 737 c
Balance of payments, current account (million US$)	- 1 006	- 417	- 1 580 c

Major trading partners						2022
Export partners (% of exports)	South Africa	13.4	France	12.9	Madagascar	9.0
Import partners (% of imports)	China	16.1	India	9.8	South Africa	9.1

Social indicators	2010	2015	2023
Population growth rate (average annual %) b	0.3	0.1	0.1 a,c
Urban population (% of total population) b	41.6	41.0	40.8 l
Urban population growth rate (average annual %) b,m	0.2	- 0.1	...
Fertility rate, total (live births per woman) b	1.6	1.4	1.4 a,c
Life expectancy at birth (females/males, years) b	77.6 / 70.6	78.2 / 71.8	77.1 / 71.0 a,c
Population age distribution (0-14/60+ years old, %) b	21.9 / 11.6	19.5 / 14.6	16.3 / 19.0 a,c
International migrant stock (000/% of total pop.) b,n	24.8 / 2.0	28.6 / 2.3	28.9 / 2.3 o
Refugees and others of concern to the UNHCR (000)	...	...	~0.0 c
Infant mortality rate (per 1 000 live births) b	12.3	12.3	13.4 a,c
Health: Current expenditure (% of GDP) p	4.6	5.7	6.7 o
Health: Physicians (per 1 000 pop.)	1.2	2.0	2.7 o
Education: Government expenditure (% of GDP)	3.6	4.8	4.7 e
Education: Primary gross enrol. ratio (f/m per 100 pop.)	103.1 / 102.5	103.8 / 102.0	104.3 / 101.5 c
Education: Lowr. sec. gross enrol. ratio (f/m per 100 pop.)	100.7 / 98.6	109.4 / 111.6	112.6 / 115.1 c
Education: Upr. sec. gross enrol. ratio (f/m per 100 pop.)	84.8 / 79.3 j	91.9 / 82.8	84.8 / 76.0 e
Intentional homicide rate (per 100 000 pop.)	2.6	1.6	2.6 e
Seats held by women in the National Parliament (%)	17.1	11.6	20.0 q

Environment and infrastructure indicators	2010	2015	2023
Individuals using the Internet (per 100 inhabitants)	28.3 r	50.1 j	67.6 e
Research & Development expenditure (% of GDP)	0.4 s,t,u	0.2 v,w,x	0.4 e
Threatened species (number)	222	249	292 c
Forested area (% of land area)	18.9	18.9	19.1 o
CO2 emission estimates (million tons/tons per capita)	3.7 / 2.9	4.0 / 3.1	3.8 / 2.9 o
Energy production, primary (Petajoules)	11	12	8 o
Energy supply per capita (Gigajoules)	49	52	44 o
Tourist/visitor arrivals at national borders (000)	935	1 151	180 o
Important sites for terrestrial biodiversity protected (%)	9.0	9.6	9.6 c
Net Official Development Assist. received (% of GNI)	1.26	0.62	2.29 e

a Projected estimate (medium fertility variant). b Including Agalega, Rodrigues and Saint Brandon. c 2022. d Excluding the islands of Saint Brandon and Agalega. e 2021. f 2018. g Excludes irrigation canals and landscaping care. h Data classified according to ISIC Rev. 4. i Excludes publishing activities, recycling. Includes irrigation canals. j Estimate. k Calculated by the UN Statistics Division from national indices. l 2019. m Data refers to a 5-year period preceding the reference year. n Refers to foreign citizens. o 2020. p Data based on calendar year (January 1 to December 31). q Data are as at 1 January of reporting year. r Population aged 5 years and over. s Based on R&D budget instead of R&D expenditure. t Overestimated or based on overestimated data. u 2005. v Break in the time series. w Excluding business enterprise. x 2012.

Mayotte

Region	Eastern Africa	Population (000, 2023)	326[a,b,c]
Pop. density (per km2, 2023)	869.6[a,b,c]	Sex ratio (m per 100 f)	90.0[a,b,c]
Capital city	Mamoudzou	National currency	Euro (EUR)
Capital city pop. (000, 2023)	6.2[d]	Exchange rate (per US$)	0.9[c]

Economic indicators

	2010	2015	2023
International trade: exports (million current US$)	6[e]	...	...
International trade: imports (million current US$)	309[e]	...	...
International trade: balance (million current US$)	- 303[e]	...	...

Social indicators

	2010	2015	2023
Population growth rate (average annual %)[a]	2.6	4.1	3.0[b,c]
Urban population (% of total population)	49.0	47.0	45.9[f]
Urban population growth rate (average annual %)[g]	2.7	2.0	...
Fertility rate, total (live births per woman)[a]	4.4	4.9	4.4[b,c]
Life expectancy at birth (females/males, years)[a]	80.4 / 74.6	80.9 / 74.3	78.5 / 71.9[b,c]
Population age distribution (0-14/60+ years old, %)[a]	44.7 / 3.9	43.9 / 4.4	44.2 / 4.6[b,c]
International migrant stock (000/% of total pop.)[h]	72.8 / 34.9	81.4 / 33.9	111.5 / 40.9[i]
Infant mortality rate (per 1 000 live births)[a]	4.8	4.1	3.7[b,c]
Intentional homicide rate (per 100 000 pop.)	5.8[i]	...	...

Environment and infrastructure indicators

	2010	2015	2023
Threatened species (number)	69	84	126[c]
Forested area (% of land area)	38.5	37.8	37.1[i]
Energy production, primary (Petajoules)	0[k]	...	...
Energy supply per capita (Gigajoules)	20[k]	...	...
Important sites for terrestrial biodiversity protected (%)	63.2	63.2	63.6[c]

a For statistical purposes, the data for France do not include this area. b Projected estimate (medium fertility variant).
c 2022. d 2018. e 2005. f 2019. g Data refers to a 5-year period preceding the reference year. h Including refugees.
i 2020. j 2009. k Data after 2010 are included in France.

Mexico

Region	Central America	
Population (000, 2023)	127 504[a,b]	
Pop. density (per km2, 2023)	65.1[a,b]	
Capital city	Mexico City	
Capital city pop. (000, 2023)	21 671.9[d,e]	

UN membership date	07 November 1945
Surface area (km2)	1 964 375[c]
Sex ratio (m per 100 f)	95.2[a,b]
National currency	Mexican Peso (MXN)
Exchange rate (per US$)	19.4[b]

Economic indicators

	2010	2015	2023
GDP: Gross domestic product (million current US$)	1 057 801	1 171 870	1 272 839[c]
GDP growth rate (annual %, const. 2015 prices)	5.1	3.3	4.7[c]
GDP per capita (current US$)	9 400.0	9 753.4	10 045.7[c]
Economy: Agriculture (% of Gross Value Added)[f,g]	3.4	3.4	4.1[c]
Economy: Industry (% of Gross Value Added)[g,h]	33.7	31.8	35.4[c]
Economy: Services and other activity (% of GVA)[g]	62.9	64.8	60.5[c]
Employment in agriculture (% of employed)	13.9	13.4	12.3[c]
Employment in industry (% of employed)	23.4[i]	25.2	17.0[i,c]
Employment in services & other sectors (% employed)	61.7	61.5	62.0[c]
Unemployment rate (% of labour force)	5.3	4.3	3.4[i]
Labour force participation rate (female/male pop. %)	42.9 / 79.4	43.7 / 78.7	45.8 / 77.6[i]
CPI: Consumer Price Index (2010=100)[j]	100	119	167[b]
Agricultural production index (2014-2016=100)	89	98	114[c]
International trade: exports (million current US$)	298 305	380 550	578 282[b]
International trade: imports (million current US$)	301 482	395 234	604 615[b]
International trade: balance (million current US$)	- 3 177	- 14 684	- 26 333[b]
Balance of payments, current account (million US$)	- 4 015	- 32 264	- 13 423[b]

Major trading partners

							2022
Export partners (% of exports)	United States	78.3	Americas n.e.s	3.7	Canada	2.7
Import partners (% of imports)	United States	43.9	China	19.6	Republic of Korea	3.7

Social indicators

	2010	2015	2023
Population growth rate (average annual %)	1.4	1.1	0.8[a,b]
Urban population (% of total population)	77.8	79.3	80.4[e]
Urban population growth rate (average annual %)[k]	2.0	1.8	...
Fertility rate, total (live births per woman)	2.3	2.1	1.8[a,b]
Life expectancy at birth (females/males, years)	77.1 / 71.3	77.7 / 71.7	78.2 / 71.5[a,b]
Population age distribution (0-14/60+ years old, %)	29.9 / 8.9	27.6 / 10.2	24.5 / 12.2[a,b]
International migrant stock (000/% of total pop.)[l]	969.7 / 0.8	1 013.7 / 0.8	1 197.6 / 0.9[m]
Refugees and others of concern to the UNHCR (000)	1.6[n]	2.2	498.2[b]
Infant mortality rate (per 1 000 live births)	16.1	13.7	10.9[a,b]
Health: Current expenditure (% of GDP)[o,p]	5.7	5.7	6.2[m]
Health: Physicians (per 1 000 pop.)	2.0	2.4	2.4[m]
Education: Government expenditure (% of GDP)	5.2	5.2	4.3[q]
Education: Primary gross enrol. ratio (f/m per 100 pop.)	109.8 / 111.4	106.5 / 106.7	104.2 / 103.2[m]
Education: Lowr. sec. gross enrol. ratio (f/m per 100 pop.)	118.3 / 108.9	134.5 / 122.8	128.5 / 115.1[m]
Education: Upr. sec. gross enrol. ratio (f/m per 100 pop.)	62.4 / 58.6	73.3 / 72.0	85.4 / 78.9[m]
Intentional homicide rate (per 100 000 pop.)	22.9	17.3	28.2[c]
Seats held by women in the National Parliament (%)	27.6	38.0	50.0[r]

Environment and infrastructure indicators

	2010	2015	2023
Individuals using the Internet (per 100 inhabitants)	31.0[s]	57.4[t]	75.6[c]
Research & Development expenditure (% of GDP)	0.5	0.4	0.3[i,m]
Threatened species (number)	943	1 109	2 437[b]
Forested area (% of land area)	34.4	34.1	33.8[m]
CO2 emission estimates (million tons/tons per capita)	448.1 / 3.9	450.1 / 3.7	404.6 / 3.1[c]
Energy production, primary (Petajoules)	9 403	8 031	6 284[m]
Energy supply per capita (Gigajoules)	67	65	59[m]
Tourist/visitor arrivals at national borders (000)[u]	23 290	32 093	31 860[c]
Important sites for terrestrial biodiversity protected (%)	33.9	35.2	37.1[b]
Pop. using safely managed sanitation (urban/rural %)	35.5 / ...	47.4 / ...	65.1 / ...[b]
Net Official Development Assist. received (% of GNI)	0.04	0.03	0.05[c]

a Projected estimate (medium fertility variant). b 2022. c 2021. d Refers to the total population in 76 municipalities of the Metropolitan Area of Mexico City. e 2019. f Excludes irrigation canals and landscaping care. g Data classified according to ISIC Rev. 4. h Excludes publishing activities, recycling. Includes irrigation canals. i Estimate. j Calculated by the UN Statistics Division from national indices. k Data refers to a 5-year period preceding the reference year. l Including refugees. m 2020. n Data as at the end of December. o Data are based on SHA2011. p Data based on calendar year (January 1 to December 31). q 2018. r Data are as at 1 January of reporting year. s Estimate to December based on ENDUTIH survey. Refers to total population. t Population aged 6 years and over. u Including nationals residing abroad.

Micronesia (Fed. States of)

Region	Micronesia	UN membership date	17 September 1991
Population (000, 2023)	114[a,b]	Surface area (km2)	702[c]
Pop. density (per km2, 2023)	163.1[a,b]	Sex ratio (m per 100 f)	101.1[a,b]
Capital city	Palikir	National currency	US Dollar (USD)
Capital city pop. (000, 2023)	7.0[d]		

Economic indicators

	2010	2015	2023
GDP: Gross domestic product (million current US$)	297	316	404[c]
GDP growth rate (annual %, const. 2015 prices)	2.3	4.6	-3.2[c]
GDP per capita (current US$)	2 760.0	2 891.3	3 572.7[c]
Economy: Agriculture (% of Gross Value Added)	26.7	27.8	23.9[c]
Economy: Industry (% of Gross Value Added)	7.8	6.5	5.2[c]
Economy: Services and other activity (% of GVA)	65.5	65.7	71.0[c]
CPI: Consumer Price Index (2010=100)	100	113	127[b]
Agricultural production index (2014-2016=100)	66	99	102[c]
International trade: exports (million current US$)	23	40[e]	224[e,b]
International trade: imports (million current US$)	168	160[e]	726[e,b]
International trade: balance (million current US$)	-145	-121[e]	-502[e,b]
Balance of payments, current account (million US$)	-25	22[f]	...

Major trading partners

2022

Export partners (% of exports)[e]	Thailand	81.5	Philippines	11.3	Japan	4.1
Import partners (% of imports)[e]	United States	40.1	China	19.3	Japan	9.7

Social indicators

	2010	2015	2023
Population growth rate (average annual %)	0.3	0.4	0.9[a,b]
Urban population (% of total population)	22.3	22.5	22.8[g]
Urban population growth rate (average annual %)[h]	-0.5	0.3	
Fertility rate, total (live births per woman)	3.2	3.0	2.7[a,b]
Life expectancy at birth (females/males, years)	74.4 / 68.2	74.8 / 68.2	74.8 / 67.3[a,b]
Population age distribution (0-14/60+ years old, %)	35.5 / 5.5	33.1 / 7.2	30.3 / 9.8[a,b]
International migrant stock (000/% of total pop.)	2.8 / 2.7	2.8 / 2.5	2.8 / 2.5[i]
Refugees and others of concern to the UNHCR (000)	...	~0.0	~0.0[i]
Infant mortality rate (per 1 000 live births)	27.0	24.0	18.9[a,b]
Health: Current expenditure (% of GDP)[k]	13.1	12.5	11.6[i]
Health: Physicians (per 1 000 pop.)	0.6[l]	0.7[m]	1.0[i]
Education: Government expenditure (% of GDP)	...	12.4	10.2[g]
Education: Primary gross enrol. ratio (f/m per 100 pop.)	113.8 / 112.4[n]	95.8 / 98.3	90.0 / 90.4[c]
Education: Lowr. sec. gross enrol. ratio (f/m per 100 pop.)	99.0 / 99.6[n]	87.7 / 85.5	79.6 / 75.6[c]
Education: Upr. sec. gross enrol. ratio (f/m per 100 pop.)	77.5 / 72.7[o]	... / ...	... / ...
Intentional homicide rate (per 100 000 pop.)	...	...	0.9[g]
Seats held by women in the National Parliament (%)	0.0	0.0	7.1[p]

Environment and infrastructure indicators

	2010	2015	2023
Threatened species (number)	148	163	188[b]
Forested area (% of land area)	91.6	91.8	92.0[i]
Energy production, primary (Petajoules)	0	0	0[i]
Energy supply per capita (Gigajoules)	14	19	19[e,i]
Tourist/visitor arrivals at national borders (000)[q]	45	31	18[g]
Important sites for terrestrial biodiversity protected (%)	~0.0	~0.0	~0.0[b]
Net Official Development Assist. received (% of GNI)	20.77	21.70	29.38[c]

a Projected estimate (medium fertility variant). **b** 2022. **c** 2021. **d** 2018. **e** Estimate. **f** 2014. **g** 2019. **h** Data refers to a 5-year period preceding the reference year. **i** 2020. **j** 2017. **k** Data refer to fiscal years beginning 1 October. **l** 2008. **m** 2012. **n** 2007. **o** 2005. **p** Data are as at 1 January of reporting year. **q** Arrivals in the States of Kosrae, Chuuk, Pohnpei and Yap; excluding FSM citizens.

Monaco

Region	Western Europe	UN membership date	28 May 1993
Population (000, 2023)	36 [a,b]	Surface area (km2)	2 [c]
Pop. density (per km2, 2023)	24 475.8 [a,b]	Sex ratio (m per 100 f)	96.1 [a,b]
Capital city	Monaco	National currency	Euro (EUR)
Capital city pop. (000, 2023)	38.9 [d]	Exchange rate (per US$)	0.9 [b]

Economic indicators	2010	2015	2023
GDP: Gross domestic product (million current US$)	5 362	6 259	8 596 [c]
GDP growth rate (annual %, const. 2015 prices)	2.1	4.9	21.6 [c]
GDP per capita (current US$)	161 623.7	170 270.2	234 317.1 [c]
Economy: Industry (% of Gross Value Added) [e,f]	12.9	17.6	12.5 [c]
Economy: Services and other activity (% of GVA) [f]	87.1	82.4	87.5 [c]

Social indicators	2010	2015	2023
Population growth rate (average annual %)	2.3	1.7	- 0.5 [a,b]
Urban population (% of total population)	100.0	100.0	100.0 [g]
Urban population growth rate (average annual %) [h]	1.9	0.6	...
Fertility rate, total (live births per woman)	2.2	2.2	2.1 [a,b]
Life expectancy at birth (females/males, years)	86.7 / 82.5	88.2 / 82.7	88.9 / 85.1 [a,b]
Population age distribution (0-14/60+ years old, %)	13.0 / 34.6	12.1 / 41.0	13.0 / 43.7 [a,b]
International migrant stock (000/% of total pop.)	21.1 / 59.3	26.0 / 68.9	26.6 / 67.8 [i]
Refugees and others of concern to the UNHCR (000)	~0.0 [j]	~0.0	~0.0 [k,b]
Infant mortality rate (per 1 000 live births)	5.0	4.5	3.6 [a,b]
Health: Current expenditure (% of GDP)	2.3	2.0	1.7 [i]
Health: Physicians (per 1 000 pop.)	...	7.8 [l]	...
Education: Government expenditure (% of GDP)	1.3	1.0 [l]	1.4 [c]
Education: Primary gross enrol. ratio (f/m per 100 pop.)	... / ...	... / ...	119.5 / 116.6 [m,b]
Education: Lowr. sec. gross enrol. ratio (f/m per 100 pop.)	... / ...	... / ...	132.8 / 125.6 [m,b]
Education: Upr. sec. gross enrol. ratio (f/m per 100 pop.)	... / ...	... / ...	136.7 / 143.9 [m,b]
Intentional homicide rate (per 100 000 pop.)	0.0 [n]	...	...
Seats held by women in the National Parliament (%)	26.1	20.8	36.4 [o]

Environment and infrastructure indicators	2010	2015	2023
Individuals using the Internet (per 100 inhabitants)	75.0	93.4 [m]	86.1 [m,c]
Research & Development expenditure (% of GDP)	~0.0 [p,q]	...	...
Threatened species (number)	11	16	48 [b]
Forested area (% of land area)	0.0	0.0	0.0 [i]
Tourist/visitor arrivals at national borders (000)	279	331	218 [c]
Pop. using safely managed drinking water (urban/rural, %)	100.0 / ...	100.0 / ...	100.0 / ... [b]
Pop. using safely managed sanitation (urban/rural %)	100.0 / ...	100.0 / ...	100.0 / ... [b]

a Projected estimate (medium fertility variant). b 2022. c 2021. d 2018. e At producers' prices. f Data classified according to ISIC Rev. 4. g 2019. h Data refers to a 5-year period preceding the reference year. i 2020. j Data as at the end of December. k Data is as of end-2021. l 2014. m Estimate. n 2008. o Data are as at 1 January of reporting year. p Partial data. q 2005.

Mongolia

Region	Eastern Asia	UN membership date	27 October 1961
Population (000, 2023)	3 398[a,b]	Surface area (km2)	1 564 116[c]
Pop. density (per km2, 2023)	2.2[a,b]	Sex ratio (m per 100 f)	98.4[a,b]
Capital city	Ulaanbaatar	National currency	Tugrik (MNT)
Capital city pop. (000, 2023)	1 552.7[d]	Exchange rate (per US$)	2 849.3[c]

Economic indicators	2010	2015	2023
GDP: Gross domestic product (million current US$)	7 189	11 620	15 098[c]
GDP growth rate (annual %, const. 2015 prices)	6.4	1.2	1.4[c]
GDP per capita (current US$)	2 660.3	3 919.4	4 509.9[c]
Economy: Agriculture (% of Gross Value Added)[e,f]	13.1	15.3	14.7[c]
Economy: Industry (% of Gross Value Added)[f,g]	37.0	34.3	41.2[c]
Economy: Services and other activity (% of GVA)[f]	50.0	50.3	44.1[c]
Employment in agriculture (% of employed)	33.5	28.5	24.3[h,c]
Employment in industry (% of employed)	16.2	20.4	20.9[h,c]
Employment in services & other sectors (% employed)	50.3	51.2	54.8[h,c]
Unemployment rate (% of labour force)	6.6	4.9	8.9[h]
Labour force participation rate (female/male pop. %)	54.2 / 64.7	53.9 / 66.0	53.1 / 67.7[h]
CPI: Consumer Price Index (2010=100)	100[i]	164[i]	124[j,i]
Agricultural production index (2014-2016=100)	63	110	129[c]
International trade: exports (million current US$)	2 908[h]	4 669	13 225[h,b]
International trade: imports (million current US$)	3 200[h]	3 797	8 592[h,b]
International trade: balance (million current US$)	- 291[h]	873	4 633[h,b]
Balance of payments, current account (million US$)	- 885	- 948	- 2 304[b]

Major trading partners							2022
Export partners (% of exports)[h]	China	82.6	Switzerland	9.4	Singapore		2.7
Import partners (% of imports)[h]	China	36.4	Russian Federation	28.6	Japan		6.6

Social indicators	2010	2015	2023
Population growth rate (average annual %)	1.3	2.2	1.5[a,b]
Urban population (% of total population)	67.6	68.2	68.5[d]
Urban population growth rate (average annual %)[k]	3.0	2.1	...
Fertility rate, total (live births per woman)	2.5	3.0	2.8[a,b]
Life expectancy at birth (females/males, years)	71.8 / 63.0	73.7 / 65.5	77.4 / 68.1[a,b]
Population age distribution (0-14/60+ years old, %)	28.1 / 5.6	29.3 / 6.1	32.5 / 8.0[a,b]
International migrant stock (000/% of total pop.)[l,m]	16.1 / 0.6	19.9 / 0.7	21.3 / 0.7[n]
Refugees and others of concern to the UNHCR (000)	0.3[o]	~0.0	~0.0[b]
Infant mortality rate (per 1 000 live births)	21.7	16.3	8.8[a,b]
Health: Current expenditure (% of GDP)	3.7	4.2	4.9[n]
Health: Physicians (per 1 000 pop.)	2.8	3.3	3.9[p]
Education: Government expenditure (% of GDP)	4.6	4.4	6.5[c]
Education: Primary gross enrol. ratio (f/m per 100 pop.)	124.3 / 127.2	99.4 / 101.3	101.2 / 103.5[c]
Education: Lowr. sec. gross enrol. ratio (f/m per 100 pop.)	94.1 / 90.3	... / ...	102.9 / 103.2[c]
Education: Upr. sec. gross enrol. ratio (f/m per 100 pop.)	96.0 / 84.8	92.2 / 87.1	106.4 / 100.9[c]
Intentional homicide rate (per 100 000 pop.)	8.8	7.2	6.2[c]
Seats held by women in the National Parliament (%)	3.9	14.9	17.1[q]

Environment and infrastructure indicators	2010	2015	2023
Individuals using the Internet (per 100 inhabitants)	10.2[r]	22.5[s]	84.3[c]
Research & Development expenditure (% of GDP)	0.2[t]	0.2[t]	0.1[u,n]
Threatened species (number)	36	36	43[b]
Forested area (% of land area)	9.1	9.1	9.1[n]
CO2 emission estimates (million tons/tons per capita)	14.4 / 5.2	17.4 / 5.7	21.0 / 6.3[n]
Energy production, primary (Petajoules)	655	655	1 169[n]
Energy supply per capita (Gigajoules)	61	92	130[n]
Tourist/visitor arrivals at national borders (000)	456	386	33[c]
Important sites for terrestrial biodiversity protected (%)	40.7	40.7	45.2[b]
Pop. using safely managed drinking water (urban/rural, %)	40.0 / 5.1	44.6 / 7.9	51.3 / 12.7[b]
Pop. using safely managed sanitation (urban/rural %)	62.0 / 35.9	66.1 / 44.5	70.3 / 56.3[b]
Net Official Development Assist. received (% of GNI)	4.34	2.22	2.17[c]

a Projected estimate (medium fertility variant). b 2022. c 2021. d 2019. e Excludes irrigation canals and landscaping care. f Data classified according to ISIC Rev. 4. g Excludes publishing activities, recycling. Includes irrigation canals. h Estimate. i Calculated by the UN Statistics Division from national indices. j Base 2020 = 100 k Data refers to a 5-year period preceding the reference year. l Refers to foreign citizens. m Including refugees. n 2020. o Data as at the end of December. p 2018. q Data are as at 1 January of reporting year. r Refers to total population. s All population. t Partial data. u Break in the time series.

Montenegro

Region	Southern Europe
Population (000, 2023)	627 [a,b]
Pop. density (per km2, 2023)	45.4 [a,b]
Capital city	Podgorica
Capital city pop. (000, 2023)	177.2 [d,e]

UN membership date	28 June 2006
Surface area (km2)	13 812 [c]
Sex ratio (m per 100 f)	94.9 [a,b]
National currency	Euro (EUR)
Exchange rate (per US$)	0.9 [b]

Economic indicators

	2010	2015	2023
GDP: Gross domestic product (million current US$)	4 139	4 053	5 809 [c]
GDP growth rate (annual %, const. 2015 prices)	2.7	3.4	13.0 [c]
GDP per capita (current US$)	6 558.9	6 393.2	9 252.3 [c]
Economy: Agriculture (% of Gross Value Added) [f,g]	9.2	9.8	7.8 [c]
Economy: Industry (% of Gross Value Added) [f,h]	20.5	17.4	18.5 [c]
Economy: Services and other activity (% of GVA) [f]	70.3	72.9	73.7 [c]
Employment in agriculture (% of employed)	6.2 [i]	7.7	7.4 [i,c]
Employment in industry (% of employed)	18.5 [i]	17.5	18.9 [i,c]
Employment in services & other sectors (% employed)	75.3 [i]	74.8	73.8 [i,c]
Unemployment rate (% of labour force)	19.6	17.6	16.1 [i]
Labour force participation rate (female/male pop. %)	42.2 / 55.9 [i]	47.7 / 60.2	50.1 / 64.5 [i]
CPI: Consumer Price Index (2010=100)	100	111	135 [j,b]
Agricultural production index (2014-2016=100)	96	98	99 [c]
International trade: exports (million current US$)	437	353	736 [b]
International trade: imports (million current US$)	2 182	2 050	3 722 [b]
International trade: balance (million current US$)	- 1 745	- 1 697	- 2 986 [b]
Balance of payments, current account (million US$)	- 852	- 443	- 825 [b]

Major trading partners

						2022
Export partners (% of exports) [i]	Serbia	21.3	Switzerland	15.4	Bosnia Herzegovina	12.9
Import partners (% of imports)	Serbia	17.4	China	9.3	Greece	8.3

Social indicators

	2010	2015	2023
Population growth rate (average annual %)	~0.0	- 0.1	- 0.1 [a,b]
Urban population (% of total population)	64.1	65.8	67.2 [k]
Urban population growth rate (average annual %) [l]	0.8	0.6	...
Fertility rate, total (live births per woman)	1.7	1.7	1.7 [a,b]
Life expectancy at birth (females/males, years)	78.9 / 73.3	79.4 / 74.0	80.3 / 73.5 [a,b]
Population age distribution (0-14/60+ years old, %)	19.3 / 18.0	18.5 / 20.2	18.1 / 22.9 [a,b]
International migrant stock (000/% of total pop.)	78.5 / 12.6	71.7 / 11.4	71.0 / 11.3 [m]
Refugees and others of concern to the UNHCR (000)	18.3 [n]	19.8	12.4 [b]
Infant mortality rate (per 1 000 live births)	5.7	2.6	1.2 [a,b]
Health: Current expenditure (% of GDP)	...	9.0	11.4 [m]
Health: Physicians (per 1 000 pop.)	2.0	2.4	2.8 [c]
Education: Primary gross enrol. ratio (f/m per 100 pop.)	110.6 / 110.3	95.5 / 95.3	102.5 / 102.0 [c]
Education: Lowr. sec. gross enrol. ratio (f/m per 100 pop.)	113.6 / 113.0	99.0 / 97.0	95.7 / 95.6 [c]
Education: Upr. sec. gross enrol. ratio (f/m per 100 pop.)	90.9 / 85.8	88.3 / 87.2	88.1 / 84.8 [c]
Intentional homicide rate (per 100 000 pop.)	2.4	2.7	2.4 [c]
Seats held by women in the National Parliament (%)	11.1	17.3	28.4 [o]

Environment and infrastructure indicators

	2010	2015	2023
Individuals using the Internet (per 100 inhabitants)	37.5 [i]	68.1	82.2 [c]
Research & Development expenditure (% of GDP)	1.1 [p]	0.4	0.4 [k]
Threatened species (number)	72	85	165 [b]
Forested area (% of land area)	61.5	61.5	61.5 [m]
CO2 emission estimates (million tons/tons per capita)	2.7 / 4.2	2.4 / 3.8	2.6 / 4.1 [m]
Energy production, primary (Petajoules)	35	30	31 [m]
Energy supply per capita (Gigajoules)	76	67	70 [m]
Tourist/visitor arrivals at national borders (000)	1 088	1 560	1 554 [c]
Important sites for terrestrial biodiversity protected (%)	17.7	17.7	25.9 [b]
Pop. using safely managed drinking water (urban/rural, %)	87.0 / ...	87.2 / ...	87.3 / ... [b]
Pop. using safely managed sanitation (urban/rural %)	31.8 / 35.3	46.3 / 39.2	64.1 / 43.1 [b]
Net Official Development Assist. received (% of GNI)	1.95	2.41	2.25 [c]

a Projected estimate (medium fertility variant). **b** 2022. **c** 2021. **d** Refers to the urban population of Podgorica municipality. **e** 2018. **f** Data classified according to ISIC Rev. 4. **g** Excludes irrigation canals and landscaping care. **h** Excludes publishing activities, recycling. Includes irrigation canals. **i** Estimate. **j** Calculated by the UN Statistics Division from national indices. **k** 2019. **l** Data refers to a 5-year period preceding the reference year. **m** 2020. **n** Data as at the end of December. **o** Data are as at 1 January of reporting year. **p** 2007.

Montserrat

Region	Caribbean	Population (000, 2023)	4[a,b,c]
Surface area (km2)	103[d]	Pop. density (per km2, 2023)	42.6[a,b,c]
Sex ratio (m per 100 f)	111.7[a,b,c]	Capital city	Brades Estate
National currency	E. Caribbean Dollar (XCD)[e]	Capital city pop. (000, 2023)	0.5[f]
Exchange rate (per US$)	2.7[c]		

Economic indicators

	2010	2015	2023
GDP: Gross domestic product (million current US$)	56	61	72[d]
GDP growth rate (annual %, const. 2015 prices)	- 6.9	1.2	5.5[d]
GDP per capita (current US$)	11 241.6	12 133.1	16 199.4[d]
Economy: Agriculture (% of Gross Value Added)	1.1	1.4	0.7[d]
Economy: Industry (% of Gross Value Added)	13.3	12.4	17.2[d]
Economy: Services and other activity (% of GVA)	85.7	86.3	82.1[d]
Unemployment rate (% of labour force)	...	5.6[g]	...
CPI: Consumer Price Index (2010=100)[h]	100	108	109[d]
International trade: exports (million current US$)	1	3[h]	7[c]
International trade: imports (million current US$)	29[h]	39[h]	39[c]
International trade: balance (million current US$)	- 28[h]	- 36[h]	- 33[c]
Balance of payments, current account (million US$)	- 19	- 1	- 13[d]

Major trading partners   2022

Export partners (% of exports)	France	78.9[h]	United States	15.7[h]	Areas nes	2.1
Import partners (% of imports)	United States	67.0	United Kingdom	7.4	Trinidad and Tobago	4.7

Social indicators

	2010	2015	2023
Population growth rate (average annual %)[b]	1.4	- 0.9	~0.0[a,c]
Urban population (% of total population)	9.2	9.0	9.1[i]
Urban population growth rate (average annual %)[j]	0.3	0.5	...
Fertility rate, total (live births per woman)[b]	1.4	1.5	1.6[a,c]
Life expectancy at birth (females/males, years)[b]	75.5 / 73.3	76.3 / 73.9	77.5 / 74.5[a,c]
Population age distribution (0-14/60+ years old, %)[b]	19.8 / 18.5	18.2 / 20.0	12.8 / 24.4[a,c]
International migrant stock (000/% of total pop.)	1.3 / 26.4	1.4 / 27.2	1.4 / 27.6[k]
Refugees and others of concern to the UNHCR (000)	~0.0[l]	...	...
Infant mortality rate (per 1 000 live births)[b]	15.7	13.1	10.3[a,c]
Education: Government expenditure (% of GDP)	5.1[m]	5.5	5.1[d]
Education: Primary gross enrol. ratio (f/m per 100 pop.)	144.0 / 145.0	101.4 / 102.1	112.4 / 99.1[i]
Education: Lowr. sec. gross enrol. ratio (f/m per 100 pop.)	156.8 / 156.2[m]	190.3 / 155.9[n]	110.4 / 97.1[i]
Education: Upr. sec. gross enrol. ratio (f/m per 100 pop.)	86.2 / 87.1[m]	160.0 / 208.8[n]	88.9 / 89.6[i]
Intentional homicide rate (per 100 000 pop.)	20.8[o]	20.1[p]	0.0[f]

Environment and infrastructure indicators

	2010	2015	2023
Individuals using the Internet (per 100 inhabitants)	35.0	54.6[g]	...
Threatened species (number)	35	54	88[c]
Forested area (% of land area)	25.0	25.0	25.0[k]
Energy production, primary (Petajoules)	...	...	0[k]
Energy supply per capita (Gigajoules)	167	146	77[k]
Tourist/visitor arrivals at national borders (000)	6	9	2[d]
Important sites for terrestrial biodiversity protected (%)	0.0	30.6	30.6[c]

a Projected estimate (medium fertility variant). **b** For statistical purposes, the data for United Kingdom do not include this area. **c** 2022. **d** 2021. **e** East Caribbean Dollar. **f** 2018. **g** 2011. **h** Estimate. **i** 2019. **j** Data refers to a 5-year period preceding the reference year. **k** 2020. **l** Data as at the end of December. **m** 2009. **n** 2014. **o** 2008. **p** 2012.

Morocco

Region	Northern Africa
Population (000, 2023)	37 458[a,b]
Pop. density (per km2, 2023)	83.9[a,b]
Capital city	Rabat
Capital city pop. (000, 2023)	1 864.9[d,e]

UN membership date	12 November 1956
Surface area (km2)	446 550[c]
Sex ratio (m per 100 f)	101.3[a,b]
National currency	Moroccan Dirham (MAD)
Exchange rate (per US$)	10.4[b]

Economic indicators	2010	2015	2023
GDP: Gross domestic product (million current US$)[f]	96 428	110 414	142 867[c]
GDP growth rate (annual %, const. 2015 prices)[f]	5.1	4.3	1.7[c]
GDP per capita (current US$)[f]	2 970.2	3 183.7	3 853.3[c]
Economy: Agriculture (% of Gross Value Added)[g]	13.7	13.2[h]	13.4[h,c]
Economy: Industry (% of Gross Value Added)[g]	28.2	28.6[i]	29.1[i,c]
Economy: Services and other activity (% of GVA)[g]	58.1	58.2	57.5[c]
Employment in agriculture (% of employed)	40.0	36.6[i]	34.6[i,c]
Employment in industry (% of employed)[j]	22.2	22.1	22.8[c]
Employment in services & other sectors (% employed)[j]	37.8	41.3	42.7[c]
Unemployment rate (% of labour force)	9.1	9.5	10.5[j]
Labour force participation rate (female/male pop. %)	25.6 / 73.8	24.4 / 70.6	21.6 / 69.2[j]
CPI: Consumer Price Index (2010=100)	100[k]	106[k]	111[l,b]
Agricultural production index (2014-2016=100)	93	108	116[c]
International trade: exports (million current US$)	17 765	22 337	42 183[b]
International trade: imports (million current US$)	35 379	38 146	72 578[b]
International trade: balance (million current US$)	- 17 614	- 15 809	- 30 394[b]
Balance of payments, current account (million US$)	- 3 925	- 2 161	- 4 775[b]

Major trading partners						2022
Export partners (% of exports)[j]	Spain	19.7	France	19.1	India	6.4
Import partners (% of imports)	Spain	14.1	France	10.6	China	10.0

Social indicators	2010	2015	2023
Population growth rate (average annual %)	1.3	1.2	1.0[a,b]
Urban population (% of total population)	58.0	60.8	63.0[e]
Urban population growth rate (average annual %)[m]	2.2	2.4	...
Fertility rate, total (live births per woman)	2.6	2.5	2.3[a,b]
Life expectancy at birth (females/males, years)	72.5 / 69.2	74.8 / 71.2	77.2 / 72.9[a,b]
Population age distribution (0-14/60+ years old, %)	28.9 / 7.9	28.0 / 9.3	26.6 / 11.9[a,b]
International migrant stock (000/% of total pop.)[n,o]	71.2 / 0.2	92.4 / 0.3	102.4 / 0.3[p]
Refugees and others of concern to the UNHCR (000)	1.1[q]	4.4	18.7[b]
Infant mortality rate (per 1 000 live births)	25.9	19.8	14.4[a,b]
Health: Current expenditure (% of GDP)[r]	5.9	5.6	6.0[j,p]
Health: Physicians (per 1 000 pop.)	0.6[s]	0.9[t]	0.7[u]
Education: Government expenditure (% of GDP)	5.3[s]	...	...
Education: Primary gross enrol. ratio (f/m per 100 pop.)	106.3 / 113.0	106.6 / 112.3	111.8 / 114.9[c]
Education: Lowr. sec. gross enrol. ratio (f/m per 100 pop.)	71.5 / 86.7	86.0 / 100.1	94.5 / 103.3[c]
Education: Upr. sec. gross enrol. ratio (f/m per 100 pop.)	46.8 / 49.2	52.5 / 57.5[v]	70.1 / 66.2[c]
Intentional homicide rate (per 100 000 pop.)	1.4	1.2	1.9[c]
Seats held by women in the National Parliament (%)	10.5	17.0	24.3[w]

Environment and infrastructure indicators	2010	2015	2023
Individuals using the Internet (per 100 inhabitants)	52.0[x,y]	57.1	88.1[c]
Research & Development expenditure (% of GDP)	0.7	...	...
Threatened species (number)	157	176	278[b]
Forested area (% of land area)	12.7	12.7	12.9[p]
CO2 emission estimates (million tons/tons per capita)	47.3 / 1.4	56.0 / 1.6	68.2 / 1.7[c,p]
Energy production, primary (Petajoules)	84	62	100[p]
Energy supply per capita (Gigajoules)	23	23	24[p]
Tourist/visitor arrivals at national borders (000)[z]	9 288	10 177	3 722[c]
Important sites for terrestrial biodiversity protected (%)	34.5	34.5	59.5[b]
Pop. using safely managed drinking water (urban/rural, %)	76.8 / 21.4	89.3 / 35.6	90.3 / 46.7[b]
Pop. using safely managed sanitation (urban/rural %)	33.2 / ...	33.7 / ...	34.4 / ...[b]
Net Official Development Assist. received (% of GNI)	1.07	1.53	0.74[c]

a Projected estimate (medium fertility variant). b 2022. c 2021. d Including Salé and Temara. e 2019. f Including Western Sahara. g Data classified according to ISIC Rev. 4. h Excludes irrigation canals and landscaping care. i Excludes publishing activities, recycling. Includes irrigation canals. j Estimate. k Calculated by the UN Statistics Division from national indices. l Base 2017 = 100. m Data refers to a 5-year period preceding the reference year. n Refers to foreign citizens. o Including refugees. p 2020. q Data as at the end of December. r Data based on calendar year (January 1 to December 31). s 2009. t 2014. u 2017. v 2012. w Data are as at 1 January of reporting year. x Population aged 6 to 74 years. y Living in electrified areas. z Including nationals residing abroad.

Mozambique

Region	Eastern Africa	UN membership date	16 September 1975
Population (000, 2023)	32 970 a,b	Surface area (km2)	799 380 c
Pop. density (per km2, 2023)	41.9 a,b	Sex ratio (m per 100 f)	96.3 a,b
Capital city	Maputo	National currency	Mozambique Metical (MZN)
Capital city pop. (000, 2023)	1 104.3 d	Exchange rate (per US$)	63.9 b

Economic indicators

	2010	2015	2023
GDP: Gross domestic product (million current US$)	11 105	15 951	15 777 c
GDP growth rate (annual %, const. 2015 prices)	6.5	6.7	2.3 c
GDP per capita (current US$)	481.3	594.2	491.8 c
Economy: Agriculture (% of Gross Value Added) e,f	29.8	25.9	30.7 c
Economy: Industry (% of Gross Value Added) f,g	18.2	20.5	24.5 c
Economy: Services and other activity (% of GVA) f	52.0	53.6	44.8 c
Employment in agriculture (% of employed)	76.5 h	72.1	70.3 h,c
Employment in industry (% of employed) h	5.3	4.9	9.3 c
Employment in services & other sectors (% employed)	18.2 h	20.1	20.5 h,c
Unemployment rate (% of labour force)	3.2 h	3.4	3.9 h
Labour force participation rate (female/male pop. %)	80.9 / 80.1 h	78.1 / 80.1	78.3 / 78.8 h
CPI: Consumer Price Index (2010=100) i	100	126	199 b
Agricultural production index (2014-2016=100)	107	97	137 c
International trade: exports (million current US$)	2 243	3 649 h	8 265 b
International trade: imports (million current US$)	3 564	7 852 h	14 665 b
International trade: balance (million current US$)	- 1 321	- 4 203 h	- 6 400 b
Balance of payments, current account (million US$)	- 1 679	- 5 948	- 6 295 b

Major trading partners

							2022
Export partners (% of exports)	India	21.1	South Africa	13.6	United Kingdom		11.9
Import partners (% of imports)	Republic of Korea	32.0	South Africa	15.6	United Arab Emirates		10.0

Social indicators

	2010	2015	2023
Population growth rate (average annual %)	2.9	3.0	2.7 a,b
Urban population (% of total population)	31.8	34.4	36.5 d
Urban population growth rate (average annual %) j	4.1	4.5	...
Fertility rate, total (live births per woman)	5.6	5.1	4.6 a,b
Life expectancy at birth (females/males, years)	55.8 / 52.4	60.4 / 55.7	62.7 / 56.5 a,b
Population age distribution (0-14/60+ years old, %)	45.4 / 4.3	45.0 / 4.2	43.5 / 4.2 a,b
International migrant stock (000/% of total pop.) k	306.5 / 1.3	321.8 / 1.2	338.8 / 1.1 l
Refugees and others of concern to the UNHCR (000)	10.0 m	18.8	901.4 b
Infant mortality rate (per 1 000 live births)	75.8	62.3	52.8 a,b
Health: Current expenditure (% of GDP) n	5.4	6.7	7.6 l
Health: Physicians (per 1 000 pop.)	~0.0	0.1 o	0.1 c
Education: Government expenditure (% of GDP)	5.4	6.0	6.9 c
Education: Primary gross enrol. ratio (f/m per 100 pop.)	105.9 / 119.2	103.4 / 113.8 h	114.9 / 121.9 l
Education: Lowr. sec. gross enrol. ratio (f/m per 100 pop.)	30.3 / 36.9	38.4 / 42.3 h	42.2 / 46.6 l
Education: Upr. sec. gross enrol. ratio (f/m per 100 000 pop.)	9.8 / 13.3	21.3 / 23.5 h	30.3 / 30.5 l
Intentional homicide rate (per 100 000 pop.)	3.8	3.6 p	...
Seats held by women in the National Parliament (%)	39.2	39.6	43.2 q

Environment and infrastructure indicators

	2010	2015	2023
Individuals using the Internet (per 100 inhabitants)	4.2	6.5 h	17.4 h,c
Research & Development expenditure (% of GDP)	0.4 r,s	0.3	...
Threatened species (number)	209	268	545 b
Forested area (% of land area)	49.6	48.2	46.7 l
CO2 emission estimates (million tons/tons per capita)	3.6 / 0.1	6.6 / 0.2	7.8 / 0.2 l
Energy production, primary (Petajoules)	397	716	746 l
Energy supply per capita (Gigajoules)	13	17	15 l
Tourist/visitor arrivals at national borders (000) t	1 718 s	1 552	492 c
Important sites for terrestrial biodiversity protected (%)	36.0	39.6	39.6 b
Pop. using safely managed sanitation (urban/rural %)	... / 9.6	... / 14.2	... / 20.9 b
Net Official Development Assist. received (% of GNI)	18.09	11.62	14.49 c

a Projected estimate (medium fertility variant). b 2022. c 2021. d 2019. e Excludes irrigation canals and landscaping care. f Data classified according to ISIC Rev. 4. g Excludes publishing activities, recycling. Includes irrigation canals. h Estimate. i Calculated by the UN Statistics Division from national indices. j Data refers to a 5-year period preceding the reference year. k Including refugees. l 2020. m Data as at the end of December. n Data based on calendar year (January 1 to December 31). o 2013. p 2011. q Data are as at 1 January of reporting year. r Excluding business enterprise. s Break in the time series. t The data of all the border posts of the country are used.

Myanmar

Region	South-eastern Asia
Population (000, 2023)	54 179[a,b]
Pop. density (per km2, 2023)	82.9[a,b]
Capital city	Nay Pyi Taw
Capital city pop. (000, 2023)	546.5[d]

UN membership date	19 April 1948
Surface area (km2)	676 577[c]
Sex ratio (m per 100 f)	99.1[a,b]
National currency	Kyat (MMK)
Exchange rate (per US$)	1 329.1[e]

Economic indicators

	2010	2015	2023
GDP: Gross domestic product (million current US$)[f]	44 847	63 835	58 582[c]
GDP growth rate (annual %, const. 2015 prices)[f]	7.8	6.4	- 17.9[c]
GDP per capita (current US$)[f]	908.0	1 239.9	1 088.9[c]
Economy: Agriculture (% of Gross Value Added)[f,g]	35.3	26.7	25.3[c]
Economy: Industry (% of Gross Value Added)[f,g]	28.3	33.9	33.8[c]
Economy: Services and other activity (% of GVA)[f]	36.5	39.4	40.9[c]
Employment in agriculture (% of employed)	52.3[h]	51.7	45.9[h,c]
Employment in industry (% of employed)	17.6[h]	16.7	18.9[h,c]
Employment in services & other sectors (% employed)	30.1[h]	31.5	35.2[h,c]
Unemployment rate (% of labour force)	0.7[h]	0.8	1.5[e]
Labour force participation rate (female/male pop. %)	52.6 / 80.1[h]	50.8 / 79.0	44.7 / 76.0[e]
CPI: Consumer Price Index (2010=100)	100	129	168[d]
Agricultural production index (2014-2016=100)	98	101	79[c]
International trade: exports (million current US$)	8 873	11 432	17 085[b]
International trade: imports (million current US$)	4 866	16 913	17 403[b]
International trade: balance (million current US$)	4 008	- 5 481	- 319[b]
Balance of payments, current account (million US$)	1 574	- 3 109	68[d]

Major trading partners

						2022
Export partners (% of exports)	Thailand	22.5	China	21.6	Japan	7.1
Import partners (% of imports)	China	32.1	Singapore	24.8	Thailand	12.4

Social indicators

	2010	2015	2023
Population growth rate (average annual %)	0.8	0.8	0.7[a,b]
Urban population (% of total population)	28.9	29.9	30.9[d]
Urban population growth rate (average annual %)[i]	1.3	1.5	...
Fertility rate, total (live births per woman)	2.3	2.2	2.1[a,b]
Life expectancy at birth (females/males, years)	66.2 / 60.6	68.7 / 62.5	70.5 / 64.2[a,b]
Population age distribution (0-14/60+ years old, %)	28.3 / 7.9	26.6 / 9.0	24.6 / 10.8[a,b]
International migrant stock (000/% of total pop.)[j]	76.4 / 0.2	73.3 / 0.1	76.4 / 0.1[e]
Refugees and others of concern to the UNHCR (000)	859.4[k]	1 466.5	1 671.2[b]
Infant mortality rate (per 1 000 live births)	48.7	40.7	32.7[a,b]
Health: Current expenditure (% of GDP)[l,m]	2.0[n]	5.5[n]	4.6[o,e]
Health: Physicians (per 1 000 pop.)	0.5	0.6[p]	0.8[d]
Education: Government expenditure (% of GDP)	...	2.2	2.1[d]
Education: Primary gross enrol. ratio (f/m per 100 pop.)	97.6 / 98.6	100.3 / 103.3[q]	109.7 / 114.8[r]
Education: Lowr. sec. gross enrol. ratio (f/m per 100 pop.)	55.2 / 53.7	60.2 / 60.3[q]	77.5 / 73.7[r]
Education: Upr. sec. gross enrol. ratio (f/m per 100 pop.)	36.7 / 33.2	36.1 / 32.4[q]	59.2 / 49.7[r]
Intentional homicide rate (per 100 000 pop.)	1.6	2.5	28.4[c]
Seats held by women in the National Parliament (%)	...	6.2	15.3[s,t,b]

Environment and infrastructure indicators

	2010	2015	2023
Individuals using the Internet (per 100 inhabitants)	0.2	10.9[h]	44.0[h,c]
Research & Development expenditure (% of GDP)	...	...	0.1[u,v,c]
Threatened species (number)	249	301	445[b]
Forested area (% of land area)	48.1	45.9	43.7[e]
CO2 emission estimates (million tons/tons per capita)[m]	11.7 / 0.2	22.7 / 0.4	34.9 / 0.6[e]
Energy production, primary (Petajoules)	967	1 177	1 147[e]
Energy supply per capita (Gigajoules)	13	16	18[e]
Tourist/visitor arrivals at national borders (000)	792	4 681	131[c]
Important sites for terrestrial biodiversity protected (%)	18.8	20.9	22.3[b]
Pop. using safely managed drinking water (urban/rural, %)	67.9 / 33.1	70.4 / 41.4	72.4 / 50.4[b]
Pop. using safely managed sanitation (urban/rural %)	60.8 / 61.1	57.1 / 62.6	52.7 / 64.3[b]
Net Official Development Assist. received (% of GNI)	0.98	1.93	2.38[c]

a Projected estimate (medium fertility variant). **b** 2022. **c** 2021. **d** 2019. **e** 2020. **f** Data compiled in accordance with the System of National Accounts 1968 (1968 SNA). **g** At producers' prices. **h** Estimate. **i** Data refers to a 5-year period preceding the reference year. **j** Refers to foreign citizens. **k** Data as at the end of December. **l** Data revision. **m** Data refer to fiscal years beginning 1 April. **n** Country is still reporting data based on SHA 1.0. **o** Data are based on SHA2011. **p** 2012. **q** 2014. **r** 2018. **s** Figures correspond to members elected at or appointed following the 2020 elections. The new parliament was unable to hold its first sitting in February 2021 due to a military take over. **t** Data are as at 1 January of reporting year. **u** Excluding private non-profit. **v** Excluding business enterprise.

Namibia

Region	Southern Africa	UN membership date	23 April 1990
Population (000, 2023)	2 567 [a,b]	Surface area (km2)	825 229 [c]
Pop. density (per km2, 2023)	3.1 [a,b]	Sex ratio (m per 100 f)	93.2 [a,b]
Capital city	Windhoek	National currency	Namibia Dollar (NAD)
Capital city pop. (000, 2023)	417.4 [d]	Exchange rate (per US$)	17.0 [b]

Economic indicators

	2010	2015	2023
GDP: Gross domestic product (million current US$)	11 282	11 335	12 236 [c]
GDP growth rate (annual %, const. 2015 prices)	6.0	4.3	2.4 [c]
GDP per capita (current US$)	5 374.3	4 965.7	4 836.2 [c]
Economy: Agriculture (% of Gross Value Added) [e,f]	9.1	7.2	10.1 [c]
Economy: Industry (% of Gross Value Added) [f,g]	29.7	29.9	26.9 [c]
Economy: Services and other activity (% of GVA) [f]	61.2	62.9	63.0 [c]
Employment in agriculture (% of employed)	31.7	24.4 [h]	22.1 [h,c]
Employment in industry (% of employed)	12.7	17.2 [h]	16.4 [h,c]
Employment in services & other sectors (% employed)	55.6	58.5 [h]	61.4 [h,c]
Unemployment rate (% of labour force)	22.1	20.9 [h]	20.6 [h]
Labour force participation rate (female/male pop. %) [h]	52.1 / 62.3	56.4 / 65.4	55.8 / 62.5
CPI: Consumer Price Index (2010=100) [i]	100	129	177 [b]
Agricultural production index (2014-2016=100)	100	100	105 [c]
International trade: exports (million current US$)	5 848	4 628	6 339 [b]
International trade: imports (million current US$)	5 980	7 697	7 905 [b]
International trade: balance (million current US$)	- 131	- 3 069	- 1 566 [b]
Balance of payments, current account (million US$)	- 448	- 1 559	- 1 569 [b]

Major trading partners

						2022
Export partners (% of exports)	South Africa	16.3	Botswana	16.1	China	11.5
Import partners (% of imports) [h]	South Africa	38.9	China	7.6	India	4.7

Social indicators

	2010	2015	2023
Population growth rate (average annual %)	1.5	1.8	1.4 [a,b]
Urban population (% of total population)	41.6	46.9	51.0 [d]
Urban population growth rate (average annual %) [j]	3.9	4.6	...
Fertility rate, total (live births per woman)	3.6	3.5	3.2 [a,b]
Life expectancy at birth (females/males, years)	58.7 / 53.3	64.0 / 57.3	61.7 / 54.6 [a,b]
Population age distribution (0-14/60+ years old, %)	37.0 / 5.3	36.3 / 5.7	36.2 / 6.1 [a,b]
International migrant stock (000/% of total pop.) [k]	103.8 / 4.9	101.6 / 4.4	109.4 / 4.3 [l]
Refugees and others of concern to the UNHCR (000)	8.8 [m]	4.4	6.9 [b]
Infant mortality rate (per 1 000 live births)	34.3	33.4	29.8 [a,b]
Health: Current expenditure (% of GDP) [n]	9.7	10.0	8.9 [b]
Health: Physicians (per 1 000 pop.)	0.4 [o]	...	0.6 [p]
Education: Government expenditure (% of GDP)	8.2	9.5	9.5 [b]
Education: Primary gross enrol. ratio (f/m per 100 pop.)	112.9 / 117.5	120.2 / 125.4	123.5 / 127.9 [c]
Education: Lowr. sec. gross enrol. ratio (f/m per 100 pop.)	93.0 / 83.4	106.7 / 98.7	108.2 / 102.8 [c]
Education: Upr. sec. gross enrol. ratio (f/m per 100 pop.)	38.3 / 34.0 [o]	... / ...	... / ...
Intentional homicide rate (per 100 000 pop.)	15.0	17.9 [q]	12.4 [c]
Seats held by women in the National Parliament (%)	26.9	41.3	44.2 [r]

Environment and infrastructure indicators

	2010	2015	2023
Individuals using the Internet (per 100 inhabitants)	11.6	25.7 [h]	53.0 [h,c]
Research & Development expenditure (% of GDP) [t]	0.1 [s]	0.3 [u]	...
Threatened species (number)	92	105	153 [b]
Forested area (% of land area)	8.9	8.5	8.1 [l]
CO2 emission estimates (million tons/tons per capita)	3.2 / 1.5	3.9 / 1.6	3.6 / 1.4 [l]
Energy production, primary (Petajoules)	17	21	29 [l]
Energy supply per capita (Gigajoules)	30	34	31 [l]
Tourist/visitor arrivals at national borders (000)	984	1 388	233 [c]
Important sites for terrestrial biodiversity protected (%)	83.5	86.2	86.2 [b]
Net Official Development Assist. received (% of GNI)	2.41	1.26	1.52 [c]

a Projected estimate (medium fertility variant). b 2022. c 2021. d 2019. e Excludes irrigation canals and landscaping care. f Data classified according to ISIC Rev. 4. g Excludes publishing activities, recycling. Includes irrigation canals. h Estimate. i Calculated by the UN Statistics Division from national indices. j Data refers to a 5-year period preceding the reference year. k Including refugees. l 2020. m Data as at the end of December. n Data refer to fiscal years beginning 1 April. o 2007. p 2018. q 2012. r Data are as at 1 January of reporting year. s Excluding government. t Partial data. u 2014.

Nauru

Region	Micronesia	UN membership date	14 September 1999
Population (000, 2023)	13 a,b	Surface area (km2)	21 c
Pop. density (per km2, 2023)	633.4 a,b	Sex ratio (m per 100 f)	103.2 a,b
Capital city	Yaren	National currency	Australian Dollar (AUD)
Capital city pop. (000, 2023)	11.3 d,e	Exchange rate (per US$)	1.5 b

Economic indicators	2010	2015	2023
GDP: Gross domestic product (million current US$)	59	104	155 c
GDP growth rate (annual %, const. 2015 prices)	13.6	36.5	0.7 c
GDP per capita (current US$)	5 788.2	9 329.7	12 390.4 c
Economy: Agriculture (% of Gross Value Added) f	4.2	2.4	2.4 c
Economy: Industry (% of Gross Value Added)	43.6	40.7	36.8 c
Economy: Services and other activity (% of GVA)	52.2	56.9	60.8 c
Unemployment rate (% of labour force)	...	23.0 g,h	...
Labour force participation rate (female/male pop. %)	... / ...	49.3 / 78.9 h	... / ...
CPI: Consumer Price Index (2010=100)	100	100 i	...
Agricultural production index (2014-2016=100)	100	100	102 c
Balance of payments, current account (million US$)	24	- 17	8 e

Social indicators	2010	2015	2023
Population growth rate (average annual %)	0.2	2.2	0.9 a,b
Urban population (% of total population)	100.0	100.0	100.0 i
Urban population growth rate (average annual %) k	- 0.2	2.3	...
Fertility rate, total (live births per woman)	3.9	3.8	3.5 a,b
Life expectancy at birth (females/males, years)	63.5 / 56.5	66.0 / 59.0	67.8 / 60.5 a,b
Population age distribution (0-14/60+ years old, %)	36.5 / 2.9	38.5 / 3.4	38.8 / 4.6 a,b
International migrant stock (000/% of total pop.) l,m	0.9 / 9.1	1.8 / 17.7	2.2 / 20.3 n
Refugees and others of concern to the UNHCR (000)	...	0.8	1.1 b
Infant mortality rate (per 1 000 live births)	26.1	19.8	15.3 a,b
Health: Current expenditure (% of GDP) o,p,q	12.7	13.7	12.0 n
Health: Physicians (per 1 000 pop.)	1.1	1.2	...
Education: Government expenditure (% of GDP)	4.2 r,s	6.4	9.5 b
Education: Primary gross enrol. ratio (f/m per 100 pop.)	93.4 / 93.8 t	104.3 / 112.1	97.1 / 94.2 n
Education: Lowr. sec. gross enrol. ratio (f/m per 100 pop.)	58.3 / 56.4 s	79.5 / 82.6 u	90.7 / 88.3 n
Education: Upr. sec. gross enrol. ratio (f/m per 100 pop.)	55.7 / 50.3 s	90.5 / 93.1 u	96.4 / 111.9 i
Seats held by women in the National Parliament (%)	0.0	5.3	10.5 v

Environment and infrastructure indicators	2010	2015	2023
Individuals using the Internet (per 100 inhabitants)	...	54.0 w,h	83.9 r,c
Threatened species (number)	74	80	94 b
Forested area (% of land area)	0.0	0.0	0.0 n
Energy production, primary (Petajoules)	0	0	0 n
Energy supply per capita (Gigajoules)	57	68 r	61 r,n
Important sites for terrestrial biodiversity protected (%)	0.0	0.0	0.0 b
Net Official Development Assist. received (% of GNI)	48.74	26.48	15.28 c

a Projected estimate (medium fertility variant). b 2022. c 2021. d Refers to Nauru. e 2018. f At producers' prices. g Break in the time series. h 2011. i 2012. j 2019. k Data refers to a 5-year period preceding the reference year. l Refers to foreign citizens. m Including refugees. n 2020. o General government expenditure (GGE) can be larger than the Gross domestic product (GDP) because government accounts for a very large part of domestic consumption and because a large part of domestic consumption in the country is accounted for by imports. p Indicators are sensitive to external funds flowing in to the country. q Data refer to fiscal years beginning 1 July. r Estimate. s 2007. t 2008. u 2014. v Data are as at 1 January of reporting year. w Population aged 15 years and over.

Nepal

Region	Southern Asia	UN membership date	14 December 1955
Population (000, 2023)	30 548 [a,b]	Surface area (km2)	147 181 [c]
Pop. density (per km2, 2023)	207.6 [a,b]	Sex ratio (m per 100 f)	92.1 [a,b]
Capital city	Kathmandu	National currency	Nepalese Rupee (NPR)
Capital city pop. (000, 2023)	1 376.1 [d,e]	Exchange rate (per US$)	131.9 [b]

Economic indicators

	2010	2015	2023
GDP: Gross domestic product (million current US$)	18 365	23 667	36 207 [c]
GDP growth rate (annual %, const. 2015 prices)	6.2	4.0	4.2 [c]
GDP per capita (current US$)	676.1	857.2	1 205.5 [c]
Economy: Agriculture (% of Gross Value Added) [f]	32.2	29.4 [g]	25.8 [g,c]
Economy: Industry (% of Gross Value Added) [f]	15.0	14.6 [h]	13.1 [h,c]
Economy: Services and other activity (% of GVA) [f]	52.8	56.0	61.1 [c]
Employment in agriculture (% of employed) [i]	67.9	65.0	62.3 [c]
Employment in industry (% of employed) [i]	14.2	14.9	16.1 [c]
Employment in services & other sectors (% employed) [i]	18.0	20.2	21.6 [c]
Unemployment rate (% of labour force) [i]	10.5	10.5	11.0
Labour force participation rate (female/male pop. %) [i]	23.6 / 58.4	26.3 / 55.3	28.8 / 53.3
CPI: Consumer Price Index (2010=100) [j]	...	104	151 [b]
Agricultural production index (2014-2016=100)	82	99	122 [c]
International trade: exports (million current US$) [k]	874	660	1 311 [i,b]
International trade: imports (million current US$) [k]	5 116	6 612	13 947 [i,b]
International trade: balance (million current US$) [k]	- 4 242	- 5 952	- 12 636 [i,b]
Balance of payments, current account (million US$)	- 128	2 447	- 2 471 [b]

Major trading partners

						2022
Export partners (% of exports) [l]	India	80.1	United States	8.0	Germany	1.8
Import partners (% of imports) [l]	India	60.5	China	15.1	Argentina	2.9

Social indicators

	2010	2015	2023
Population growth rate (average annual %)	0.5	0.7	1.2 [a,b]
Urban population (% of total population)	16.8	18.6	20.2 [e]
Urban population growth rate (average annual %) [l]	3.1	3.2	...
Fertility rate, total (live births per woman)	2.5	2.2	2.0 [a,b]
Life expectancy at birth (females/males, years)	68.6 / 65.1	69.1 / 65.8	72.4 / 68.6 [a,b]
Population age distribution (0-14/60+ years old, %)	36.2 / 7.4	33.4 / 8.5	28.9 / 9.0 [a,b]
International migrant stock (000/% of total pop.) [m]	581.9 / 2.2	509.5 / 1.9	487.6 / 1.7 [n]
Refugees and others of concern to the UNHCR (000)	891.3 [o]	36.8	20.3 [b]
Infant mortality rate (per 1 000 live births)	36.7	29.6	20.3 [a,b]
Health: Current expenditure (% of GDP) [p]	4.4	5.5	5.2 [n]
Health: Physicians (per 1 000 pop.)	...	0.6 [q]	0.9 [c]
Education: Government expenditure (% of GDP)	3.6	3.3	4.0 [c]
Education: Primary gross enrol. ratio (f/m per 100 pop.)	143.7 / 145.1	149.2 / 139.3	122.3 / 132.4 [b]
Education: Lowr. sec. gross enrol. ratio (f/m per 100 pop.)	75.7 / 75.3	98.4 / 89.8	102.0 / 106.3 [b]
Education: Upr. sec. gross enrol. ratio (f/m per 100 pop.)	41.5 / 43.9 [i]	49.6 / 48.7 [i]	72.9 / 71.7 [b]
Intentional homicide rate (per 100 000 pop.)	3.0	2.0	2.3 [e]
Seats held by women in the National Parliament (%)	33.2	29.5	33.1 [r]

Environment and infrastructure indicators

	2010	2015	2023
Individuals using the Internet (per 100 inhabitants)	7.9 [s]	17.6 [i]	51.6 [i,c]
Research & Development expenditure (% of GDP)	0.3 [t,u]	...	...
Threatened species (number)	93	105	131 [b]
Forested area (% of land area)	41.6	41.6	41.6 [n]
CO2 emission estimates (million tons/tons per capita)	7.3 / 0.2	9.1 / 0.2	15.9 / 0.4 [n]
Energy production, primary (Petajoules)	384	424	465 [n]
Energy supply per capita (Gigajoules)	16	18	22 [n]
Tourist/visitor arrivals at national borders (000) [v]	603	539	151 [c]
Important sites for terrestrial biodiversity protected (%)	51.7	51.7	51.7 [b]
Pop. using safely managed drinking water (urban/rural, %)	37.9 / 27.6	33.0 / 23.8	23.2 / 14.2 [b]
Pop. using safely managed sanitation (urban/rural %)	28.5 / 26.7	35.4 / 37.6	44.6 / 52.2 [b]
Net Official Development Assist. received (% of GNI)	4.76	4.96	4.38 [c]

a Projected estimate (medium fertility variant). b 2022. c 2021. d Refers to the municipality. e 2019. f Data classified according to ISIC Rev. 4. g Excludes irrigation canals and landscaping care. h Excludes publishing activities, recycling. Includes irrigation canals. i Estimate. j Index base: 2014/2015=100. k Merchandise trade data up to 2009 reported by fiscal year and beginning 2010 reported by calendar year. l Data refers to a 5-year period preceding the reference year. m Including refugees. n 2020. o Data as at the end of December. p Data refer to fiscal years beginning 16 July. q 2013. r Data are as at 1 January of reporting year. s December. t Partial data. u Based on R&D budget instead of R&D expenditure. v Including arrivals from India.

Netherlands (Kingdom of the)

Region	Western Europe	UN membership date	10 December 1945
Population (000, 2023)	17 564 [a,b,c]	Surface area (km2)	41 543 [d]
Pop. density (per km2, 2023)	521.6 [a,b,c]	Sex ratio (m per 100 f)	98.8 [a,b,c]
Capital city	Amsterdam [e]	National currency	Euro (EUR)
Capital city pop. (000, 2023)	1 140.3 [f]	Exchange rate (per US$)	0.9 [c]

Economic indicators	2010	2015	2023
GDP: Gross domestic product (million current US$)	846 555	765 265	1 012 847 [d]
GDP growth rate (annual %, const. 2015 prices)	1.3	2.0	4.9 [d]
GDP per capita (current US$)	50 944.8	44 907.0	57 871.3 [d]
Economy: Agriculture (% of Gross Value Added) [g,h]	2.0	1.9	1.7 [d]
Economy: Industry (% of Gross Value Added) [h,i]	21.9	20.2	20.3 [d]
Economy: Services and other activity (% of GVA) [h]	76.1	77.9	78.0 [d]
Employment in agriculture (% of employed)	3.1	2.3	2.3 [d]
Employment in industry (% of employed)	10.9 [j]	16.3	14.0 [d]
Employment in services & other sectors (% employed)	79.2	81.2	83.8 [d]
Unemployment rate (% of labour force)	5.0	6.9	3.8 [d]
Labour force participation rate (female/male pop. %)	58.7 / 71.2	58.8 / 70.1	60.8 / 70.9 [j]
CPI: Consumer Price Index (2010=100)	100	109	133 [c]
Agricultural production index (2014-2016=100)	90	101	104 [d]
International trade: exports (million current US$)	492 646	464 697	770 307 [c]
International trade: imports (million current US$)	439 987	412 644	712 802 [c]
International trade: balance (million current US$)	52 659	52 053	57 505 [c]
Balance of payments, current account (million US$)	61 803	40 162	43 588 [c]

Major trading partners						2022
Export partners (% of exports)	Germany	24.5	Belgium	12.0	France	8.1
Import partners (% of imports)	Germany	15.3	Belgium	10.1	China	9.5

Social indicators	2010	2015	2023
Population growth rate (average annual %) [a]	0.5	0.5	0.3 [b,c]
Urban population (% of total population)	87.1	90.2	91.9 [f]
Urban population growth rate (average annual %) [k]	1.4	1.0	...
Fertility rate, total (live births per woman) [a]	1.8	1.7	1.6 [b,c]
Life expectancy at birth (females/males, years) [a]	82.7 / 78.8	83.1 / 79.7	83.9 / 80.9 [b,c]
Population age distribution (0-14/60+ years old, %) [a]	17.5 / 22.0	16.6 / 24.1	15.4 / 27.0 [b,c]
International migrant stock (000/% of total pop.)	1 832.5 / 11.0	1 996.3 / 11.8	2 358.3 / 13.8 [l]
Refugees and others of concern to the UNHCR (000)	90.1 [m]	92.5	221.4 [n,c]
Infant mortality rate (per 1 000 live births) [a]	3.8	3.2	3.0 [b,c]
Health: Current expenditure (% of GDP)	10.2	10.3	11.2 [d]
Health: Physicians (per 1 000 pop.)	3.0	3.5	3.8 [l]
Education: Government expenditure (% of GDP)	5.5	5.3	5.2 [f]
Education: Primary gross enrol. ratio (f/m per 100 pop.)	108.1 / 108.5	102.7 / 102.7	106.2 / 106.4 [l]
Education: Lowr. sec. gross enrol. ratio (f/m per 100 pop.)	124.1 / 130.5	99.4 / 102.7	96.2 / 100.5 [l]
Education: Upr. sec. gross enrol. ratio (f/m per 100 pop.)	118.4 / 115.4	136.0 / 127.7	141.5 / 131.9 [l]
Intentional homicide rate (per 100 000 pop.)	0.9	0.6	0.7 [d]
Seats held by women in the National Parliament (%)	42.0	37.3	40.7 [o]

Environment and infrastructure indicators	2010	2015	2023
Individuals using the Internet (per 100 inhabitants)	90.7 [p,q]	91.7	92.1 [r,d]
Research & Development expenditure (% of GDP)	1.7	2.1	2.3 [l]
Threatened species (number)	24	29	83 [c]
Forested area (% of land area)	11.1	10.8	11.0 [l]
CO2 emission estimates (million tons/tons per capita)	172.3 / 10.3	158.6 / 9.3	137.5 / 7.8 [d]
Energy production, primary (Petajoules) [s]	2 979	2 012	1 136 [l]
Energy supply per capita (Gigajoules) [s]	207	176	165 [l]
Tourist/visitor arrivals at national borders (000)	10 883	15 007	6 248 [d]
Important sites for terrestrial biodiversity protected (%)	68.2	76.2	79.6 [c]
Pop. using safely managed sanitation (urban/rural %)	97.5 / 97.4	97.5 / 97.5	97.5 / 97.5 [c]
Net Official Development Assist. disbursed (% of GNI) [t]	1.67	8.91	- 0.82 [d]

a For statistical purposes, the data for Netherlands do not include Aruba, Bonaire, Sint Eustatius and Saba, Curaçao, and Sint Maarten (Dutch part). **b** Projected estimate (medium fertility variant). **c** 2022. **d** 2021. **e** Amsterdam is the capital and The Hague is the seat of government. **f** 2019. **g** Excludes irrigation canals and landscaping care. **h** Data classified according to ISIC Rev. 4. **i** Excludes publishing activities, recycling. Includes irrigation canals. **j** Estimate. **k** Data refers to a 5-year period preceding the reference year. **l** 2020. **m** Data as at the end of December. **n** Number of refugees is based on government data as of start-2022. **o** Data are as at 1 January of reporting year. **p** Users in the last 12 months. **q** Population aged 16 to 74 years. **r** Users in the last 3 months. **s** Data exclude Suriname and the Netherlands Antilles (former) **t** Development Assistance Committee member (OECD).

New Caledonia

Region	Melanesia	Population (000, 2023)	290 [a,b,c]
Surface area (km2)	19 100 [d]	Pop. density (per km2, 2023)	15.9 [a,b,c]
Sex ratio (m per 100 f)	98.9 [a,b,c]	Capital city	Nouméa
National currency	CFP Franc (XPF) [e]	Capital city pop. (000, 2023)	197.8 [f]
Exchange rate (per US$)	111.9 [c]		

Economic indicators	2010	2015	2023
GDP: Gross domestic product (million current US$)	9 355	8 735	10 071 [d]
GDP growth rate (annual %, const. 2015 prices)	6.9	0.8	- 2.1 [d]
GDP per capita (current US$)	35 785.4	30 861.1	34 994.3 [d]
Economy: Agriculture (% of Gross Value Added)	1.5	2.1	2.1 [d]
Economy: Industry (% of Gross Value Added)	28.3	24.0	22.9 [d]
Economy: Services and other activity (% of GVA)	70.2	73.9	74.9 [d]
Employment in agriculture (% of employed) [g]	4.0	4.0	3.6 [d]
Employment in industry (% of employed) [g]	31.5	29.3	27.4 [d]
Employment in services & other sectors (% employed) [g]	64.6	66.7	69.0 [d]
Unemployment rate (% of labour force) [g]	13.7	13.9	12.3
Labour force participation rate (female/male pop. %) [g]	58.9 / 69.6	57.8 / 67.7	52.3 / 60.9
CPI: Consumer Price Index (2010=100) [h]	100	106	114 [c]
Agricultural production index (2014-2016=100)	86	111	98 [d]
International trade: exports (million current US$)	1 268	1 239	1 752 [g,c]
International trade: imports (million current US$)	3 303	2 529	3 814 [g,c]
International trade: balance (million current US$)	- 2 036	- 1 291	- 2 061 [g,c]
Balance of payments, current account (million US$)	- 1 360	- 1 119	- 654 [i]

Major trading partners							2022
Export partners (% of exports) [g]	China	62.1	Republic of Korea	13.4	Japan	12.1
Import partners (% of imports) [g]	France	30.3	Australia	22.7	Singapore	13.7

Social indicators	2010	2015	2023
Population growth rate (average annual %) [a]	1.8	0.3	1.1 [b,c]
Urban population (% of total population)	67.1	69.4	71.1 [j]
Urban population growth rate (average annual %) [k]	2.5	2.1	...
Fertility rate, total (live births per woman) [a]	2.2	2.1	2.0 [b,c]
Life expectancy at birth (females/males, years) [a]	82.6 / 74.3	82.7 / 74.9	84.6 / 77.5 [b,c]
Population age distribution (0-14/60+ years old, %) [a]	25.8 / 11.3	24.1 / 12.6	22.2 / 15.8 [b,c]
International migrant stock (000/% of total pop.)	61.2 / 24.1	68.9 / 25.4	73.1 / 25.6 [i]
Infant mortality rate (per 1 000 live births) [a]	14.0	12.2	9.4 [b,c]
Intentional homicide rate (per 100 000 pop.)	3.1 [m]	...	...

Environment and infrastructure indicators	2010	2015	2023
Individuals using the Internet (per 100 inhabitants) [g]	42.0	74.0	82.0 [n]
Threatened species (number)	415	493	1 002 [c]
Forested area (% of land area)	45.9	45.9	45.8 [i]
Energy production, primary (Petajoules)	1	2	2 [i]
Energy supply per capita (Gigajoules)	177	217	220 [i]
Tourist/visitor arrivals at national borders (000) [o]	99	114	12 [d]
Important sites for terrestrial biodiversity protected (%)	27.9	37.8	42.2 [c]

a For statistical purposes, the data for France do not include this area. b Projected estimate (medium fertility variant). c 2022. d 2021. e Communauté financière du Pacifique (CFP) Franc. f 2018. g Estimate. h Calculated by the UN Statistics Division from national indices. i 2016. j 2019. k Data refers to a 5-year period preceding the reference year. l 2020. m 2009. n 2017. o Including nationals residing abroad.

New Zealand

Region	Oceania	
Population (000, 2023)	5 185 [a,b,c]	
Pop. density (per km2, 2023)	19.6 [a,b,c]	
Capital city	Wellington	
Capital city pop. (000, 2023)	413.0 [e]	

UN membership date	24 October 1945
Surface area (km2)	268 107 [d]
Sex ratio (m per 100 f)	98.3 [a,b,c]
National currency	New Zealand Dollar (NZD)
Exchange rate (per US$)	1.6 [c]

Economic indicators

	2010	2015	2023
GDP: Gross domestic product (million current US$)	146 518	178 064	250 451 [d]
GDP growth rate (annual %, const. 2015 prices)	0.9	4.2	3.7 [d]
GDP per capita (current US$)	33 710.6	38 789.0	48 823.5 [d]
Economy: Agriculture (% of Gross Value Added) [f,g]	7.1	4.9	6.2 [d]
Economy: Industry (% of Gross Value Added) [g,h]	23.0	23.1	22.2 [d]
Economy: Services and other activity (% of GVA) [g]	69.9	72.0	71.6 [d]
Employment in agriculture (% of employed)	6.9	6.1	6.1 [d]
Employment in industry (% of employed)	20.9	22.0	20.0 [d]
Employment in services & other sectors (% employed)	72.1	71.9	74.0 [d]
Unemployment rate (% of labour force)	6.6	5.4	3.3 [i]
Labour force participation rate (female/male pop. %)	61.6 / 74.1	63.4 / 74.5	66.0 / 75.1 [i]
CPI: Consumer Price Index (2010=100) [j]	100	108	129 [k,c]
Agricultural production index (2014-2016=100)	87	101	103 [d]
International trade: exports (million current US$)	31 393	34 357	45 615 [c]
International trade: imports (million current US$)	30 616	36 528	54 850 [c]
International trade: balance (million current US$)	777	- 2 171	- 9 235 [c]
Balance of payments, current account (million US$)	- 3 429	- 4 663	- 21 262 [c]

Major trading partners

						2022
Export partners (% of exports)	China	28.0	Australia	12.1	United States	10.8
Import partners (% of imports)	China	23.1	Australia	11.1	United States	8.9

Social indicators

	2010	2015	2023
Population growth rate (average annual %) [a]	0.9	1.7	0.8 [b,c]
Urban population (% of total population)	86.2	86.3	86.6 [e]
Urban population growth rate (average annual %) [l]	1.1	1.1	...
Fertility rate, total (live births per woman) [a]	2.2	2.0	1.8 [b,c]
Life expectancy at birth (females/males, years) [a]	83.0 / 79.2	83.7 / 80.1	84.7 / 81.3 [b,c]
Population age distribution (0-14/60+ years old, %) [a]	20.9 / 18.3	20.0 / 20.0	18.7 / 22.2 [b,c]
International migrant stock (000/% of total pop.)	947.4 / 21.7	1 039.7 / 22.5	1 381.7 / 28.7 [m]
Refugees and others of concern to the UNHCR (000)	2.5 [n]	1.6	2.4 [c]
Infant mortality rate (per 1 000 live births) [a]	5.0	4.4	3.5 [b,c]
Health: Current expenditure (% of GDP)	9.6	9.3	10.0 [m]
Health: Physicians (per 1 000 pop.)	2.6	3.0	3.5 [d]
Education: Government expenditure (% of GDP)	7.0	6.3	5.2 [e]
Education: Primary gross enrol. ratio (f/m per 100 pop.)	101.3 / 101.0	98.2 / 97.7	102.4 / 102.2 [m]
Education: Lowr. sec. gross enrol. ratio (f/m per 100 pop.)	103.6 / 105.0	102.0 / 102.4	105.1 / 105.4 [m]
Education: Upr. sec. gross enrol. ratio (f/m per 100 pop.)	144.6 / 130.7	138.6 / 122.9	149.0 / 134.8 [m]
Intentional homicide rate (per 100 000 pop.)	1.0	1.0	2.6 [e]
Seats held by women in the National Parliament (%)	33.6	31.4	50.0 [o]

Environment and infrastructure indicators

	2010	2015	2023
Individuals using the Internet (per 100 inhabitants) [i]	80.5	85.2	95.9 [d]
Research & Development expenditure (% of GDP)	1.3 [p]	1.2	1.4 [q,e]
Threatened species (number)	153	197	277 [c]
Forested area (% of land area)	37.4	37.4	37.6 [m]
CO2 emission estimates (million tons/tons per capita)	31.0 / 7.0	32.0 / 6.8	35.1 / 6.7 [d]
Energy production, primary (Petajoules)	773	790	727 [m]
Energy supply per capita (Gigajoules)	193	210	185 [m]
Tourist/visitor arrivals at national borders (000)	2 435	3 039	205 [d]
Important sites for terrestrial biodiversity protected (%)	45.4	46.2	46.2 [c]
Net Official Development Assist. disbursed (% of GNI) [r]	0.32	0.37	0.36 [d]

a For statistical purposes, the data for New Zealand do not include Cook Islands, Niue, and Tokelau. **b** Projected estimate (medium fertility variant). **c** 2022. **d** 2021. **e** 2019. **f** Excludes irrigation canals and landscaping care. **g** Data classified according to ISIC Rev. 4. **h** Excludes publishing activities, recycling. Includes irrigation canals. **i** Estimate. **j** Calculated by the UN Statistics Division from national indices. **k** Monthly average for quarter or index for quarter. **l** Data refers to a 5-year period preceding the reference year. **m** 2020. **n** Data as at the end of December. **o** Data are as at 1 January of reporting year. **p** 2009. **q** Provisional data. **r** Development Assistance Committee member (OECD).

Nicaragua

Region	Central America	UN membership date	24 October 1945
Population (000, 2023)	6 948 [a,b]	Surface area (km2)	130 374 [c]
Pop. density (per km2, 2023)	57.7 [a,b]	Sex ratio (m per 100 f)	97.1 [a,b]
Capital city	Managua	National currency	Cordoba Oro (NIO)
Capital city pop. (000, 2023)	1 055.5 [d]	Exchange rate (per US$)	36.2 [b]

Economic indicators

	2010	2015	2023
GDP: Gross domestic product (million current US$)	8 759	12 757	14 013 [c]
GDP growth rate (annual %, const. 2015 prices)	4.4	4.8	10.3 [c]
GDP per capita (current US$)	1 495.7	2 025.3	2 045.5 [c]
Economy: Agriculture (% of Gross Value Added)	18.7	17.8	17.4 [c]
Economy: Industry (% of Gross Value Added)	24.2	28.5	30.6 [c]
Economy: Services and other activity (% of GVA)	57.0	53.7	52.0 [c]
Employment in agriculture (% of employed) [e]	29.7	30.9	28.7 [c]
Employment in industry (% of employed) [e]	17.8	17.9	18.4 [c]
Employment in services & other sectors (% employed) [e]	52.5	51.2	52.9 [c]
Unemployment rate (% of labour force)	7.8	4.7	5.9 [e]
Labour force participation rate (female/male pop. %) [e]	44.4 / 84.0	48.3 / 82.9	49.4 / 83.5
CPI: Consumer Price Index (2010=100)	100	137	196 [b]
Agricultural production index (2014-2016=100)	83	97	128 [c]
International trade: exports (million current US$)	1 848	4 667	7 360 [b]
International trade: imports (million current US$)	4 191	5 866	11 247 [b]
International trade: balance (million current US$)	- 2 343	- 1 199	- 3 887 [b]
Balance of payments, current account (million US$)	- 777	- 1 260	- 216 [b]

Major trading partners

						2022
Export partners (% of exports)	United States	52.3	Mexico	12.9	Honduras	7.3
Import partners (% of imports)	United States	26.9	China	12.3	Honduras	9.1

Social indicators

	2010	2015	2023
Population growth rate (average annual %)	1.5	1.4	1.4 [a,b]
Urban population (% of total population)	56.9	57.9	58.8 [d]
Urban population growth rate (average annual %) [f]	1.6	1.5	...
Fertility rate, total (live births per woman)	2.6	2.5	2.3 [a,b]
Life expectancy at birth (females/males, years)	75.1 / 68.9	75.9 / 70.0	77.6 / 71.6 [a,b]
Population age distribution (0-14/60+ years old, %)	34.4 / 5.9	32.1 / 6.8	29.7 / 7.9 [a,b]
International migrant stock (000/% of total pop.) [g]	37.3 / 0.6	40.3 / 0.6	42.2 / 0.6 [h]
Refugees and others of concern to the UNHCR (000)	0.1 [i]	0.4	1.0 [b]
Infant mortality rate (per 1 000 live births)	20.0	16.3	12.3 [a,b]
Health: Current expenditure (% of GDP) [e,j]	7.7	8.0	8.6 [h]
Health: Physicians (per 1 000 pop.)	0.7	0.9	0.7 [k]
Education: Government expenditure (% of GDP)	4.5	4.1 [e]	4.1 [c]
Education: Primary gross enrol. ratio (f/m per 100 pop.)	120.1 / 121.1	110.5 / 110.6	111.8 / 112.5 [h]
Education: Lowr. sec. gross enrol. ratio (f/m per 100 pop.)	87.1 / 81.5	... / ...	... / ...
Education: Upr. sec. gross enrol. ratio (f/m per 100 pop.)	64.4 / 50.6	... / ...	... / ...
Intentional homicide rate (per 100 000 pop.)	13.4	8.3	11.0 [c]
Seats held by women in the National Parliament (%)	20.7	39.1	51.6 [l]

Environment and infrastructure indicators

	2010	2015	2023
Individuals using the Internet (per 100 inhabitants) [e]	10.0	19.7	57.1 [c]
Research & Development expenditure (% of GDP)	...	0.1 [m]	...
Threatened species (number)	121	141	303 [b]
Forested area (% of land area)	34.8	32.5	28.3 [h]
CO2 emission estimates (million tons/tons per capita)	4.7 / 0.7	5.5 / 0.8	4.9 / 0.7 [h]
Energy production, primary (Petajoules)	69	88	94 [h]
Energy supply per capita (Gigajoules)	22	26	24 [h]
Tourist/visitor arrivals at national borders (000) [n]	1 011	1 386	222 [c]
Important sites for terrestrial biodiversity protected (%)	66.1	67.6	67.6 [b]
Pop. using safely managed drinking water (urban/rural, %)	66.6 / 31.9	67.2 / 38.6	67.3 / 38.5 [h]
Net Official Development Assist. received (% of GNI)	6.00	3.73	5.71 [c]

a Projected estimate (medium fertility variant). **b** 2022. **c** 2021. **d** 2019. **e** Estimate. **f** Data refers to a 5-year period preceding the reference year. **g** Including refugees. **h** 2020. **i** Data as at the end of December. **j** Data based on calendar year (January 1 to December 31). **k** 2018. **l** Data are as at 1 January of reporting year. **m** Higher Education only. **n** Including nationals residing abroad.

Niger

Region	Western Africa		UN membership date		20 September 1960
Population (000, 2023)	26 208[a,b]		Surface area (km2)		1 267 000[c]
Pop. density (per km2, 2023)	20.7[a,b]		Sex ratio (m per 100 f)		102.9[a,b]
Capital city	Niamey		National currency		CFA Franc, BCEAO (XOF)[d]
Capital city pop. (000, 2023)	1 251.5[e]		Exchange rate (per US$)		615.0[b]

Economic indicators

	2010	2015	2023
GDP: Gross domestic product (million current US$)	7 631	9 677	14 915[c]
GDP growth rate (annual %, const. 2015 prices)	8.7	4.8	1.4[c]
GDP per capita (current US$)	458.4	480.7	590.6[c]
Economy: Agriculture (% of Gross Value Added)[f,g]	39.5	34.7	38.7[c]
Economy: Industry (% of Gross Value Added)[g,h]	20.9	24.1	22.1[c]
Economy: Services and other activity (% of GVA)[g]	39.7	41.2	39.3[c]
Employment in agriculture (% of employed)[i]	77.2	73.0	70.7[c]
Employment in industry (% of employed)[i]	7.3	7.2	7.6[c]
Employment in services & other sectors (% employed)[i]	15.5	19.7	21.6[c]
Unemployment rate (% of labour force)	0.8	0.5	0.5
Labour force participation rate (female/male pop. %)[i]	68.6 / 90.2	62.1 / 84.7	62.5 / 84.2
CPI: Consumer Price Index (2010=100)[k]	...	107[j,l]	113[m,b]
Agricultural production index (2014-2016=100)	86	102	114[c]
International trade: exports (million current US$)	479	790	423[b]
International trade: imports (million current US$)	2 273	2 458	3 779[b]
International trade: balance (million current US$)	- 1 794	- 1 669	- 3 356[b]
Balance of payments, current account (million US$)	- 1 137	- 1 486	- 2 099[c]

Major trading partners

						2022
Export partners (% of exports)	France	33.2	Mali	18.7	Nigeria	16.0
Import partners (% of imports)	China	23.9	France	21.0	India	10.3

Social indicators

	2010	2015	2023
Population growth rate (average annual %)	3.7	3.9	3.7[a,b]
Urban population (% of total population)	16.2	16.2	16.5[e]
Urban population growth rate (average annual %)[n]	3.7	3.9	...
Fertility rate, total (live births per woman)	7.5	7.2	6.7[a,b]
Life expectancy at birth (females/males, years)	59.0 / 57.7	62.1 / 60.1	63.4 / 60.8[a,b]
Population age distribution (0-14/60+ years old, %)	49.1 / 3.8	49.1 / 3.9	48.8 / 3.9[a,b]
International migrant stock (000/% of total pop.)[o]	126.5 / 0.8	253.0 / 1.3	348.1 / 1.4[p]
Refugees and others of concern to the UNHCR (000)	0.3[q]	202.2	595.0[b]
Infant mortality rate (per 1 000 live births)	61.8	50.4	40.1[a,b]
Health: Current expenditure (% of GDP)[r]	5.0	5.3	6.2[p]
Health: Physicians (per 1 000 pop.)	~0.0[s]	~0.0	~0.0[p]
Education: Government expenditure (% of GDP)	2.7	4.5	3.5[t]
Education: Primary gross enrol. ratio (f/m per 100 pop.)	55.9 / 69.2	65.6 / 77.4	61.8 / 67.7[c]
Education: Lowr. sec. gross enrol. ratio (f/m per 100 pop.)	15.5 / 21.5	22.2 / 30.8	28.1 / 36.6[u]
Education: Upr. sec. gross enrol. ratio (f/m per 100 pop.)	3.1 / 5.5	8.7 / 11.0	9.1 / 13.6[u]
Intentional homicide rate (per 100 000 pop.)	...	4.4[v]	...
Seats held by women in the National Parliament (%)	9.7	13.3	30.7[w]

Environment and infrastructure indicators

	2010	2015	2023
Individuals using the Internet (per 100 inhabitants)[i]	0.8	2.5	22.4[c]
Threatened species (number)	26	31	43[b]
Forested area (% of land area)	1.0	0.9	0.9[p]
CO2 emission estimates (million tons/tons per capita)	2.0 / 0.1	2.8 / 0.1	3.1 / 0.1[p]
Energy production, primary (Petajoules)	56	100	115[i,p]
Energy supply per capita (Gigajoules)	4	5	5[i,p]
Tourist/visitor arrivals at national borders (000)	74	135	85[p]
Important sites for terrestrial biodiversity protected (%)	23.4	23.4	54.7[b]
Pop. using safely managed sanitation (urban/rural %)	15.2 / 3.5	17.4 / 4.4	20.6 / 5.6[b]
Net Official Development Assist. received (% of GNI)	8.95	8.56	11.90[c]

a Projected estimate (medium fertility variant). b 2022. c 2021. d African Financial Community (CFA) Franc, Central Bank of West African States (BCEAO). e 2019. f Excludes irrigation canals and landscaping care. g Data classified according to ISIC Rev. 4. h Excludes publishing activities, recycling. Includes irrigation canals. i Estimate. j Index base: 2008=100. k WAEMU harmonized consumer price index. l Niamey m Index base: 2014=100. n Data refers to a 5-year period preceding the reference year. o Including refugees. p 2020. q Data as at the end of December. r Data based on calendar year (January 1 to December 31). s 2009. t 2018. u 2017. v 2012. w Data are as at 1 January of reporting year.

Nigeria

Region	Western Africa	UN membership date	07 October 1960
Population (000, 2023)	218 541 [a,b]	Surface area (km2)	923 768 [c]
Pop. density (per km2, 2023)	240.0 [a,b]	Sex ratio (m per 100 f)	102.2 [a,b]
Capital city	Abuja	National currency	Naira (NGN)
Capital city pop. (000, 2023)	3 095.1 [d,e]	Exchange rate (per US$)	460.0 [b]

Economic indicators

	2010	2015	2023
GDP: Gross domestic product (million current US$)	363 360	494 583	430 923 [c]
GDP growth rate (annual %, const. 2015 prices)	8.0	2.7	3.6 [c]
GDP per capita (current US$)	2 257.6	2 688.0	2 019.3 [c]
Economy: Agriculture (% of Gross Value Added) [f,g]	23.9	20.9	23.7 [c]
Economy: Industry (% of Gross Value Added) [g,h]	25.3	20.4	31.9 [c]
Economy: Services and other activity (% of GVA) [g]	50.8	58.8	44.4 [c]
Employment in agriculture (% of employed) [i]	41.3	37.0	35.2 [c]
Employment in industry (% of employed) [i]	10.2	12.2	12.7 [c]
Employment in services & other sectors (% employed) [i]	48.4	50.9	52.2 [c]
Unemployment rate (% of labour force) [i]	3.8	4.2	5.8
Labour force participation rate (female/male pop. %) [i]	56.8 / 64.0	51.7 / 61.2	52.2 / 65.6
CPI: Consumer Price Index (2010=100) [j]	100	159	421 [k,b]
Agricultural production index (2014-2016=100)	87	99	108 [c]
International trade: exports (million current US$)	86 568	48 433	52 610 [i,b]
International trade: imports (million current US$)	44 235	33 831	55 148 [i,b]
International trade: balance (million current US$)	42 333	14 602	- 2 538 [i,b]
Balance of payments, current account (million US$)	13 111	- 15 439	1 019 [b]

Major trading partners

						2022
Export partners (% of exports) [i]	India	16.4	Spain	11.8	France	6.3
Import partners (% of imports) [i]	China	24.7	Netherlands	10.3	India	8.8

Social indicators

	2010	2015	2023
Population growth rate (average annual %)	2.8	2.5	2.4 [a,b]
Urban population (% of total population)	43.5	47.8	51.2 [e]
Urban population growth rate (average annual %) [i]	4.8	4.6	...
Fertility rate, total (live births per woman)	6.0	5.6	5.1 [a,b]
Life expectancy at birth (females/males, years)	51.4 / 50.5	52.2 / 51.5	54.0 / 53.3 [a,b]
Population age distribution (0-14/60+ years old, %)	44.3 / 4.9	44.3 / 4.8	43.0 / 4.7 [a,b]
International migrant stock (000/% of total pop.) [m,n]	990.5 / 0.6	1 199.1 / 0.7	1 308.6 / 0.6 [o]
Refugees and others of concern to the UNHCR (000)	10.6 [p]	1 510.2	3 216.8 [b]
Infant mortality rate (per 1 000 live births)	86.4	81.6	71.9 [a,b]
Health: Current expenditure (% of GDP) [q]	3.3	3.6	3.4 [o]
Health: Physicians (per 1 000 pop.)	0.4 [r]	0.4 [s]	0.4 [c]
Education: Primary gross enrol. ratio (f/m per 100 pop.)	81.0 / 89.1 [i]	83.6 / 89.2	86.2 / 85.3 [e]
Education: Lowr. sec. gross enrol. ratio (f/m per 100 pop.)	43.7 / 49.6	47.4 / 51.0	48.9 / 50.4 [t]
Education: Upr. sec. gross enrol. ratio (f/m per 100 pop.)	38.4 / 44.5	41.6 / 46.3	35.2 / 38.1 [t]
Intentional homicide rate (per 100 000 pop.)	...	...	21.7 [e]
Seats held by women in the National Parliament (%)	7.0	6.7	3.6 [u]

Environment and infrastructure indicators

	2010	2015	2023
Individuals using the Internet (per 100 inhabitants) [i]	11.5	24.5	55.4 [c]
Research & Development expenditure (% of GDP)	0.1 [v,w]	...	...
Threatened species (number)	297	333	461 [b]
Forested area (% of land area)	25.5	24.6	23.7 [o]
CO2 emission estimates (million tons/tons per capita)	89.0 / 0.4	121.8 / 0.5	128.5 / 0.4 [o]
Energy production, primary (Petajoules)	10 591	10 636	9 932 [o]
Energy supply per capita (Gigajoules)	33	33	32 [o]
Tourist/visitor arrivals at national borders (000)	1 555	1 255	518 [c]
Important sites for terrestrial biodiversity protected (%)	79.9	79.9	79.9 [b]
Pop. using safely managed drinking water (urban/rural, %)	30.7 / 13.9	33.9 / 16.8	35.7 / 21.2 [b]
Pop. using safely managed sanitation (urban/rural, %)	25.6 / 24.1	30.0 / 25.2	36.6 / 26.6 [b]
Net Official Development Assist. received (% of GNI)	0.60	0.51	0.83 [c]

a Projected estimate (medium fertility variant). b 2022. c 2021. d Data refers to the urban agglomeration. e 2019. f Excludes irrigation canals and landscaping care. g Data classified according to ISIC Rev. 4. h Excludes publishing activities, recycling. Includes irrigation canals. i Estimate. j Rural and urban areas. k Calculated by the UN Statistics Division from national indices. l Data refers to a 5-year period preceding the reference year. m Refers to foreign citizens. n Including refugees. o 2020. p Data as at the end of December. q Data based on calendar year (January 1 to December 31). r 2009. s 2013. t 2018. u Data are as at 1 January of reporting year. v Excluding business enterprise. w 2007.

Niue

Region	Polynesia	Population (000, 2023)	2 [a,b,c]
Surface area (km2)	260 [d]	Pop. density (per km2, 2023)	7.4 [a,b,c]
Sex ratio (m per 100 f)	88.4 [a,b,c]	Capital city	Alofi
National currency	New Zealand Dollar (NZD)	Capital city pop. (000, 2023)	0.7 [e]
Exchange rate (per US$)	1.6 [c]		

Economic indicators	2010	2015	2023
Agricultural production index (2014-2016=100)	99	97	99 [d]

Social indicators	2010	2015	2023
Population growth rate (average annual %) [b]	0.2	1.2	0.3 [a,c]
Urban population (% of total population)	38.7	42.6	45.5 [f]
Urban population growth rate (average annual %) [g]	1.2	1.9	...
Fertility rate, total (live births per woman) [b]	2.9	2.7	2.4 [a,c]
Life expectancy at birth (females/males, years) [b]	70.5 / 66.6	71.6 / 68.7	72.9 / 69.5 [a,c]
Population age distribution (0-14/60+ years old, %) [b]	26.2 / 16.6	27.0 / 18.6	26.1 / 21.0 [a,c]
International migrant stock (000/% of total pop.)	0.6 / 36.3	0.6 / 36.5	0.6 / 36.3 [h]
Infant mortality rate (per 1 000 live births) [b]	27.4	23.9	19.4 [a,c]
Health: Current expenditure (% of GDP) [i,j,k]	15.5	8.7	7.8 [h]
Health: Physicians (per 1 000 pop.)	1.7 [l]	...	...
Education: Primary gross enrol. ratio (f/m per 100 pop.)	100.0 / 103.5 [m]	127.8 / 127.7	131.6 / 134.1 [d]
Education: Lowr. sec. gross enrol. ratio (f/m per 100 pop.)	... / ...	130.4 / 90.2	153.1 / 137.7 [d]
Education: Upr. sec. gross enrol. ratio (f/m per 100 pop.)	... / ...	80.0 / 88.6	123.1 / 124.3 [d]

Environment and infrastructure indicators	2010	2015	2023
Individuals using the Internet (per 100 inhabitants) [n]	77.0	79.6 [o]	...
Threatened species (number)	43	50	63 [c]
Forested area (% of land area)	72.2	72.4	72.6 [h]
Energy production, primary (Petajoules)	0	0	0 [n,h]
Energy supply per capita (Gigajoules)	47	56	55 [n,h]
Tourist/visitor arrivals at national borders (000) [p]	6	8	~0 [d]
Important sites for terrestrial biodiversity protected (%)	95.3	95.3	95.3 [c]

a Projected estimate (medium fertility variant). b For statistical purposes, the data for New Zealand do not include this area. c 2022. d 2021. e 2018. f 2019. g Data refers to a 5-year period preceding the reference year. h 2020. i General government expenditure (GGE) can be larger than the Gross domestic product (GDP) because government accounts for a very large part of domestic consumption and because a large part of domestic consumption in the country is accounted for by imports. j Indicators are sensitive to external funds flowing in to the country. k Data refer to fiscal years beginning 1 July. l 2008. m 2005. n Estimate. o 2011. p Including Niueans residing usually in New Zealand.

North Macedonia

Region	Southern Europe	UN membership date	08 April 1993
Population (000, 2023)	2 094 [a,b]	Surface area (km2)	25 713 [a]
Pop. density (per km2, 2023)	84.0 [a,b]	Sex ratio (m per 100 f)	99.4 [a,b]
Capital city	Skopje	National currency	Denar (MKD)
Capital city pop. (000, 2023)	589.8 [d]	Exchange rate (per US$)	57.7 [b]

Economic indicators	2010	2015	2023
GDP: Gross domestic product (million current US$)	9 407	10 065	13 881 [c]
GDP growth rate (annual %, const. 2015 prices)	3.4	3.9	4.0 [c]
GDP per capita (current US$)	4 492.8	4 774.5	6 599.6 [c]
Economy: Agriculture (% of Gross Value Added) [e,f]	11.7	11.1	9.0 [c]
Economy: Industry (% of Gross Value Added) [f,g]	24.4	27.4	25.3 [c]
Economy: Services and other activity (% of GVA) [f]	63.9	61.5	65.7 [c]
Employment in agriculture (% of employed)	18.1	17.9	10.8 [c]
Employment in industry (% of employed)	29.4	26.7 [h]	24.1 [h,c]
Employment in services & other sectors (% employed)	52.5	51.6	58.3 [c]
Unemployment rate (% of labour force)	33.1	26.4	16.1 [h]
Labour force participation rate (female/male pop. %)	43.0 / 68.6	43.5 / 67.5	43.7 / 65.8 [h]
CPI: Consumer Price Index (2010=100)	100	110	135 [b]
Agricultural production index (2014-2016=100)	97	102	95 [c]
International trade: exports (million current US$)	3 351	4 530	8 729 [b]
International trade: imports (million current US$)	5 474	6 427	12 755 [b]
International trade: balance (million current US$)	- 2 123	- 1 897	- 4 026 [b]
Balance of payments, current account (million US$)	- 198	- 172	- 840 [b]

Major trading partners						2022
Export partners (% of exports)	Germany	45.1	Serbia	9.2	Bulgaria	5.0
Import partners (% of imports)	United Kingdom	15.8	Greece	11.2	Germany	8.6

Social indicators	2010	2015	2023
Population growth rate (average annual %)	0.2	0.1	- 0.5 [a,b]
Urban population (% of total population)	57.1	57.4	58.2 [d]
Urban population growth rate (average annual %) [i]	- 0.1	0.2	...
Fertility rate, total (live births per woman)	1.5	1.5	1.4 [a,b]
Life expectancy at birth (females/males, years)	77.5 / 72.8	78.2 / 73.8	76.2 / 71.7 [a,b]
Population age distribution (0-14/60+ years old, %)	18.5 / 16.5	17.1 / 18.6	16.0 / 21.3 [a,b]
International migrant stock (000/% of total pop.)	129.7 / 6.3	130.7 / 6.3	131.3 / 6.3 [i]
Refugees and others of concern to the UNHCR (000)	3.3 [k]	1.6	2.0 [b]
Infant mortality rate (per 1 000 live births)	6.8	6.9	4.9 [a,b]
Health: Current expenditure (% of GDP)	6.7	6.3	7.9 [j]
Health: Physicians (per 1 000 pop.)	2.6	2.8	...
Education: Primary gross enrol. ratio (f/m per 100 pop.)	86.7 / 88.0	94.0 / 93.7	95.5 / 95.5 [j]
Education: Lowr. sec. gross enrol. ratio (f/m per 100 pop.)	88.2 / 90.4	84.5 / 85.9	87.8 / 88.0 [j]
Education: Upr. sec. gross enrol. ratio (f/m per 100 pop.)	74.6 / 77.1	78.1 / 79.5	71.0 / 72.8 [j]
Intentional homicide rate (per 100 000 pop.)	2.1	1.2	1.1 [d]
Seats held by women in the National Parliament (%)	32.5	33.3	41.7 [l]

Environment and infrastructure indicators	2010	2015	2023
Individuals using the Internet (per 100 inhabitants)	51.9 [m]	70.4 [n]	83.0 [h,c]
Research & Development expenditure (% of GDP)	0.2	0.4	0.4 [c]
Threatened species (number)	90	100	147 [b]
Forested area (% of land area)	38.1	39.4	39.7 [j]
CO2 emission estimates (million tons/tons per capita)	8.5 / 4.0	7.3 / 3.4	6.9 / 3.3 [c,j]
Energy production, primary (Petajoules)	68	58	50 [j]
Energy supply per capita (Gigajoules)	58	55	55 [j]
Tourist/visitor arrivals at national borders (000)	262	486	294 [c]
Important sites for terrestrial biodiversity protected (%)	24.4	24.4	27.1 [b]
Pop. using safely managed drinking water (urban/rural, %)	84.7 / 74.5	84.7 / 74.6	84.6 / 74.4 [b]
Pop. using safely managed sanitation (urban/rural %)	9.4 / 17.2	8.7 / 17.6	8.2 / 18.0 [b]
Net Official Development Assist. received (% of GNI)	2.10	2.20	2.56 [c]

a Projected estimate (medium fertility variant). **b** 2022. **c** 2021. **d** 2019. **e** Excludes irrigation canals and landscaping care. **f** Data classified according to ISIC Rev. 4. **g** Excludes publishing activities, recycling. Includes irrigation canals. **h** Estimate. **i** Data refers to a 5-year period preceding the reference year. **j** 2020. **k** Data as at the end of December. **l** Data are as at 1 January of reporting year. **m** Population aged 15 to 74 years. **n** Users in the last 3 months.

Northern Mariana Islands

Region	Micronesia	Population (000, 2023)	50 [a,b,c]
Surface area (km2)	457 [d]	Pop. density (per km2, 2023)	108.4 [a,b,c]
Sex ratio (m per 100 f)	116.2 [a,b,c]	Capital city	Garapan
National currency	US Dollar (USD)	Capital city pop. (000)	4.0 [e]

Economic indicators

	2010	2015	2023
Unemployment rate (% of labour force)	11.2 [f,g]	...	...
Labour force participation rate (female/male pop. %)	66.6 / 77.6 [f,g]	... / ...	... / ...
International trade: exports (million current US$) [h]	1 453	1 685	2 072 [c]
International trade: imports (million current US$) [h]	2 867	4 215	7 225 [c]
International trade: balance (million current US$) [h]	- 1 414	- 2 530	- 5 153 [c]

Major trading partners

2022

Export partners (% of exports) [h]	Republic of Korea	43.1	Other Asia, nes	13.1	Japan	9.2
Import partners (% of imports) [h]	Singapore	43.6	Japan	21.4	Republic of Korea	11.3

Social indicators

	2010	2015	2023
Population growth rate (average annual %) [a]	- 5.5	- 0.7	0.5 [b,c]
Urban population (% of total population)	90.9	91.4	91.7 [i]
Urban population growth rate (average annual %) [j]	- 3.1	0.2	...
Fertility rate, total (live births per woman) [a]	2.9	2.5	2.1 [b,c]
Life expectancy at birth (females/males, years) [a]	79.4 / 75.8	78.8 / 75.3	79.5 / 75.9 [b,c]
Population age distribution (0-14/60+ years old, %) [a]	27.3 / 6.0	24.2 / 9.9	21.2 / 18.8 [b,c]
International migrant stock (000/% of total pop.)	24.2 / 44.8	21.6 / 38.8	21.8 / 38.0 [k]
Infant mortality rate (per 1 000 live births) [a]	5.7	7.3	5.9 [b,c]

Environment and infrastructure indicators

	2010	2015	2023
Threatened species (number)	85	99	108 [c]
Forested area (% of land area)	65.9	64.1	53.0 [k]
Energy production, primary (Petajoules)	...	...	0 [h,k]
Energy supply per capita (Gigajoules) [h]	138	151	110 [k]
Tourist/visitor arrivals at national borders (000)	379	479	13 [d]
Important sites for terrestrial biodiversity protected (%)	40.6	40.6	40.6 [c]

a For statistical purposes, the data for United States of America do not include this area. **b** Projected estimate (medium fertility variant). **c** 2022. **d** 2021. **e** 2010. **f** Break in the time series. **g** Population aged 16 years and over. **h** Estimate. **i** 2019. **j** Data refers to a 5-year period preceding the reference year. **k** 2020.

Norway

Region	Northern Europe	UN membership date	27 November 1945
Population (000, 2023)	5 434[a,b,c]	Surface area (km2)	323 772[d]
Pop. density (per km2, 2023)	17.9[a,b,c]	Sex ratio (m per 100 f)	101.9[a,b,c]
Capital city	Oslo	National currency	Norwegian Krone (NOK)
Capital city pop. (000, 2023)	1 026.8[e]	Exchange rate (per US$)	9.9[c]

Economic indicators

	2010	2015	2023
GDP: Gross domestic product (million current US$)	428 757	385 802	482 175[d]
GDP growth rate (annual %, const. 2015 prices)	0.7	2.0	3.9[d]
GDP per capita (current US$)	87 685.0	74 330.5	89 241.7[d]
Economy: Agriculture (% of Gross Value Added)[f,g]	1.8	1.7	1.8[d]
Economy: Industry (% of Gross Value Added)[g,h]	39.0	34.8	39.6[d]
Economy: Services and other activity (% of GVA)[g]	59.2	63.4	58.6[d]
Employment in agriculture (% of employed)	2.5	0.1[i]	2.3[d]
Employment in industry (% of employed)	16.8[i]	20.1	19.1[d]
Employment in services & other sectors (% employed)	77.8	77.9	78.5[d]
Unemployment rate (% of labour force)	3.5	4.3	3.0[i]
Labour force participation rate (female/male pop. %)	61.7 / 69.6[i]	61.4 / 68.4	63.7 / 65.1[i]
CPI: Consumer Price Index (2010=100)	100	109	133[c]
Agricultural production index (2014-2016=100)	97	100	102[d]
International trade: exports (million current US$)	130 657	103 785	273 734[c]
International trade: imports (million current US$)	77 330	76 399	107 197[c]
International trade: balance (million current US$)	53 327	27 386	166 536[c]
Balance of payments, current account (million US$)	50 258	31 106	175 372[c]

Major trading partners

						2022
Export partners (% of exports)	Germany	28.0	United Kingdom	21.4	France	9.4
Import partners (% of imports)	Sweden	12.6	China	12.3	Germany	11.4

Social indicators

	2010	2015	2023
Population growth rate (average annual %)[b]	1.3	0.9	0.7[a,c]
Urban population (% of total population)[b]	79.1	81.1	82.6[e]
Urban population growth rate (average annual %)[b,j]	1.4	1.7	...
Fertility rate, total (live births per woman)[b]	1.9	1.7	1.5[a,c]
Life expectancy at birth (females/males, years)[b]	83.2 / 78.8	84.1 / 80.4	85.1 / 81.7[a,c]
Population age distribution (0-14/60+ years old, %)[b]	18.8 / 21.0	18.0 / 21.9	16.7 / 24.2[a,c]
International migrant stock (000/% of total pop.)[b]	524.6 / 10.7	746.4 / 14.4	852.2 / 15.7[k]
Refugees and others of concern to the UNHCR (000)	55.9[l]	54.9	69.5[c]
Infant mortality rate (per 1 000 live births)[b]	2.8	2.3	1.9[a,c]
Health: Current expenditure (% of GDP)	8.9	10.1	10.1[d]
Health: Physicians (per 1 000 pop.)	4.1	4.5	5.2[d]
Education: Government expenditure (% of GDP)	6.7	7.6	7.9[e]
Education: Primary gross enrol. ratio (f/m per 100 pop.)	99.2 / 98.9	99.8 / 100.0	100.1 / 99.8[k]
Education: Lowr. sec. gross enrol. ratio (f/m per 100 pop.)	99.2 / 99.3	103.9 / 102.0	106.3 / 104.7[k]
Education: Upr. sec. gross enrol. ratio (f/m per 100 pop.)	124.1 / 127.8	122.1 / 129.4	125.5 / 138.8[k]
Intentional homicide rate (per 100 000 pop.)	0.6	0.5	0.5[d]
Seats held by women in the National Parliament (%)	39.6	39.6	46.2[m]

Environment and infrastructure indicators

	2010	2015	2023
Individuals using the Internet (per 100 inhabitants)	93.4[n]	96.8[o]	99.0[d]
Research & Development expenditure (% of GDP)	1.6	1.9	2.3[k]
Threatened species (number)	36	44	135[c]
Forested area (% of land area)	33.1	33.2	33.4[k]
CO2 emission estimates (million tons/tons per capita)	39.4 / 7.9	39.5 / 7.5	40.3 / 7.3[d]
Energy production, primary (Petajoules)[b]	8 727	8 814	8 727[k]
Energy supply per capita (Gigajoules)[b]	279	238	212[k]
Tourist/visitor arrivals at national borders (000)	4 767[p]	5 361[q]	1 435[q,d]
Important sites for terrestrial biodiversity protected (%)	52.7	54.5	56.8[c]
Net Official Development Assist. disbursed (% of GNI)[r]	1.41	1.12	1.22[d]

a Projected estimate (medium fertility variant). b Including Svalbard and Jan Mayen Islands. c 2022. d 2021. e 2019. f Excludes irrigation canals and landscaping care. g Data classified according to ISIC Rev. 4. h Excludes publishing activities, recycling. Includes irrigation canals. i Estimate. j Data refers to a 5-year period preceding the reference year. k 2020. l Data as at the end of December. m Data are as at 1 January of reporting year. n Population aged 16 to 74 years. o Users in the last 3 months. p Arrivals of non-resident tourists at national borders. q Non-resident tourists staying in all types of accommodation establishments. r Development Assistance Committee member (OECD).

Oman

Region	Western Asia	UN membership date	07 October 1971
Population (000, 2023)	4 576[a,b]	Surface area (km2)	309 980[c]
Pop. density (per km2, 2023)	14.8[a,b]	Sex ratio (m per 100 f)	155.5[a,b]
Capital city	Muscat	National currency	Rial Omani (OMR)
Capital city pop. (000, 2023)	1 501.6[d,e]	Exchange rate (per US$)	0.4[b]

Economic indicators	2010	2015	2023
GDP: Gross domestic product (million current US$)	64 994	78 711	88 192[c]
GDP growth rate (annual %, const. 2015 prices)	2.5	5.0	3.1[c]
GDP per capita (current US$)	22 552.2	18 777.5	19 509.5[c]
Economy: Agriculture (% of Gross Value Added)[f]	1.2	1.6	2.1[c]
Economy: Industry (% of Gross Value Added)[g]	60.6	50.6	49.0[c]
Economy: Services and other activity (% of GVA)	38.2	47.8	48.9[c]
Employment in agriculture (% of employed)	5.2	5.2[h]	4.1[h,c]
Employment in industry (% of employed)	36.9	37.3[h]	48.2[h,c]
Employment in services & other sectors (% employed)	57.9	57.4[h]	47.6[h,c]
Unemployment rate (% of labour force)[h]	4.0	3.4	2.5
Labour force participation rate (female/male pop. %)[h]	26.5 / 80.8	29.8 / 87.4	33.3 / 87.6
CPI: Consumer Price Index (2010=100)	100	109	117[b]
Agricultural production index (2014-2016=100)	84	101	144[c]
International trade: exports (million current US$)	36 600	35 686	53 960[h,b]
International trade: imports (million current US$)	19 775	29 007	39 869[h,b]
International trade: balance (million current US$)	16 825	6 679	14 091[h,b]
Balance of payments, current account (million US$)	4 634	- 10 954	- 4 288[c]

Major trading partners					2022
Export partners (% of exports)[h]	China	45.8	United Arab Emirates	9.1	India	8.0
Import partners (% of imports)[h]	United Arab Emirates	35.6	China	7.0	India	6.6

Social indicators	2010	2015	2023
Population growth rate (average annual %)	11.2	5.1	1.4[a,b]
Urban population (% of total population)	75.2	81.4	85.4[e]
Urban population growth rate (average annual %)[i]	4.6	8.0	...
Fertility rate, total (live births per woman)	2.9	3.0	2.6[a,b]
Life expectancy at birth (females/males, years)	78.5 / 74.6	79.5 / 76.3	76.0 / 72.4[a,b]
Population age distribution (0-14/60+ years old, %)	26.9 / 3.9	22.3 / 3.9	27.0 / 4.5[a,b]
International migrant stock (000/% of total pop.)[j,k]	816.2 / 26.8	1 856.2 / 43.5	2 372.8 / 46.5[l]
Refugees and others of concern to the UNHCR (000)	0.1[m]	0.4	0.8[b]
Infant mortality rate (per 1 000 live births)	10.0	9.6	8.6[a,b]
Health: Current expenditure (% of GDP)[n]	2.8	4.7	5.3[h,l]
Health: Physicians (per 1 000 pop.)	2.0	2.1	2.0[l]
Education: Government expenditure (% of GDP)	4.2[o]	4.4[p]	...
Education: Primary gross enrol. ratio (f/m per 100 pop.)	100.8 / 105.4[o]	110.7 / 106.0	103.9 / 104.2[c]
Education: Lowr. sec. gross enrol. ratio (f/m per 100 pop.)	101.7 / 112.8[o]	106.5 / 109.9	103.1 / 101.3[c]
Education: Upr. sec. gross enrol. ratio (f/m per 100 pop.)	92.8 / 93.1[o]	98.3 / 98.6	100.5 / 153.8[c]
Intentional homicide rate (per 100 000 pop.)	1.7	0.4	0.2[c]
Seats held by women in the National Parliament (%)	0.0	1.2	2.3[q]

Environment and infrastructure indicators	2010	2015	2023
Individuals using the Internet (per 100 inhabitants)	35.8[r]	73.5[h]	96.4[h,c]
Research & Development expenditure (% of GDP)	...	0.2	0.3[c]
Threatened species (number)	79	90	147[b]
Forested area (% of land area)	~0.0	~0.0	~0.0[l]
CO2 emission estimates (million tons/tons per capita)	42.8 / 14.0	64.2 / 14.9	64.5 / 12.6[l]
Energy production, primary (Petajoules)	2 793	3 228	3 341[l]
Energy supply per capita (Gigajoules)	286	262	248[l]
Tourist/visitor arrivals at national borders (000)	1 441	1 909	464[c]
Important sites for terrestrial biodiversity protected (%)	19.8	22.8	23.3[b]
Net Official Development Assist. received (% of GNI)	- 0.04	...	...

a Projected estimate (medium fertility variant). **b** 2022. **c** 2021. **d** Refers to Muscat governorate. **e** 2019. **f** Excludes irrigation canals and landscaping care. **g** Excludes publishing activities, recycling. Includes irrigation canals. **h** Estimate. **i** Data refers to a 5-year period preceding the reference year. **j** Including refugees. **k** Refers to foreign citizens. **l** 2020. **m** Data as at the end of December. **n** Data based on calendar year (January 1 to December 31). **o** 2009. **p** 2013. **q** Data are as at 1 January of reporting year. **r** Population aged 5 years and over.

Pakistan

Region	Southern Asia
Population (000, 2023)	235 825[a,b]
Pop. density (per km2, 2023)	305.9[a,b]
Capital city	Islamabad
Capital city pop. (000, 2023)	1 095.1[d]

UN membership date	30 September 1947
Surface area (km2)	796 095[c]
Sex ratio (m per 100 f)	101.8[a,b]
National currency	Pakistan Rupee (PKR)
Exchange rate (per US$)	226.5[b]

Economic indicators	2010	2015	2023
GDP: Gross domestic product (million current US$)	182 960	297 019	342 501[c]
GDP growth rate (annual %, const. 2015 prices)	2.8	6.0	6.5[c]
GDP per capita (current US$)	940.9	1 407.9	1 480.1[c]
Economy: Agriculture (% of Gross Value Added)[e,f]	24.1	24.5	24.2[c]
Economy: Industry (% of Gross Value Added)[f,g]	20.5	20.1	20.1[c]
Economy: Services and other activity (% of GVA)[f]	55.4	55.5	55.7[c]
Employment in agriculture (% of employed)	43.4	41.0	37.5[h,c]
Employment in industry (% of employed)[h]	14.7	23.0	25.2[c]
Employment in services & other sectors (% employed)	35.2	35.0	37.3[h,c]
Unemployment rate (% of labour force)	0.6	3.6	6.7[h]
Labour force participation rate (female/male pop. %)	22.0 / 78.5	24.0 / 78.9	24.6 / 80.7[h]
CPI: Consumer Price Index (2010=100)	100[i]	145	263[b]
Agricultural production index (2014-2016=100)	81	99	122[c]
International trade: exports (million current US$)	21 413	22 089	30 138[h,b]
International trade: imports (million current US$)	37 537	43 990	74 152[h,b]
International trade: balance (million current US$)	- 16 124	- 21 901	- 44 013[h,b]
Balance of payments, current account (million US$)	- 1 354	- 2 803	- 12 129[b]

Major trading partners						2022
Export partners (% of exports)[h]	United States	21.1	China	10.5	United Kingdom	7.3
Import partners (% of imports)[h]	China	28.3	United Arab Emirates	10.1	Indonesia	5.8

Social indicators	2010	2015	2023
Population growth rate (average annual %)	2.2	1.2	2.0[a,b]
Urban population (% of total population)	35.0	36.0	36.9[d]
Urban population growth rate (average annual %)[j]	2.6	2.7	...
Fertility rate, total (live births per woman)	4.3	3.9	3.4[a,b]
Life expectancy at birth (females/males, years)	66.9 / 62.3	68.2 / 63.5	68.9 / 64.1[a,b]
Population age distribution (0-14/60+ years old, %)	39.2 / 5.7	38.4 / 6.0	36.6 / 6.8[a,b]
International migrant stock (000/% of total pop.)[k]	3 943.7 / 2.2	3 506.5 / 1.8	3 276.6 / 1.5[l]
Refugees and others of concern to the UNHCR (000)	4 151.0[m]	3 440.0	1 690.9[b]
Infant mortality rate (per 1 000 live births)	70.5	62.1	51.8[a,b]
Health: Current expenditure (% of GDP)[n,o]	2.4	2.5	2.8[h,l]
Health: Physicians (per 1 000 pop.)	0.7	0.9	1.1[d]
Education: Government expenditure (% of GDP)	2.3	2.6	2.1[c]
Education: Primary gross enrol. ratio (f/m per 100 pop.)	77.6 / 91.0	78.3 / 91.4	89.2 / 101.3[d]
Education: Lowr. sec. gross enrol. ratio (f/m per 100 pop.)	37.8 / 47.8	44.6 / 53.9	51.2 / 58.4[d]
Education: Upr. sec. gross enrol. ratio (f/m per 100 pop.)	21.8 / 29.0	27.4 / 36.2	34.0 / 39.7[d]
Intentional homicide rate (per 100 000 pop.)	6.8	4.5	4.0[c]
Seats held by women in the National Parliament (%)	22.2	20.7	20.5[p]

Environment and infrastructure indicators	2010	2015	2023
Individuals using the Internet (per 100 inhabitants)[h]	8.0	11.0	21.0[c]
Research & Development expenditure (% of GDP)[q,r]	0.4[s]	0.2	0.2[c]
Threatened species (number)	109	129	233[b]
Forested area (% of land area)	5.3	5.1	4.8[l]
CO2 emission estimates (million tons/tons per capita)	140.3 / 0.7	163.3 / 0.8	180.0 / 0.8[l]
Energy production, primary (Petajoules)	2 252	2 302	2 220[l]
Energy supply per capita (Gigajoules)	16	16	16[l]
Tourist/visitor arrivals at national borders (000)	907	966[t]	...
Important sites for terrestrial biodiversity protected (%)	34.8	34.8	34.8[b]
Pop. using safely managed drinking water (urban/rural, %)	49.8 / 32.4	52.7 / 38.3	56.8 / 46.9[b]
Pop. using safely managed sanitation (urban/rural %)	... / 19.6	... / 28.3	... / 40.2[b]
Net Official Development Assist. received (% of GNI)	1.69	1.42	0.86[c]

a Projected estimate (medium fertility variant). b 2022. c 2021. d 2019. e Excludes irrigation canals and landscaping care. f Data classified according to ISIC Rev. 4. g Excludes publishing activities, recycling. Includes irrigation canals. h Estimate. i Break in the time series. j Data refers to a 5-year period preceding the reference year. k Including refugees. l 2020. m Data as at the end of December. n Health expenditure data for even years (2006, 2008, 2010, 2012, 2014, 2016 and 2018) are based on SHA 1.0 health accounts produced by the country, adjusted to separate current health expenditure from capital health expenditure. o Data refer to fiscal years beginning 1 July. p Data are as at 1 January of reporting year. q Excluding private non-profit. r Excluding business enterprise. s 2009. t 2012.

Palau

Region	Micronesia	UN membership date	15 December 1994
Population (000, 2023)	18[a,b]	Surface area (km2)	459[c]
Pop. density (per km2, 2023)	39.2[a,b]	Sex ratio (m per 100 f)	108.0[a,b]
Capital city	Melekeok	National currency	US Dollar (USD)
Capital city pop. (000, 2023)	11.4[d,e]		

Economic indicators

	2010	2015	2023
GDP: Gross domestic product (million current US$)	183	280	218[c]
GDP growth rate (annual %, const. 2015 prices)	0.4	8.8	- 13.3[c]
GDP per capita (current US$)	9 883.1	15 760.2	12 084.1[c]
Economy: Agriculture (% of Gross Value Added)[f,g]	4.8	3.5	4.3[c]
Economy: Industry (% of Gross Value Added)[f,h]	11.0	9.2	13.6[c]
Economy: Services and other activity (% of GVA)[f]	84.2	87.3	82.1[c]
Employment in agriculture (% of employed)	2.4[i,j,k]	...	...
Employment in industry (% of employed)	11.8[i,j,k]	...	...
Employment in services & other sectors (% employed)	85.9[i,j,k]	...	...
Unemployment rate (% of labour force)	4.2[i,l]	...	...
Labour force participation rate (female/male pop. %)	58.1 / 75.4[i,l]	... / ...	... / ...
CPI: Consumer Price Index (2010=100)	100	118	140[b]
International trade: exports (million current US$)	12[m]	6	4[m,b]
International trade: imports (million current US$)	107	150	297[m,b]
International trade: balance (million current US$)	- 96	- 144	- 293[m,b]
Balance of payments, current account (million US$)	- 19	- 24	- 64[c]

Major trading partners

							2022
Export partners (% of exports)[m]	Greece	26.3	Japan	24.8	France	16.2
Import partners (% of imports)[m]	China	31.1	United States	14.1	Singapore	13.9

Social indicators

	2010	2015	2023
Population growth rate (average annual %)	- 1.6	0.1	~0.0[a,b]
Urban population (% of total population)	74.8	78.2	80.5[n]
Urban population growth rate (average annual %)[o]	1.6	1.7	...
Fertility rate, total (live births per woman)	2.0	2.1	2.4[a,b]
Life expectancy at birth (females/males, years)	68.7 / 63.0	66.7 / 61.3	69.3 / 62.2[a,b]
Population age distribution (0-14/60+ years old, %)	21.3 / 9.8	20.6 / 12.2	21.0 / 15.6[a,b]
International migrant stock (000/% of total pop.)	5.5 / 30.6	4.9 / 27.9	5.1 / 28.1[p]
Refugees and others of concern to the UNHCR (000)	...	~0.0	~0.0[q]
Infant mortality rate (per 1 000 live births)	20.8	17.9	14.6[a,b]
Health: Current expenditure (% of GDP)[r]	11.7	11.1	18.4[p]
Health: Physicians (per 1 000 pop.)	1.6	1.4[s]	1.8[p]
Education: Primary gross enrol. ratio (f/m per 100 pop.)	... / ...	105.2 / 119.6[s]	102.7 / 106.0[c]
Education: Lowr. sec. gross enrol. ratio (f/m per 100 pop.)	... / ...	109.3 / 106.4[s]	121.6 / 96.8[c]
Education: Upr. sec. gross enrol. ratio (f/m per 100 pop.)	89.4 / 86.0[t]	129.8 / 112.9[s]	97.4 / 97.5[c]
Intentional homicide rate (per 100 000 pop.)	...	16.9	11.2[e]
Seats held by women in the National Parliament (%)	0.0	0.0	6.2[u]

Environment and infrastructure indicators

	2010	2015	2023
Threatened species (number)	128	177	198[b]
Forested area (% of land area)	88.2	89.1	90.0[p]
Energy production, primary (Petajoules)	...	0	0[m,p]
Energy supply per capita (Gigajoules)	156	159[m]	164[m,p]
Tourist/visitor arrivals at national borders (000)[v]	85	162	18[p]
Important sites for terrestrial biodiversity protected (%)	46.3	48.1	48.1[b]
Pop. using safely managed drinking water (urban/rural, %)	82.6 / 55.8	88.9 / 56.5	97.7 / 57.5[b]
Net Official Development Assist. received (% of GNI)	14.31	4.61	25.28[p]

a Projected estimate (medium fertility variant). b 2022. c 2021. d Refers to Koror. e 2018. f Data classified according to ISIC Rev. 4. g Excludes irrigation canals and landscaping care. h Excludes publishing activities, recycling. Includes irrigation canals. i Population aged 16 years and over. j Data classified according to ISIC Rev. 3. k 2008. l 2005. m Estimate. n 2019. o Data refers to a 5-year period preceding the reference year. p 2020. q 2017. r Data refer to fiscal years beginning 1 October. s 2014. t 2007. u Data are as at 1 January of reporting year. v Air arrivals (Palau International Airport).

Panama

Region	Central America	UN membership date	13 November 1945
Population (000, 2023)	4 409[a,b]	Surface area (km2)	75 320[c]
Pop. density (per km2, 2023)	59.4[a,b]	Sex ratio (m per 100 f)	100.0[a,b]
Capital city	Panama City	National currency	Balboa (PAB)
Capital city pop. (000, 2023)	1 821.7[d,e]	Exchange rate (per US$)	1.0[b]

Economic indicators

	2010	2015	2023
GDP: Gross domestic product (million current US$)	29 440	54 092	63 605[c]
GDP growth rate (annual %, const. 2015 prices)	5.8	5.7	15.3[c]
GDP per capita (current US$)	8 124.6	13 669.5	14 617.6[c]
Economy: Agriculture (% of Gross Value Added)	3.8	2.9	2.7[c]
Economy: Industry (% of Gross Value Added)	20.1	28.7	28.7[c]
Economy: Services and other activity (% of GVA)	76.2	68.4	68.6[c]
Employment in agriculture (% of employed)	17.4	14.7	15.7[c]
Employment in industry (% of employed)	18.7	8.2[f]	16.8[c]
Employment in services & other sectors (% employed)	63.9	66.6	67.5[c]
Unemployment rate (% of labour force)	5.9	4.4	9.3[f]
Labour force participation rate (female/male pop. %)	46.8 / 79.5	50.0 / 77.5	55.6 / 77.2[f]
CPI: Consumer Price Index (2010=100)[g]	100	120	126[b]
Agricultural production index (2014-2016=100)	90	100	112[c]
International trade: exports (million current US$)[h]	10 987	11 348	3 590[f,b]
International trade: imports (million current US$)[h]	16 737	10 375	15 186[f,b]
International trade: balance (million current US$)[h]	- 5 751	973	- 11 596[f,b]
Balance of payments, current account (million US$)	- 3 121	- 4 848	- 2 051[c]

Major trading partners
2022

Export partners (% of exports)[f]	China	31.7	Japan	13.2	Republic of Korea	10.2
Import partners (% of imports)[f]	United States	29.0	China	17.9	Free Zones	9.4

Social indicators

	2010	2015	2023
Population growth rate (average annual %)	1.8	1.7	1.3[a,b]
Urban population (% of total population)	65.1	66.7	68.1[e]
Urban population growth rate (average annual %)[i]	2.2	2.2	...
Fertility rate, total (live births per woman)	2.6	2.6	2.3[a,b]
Life expectancy at birth (females/males, years)	79.7 / 73.3	80.5 / 74.5	80.1 / 73.7[a,b]
Population age distribution (0-14/60+ years old, %)	29.2 / 9.4	28.0 / 10.6	26.1 / 12.7[a,b]
International migrant stock (000/% of total pop.)[j]	157.8 / 4.3	184.7 / 4.7	313.2 / 7.3[k]
Refugees and others of concern to the UNHCR (000)	17.6[l]	19.3	155.9[b]
Infant mortality rate (per 1 000 live births)	16.9	15.1	12.7[a,b]
Health: Current expenditure (% of GDP)[m]	7.5	7.2	9.7[f,k]
Health: Physicians (per 1 000 pop.)	1.4	1.6	1.6[k]
Education: Government expenditure (% of GDP)	3.5[n]	3.0	3.5[c]
Education: Primary gross enrol. ratio (f/m per 100 pop.)	103.1 / 107.0	94.9 / 97.2	100.4 / 101.9[c]
Education: Lowr. sec. gross enrol. ratio (f/m per 100 pop.)	90.0 / 89.3	93.2 / 92.2	94.2 / 94.2[c]
Education: Upr. sec. gross enrol. ratio (f/m per 100 pop.)	56.3 / 48.3	62.5 / 55.3	73.4 / 66.7[c]
Intentional homicide rate (per 100 000 pop.)	12.7	11.9	12.7[c]
Seats held by women in the National Parliament (%)	8.5	19.3	22.5[o]

Environment and infrastructure indicators

	2010	2015	2023
Individuals using the Internet (per 100 inhabitants)	40.1[p]	51.2	67.5[f,c]
Research & Development expenditure (% of GDP)	0.1	0.1	0.2[c]
Threatened species (number)	347	373	561[b]
Forested area (% of land area)	58.2	57.6	56.8[k]
CO2 emission estimates (million tons/tons per capita)	8.8 / 2.4	10.1 / 2.5	9.5 / 2.2[k]
Energy production, primary (Petajoules)[q]	26	36	41[k]
Energy supply per capita (Gigajoules)[q]	40	43	41[k]
Tourist/visitor arrivals at national borders (000)	1 324	2 110	618[c]
Important sites for terrestrial biodiversity protected (%)	54.3	54.3	54.9[b]
Pop. using safely managed sanitation (urban/rural %)	12.2 / ...	28.6 / ...	50.0 / ...[b]
Net Official Development Assist. received (% of GNI)	0.48	0.02	0.15[c]

a Projected estimate (medium fertility variant). b 2022. c 2021. d Refers to the metropolitan area of Panama City. e 2019. f Estimate. g Urban areas. h From 2004 to 2020 merchandise data including Zona Libre de Colon. i Data refers to a 5-year period preceding the reference year. j Including refugees. k 2020. l Data as at the end of December. m Data based on calendar year (January 1 to December 31). n 2008. o Data are as at 1 January of reporting year. p Multipliers were applied to residential and commercial subscriptions, taking into account the average size of households and employees per business. q Includes the Panama Canal Zone.

Papua New Guinea

Region	Melanesia	UN membership date		10 October 1975
Population (000, 2023)	10 143[a,b]	Surface area (km2)		462 840[c]
Pop. density (per km2, 2023)	22.4[a,b]	Sex ratio (m per 100 f)		106.6[a,b]
Capital city	Port Moresby	National currency		Kina (PGK)
Capital city pop. (000, 2023)	374.5[d]	Exchange rate (per US$)		3.5[c]

Economic indicators

	2010	2015	2023
GDP: Gross domestic product (million current US$)	14 251	21 723	26 595[c]
GDP growth rate (annual %, const. 2015 prices)	10.1	6.6	1.1[c]
GDP per capita (current US$)	1 879.2	2 502.1	2 673.0[c]
Economy: Agriculture (% of Gross Value Added)[e,f]	20.2	18.3	20.2[c]
Economy: Industry (% of Gross Value Added)[f,g]	34.2	36.4	35.8[c]
Economy: Services and other activity (% of GVA)[f]	45.5	45.3	44.0[c]
Employment in agriculture (% of employed)	25.7	21.1[h]	17.2[h,c]
Employment in industry (% of employed)	7.6	8.8[h]	9.9[h,c]
Employment in services & other sectors (% employed)	66.7	70.1[h]	72.9[h,c]
Unemployment rate (% of labour force)	2.0	2.4[h]	2.7[h]
Labour force participation rate (female/male pop. %)	47.7 / 49.0	46.9 / 48.4[h]	46.2 / 47.5[h]
CPI: Consumer Price Index (2010=100)	100[i]	128	171[c]
Agricultural production index (2014-2016=100)	88	100	104[c]
International trade: exports (million current US$)[h]	5 742	8 425	9 593[b]
International trade: imports (million current US$)[h]	3 950	2 537	6 690[b]
International trade: balance (million current US$)[h]	1 792	5 888	2 904[b]
Balance of payments, current account (million US$)	- 642	1 892	4 499[c]

Major trading partners

						2022
Export partners (% of exports)[h]	Japan	30.3	China	25.5	Australia	11.5
Import partners (% of imports)[h]	China	26.6	Australia	24.9	Singapore	16.2

Social indicators

	2010	2015	2023
Population growth rate (average annual %)	3.0	2.5	1.9[a,b]
Urban population (% of total population)	13.0	13.0	13.2[d]
Urban population growth rate (average annual %)[j]	2.2	2.2	...
Fertility rate, total (live births per woman)	3.9	3.6	3.2[a,b]
Life expectancy at birth (females/males, years)	65.3 / 61.3	67.8 / 62.3	69.2 / 63.4[a,b]
Population age distribution (0-14/60+ years old, %)	37.9 / 4.3	36.5 / 4.6	34.2 / 5.5[a,b]
International migrant stock (000/% of total pop.)[k,l]	30.4 / 0.4	30.9 / 0.4	31.1 / 0.3[m]
Refugees and others of concern to the UNHCR (000)	9.7[n]	9.9	36.1[b]
Infant mortality rate (per 1 000 live births)	44.9	40.0	33.8[a,b]
Health: Current expenditure (% of GDP)	2.1	1.8	2.5[m]
Health: Physicians (per 1 000 pop.)	~0.0	...	0.1[c]
Education: Government expenditure (% of GDP)	...	...	1.9[h,o]
Education: Primary gross enrol. ratio (f/m per 100 pop.)	54.3 / 61.4[p]	95.7 / 107.9[q]	111.8 / 119.9[o]
Education: Lowr. sec. gross enrol. ratio (f/m per 100 pop.)	... / ...	62.0 / 78.0[q]	54.0 / 65.8[o]
Education: Upr. sec. gross enrol. ratio (f/m per 100 pop.)	... / ...	17.2 / 25.4[q]	15.6 / 23.1[o]
Intentional homicide rate (per 100 000 pop.)	9.4	...	...
Seats held by women in the National Parliament (%)	0.9	2.7	1.7[r]

Environment and infrastructure indicators

	2010	2015	2023
Individuals using the Internet (per 100 inhabitants)	1.3[s]	7.9[h]	32.1[h,c]
Research & Development expenditure (% of GDP)	...	...	~0.0[t,u,v]
Threatened species (number)	453	478	1 133[b]
Forested area (% of land area)	79.9	79.5	79.2[m]
Energy production, primary (Petajoules)	95	543	596[m]
Energy supply per capita (Gigajoules)	19	21	21[m]
Tourist/visitor arrivals at national borders (000)	140	183	17[c]
Important sites for terrestrial biodiversity protected (%)	7.2	7.2	7.3[b]
Pop. using safely managed sanitation (urban/rural %)	29.8[q] / ...	29.1[q] / ...	28.3[q] / ...[b]
Net Official Development Assist. received (% of GNI)	3.90	2.77	4.57[c]

a Projected estimate (medium fertility variant). b 2022. c 2021. d 2019. e Excludes irrigation canals and landscaping care. f Data classified according to ISIC Rev. 4. g Excludes publishing activities, recycling. Includes irrigation canals. h Estimate. i Break in the time series. j Data refers to a 5-year period preceding the reference year. k Refers to foreign citizens. l Including refugees. m 2020. n Data as at the end of December. o 2018. p 2008. q 2012. r Data are as at 1 January of reporting year. s Population aged 10 years and over. t Partial data. u Excluding business enterprise. v 2016.

Paraguay

Region	South America	
Population (000, 2023)	6 781 [a,b]	
Pop. density (per km2, 2023)	16.8 [a,b]	
Capital city	Asunción	
Capital city pop. (000, 2023)	3 279.2 [d,e]	

UN membership date	24 October 1945
Surface area (km2)	406 752 [c]
Sex ratio (m per 100 f)	100.7 [a,b]
National currency	Guarani (PYG)
Exchange rate (per US$)	7 331.3 [b]

Economic indicators

	2010	2015	2023
GDP: Gross domestic product (million current US$)	27 261	36 211	40 458 [c]
GDP growth rate (annual %, const. 2015 prices)	11.1	3.0	5.0 [c]
GDP per capita (current US$)	4 725.7	5 861.4	6 035.1 [c]
Economy: Agriculture (% of Gross Value Added) [f,g]	14.0	10.2	11.2 [c]
Economy: Industry (% of Gross Value Added) [f]	37.2	37.3	38.4 [c]
Economy: Services and other activity (% of GVA) [f]	48.8	52.5	50.5 [c]
Employment in agriculture (% of employed)	25.6	19.7	19.7 [c]
Employment in industry (% of employed)	19.2	19.8	19.5 [c]
Employment in services & other sectors (% employed)	55.2	60.5	60.8 [c]
Unemployment rate (% of labour force)	4.6	4.6	6.5 [h]
Labour force participation rate (female/male pop. %)	53.1 / 82.4	54.8 / 81.1	60.1 / 83.5 [h]
CPI: Consumer Price Index (2010=100) [i,j]	100	125	168 [b]
Agricultural production index (2014-2016=100)	81	99	111 [c]
International trade: exports (million current US$)	6 517	8 328	9 948 [b]
International trade: imports (million current US$)	10 033	10 291	15 853 [b]
International trade: balance (million current US$)	- 3 517	- 1 964	- 5 904 [b]
Balance of payments, current account (million US$)	- 289	- 25	- 2 713 [b]

Major trading partners
2022

Export partners (% of exports)	Brazil	36.9	Argentina	19.3	Chile	11.6
Import partners (% of imports)	China	29.6	Brazil	23.2	United States	9.6

Social indicators

	2010	2015	2023
Population growth rate (average annual %)	1.3	1.4	1.1 [a,b]
Urban population (% of total population)	59.3	60.8	61.9 [e]
Urban population growth rate (average annual %) [k]	1.9	1.8	...
Fertility rate, total (live births per woman)	2.7	2.6	2.4 [a,b]
Life expectancy at birth (females/males, years)	74.8 / 69.2	76.0 / 70.5	73.6 / 67.6 [a,b]
Population age distribution (0-14/60+ years old, %)	33.0 / 7.5	30.5 / 8.2	28.9 / 9.4 [a,b]
International migrant stock (000/% of total pop.) [l]	160.3 / 2.6	156.5 / 2.3	169.6 / 2.4 [m]
Refugees and others of concern to the UNHCR (000)	0.1 [n]	0.2	7.5 [b]
Infant mortality rate (per 1 000 live births)	21.7	18.6	16.4 [a,b]
Health: Current expenditure (% of GDP) [h,o,p]	5.5	6.7	7.6 [m]
Health: Physicians (per 1 000 pop.)	...	1.4 [q]	3.2 [c]
Education: Government expenditure (% of GDP)	2.8	3.3	3.4 [c]
Education: Primary gross enrol. ratio (f/m per 100 pop.)	100.9 / 104.3	88.3 / 91.1	... / ...
Education: Lowr. sec. gross enrol. ratio (f/m per 100 pop.)	80.5 / 77.0	85.5 / 81.6 [q]	... / ...
Education: Upr. sec. gross enrol. ratio (f/m per 100 pop.)	58.7 / 53.9	63.9 / 58.1	84.3 / 70.6 [c]
Intentional homicide rate (per 100 000 pop.)	12.8	10.0	7.8 [c]
Seats held by women in the National Parliament (%)	12.5	15.0	18.8 [r]

Environment and infrastructure indicators

	2010	2015	2023
Individuals using the Internet (per 100 inhabitants)	19.8 [s,t]	49.7	77.0 [c]
Research & Development expenditure (% of GDP)	~0.0 [u]	0.1 [v]	0.2 [v,m]
Threatened species (number)	48	58	83 [b]
Forested area (% of land area)	49.3	44.0	40.5 [m]
CO2 emission estimates (million tons/tons per capita)	5.3 / 0.8	6.6 / 0.9	8.0 / 1.0 [m]
Energy production, primary (Petajoules)	352	350	293 [m]
Energy supply per capita (Gigajoules)	45	45	44 [m]
Tourist/visitor arrivals at national borders (000) [w,x]	465	1 215	95 [c]
Important sites for terrestrial biodiversity protected (%)	36.2	36.3	36.3 [b]
Pop. using safely managed drinking water (urban/rural, %)	70.2 / 40.4	71.4 / 46.8	72.2 / 50.7 [b]
Pop. using safely managed sanitation (urban/rural, %)	51.7 / 44.8	52.3 / 50.8	53.0 / 59.0 [b]
Net Official Development Assist. received (% of GNI)	0.44	0.17	0.46 [c]

a Projected estimate (medium fertility variant). b 2022. c 2021. d Refers to the district of Asunción and the 19 districts of Central Department. e 2019. f Data classified according to ISIC Rev. 4. g Excludes irrigation canals and landscaping care. h Estimate. i Calculated by the UN Statistics Division from national indices. j For Greater Asuncion only. k Data refers to a 5-year period preceding the reference year. l Including refugees. m 2020. n Data as at the end of December. o Data based on calendar year (January 1 to December 31). p Data are based on SHA2011. q 2012. r Data are as at 1 January of reporting year. s Population aged 10 years and over. t Users in the last 3 months. u 2008. v Excluding business enterprise. w E/D cards in the "Silvio Petirossi" airport and passenger counts at the national border crossings - National Police and SENATUR. x Excluding nationals residing abroad and crew members.

Peru

		UN membership date	31 October 1945
Region	South America	UN membership date	31 October 1945
Population (000, 2023)	34 050 [a,b]	Surface area (km2)	1 285 216 [c]
Pop. density (per km2, 2023)	26.6 [a,b]	Sex ratio (m per 100 f)	98.0 [a,b]
Capital city	Lima	National currency	Sol (PEN)
Capital city pop. (000, 2023)	10 554.7 [d,e]	Exchange rate (per US$)	3.8 [b]

Economic indicators

	2010	2015	2023
GDP: Gross domestic product (million current US$)	147 528	189 803	223 252 [c]
GDP growth rate (annual %, const. 2015 prices)	8.3	3.3	13.3 [c]
GDP per capita (current US$)	5 047.2	6 180.1	6 621.7 [c]
Economy: Agriculture (% of Gross Value Added) [f,g]	7.5	7.7	7.6 [c]
Economy: Industry (% of Gross Value Added) [f,h]	39.1	33.2	38.4 [c]
Economy: Services and other activity (% of GVA) [f]	53.5	59.1	53.9 [c]
Employment in agriculture (% of employed)	26.8	27.0	27.9 [c]
Employment in industry (% of employed)	17.4	17.4	17.0 [c]
Employment in services & other sectors (% of employed)	55.8	55.6	55.1 [c]
Unemployment rate (% of labour force)	3.6	3.3	3.6 [i]
Labour force participation rate (female/male pop. %)	72.1 / 86.6	67.7 / 84.4	64.4 / 76.6 [i]
CPI: Consumer Price Index (2010=100) [j]	100	118	150 [b]
Agricultural production index (2014-2016=100)	84	99	123 [c]
International trade: exports (million current US$)	35 807	33 667	66 432 [i,b]
International trade: imports (million current US$)	29 966	38 026	60 571 [i,b]
International trade: balance (million current US$)	5 842	- 4 359	5 860 [i,b]
Balance of payments, current account (million US$)	- 3 564	- 8 776	- 9 908 [b]

Major trading partners
2022

Export partners (% of exports) [i]	China	32.0	United States	12.8	Republic of Korea	5.0
Import partners (% of imports) [i]	China	28.6	United States	18.7	Brazil	6.7

Social indicators

	2010	2015	2023
Population growth rate (average annual %)	0.8	1.2	0.8 [a,b]
Urban population (% of total population)	76.4	77.4	78.1 [e]
Urban population growth rate (average annual %) [k]	1.6	1.6	...
Fertility rate, total (live births per woman)	2.6	2.3	2.2 [a,b]
Life expectancy at birth (females/males, years)	75.9 / 71.6	77.7 / 73.6	75.5 / 71.3 [a,b]
Population age distribution (0-14/60+ years old, %)	29.8 / 10.1	28.4 / 11.2	26.0 / 12.0 [a,b]
International migrant stock (000/% of total pop.) [l]	104.7 / 0.4	154.8 / 0.5	1 224.5 / 3.7 [m]
Refugees and others of concern to the UNHCR (000)	1.4 [n]	1.8	1 497.7 [b]
Infant mortality rate (per 1 000 live births)	15.7	12.6	9.7 [a,b]
Health: Current expenditure (% of GDP) [o]	4.7 [p]	5.0 [q]	6.3 [q,m]
Health: Physicians (per 1 000 pop.)	0.9 [r]	1.1 [s]	1.6 [c]
Education: Government expenditure (% of GDP)	2.9	4.0	4.0 [c]
Education: Primary gross enrol. ratio (f/m per 100 pop.)	110.0 / 109.8	100.3 / 100.2	120.1 / 123.8 [c]
Education: Lowr. sec. gross enrol. ratio (f/m per 100 pop.)	102.2 / 103.3	101.4 / 102.4	107.6 / 113.3 [c]
Education: Upr. sec. gross enrol. ratio (f/m per 100 pop.)	80.2 / 73.5	91.4 / 90.9	107.8 / 113.8 [c]
Intentional homicide rate (per 100 000 pop.)	...	7.3	5.7 [m]
Seats held by women in the National Parliament (%)	27.5	22.3	38.8 [t]

Environment and infrastructure indicators

	2010	2015	2023
Individuals using the Internet (per 100 inhabitants)	34.8 [u]	40.9	71.1 [v,w,c]
Research & Development expenditure (% of GDP)	...	0.1	0.2 [m]
Threatened species (number)	551	643	985 [b]
Forested area (% of land area)	57.9	57.2	56.5 [m]
CO2 emission estimates (million tons/tons per capita)	43.1 / 1.4	51.1 / 1.6	43.9 / 1.3 [m]
Energy production, primary (Petajoules)	810	953	890 [m]
Energy supply per capita (Gigajoules)	28	29	26 [m]
Tourist/visitor arrivals at national borders (000) [x,y]	2 299	3 456	444 [c]
Important sites for terrestrial biodiversity protected (%)	24.9	26.8	28.4 [b]
Pop. using safely managed drinking water (urban/rural, %)	57.9 / 18.0	58.7 / 20.1	59.8 / 23.0 [b]
Pop. using safely managed sanitation (urban/rural %)	32.3 / ...	44.0 / ...	61.6 / ... [b]
Net Official Development Assist. received (% of GNI)	- 0.22	0.18	0.15 [c]

a Projected estimate (medium fertility variant). b 2022. c 2021. d Refers to the Province of Lima and the Constitutional Province of Callao. e 2019. f Data classified according to ISIC Rev. 4. g Excludes irrigation canals and landscaping care. h Excludes publishing activities, recycling. Includes irrigation canals. i Estimate. j Metropolitan Lima. k Data refers to a 5-year period preceding the reference year. l Including refugees. m 2020. n Data as at the end of December. o Data based on calendar year (January 1 to December 31). p Country is still reporting data based on SHA 1.0. q Data are based on SHA2011. r 2009. s 2012. t Data are as at 1 January of reporting year. u Population aged 6 years and over. v Population aged 14 years and over. w Users in the last month. x Including tourists with identity document other than a passport. y Including nationals residing abroad.

Philippines

Region	South-eastern Asia	UN membership date	24 October 1945
Population (000, 2023)	115 559 [a,b]	Surface area (km2)	300 000 [c]
Pop. density (per km2, 2023)	385.2 [a,b]	Sex ratio (m per 100 f)	103.2 [a,b]
Capital city	Manila	National currency	Philippine Piso (PHP)
Capital city pop. (000, 2023)	13 698.9 [d,e]	Exchange rate (per US$)	56.1 [b]

Economic indicators

	2010	2015	2023
GDP: Gross domestic product (million current US$)	208 369	306 446	394 086 [c]
GDP growth rate (annual %, const. 2015 prices)	7.3	6.3	5.7 [c]
GDP per capita (current US$)	2 201.8	2 974.3	3 460.5 [c]
Economy: Agriculture (% of Gross Value Added) [f,g,h]	13.7	11.0	10.1 [c]
Economy: Industry (% of Gross Value Added) [f,g,i]	32.3	30.5	28.9 [c]
Economy: Services and other activity (% of GVA) [f]	53.9	58.5	61.0 [c]
Employment in agriculture (% of employed)	33.0 [j]	29.2	24.3 [j,c]
Employment in industry (% of employed) [j]	15.5	8.6	18.6 [c]
Employment in services & other sectors (% employed)	51.5 [j]	54.7	57.0 [j,c]
Unemployment rate (% of labour force)	3.6	3.1	2.2 [j]
Labour force participation rate (female/male pop. %)	48.0 / 74.9	48.5 / 74.2	46.3 / 71.0 [j]
CPI: Consumer Price Index (2010=100)	...	107 [k]	115 [l,b]
Agricultural production index (2014-2016=100)	92	101	100 [c]
International trade: exports (million current US$)	51 498	58 648	78 929 [b]
International trade: imports (million current US$)	58 468	70 153	145 880 [b]
International trade: balance (million current US$)	- 6 970	- 11 505	- 66 951 [b]
Balance of payments, current account (million US$)	7 179	7 266	- 17 832 [b]

Major trading partners 2022

Export partners (% of exports)	United States	15.8	Japan	14.1	China	13.9
Import partners (% of imports)	China	20.4	Indonesia	9.6	Japan	9.0

Social indicators

	2010	2015	2023
Population growth rate (average annual %)	1.8	1.8	1.5 [a,b]
Urban population (% of total population)	45.3	46.3	47.1 [e]
Urban population growth rate (average annual %) [m]	1.5	2.1	...
Fertility rate, total (live births per woman)	3.3	3.0	2.7 [a,b]
Life expectancy at birth (females/males, years)	72.4 / 69.1	73.0 / 69.5	74.2 / 70.2 [a,b]
Population age distribution (0-14/60+ years old, %)	34.5 / 6.6	32.6 / 7.4	30.3 / 8.6 [a,b]
International migrant stock (000/% of total pop.) [n,o]	208.6 / 0.2	211.9 / 0.2	225.5 / 0.2 [p]
Refugees and others of concern to the UNHCR (000)	139.9 [q]	386.2	307.3 [r,b]
Infant mortality rate (per 1 000 live births)	26.3	24.7	21.6 [a,b]
Health: Current expenditure (% of GDP)	4.1 [s]	3.9	5.6 [c]
Health: Physicians (per 1 000 pop.)	1.3	...	0.8 [c]
Education: Government expenditure (% of GDP)	2.5 [t]	3.5	3.9 [c]
Education: Primary gross enrol. ratio (f/m per 100 pop.)	107.1 / 108.3 [t]	110.5 / 113.9	91.3 / 93.5 [c]
Education: Lowr. sec. gross enrol. ratio (f/m per 100 pop.)	89.3 / 84.9 [t]	94.3 / 87.8	99.1 / 94.9 [c]
Education: Upr. sec. gross enrol. ratio (f/m per 100 pop.)	78.2 / 68.1	83.1 / 74.3	84.1 / 70.6 [c]
Intentional homicide rate (per 100 000 pop.)	9.1	8.7 [u]	4.3 [e]
Seats held by women in the National Parliament (%)	21.0	27.2	27.3 [v]

Environment and infrastructure indicators

	2010	2015	2023
Individuals using the Internet (per 100 inhabitants)	25.0	36.9 [j]	52.7 [j,c]
Research & Development expenditure (% of GDP)	0.1 [t]	0.2	0.3 [w]
Threatened species (number)	697	767	1 624 [b]
Forested area (% of land area)	22.9	23.5	24.1 [p]
CO2 emission estimates (million tons/tons per capita)	78.5 / 0.8	104.7 / 1.0	127.8 / 1.1 [p]
Energy production, primary (Petajoules)	999	1 092	1 229 [p]
Energy supply per capita (Gigajoules)	18	21	21 [p]
Tourist/visitor arrivals at national borders (000) [x]	3 520	5 361	164 [c]
Important sites for terrestrial biodiversity protected (%)	25.4	26.9	42.8 [b]
Pop. using safely managed drinking water (urban/rural, %)	60.7 / 32.4	61.2 / 33.5	61.9 / 35.0 [b]
Pop. using safely managed sanitation (urban/rural %)	49.4 / 52.3	52.1 / 58.9	56.2 / 68.8 [b]
Net Official Development Assist. received (% of GNI)	0.25	0.15	0.40 [c]

a Projected estimate (medium fertility variant). b 2022. c 2021. d Refers to the National Capital Region. e 2019. f Data classified according to ISIC Rev. 4. g Includes taxes less subsidies on production and imports. h Excludes irrigation canals and landscaping care. i Excludes publishing activities, recycling. Includes irrigation canals. j Estimate. k Base: 2012=100. l Base: 2018=100. m Data refers to a 5-year period preceding the reference year. n Refers to foreign citizens. o Including refugees. p 2020. q Data as at the end of December. r Updated figure is based on improved information concerning persons of Indonesian descent who have acquired nationality. s Data revision. t 2009. u 2012. v Data are as at 1 January of reporting year. w 2018. x Including nationals residing abroad.

Poland

Region	Eastern Europe	UN membership date	24 October 1945	
Population (000, 2023)	39 857 a,b	Surface area (km2)	312 679 c	
Pop. density (per km2, 2023)	130.2 a,b	Sex ratio (m per 100 f)	93.8 a,b	
Capital city	Warsaw	National currency	Zloty (PLN)	
Capital city pop. (000, 2023)	1 775.9 d	Exchange rate (per US$)	4.4 b	

Economic indicators

	2010	2015	2023
GDP: Gross domestic product (million current US$)	475 697	477 111	679 442 c
GDP growth rate (annual %, const. 2015 prices)	2.9	4.4	6.8 c
GDP per capita (current US$)	12 324.6	12 375.4	17 736.4 c
Economy: Agriculture (% of Gross Value Added) e,f	3.2	2.7	2.6 c
Economy: Industry (% of Gross Value Added) e,g	32.8	34.0	32.0 c
Economy: Services and other activity (% of GVA) e	64.0	63.4	65.4 c
Employment in agriculture (% of employed)	13.1	11.5	8.4 c
Employment in industry (% of employed)	30.3	30.5	23.2 h,c
Employment in services & other sectors (% employed)	56.6	57.9	60.7 c
Unemployment rate (% of labour force)	9.6	7.5	2.9 h
Labour force participation rate (female/male pop. %)	48.3 / 64.3	49.1 / 65.1	50.7 / 66.6 h
CPI: Consumer Price Index (2010=100) i	100	108	141 b
Agricultural production index (2014-2016=100)	91	97	111 c
International trade: exports (million current US$)	157 065	194 461	342 845 b
International trade: imports (million current US$)	174 128	189 696	358 593 b
International trade: balance (million current US$)	- 17 063	4 765	- 15 748 b
Balance of payments, current account (million US$)	- 24 627	- 6 170	- 20 651 b

Major trading partners

						2022
Export partners (% of exports)	Germany	27.8	Czechia	6.6	France	5.7
Import partners (% of imports)	Germany	20.9	China	13.1	Italy	4.6

Social indicators

	2010	2015	2023
Population growth rate (average annual %)	0.1	- 0.1	8.1 a,b
Urban population (% of total population)	60.9	60.3	60.0 d
Urban population growth rate (average annual %) j	- 0.2	- 0.2	...
Fertility rate, total (live births per woman)	1.4	1.3	1.5 a,b
Life expectancy at birth (females/males, years)	80.5 / 72.2	81.3 / 73.5	80.8 / 73.2 a,b
Population age distribution (0-14/60+ years old, %)	15.2 / 19.3	15.0 / 22.6	15.2 / 25.0 a,b
International migrant stock (000/% of total pop.)	642.4 / 1.7	611.9 / 1.6	817.3 / 2.2 k
Refugees and others of concern to the UNHCR (000)	18.4 l	29.0	1 215.4 b
Infant mortality rate (per 1 000 live births)	4.9	4.0	3.4 a,b
Health: Current expenditure (% of GDP)	6.4 m	6.4	6.6 c
Health: Physicians (per 1 000 pop.)	2.2	2.3	3.7 k
Education: Government expenditure (% of GDP)	5.1	4.8	4.7 d
Education: Primary gross enrol. ratio (f/m per 100 pop.)	96.1 / 96.9	100.3 / 100.0 n	82.5 / 85.6 k
Education: Lowr. sec. gross enrol. ratio (f/m per 100 pop.)	94.4 / 96.4	98.4 / 102.0	113.4 / 113.7 k
Education: Upr. sec. gross enrol. ratio (f/m per 100 pop.)	96.8 / 96.1	112.1 / 116.6	115.6 / 118.6 k
Intentional homicide rate (per 100 000 pop.)	1.0	0.8	0.7 c
Seats held by women in the National Parliament (%)	20.0	24.1	28.3 o

Environment and infrastructure indicators

	2010	2015	2023
Individuals using the Internet (per 100 inhabitants) p	62.3	68.0 q	85.4 c
Research & Development expenditure (% of GDP)	0.7	1.0	1.4 k
Threatened species (number)	37	51	113 b
Forested area (% of land area)	30.5	30.8	31.0 k
CO2 emission estimates (million tons/tons per capita)	314.3 / 8.0	288.7 / 7.4	301.8 / 7.7 c
Energy production, primary (Petajoules)	2 809	2 843	2 423 k
Energy supply per capita (Gigajoules)	110	104	112 k
Tourist/visitor arrivals at national borders (000)	12 470 r	16 728	9 722 c
Important sites for terrestrial biodiversity protected (%)	85.6	88.7	88.7 b
Net Official Development Assist. disbursed (% of GNI) s	0.08	0.11	0.15 c

a Projected estimate (medium fertility variant). b 2022. c 2021. d 2019. e Data classified according to ISIC Rev. 4. f Excludes irrigation canals and landscaping care. g Excludes publishing activities, recycling. Includes irrigation canals. h Estimate. i Calculated by the UN Statistics Division from national indices. j Data refers to a 5-year period preceding the reference year. k 2020. l Data as at the end of December. m Break in the time series. n 2014. o Data are as at 1 January of reporting year. p Population aged 16 to 74 years. q Users in the last 3 months. r Based on surveys by the Institute of Tourism. s Development Assistance Committee member (OECD).

Portugal

Region	Southern Europe	UN membership date	14 December 1955
Population (000, 2023)	10 271 [a,b]	Surface area (km2)	92 226 [b]
Pop. density (per km2, 2023)	111.7 [a,b]	Sex ratio (m per 100 f)	89.3 [a,b]
Capital city	Lisbon	National currency	Euro (EUR)
Capital city pop. (000, 2023)	2 942.1 [d,e]	Exchange rate (per US$)	0.9 [b]

Economic indicators	2010	2015	2023
GDP: Gross domestic product (million current US$)	237 881	199 314	253 663 [c]
GDP growth rate (annual %, const. 2015 prices)	1.7	1.8	5.5 [c]
GDP per capita (current US$)	22 466.2	19 228.7	24 651.2 [c]
Economy: Agriculture (% of Gross Value Added) [f,g]	2.2	2.4	2.5 [c]
Economy: Industry (% of Gross Value Added) [f,h]	22.7	22.3	22.7 [c]
Economy: Services and other activity (% of GVA) [f]	75.1	75.2	74.8 [c]
Employment in agriculture (% of employed)	11.2	7.5	5.2 [i,c]
Employment in industry (% of employed)	27.3	24.3	23.9 [c]
Employment in services & other sectors (% employed)	61.5	68.1	70.9 [c]
Unemployment rate (% of labour force)	10.8	12.4	6.1 [i]
Labour force participation rate (female/male pop. %)	55.9 / 67.2	53.7 / 64.1	54.6 / 63.5 [i]
CPI: Consumer Price Index (2010=100) [j,k]	100	107	121 [b]
Agricultural production index (2014-2016=100)	97	108	127 [c]
International trade: exports (million current US$)	49 414	55 045	82 354 [b]
International trade: imports (million current US$)	77 682	66 909	115 036 [b]
International trade: balance (million current US$)	- 28 268	- 11 864	- 32 682 [b]
Balance of payments, current account (million US$)	- 24 407	471	- 2 987 [c]

Major trading partners						2022
Export partners (% of exports)	Spain	26.0	France	12.4	Germany	10.9
Import partners (% of imports)	Spain	32.1	Germany	11.2	France	6.1

Social indicators	2010	2015	2023
Population growth rate (average annual %)	- 0.2	- 0.3	- 0.2 [a,b]
Urban population (% of total population)	60.6	63.5	65.8 [e]
Urban population growth rate (average annual %) [l]	1.2	0.5	...
Fertility rate, total (live births per woman)	1.4	1.3	1.4 [a,b]
Life expectancy at birth (females/males, years)	83.1 / 76.8	84.1 / 78.1	84.9 / 79.3 [a,b]
Population age distribution (0-14/60+ years old, %)	15.2 / 24.4	14.2 / 26.8	13.2 / 29.7 [a,b]
International migrant stock (000/% of total pop.)	762.8 / 7.2	864.8 / 8.3	1 002.0 / 9.8 [m]
Refugees and others of concern to the UNHCR (000)	0.5 [n]	1.4	51.6 [b]
Infant mortality rate (per 1 000 live births)	2.6	3.0	2.4 [a,b]
Health: Current expenditure (% of GDP)	10.0	9.3	11.2 [c]
Health: Physicians (per 1 000 pop.)	4.0	4.8	5.6 [m]
Education: Government expenditure (% of GDP)	5.4	4.9	4.6 [e]
Education: Primary gross enrol. ratio (f/m per 100 pop.)	109.9 / 113.2	104.9 / 109.0	107.1 / 108.4 [m]
Education: Lowr. sec. gross enrol. ratio (f/m per 100 pop.)	111.4 / 114.1	116.1 / 121.1	113.1 / 116.3 [m]
Education: Upr. sec. gross enrol. ratio (f/m per 100 pop.)	105.2 / 96.6	117.7 / 120.1	126.7 / 122.5 [m]
Intentional homicide rate (per 100 000 pop.)	1.2	1.0	0.8 [c]
Seats held by women in the National Parliament (%)	27.4	31.3	36.1 [o]

Environment and infrastructure indicators	2010	2015	2023
Individuals using the Internet (per 100 inhabitants)	53.3 [p]	68.6	82.3 [c]
Research & Development expenditure (% of GDP)	1.5	1.2	1.6 [m]
Threatened species (number)	171	256	540 [b]
Forested area (% of land area)	35.5	36.2	36.2 [m]
CO2 emission estimates (million tons/tons per capita) [q]	48.5 / 4.5	47.9 / 4.5	35.3 / 3.3 [c]
Energy production, primary (Petajoules) [r]	242	222	254 [m]
Energy supply per capita (Gigajoules) [r]	93	89	82 [m]
Tourist/visitor arrivals at national borders (000) [s]	6 756	11 723 [t]	6 345 [t,c]
Important sites for terrestrial biodiversity protected (%)	73.9	77.0	77.3 [b]
Pop. using safely managed drinking water (urban/rural, %)	97.0 / 89.6	97.1 / 90.3	97.1 / 91.2 [b]
Pop. using safely managed sanitation (urban/rural %)	73.6 / 63.4	87.0 / 74.9	95.9 / 86.3 [b]
Net Official Development Assist. disbursed (% of GNI) [u]	0.07	0.27	- 0.10 [c]

a Projected estimate (medium fertility variant). b 2022. c 2021. d Refers to Grande Lisboa, the Peninsula of Setúbal, and the municipality Azambuja. e 2019. f Data classified according to ISIC Rev. 4. g Excludes irrigation canals and landscaping care. h Excludes publishing activities, recycling. Includes irrigation canals. i Estimate. j Excluding rent. k Calculated by the UN Statistics Division from national indices. l Data refers to a 5-year period preceding the reference year. m 2020. n Data as at the end of December. o Data are as at 1 January of reporting year. p Population aged 16 to 74 years. q Data includes the Azores and Madeira. r Including the Azores and Madeira Islands. s Non-resident tourists staying in all types of accommodation establishments. t Include hotels, apartment hotels, "pousadas", tourist apartments, tourist villages, camping sites, recreation centres, tourism in rural areas and local accommodation. u Development Assistance Committee member (OECD).

Puerto Rico

Region	Caribbean	Population (000, 2023)	3 252 a,b
Surface area (km2)	8 868 c	Pop. density (per km2, 2023)	374.2 a,b
Sex ratio (m per 100 f)	89.3 a,b	Capital city	San Juan
National currency	US Dollar (USD)	Capital city pop. (000, 2023)	2 451.4 d,e

Economic indicators	2010	2015	2023
GDP: Gross domestic product (million current US$)[f]	98 381	103 376	106 526 c
GDP growth rate (annual %, const. 2015 prices)[f]	- 0.4	- 1.0	0.2 c
GDP per capita (current US$)[f]	26 461.4	29 558.4	32 716.5 c
Economy: Agriculture (% of Gross Value Added)[f,g]	0.8	0.8	0.7 c
Economy: Industry (% of Gross Value Added)[f,g]	50.7	51.1	50.6 c
Economy: Services and other activity (% of GVA)[f]	48.4	48.0	48.7 c
Employment in agriculture (% of employed)	1.5	1.4 h	1.2 h,c
Employment in industry (% of employed)[h]	6.3	13.6	12.2 c
Employment in services & other sectors (% employed)	83.6	85.0 h	86.7 h,c
Unemployment rate (% of labour force)	16.1	12.0	5.6 h
Labour force participation rate (female/male pop. %)	33.9 / 50.9	31.9 / 49.2	31.0 / 50.0 h
CPI: Consumer Price Index (2010=100)[i]	100	105	107 j
Agricultural production index (2014-2016=100)	119	102	94 c

Social indicators	2010	2015	2023
Population growth rate (average annual %)	- 0.6	- 1.8	0.2 a,b
Urban population (% of total population)	93.8	93.6	93.6 e
Urban population growth rate (average annual %)[k]	- 0.3	- 0.3	...
Fertility rate, total (live births per woman)	1.6	1.4	1.3 a,b
Life expectancy at birth (females/males, years)	82.1 / 74.0	83.8 / 75.7	83.9 / 75.6 a,b
Population age distribution (0-14/60+ years old, %)	19.6 / 20.5	16.7 / 24.3	13.4 / 30.0 a,b
International migrant stock (000/% of total pop.)	305.0 / 8.5	280.5 / 8.3	247.1 / 8.6 l
Infant mortality rate (per 1 000 live births)	7.2	6.8	6.8 a,b
Education: Government expenditure (% of GDP)	...	4.7	3.6 c
Education: Primary gross enrol. ratio (f/m per 100 pop.)	99.3 / 95.7	91.6 / 90.2 m	... / ...
Education: Lowr. sec. gross enrol. ratio (f/m per 100 pop.)	95.9 / 92.3	96.1 / 90.9 m	... / ...
Education: Upr. sec. gross enrol. ratio (f/m per 100 pop.)	81.1 / 75.0	83.8 / 76.2 m	... / ...
Intentional homicide rate (per 100 000 pop.)	27.7	17.6	17.0 l

Environment and infrastructure indicators	2010	2015	2023
Individuals using the Internet (per 100 inhabitants)	45.3 n	63.5	77.7 e
Research & Development expenditure (% of GDP)	0.5 o	0.4	...
Threatened species (number)	103	127	197 b
Forested area (% of land area)	55.4	55.7	56.0 l
Energy production, primary (Petajoules)	1	1	2 l
Energy supply per capita (Gigajoules)	7	16	15 l
Tourist/visitor arrivals at national borders (000)[p,q]	3 186	3 542	2 755 c
Important sites for terrestrial biodiversity protected (%)	33.0	33.0	33.0 b

a Projected estimate (medium fertility variant). b 2022. c 2021. d Refers to the Metropolitan Statistical Area. e 2019. f Data compiled in accordance with the System of National Accounts 1968 (1968 SNA). g At producers' prices. h Estimate. i Calculated by the UN Statistics Division from national indices. j 2017. k Data refers to a 5-year period preceding the reference year. l 2020. m 2013. n Population aged 12 years and over. o 2009. p Data refer to fiscal years beginning 1 July. q Arrivals of non-resident tourists by air.

Qatar

Region	Western Asia	UN membership date	21 September 1971
Population (000, 2023)	2 695 a,b	Surface area (km2)	11 627 c
Pop. density (per km2, 2023)	232.6 a,b	Sex ratio (m per 100 f)	263.8 a,b
Capital city	Doha	National currency	Qatari Rial (QAR)
Capital city pop. (000, 2023)	637.3 d,e	Exchange rate (per US$)	3.6 b

Economic indicators

	2010	2015	2023
GDP: Gross domestic product (million current US$)	125 122	161 740	179 571 c
GDP growth rate (annual %, const. 2015 prices)	16.7	4.8	1.5 c
GDP per capita (current US$)	73 021.3	66 984.9	66 798.8 c
Economy: Agriculture (% of Gross Value Added) f,g,h	0.1	0.2	0.3 c
Economy: Industry (% of Gross Value Added) f,g,i	67.5	55.4	57.2 c
Economy: Services and other activity (% of GVA) f	32.4	44.4	42.6 c
Employment in agriculture (% of employed)	1.5 i	1.2	1.2 i,c
Employment in industry (% of employed) j	56.4	47.5	54.0 c
Employment in services & other sectors (% employed)	42.1 i	44.6	44.8 i,c
Unemployment rate (% of labour force)	0.4	0.2	0.1 i
Labour force participation rate (female/male pop. %)	50.7 / 95.8	56.3 / 95.6	60.6 / 96.9 i
CPI: Consumer Price Index (2010=100)	...	105 k	104 l,b
Agricultural production index (2014-2016=100)	70	113	162 c
International trade: exports (million current US$)	74 964	77 971	130 964 b
International trade: imports (million current US$)	23 240	32 610	33 479 b
International trade: balance (million current US$)	51 725	45 361	97 485 b
Balance of payments, current account (million US$)	...	13 751	63 118 b

Major trading partners

						2022
Export partners (% of exports)	China	15.9	India	11.6	Republic of Korea	10.9
Import partners (% of imports)	China	16.2	United States	14.6	India	6.2

Social indicators

	2010	2015	2023
Population growth rate (average annual %)	4.7	8.3	0.8 a,b
Urban population (% of total population)	98.5	98.9	99.2 e
Urban population growth rate (average annual %) m	14.7	6.7	...
Fertility rate, total (live births per woman)	2.1	1.9	1.8 a,b
Life expectancy at birth (females/males, years)	80.5 / 77.4	81.7 / 79.2	83.1 / 80.6 a,b
Population age distribution (0-14/60+ years old, %)	13.8 / 1.8	13.9 / 2.2	15.8 / 3.3 a,b
International migrant stock (000/% of total pop.) n	1 456.4 / 78.5	1 687.6 / 65.8	2 226.2 / 77.3 o
Refugees and others of concern to the UNHCR (000)	1.3 p	1.4	1.7 b
Infant mortality rate (per 1 000 live births)	7.8	6.7	5.0 a,b
Health: Current expenditure (% of GDP) q,r	1.9	3.7 j	4.2 j,o
Health: Physicians (per 1 000 pop.)	4.0	1.9 s	2.5 t
Education: Government expenditure (% of GDP)	4.5	3.6 s	3.2 o
Education: Primary gross enrol. ratio (f/m per 100 pop.)	104.4 / 100.9	103.0 / 102.2	103.4 / 101.0 c
Education: Lower sec. gross enrol. ratio (f/m per 100 pop.)	104.4 / 116.3	102.5 / 99.8	95.8 / 97.6 c
Education: Upr. sec. gross enrol. ratio (f/m per 100 pop.)	100.9 / 100.3	... / ...	... / ...
Intentional homicide rate (per 100 000 pop.)	0.2	0.2	0.3 c
Seats held by women in the National Parliament (%)	0.0	0.0	4.4 u

Environment and infrastructure indicators

	2010	2015	2023
Individuals using the Internet (per 100 inhabitants)	69.0 v	92.9	100.0 j,c
Research & Development expenditure (% of GDP)	...	0.5	0.7 c
Threatened species (number)	32	35	71 b
Forested area (% of land area)	0.0	0.0	0.0 o
CO2 emission estimates (million tons/tons per capita)	56.1 / 30.1	80.9 / 31.4	84.5 / 29.2 o
Energy production, primary (Petajoules)	7 428	9 402	9 216 o
Energy supply per capita (Gigajoules)	680	640	635 o
Tourist/visitor arrivals at national borders (000)	1 700	2 941	611 c
Important sites for terrestrial biodiversity protected (%)	60.0	60.0	60.0 b
Net Official Development Assist. disbursed (% of GNI)	...	...	0.38 o

a Projected estimate (medium fertility variant). b 2022. c 2021. d Does not include the populations from the industrial area and zone 58. e 2019. f Data classified according to ISIC Rev. 4. g At producers' prices. h Excludes irrigation canals and landscaping care. i Excludes publishing activities, recycling. Includes irrigation canals. j Estimate. k Index base: 2013=100. l Base: 2018=100. m Data refers to a 5-year period preceding the reference year. n Refers to foreign citizens. o 2020. p Data as at the end of December. q Data based on calendar year (January 1 to December 31). r Estimates should be viewed with caution as these are derived from scarce data. s 2014. t 2018. u Data are as at 1 January of reporting year. v Refers to total population.

Republic of Korea

Region	Eastern Asia	UN membership date	17 September 1991
Population (000, 2023)	51 816 [a,b]	Surface area (km2)	100 401 [c]
Pop. density (per km2, 2023)	523.7 [a,b]	Sex ratio (m per 100 f)	99.7 [a,b]
Capital city	Seoul	National currency	South Korean Won (KRW)
Capital city pop. (000, 2023)	9 962.4 [d,e]	Exchange rate (per US$)	1 267.3 [b]

Economic indicators	2010	2015	2023
GDP: Gross domestic product (million current US$) [f]	1 144 067	1 465 773	1 810 966 [c]
GDP growth rate (annual %, const. 2015 prices) [f]	6.8	2.8	4.1 [c]
GDP per capita (current US$) [f]	23 437.7	28 743.8	34 940.4 [c]
Economy: Agriculture (% of Gross Value Added) [g,h]	2.4	2.2	2.0 [c]
Economy: Industry (% of Gross Value Added) [h,i]	37.5	37.2	35.6 [c]
Economy: Services and other activity (% of GVA) [h]	60.1	60.6	62.5 [c]
Employment in agriculture (% of employed)	6.5	5.2	5.3 [c]
Employment in industry (% of employed)	24.8	25.5	24.6 [c]
Employment in services & other sectors (% of employed)	68.7	69.3	70.1 [c]
Unemployment rate (% of labour force)	3.3	3.6	2.9 [i]
Labour force participation rate (female/male pop. %)	49.9 / 73.0	52.3 / 74.1	53.6 / 72.4 [i]
CPI: Consumer Price Index (2010=100) [k]	100	110	125 [b]
Agricultural production index (2014-2016=100)	94	100	102 [c]
International trade: exports (million current US$)	466 381	526 753	683 596 [i,b]
International trade: imports (million current US$)	425 208	436 487	731 275 [i,b]
International trade: balance (million current US$)	41 173	90 266	- 47 679 [i,b]
Balance of payments, current account (million US$)	27 950	105 119	29 831 [b]

Major trading partners						2022
Export partners (% of exports) [j]	China	25.3	United States	14.9	Viet Nam	8.8
Import partners (% of imports) [j]	China	22.5	United States	12.0	Japan	8.9

Social indicators	2010	2015	2023
Population growth rate (average annual %)	0.5	0.8	- 0.1 [a,b]
Urban population (% of total population)	81.9	81.6	81.4 [e]
Urban population growth rate (average annual %) [l]	0.5	0.3	...
Fertility rate, total (live births per woman)	1.2	1.2	0.9 [a,b]
Life expectancy at birth (females/males, years)	84.2 / 77.1	85.8 / 79.0	87.1 / 80.7 [a,b]
Population age distribution (0-14/60+ years old, %)	16.4 / 15.5	13.8 / 18.3	11.6 / 25.5 [a,b]
International migrant stock (000/% of total pop.) [m,n]	920.0 / 1.9	1 370.9 / 2.7	1 728.2 / 3.4 [o]
Refugees and others of concern to the UNHCR (000)	1.2 [p]	6.6	15.9 [q,b]
Infant mortality rate (per 1 000 live births)	3.5	2.9	2.3 [a,b]
Health: Current expenditure (% of GDP)	5.9	6.7	8.4 [o]
Health: Physicians (per 1 000 pop.)	2.0	2.2	2.5 [o]
Education: Government expenditure (% of GDP)	3.5	...	4.7 [e]
Education: Primary gross enrol. ratio (f/m per 100 pop.)	101.8 / 101.7	98.7 / 98.9	99.1 / 99.3 [o]
Education: Lowr. sec. gross enrol. ratio (f/m per 100 pop.)	100.2 / 100.6	103.3 / 104.2	97.0 / 97.1 [o]
Education: Upr. sec. gross enrol. ratio (f/m per 100 pop.)	92.2 / 93.0	96.6 / 97.1	94.6 / 95.6 [o]
Intentional homicide rate (per 100 000 pop.)	1.0	0.7	0.5 [c]
Seats held by women in the National Parliament (%)	14.7	16.3	19.1 [r]

Environment and infrastructure indicators	2010	2015	2023
Individuals using the Internet (per 100 inhabitants)	83.7 [s]	89.9 [t]	97.6 [c]
Research & Development expenditure (% of GDP)	3.3	4.0	4.8 [o]
Threatened species (number)	64	76	175 [b]
Forested area (% of land area)	65.7	65.0	64.4 [o]
CO2 emission estimates (million tons/tons per capita)	555.4 / 11.1	587.2 / 11.4	586.9 / 11.2 [c]
Energy production, primary (Petajoules)	1 863	2 123	2 169 [o]
Energy supply per capita (Gigajoules)	215	224	223 [o]
Tourist/visitor arrivals at national borders (000) [u]	8 798	13 232	967 [c]
Important sites for terrestrial biodiversity protected (%)	33.8	36.4	37.6 [b]
Net Official Development Assist. disbursed (% of GNI) [v]	1.17	0.89	0.81 [c]

a Projected estimate (medium fertility variant). b 2022. c 2021. d Refers to Seoul Special City. e 2019. f Data compiled in accordance with the System of National Accounts 1968 (1968 SNA). g Excludes irrigation canals and landscaping care. h Data classified according to ISIC Rev. 4. i Excludes publishing activities, recycling. Includes irrigation canals. j Estimate. k Calculated by the UN Statistics Division from national indices. l Data refers to a 5-year period preceding the reference year. m Including refugees. n Refers to foreign citizens. o Data as at the end of December. p Data is as of end-2021. q Data are as at 1 January of reporting year. r Data are as at 1 January of reporting year. s Population aged 3 years and over. t Population aged 16 to 74 years. u Including nationals residing abroad and crew members. v Development Assistance Committee member (OECD).

Republic of Moldova

Region	Eastern Europe	UN membership date	02 March 1992
Population (000, 2023)	3 273[a,b,c]	Surface area (km2)	33 847[d]
Pop. density (per km2, 2023)	99.5[a,b,c]	Sex ratio (m per 100 f)	90.9[a,b,c]
Capital city	Chisinau	National currency	Moldovan Leu (MDL)
Capital city pop. (000, 2023)	504.3[e]	Exchange rate (per US$)	19.2[c]

Economic indicators

	2010	2015	2023
GDP: Gross domestic product (million current US$)	6 975	7 745	13 680[d]
GDP growth rate (annual %, const. 2015 prices)	7.1	- 0.3	13.9[d]
GDP per capita (current US$)	1 896.3	2 363.2	4 468.4[d]
Economy: Agriculture (% of Gross Value Added)[f,g]	13.0	13.2	12.1[d]
Economy: Industry (% of Gross Value Added)[g,h]	23.7	26.0	24.0[d]
Economy: Services and other activity (% of GVA)[g]	63.3	60.8	63.9[d]
Employment in agriculture (% of employed)	27.5	34.2	37.6[i,d]
Employment in industry (% of employed)	18.7	17.1	16.5[i,d]
Employment in services & other sectors (% employed)	53.8	48.7	45.9[i,d]
Unemployment rate (% of labour force)	7.4	4.7	2.3[i]
Labour force participation rate (female/male pop. %)	38.6 / 45.0	41.2 / 48.2	38.4 / 46.3[i]
CPI: Consumer Price Index (2010=100)[j,k]	100	136	234[c]
Agricultural production index (2014-2016=100)	89	91	125[d]
International trade: exports (million current US$)	1 541	1 967	4 335[c]
International trade: imports (million current US$)	3 855	3 987	9 219[c]
International trade: balance (million current US$)	- 2 314	- 2 020	- 4 884[c]
Balance of payments, current account (million US$)	- 481	- 463	- 2 275[c]

Major trading partners

					2022
Export partners (% of exports)	Romania	28.6[i]	Ukraine 16.6	Italy	7.6
Import partners (% of imports)	Romania	17.9	Russian Federation 12.4	China	10.3

Social indicators

	2010	2015	2023
Population growth rate (average annual %)[a]	- 2.2	- 1.7	13.7[b,c]
Urban population (% of total population)[a]	42.6	42.5	42.7[e]
Urban population growth rate (average annual %)[a,l]	- 0.4	- 0.2	...
Fertility rate, total (live births per woman)[a]	1.7	1.9	1.8[b,c]
Life expectancy at birth (females/males, years)[a]	73.8 / 65.0	73.8 / 64.8	73.3 / 64.2[b,c]
Population age distribution (0-14/60+ years old, %)[a]	18.0 / 15.1	18.2 / 17.7	19.3 / 19.4[b,c]
International migrant stock (000/% of total pop.)[a]	129.5 / 3.2	106.4 / 2.6	104.4 / 2.6[m]
Refugees and others of concern to the UNHCR (000)	2.3[n]	6.8	89.3[c]
Infant mortality rate (per 1 000 live births)[a]	14.6	13.4	12.4[b,c]
Health: Current expenditure (% of GDP)	10.1	8.6	6.8[m]
Health: Physicians (per 1 000 pop.)	2.6	3.1	4.1[m]
Education: Government expenditure (% of GDP)	7.6	5.8	5.8[d]
Education: Primary gross enrol. ratio (f/m per 100 pop.)[i]	... / ...	105.1 / 106.2	107.2 / 108.4[d]
Education: Lowr. sec. gross enrol. ratio (f/m per 100 pop.)[i]	... / ...	105.9 / 105.8	104.6 / 105.8[d]
Education: Upr. sec. gross enrol. ratio (f/m per 100 pop.)[i]	... / ...	105.7 / 101.2	82.6 / 82.3[d]
Intentional homicide rate (per 100 000 pop.)	7.2	5.8	3.0[m]
Seats held by women in the National Parliament (%)	23.8	20.8	38.6[o]

Environment and infrastructure indicators

	2010	2015	2023
Individuals using the Internet (per 100 inhabitants)[i]	29.7	43.1	61.3[d]
Research & Development expenditure (% of GDP)	0.4	0.3	0.2[d]
Threatened species (number)	27	29	36[c]
Forested area (% of land area)	11.4	11.8	11.8[m]
CO2 emission estimates (million tons/tons per capita)	8.2 / 2.8	7.9 / 2.7	9.2 / 3.1[d,m]
Energy production, primary (Petajoules)[p]	8	28	29[m]
Energy supply per capita (Gigajoules)[p]	25	33	37[m]
Tourist/visitor arrivals at national borders (000)[k,q]	64	94	69[d]
Important sites for terrestrial biodiversity protected (%)	62.2	71.9	78.4[c]
Pop. using safely managed sanitation (urban/rural %)	76.4 / ...	79.8 / ...	84.6 / ...[c]
Net Official Development Assist. received (% of GNI)	6.32	3.82	4.24[d]

a Including the Transnistria region. b Projected estimate (medium fertility variant). c 2022. d 2021. e 2019. f Excludes irrigation canals and landscaping care. g Data classified according to ISIC Rev. 4. h Excludes publishing activities, recycling. Includes irrigation canals. i Estimate. j Data refer to 8 cities only. k Excluding the left side of the river Nistru and the municipality of Bender. l Data refers to a 5-year period preceding the reference year. m 2020. n Data as at the end of December. o Data are as at 1 January of reporting year. p Data exclude Transnistria and the municipality of Bender. q Non-resident tourists staying in all types of accommodation establishments.

Réunion

Region	Eastern Africa	Population (000, 2023)	974[a,b,c]
Surface area (km2)	2 510[d]	Pop. density (per km2, 2023)	389.6[a,b,c]
Sex ratio (m per 100 f)	93.2[a,b,c]	Capital city	Saint-Denis
National currency	Euro (EUR)	Capital city pop. (000, 2023)	147.2[e]
Exchange rate (per US$)	0.9[c]		

Economic indicators	2010	2015	2023
Employment in agriculture (% of employed)[f]	4.2[g]	4.3[h,i]	...
Employment in industry (% of employed)[f]	14.1[g]	12.7[h,i]	...
Employment in services & other sectors (% employed)[f]	67.1[g]	81.7[h,i]	...
Unemployment rate (% of labour force)[f]	28.9	28.9[h,i]	...
Labour force participation rate (female/male pop. %)	45.3 / 59.9[f]	49.1 / 61.3[f,h,i]	... / ...
CPI: Consumer Price Index (2010=100)[k]	100	105	113[c]

Social indicators	2010	2015	2023
Population growth rate (average annual %)[b]	0.7	0.5	0.8[a,c]
Urban population (% of total population)	98.5	99.3	99.6[l]
Urban population growth rate (average annual %)[m]	1.4	0.9	...
Fertility rate, total (live births per woman)[b]	2.4	2.5	2.2[a,c]
Life expectancy at birth (females/males, years)[b]	83.4 / 76.3	84.3 / 78.1	85.4 / 79.7[a,c]
Population age distribution (0-14/60+ years old, %)[b]	26.4 / 12.2	25.0 / 14.8	22.8 / 18.8[a,c]
International migrant stock (000/% of total pop.)	123.0 / 14.8	127.2 / 14.7	131.8 / 14.7[n]
Infant mortality rate (per 1 000 live births)[b]	6.5	5.6	4.7[a,c]
Intentional homicide rate (per 100 000 pop.)	1.7[o]	...	...

Environment and infrastructure indicators	2010	2015	2023
Individuals using the Internet (per 100 inhabitants)	36.3[p,o]	...	...
Threatened species (number)	104	126	158[c]
Forested area (% of land area)	37.6	38.3	39.2[n]
Energy production, primary (Petajoules)	8[q]	...	...
Energy supply per capita (Gigajoules)	65[q]	...	...
Tourist/visitor arrivals at national borders (000)[r]	420	426	251[d]
Important sites for terrestrial biodiversity protected (%)	45.2	45.2	46.3[c]

a Projected estimate (medium fertility variant). b For statistical purposes, the data for France do not include this area. c 2022. d 2021. e 2018. f Excluding the institutional population. g Population aged 15 to 64 years. h Break in the time series. i 2012. j 2013. k Calculated by the UN Statistics Division from national indices. l 2019. m Data refers to a 5-year period preceding the reference year. n 2020. o 2009. p Estimate. q Data after 2010 are included in France. r Arrivals by air only.

Romania

Region	Eastern Europe	UN membership date	14 December 1955
Population (000, 2023)	19 659[a,b]	Surface area (km2)	238 391[c]
Pop. density (per km2, 2023)	85.4[a,b]	Sex ratio (m per 100 f)	93.7[a,b]
Capital city	Bucharest	National currency	Romanian Leu (RON)
Capital city pop. (000, 2023)	1 812.3[d]	Exchange rate (per US$)	4.6[b]

Economic indicators

Economic indicators	2010	2015	2023
GDP: Gross domestic product (million current US$)	170 029	177 884	284 086[c]
GDP growth rate (annual %, const. 2015 prices)	- 3.9	3.2	5.1[c]
GDP per capita (current US$)	8 361.3	8 936.2	14 697.8[c]
Economy: Agriculture (% of Gross Value Added)[e,f]	5.8	5.0	4.8[c]
Economy: Industry (% of Gross Value Added)[e,g]	42.8	35.1	30.8[c]
Economy: Services and other activity (% of GVA)[e]	51.4	59.9	64.4[c]
Employment in agriculture (% of employed)	31.0	25.6	18.6[h,c]
Employment in industry (% of employed)	28.3	28.5	30.4[c]
Employment in services & other sectors (% employed)	40.7	46.0	51.0[c]
Unemployment rate (% of labour force)	7.0	6.8	5.3[h]
Labour force participation rate (female/male pop. %)	46.2 / 64.3	45.3 / 64.6	44.2 / 64.6[h]
CPI: Consumer Price Index (2010=100)	100[i]	114[i]	152[i,b]
Agricultural production index (2014-2016=100)	93	96	106[c]
International trade: exports (million current US$)	49 413	60 605	96 830[b]
International trade: imports (million current US$)	62 007	69 858	132 700[b]
International trade: balance (million current US$)	- 12 593	- 9 253	- 35 870[b]
Balance of payments, current account (million US$)	- 8 478	- 1 396	- 27 979[b]

Major trading partners

Major trading partners						2022
Export partners (% of exports)	Germany	19.8	Italy	10.1	Hungary	7.3
Import partners (% of imports)	Germany	17.8	Italy	8.2	Bulgaria	7.1

Social indicators

Social indicators	2010	2015	2023
Population growth rate (average annual %)	- 0.7	- 0.5	4.0[a,b]
Urban population (% of total population)	53.8	53.9	54.1[d]
Urban population growth rate (average annual %)[k]	- 0.7	- 0.5	...
Fertility rate, total (live births per woman)	1.6	1.6	1.7[a,b]
Life expectancy at birth (females/males, years)	77.7 / 70.4	78.2 / 71.4	77.6 / 70.7[a,b]
Population age distribution (0-14/60+ years old, %)	15.8 / 21.3	15.7 / 23.5	15.9 / 24.5[a,b]
International migrant stock (000/% of total pop.)	177.2 / 0.9	281.0 / 1.4	705.3 / 3.7[l]
Refugees and others of concern to the UNHCR (000)	1.7[m]	2.9	89.2[b]
Infant mortality rate (per 1 000 live births)	10.3	7.9	5.4[a,b]
Health: Current expenditure (% of GDP)	5.8	4.9	6.3[n,l]
Health: Physicians (per 1 000 pop.)	2.5	2.6[o]	3.0[p]
Education: Government expenditure (% of GDP)	3.4	3.1	3.6[d]
Education: Primary gross enrol. ratio (f/m per 100 pop.)	99.1 / 100.8	88.5 / 89.8	87.4 / 88.2[l]
Education: Lowr. sec. gross enrol. ratio (f/m per 100 pop.)	97.4 / 98.5	95.0 / 97.0	82.9 / 84.4[l]
Education: Upr. sec. gross enrol. ratio (f/m per 100 pop.)	97.1 / 97.7	91.0 / 89.1	92.1 / 89.6[l]
Intentional homicide rate (per 100 000 pop.)	1.3	1.7	1.3[c]
Seats held by women in the National Parliament (%)	11.4	13.7	19.1[q]

Environment and infrastructure indicators

Environment and infrastructure indicators	2010	2015	2023
Individuals using the Internet (per 100 inhabitants)	39.9[r]	55.8[s]	83.6[r,c]
Research & Development expenditure (% of GDP)	0.4	0.5	0.5[l]
Threatened species (number)	64	85	170[b]
Forested area (% of land area)	28.3	30.0	30.1[l]
CO2 emission estimates (million tons/tons per capita)	76.7 / 3.7	71.7 / 3.5	73.6 / 3.4[c,l]
Energy production, primary (Petajoules)	1 155	1 116	941[l]
Energy supply per capita (Gigajoules)	72	67	70[l]
Tourist/visitor arrivals at national borders (000)	7 498	9 331	6 789[c]
Important sites for terrestrial biodiversity protected (%)	65.0	75.9	76.0[b]
Pop. using safely managed drinking water (urban/rural, %)	95.0 / 66.7	95.0 / 66.7	95.0 / 66.7[b]
Net Official Development Assist. disbursed (% of GNI)	...	0.07[o]	0.15[c]

a Projected estimate (medium fertility variant). **b** 2022. **c** 2021. **d** 2019. **e** Data classified according to ISIC Rev. 4. **f** Excludes irrigation canals and landscaping care. **g** Excludes publishing activities, recycling. Includes irrigation canals. **h** Estimate. **i** Break in the time series. **j** Calculated by the UN Statistics Division from national indices. **k** Data refers to a 5-year period preceding the reference year. **l** 2020. **m** Data as at the end of December. **n** Beginning with 2016, the legislative norms in the insurance field changed in order to comply with Solvency II EU Directive. As a result, the data reported by health services and providers showed a increase in insurance benefits sum. **o** 2013. **p** 2017. **q** Data are as at 1 January of reporting year. **r** Population aged 16 to 74 years. **s** Users in the last 3 months.

Russian Federation

Region	Eastern Europe	UN membership date	24 October 1945
Population (000, 2023)	144 713[a,b]	Surface area (km2)	17 098 246[c]
Pop. density (per km2, 2023)	8.8[a,b]	Sex ratio (m per 100 f)	86.7[a,b]
Capital city	Moscow	National currency	Russian Ruble (RUB)
Capital city pop. (000, 2023)	12 476.2[d]	Exchange rate (per US$)	70.3[b]

Economic indicators

	2010	2015	2023
GDP: Gross domestic product (million current US$)	1 539 845	1 363 482	1 778 782[c]
GDP growth rate (annual %, const. 2015 prices)	4.5	- 2.0	4.7[c]
GDP per capita (current US$)	10 749.9	9 424.9	12 258.8[c]
Economy: Agriculture (% of Gross Value Added)[e]	3.8	4.3	4.2[c]
Economy: Industry (% of Gross Value Added)[e]	34.8	33.1	36.9[c]
Economy: Services and other activity (% of GVA)[e]	61.4	62.6	58.9[c]
Employment in agriculture (% of employed)	7.7	6.7	5.8[f,c]
Employment in industry (% of employed)	27.8	27.3	26.9[f,c]
Employment in services & other sectors (% employed)	64.4	66.0	67.3[f,c]
Unemployment rate (% of labour force)	7.4	5.6	4.7[c]
Labour force participation rate (female/male pop. %)	56.0 / 70.6[f]	55.6 / 71.3[f]	55.3 / 70.4[c]
CPI: Consumer Price Index (2010=100)	100	152	227[b]
Agricultural production index (2014-2016=100)	74	100	112[b]
International trade: exports (million current US$)[g]	397 068	343 908	572 780[f,b]
International trade: imports (million current US$)[g]	228 912	182 782	200 918[f,b]
International trade: balance (million current US$)[g]	168 156	161 126	371 862[f,b]
Balance of payments, current account (million US$)	67 452	67 777	233 018[b]

Major trading partners

							2022
Export partners (% of exports)[g,f]	China	14.0	Netherlands	8.6	Germany	6.0
Import partners (% of imports)[g,f]	China	24.8	Germany	9.3	United States	5.9

Social indicators

	2010	2015	2023
Population growth rate (average annual %)	~0.0	0.3	~-0.0[a,b]
Urban population (% of total population)	73.7	74.0	74.6[d]
Urban population growth rate (average annual %)[h]	~-0.0	0.2	...
Fertility rate, total (live births per woman)	1.6	1.8	1.5[a,b]
Life expectancy at birth (females/males, years)	75.3 / 63.5	77.4 / 66.6	75.7 / 64.7[a,b]
Population age distribution (0-14/60+ years old, %)	15.2 / 18.1	16.9 / 20.0	17.7 / 22.8[a,b]
International migrant stock (000/% of total pop.)	11 194.7 / 7.8	11 643.3 / 8.0	11 636.9 / 8.0[i]
Refugees and others of concern to the UNHCR (000)	132.6[j]	431.2	1 515.2[b]
Infant mortality rate (per 1 000 live births)	7.9	6.0	4.0[a,b]
Health: Current expenditure (% of GDP)	5.0	5.3	7.6[i]
Health: Physicians (per 1 000 pop.)	5.0	3.9	3.8[i]
Education: Government expenditure (% of GDP)	3.8	3.8	3.5[d]
Education: Primary gross enrol. ratio (f/m per 100 pop.)	99.6 / 99.1[k]	99.5 / 98.7	103.7 / 104.7[d]
Education: Lowr. sec. gross enrol. ratio (f/m per 100 pop.)	87.1 / 85.2[k]	99.7 / 98.7	100.6 / 101.4[d]
Education: Upr. sec. gross enrol. ratio (f/m per 100 pop.)	78.3 / 85.9[k]	104.2 / 115.3	106.5 / 114.9[d]
Intentional homicide rate (per 100 000 pop.)	11.7	11.5	6.8[c]
Seats held by women in the National Parliament (%)	14.0	13.6	16.4[l]

Environment and infrastructure indicators

	2010	2015	2023
Individuals using the Internet (per 100 inhabitants)	49.0[m]	70.1[n,o,p]	88.2[c]
Research & Development expenditure (% of GDP)	1.1	1.1	1.1[i]
Threatened species (number)	126	217	316[b]
Forested area (% of land area)	49.8	49.8	49.8[i]
CO2 emission estimates (million tons/tons per capita)	1 538.7 / 10.7	1 543.5 / 10.6	1 713.4 / 10.8[c,i]
Energy production, primary (Petajoules)	53 679	56 024	60 041[i]
Energy supply per capita (Gigajoules)	202	200	216[i]
Tourist/visitor arrivals at national borders (000)	22 281	33 729	6 359[i]
Important sites for terrestrial biodiversity protected (%)	22.8	24.6	25.5[b]
Pop. using safely managed sanitation (urban/rural %)	62.4 / ...	63.3 / ...	64.2 / ...[b]

a Projected estimate (medium fertility variant). b 2022. c 2021. d 2019. e Data classified according to ISIC Rev. 4. f Estimate. g Russian data provided by the Russian Federation. Includes statistical data for the Autonomous Republic of Crimea and the city of Sevastopol, Ukraine, temporarily occupied by the Russian Federation. h Data refers to a 5-year period preceding the reference year. i 2020. j Data as at the end of December. k 2009. l Data are as at 1 January of reporting year. m Population aged 16 to 74 years. n Break in the time series. o Population aged 15 to 72 years. p Users in the last 3 months.

Rwanda

Region	Eastern Africa	UN membership date	18 September 1962
Population (000, 2023)	13 777 a,b	Surface area (km2)	26 338 c
Pop. density (per km2, 2023)	569.0 a,b	Sex ratio (m per 100 f)	95.8 a,b
Capital city	Kigali	National currency	Rwanda Franc (RWF)
Capital city pop. (000, 2023)	1 094.8 d	Exchange rate (per US$)	1 070.7 b

Economic indicators

	2010	2015	2023
GDP: Gross domestic product (million current US$)	6 120	8 526	11 070 c
GDP growth rate (annual %, const. 2015 prices)	7.3	8.9	10.9 c
GDP per capita (current US$)	593.7	732.3	822.3 c
Economy: Agriculture (% of Gross Value Added) e,f	26.9	26.3	26.1 c
Economy: Industry (% of Gross Value Added) f,g	18.0	19.1	22.1 c
Economy: Services and other activity (% of GVA) f	55.1	54.5	51.8 c
Employment in agriculture (% of employed) h	79.3	65.6	54.7 c
Employment in industry (% of employed) h	5.7	9.5	18.7 c
Employment in services & other sectors (% employed) h	15.0	24.9	26.6 c
Unemployment rate (% of labour force) h	11.9	11.8	12.7
Labour force participation rate (female/male pop. %) h	54.3 / 68.4	54.6 / 67.3	47.8 / 60.9
CPI: Consumer Price Index (2010=100) i,j	100	122	174 b
Agricultural production index (2014-2016=100)	106	101	129 c
International trade: exports (million current US$)	242	594	2 019 b
International trade: imports (million current US$)	1 405	2 370	5 125 b
International trade: balance (million current US$)	- 1 163	- 1 777	- 3 105 b
Balance of payments, current account (million US$)	- 399	- 1 084	- 1 306 b

Major trading partners

					2022
Export partners (% of exports)	Dem. Rep. of Congo	38.0	United Arab Emirates	29.2	China 4.8
Import partners (% of imports)	China	21.0	United Rep. Tanzania	11.1	Kenya 9.3

Social indicators

	2010	2015	2023
Population growth rate (average annual %)	2.6	2.4	2.3 a,b
Urban population (% of total population)	16.9	17.0	17.3 d
Urban population growth rate (average annual %) k	2.6	2.6	...
Fertility rate, total (live births per woman)	4.5	4.1	3.7 a,b
Life expectancy at birth (females/males, years)	64.2 / 60.7	67.2 / 63.2	69.2 / 64.8 a,b
Population age distribution (0-14/60+ years old, %)	42.2 / 4.6	41.2 / 4.8	38.5 / 5.2 a,b
International migrant stock (000/% of total pop.) l	426.9 / 4.3	514.6 / 4.5	513.9 / 4.0 m
Refugees and others of concern to the UNHCR (000)	55.7 n	135.6	138.6 b
Infant mortality rate (per 1 000 live births)	44.9	34.8	28.3 a,b
Health: Current expenditure (% of GDP) o	8.1	6.7	7.3 m
Health: Physicians (per 1 000 pop.)	...	0.1	0.1 d
Education: Government expenditure (% of GDP)	4.6	3.6 h	4.0 b
Education: Primary gross enrol. ratio (f/m per 100 pop.)	150.1 / 146.4	140.6 / 138.7	140.3 / 141.1 c
Education: Lowr. sec. gross enrol. ratio (f/m per 100 pop.)	44.1 / 41.8	46.2 / 40.4	63.3 / 54.1 c
Education: Upr. sec. gross enrol. ratio (f/m per 100 pop.)	18.4 / 20.6	32.1 / 31.9	33.7 / 30.7 c
Intentional homicide rate (per 100 000 pop.)	2.8	2.5	3.6 m
Seats held by women in the National Parliament (%)	56.2	63.8	61.2 p

Environment and infrastructure indicators

	2010	2015	2023
Individuals using the Internet (per 100 inhabitants)	8.0	12.5 h	30.5 h,c
Research & Development expenditure (% of GDP)	...	...	0.8 d
Threatened species (number)	55	61	195 b
Forested area (% of land area)	10.7	10.9	11.2 m
CO2 emission estimates (million tons/tons per capita)	1.4 / 0.1	1.8 / 0.1	2.1 / 0.1 m
Energy production, primary (Petajoules)	76	86 h	89 h,m
Energy supply per capita (Gigajoules)	8	8 h	8 h,m
Tourist/visitor arrivals at national borders (000) q	605	1 217	480 c
Important sites for terrestrial biodiversity protected (%)	47.1	51.2	51.2 b
Pop. using safely managed drinking water (urban/rural, %)	37.0 / ...	44.6 / ...	54.6 / ... b
Pop. using safely managed sanitation (urban/rural %)	... / 43.8	... / 50.2	... / 57.9 b
Net Official Development Assist. received (% of GNI)	17.02	13.00	12.27 c

a Projected estimate (medium fertility variant). b 2022. c 2021. d 2019. e Excludes irrigation canals and landscaping care. f Data classified according to ISIC Rev. 4. g Excludes publishing activities, recycling. Includes irrigation canals. h Estimate. i Calculated by the UN Statistics Division from national indices. j For urban population only. k Data refers to a 5-year period preceding the reference year. l Including refugees. m 2020. n Data as at the end of December. o Data based on calendar year (January 1 to December 31). p Data are as at 1 January of reporting year. q January-November.

Saint Helena

Region	Western Africa	Population (000, 2023)	5 [a,b,c]
Surface area (km2)	309 [d,e,f]	Pop. density (per km2, 2023)	13.8 [a,b,c]
Sex ratio (m per 100 f)	93.4 [a,b,c]	Capital city	Jamestown
National currency	Saint Helena Pound (SHP)	Capital city pop. (000, 2023)	0.6 [g]
Exchange rate (per US$)	0.8 [c]		

Economic indicators	2010	2015	2023
Employment in agriculture (% of employed)	7.3 [h,i,j]	...	...
Employment in industry (% of employed)	20.0 [h,i,j]	...	...
Employment in services & other sectors (% employed)	72.7 [h,i,j]	...	...
International trade: exports (million current US$) [k]	~0	~0	~0 [f]
International trade: imports (million current US$) [k]	20	41	93 [f]
International trade: balance (million current US$) [k]	- 20	- 40	- 93 [f]

Major trading partners						2022
Export partners (% of exports)	United States	...	Japan	...	Greece	...
Import partners (% of imports)	United Kingdom	...	United States	...	South Africa	...

Social indicators	2010	2015	2023
Population growth rate (average annual %) [a]	0.7	0.7	- 1.0 [b,c]
Urban population (% of total population) [d]	39.5	39.5	39.9 [l]
Urban population growth rate (average annual %) [d,m]	- 0.7	- 0.7	
Fertility rate, total (live births per woman) [a]	1.6	1.6	1.6 [b,c]
Life expectancy at birth (females/males, years) [a]	80.3 / 73.4	78.6 / 72.6	80.9 / 74.4 [b,c]
Population age distribution (0-14/60+ years old, %) [a]	14.3 / 26.8	13.6 / 27.9	14.1 / 38.2 [b,c]
International migrant stock (000/% of total pop.) [a,n]	0.2 / 4.8	0.4 / 6.4	0.4 / 7.2 [o]
Infant mortality rate (per 1 000 live births) [a]	12.8	14.6	11.1 [b,c]
Intentional homicide rate (per 100 000 pop.)	0.0 [p]	...	...

Environment and infrastructure indicators	2010	2015	2023
Individuals using the Internet (per 100 inhabitants)	24.9	37.6 [k,q]	...
Threatened species (number) [d]	60	80	189 [c]
Forested area (% of land area)	5.1	5.1	5.1 [o]
Energy production, primary (Petajoules)	0	0	0 [o]
Energy supply per capita (Gigajoules)	30	29	45 [k,o]
Important sites for terrestrial biodiversity protected (%)	15.4	38.5	38.5 [c]

a Including Ascension and Tristan da Cunha. For statistical purposes, the data for United Kingdom do not include this area. **b** Projected estimate (medium fertility variant). **c** 2022. **d** Including Ascension and Tristan da Cunha. **e** St. Helena Island has no substantial natural inland waters however there are 15 reservoirs and similar open water storage features on island. **f** 2021. **g** 2018. **h** Data classified according to ISIC Rev. 3. **i** Population aged 15 to 69 years. **j** 2008. **k** Estimate. **l** 2019. **m** Data refers to a 5-year period preceding the reference year. **n** Refers to foreign citizens. **o** 2020. **p** 2009. **q** 2012.

Saint Kitts and Nevis

Region	Caribbean	UN membership date	23 September 1983
Population (000, 2023)	48 a,b	Surface area (km2)	261 c
Pop. density (per km2, 2023)	183.3 a,b	Sex ratio (m per 100 f)	93.4 a,b
Capital city	Basseterre	National currency	E. Caribbean Dollar (XCD) d
Capital city pop. (000, 2023)	14.4 e	Exchange rate (per US$)	2.7 b

Economic indicators

	2010	2015	2023
GDP: Gross domestic product (million current US$)	779	957	861 c
GDP growth rate (annual %, const. 2015 prices)	- 0.1	0.7	- 0.9 c
GDP per capita (current US$)	16 427.6	20 025.9	18 082.7 c
Economy: Agriculture (% of Gross Value Added)	1.4	1.0	1.6 c
Economy: Industry (% of Gross Value Added)	25.2	26.0	25.5 c
Economy: Services and other activity (% of GVA)	73.4	73.0	72.9 c
CPI: Consumer Price Index (2010=100) f	100	106	107 b
Agricultural production index (2014-2016=100)	105	100	99 c
International trade: exports (million current US$)	32	32	26 g,b
International trade: imports (million current US$)	270	297	325 g,b
International trade: balance (million current US$)	- 238	- 265	- 300 g,b
Balance of payments, current account (million US$)	- 139	- 80	- 50 c

Major trading partners
2022

Export partners (% of exports) g	United States	58.3	India	5.6	Saint Lucia	4.9
Import partners (% of imports) g	United States	46.0	Trinidad and Tobago	10.9	Italy	7.5

Social indicators

	2010	2015	2023
Population growth rate (average annual %)	0.2	-0.0	0.2 a,b
Urban population (% of total population)	31.3	30.8	30.8 h
Urban population growth rate (average annual %) i	0.7	0.8	...
Fertility rate, total (live births per woman)	1.8	1.6	1.5 a,b
Life expectancy at birth (females/males, years)	74.4 / 68.4	74.9 / 67.1	75.7 / 68.7 a,b
Population age distribution (0-14/60+ years old, %)	23.7 / 10.3	21.4 / 11.8	19.5 / 16.0 a,b
International migrant stock (000/% of total pop.) j	7.2 / 14.8	7.4 / 14.5	7.7 / 14.5 k
Refugees and others of concern to the UNHCR (000)	...	~0.0	0.1 b
Infant mortality rate (per 1 000 live births)	12.8	14.6	7.8 a,b
Health: Current expenditure (% of GDP) g,l	5.2	5.1	5.4 k
Health: Physicians (per 1 000 pop.)	...	2.9	3.0 e
Education: Government expenditure (% of GDP)	4.2 m	2.5	2.8 c
Education: Primary gross enrol. ratio (f/m per 100 pop.)	110.6 / 116.5	107.9 / 108.7	107.9 / 113.8 c
Education: Lowr. sec. gross enrol. ratio (f/m per 100 pop.)	108.4 / 117.1 g	112.9 / 114.0	112.6 / 112.1 c
Education: Upr. sec. gross enrol. ratio (f/m per 100 pop.)	100.0 / 92.8 g	99.9 / 100.1	102.2 / 105.5 c
Intentional homicide rate (per 100 000 pop.)	44.3	37.7 n	29.4 c
Seats held by women in the National Parliament (%)	6.7	6.7	31.2 o

Environment and infrastructure indicators

	2010	2015	2023
Individuals using the Internet (per 100 inhabitants)	63.0	75.7 g	79.5 g,c
Threatened species (number)	36	51	88 b
Forested area (% of land area)	42.3	42.3	42.3 k
Energy production, primary (Petajoules)	0	0	0 k
Energy supply per capita (Gigajoules)	67	70 g	70 g,k
Tourist/visitor arrivals at national borders (000) p	98	118	20 c
Important sites for terrestrial biodiversity protected (%)	22.3	23.3	56.8 b
Net Official Development Assist. received (% of GNI)	1.57	3.64 q	...

a Projected estimate (medium fertility variant). b 2022. c 2021. d East Caribbean Dollar. e 2018. f Calculated by the UN Statistics Division from national indices. g Estimate. h 2019. i Data refers to a 5-year period preceding the reference year. j Including refugees. k 2020. l Data based on calendar year (January 1 to December 31). m 2007. n 2012. o Data are as at 1 January of reporting year. p Arrivals of non-resident tourists by air. q 2013.

Saint Lucia

Region	Caribbean	UN membership date	18 September 1979
Population (000, 2023)	180 [a,b]	Surface area (km2)	616 [c]
Pop. density (per km2, 2023)	292.0 [a,b]	Sex ratio (m per 100 f)	97.8 [a,b]
Capital city	Castries	National currency	E. Caribbean Dollar (XCD) [d]
Capital city pop. (000, 2023)	22.3 [e]	Exchange rate (per US$)	2.7 [b]

Economic indicators

	2010	2015	2023
GDP: Gross domestic product (million current US$)	1 487	1 810	1 765 [c]
GDP growth rate (annual %, const. 2015 prices)	0.5	0.1	6.6 [c]
GDP per capita (current US$)	8 697.1	10 306.0	9 824.1 [c]
Economy: Agriculture (% of Gross Value Added) [f,g]	3.0	2.5	2.2 [c]
Economy: Industry (% of Gross Value Added) [f,h]	13.5	12.7	12.9 [c]
Economy: Services and other activity (% of GVA) [f]	83.4	84.8	85.0 [c]
Employment in agriculture (% of employed)	12.6 [i]	11.0 [i]	10.5 [c]
Employment in industry (% of employed) [i]	19.2	16.9	14.8 [c]
Employment in services & other sectors (% of employed)	68.4 [i]	72.0 [i]	73.6 [c]
Unemployment rate (% of labour force) [i]	17.1	20.6	16.3
Labour force participation rate (female/male pop. %) [i]	60.9 / 72.8	64.0 / 75.7	65.4 / 73.9
CPI: Consumer Price Index (2010=100) [j]	100	111	119 [b]
Agricultural production index (2014-2016=100)	107	101	76 [c]
International trade: exports (million current US$)	215	181	79 [i,b]
International trade: imports (million current US$)	647	583	1 965 [i,b]
International trade: balance (million current US$)	- 432	- 403	- 1 886 [i,b]
Balance of payments, current account (million US$)	- 203	- 12	- 132 [c]

Major trading partners

						2022
Export partners (% of exports) [i]	United States	28.0	Trinidad and Tobago	12.0	United Kingdom	9.0
Import partners (% of imports) [i]	United States	39.8	Trinidad and Tobago	14.1	United Kingdom	6.4

Social indicators

	2010	2015	2023
Population growth rate (average annual %)	0.8	0.5	0.1 [a,b]
Urban population (% of total population)	18.4	18.5	18.8 [k]
Urban population growth rate (average annual %) [l]	- 3.4	0.6	...
Fertility rate, total (live births per woman)	1.5	1.5	1.4 [a,b]
Life expectancy at birth (females/males, years)	75.7 / 69.9	76.4 / 70.1	74.9 / 68.0 [a,b]
Population age distribution (0-14/60+ years old, %)	24.1 / 11.1	20.6 / 11.9	18.0 / 14.2 [a,b]
International migrant stock (000/% of total pop.) [m]	9.0 / 5.2	8.7 / 4.8	8.3 / 4.5 [n]
Refugees and others of concern to the UNHCR (000)	~0.0 [o]	0.1	~0.0 [n]
Infant mortality rate (per 1 000 live births)	16.5	14.6	11.9 [a,b]
Health: Current expenditure (% of GDP) [i,p]	5.0	4.6	6.7 [n]
Health: Physicians (per 1 000 pop.)	1.7	1.9 [q]	0.7 [r]
Education: Government expenditure (% of GDP)	3.5 [i]	3.9	4.9 [b]
Education: Primary gross enrol. ratio (f/m per 100 pop.)	98.0 / 103.2 [s]	99.5 / 102.8	102.4 / 99.9 [n]
Education: Lowr. sec. gross enrol. ratio (f/m per 100 pop.)	93.0 / 98.0	91.7 / 94.3	94.2 / 93.4 [n]
Education: Upr. sec. gross enrol. ratio (f/m per 100 pop.)	93.6 / 89.1	83.3 / 81.5	86.7 / 92.0 [n]
Intentional homicide rate (per 100 000 pop.)	25.7	15.9	39.0 [c]
Seats held by women in the National Parliament (%)	11.1	16.7	11.1 [t]

Environment and infrastructure indicators

	2010	2015	2023
Individuals using the Internet (per 100 inhabitants) [i]	32.5	57.3	78.1 [c]
Threatened species (number)	46	58	105 [b]
Forested area (% of land area)	34.0	34.0	34.0 [n]
Energy production, primary (Petajoules) [i]	1	1	1 [n]
Energy supply per capita (Gigajoules)	46	43	42 [i,n]
Tourist/visitor arrivals at national borders (000) [u]	306	345	199 [c]
Important sites for terrestrial biodiversity protected (%)	45.6	45.6	45.6 [b]
Net Official Development Assist. received (% of GNI)	2.84	0.83	5.76 [c]

a Projected estimate (medium fertility variant). b 2022. c 2021. d East Caribbean Dollar. e 2018. f Data classified according to ISIC Rev. 4. g Excludes irrigation canals and landscaping care. h Excludes publishing activities, recycling. Includes irrigation canals. i Estimate. j Calculated by the UN Statistics Division from national indices. k 2019. l Data refers to a 5-year period preceding the reference year. m Including refugees. n 2020. o Data as at the end of December. p Data refer to fiscal years beginning 1 April. q 2014. r 2017. s 2007. t Data are as at 1 January of reporting year. u Excluding nationals residing abroad.

Saint Pierre and Miquelon

Region	Northern America	Population (000, 2023)	6 [a,b,c]
Surface area (km2)	242 [d]	Pop. density (per km2, 2023)	25.5 [a,b,c]
Sex ratio (m per 100 f)	98.9 [a,b,c]	Capital city	Saint-Pierre
National currency	Euro (EUR)	Capital city pop. (000, 2023)	5.7 [e]
Exchange rate (per US$)	0.9 [c]		

Economic indicators	2010	2015	2023
International trade: exports (million current US$) [f]	137	533	1 587 [d]
International trade: imports (million current US$) [f]	747	2 259	5 008 [d]
International trade: balance (million current US$) [f]	- 610	- 1 726	- 3 421 [d]

Major trading partners						2022
Export partners (% of exports)	Canada	...	France	...	Ireland	...
Import partners (% of imports)	France	...	Canada	...	Netherlands	...

Social indicators	2010	2015	2023
Population growth rate (average annual %) [b]	0.0	- 0.2	- 0.3 [a,c]
Urban population (% of total population)	89.9	89.9	89.9 [g]
Urban population growth rate (average annual %) [h]	~0.0	0.1	...
Fertility rate, total (live births per woman) [b]	1.8	1.6	1.6 [a,c]
Life expectancy at birth (females/males, years) [b]	81.0 / 72.9	81.2 / 73.1	81.7 / 74.0 [a,c]
Population age distribution (0-14/60+ years old, %) [b]	17.9 / 20.2	17.6 / 23.1	16.9 / 23.8 [a,c]
International migrant stock (000/% of total pop.)	1.0 / 16.0	1.0 / 16.5	1.0 / 17.2 [i]
Infant mortality rate (per 1 000 live births) [b]	9.2	8.8	7.8 [a,c]
Intentional homicide rate (per 100 000 pop.)	16.5 [j]	...	...

Environment and infrastructure indicators	2010	2015	2023
Threatened species (number)	4	7	26 [c]
Forested area (% of land area)	6.3	5.8	5.3 [i]
Energy production, primary (Petajoules)	0	0	0 [i]
Energy supply per capita (Gigajoules) [f]	151	153	148 [i]
Important sites for terrestrial biodiversity protected (%)	0.8	1.6	1.6 [c]

a Projected estimate (medium fertility variant). **b** For statistical purposes, the data for France do not include this area. **c** 2022. **d** 2021. **e** 2018. **f** Estimate. **g** 2019. **h** Data refers to a 5-year period preceding the reference year. **i** 2020. **j** 2009.

Saint Vincent & Grenadines

Region	Caribbean	UN membership date	16 September 1980
Population (000, 2023)	104[a,b]	Surface area (km2)	389[c]
Pop. density (per km2, 2023)	266.5[a,b]	Sex ratio (m per 100 f)	103.7[a,b]
Capital city	Kingstown	National currency	E. Caribbean Dollar (XCD)[d]
Capital city pop. (000, 2023)	26.6[e]	Exchange rate (per US$)	2.7[b]

Economic indicators

	2010	2015	2023
GDP: Gross domestic product (million current US$)	720	787	881[c]
GDP growth rate (annual %, const. 2015 prices)	- 4.5	2.8	0.5[c]
GDP per capita (current US$)	6 591.0	7 386.7	8 440.0[c]
Economy: Agriculture (% of Gross Value Added)[f]	7.3	7.3	7.7[c]
Economy: Industry (% of Gross Value Added)[g]	18.5	17.4	16.1[c]
Economy: Services and other activity (% of GVA)	74.3	75.3	76.2[c]
Employment in agriculture (% of employed)[h]	12.4	11.3	10.3[c]
Employment in industry (% of employed)[h]	20.7	20.3	20.7[c]
Employment in services & other sectors (% employed)[h]	66.9	68.8	68.9[c]
Unemployment rate (% of labour force)[h]	19.0	19.0	18.8
Labour force participation rate (female/male pop. %)[h]	53.2 / 75.7	53.9 / 75.5	54.9 / 74.3
CPI: Consumer Price Index (2010=100)[h]	100[i]	105	118[b]
Agricultural production index (2014-2016=100)	94	100	104[c]
International trade: exports (million current US$)	42	47	47[h,b]
International trade: imports (million current US$)	379	334	482[h,b]
International trade: balance (million current US$)	- 338	- 287	- 435[h,b]
Balance of payments, current account (million US$)	- 208	- 116	- 200[c]

Major trading partners

						2022
Export partners (% of exports)[h]	Barbados	16.5	Saint Lucia	16.3	United States	14.6
Import partners (% of imports)[h]	United States	46.8	Trinidad and Tobago	9.4	China	6.6

Social indicators

	2010	2015	2023
Population growth rate (average annual %)	- 0.5	- 0.4	- 0.3[a,b]
Urban population (% of total population)	49.0	51.0	52.6[j]
Urban population growth rate (average annual %)[k]	0.9	0.8	...
Fertility rate, total (live births per woman)	2.1	2.1	1.8[a,b]
Life expectancy at birth (females/males, years)	77.6 / 72.2	77.3 / 72.0	71.7 / 66.7[a,b]
Population age distribution (0-14/60+ years old, %)	25.7 / 11.6	23.6 / 13.5	21.9 / 16.2[a,b]
International migrant stock (000/% of total pop.)[l]	4.6 / 4.2	4.6 / 4.2	4.7 / 4.3[m]
Refugees and others of concern to the UNHCR (000)	...	...	~0.0[b]
Infant mortality rate (per 1 000 live births)	16.8	14.3	12.5[a,b]
Health: Current expenditure (% of GDP)[h,n,o]	4.3	4.1	4.8[m]
Health: Physicians (per 1 000 pop.)	0.7	0.9[p]	...
Education: Government expenditure (% of GDP)	4.8	5.0	6.6[m]
Education: Primary gross enrol. ratio (f/m per 100 pop.)	106.2 / 111.9	109.7 / 110.7	111.6 / 114.0[m]
Education: Lowr. sec. gross enrol. ratio (f/m per 100 pop.)	116.1 / 121.3	117.3 / 125.2	112.7 / 120.1[e]
Education: Upr. sec. gross enrol. ratio (f/m per 100 pop.)	102.5 / 81.6	94.0 / 80.9	102.8 / 85.3[e]
Intentional homicide rate (per 100 000 pop.)	22.9	...	30.7[c]
Seats held by women in the National Parliament (%)	21.7	13.0	18.2[q]

Environment and infrastructure indicators

	2010	2015	2023
Individuals using the Internet (per 100 inhabitants)[h]	33.7	49.4	84.9[c]
Threatened species (number)	38	54	95[b]
Forested area (% of land area)	73.2	73.2	73.2[m]
Energy production, primary (Petajoules)	0	0	0[m]
Energy supply per capita (Gigajoules)	31	33	35[m]
Tourist/visitor arrivals at national borders (000)[r]	72	75	24[c]
Important sites for terrestrial biodiversity protected (%)	45.6	45.6	45.6[b]
Net Official Development Assist. received (% of GNI)	2.38	1.76	14.29[c]

a Projected estimate (medium fertility variant). **b** 2022. **c** 2021. **d** East Caribbean Dollar. **e** 2018. **f** Excludes irrigation canals and landscaping care. **g** Excludes publishing activities, recycling. Includes irrigation canals. **h** Estimate. **i** Break in the time series. **j** 2019. **k** Data refers to a 5-year period preceding the reference year. **l** Including refugees. **m** 2020. **n** Data based on calendar year (January 1 to December 31). **o** Estimates should be viewed with caution as these are derived from scarce data. **p** 2012. **q** Data are as at 1 January of reporting year. **r** Arrivals of non-resident tourists by air.

Samoa

Region	Polynesia	UN membership date	15 December 1976
Population (000, 2023)	222 [a,b]	Surface area (km2)	2 842 [c]
Pop. density (per km2, 2023)	78.6 [a,b]	Sex ratio (m per 100 f)	104.0 [a,b]
Capital city	Apia	National currency	Tala (WST)
Capital city pop. (000, 2023)	36.1 [d]	Exchange rate (per US$)	2.7 [b]

Economic indicators

	2010	2015	2023
GDP: Gross domestic product (million current US$)	699	826	857 [c]
GDP growth rate (annual %, const. 2015 prices)	1.6	6.1	- 2.3 [c]
GDP per capita (current US$)	3 589.3	4 055.4	3 918.7 [c]
Economy: Agriculture (% of Gross Value Added) [e,g]	9.3 [f]	9.2	10.2 [c]
Economy: Industry (% of Gross Value Added) [e]	16.9	16.2	12.8 [c]
Economy: Services and other activity (% of GVA) [e]	73.8	74.6	76.9 [c]
Employment in agriculture (% of employed) [h]	30.8	27.3	24.1 [c]
Employment in industry (% of employed) [h]	14.5	15.1	16.6 [c]
Employment in services & other sectors (% employed) [h]	54.5	57.6	59.5 [c]
Unemployment rate (% of labour force) [h]	5.7	8.8	9.9
Labour force participation rate (female/male pop. %) [h]	41.2 / 66.8	41.2 / 66.9	41.0 / 66.2
CPI: Consumer Price Index (2010=100) [h,i]	100	108	132 [b]
Agricultural production index (2014-2016=100)	119	91	84 [c]
International trade: exports (million current US$)	70	59	34 [h,b]
International trade: imports (million current US$)	310	371	459 [h,b]
International trade: balance (million current US$)	- 240	- 312	- 425 [h,b]
Balance of payments, current account (million US$)	- 62	- 13	- 78 [b]

Major trading partners

							2022
Export partners (% of exports) [h]	New Zealand	23.3	American Samoa	21.1	United States	18.6
Import partners (% of imports) [h]	New Zealand	23.2	Singapore	16.0	China	13.5

Social indicators

	2010	2015	2023
Population growth rate (average annual %)	0.8	0.9	1.5 [a,b]
Urban population (% of total population)	20.1	18.9	18.1 [j]
Urban population growth rate (average annual %) [k]	- 0.4	- 0.4	...
Fertility rate, total (live births per woman)	4.6	4.4	3.9 [a,b]
Life expectancy at birth (females/males, years)	75.0 / 69.7	75.2 / 70.1	75.3 / 70.1 [a,b]
Population age distribution (0-14/60+ years old, %)	39.0 / 6.8	38.4 / 7.2	37.6 / 8.1 [a,b]
International migrant stock (000/% of total pop.) [l]	5.1 / 2.8	4.3 / 2.2	4.0 / 2.0 [m]
Refugees and others of concern to the UNHCR (000)	...	...	~0.0 [m]
Infant mortality rate (per 1 000 live births)	16.3	15.7	15.1 [a,b]
Health: Current expenditure (% of GDP) [n]	5.3	5.8	5.3 [m]
Health: Physicians (per 1 000 pop.)	0.3	0.5 [o]	0.6 [m]
Education: Government expenditure (% of GDP)	5.1 [p]	4.9	4.8 [m]
Education: Primary gross enrol. ratio (f/m per 100 pop.)	109.9 / 111.5	106.4 / 106.4	122.3 / 121.8 [c]
Education: Lowr. sec. gross enrol. ratio (f/m per 100 pop.)	108.3 / 110.4	109.9 / 114.0	111.1 / 107.9 [c]
Education: Upr. sec. gross enrol. ratio (f/m per 100 pop.)	87.3 / 70.3	94.5 / 79.0	92.3 / 79.6 [q]
Intentional homicide rate (per 100 000 pop.)	8.2	3.0 [o]	6.2 [d]
Seats held by women in the National Parliament (%)	8.2	6.1	13.0 [r]

Environment and infrastructure indicators

	2010	2015	2023
Individuals using the Internet (per 100 inhabitants) [h]	7.0	25.4	78.2 [c]
Threatened species (number)	78	90	116 [b]
Forested area (% of land area)	58.8	58.0	58.2 [m]
Energy production, primary (Petajoules)	2	2	2 [h,m]
Energy supply per capita (Gigajoules)	22	25	24 [h,m]
Tourist/visitor arrivals at national borders (000)	122	128	3 [c]
Important sites for terrestrial biodiversity protected (%)	47.0	47.0	47.1 [b]
Pop. using safely managed drinking water (urban/rural, %)	85.5 / 54.9	88.6 / 55.4	90.2 / 56.2 [b]
Pop. using safely managed sanitation (urban/rural %)	42.9 / 50.7	40.1 / 48.4	36.7 / 44.3 [b]
Net Official Development Assist. received (% of GNI)	19.35	12.16	10.92 [c]

a Projected estimate (medium fertility variant). b 2022. c 2021. d 2018. e Data classified according to ISIC Rev. 4. f Includes taxes less subsidies on production and imports. g Excludes irrigation canals and landscaping care. h Estimate. i Excluding rent. j 2019. k Data refers to a 5-year period preceding the reference year. l Including refugees. m 2020. n Data refer to fiscal years beginning 1 July. o 2013. p 2008. q 2016. r Data are as at 1 January of reporting year.

San Marino

Region	Southern Europe
Population (000, 2023)	34 [a,b]
Pop. density (per km2, 2023)	551.8 [a,b]
Capital city	San Marino
Capital city pop. (000, 2023)	4.5 [d]

UN membership date	02 March 1992
Surface area (km2)	61 [c]
Sex ratio (m per 100 f)	94.8 [a,b]
National currency	Euro (EUR)
Exchange rate (per US$)	0.9 [b]

Economic indicators	2010	2015	2023
GDP: Gross domestic product (million current US$)	2 139	1 419	1 702 [c]
GDP growth rate (annual %, const. 2015 prices)	- 4.6	- 6.2	5.4 [c]
GDP per capita (current US$)	67 683.6	42 264.8	50 425.1 [c]
Economy: Agriculture (% of Gross Value Added) [e,f]	~0.0	~0.0	~0.0 [c]
Economy: Industry (% of Gross Value Added) [e,g,h,i]	36.1	35.1	39.5 [c]
Economy: Services and other activity (% of GVA) [e]	63.9	64.9	60.5 [c]
Employment in agriculture (% of employed)	0.3 [i]	...	...
Employment in industry (% of employed)	34.3 [i]	...	...
Employment in services & other sectors (% employed)	65.4 [i]	...	...
Unemployment rate (% of labour force)	4.4	6.6 [j,k,l]	...
CPI: Consumer Price Index (2010=100) [m]	...	108	122 [b]
Balance of payments, current account (million US$)	...	...	280 [c]

Social indicators	2010	2015	2023
Population growth rate (average annual %)	2.2	0.8	- 0.1 [a,b]
Urban population (% of total population)	95.7	96.7	97.4 [n]
Urban population growth rate (average annual %) [o]	1.5	1.4	...
Fertility rate, total (live births per woman)	1.5	1.2	1.1 [a,b]
Life expectancy at birth (females/males, years)	84.3 / 80.9	84.3 / 81.4	84.7 / 82.0 [a,b]
Population age distribution (0-14/60+ years old, %)	15.4 / 23.0	14.9 / 24.1	12.7 / 27.8 [a,b]
International migrant stock (000/% of total pop.) [p]	4.9 / 15.6	5.2 / 15.6	5.5 / 16.3 [q]
Infant mortality rate (per 1 000 live births)	3.0	2.8	2.4 [a,b]
Health: Current expenditure (% of GDP)	6.3	8.6 [r]	8.7 [r,q]
Health: Physicians (per 1 000 pop.)	...	6.0 [l]	...
Education: Government expenditure (% of GDP)	2.6	3.4	3.4 [q]
Education: Primary gross enrol. ratio (f/m per 100 pop.)	... / ...	... / ...	96.9 / 97.8 [s,c]
Education: Lowr. sec. gross enrol. ratio (f/m per 100 pop.)	... / ...	... / ...	96.0 / 88.7 [s,c]
Education: Upr. sec. gross enrol. ratio (f/m per 100 pop.)	... / ...	... / ...	33.6 / 45.4 [s,c]
Intentional homicide rate (per 100 000 pop.)	0.0	0.0 [t]	...
Seats held by women in the National Parliament (%)	16.7	16.7	33.3 [u]

Environment and infrastructure indicators	2010	2015	2023
Individuals using the Internet (per 100 inhabitants)	54.2 [v]	49.6 [t]	74.9 [s,c]
Threatened species (number)	0	1	5 [b]
Forested area (% of land area)	16.7	16.7	16.7 [q]
Tourist/visitor arrivals at national borders (000) [w]	120	54	94 [c]

a Projected estimate (medium fertility variant). b 2022. c 2021. d 2018. e Data classified according to ISIC Rev. 4. f Excludes irrigation canals and landscaping care. g Includes mining and quarrying. h Includes Electricity, gas and water supply. i Excludes publishing activities, recycling. Includes irrigation canals. j Break in the time series. k Population aged 14 years and over. l 2014. m Index base: December 2010=100. n 2019. o Data refers to a 5-year period preceding the reference year. p Refers to foreign citizens. q 2020. r Provisional data. s Estimate. t 2011. u Data are as at 1 January of reporting year. v 2009. w Including Italian visitors.

Sao Tome and Principe

Region	Middle Africa	UN membership date	16 September 1975
Population (000, 2023)	227 a,b	Surface area (km2)	964 c
Pop. density (per km2, 2023)	236.9 a,b	Sex ratio (m per 100 f)	99.5 a,b
Capital city	Sao Tome	National currency	Dobra (STN)
Capital city pop. (000, 2023)	80.1 d	Exchange rate (per US$)	21.7 c

Economic indicators

	2010	2015	2023
GDP: Gross domestic product (million current US$)	197	318	555 c
GDP growth rate (annual %, const. 2015 prices)	6.7	3.9	1.8 c
GDP per capita (current US$)	1 084.1	1 582.4	2 485.8 c
Economy: Agriculture (% of Gross Value Added)	11.8	12.2	12.7 c
Economy: Industry (% of Gross Value Added)	18.2	15.7	13.9 c
Economy: Services and other activity (% of GVA)	70.1	72.1	73.4 c
Employment in agriculture (% of employed) e	23.1	20.1	18.0 c
Employment in industry (% of employed) e	18.0	19.6	20.2 c
Employment in services & other sectors (% of employed) e	59.2	60.6	61.6 c
Unemployment rate (% of labour force) e	14.6	13.8	15.5
Labour force participation rate (female/male pop. %) e	37.6 / 71.7	37.5 / 71.6	38.0 / 69.9
CPI: Consumer Price Index (2010=100)	100	154	185 d
Agricultural production index (2014-2016=100)	103	90	104 c
International trade: exports (million current US$)	6	9	23 b
International trade: imports (million current US$)	112	142	196 b
International trade: balance (million current US$)	- 106	- 133	- 174 b
Balance of payments, current account (million US$)	- 88	- 69	- 95 c

Major trading partners

						2022
Export partners (% of exports)	Netherlands	38.6	Areas nes	22.1	Belgium	13.9
Import partners (% of imports)	Portugal	40.3	Angola	16.0	Togo	15.4

Social indicators

	2010	2015	2023
Population growth rate (average annual %)	2.2	1.8	2.0 a,b
Urban population (% of total population)	65.0	70.2	73.6 f
Urban population growth rate (average annual %) g	4.2	3.8	...
Fertility rate, total (live births per woman)	4.7	4.4	3.8 a,b
Life expectancy at birth (females/males, years)	67.8 / 62.9	70.2 / 64.6	71.9 / 66.1 a,b
Population age distribution (0-14/60+ years old, %)	42.1 / 5.1	42.3 / 5.2	39.5 / 5.9 a,b
International migrant stock (000/% of total pop.) h	2.7 / 1.5	2.4 / 1.2	2.1 / 1.0 i
Infant mortality rate (per 1 000 live births)	26.8	17.8	12.6 a,b
Health: Current expenditure (% of GDP) j	6.8	5.3	4.9 i
Health: Physicians (per 1 000 pop.)	...	0.3	0.5 f
Education: Government expenditure (% of GDP)	9.7	3.9	5.3 c
Education: Primary gross enrol. ratio (f/m per 100 pop.)	116.2 / 117.0	103.2 / 107.3	105.0 / 108.5 k
Education: Lowr. sec. gross enrol. ratio (f/m per 100 pop.)	73.5 / 68.8	106.2 / 96.8	111.1 / 100.1 k
Education: Upr. sec. gross enrol. ratio (f/m per 100 pop.)	17.8 / 22.6	64.3 / 56.4	78.2 / 63.0 k
Intentional homicide rate (per 100 000 pop.)	3.3	3.2 l	...
Seats held by women in the National Parliament (%)	7.3	18.2	14.6 m

Environment and infrastructure indicators

	2010	2015	2023
Individuals using the Internet (per 100 inhabitants)	18.8	25.8 e	51.2 e,c
Threatened species (number)	70	81	141 b
Forested area (% of land area)	60.5	57.3	54.1 i
Energy production, primary (Petajoules)	1	1	1 i
Energy supply per capita (Gigajoules)	14	15	14 e,i
Tourist/visitor arrivals at national borders (000)	8	26	15 c
Important sites for terrestrial biodiversity protected (%)	86.3	86.3	86.3 b
Pop. using safely managed drinking water (urban/rural, %)	36.2 / 21.0	38.3 / 22.3	40.3 / 23.8 b
Pop. using safely managed sanitation (urban/rural %)	25.5 / 18.6	29.7 / 24.2	34.8 / 31.5 b
Net Official Development Assist. received (% of GNI)	25.48	15.55	13.07 c

a Projected estimate (medium fertility variant). b 2022. c 2021. d 2018. e Estimate. f 2019. g Data refers to a 5-year period preceding the reference year. h Refers to foreign citizens. i 2020. j Data based on calendar year (January 1 to December 31). k 2017. l 2011. m Data are as at 1 January of reporting year.

Saudi Arabia

Region	Western Asia	
Population (000, 2023)	36 409[a,b]	
Pop. density (per km2, 2023)	16.9[a,b]	
Capital city	Riyadh	
Capital city pop. (000, 2023)	7 070.7[d]	

UN membership date	24 October 1945	
Surface area (km2)	2 206 714[c]	
Sex ratio (m per 100 f)	136.0[a,b]	
National currency	Saudi Riyal (SAR)	
Exchange rate (per US$)	3.8[b]	

Economic indicators	2010	2015	2023
GDP: Gross domestic product (million current US$)	528 207	654 270	833 541[c]
GDP growth rate (annual %, const. 2015 prices)	5.0	4.1	3.2[c]
GDP per capita (current US$)	17 958.9	19 977.8	23 185.9[c]
Economy: Agriculture (% of Gross Value Added)[e,f]	2.6	2.6	2.4[c]
Economy: Industry (% of Gross Value Added)[e,g]	58.2	45.3	48.2[c]
Economy: Services and other activity (% of GVA)[e]	39.1	52.0	49.4[c]
Employment in agriculture (% of employed)	6.3[h]	5.9	2.7[c]
Employment in industry (% of employed)	23.5[h]	23.8	20.0[c]
Employment in services & other sectors (% employed)	70.2[h]	70.3	77.3[c]
Unemployment rate (% of labour force)	5.6	5.6	5.6[h]
Labour force participation rate (female/male pop. %)	19.2 / 76.0[h]	22.2 / 79.9	28.1 / 80.2[h]
CPI: Consumer Price Index (2010=100)	100[i]	96[j]	107[j,b]
Agricultural production index (2014-2016=100)	101	101	159[c]
International trade: exports (million current US$)	250 577	203 689	419 391[h,b]
International trade: imports (million current US$)	103 622	174 786	187 971[h,b]
International trade: balance (million current US$)	146 955	28 903	231 420[h,b]
Balance of payments, current account (million US$)	66 751	- 56 724	150 753[b]

Major trading partners						2022
Export partners (% of exports)[h]	China	18.2	India	10.4	Japan	9.5
Import partners (% of imports)[h]	China	19.8	United States	10.6	United Arab Emirates	8.2

Social indicators	2010	2015	2023
Population growth rate (average annual %)	2.7	1.9	1.5[a,b]
Urban population (% of total population)	82.1	83.2	84.1[d]
Urban population growth rate (average annual %)[k]	3.0	3.1	...
Fertility rate, total (live births per woman)	2.9	2.6	2.4[a,b]
Life expectancy at birth (females/males, years)	77.6 / 74.5	78.6 / 75.8	79.5 / 76.7[a,b]
Population age distribution (0-14/60+ years old, %)	29.5 / 3.2	27.5 / 4.1	25.9 / 5.3[a,b]
International migrant stock (000/% of total pop.)[l]	8 430.0 / 30.7	10 771.4 / 34.0	13 454.8 / 38.6[m]
Refugees and others of concern to the UNHCR (000)	70.7	70.3	83.8[b]
Infant mortality rate (per 1 000 live births)	10.5	7.8	5.5[a,b]
Health: Current expenditure (% of GDP)	3.6	6.0	5.5[n,o]
Health: Physicians (per 1 000 pop.)	1.9	2.2	2.8[c]
Education: Government expenditure (% of GDP)	5.1[p]	...	...
Education: Primary gross enrol. ratio (f/m per 100 pop.)	106.2 / 107.1	112.1 / 108.7	102.8 / 101.3[c]
Education: Lowr. sec. gross enrol. ratio (f/m per 100 pop.)	94.8 / 108.0[q,h]	113.5 / 113.2	105.9 / 106.7[c]
Education: Upr. sec. gross enrol. ratio (f/m per 100 pop.)	83.1 / 92.8[q]	116.5 / 122.7	112.3 / 120.8[c]
Intentional homicide rate (per 100 000 pop.)	1.0[r]	...	0.8[d]
Seats held by women in the National Parliament (%)	0.0	19.9	19.9[s]

Environment and infrastructure indicators	2010	2015	2023
Individuals using the Internet (per 100 inhabitants)	41.0	69.6[t]	100.0[c]
Research & Development expenditure (% of GDP)	0.9[u,v,w]	0.8[u,v,x]	0.5[y,c]
Threatened species (number)	103	119	171[b]
Forested area (% of land area)	0.5	0.5	0.5[m]
CO2 emission estimates (million tons/tons per capita)	421.7 / 15.2	536.1 / 16.8	487.5 / 13.9[m]
Energy production, primary (Petajoules)	22 115	27 723	25 618[m]
Energy supply per capita (Gigajoules)	262	315	262[m]
Tourist/visitor arrivals at national borders (000)	10 850	17 994	3 477[c]
Important sites for terrestrial biodiversity protected (%)	22.0	22.0	22.0[b]
Pop. using safely managed sanitation (urban/rural %)	82.4 / ...	82.4 / ...	82.4 / ...[b]
Net Official Development Assist. disbursed (% of GNI)	...	...	0.99[c]
Net Official Development Assist. received (% of GNI)	- 0.03[r]	...	...

a Projected estimate (medium fertility variant). b 2022. c 2021. d 2019. e Data classified according to ISIC Rev. 4. f Excludes irrigation canals and landscaping care. g Excludes publishing activities, recycling. Includes irrigation canals. h Estimate. i Calculated by the UN Statistics Division from national indices. j Base: 2018=100. k Data refers to a 5-year period preceding the reference year. l Including refugees. Refers to foreign citizens. m 2020. n Data are based on SHA2011. o 2018. p 2008. q 2009. r 2007. s Data are as at 1 January of reporting year. t This number is reflecting the whole population, based on the age range 12-65 years for the study it is 70% of the population. u Based on R&D budget instead of R&D expenditure. v Overestimated or based on overestimated data. w Break in the time series. x 2013. y Excluding private non-profit.

Senegal

Region	Western Africa	UN membership date	28 September 1960
Population (000, 2023)	17 316[a,b]	Surface area (km2)	196 712[c]
Pop. density (per km2, 2023)	89.9[a,b]	Sex ratio (m per 100 f)	96.8[a,b]
Capital city	Dakar	National currency	CFA Franc, BCEAO (XOF)[d]
Capital city pop. (000, 2023)	3 057.1[e,f]	Exchange rate (per US$)	615.0[b]

Economic indicators

	2010	2015	2023
GDP: Gross domestic product (million current US$)	16 106	17 761	27 625[c]
GDP growth rate (annual %, const. 2015 prices)	3.4	6.4	6.1[c]
GDP per capita (current US$)	1 285.4	1 237.2	1 636.9[c]
Economy: Agriculture (% of Gross Value Added)[g,h]	17.7	16.0	17.1[c]
Economy: Industry (% of Gross Value Added)[g,i]	24.2	26.4	27.5[c]
Economy: Services and other activity (% of GVA)[g]	58.2	57.6	55.4[c]
Employment in agriculture (% of employed)	38.2[j]	31.3	21.6[j,c]
Employment in industry (% of employed)[j]	18.2	18.4	22.6[c]
Employment in services & other sectors (% employed)	43.6[j]	50.4	55.7[j,c]
Unemployment rate (% of labour force)	10.2[j]	6.8	3.4[j]
Labour force participation rate (female/male pop. %)	33.8 / 63.4[j]	34.3 / 57.7	38.8 / 64.9[j]
CPI: Consumer Price Index (2010=100)[k]	100	105	126[l,b]
Agricultural production index (2014-2016=100)	96	110	177[c]
International trade: exports (million current US$)	2 086	2 612	5 790[j,b]
International trade: imports (million current US$)	4 777	5 595	12 057[j,b]
International trade: balance (million current US$)	- 2 691	- 2 984	- 6 267[j,b]
Balance of payments, current account (million US$)	- 589	- 945	- 2 215[m]

Major trading partners

						2022
Export partners (% of exports)[j]	Mali	20.2	Switzerland	14.4	India	9.8
Import partners (% of imports)[j]	France	11.8	China	9.7	India	7.1

Social indicators

	2010	2015	2023
Population growth rate (average annual %)	2.7	2.7	2.5[a,b]
Urban population (% of total population)	43.8	45.9	47.7[f]
Urban population growth rate (average annual %)[n]	3.7	3.9	...
Fertility rate, total (live births per woman)	5.1	4.8	4.3[a,b]
Life expectancy at birth (females/males, years)	66.3 / 62.8	69.1 / 64.5	70.2 / 65.5[a,b]
Population age distribution (0-14/60+ years old, %)	43.2 / 4.9	43.1 / 4.8	41.5 / 4.9[a,b]
International migrant stock (000/% of total pop.)[o]	256.1 / 2.0	266.5 / 1.8	274.9 / 1.6[p]
Refugees and others of concern to the UNHCR (000)	24.2[q]	17.3	12.0[b]
Infant mortality rate (per 1 000 live births)	40.0	31.5	21.0[a,b]
Health: Current expenditure (% of GDP)[r]	4.0	4.4	5.2[p]
Health: Physicians (per 1 000 pop.)	0.1[s]	...	0.1[p]
Education: Government expenditure (% of GDP)	5.2	5.5	5.6[c]
Education: Primary gross enrol. ratio (f/m per 100 pop.)	86.4 / 81.7	89.8 / 80.2	87.5 / 75.2[c]
Education: Lowr. sec. gross enrol. ratio (f/m per 100 pop.)	36.0 / 43.3[s]	62.3 / 59.2[j,t]	59.5 / 48.5[c]
Education: Upr. sec. gross enrol. ratio (f/m per 100 pop.)	13.4 / 19.9[s]	32.4 / 37.3[j,t]	38.8 / 33.9[c]
Seats held by women in the National Parliament (%)	22.7	42.7	46.1[u]

Environment and infrastructure indicators

	2010	2015	2023
Individuals using the Internet (per 100 inhabitants)[j]	8.0[v]	21.7	58.1[c]
Research & Development expenditure (% of GDP)	0.4	0.6[w]	...
Threatened species (number)	82	106	181[b]
Forested area (% of land area)	44.0	42.9	41.9[p]
CO2 emission estimates (million tons/tons per capita)	5.9 / 0.4	7.9 / 0.5	8.4 / 0.5[p]
Energy production, primary (Petajoules)	86	69	86[p]
Energy supply per capita (Gigajoules)	13	12	12[p]
Tourist/visitor arrivals at national borders (000)[j]	900	1 007	1 365[x]
Important sites for terrestrial biodiversity protected (%)	42.5	42.7	45.4[b]
Pop. using safely managed drinking water (urban/rural, %)	40.0 / 9.7	40.5 / 10.9	41.3 / 12.6[b]
Pop. using safely managed sanitation (urban/rural, %)	19.9 / 19.4	17.0 / 17.2	13.9 / 14.2[b]
Net Official Development Assist. received (% of GNI)	5.86	5.02	5.14[c]

a Projected estimate (medium fertility variant). b 2022. c 2021. d African Financial Community (CFA) Franc, Central Bank of West African States (BCEAO). e Refers to the sum of the Departments of Dakar, Pikinie and Guédiawaye, in Dakar Region. f 2019. g Data classified according to ISIC Rev. 4. h Excludes irrigation canals and landscaping care. i Excludes publishing activities, recycling. Includes irrigation canals. j Estimate. k WAEMU harmonized consumer price index. l Calculated by the UN Statistics Division from national indices. m 2018. n Data refers to a 5-year period preceding the reference year. o Including refugees. p 2020. q Data as at the end of December. r Data based on calendar year (January 1 to December 31). s 2008. t 2014. u Data are as at 1 January of reporting year. v Refers to total population. Survey result: 16% for population age 12+. w Excluding business enterprise. x 2017.

Serbia

Region	Southern Europe	UN membership date	01 November 2000
Population (000, 2023)	7 221 [a,b,c]	Surface area (km2)	88 444 [d]
Pop. density (per km2, 2023)	94.1 [a,b,c]	Sex ratio (m per 100 f)	92.1 [a,b,c]
Capital city	Belgrade	National currency	Serbian Dinar (RSD)
Capital city pop. (000, 2023)	1 393.7 [e,f]	Exchange rate (per US$)	110.2 [c]

Economic indicators

	2010	2015	2023
GDP: Gross domestic product (million current US$)	41 819	39 656	63 068 [d]
GDP growth rate (annual %, const. 2015 prices)	0.7	1.8	7.4 [d]
GDP per capita (current US$)	5 463.9	5 273.8	8 643.3 [d]
Economy: Agriculture (% of Gross Value Added) [g,h]	7.9	8.1	7.8 [d]
Economy: Industry (% of Gross Value Added) [g,i]	30.3	30.9	30.3 [d]
Economy: Services and other activity (% of GVA) [g]	61.8	61.0	61.9 [d]
Employment in agriculture (% of employed)	22.3	19.4	13.9 [j,d]
Employment in industry (% of employed)	20.8 [j]	24.4	28.9 [j,d]
Employment in services & other sectors (% of employed)	52.1	56.1	57.1 [j,d]
Unemployment rate (% of labour force)	19.2	17.7	10.3 [j]
Labour force participation rate (female/male pop. %)	41.7 / 58.6	43.3 / 60.8	48.5 / 65.3 [j]
CPI: Consumer Price Index (2010=100)	100	133	170 [c]
Agricultural production index (2014-2016=100)	100	94	104 [c]
International trade: exports (million current US$) [k]	9 795	13 379	29 058 [c]
International trade: imports (million current US$) [k]	16 735	18 210	41 138 [c]
International trade: balance (million current US$) [k]	- 6 940	- 4 831	- 12 079 [c]
Balance of payments, current account (million US$)	- 2 692	- 1 370	- 4 434 [c]

Major trading partners

						2022
Export partners (% of exports)	Germany	13.7	Bosnia Herzegovina	7.5	Italy	7.2
Import partners (% of imports)	China	12.1	Germany	11.4	Russian Federation	7.5

Social indicators

	2010	2015	2023
Population growth rate (average annual %) [a]	- 0.4	- 0.3	- 1.1 [b,c]
Urban population (% of total population) [l]	55.0	55.7	56.3 [f]
Urban population growth rate (average annual %) [l,m]	-0.0	- 0.1	...
Fertility rate, total (live births per woman) [a]	1.4	1.5	1.5 [b,c]
Life expectancy at birth (females/males, years) [a]	77.3 / 71.4	78.7 / 72.8	77.0 / 71.3 [b,c]
Population age distribution (0-14/60+ years old, %) [a]	14.3 / 24.5	14.3 / 26.4	14.4 / 27.1 [b,c]
International migrant stock (000/% of total pop.) [l]	826.3 / 9.2	807.4 / 9.1	823.0 / 9.4 [n]
Refugees and others of concern to the UNHCR (000)	312.6 [l,o]	259.7 [l]	245.9 [c]
Infant mortality rate (per 1 000 live births) [a]	5.9	4.6	4.4 [b,c]
Health: Current expenditure (% of GDP)	9.5	8.8	8.7 [n]
Health: Physicians (per 1 000 pop.)	2.9	2.9	3.7 [p]
Education: Government expenditure (% of GDP)	3.9	3.8 [q]	3.6 [f]
Education: Primary gross enrol. ratio (f/m per 100 pop.) [j]	95.6 / 96.1	101.2 / 101.5	97.0 / 96.7 [d]
Education: Lowr. sec. gross enrol. ratio (f/m per 100 pop.) [j]	98.3 / 98.7	101.7 / 102.4	97.0 / 97.0 [d]
Education: Upr. sec. gross enrol. ratio (f/m per 100 pop.) [j]	86.9 / 83.1	93.1 / 89.7	89.6 / 86.5 [d]
Intentional homicide rate (per 100 000 pop.)	1.7	1.3	1.1 [d]
Seats held by women in the National Parliament (%)	21.6	34.0	34.8 [r]

Environment and infrastructure indicators

	2010	2015	2023
Individuals using the Internet (per 100 inhabitants)	40.9	65.3	81.2 [d]
Research & Development expenditure (% of GDP)	0.7 [s]	0.8 [s]	1.0 [d]
Threatened species (number)	46	56	121 [c]
Forested area (% of land area)	31.0	31.1	31.1 [n]
CO2 emission estimates (million tons/tons per capita)	46.8 / 6.3	45.4 / 6.3	47.1 / 6.6 [d,n]
Energy production, primary (Petajoules) [a]	440	449	458 [n]
Energy supply per capita (Gigajoules) [a]	85	81	89 [n]
Tourist/visitor arrivals at national borders (000) [t,u]	683	1 132	871 [d]
Important sites for terrestrial biodiversity protected (%)	21.5	26.7	29.4 [c]
Pop. using safely managed drinking water (urban/rural, %)	81.5 / 66.5	81.5 / 66.5	81.5 / 66.6 [c]
Pop. using safely managed sanitation (urban/rural %)	26.3 / 30.6	24.8 / 30.1	22.4 / 29.3 [c]
Net Official Development Assist. received (% of GNI)	1.62	0.83	0.88 [d]

a Excluding Kosovo. b Projected estimate (medium fertility variant). c 2022. d 2021. e Refers to the urban population of Belgrade area. f 2019. g Data classified according to ISIC Rev. 4. h Excludes irrigation canals and landscaping care. i Excludes publishing activities, recycling. Includes irrigation canals. j Estimate. k Special trade system up to 2008. l Including Kosovo. m Data refers to a 5-year period preceding the reference year. n 2020. o Data as at the end of December. p 2016. q 2012. r Data are as at 1 January of reporting year. s Excluding data from some regions, provinces or states. t Excluding Kosovo and Metohija. u Tourists staying in visitor accommodation establishments.

Seychelles

Region	Eastern Africa	
Population (000, 2023)	107 [a,b]	
Pop. density (per km2, 2023)	234.4 [a,b]	
Capital city	Victoria	
Capital city pop. (000, 2023)	28.1 [d]	

UN membership date	21 September 1976	
Surface area (km2)	457 [c]	
Sex ratio (m per 100 f)	111.2 [a,b]	
National currency	Seychelles Rupee (SCR)	
Exchange rate (per US$)	14.1 [b]	

Economic indicators

	2010	2015	2023
GDP: Gross domestic product (million current US$)	986	1 391	1 287 [c]
GDP growth rate (annual %, const. 2015 prices)	6.4	4.2	2.4 [c]
GDP per capita (current US$)	10 669.4	14 020.6	12 084.6 [c]
Economy: Agriculture (% of Gross Value Added) [e,f]	2.7	2.8	3.4 [c]
Economy: Industry (% of Gross Value Added) [e,g]	19.2	17.1	16.2 [c]
Economy: Services and other activity (% of GVA) [e]	78.1	80.1	80.3 [c]
Employment in agriculture (% of employed)	...	3.6 [h,i,j]	...
Employment in industry (% of employed)	...	17.9 [h,i,j]	...
Employment in services & other sectors (% employed)	...	78.2 [h,i,j]	...
Unemployment rate (% of labour force)	5.5 [k]	4.1 [h,i,j]	...
Labour force participation rate (female/male pop. %)	... / ...	61.9 / 68.3 [h,i,l,j]	... / ...
CPI: Consumer Price Index (2010=100) [m]	100	121	148 [b]
Agricultural production index (2014-2016=100)	100	99	95 [c]
International trade: exports (million current US$) [n]	418	474	1 865 [o,b]
International trade: imports (million current US$) [n]	1 180	975	2 270 [o,b]
International trade: balance (million current US$) [n]	- 763	- 501	- 405 [o,b]
Balance of payments, current account (million US$)	- 214	- 256	- 154 [c]

Major trading partners

						2022
Export partners (% of exports) [o]	Gibraltar	33.0	Îles Caïmanes	15.4	Bermuda	12.0
Import partners (% of imports) [o]	South Africa	18.7	Netherlands	16.4	United Arab Emirates	15.8

Social indicators

	2010	2015	2023
Population growth rate (average annual %)	1.5	1.2	0.4 [a,b]
Urban population (% of total population)	53.3	55.4	57.1 [p]
Urban population growth rate (average annual %) [q]	1.2	1.3	...
Fertility rate, total (live births per woman)	2.2	2.3	2.3 [a,b]
Life expectancy at birth (females/males, years)	77.6 / 68.8	78.3 / 69.7	76.0 / 68.2 [a,b]
Population age distribution (0-14/60+ years old, %)	24.3 / 9.2	23.3 / 10.2	23.1 / 13.1 [a,b]
International migrant stock (000/% of total pop.)	11.4 / 12.5	12.8 / 13.5	13.0 / 13.3 [r]
Refugees and others of concern to the UNHCR (000)	...	...	~0.0 [d]
Infant mortality rate (per 1 000 live births)	12.0	12.6	11.4 [a,b]
Health: Current expenditure (% of GDP) [s]	4.8	4.5	6.4 [r]
Health: Physicians (per 1 000 pop.)	1.1	1.0 [t]	2.1 [p]
Education: Government expenditure (% of GDP)	3.5	5.0	5.5 [c]
Education: Primary gross enrol. ratio (f/m per 100 pop.)	112.1 / 108.8	106.0 / 102.8	100.9 / 97.8 [c]
Education: Lowr. sec. gross enrol. ratio (f/m per 100 pop.)	107.3 / 109.7	112.7 / 109.7	106.0 / 97.0 [c]
Education: Upr. sec. gross enrol. ratio (f/m per 100 pop.)	56.0 / 47.5 [o]	63.3 / 55.9	61.1 / 56.2 [c]
Intentional homicide rate (per 100 000 pop.)	9.7	7.1	4.7 [c]
Seats held by women in the National Parliament (%)	23.5	43.8	22.9 [u]

Environment and infrastructure indicators

	2010	2015	2023
Individuals using the Internet (per 100 inhabitants) [o]	41.0	54.3	81.6 [c]
Research & Development expenditure (% of GDP)	0.3 [k]	...	0.2 [l,v]
Threatened species (number)	190	435	461 [b]
Forested area (% of land area)	73.3	73.3	73.3 [r]
Energy production, primary (Petajoules)	0	0	0 [r]
Energy supply per capita (Gigajoules)	66	70	80 [o,r]
Tourist/visitor arrivals at national borders (000)	175	276	183 [c]
Important sites for terrestrial biodiversity protected (%)	24.3	24.3	52.8 [b]
Net Official Development Assist. received (% of GNI)	5.88	0.52	1.15 [w]

a Projected estimate (medium fertility variant). **b** 2022. **c** 2021. **d** 2018. **e** Data classified according to ISIC Rev. 4. **f** Excludes irrigation canals and landscaping care. **g** Excludes publishing activities, recycling. Includes irrigation canals. **h** Excluding some areas. **i** Excluding the institutional population. **j** 2011. **k** 2005. **l** Break in the time series. **m** Calculated by the UN Statistics Division from national indices. **n** As of 2010, trade in services data reflect improvement of the coverage of balance of payment statistics. **o** Estimate. **p** 2019. **q** Data refers to a 5-year period preceding the reference year. **r** 2020. **s** Data based on calendar year (January 1 to December 31). **t** 2012. **u** Data are as at 1 January of reporting year. **v** 2016. **w** 2017.

Sierra Leone

Region	Western Africa	UN membership date	27 September 1961
Population (000, 2023)	8 606 [a,b]	Surface area (km2)	72 300 [c]
Pop. density (per km2, 2023)	120.0 [a,b]	Sex ratio (m per 100 f)	100.4 [a,b]
Capital city	Freetown	National currency	Leone (SLL)
Capital city pop. (000, 2023)	1 168.4 [d]	Exchange rate (per US$)	18.8 [b]

Economic indicators

	2010	2015	2023
GDP: Gross domestic product (million current US$)	2 578	4 248	4 249 [c]
GDP growth rate (annual %, const. 2015 prices)	5.3	- 20.5	4.1 [c]
GDP per capita (current US$)	400.5	580.8	504.6 [c]
Economy: Agriculture (% of Gross Value Added)	55.2	60.5	60.0 [c]
Economy: Industry (% of Gross Value Added)	8.1	4.6	6.2 [c]
Economy: Services and other activity (% of GVA)	36.7	34.9	33.8 [c]
Employment in agriculture (% of employed) [e]	65.2	57.0	42.7 [c]
Employment in industry (% of employed) [e]	5.2	6.7	11.9 [c]
Employment in services & other sectors (% employed) [e]	29.7	36.4	45.4 [c]
Unemployment rate (% of labour force) [e]	4.2	4.4	3.7
Labour force participation rate (female/male pop. %) [e]	60.2 / 61.2	55.1 / 57.3	51.0 / 55.4
CPI: Consumer Price Index (2010=100) [f]	100	134	378 [b]
Agricultural production index (2014-2016=100)	101	96	130 [c]
International trade: exports (million current US$)	319 [e]	93	491 [e,b]
International trade: imports (million current US$)	776 [e]	1 759	1 907 [e,b]
International trade: balance (million current US$)	- 457 [e]	- 1 666	- 1 416 [e,b]
Balance of payments, current account (million US$)	- 585	- 1 003	- 358 [c]

Major trading partners

							2022
Export partners (% of exports) [e]	China	56.4	Belgium	11.0	United Arab Emirates	6.3
Import partners (% of imports) [e]	China	31.4	India	11.0	Türkiye	8.6

Social indicators

	2010	2015	2023
Population growth rate (average annual %)	2.7	2.4	2.1 [a,b]
Urban population (% of total population)	38.9	40.8	42.5 [d]
Urban population growth rate (average annual %) [g]	3.7	3.3	...
Fertility rate, total (live births per woman)	5.3	4.5	3.9 [a,b]
Life expectancy at birth (females/males, years)	54.5 / 52.9	58.2 / 56.2	61.7 / 59.1 [a,b]
Population age distribution (0-14/60+ years old, %)	43.2 / 5.0	41.8 / 4.9	39.0 / 5.1 [a,b]
International migrant stock (000/% of total pop.) [h]	79.3 / 1.2	58.8 / 0.8	53.7 / 0.7 [i]
Refugees and others of concern to the UNHCR (000)	8.6 [i]	1.4	~0.0 [b]
Infant mortality rate (per 1 000 live births)	104.4	88.1	70.0 [a,b]
Health: Current expenditure (% of GDP) [k]	10.9	20.4	8.8 [i]
Health: Physicians (per 1 000 pop.)	~0.0	~0.0 [i]	0.1 [i]
Education: Government expenditure (% of GDP)	2.8	3.2	3.3 [c]
Education: Primary gross enrol. ratio (f/m per 100 pop.)	... / ...	116.9 / 115.3	159.4 / 153.5 [c]
Education: Lowr. sec. gross enrol. ratio (f/m per 100 pop.)	... / ...	53.7 / 57.4	93.5 / 90.2 [c]
Education: Upr. sec. gross enrol. ratio (f/m per 100 pop.)	... / ...	22.3 / 28.5	26.4 / 29.2 [m]
Intentional homicide rate (per 100 000 pop.)	2.5	1.7	2.1 [i]
Seats held by women in the National Parliament (%)	13.2	12.4	13.0 [n]

Environment and infrastructure indicators

	2010	2015	2023
Individuals using the Internet (per 100 inhabitants) [e]	0.6	6.3	18.0 [i]
Threatened species (number)	131	158	295 [b]
Forested area (% of land area)	37.9	36.5	35.1 [i]
Energy production, primary (Petajoules)	52	54	56 [i]
Energy supply per capita (Gigajoules)	9	9	9 [i]
Tourist/visitor arrivals at national borders (000) [o]	39	24	40 [c]
Important sites for terrestrial biodiversity protected (%)	62.1	65.3	65.3 [b]
Pop. using safely managed drinking water (urban/rural, %)	11.4 / 4.5	11.8 / 6.1	12.2 / 8.7 [b]
Pop. using safely managed sanitation (urban/rural, %)	13.9 / 4.8	16.7 / 6.7	22.5 / 9.8 [b]
Net Official Development Assist. received (% of GNI)	17.59	22.75	17.49 [c]

a Projected estimate (medium fertility variant). **b** 2022. **c** 2021. **d** 2019. **e** Estimate. **f** Calculated by the UN Statistics Division from national indices. **g** Data refers to a 5-year period preceding the reference year. **h** Including refugees. **i** 2020. **j** Data as at the end of December. **k** Data based on calendar year (January 1 to December 31). **l** 2011. **m** 2017. **n** Data are as at 1 January of reporting year. **o** Arrivals by air.

Singapore

Region	South-eastern Asia	UN membership date	21 September 1965
Population (000, 2023)	5 976 [a,b]	Surface area (km2)	728 [c,d]
Pop. density (per km2, 2023)	8 749.2 [a,b]	Sex ratio (m per 100 f)	109.6 [a,b]
Capital city	Singapore	National currency	Singapore Dollar (SGD)
Capital city pop. (000, 2023)	5 868.1 [e]	Exchange rate (per US$)	1.3 [b]

Economic indicators	2010	2015	2023
GDP: Gross domestic product (million current US$)	239 808	307 999	396 992 [d]
GDP growth rate (annual %, const. 2015 prices)	14.7	3.0	7.6 [d]
GDP per capita (current US$)	46 442.1	54 512.8	66 821.7 [d]
Economy: Agriculture (% of Gross Value Added) [f,g,h]	~0.0	~0.0	~0.0 [d]
Economy: Industry (% of Gross Value Added) [h,i,j]	28.2	25.8	26.4 [d]
Economy: Services and other activity (% of GVA) [h]	71.8	74.2	73.6 [d]
Employment in agriculture (% of employed) [k]	0.9	0.6	0.3 [d]
Employment in industry (% of employed) [k]	23.6	17.1	14.5 [d]
Employment in services & other sectors (% employed)	75.6 [k]	82.3	85.3 [k,d]
Unemployment rate (% of labour force)	4.1	3.8	3.1 [b]
Labour force participation rate (female/male pop. %)	57.9 / 78.6 [k]	62.3 / 79.2	62.2 / 75.7 [k]
CPI: Consumer Price Index (2010=100)	100	113	124 [b]
Agricultural production index (2014-2016=100)	76	99	112 [d]
International trade: exports (million current US$)	353 240	357 941	514 966 [b]
International trade: imports (million current US$)	313 071	308 122	475 413 [b]
International trade: balance (million current US$)	40 169	49 820	39 553 [b]
Balance of payments, current account (million US$)	54 996	57 574	90 239 [b]

Major trading partners					2022
Export partners (% of exports)	China	12.4	China, Hong Kong SAR	11.2	Malaysia 10.0
Import partners (% of imports)	China	13.2	Malaysia	12.5	Other Asia, nes 12.1

Social indicators	2010	2015	2023
Population growth rate (average annual %)	2.6	1.2	0.7 [a,b]
Urban population (% of total population)	100.0	100.0	100.0 [e]
Urban population growth rate (average annual %) [l]	2.4	1.7	...
Fertility rate, total (live births per woman)	1.2	1.2	1.0 [a,b]
Life expectancy at birth (females/males, years)	84.0 / 79.3	85.0 / 80.6	86.3 / 82.0 [a,b]
Population age distribution (0-14/60+ years old, %)	14.3 / 12.4	12.7 / 15.5	11.8 / 23.0 [a,b]
International migrant stock (000/% of total pop.)	2 164.8 / 42.2	2 483.4 / 44.4	2 523.6 / 43.1 [m]
Refugees and others of concern to the UNHCR (000)	~0.0 [n]	~0.0	1.1 [b]
Infant mortality rate (per 1 000 live births)	2.2	2.1	1.7 [a,b]
Health: Current expenditure (% of GDP) [o,p]	3.2	4.2	6.1 [m]
Health: Physicians (per 1 000 pop.)	1.7	2.2	2.4 [e]
Education: Government expenditure (% of GDP)	3.1	2.9	2.5 [b]
Education: Primary gross enrol. ratio (f/m per 100 pop.)	... / ...	... / ...	100.5 / 100.6 [k,m]
Education: Lowr. sec. gross enrol. ratio (f/m per 100 pop.)	... / ...	... / ...	99.8 / 100.1 [k,m]
Education: Upr. sec. gross enrol. ratio (f/m per 100 pop.)	... / ...	... / ...	105.7 / 107.3 [k,m]
Intentional homicide rate (per 100 000 pop.)	0.4	0.2	0.1 [d]
Seats held by women in the National Parliament (%)	23.4	25.3	29.1 [q]

Environment and infrastructure indicators	2010	2015	2023
Individuals using the Internet (per 100 inhabitants)	71.0 [r]	83.2	91.1 [k,d]
Research & Development expenditure (% of GDP)	1.9	2.2	1.9 [e]
Threatened species (number)	277	287	365 [b]
Forested area (% of land area)	25.3	23.2	21.7 [m]
CO2 emission estimates (million tons/tons per capita)	42.7 / 8.4	45.7 / 8.2	44.0 / 7.7 [m]
Energy production, primary (Petajoules)	25	26	26 [m]
Energy supply per capita (Gigajoules)	171	215	192 [m]
Tourist/visitor arrivals at national borders (000) [s]	9 161	12 052	325 [d]
Important sites for terrestrial biodiversity protected (%)	21.1	21.1	21.1 [b]
Pop. using safely managed drinking water (urban/rural, %)	100.0 / ...	100.0 / ...	100.0 / ... [b]
Pop. using safely managed sanitation (urban/rural %)	100.0 / ...	100.0 / ...	100.0 / ... [b]

a Projected estimate (medium fertility variant). b 2022. c The land area of Singapore comprises the mainland and other islands. d 2021. e 2019. f Includes quarrying. g Excludes irrigation canals and landscaping care. h Data classified according to ISIC Rev. 4. i Excluding quarrying. j Excludes publishing activities, recycling. Includes irrigation canals. k Estimate. l Data refers to a 5-year period preceding the reference year. m 2020. n Data as at the end of December. o Medisave is classified as Social insurance scheme, considering that it is a compulsory payment. p Data refer to fiscal years beginning 1 April. q Data are as at 1 January of reporting year. r Population aged 7 years and over. s Excluding Malaysian citizens arriving by land.

Sint Maarten (Dutch part)

Region	Caribbean	Population (000, 2023)	44 [a,b,c]
Surface area (km2)	34 [d]	Pop. density (per km2, 2023)	1 299.3 [a,b,c]
Sex ratio (m per 100 f)	115.2 [a,b,c]	Capital city	Philipsburg
National currency	Neth. Ant. Guilder (ANG) [e]	Capital city pop. (000, 2023)	40.6 [f,g]
Exchange rate (per US$)	1.8 [c]		

Economic indicators	2010	2015	2023
GDP: Gross domestic product (million current US$)	896	1 367	1 154 [d]
GDP growth rate (annual %, const. 2015 prices)	1.1	0.5	4.0 [d]
GDP per capita (current US$)	27 138.5	34 000.3	26 198.7 [d]
Economy: Industry (% of Gross Value Added) [h,i]	13.5	5.5	6.8 [d]
Economy: Services and other activity (% of GVA)	86.5	94.5	93.2 [d]
Balance of payments, current account (million US$)	...	18	- 294 [d]

Social indicators	2010	2015	2023
Population growth rate (average annual %) [a]	0.7	2.9	~0.0 [b,c]
Urban population (% of total population)	100.0	100.0	100.0 [j]
Urban population growth rate (average annual %) [k]	0.4	3.1	...
Fertility rate, total (live births per woman) [a]	1.8	1.7	1.6 [b,c]
Life expectancy at birth (females/males, years) [a]	78.0 / 72.5	80.6 / 74.0	77.1 / 72.0 [b,c]
Population age distribution (0-14/60+ years old, %) [a]	22.6 / 9.2	19.2 / 11.3	11.0 / 19.7 [b,c]
International migrant stock (000/% of total pop.) [l]	26.2 / 76.7	27.3 / 68.3	28.8 / 67.3 [m]
Refugees and others of concern to the UNHCR (000)	~0.0 [n]	~0.0	0.1 [c]
Infant mortality rate (per 1 000 live births) [a]	15.1	11.9	13.9 [b,c]
Education: Primary gross enrol. ratio (f/m per 100 pop.)	... / ...	128.9 / 127.5 [o]	... / ...
Education: Lowr. sec. gross enrol. ratio (f/m per 100 pop.)	... / ...	109.2 / 105.4 [o]	... / ...
Education: Upr. sec. gross enrol. ratio (f/m per 100 pop.)	... / ...	76.4 / 84.9 [o]	... / ...

Environment and infrastructure indicators	2010	2015	2023
Threatened species (number)	...	49	80 [c]
Forested area (% of land area)	...	2.3	10.9 [m]
Energy supply per capita (Gigajoules) [p]	...	289	238 [m]
Tourist/visitor arrivals at national borders (000) [q]	443	505	249 [d]
Important sites for terrestrial biodiversity protected (%)	5.1	5.1	5.1 [c]

a For statistical purposes, the data for Netherlands do not include this area. **b** Projected estimate (medium fertility variant). **c** 2022. **d** 2021. **e** Netherlands Antillean Guilder. **f** Refers to the total population of Sint Maarten. **g** 2018. **h** Excludes publishing activities, recycling. Includes irrigation canals. **i** Agricultural services and related activities such as cotton ginning and pressing are included in Manufacturing. **j** 2019. **k** Data refers to a 5-year period preceding the reference year. **l** Including refugees. **m** 2020. **n** Data as at the end of December. **o** 2014. **p** Estimate. **q** Arrivals by air. Including arrivals to Saint Martin (French part).

Slovakia

Region	Eastern Europe	UN membership date	19 January 1993
Population (000, 2023)	5 644 a,b	Surface area (km2)	49 035 c
Pop. density (per km2, 2023)	115.1 a,b	Sex ratio (m per 100 f)	95.6 a,b
Capital city	Bratislava	National currency	Euro (EUR)
Capital city pop. (000, 2023)	432.5 d	Exchange rate (per US$)	0.9 b

Economic indicators

	2010	2015	2023
GDP: Gross domestic product (million current US$)	91 074	88 865	116 527 c
GDP growth rate (annual %, const. 2015 prices)	6.7	5.2	3.0 c
GDP per capita (current US$)	16 876.7	16 382.3	21 390.5 c
Economy: Agriculture (% of Gross Value Added) e,f	1.7	2.4	2.0 c
Economy: Industry (% of Gross Value Added) e,g	33.8	34.0	31.6 c
Economy: Services and other activity (% of GVA) e	64.5	63.6	66.4 c
Employment in agriculture (% of employed)	3.2	3.2	2.5 c
Employment in industry (% of employed)	37.1	36.1	36.7 c
Employment in services & other sectors (% employed)	59.7	60.7	60.9 c
Unemployment rate (% of labour force)	14.4	11.5	6.1 h
Labour force participation rate (female/male pop. %)	50.8 / 67.8	51.9 / 67.9	55.6 / 68.3 h
CPI: Consumer Price Index (2010=100)	100	109	137 b
Agricultural production index (2014-2016=100)	87	90	97 c
International trade: exports (million current US$)	65 306	74 970	108 013 b
International trade: imports (million current US$)	65 644	73 053	115 215 b
International trade: balance (million current US$)	- 338	1 916	- 7 203 b
Balance of payments, current account (million US$)	- 4 210	- 1 849	- 9 385 b

Major trading partners

						2022
Export partners (% of exports)	Germany	21.0	Czechia	12.0	Hungary	8.7
Import partners (% of imports)	Germany	14.0	Other Europe, nes	11.3	Czechia	9.0

Social indicators

	2010	2015	2023
Population growth rate (average annual %)	0.1	0.1	7.2 a,b
Urban population (% of total population)	54.7	53.9	53.7 d
Urban population growth rate (average annual %) i	- 0.3	- 0.2	...
Fertility rate, total (live births per woman)	1.4	1.4	1.6 a,b
Life expectancy at birth (females/males, years)	79.2 / 71.7	80.1 / 73.1	78.8 / 71.9 a,b
Population age distribution (0-14/60+ years old, %)	15.4 / 18.0	15.3 / 20.9	15.7 / 23.1 a,b
International migrant stock (000/% of total pop.)	146.3 / 2.7	177.6 / 3.3	197.2 / 3.6 i
Refugees and others of concern to the UNHCR (000)	1.6 k	2.5	87.9 b
Infant mortality rate (per 1 000 live births)	5.7	5.1	4.7 a,b
Health: Current expenditure (% of GDP)	7.7	6.8	7.2 i
Health: Physicians (per 1 000 pop.)	3.4	3.5	4.6 c
Education: Government expenditure (% of GDP)	4.0	4.6	4.3 d
Education: Primary gross enrol. ratio (f/m per 100 pop.)	101.0 / 101.9	98.1 / 98.9	101.9 / 102.3 i
Education: Lowr. sec. gross enrol. ratio (f/m per 100 pop.)	92.6 / 94.0	95.7 / 96.8	93.7 / 94.8 i
Education: Upr. sec. gross enrol. ratio (f/m per 100 pop.)	93.0 / 89.5	86.8 / 83.5	87.7 / 83.8 i
Intentional homicide rate (per 100 000 pop.)	1.6	0.9	1.0 c
Seats held by women in the National Parliament (%)	18.0	18.7	22.0 i

Environment and infrastructure indicators

	2010	2015	2023
Individuals using the Internet (per 100 inhabitants)	75.7 m,n	77.6 m,n	88.9 c
Research & Development expenditure (% of GDP)	0.6	1.2	0.9 i
Threatened species (number)	34	45	134 b
Forested area (% of land area)	39.9	40.0	40.1 i
CO2 emission estimates (million tons/tons per capita)	34.9 / 6.4	29.8 / 5.4	31.6 / 5.7 c
Energy production, primary (Petajoules)	250	265	280 i
Energy supply per capita (Gigajoules)	136	124	125 i
Tourist/visitor arrivals at national borders (000) o	1 327	4 869	5 630 d
Important sites for terrestrial biodiversity protected (%)	73.7	85.3	85.8 b
Pop. using safely managed sanitation (urban/rural %)	88.9 / 76.5	88.5 / 75.5	88.5 / 75.5 b
Net Official Development Assist. disbursed (% of GNI) p	0.09	0.10	0.15 c

a Projected estimate (medium fertility variant). b 2022. c 2021. d 2019. e Data classified according to ISIC Rev. 4. f Excludes irrigation canals and landscaping care. g Excludes publishing activities, recycling. Includes irrigation canals. h Estimate. i Data refers to a 5-year period preceding the reference year. j 2020. k Data as at the end of December. l Data are as at 1 January of reporting year. m Users in the last 3 months. n Population aged 16 to 74 years. o The number of inbound arrivals is based on a combination of accommodation statistics and border survey statistics (as calculated within Tourism Satellite Account). p Development Assistance Committee member (OECD).

Slovenia

Region	Southern Europe	UN membership date	22 May 1992	
Population (000, 2023)	2 120[a,b]	Surface area (km2)	20 273[c]	
Pop. density (per km2, 2023)	105.3[a,b]	Sex ratio (m per 100 f)	101.1[a,b]	
Capital city	Ljubljana	National currency	Euro (EUR)	
Capital city pop. (000, 2023)	286.5[d]	Exchange rate (per US$)	0.9[b]	

Economic indicators

	2010	2015	2023
GDP: Gross domestic product (million current US$)	48 161	43 090	61 749[c]
GDP growth rate (annual %, const. 2015 prices)	1.3	2.2	8.2[c]
GDP per capita (current US$)	23 410.1	20 707.8	29 134.8[c]
Economy: Agriculture (% of Gross Value Added)[e,f]	2.2	2.4	1.9[c]
Economy: Industry (% of Gross Value Added)[f,g]	30.4	32.4	32.4[c]
Economy: Services and other activity (% of GVA)[f]	67.4	65.2	65.7[c]
Employment in agriculture (% of employed)	8.8	7.1	4.1[c]
Employment in industry (% of employed)	26.8[h]	32.0	30.0[c]
Employment in services & other sectors (% employed)	58.6	61.0	65.9[c]
Unemployment rate (% of labour force)	7.2	9.0	4.2[h]
Labour force participation rate (female/male pop. %)	53.3 / 65.3	51.9 / 62.9	53.8 / 62.5[h]
CPI: Consumer Price Index (2010=100)	100	106	123[b]
Agricultural production index (2014-2016=100)	104	102	97[c]
International trade: exports (million current US$)	24 435	26 587	55 479[b]
International trade: imports (million current US$)	26 592	25 870	59 723[b]
International trade: balance (million current US$)	- 2 157	717	- 4 244[b]
Balance of payments, current account (million US$)	- 366	1 646	- 284[b]

Major trading partners

						2022
Export partners (% of exports)[h]	Switzerland	21.0	Germany	14.6	Italy	10.7
Import partners (% of imports)[h]	Switzerland	15.3	China	11.9	Germany	10.6

Social indicators

	2010	2015	2023
Population growth rate (average annual %)	0.6	0.5	~0.0[a,b]
Urban population (% of total population)	52.7	53.8	54.8[i]
Urban population growth rate (average annual %)[j]	0.9	0.7	...
Fertility rate, total (live births per woman)	1.6	1.6	1.6[a,b]
Life expectancy at birth (females/males, years)	82.7 / 76.5	83.6 / 78.0	84.6 / 79.6[a,b]
Population age distribution (0-14/60+ years old, %)	14.2 / 21.9	14.9 / 24.7	15.1 / 27.7[a,b]
International migrant stock (000/% of total pop.)	253.8 / 12.4	237.6 / 11.5	278.0 / 13.4[k]
Refugees and others of concern to the UNHCR (000)	4.6[l]	0.3	8.6[b]
Infant mortality rate (per 1 000 live births)	2.5	1.7	1.4[a,b]
Health: Current expenditure (% of GDP)	8.6	8.5	9.2[c]
Health: Physicians (per 1 000 pop.)	2.4	2.8	3.3[k]
Education: Government expenditure (% of GDP)	5.5	4.9	4.9[i]
Education: Primary gross enrol. ratio (f/m per 100 pop.)	99.5 / 99.5	100.3 / 99.6	103.2 / 103.4[k]
Education: Lower. sec. gross enrol. ratio (f/m per 100 pop.)	96.8 / 96.8	101.6 / 101.2	99.0 / 98.9[k]
Education: Upr. sec. gross enrol. ratio (f/m per 100 pop.)	99.8 / 101.0	117.7 / 115.7	124.2 / 121.2[k]
Intentional homicide rate (per 100 000 pop.)	0.7	1.0	0.4[c]
Seats held by women in the National Parliament (%)	14.4	36.7	37.8[m]

Environment and infrastructure indicators

	2010	2015	2023
Individuals using the Internet (per 100 inhabitants)	70.0[n]	73.1	89.0[n,c]
Research & Development expenditure (% of GDP)	2.1	2.2	2.1[k]
Threatened species (number)	95	125	211[b]
Forested area (% of land area)	61.9	62.0	61.5[k]
CO2 emission estimates (million tons/tons per capita)	15.8 / 7.5	13.1 / 6.2	12.3 / 5.7[c]
Energy production, primary (Petajoules)	158	143	151[k]
Energy supply per capita (Gigajoules)	149	133	127[k]
Tourist/visitor arrivals at national borders (000)	2 049	3 022	1 832[c]
Important sites for terrestrial biodiversity protected (%)	71.0	73.4	73.9[b]
Net Official Development Assist. disbursed (% of GNI)[o]	0.13	0.37	0.63[c]

a Projected estimate (medium fertility variant). **b** 2022. **c** 2021. **d** 2018. **e** Excludes irrigation canals and landscaping care. **f** Data classified according to ISIC Rev. 4. **g** Excludes publishing activities, recycling. Includes irrigation canals. **h** Estimate. **i** 2019. **j** Data refers to a 5-year period preceding the reference year. **k** 2020. **l** Data as at the end of December. **m** Data are as at 1 January of reporting year. **n** Population aged 16 to 74 years. **o** Development Assistance Committee member (OECD).

Solomon Islands

Region	Melanesia	UN membership date	19 September 1978
Population (000, 2023)	724[a,b]	Surface area (km2)	28 896[c]
Pop. density (per km2, 2023)	25.2[a,b]	Sex ratio (m per 100 f)	104.4[a,b]
Capital city	Honiara	National currency	Solomon Is. Dollar (SBD)[d]
Capital city pop. (000, 2023)	81.8[e]	Exchange rate (per US$)	8.3[b]

Economic indicators

	2010	2015	2023
GDP: Gross domestic product (million current US$)	898	1 308	1 632[c]
GDP growth rate (annual %, const. 2015 prices)	9.7	1.7	- 0.2[c]
GDP per capita (current US$)	1 662.0	2 134.8	2 306.0[c]
Economy: Agriculture (% of Gross Value Added)	34.6	33.3	33.6[c]
Economy: Industry (% of Gross Value Added)	13.8	15.6	17.7[c]
Economy: Services and other activity (% of GVA)	51.6	51.2	48.7[c]
Employment in agriculture (% of employed)[f]	44.3	40.7	38.0[c]
Employment in industry (% of employed)[f]	8.5	9.5	10.9[c]
Employment in services & other sectors (% employed)[f]	47.3	49.8	51.0[c]
Unemployment rate (% of labour force)[f]	1.6	0.7	1.5
Labour force participation rate (female/male pop. %)[f]	82.5 / 86.0	82.5 / 85.8	82.2 / 85.2
CPI: Consumer Price Index (2010=100)	100	125	137[c]
Agricultural production index (2014-2016=100)	92	100	105[c]
International trade: exports (million current US$)	215	400	379[f,b]
International trade: imports (million current US$)	328	466	643[f,b]
International trade: balance (million current US$)	- 112	- 65	- 265[f,b]
Balance of payments, current account (million US$)	- 144	- 36	- 219[b]

Major trading partners

2022

Export partners (% of exports)[f]	China	51.5	Italy	8.4	India	7.7
Import partners (% of imports)[f]	China	37.0	Singapore	15.8	Australia	10.9

Social indicators

	2010	2015	2023
Population growth rate (average annual %)	2.4	2.5	2.2[a,b]
Urban population (% of total population)	20.0	22.4	24.2[g]
Urban population growth rate (average annual %)[h]	4.7	4.3	...
Fertility rate, total (live births per woman)	4.4	4.4	3.9[a,b]
Life expectancy at birth (females/males, years)	70.6 / 67.1	71.2 / 68.1	72.4 / 69.3[a,b]
Population age distribution (0-14/60+ years old, %)	41.2 / 5.2	40.5 / 5.2	39.1 / 5.5[a,b]
International migrant stock (000/% of total pop.)[i]	2.8 / 0.5	2.6 / 0.4	2.5 / 0.4[i]
Refugees and others of concern to the UNHCR (000)	...	~0.0	~0.0[g]
Infant mortality rate (per 1 000 live births)	22.0	19.1	15.6[a,b]
Health: Current expenditure (% of GDP)	4.7	4.4	4.4[i]
Health: Physicians (per 1 000 pop.)	0.2[k]	0.2[l]	0.2[m]
Education: Government expenditure (% of GDP)	7.5	...	...
Education: Primary gross enrol. ratio (f/m per 100 pop.)	113.2 / 116.0	113.0 / 114.2	103.9 / 104.7[g]
Education: Lowr. sec. gross enrol. ratio (f/m per 100 pop.)	67.0 / 70.0	78.0 / 76.4	76.4 / 72.9[g]
Education: Upr. sec. gross enrol. ratio (f/m per 100 pop.)	26.4 / 36.6	26.5 / 30.7[n]	... / ...
Intentional homicide rate (per 100 000 pop.)	3.7[k]	...	...
Seats held by women in the National Parliament (%)	0.0	2.0	8.0[o]

Environment and infrastructure indicators

	2010	2015	2023
Individuals using the Internet (per 100 inhabitants)[f]	5.0	10.0	36.1[c]
Threatened species (number)	220	238	303[b]
Forested area (% of land area)	90.4	90.3	90.1[i]
Energy production, primary (Petajoules)[f]	3	3	3[i]
Energy supply per capita (Gigajoules)	15[f]	12	11[f,i]
Tourist/visitor arrivals at national borders (000)[p]	20	22	1[c]
Important sites for terrestrial biodiversity protected (%)	4.5	4.6	4.8[b]
Net Official Development Assist. received (% of GNI)	41.50	14.82	15.97[c]

a Projected estimate (medium fertility variant). b 2022. c 2021. d Solomon Islands Dollar. e 2018. f Estimate. g 2019. h Data refers to a 5-year period preceding the reference year. i Including refugees. j 2020. k 2008. l 2013. m 2016. n 2012. o Data are as at 1 January of reporting year. p Arrivals by air.

Somalia

Region	Eastern Africa	
Population (000, 2023)	17 598 [a,b]	
Pop. density (per km2, 2023)	28.1 [a,b]	
Capital city	Mogadishu	
Capital city pop. (000, 2023)	2 179.9 [d,e]	

UN membership date	20 September 1960
Surface area (km2)	637 657 [c]
Sex ratio (m per 100 f)	100.5 [a,b]
National currency	Somali Shilling (SOS)
Exchange rate (per US$)	24 300.0 [f,b]

Economic indicators

	2010	2015	2023
GDP: Gross domestic product (million current US$)	2 688	5 335	7 628 [c]
GDP growth rate (annual %, const. 2015 prices)	6.7	15.0	2.9 [c]
GDP per capita (current US$)	223.5	387.6	447.0 [c]
Economy: Agriculture (% of Gross Value Added)	60.2	60.2	60.2 [c]
Economy: Industry (% of Gross Value Added)	7.3	7.3	7.4 [c]
Economy: Services and other activity (% of GVA)	32.5	32.5	32.5 [c]
Employment in agriculture (% of employed) [g]	35.8	31.0	26.3 [c]
Employment in industry (% of employed) [g]	16.4	16.7	17.7 [c]
Employment in services & other sectors (% employed) [g]	47.7	52.3	56.1 [c]
Unemployment rate (% of labour force) [g]	19.2	18.9	20.4
Labour force participation rate (female/male pop. %) [g]	20.6 / 48.9	20.9 / 47.9	21.2 / 46.9
Agricultural production index (2014-2016=100)	107	102	99 [c]
International trade: exports (million current US$) [g]	568	853	639 [b]
International trade: imports (million current US$) [g]	496	525	3 871 [b]
International trade: balance (million current US$) [g]	72	328	- 3 232 [b]

Major trading partners

						2022
Export partners (% of exports) [g]	Oman	40.6	United Arab Emirates	28.8	Saudi Arabia	9.7
Import partners (% of imports) [g]	United Arab Emirates	32.1	China	15.9	India	13.9

Social indicators

	2010	2015	2023
Population growth rate (average annual %)	2.5	3.3	3.0 [a,b]
Urban population (% of total population)	39.3	43.2	45.6 [e]
Urban population growth rate (average annual %) [h]	4.5	4.8	...
Fertility rate, total (live births per woman)	7.3	7.0	6.2 [a,b]
Life expectancy at birth (females/males, years)	52.5 / 48.7	56.9 / 52.9	58.2 / 54.1 [a,b]
Population age distribution (0-14/60+ years old, %)	48.3 / 4.0	47.8 / 4.1	47.2 / 4.1 [a,b]
International migrant stock (000/% of total pop.) [g,i]	48.1 / 0.4	41.0 / 0.3	58.6 / 0.4 [j]
Refugees and others of concern to the UNHCR (000)	1 489.8 [k]	1 165.0	3 002.3 [b]
Infant mortality rate (per 1 000 live births)	102.5	83.9	66.2 [a,b]
Health: Physicians (per 1 000 pop.)	~0.0 [l]	~0.0 [m]	...
Education: Government expenditure (% of GDP)	...	...	0.0 [c]
Education: Primary gross enrol. ratio (f/m per 100 pop.)	16.6 / 30.1 [n]	... / ...	... / ...
Education: Lowr. sec. gross enrol. ratio (f/m per 100 pop.)	4.7 / 10.2 [n]	... / ...	... / ...
Education: Upr. sec. gross enrol. ratio (f/m per 100 pop.)	3.2 / 6.9 [n]	... / ...	... / ...
Seats held by women in the National Parliament (%)	6.9	13.8	19.7 [o]

Environment and infrastructure indicators

	2010	2015	2023
Individuals using the Internet (per 100 inhabitants) [g]	1.2 [p]	1.8	2.0 [q]
Threatened species (number)	128	165	232 [b]
Forested area (% of land area)	10.8	10.1	9.5 [i]
Energy production, primary (Petajoules)	124	129	151 [i]
Energy supply per capita (Gigajoules)	10	10	10 [i]
Important sites for terrestrial biodiversity protected (%)	0.0	0.0	0.0 [b]
Pop. using safely managed sanitation (urban/rural %)	38.4 / 12.5	41.1 / 16.4	44.5 / 21.8 [b]
Net Official Development Assist. received (% of GNI)	...	23.77	33.20 [c]

a Projected estimate (medium fertility variant). b 2022. c 2021. d Data refers to the urban agglomeration. e 2019. f UN operational exchange rate. g Estimate. h Data refers to a 5-year period preceding the reference year. i Including refugees. j 2020. k Data as at the end of December. l 2006. m 2014. n 2007. o Data are as at 1 January of reporting year. p 2009. q 2017.

South Africa

Region	Southern Africa	UN membership date	07 November 1945
Population (000, 2023)	59 894 a,b	Surface area (km2)	1 221 037 c
Pop. density (per km2, 2023)	49.1 a,b	Sex ratio (m per 100 f)	94.9 a,b
Capital city	Pretoria d	National currency	Rand (ZAR)
Capital city pop. (000, 2023)	2 472.6 e	Exchange rate (per US$)	17.0 b

Economic indicators

	2010	2015	2023
GDP: Gross domestic product (million current US$)	417 364	346 486	419 016 c
GDP growth rate (annual %, const. 2015 prices)	3.0	1.3	4.9 c
GDP per capita (current US$)	8 059.6	6 200.9	7 055.1 c
Economy: Agriculture (% of Gross Value Added)	2.3	2.5	2.7 c
Economy: Industry (% of Gross Value Added)	27.6	26.3	27.2 c
Economy: Services and other activity (% of GVA)	70.1	71.2	70.0 c
Employment in agriculture (% of employed)	16.6 f	15.5	21.3 c
Employment in industry (% of employed)	21.6	21.4	17.3 c
Employment in services & other sectors (% employed)	61.9	63.1	61.4 c
Unemployment rate (% of labour force)	23.2	22.9	29.9 f
Labour force participation rate (female/male pop. %)	47.0 / 62.2	51.0 / 65.0	51.9 / 64.7 f
CPI: Consumer Price Index (2010=100) g,h	100	130	183 b
Agricultural production index (2014-2016=100)	90	101	114 c
International trade: exports (million current US$)	82 631	80 264	121 616 b
International trade: imports (million current US$)	83 100	85 511	111 880 b
International trade: balance (million current US$)	- 469	- 5 246	9 736 b
Balance of payments, current account (million US$)	- 5 422	- 14 944	- 1 789 b

Major trading partners 2022

Export partners (% of exports) f	China	11.2	United States	8.9	Germany	7.3
Import partners (% of imports) f	China	20.1	India	7.5	United States	7.5

Social indicators

	2010	2015	2023
Population growth rate (average annual %)	1.2	2.4	0.8 a,b
Urban population (% of total population)	62.2	64.8	66.9 e
Urban population growth rate (average annual %) i	2.0	2.2	...
Fertility rate, total (live births per woman)	2.4	2.4	2.3 a,b
Life expectancy at birth (females/males, years)	61.3 / 56.1	66.8 / 60.7	64.2 / 58.6 a,b
Population age distribution (0-14/60+ years old, %)	28.7 / 7.6	28.3 / 8.1	28.6 / 8.7 a,b
International migrant stock (000/% of total pop.) j	2 114.8 / 4.1	3 231.7 / 5.8	2 860.5 / 4.8 k
Refugees and others of concern to the UNHCR (000)	229.7 l	912.6	240.1 b
Infant mortality rate (per 1 000 live births)	35.1	27.8	28.1 a,b
Health: Current expenditure (% of GDP) m	7.8	8.1	8.6 k
Health: Physicians (per 1 000 pop.)	...	...	0.8 c
Education: Government expenditure (% of GDP)	5.1	5.5	6.6 b
Education: Primary gross enrol. ratio (f/m per 100 pop.)	102.7 / 106.8	101.9 / 109.2	95.4 / 99.4 k
Education: Lowr. sec. gross enrol. ratio (f/m per 100 pop.)	103.2 / 101.9	106.5 / 105.4	104.3 / 103.7 k
Education: Upr. sec. gross enrol. ratio (f/m per 100 pop.)	92.3 / 83.9	110.2 / 113.2	108.1 / 93.6 k
Intentional homicide rate (per 100 000 pop.)	30.7	33.4	41.9 c
Seats held by women in the National Parliament (%)	44.5	41.5	46.2 n

Environment and infrastructure indicators

	2010	2015	2023
Individuals using the Internet (per 100 inhabitants) f	24.0	51.9	72.3 c
Research & Development expenditure (% of GDP)	0.7	0.7	0.6 e
Threatened species (number)	441	527	905 b
Forested area (% of land area)	14.4	14.2	14.1 k
CO2 emission estimates (million tons/tons per capita)	425.6 / 8.2	425.3 / 7.6	393.1 / 6.5 k
Energy production, primary (Petajoules)	6 617	6 442	6 313 k
Energy supply per capita (Gigajoules)	113	100	94 k
Tourist/visitor arrivals at national borders (000)	8 074 o	8 904 o,p	2 256 p,c
Important sites for terrestrial biodiversity protected (%)	30.9	32.7	36.5 b
Pop. using safely managed drinking water (urban/rural, %)	87.0 / ...	84.3 / ...	80.5 / ... b
Pop. using safely managed sanitation (urban/rural %)	69.3 / ...	70.9 / ...	73.1 / ... b
Net Official Development Assist. received (% of GNI)	0.25	0.42	0.25 c

a Projected estimate (medium fertility variant). b 2022. c 2021. d Pretoria is the administrative capital, Cape Town is the legislative capital and Bloemfontein is the judiciary capital. e 2019. f Estimate. g All urban consumers. h Calculated by the UN Statistics Division from national indices. i Data refers to a 5-year period preceding the reference year. j Including refugees. k 2020. l Data as at the end of December. m Data refer to fiscal years beginning 1 April. n Data are as at 1 January of reporting year. o Break in the time series. p Excluding transit.

South Sudan

Region	Eastern Africa		UN membership date		14 July 2011
Population (000, 2023)	10 913[a,b]		Surface area (km2)		658 841[c]
Pop. density (per km2, 2023)	19.3[a,b]		Sex ratio (m per 100 f)		98.1[a,b]
Capital city	Juba		National currency		S. Sudanese Pound (SSP)[d]
Capital city pop. (000, 2023)	385.8[e]		Exchange rate (per US$)		432.0[f]

Economic indicators	2010	2015	2023
GDP: Gross domestic product (million current US$)	14 925	6 231	4 304[f]
GDP growth rate (annual %, const. 2015 prices)	- 0.5	6.9	- 2.3[f]
GDP per capita (current US$)	1 536.4	556.6	400.4[f]
Economy: Agriculture (% of Gross Value Added)	5.1	4.2	4.0[f]
Economy: Industry (% of Gross Value Added)	55.4	45.0	52.0[f]
Economy: Services and other activity (% of GVA)	39.4	50.9	44.0[f]
Employment in agriculture (% of employed)[g]	62.1	62.0	62.1[f]
Employment in industry (% of employed)[g]	15.5	12.8	13.1[f]
Employment in services & other sectors (% employed)[g]	22.4	25.2	24.8[f]
Unemployment rate (% of labour force)[g]	12.1	12.3	12.7
Labour force participation rate (female/male pop. %)[g]	69.6 / 72.8	69.9 / 71.8	71.2 / 71.2
CPI: Consumer Price Index (2010=100)	100	332	22 571[f]
Agricultural production index (2014-2016=100)	...	101	113[f]
International trade: exports (million current US$)[g]	...	3 103	522[b]
International trade: imports (million current US$)[g]	...	635	1 312[b]
International trade: balance (million current US$)[g]	...	2 468	- 791[b]
Balance of payments, current account (million US$)	...	- 500	- 7[f]

Major trading partners					2022
Export partners (% of exports)[g]	China	37.4	Italy	22.3	Uganda	17.0
Import partners (% of imports)[g]	United Arab Emirates	33.6	Uganda	22.1	Kenya	12.0

Social indicators	2010	2015	2023
Population growth rate (average annual %)	5.9	1.1	1.5[a,b]
Urban population (% of total population)	17.9	18.9	19.9[e]
Urban population growth rate (average annual %)[h]	5.1	4.4	...
Fertility rate, total (live births per woman)	5.4	4.9	4.3[a,b]
Life expectancy at birth (females/males, years)	55.8 / 53.7	57.2 / 53.9	57.0 / 54.0[a,b]
Population age distribution (0-14/60+ years old, %)	43.0 / 4.0	43.5 / 4.1	43.9 / 4.8[a,b]
International migrant stock (000/% of total pop.)[i]	230.7 / 2.4	844.1 / 7.9	882.3 / 7.9[i]
Refugees and others of concern to the UNHCR (000)	...	2 058.5	2 667.7[b]
Infant mortality rate (per 1 000 live births)	69.4	63.8	60.7[a,b]
Health: Current expenditure (% of GDP)	...	...	5.3[k,j]
Health: Physicians (per 1 000 pop.)	...	...	~0.0[l]
Education: Government expenditure (% of GDP)	...	1.5	1.6[m]
Education: Primary gross enrol. ratio (f/m per 100 pop.)	... / ...	60.4 / 85.3	... / ...
Education: Lower. sec. gross enrol. ratio (f/m per 100 pop.)	... / ...	15.4 / 26.0	... / ...
Education: Upr. sec. gross enrol. ratio (f/m per 100 pop.)	... / ...	3.6 / 8.0	6.5 / 11.6[l]
Intentional homicide rate (per 100 000 pop.)	...	14.1[n]	...
Seats held by women in the National Parliament (%)	...	26.5	32.4[o]

Environment and infrastructure indicators	2010	2015	2023
Individuals using the Internet (per 100 inhabitants)[g]	...	3.0	6.5[j]
Threatened species (number)	...	42	68[b]
Forested area (% of land area)	...	41.7	11.3[j]
CO2 emission estimates (million tons/tons per capita)	... / ...	2.1 / 0.2	1.8 / 0.2[j]
Energy production, primary (Petajoules)	...	321	358[j]
Energy supply per capita (Gigajoules)	...	3	3[j]
Important sites for terrestrial biodiversity protected (%)	33.6	33.6	33.6[b]
Net Official Development Assist. received (% of GNI)	...	15.92	...

a Projected estimate (medium fertility variant). b 2022. c 2017. d South Sudanese Pound. e 2019. f 2021. g Estimate. h Data refers to a 5-year period preceding the reference year. i Including refugees. j 2020. k The country did not exist before 2012 (independence from Sudan on July 9, 2011, which corresponds to fiscal year 2011/12, converted in 2012). l 2018. m 2016. n 2012. o Data are as at 1 January of reporting year.

Spain

Region	Southern Europe	UN membership date	14 December 1955
Population (000, 2023)	47 559[a,b,c]	Surface area (km2)	506 008[d]
Pop. density (per km2, 2023)	94.7[a,b,c]	Sex ratio (m per 100 f)	96.1[a,b,c]
Capital city	Madrid	National currency	Euro (EUR)
Capital city pop. (000, 2023)	6 559.0[e]	Exchange rate (per US$)	0.9[c]

Economic indicators	2010	2015	2023
GDP: Gross domestic product (million current US$)	1 420 722	1 195 676	1 427 381[d]
GDP growth rate (annual %, const. 2015 prices)	0.2	3.8	5.5[d]
GDP per capita (current US$)	30 505.4	25 751.5	30 058.4[d]
Economy: Agriculture (% of Gross Value Added)[f,g]	2.6	3.0	2.9[d]
Economy: Industry (% of Gross Value Added)[f,h]	25.2	22.1	22.5[d]
Economy: Services and other activity (% of GVA)[f]	72.1	74.9	74.6[d]
Employment in agriculture (% of employed)	4.2	4.1	4.1[d]
Employment in industry (% of employed)	22.9	14.2[i]	20.2[d]
Employment in services & other sectors (% employed)	72.9	76.0	75.8[d]
Unemployment (% of labour force)	19.9	22.1	13.9[i]
Labour force participation rate (female/male pop. %)	51.7 / 67.2	52.6 / 64.6	52.5 / 62.9[i]
CPI: Consumer Price Index (2010=100)[j]	100	107	124[c]
Agricultural production index (2014-2016=100)	95	99	117[d]
International trade: exports (million current US$)	246 265	276 959	424 286[c]
International trade: imports (million current US$)	315 547	304 708	499 055[c]
International trade: balance (million current US$)	- 69 282	- 27 750	- 74 769[c]
Balance of payments, current account (million US$)	- 52 250	24 108	7 575[c]

Major trading partners						2022
Export partners (% of exports)	France	14.9	Germany	9.3	Portugal	8.0
Import partners (% of imports)	China	10.5	Germany	9.1	France	8.6

Social indicators	2010	2015	2023
Population growth rate (average annual %)[b]	0.4	~-0.0	- 0.1[a,c]
Urban population (% of total population)[b]	78.4	79.6	80.6[e]
Urban population growth rate (average annual %)[b,k]	1.5	0.1	...
Fertility rate, total (live births per woman)[b]	1.4	1.3	1.3[a,c]
Life expectancy at birth (females/males, years)[b]	85.0 / 79.0	85.4 / 79.9	86.5 / 81.2[a,c]
Population age distribution (0-14/60+ years old, %)[b]	15.0 / 22.2	15.2 / 24.1	13.8 / 26.8[a,c]
International migrant stock (000/% of total pop.)[b]	6 280.1 / 13.4	5 891.2 / 12.6	6 842.2 / 14.6[i]
Refugees and others of concern to the UNHCR (000)	6.6[m]	17.3	394.3[c]
Infant mortality rate (per 1 000 live births)[b]	3.2	2.6	2.2[a,c]
Health: Current expenditure (% of GDP)	9.1[n]	9.1	10.7[l]
Health: Physicians (per 1 000 pop.)	3.8	3.8	4.6[l]
Education: Government expenditure (% of GDP)	4.9	4.3	4.2[e]
Education: Primary gross enrol. ratio (f/m per 100 pop.)	103.6 / 104.4	107.2 / 105.6	103.9 / 102.9[l]
Education: Lowr. sec. gross enrol. ratio (f/m per 100 pop.)	113.7 / 114.7	121.1 / 126.0	116.4 / 117.4[l]
Education: Upr. sec. gross enrol. ratio (f/m per 100 pop.)	134.3 / 123.1	128.0 / 124.7	137.9 / 129.3[l]
Intentional homicide rate (per 100 000 pop.)	0.9	0.7	0.6[d]
Seats held by women in the National Parliament (%)	36.6	41.1	42.4[o]

Environment and infrastructure indicators	2010	2015	2023
Individuals using the Internet (per 100 inhabitants)	65.8[p]	78.7[q]	93.9[d]
Research & Development expenditure (% of GDP)	1.4	1.2	1.4[l]
Threatened species (number)	240	551	854[c]
Forested area (% of land area)	37.1	37.1	37.2[l]
CO2 emission estimates (million tons/tons per capita)	267.0 / 5.6	251.7 / 5.3	214.2 / 4.4[d]
Energy production, primary (Petajoules)[r]	1 418	1 372	1 407[l]
Energy supply per capita (Gigajoules)[r]	115	106	96[l]
Tourist/visitor arrivals at national borders (000)	52 677	68 175	31 181[d]
Important sites for terrestrial biodiversity protected (%)	51.3	57.3	57.6[c]
Pop. using safely managed drinking water (urban/rural, %)	99.9 / 98.6	99.8 / 98.6	99.8 / 98.6[c]
Net Official Development Assist. disbursed (% of GNI)[s]	0.74	1.84	0.52[d]

a Projected estimate (medium fertility variant). **b** Including Canary Islands, Ceuta and Melilla. **c** 2022. **d** 2021. **e** 2019. **f** Data classified according to ISIC Rev. 4. **g** Excludes irrigation canals and landscaping care. **h** Excludes publishing activities, recycling. Includes irrigation canals. **i** Estimate. **j** Calculated by the UN Statistics Division from national indices. **k** Data refers to a 5-year period preceding the reference year. **l** 2020. **m** Data as at the end of December. **n** Break in the time series. **o** Data are as at 1 January of reporting year. **p** Population aged 10 years and over. **q** Users in the last 3 months. **r** Data include the Canary Islands. **s** Development Assistance Committee member (OECD).

Sri Lanka

Region	Southern Asia	UN membership date	14 December 1955	
Population (000, 2023)	21 832[a,b]	Surface area (km2)	65 610[c]	
Pop. density (per km2, 2023)	348.2[a,b]	Sex ratio (m per 100 f)	92.9[a,b]	
Capital city	Colombo[d]	National currency	Sri Lanka Rupee (LKR)	
Capital city pop. (000, 2023)	606.2[e]	Exchange rate (per US$)	200.4[c]	

Economic indicators

	2010	2015	2023
GDP: Gross domestic product (million current US$)	56 726	80 604	85 309[c]
GDP growth rate (annual %, const. 2015 prices)	8.0	5.0	3.7[c]
GDP per capita (current US$)	2 744.5	3 777.7	3 918.0[c]
Economy: Agriculture (% of Gross Value Added)[f,g]	9.5	8.8	9.6[c]
Economy: Industry (% of Gross Value Added)[f,h]	29.7	29.3	29.5[c]
Economy: Services and other activity (% of GVA)[f]	60.9	61.9	60.9[c]
Employment in agriculture (% of employed)	30.9	28.7	25.7[i,c]
Employment in industry (% of employed)	24.8	25.8	27.9[i,c]
Employment in services & other sectors (% employed)	44.2	45.6	46.3[i,c]
Unemployment rate (% of labour force)	4.8	4.5	7.2[i]
Labour force participation rate (female/male pop. %)	34.0 / 74.2	35.4 / 73.8	33.0 / 70.3[i]
CPI: Consumer Price Index (2010=100)	100[j,k]	110[l]	221[l,b]
Agricultural production index (2014-2016=100)	96	104	116[c]
International trade: exports (million current US$)	8 304	10 440	13 592[b]
International trade: imports (million current US$)	12 354	18 967	17 560[b]
International trade: balance (million current US$)	- 4 050	- 8 528	- 3 967[b]
Balance of payments, current account (million US$)	- 1 075	- 1 883	- 1 083[m]

Major trading partners

						2022
Export partners (% of exports)	United States	25.5	United Kingdom	7.4	India	6.7
Import partners (% of imports)	India	26.4	China	20.0	United Arab Emirates	5.5

Social indicators

	2010	2015	2023
Population growth rate (average annual %)	0.9	0.4	0.3[a,b]
Urban population (% of total population)	18.2	18.3	18.6[e]
Urban population growth rate (average annual %)[n]	0.6	0.5	...
Fertility rate, total (live births per woman)	2.2	2.1	2.0[a,b]
Life expectancy at birth (females/males, years)	77.6 / 69.2	79.0 / 71.0	80.2 / 72.9[a,b]
Population age distribution (0-14/60+ years old, %)	25.5 / 11.8	25.0 / 13.6	22.8 / 16.7[a,b]
International migrant stock (000/% of total pop.)[o]	39.0 / 0.2	39.7 / 0.2	40.3 / 0.2[m]
Refugees and others of concern to the UNHCR (000)	435.3[p]	51.8	9.9[b]
Infant mortality rate (per 1 000 live births)	9.7	7.5	5.5[a,b]
Health: Current expenditure (% of GDP)	3.9	3.9	4.1[i,m]
Health: Physicians (per 1 000 pop.)	0.7	0.8	1.2[c]
Education: Government expenditure (% of GDP)	1.7	2.1	2.0[q]
Education: Primary gross enrol. ratio (f/m per 100 pop.)	98.2 / 100.7	100.6 / 102.7	100.3 / 100.3[m]
Education: Lowr. sec. gross enrol. ratio (f/m per 100 pop.)	96.8 / 100.8	97.7 / 99.0	101.7 / 101.5[m]
Education: Upr. sec. gross enrol. ratio (f/m per 100 pop.)	98.2 / 91.7	103.9 / 94.0[r]	105.3 / 95.2[q]
Intentional homicide rate (per 100 000 pop.)	3.7	2.3	3.4[e]
Seats held by women in the National Parliament (%)	5.8	5.8	5.3[s]

Environment and infrastructure indicators

	2010	2015	2023
Individuals using the Internet (per 100 inhabitants)	3.9[t]	15.3[i,u,v]	66.7[i,c]
Research & Development expenditure (% of GDP)	0.1	0.1	0.1[q]
Threatened species (number)	552	580	820[b]
Forested area (% of land area)	33.5	34.4	34.2[m]
CO2 emission estimates (million tons/tons per capita)	14.0 / 0.6	19.6 / 0.9	22.0 / 1.0[m]
Energy production, primary (Petajoules)	163	159	151[i,m]
Energy supply per capita (Gigajoules)	16	19	19[m]
Tourist/visitor arrivals at national borders (000)[w]	654	1 798	194[c]
Important sites for terrestrial biodiversity protected (%)	41.4	43.7	43.7[b]
Pop. using safely managed drinking water (urban/rural, %)	88.1 / 37.0	90.3 / 37.7	83.0 / 38.7[b]
Net Official Development Assist. received (% of GNI)	1.00	0.57	0.19[c]

a Projected estimate (medium fertility variant). b 2022. c 2021. d Colombo is the capital and Sri Jayewardenepura Kotte is the legislative capital. e 2019. f Data classified according to ISIC Rev. 4. g Excludes irrigation canals and landscaping care. h Excludes publishing activities, recycling. Includes irrigation canals. i Estimate. j Colombo k Calculated by the UN Statistics Division from national indices. l Index base: 2013=100. m 2020. n Data refers to a 5-year period preceding the reference year. o Including refugees. p Data as at the end of December. q 2018. r 2013. s Data are as at 1 January of reporting year. t 2007. u Users in the last 12 months. v Population aged 5 to 69 years. w Excluding nationals residing abroad.

State of Palestine

Region	Western Asia	Population (000, 2023)	5 250[a,b,c]
Surface area (km2)	6 025[d]	Pop. density (per km2, 2023)	872.1[a,b,c]
Sex ratio (m per 100 f)	99.6[a,b,c]	Capital city	East Jerusalem[e]
Capital city pop. (000, 2023)	275.1[e,f]		

Economic indicators

	2010	2015	2023
GDP: Gross domestic product (million current US$)	9 682	13 972	18 037[d]
GDP growth rate (annual %, const. 2015 prices)	5.8	3.7	7.1[d]
GDP per capita (current US$)	2 425.1	3 115.6	3 513.6[d]
Economy: Agriculture (% of Gross Value Added)[g,h]	10.6	8.7	8.3[d]
Economy: Industry (% of Gross Value Added)[h,i]	21.8	19.2	21.2[d]
Economy: Services and other activity (% of GVA)[h]	67.6	72.1	70.4[d]
Employment in agriculture (% of employed)	11.8	8.7	6.7[d]
Employment in industry (% of employed)	14.1[j]	28.7	19.9[j,d]
Employment in services & other sectors (% employed)	63.5	62.6	61.5[d]
Unemployment rate (% of labour force)	21.4	23.0	25.6[j]
Labour force participation (female/male pop. %)	14.1 / 66.7	18.0 / 70.8	19.2 / 71.6[j]
CPI: Consumer Price Index (2010=100)	100	111	117[k,c]
Agricultural production index (2014-2016=100)	102	90	104[d]
International trade: exports (million current US$)	576	958	1 475[j,c]
International trade: imports (million current US$)	3 959	5 225	9 996[j,c]
International trade: balance (million current US$)	- 3 383	- 4 268	- 8 520[j,c]
Balance of payments, current account (million US$)	- 1 307	- 1 939	- 2 865[c]

Major trading partners   2022

Export partners (% of exports)[j]	Israel	86.1	Jordan	5.1	United Arab Emirates	1.5
Import partners (% of imports)[j]	Israel	53.1	Türkiye	10.3	China	6.8

Social indicators

	2010	2015	2023
Population growth rate (average annual %)[b]	2.4	2.4	2.3[a,c]
Urban population (% of total population)[b]	74.1	75.4	76.4[l]
Urban population growth rate (average annual %)[b,m]	2.9	3.1	...
Fertility rate, total (live births per woman)[b]	4.4	4.0	3.4[a,c]
Life expectancy at birth (females/males, years)[b]	75.1 / 70.9	76.4 / 72.4	75.9 / 71.0[a,c]
Population age distribution (0-14/60+ years old, %)[b]	42.4 / 4.3	40.6 / 4.8	38.8 / 5.5[a,c]
International migrant stock (000/% of total pop.)[b]	273.8 / 6.8	273.2 / 6.0	272.8 / 5.3[n]
Refugees and others of concern to the UNHCR (000)	...	~0.0	...
Infant mortality rate (per 1 000 live births)[b]	18.6	16.4	13.9[a,c]
Health: Physicians (per 1 000 pop.)	...	...	2.2[f]
Education: Government expenditure (% of GDP)	6.2	4.7	5.5[d]
Education: Primary gross enrol. ratio (f/m per 100 pop.)	90.4 / 92.2	97.5 / 97.5	93.7 / 94.2[d]
Education: Lowr. sec. gross enrol. ratio (f/m per 100 pop.)	90.1 / 86.3	94.0 / 89.4	98.8 / 96.1[d]
Education: Upr. sec. gross enrol. ratio (f/m per 100 pop.)	85.9 / 70.2	77.4 / 59.0	92.0 / 73.5[d]
Intentional homicide rate (per 100 000 pop.)	1.0	1.2	0.9[d]

Environment and infrastructure indicators

	2010	2015	2023
Individuals using the Internet (per 100 inhabitants)	37.4[j,o]	56.7[j]	70.6[l]
Research & Development expenditure (% of GDP)[p]	0.4	0.5[q]	...
Threatened species (number)	18	24	55[c]
Forested area (% of land area)	1.7	1.7	1.7[n]
Energy production, primary (Petajoules)	9	9	9[n]
Energy supply per capita (Gigajoules)	13	16	16[n]
Tourist/visitor arrivals at national borders (000)	522	432[r]	170[r,n]
Important sites for terrestrial biodiversity protected (%)	17.5	19.6	20.9[c]
Pop. using safely managed drinking water (urban/rural, %)	78.1 / 71.6	79.5 / 73.6	81.5 / 76.4[c]
Pop. using safely managed sanitation (urban/rural %)	60.8 / 25.4	66.4 / 37.2	74.6 / 54.7[c]
Net Official Development Assist. received (% of GNI)	24.44	11.94	10.08[d]

a Projected estimate (medium fertility variant). **b** Including East Jerusalem. **c** 2022. **d** 2021. **e** Designation and data provided by the State of Palestine. The position of the UN on Jerusalem is stated in A/RES/181 (II) and subsequent General Assembly and Security Council resolutions. **f** 2018. **g** Excludes irrigation canals and landscaping care. **h** Data classified according to ISIC Rev. 4. **i** Excludes publishing activities, recycling. Includes irrigation canals. **j** Estimate. **k** Calculated by the UN Statistics Division from national indices. **l** 2019. **m** Data refers to a 5-year period preceding the reference year. **n** 2020. **o** Refers to total population. **p** Excluding business enterprise. **q** 2013. **r** Represent the data on hotel activity in the West Bank only.

Sudan

Region	Northern Africa	UN membership date	12 November 1956
Population (000, 2023)	46 874[a,b]	Pop. density (per km2, 2023)	26.6[a,b]
Sex ratio (m per 100 f)	99.9[a,b]	Capital city	Khartoum
National currency	Sudanese Pound (SDG)	Capital city pop. (000, 2023)	5 677.9[c]
Exchange rate (per US$)	578.2[b]		

Economic indicators

	2010	2015	2023
GDP: Gross domestic product (million current US$)[d]	54 740	83 934	35 867[e]
GDP growth rate (annual %, const. 2015 prices)[d]	8.3	4.0	0.1[e]
GDP per capita (current US$)[d]	1 622.4	2 198.9	785.6[e]
Economy: Agriculture (% of Gross Value Added)[d]	42.6	32.0	19.7[e]
Economy: Industry (% of Gross Value Added)[d]	14.1	16.3	22.3[e]
Economy: Services and other activity (% of GVA)[d]	43.4	51.8	58.0[e]
Employment in agriculture (% of employed)[f]	45.9	42.8	40.6[e]
Employment in industry (% of employed)[f]	14.9	14.7	14.6[e]
Employment in services & other sectors (% employed)[f]	39.1	42.5	44.8[e]
Unemployment rate (% of labour force)[f]	15.1	17.4	18.5
Labour force participation rate (female/male pop. %)[f]	28.3 / 70.4	28.4 / 69.3	29.5 / 68.6
CPI: Consumer Price Index (2010=100)[f]	100	350	55 732[b]
Agricultural production index (2014-2016=100)	...	92	115[e]
International trade: exports (million current US$)[g]	...	5 588	3 102[f,b]
International trade: imports (million current US$)[g]	...	8 413	16 828[f,b]
International trade: balance (million current US$)[g]	...	- 2 826	- 13 726[f,b]
Balance of payments, current account (million US$)	- 1 725	- 5 461	- 4 443[b]

Major trading partners

						2022
Export partners (% of exports)[f]	United Arab Emirates	50.1	China	12.4	Italy	7.6
Import partners (% of imports)[f]	China	17.8	United Arab Emirates	16.5	Saudi Arabia	15.0

Social indicators

	2010	2015	2023
Population growth rate (average annual %)	2.0	3.1	2.6[a,b]
Urban population (% of total population)	33.1	33.9	34.9[c]
Urban population growth rate (average annual %)[h]	2.3	2.8	...
Fertility rate, total (live births per woman)	5.0	4.9	4.4[a,b]
Life expectancy at birth (females/males, years)	65.5 / 60.7	67.3 / 62.1	68.2 / 63.0[a,b]
Population age distribution (0-14/60+ years old, %)	42.1 / 4.1	42.0 / 4.9	40.9 / 5.5[a,b]
International migrant stock (000/% of total pop.)[i]	618.7 / 1.8	620.5 / 1.6	1 379.1 / 3.1[i]
Refugees and others of concern to the UNHCR (000)	1 951.5[k]	2 767.9	4 181.3[b]
Infant mortality rate (per 1 000 live births)	50.7	45.3	37.5[a,b]
Health: Current expenditure (% of GDP)[l,n]	5.1[m]	7.3	3.0[f,o,j]
Health: Physicians (per 1 000 pop.)	0.3[p]	0.4	0.3[q]
Education: Government expenditure (% of GDP)	2.0[r]	...	...
Education: Primary gross enrol. ratio (f/m per 100 pop.)	67.8 / 75.6	69.8 / 76.4	76.1 / 81.7[s]
Education: Lowr. sec. gross enrol. ratio (f/m per 100 pop.)	50.5 / 61.5	52.3 / 56.9	54.4 / 56.4[s]
Education: Upr. sec. gross enrol. ratio (f/m per 100 pop.)	31.5 / 34.0	40.3 / 38.2	40.6 / 37.6[s]
Seats held by women in the National Parliament (%)	...	24.3	27.7[c]

Environment and infrastructure indicators

	2010	2015	2023
Individuals using the Internet (per 100 inhabitants)	8.7[t]	...	28.4[f,j]
Research & Development expenditure (% of GDP)	0.2[f,u,v]	...	...
Threatened species (number)	112	123	172[b]
Forested area (% of land area)	...	905.1	9.8[j]
CO2 emission estimates (million tons/tons per capita)	17.4 / 0.3	19.2 / 0.4	21.2 / 0.4[j]
Energy production, primary (Petajoules)	...	461	405[j]
Energy supply per capita (Gigajoules)	...	13	12[j]
Tourist/visitor arrivals at national borders (000)[w]	495	741	836[s]
Important sites for terrestrial biodiversity protected (%)	9.1	9.1	17.8[b]
Net Official Development Assist. received (% of GNI)	2.94	1.17	11.74[e]

a Projected estimate (medium fertility variant). b 2022. c 2019. d Data compiled in accordance with the System of National Accounts 1968 (1968 SNA). e 2021. f Estimate. g Data up to 2011 refer to former Sudan (including South Sudan) and data beginning 2012 is attributed to Sudan without South Sudan. h Data refers to a 5-year period preceding the reference year. i Including refugees. j 2020. k Data as at the end of December. l Data based on calendar year (January 1 to December 31). m Including South Sudan. n Estimates should be viewed with caution as these are derived from scarce data. o Data are based on SHA2011. p 2008. q 2017. r 2009. s 2018. t 2007. u Overestimated or based on overestimated data. v 2005. w Including nationals residing abroad.

Suriname

Region	South America	UN membership date	04 December 1975
Population (000, 2023)	618[a,b]	Surface area (km2)	163 820[c]
Pop. density (per km2, 2023)	4.0[a,b]	Sex ratio (m per 100 f)	99.1[a,b]
Capital city	Paramaribo	National currency	Surinam Dollar (SRD)
Capital city pop. (000, 2023)	239.5[d,e]	Exchange rate (per US$)	31.8[b]

Economic indicators	2010	2015	2023
GDP: Gross domestic product (million current US$)	4 482	5 126	3 224[c]
GDP growth rate (annual %, const. 2015 prices)	6.1	- 2.6	- 2.7[c]
GDP per capita (current US$)	8 207.3	8 907.8	5 259.3[c]
Economy: Agriculture (% of Gross Value Added)[f]	10.7	11.3[g]	9.4[a,c]
Economy: Industry (% of Gross Value Added)[f]	39.2	29.6	37.6[c]
Economy: Services and other activity (% of GVA)[f]	50.1	59.1	53.0[c]
Employment in agriculture (% of employed)[h]	7.2	7.3	7.9[c]
Employment in industry (% of employed)[h]	24.8	27.1	26.7[c]
Employment in services & other sectors (% employed)[h]	68.2	65.6	65.6[c]
Unemployment rate (% of labour force)	7.2	7.2	8.2[h]
Labour force participation rate (female/male pop. %)[h]	40.7 / 64.8	44.4 / 66.8	46.0 / 65.7
CPI: Consumer Price Index (2010=100)[i]	100	139	965[b]
Agricultural production index (2014-2016=100)	92	98	88[c]
International trade: exports (million current US$)	2 026	1 814	2 579[b]
International trade: imports (million current US$)	1 397	1 904	1 803[b]
International trade: balance (million current US$)	628	- 90	776[b]
Balance of payments, current account (million US$)	651	- 786	67[b]

Major trading partners					2022
Export partners (% of exports)	Switzerland	44.6	United Arab Emirates	23.2[h]	Belgium	5.0[h]
Import partners (% of imports)	United States	24.5	Netherlands	14.0	Trinidad and Tobago	13.9

Social indicators	2010	2015	2023
Population growth rate (average annual %)	1.1	1.0	0.8[a,b]
Urban population (% of total population)	66.3	66.1	66.1[j]
Urban population growth rate (average annual %)[k]	1.0	0.9	...
Fertility rate, total (live births per woman)	2.6	2.5	2.3[a,b]
Life expectancy at birth (females/males, years)	73.6 / 66.5	74.2 / 67.6	73.6 / 67.2[a,b]
Population age distribution (0-14/60+ years old, %)	29.9 / 8.6	28.5 / 9.5	26.2 / 11.4[a,b]
International migrant stock (000/% of total pop.)[l,m]	39.7 / 7.5	43.1 / 7.7	47.8 / 8.1[n]
Refugees and others of concern to the UNHCR (000)	~0.0[o]	~0.0	2.5[b]
Infant mortality rate (per 1 000 live births)	20.5	18.1	16.1[a,b]
Health: Current expenditure (% of GDP)[h,q]	4.7[p]	5.8[p]	6.8[n]
Health: Physicians (per 1 000 pop.)	0.7[r]	1.0	0.8[e]
Education: Government expenditure (% of GDP)	...	5.5	4.0[c]
Education: Primary gross enrol. ratio (f/m per 100 pop.)	113.8 / 114.2	116.4 / 115.2	100.2 / 101.2[c]
Education: Lowr. sec. gross enrol. ratio (f/m per 100 pop.)	90.2 / 80.5	104.7 / 89.2	96.2 / 83.9[c]
Education: Upr. sec. gross enrol. ratio (f/m per 100 pop.)	67.7 / 37.8	66.9 / 36.8	53.1 / 37.1[c]
Intentional homicide rate (per 100 000 pop.)	8.1[s]	5.9	5.7[c]
Seats held by women in the National Parliament (%)	25.5	11.8	29.4[t]

Environment and infrastructure indicators	2010	2015	2023
Individuals using the Internet (per 100 inhabitants)	31.6	42.8[h]	65.9[h,c]
Threatened species (number)	65	76	129[b]
Forested area (% of land area)	98.1	97.8	97.4[n]
CO2 emission estimates (million tons/tons per capita)	1.8 / 3.3	2.7 / 4.8	2.6 / 4.4[n]
Energy production, primary (Petajoules)	43	45	43[n]
Energy supply per capita (Gigajoules)	73	75	74[n]
Tourist/visitor arrivals at national borders (000)	205	228	278[u]
Important sites for terrestrial biodiversity protected (%)	51.2	51.2	51.2[b]
Pop. using safely managed drinking water (urban/rural, %)	62.9 / 35.6	63.1 / 38.2	63.4 / 40.8[b]
Pop. using safely managed sanitation (urban/rural, %)	23.6 / 38.3	22.0 / 36.2	20.7 / 33.9[b]
Net Official Development Assist. received (% of GNI)	2.36	0.31	1.16[c]

a Projected estimate (medium fertility variant). b 2022. c 2021. d Refers to the total population of the District of Paramaribo. e 2018. f Data classified according to ISIC Rev. 4. g Excludes irrigation canals and landscaping care. h Estimate. i Calculated by the UN Statistics Division from national indices. j 2019. k Data refers to a 5-year period preceding the reference year. l Refers to foreign citizens. m Including refugees. n 2020. o Data as at the end of December. p Estimates should be viewed with caution as these are derived from scarce data. q Data based on calendar year (January 1 to December 31). r 2009. s 2008. t Data are as at 1 January of reporting year. u 2017.

Sweden

Region	Northern Europe	UN membership date	19 November 1946	
Population (000, 2023)	10 549[a,b]	Surface area (km2)	438 574[c]	
Pop. density (per km2, 2023)	25.9[a,b]	Sex ratio (m per 100 f)	101.6[a,b]	
Capital city	Stockholm	National currency	Swedish Krona (SEK)	
Capital city pop. (000, 2023)	1 608.0[d,e]	Exchange rate (per US$)	10.4[b]	

Economic indicators	2010	2015	2023
GDP: Gross domestic product (million current US$)	495 813	505 104	635 664[c]
GDP growth rate (annual %, const. 2015 prices)	6.0	4.5	5.1[c]
GDP per capita (current US$)	52 848.7	51 283.0	60 729.7[c]
Economy: Agriculture (% of Gross Value Added)[f,g]	1.9	1.6	1.5[c]
Economy: Industry (% of Gross Value Added)[g,h]	26.9	24.9	25.5[c]
Economy: Services and other activity (% of GVA)[g]	71.2	73.4	73.0[c]
Employment in agriculture (% of employed)	2.1	0.1[i]	0.1[i,c]
Employment in industry (% of employed)	19.9	18.3	18.1[c]
Employment in services & other sectors (% employed)	78.0	79.6	79.9[c]
Unemployment rate (% of labour force)	8.6	7.4	7.5[i]
Labour force participation rate (female/male pop. %)[i]	59.0 / 67.5	60.6 / 67.3	61.5 / 67.7
CPI: Consumer Price Index (2010=100)	100	104	123[b]
Agricultural production index (2014-2016=100)	91	102	96[c]
International trade: exports (million current US$)	158 411	140 001	197 575[b]
International trade: imports (million current US$)	148 788	138 361	202 093[b]
International trade: balance (million current US$)	9 622	1 641	- 4 518[b]
Balance of payments, current account (million US$)	29 196	16 159	25 015[b]

Major trading partners						2022
Export partners (% of exports)	Germany	11.1	Norway	10.9	United States	9.2
Import partners (% of imports)	Germany	15.3	Norway	11.7	Netherlands	10.5

Social indicators	2010	2015	2023
Population growth rate (average annual %)	0.9	1.0	0.6[a,b]
Urban population (% of total population)	85.1	86.6	87.7[e]
Urban population growth rate (average annual %)[j]	0.9	1.1	...
Fertility rate, total (live births per woman)	2.0	1.8	1.7[a,b]
Life expectancy at birth (females/males, years)	83.5 / 79.5	84.0 / 80.3	85.1 / 81.9[a,b]
Population age distribution (0-14/60+ years old, %)	16.6 / 24.9	17.4 / 25.3	17.6 / 25.7[a,b]
International migrant stock (000/% of total pop.)	1 337.2 / 14.2	1 602.5 / 16.4	2 003.9 / 19.8[k]
Refugees and others of concern to the UNHCR (000)	110.8[l]	225.5	315.1[b]
Infant mortality rate (per 1 000 live births)	2.6	2.4	1.8[a,b]
Health: Current expenditure (% of GDP)	8.3	10.8	11.3[c]
Health: Physicians (per 1 000 pop.)	3.8	4.2	7.1[k]
Education: Government expenditure (% of GDP)	6.5	7.4	7.6[e]
Education: Primary gross enrol. ratio (f/m per 100 pop.)	101.2 / 101.7	125.5 / 120.5	129.0 / 122.5[k]
Education: Lowr. sec. gross enrol. ratio (f/m per 100 pop.)	95.9 / 96.4	118.6 / 112.4	121.4 / 117.2[k]
Education: Upr. sec. gross enrol. ratio (f/m per 100 pop.)	99.1 / 100.5	179.1 / 149.2	183.6 / 163.7[k]
Intentional homicide rate (per 100 000 pop.)	1.0	1.1	1.1[c]
Seats held by women in the National Parliament (%)	46.4	43.6	46.4[m]

Environment and infrastructure indicators	2010	2015	2023
Individuals using the Internet (per 100 inhabitants)	90.0[n]	90.6	88.3[c]
Research & Development expenditure (% of GDP)	3.2[i]	3.2[o]	3.5[k]
Threatened species (number)	29	36	117[b]
Forested area (% of land area)	68.9	68.7	68.7[b]
CO2 emission estimates (million tons/tons per capita)	48.4 / 5.0	39.4 / 3.8	35.6 / 3.2[c]
Energy production, primary (Petajoules)	1 343	1 398	1 411[k]
Energy supply per capita (Gigajoules)	224	186	176[k]
Tourist/visitor arrivals at national borders (000)	5 183	6 482	2 990[c]
Important sites for terrestrial biodiversity protected (%)	56.5	58.0	59.2[b]
Pop. using safely managed sanitation (urban/rural %)	95.9 / 91.4	96.0 / 91.6	96.0 / 91.8[b]
Net Official Development Assist. disbursed (% of GNI)[p]	1.10	2.05	1.60[c]

a Projected estimate (medium fertility variant). b 2022. c 2021. d Refers to "tätort" (according to the administrative divisions of 2005). e 2019. f Excludes irrigation canals and landscaping care. g Data classified according to ISIC Rev. 4. h Excludes publishing activities, recycling. Includes irrigation canals. i Estimate. j Data refers to a 5-year period preceding the reference year. k 2020. l Data as at the end of December. m Data are as at 1 January of reporting year. n Population aged 16 to 75 years. o The sum of the breakdown does not add to the total. p Development Assistance Committee member (OECD).

Switzerland

Region	Western Europe	UN membership date	10 September 2002
Population (000, 2023)	8 740[a,b]	Surface area (km2)	41 291[c]
Pop. density (per km2, 2023)	218.6[a,b]	Sex ratio (m per 100 f)	98.6[a,b]
Capital city	Bern	National currency	Swiss Franc (CHF)
Capital city pop. (000, 2023)	426.0[d]	Exchange rate (per US$)	0.9[b]

Economic indicators

	2010	2015	2023
GDP: Gross domestic product (million current US$)	603 434	702 150	812 867[c]
GDP growth rate (annual %, const. 2015 prices)	3.3	1.7	3.7[c]
GDP per capita (current US$)	77 141.5	84 782.9	93 525.4[c]
Economy: Agriculture (% of Gross Value Added)[e,f]	0.7	0.6	0.6[c]
Economy: Industry (% of Gross Value Added)[e,g]	25.8	25.3	26.4[c]
Economy: Services and other activity (% of GVA)[e]	73.5	74.1	73.0[c]
Employment in agriculture (% of employed)	3.5	3.4	2.2[c]
Employment in industry (% of employed)	21.5[h]	19.7[h]	19.9[c]
Employment in services & other sectors (% employed)	74.0	75.8	78.0[c]
Unemployment rate (% of labour force)	4.8	4.8	4.2[h]
Labour force participation rate (female/male pop. %)	60.0 / 74.3	62.3 / 74.2	62.2 / 72.3[h]
CPI: Consumer Price Index (2010=100)[i]	100	98	102[b]
Agricultural production index (2014-2016=100)	99	99	95[c]
International trade: exports (million current US$)	195 609	291 959	400 057[b]
International trade: imports (million current US$)	176 281	253 152	356 235[b]
International trade: balance (million current US$)	19 329	38 807	43 822[b]
Balance of payments, current account (million US$)	78 050	61 631	81 459[b]

Major trading partners 2022

Export partners (% of exports)	United States	16.3	Germany	13.3	China	11.0
Import partners (% of imports)	Germany	19.5	United States	11.0	Italy	7.0

Social indicators

	2010	2015	2023
Population growth rate (average annual %)	1.2	1.1	0.7[a,b]
Urban population (% of total population)	73.6	73.7	73.8[d]
Urban population growth rate (average annual %)[j]	1.1	1.2	...
Fertility rate, total (live births per woman)	1.5	1.5	1.5[a,b]
Life expectancy at birth (females/males, years)	84.4 / 80.0	84.9 / 80.7	85.9 / 82.5[a,b]
Population age distribution (0-14/60+ years old, %)	15.2 / 22.7	14.9 / 23.5	15.0 / 25.7[a,b]
International migrant stock (000/% of total pop.)	2 075.2 / 26.6	2 258.2 / 27.2	2 491.2 / 28.8[k]
Refugees and others of concern to the UNHCR (000)	61.9[l]	86.6	121.1[b]
Infant mortality rate (per 1 000 live births)	3.9	4.0	3.1[a,b]
Health: Current expenditure (% of GDP)	9.9	11.0	11.8[k]
Health: Physicians (per 1 000 pop.)	3.8	4.2	4.4[c]
Education: Government expenditure (% of GDP)	4.8	5.0	5.1[d]
Education: Primary gross enrol. ratio (f/m per 100 pop.)	102.6 / 103.1	104.0 / 104.3	105.8 / 106.5[k]
Education: Lowr. sec. gross enrol. ratio (f/m per 100 pop.)	111.5 / 108.6	106.0 / 106.7	105.1 / 105.7[k]
Education: Upr. sec. gross enrol. ratio (f/m per 100 pop.)	82.6 / 89.5	95.3 / 100.8	95.9 / 105.0[k]
Intentional homicide rate (per 100 000 pop.)	0.7	0.7	0.5[c]
Seats held by women in the National Parliament (%)	29.0	30.5	41.7[m]

Environment and infrastructure indicators

	2010	2015	2023
Individuals using the Internet (per 100 inhabitants)	83.9[n,o]	87.5	95.6[p,c]
Research & Development expenditure (% of GDP)	2.7[q]	3.1	3.2[d]
Threatened species (number)	45	62	171[b]
Forested area (% of land area)	31.2	31.7	32.1[k]
CO2 emission estimates (million tons/tons per capita)	44.2 / 5.5	38.3 / 4.5	33.8 / 3.8[c]
Energy production, primary (Petajoules)	516	495	519[k]
Energy supply per capita (Gigajoules)	139	122	112[k]
Tourist/visitor arrivals at national borders (000)	8 628[r]	9 305[r]	4 390[s,c]
Important sites for terrestrial biodiversity protected (%)	34.6	34.6	37.1[b]
Pop. using safely managed sanitation (urban/rural %)	99.8 / 95.5	99.9 / 97.4	99.9 / 99.6[b]
Net Official Development Assist. disbursed (% of GNI)[t]	4.01	0.94	0.50[c]

a Projected estimate (medium fertility variant). **b** 2022. **c** 2021. **d** 2019. **e** Data classified according to ISIC Rev. 4. **f** Excludes irrigation canals and landscaping care. **g** Excludes publishing activities, recycling. Includes irrigation canals. **h** Estimate. **i** Calculated by the UN Statistics Division from national indices. **j** Data refers to a 5-year period preceding the reference year. **k** 2020. **l** Data as at the end of December. **m** Data are as at 1 January of reporting year. **n** Population aged 14 years and over. **o** Users in the last 6 months. **p** Population aged 15 to 88 years. **q** 2008. **r** Hotels and similar establishments (including health establishments). **s** All collective tourism establishments. **t** Development Assistance Committee member (OECD).

Syrian Arab Republic

Region	Western Asia	UN membership date	24 October 1945
Population (000, 2023)	22 125[a,b]	Surface area (km2)	185 180[c]
Pop. density (per km2, 2023)	120.4[a,b]	Sex ratio (m per 100 f)	100.3[a,b]
Capital city	Damascus	National currency	Syrian Pound (SYP)
Capital city pop. (000, 2023)	2 353.6[d,e]	Exchange rate (per US$)	3 000.0[f,b]

Economic indicators	2010	2015	2023
GDP: Gross domestic product (million current US$)	60 465	19 967	19 719[c]
GDP growth rate (annual %, const. 2015 prices)	3.4	- 3.2	- 2.9[c]
GDP per capita (current US$)	2 706.9	1 039.6	924.7[c]
Economy: Agriculture (% of Gross Value Added)[g]	19.7	20.7	20.6[c]
Economy: Industry (% of Gross Value Added)[g]	30.7	30.0	30.1[c]
Economy: Services and other activity (% of GVA)	49.6	49.3	49.3[c]
Employment in agriculture (% of employed)	14.8	14.2[h]	12.5[h,c]
Employment in industry (% of employed)[h]	33.7	22.3	22.2[c]
Employment in services & other sectors (% employed)	51.6	63.5[h]	65.4[h,c]
Unemployment rate (% of labour force)	8.6	8.7[h]	9.5[h]
Labour force participation rate (female/male pop. %)	13.0 / 72.3	15.9 / 72.5[h]	17.1 / 72.6[h]
CPI: Consumer Price Index (2010=100)	100	449	896[e]
Agricultural production index (2014-2016=100)	126	108	103[c]
International trade: exports (million current US$)	11 353	1 688[h]	4 514[h,b]
International trade: imports (million current US$)	17 562	3 206[h]	5 846[h,b]
International trade: balance (million current US$)	- 6 209	- 1 518[h]	- 1 332[h,b]
Balance of payments, current account (million US$)	- 367	...	...

Major trading partners						2022
Export partners (% of exports)[h]	Saudi Arabia	35.1	Türkiye	20.6	Lebanon	9.7
Import partners (% of imports)[h]	Türkiye	38.5	Russian Federation	11.9	United Arab Emirates	10.9

Social indicators	2010	2015	2023
Population growth rate (average annual %)	2.3	- 3.0	4.8[a,b]
Urban population (% of total population)	55.6	52.2	54.8[e]
Urban population growth rate (average annual %)[i]	3.4	- 3.6	...
Fertility rate, total (live births per woman)	3.4	3.0	2.7[a,b]
Life expectancy at birth (females/males, years)	76.7 / 71.4	70.4 / 60.6	76.1 / 68.7[a,b]
Population age distribution (0-14/60+ years old, %)	36.4 / 5.2	41.1 / 6.3	31.4 / 7.2[a,b]
International migrant stock (000/% of total pop.)[j,k]	1 783.6 / 8.3	835.7 / 4.6	868.7 / 5.0[l]
Refugees and others of concern to the UNHCR (000)	1 308.1[m]	7 946.5	7 070.6[b]
Infant mortality rate (per 1 000 live births)	15.9	25.1	16.3[a,b]
Health: Current expenditure (% of GDP)[n]	3.3	3.0[o]	...
Health: Physicians (per 1 000 pop.)	1.4	1.4[p]	1.2[q]
Education: Government expenditure (% of GDP)	5.1[r]	...	...
Education: Primary gross enrol. ratio (f/m per 100 pop.)	114.7 / 118.8	80.2 / 83.1[s]	101.9 / 103.2[b]
Education: Lowr. sec. gross enrol. ratio (f/m per 100 pop.)	90.6 / 92.0	63.0 / 65.3[s]	85.1 / 78.5[b]
Education: Upr. sec. gross enrol. ratio (f/m per 100 pop.)	38.8 / 35.8	33.7 / 30.5[s]	50.8 / 42.9[b]
Intentional homicide rate (per 100 000 pop.)	2.1	...	...
Seats held by women in the National Parliament (%)	12.4	12.4	10.8[t]

Environment and infrastructure indicators	2010	2015	2023
Individuals using the Internet (per 100 inhabitants)	20.7	30.0[h]	35.8[h,l]
Research & Development expenditure (% of GDP)	...	~0.0[u,v]	...
Threatened species (number)	78	108	174[b]
Forested area (% of land area)	2.7	2.8	2.8[l]
CO2 emission estimates (million tons/tons per capita)	57.7 / 2.7	23.9 / 1.3	22.5 / 1.3[l]
Energy production, primary (Petajoules)	1 165	197	191[l]
Energy supply per capita (Gigajoules)	41	22	18[l]
Tourist/visitor arrivals at national borders (000)[w]	8 546	5 070[x]	...
Important sites for terrestrial biodiversity protected (%)	0.0	0.0	0.0[b]
Net Official Development Assist. received (% of GNI)	0.06	29.02	48.40[y]

a Projected estimate (medium fertility variant). b 2022. c 2021. d Estimates should be viewed with caution as these are derived from scarce data. e 2019. f UN operational exchange rate. g Includes taxes less subsidies on production and imports. h Estimate. i Data refers to a 5-year period preceding the reference year. j Including refugees. k Refers to foreign citizens. l 2020. m Data as at the end of December. n Data based on calendar year (January 1 to December 31). o 2012. p 2014. q 2016. r 2009. s 2013. t Data are as at 1 January of reporting year. u Excluding business enterprise. v Excluding private non-profit. w Including Iraqi nationals. x 2011. y 2018.

Tajikistan

Region	Central Asia	UN membership date	02 March 1992
Population (000, 2023)	9 953[a,b]	Surface area (km2)	141 400[c]
Pop. density (per km2, 2023)	69.6[a,b]	Sex ratio (m per 100 f)	101.3[a,b]
Capital city	Dushanbe	National currency	Somoni (TJS)
Capital city pop. (000, 2023)	893.8[d]	Exchange rate (per US$)	10.2[b]

Economic indicators

	2010	2015	2023
GDP: Gross domestic product (million current US$)	5 642	8 271	8 746[c]
GDP growth rate (annual %, const. 2015 prices)	6.5	6.0	9.2[c]
GDP per capita (current US$)	740.3	970.4	897.1[c]
Economy: Agriculture (% of Gross Value Added)[e]	21.8	23.9	26.8[f,c]
Economy: Industry (% of Gross Value Added)[e]	27.9	30.8	29.1[g,c]
Economy: Services and other activity (% of GVA)[e]	50.3	45.3	44.1[c]
Employment in agriculture (% of employed)[h]	52.3	47.3	42.6[c]
Employment in industry (% of employed)[h]	15.8	17.8	20.1[c]
Employment in services & other sectors (% employed)[h]	31.9	34.9	37.4[c]
Unemployment rate (% of labour force)[h]	10.9	7.6	8.4
Labour force participation rate (female/male pop. %)[h]	29.4 / 55.9	31.9 / 53.1	31.1 / 50.8
CPI: Consumer Price Index (2010=100)[i]	100	140	225[b]
Agricultural production index (2014-2016=100)	66	110	132[c]
International trade: exports (million current US$)[h]	1 206	891	1 491[b]
International trade: imports (million current US$)[h]	2 659	3 435	5 596[b]
International trade: balance (million current US$)[h]	- 1 453	- 2 544	- 4 105[b]
Balance of payments, current account (million US$)	- 581	- 477	1 635[b]

Major trading partners

							2022
Export partners (% of exports)[h]	Kazakhstan	24.4	Switzerland	24.0	Türkiye	15.7
Import partners (% of imports)[h]	Russian Federation	30.4	Kazakhstan	19.4	China	16.1

Social indicators

	2010	2015	2023
Population growth rate (average annual %)	2.1	2.4	1.9[a,b]
Urban population (% of total population)	26.5	26.7	27.3[d]
Urban population growth rate (average annual %)[j]	2.2	2.4	...
Fertility rate, total (live births per woman)	3.5	3.5	3.1[a,b]
Life expectancy at birth (females/males, years)	70.4 / 65.4	71.9 / 67.0	73.5 / 69.2[a,b]
Population age distribution (0-14/60+ years old, %)	36.8 / 4.6	36.6 / 4.9	36.3 / 6.2[a,b]
International migrant stock (000/% of total pop.)[k]	279.8 / 3.7	275.1 / 3.3	276.0 / 2.9[l]
Refugees and others of concern to the UNHCR (000)	7.1[m]	11.9	16.2[b]
Infant mortality rate (per 1 000 live births)	36.5	32.1	23.4[a,b]
Health: Current expenditure (% of GDP)	5.7	6.9	8.2[l]
Health: Physicians (per 1 000 pop.)	1.7	1.7[n]	...
Education: Government expenditure (% of GDP)	4.0	5.0	5.7[c]
Education: Primary gross enrol. ratio (f/m per 100 pop.)	100.2 / 102.7	97.1 / 98.1	100.3 / 101.4[o]
Education: Lowr. sec. gross enrol. ratio (f/m per 100 pop.)	91.3 / 98.0	97.6 / 101.3	97.3 / 100.0[o]
Education: Upr. sec. gross enrol. ratio (f/m per 100 pop.)	47.8 / 71.0	58.5 / 77.7[p]	... / ...
Intentional homicide rate (per 100 000 pop.)	2.4	1.6[q]	0.9[l]
Seats held by women in the National Parliament (%)	17.5	16.9	27.0[r]

Environment and infrastructure indicators

	2010	2015	2023
Individuals using the Internet (per 100 inhabitants)[h]	11.6	19.0	22.0[o]
Research & Development expenditure (% of GDP)[s,t]	0.1	0.1	0.1[l]
Threatened species (number)	40	41	59[b]
Forested area (% of land area)	2.9	3.0	3.1[l]
CO2 emission estimates (million tons/tons per capita)	2.3 / 0.3	4.3 / 0.5	7.4 / 0.8[l]
Energy production, primary (Petajoules)	115	131[h]	155[l]
Energy supply per capita (Gigajoules)	19	20	21[l]
Tourist/visitor arrivals at national borders (000)	160	414	296[c]
Important sites for terrestrial biodiversity protected (%)	15.8	16.8	16.8[b]
Pop. using safely managed sanitation (urban/rural %)	... / 57.4	... / 58.4	... / 59.3[b]
Net Official Development Assist. received (% of GNI)	5.57	4.41	5.21[c]

a Projected estimate (medium fertility variant). **b** 2022. **c** 2021. **d** 2019. **e** Data classified according to ISIC Rev. 4. **f** Excludes irrigation canals and landscaping care. **g** Excludes publishing activities, recycling. Includes irrigation canals. **h** Estimate. **i** Calculated by the UN Statistics Division from national indices. **j** Data refers to a 5-year period preceding the reference year. **k** Including refugees. **l** 2020. **m** Data as at the end of December. **n** 2014. **o** 2017. **p** 2013. **q** 2011. **r** Data are as at 1 January of reporting year. **s** Excluding private non-profit. **t** Excluding business enterprise.

Thailand

Region	South-eastern Asia	
Population (000, 2023)	71 697 [a,b]	
Pop. density (per km2, 2023)	140.3 [a,b]	
Capital city	Bangkok	
Capital city pop. (000, 2023)	10 350.2 [d]	

UN membership date	16 December 1946	
Surface area (km2)	513 140 [c]	
Sex ratio (m per 100 f)	94.3 [a,b]	
National currency	Baht (THB)	
Exchange rate (per US$)	34.6 [b]	

Economic indicators

	2010	2015	2023
GDP: Gross domestic product (million current US$)	341 105	401 296	505 982 [c]
GDP growth rate (annual %, const. 2015 prices)	7.5	3.1	1.6 [c]
GDP per capita (current US$)	4 996.4	5 708.8	7 066.7 [c]
Economy: Agriculture (% of Gross Value Added) [e,f,g]	10.5	8.9	8.5 [c]
Economy: Industry (% of Gross Value Added) [e,g,h]	39.9	36.2	34.8 [c]
Economy: Services and other activity (% of GVA) [g]	49.6	54.9	56.7 [c]
Employment in agriculture (% of employed)	38.2	32.3	31.6 [c]
Employment in industry (% of employed)	20.7	18.0 [i]	22.5 [c]
Employment in services & other sectors (% employed)	41.2	43.9	45.9 [c]
Unemployment rate (% of labour force)	0.6	0.6	0.8 [i]
Labour force participation rate (female/male pop. %)	63.7 / 80.0	61.1 / 77.9	57.9 / 74.0 [i]
CPI: Consumer Price Index (2010=100) [j]	100	110	121 [b]
Agricultural production index (2014-2016=100)	90	97	100 [c]
International trade: exports (million current US$)	195 312	214 309	283 912 [i,b]
International trade: imports (million current US$)	182 393	202 642	305 288 [i,b]
International trade: balance (million current US$)	12 918	11 667	- 21 376 [i,b]
Balance of payments, current account (million US$)	11 486	27 753	- 17 230 [b]

Major trading partners
							2022
Export partners (% of exports) [i]	United States	15.5	China	13.7	Japan		9.2
Import partners (% of imports) [i]	China	24.8	Japan	13.3	United States		5.4

Social indicators

	2010	2015	2023
Population growth rate (average annual %)	0.6	0.4	0.2 [a,b]
Urban population (% of total population)	43.9	47.7	50.7 [d]
Urban population growth rate (average annual %) [k]	3.7	2.1	...
Fertility rate, total (live births per woman)	1.6	1.5	1.3 [a,b]
Life expectancy at birth (females/males, years)	80.4 / 72.1	82.0 / 73.5	83.9 / 75.5 [a,b]
Population age distribution (0-14/60+ years old, %)	19.3 / 13.2	17.4 / 16.3	15.5 / 22.0 [a,b]
International migrant stock (000/% of total pop.) [l]	3 234.4 / 4.8	3 470.2 / 5.1	3 632.5 / 5.2 [m]
Refugees and others of concern to the UNHCR (000)	649.4 [n]	625.3	663.9 [b]
Infant mortality rate (per 1 000 live births)	11.6	9.2	7.1 [a,b]
Health: Current expenditure (% of GDP) [o]	3.4	3.9 [p]	4.4 [p,m]
Health: Physicians (per 1 000 pop.)	0.4	0.5	0.9 [m]
Education: Government expenditure (% of GDP)	3.5	3.9	3.0 [c]
Education: Primary gross enrol. ratio (f/m per 100 pop.)	96.3 / 97.4	97.6 / 103.5	101.3 / 102.1 [b]
Education: Lowr. sec. gross enrol. ratio (f/m per 100 pop.)	97.7 / 97.3	116.1 / 125.7	111.1 / 99.4 [b]
Education: Upr. sec. gross enrol. ratio (f/m per 100 pop.)	73.5 / 62.4	120.2 / 120.3	96.0 / 95.3 [b]
Intentional homicide rate (per 100 000 pop.)	5.4	4.8 [q]	...
Seats held by women in the National Parliament (%)	13.3	6.1	16.6 [r]

Environment and infrastructure indicators

	2010	2015	2023
Individuals using the Internet (per 100 inhabitants)	22.4	39.3 [s]	85.3 [c]
Research & Development expenditure (% of GDP)	0.2 [t]	0.6	1.3 [m]
Threatened species (number)	477	595	802 [b]
Forested area (% of land area)	39.3	39.3	38.9 [m]
CO2 emission estimates (million tons/tons per capita)	226.7 / 3.3	253.4 / 3.6	247.9 / 3.5 [m]
Energy production, primary (Petajoules)	2 928	3 131	2 598 [m]
Energy supply per capita (Gigajoules)	72	81	73 [m]
Tourist/visitor arrivals at national borders (000)	15 936	29 923	428 [c]
Important sites for terrestrial biodiversity protected (%)	66.7	67.6	68.0 [b]
Pop. using safely managed sanitation (urban/rural %)	25.9 / 20.0	27.7 / 21.1	30.0 / 22.2 [b]
Net Official Development Assist. disbursed (% of GNI)	...	0.02 [u]	0.02 [c]
Net Official Development Assist. received (% of GNI)	- 0.01	0.02	0.03 [c]

a Projected estimate (medium fertility variant). b 2022. c 2021. d 2019. e At producers' prices. f Excludes irrigation canals and landscaping care. g Data classified according to ISIC Rev. 4. h Excludes publishing activities, recycling. Includes irrigation canals. i Estimate. j Calculated by the UN Statistics Division from national indices. k Data refers to a 5-year period preceding the reference year. l Including refugees. m 2020. n Data as at the end of December. o Data revision. p Data refer to fiscal years beginning 1 October. q 2011. r Data are as at 1 January of reporting year. s Population aged 6 years and over. t 2009. u 2014.

Timor-Leste

Region	South-eastern Asia	UN membership date	27 September 2002
Population (000, 2023)	1 341 a,b	Surface area (km2)	14 919 c
Pop. density (per km2, 2023)	90.2 a,b	Sex ratio (m per 100 f)	104.0 a,b
Capital city	Dili	National currency	US Dollar (USD)
Capital city pop. (000, 2023)	281.1 d		

Economic indicators	2010	2015	2023
GDP: Gross domestic product (million current US$)	882	1 594	2 004 c
GDP growth rate (annual %, const. 2015 prices)	9.6	2.8	1.5 c
GDP per capita (current US$)	810.1	1 322.3	1 517.2 c
Economy: Agriculture (% of Gross Value Added) e,f	24.7	17.8	15.8 c
Economy: Industry (% of Gross Value Added) e,g	8.8	18.4	24.3 c
Economy: Services and other activity (% of GVA) e	66.5	63.8	59.9 c
Employment in agriculture (% of employed) h	48.5	47.2	41.6 c
Employment in industry (% of employed)	9.3	9.9 h	14.4 h,c
Employment in services & other sectors (% employed) h	42.2	42.9	43.9 c
Unemployment rate (% of labour force)	3.3	4.5 h	4.8 h
Labour force participation rate (female/male pop. %) h	62.1 / 73.1	61.5 / 72.7	61.7 / 72.5
CPI: Consumer Price Index (2010=100) h	100	143	146 i
Agricultural production index (2014-2016=100)	115	104	87 c
International trade: exports (million current US$) h	42	45	322 b
International trade: imports (million current US$) h	246	578	1 427 b
International trade: balance (million current US$) h	- 205	- 533	- 1 105 b
Balance of payments, current account (million US$)	1 671	225	1 022 c

Major trading partners						2022
Export partners (% of exports) h	China	47.4	Japan	23.6	Malaysia	10.6
Import partners (% of imports) h	Indonesia	33.6	China	31.1	Singapore	9.9

Social indicators	2010	2015	2023
Population growth rate (average annual %)	2.2	1.6	1.4 a,b
Urban population (% of total population)	27.7	29.5	30.9 i
Urban population growth rate (average annual %) j	2.8	3.5	...
Fertility rate, total (live births per woman)	4.8	3.9	3.0 a,b
Life expectancy at birth (females/males, years)	67.0 / 63.8	68.9 / 65.5	70.8 / 67.4 a,b
Population age distribution (0-14/60+ years old, %)	41.4 / 7.6	39.0 / 7.9	34.7 / 7.3 a,b
International migrant stock (000/% of total pop.) k	11.5 / 1.1	8.5 / 0.7	8.4 / 0.6 l
Refugees and others of concern to the UNHCR (000)	~0.0 m	~0.0	~0.0 l
Infant mortality rate (per 1 000 live births)	47.3	39.8	30.9 a,b
Health: Current expenditure (% of GDP)	6.5	7.7 n	9.9 n,l
Health: Physicians (per 1 000 pop.)	...	0.7	0.8 l
Education: Government expenditure (% of GDP)	11.1	6.3	5.5 c
Education: Primary gross enrol. ratio (f/m per 100 pop.)	119.2 / 126.1	126.6 / 129.8	109.6 / 111.8 l
Education: Lowr. sec. gross enrol. ratio (f/m per 100 pop.)	73.1 / 72.3	85.0 / 80.6	99.2 / 92.1 l
Education: Upr. sec. gross enrol. ratio (f/m per 100 pop.)	50.6 / 52.5	62.5 / 59.2	83.1 / 73.0 l
Intentional homicide rate (per 100 000 pop.)	3.6	4.1	...
Seats held by women in the National Parliament (%)	29.2	38.5	40.0 o

Environment and infrastructure indicators	2010	2015	2023
Individuals using the Internet (per 100 inhabitants) h	3.0	18.6	39.5 c
Threatened species (number)	18	21	59 b
Forested area (% of land area)	62.9	62.4	61.9 l
Energy production, primary (Petajoules)	318	281	197 l
Energy supply per capita (Gigajoules)	4	6	7 l
Tourist/visitor arrivals at national borders (000) p	40	62	6 c
Important sites for terrestrial biodiversity protected (%)	40.7	40.7	45.6 b
Net Official Development Assist. received (% of GNI)	8.72	7.60	10.74 c

a Projected estimate (medium fertility variant). b 2022. c 2021. d 2018. e Data classified according to ISIC Rev. 4. f Excludes irrigation canals and landscaping care. g Excludes publishing activities, recycling. Includes irrigation canals. h Estimate. i 2019. j Data refers to a 5-year period preceding the reference year. k Including refugees. l 2020. m Data as at the end of December. n Data revision. o Data are as at 1 January of reporting year. p Arrivals by air at Dili Airport.

Togo

Region	Western Africa	UN membership date	20 September 1960
Population (000, 2023)	8 849 [a,b]	Surface area (km2)	56 785 [c]
Pop. density (per km2, 2023)	162.7 [a,b]	Sex ratio (m per 100 f)	101.1 [a,b]
Capital city	Lomé	National currency	CFA Franc, BCEAO (XOF) [d]
Capital city pop. (000, 2023)	1 785.3 [e]	Exchange rate (per US$)	615.0 [b]

Economic indicators

	2010	2015	2023
GDP: Gross domestic product (million current US$)	4 742	5 751	8 160 [c]
GDP growth rate (annual %, const. 2015 prices)	5.9	5.5	5.3 [c]
GDP per capita (current US$)	721.5	769.6	943.9 [c]
Economy: Agriculture (% of Gross Value Added) [f,g]	22.9	20.8	21.1 [c]
Economy: Industry (% of Gross Value Added) [g,h]	22.1	25.1	22.5 [c]
Economy: Services and other activity (% of GVA) [g]	55.0	54.1	56.4 [c]
Employment in agriculture (% of employed) [i]	39.9	36.4	30.9 [c]
Employment in industry (% of employed) [i]	18.0	18.7	20.4 [c]
Employment in services & other sectors (% employed) [i]	42.1	37.2	48.7 [c]
Unemployment rate (% of labour force)	2.4 [i]	2.2	4.0 [i]
Labour force participation rate (female/male pop. %) [i]	55.3 / 61.6	55.6 / 60.9	56.4 / 59.6
CPI: Consumer Price Index (2010=100)	100	111	115 [j]
Agricultural production index (2014-2016=100)	90	97	112 [c]
International trade: exports (million current US$)	741	792	1 348 [b]
International trade: imports (million current US$)	1 350	1 877	2 769 [b]
International trade: balance (million current US$)	- 609	- 1 085	- 1 421 [b]
Balance of payments, current account (million US$)	- 200	- 461	- 21 [j]

Major trading partners

						2022
Export partners (% of exports)	India	17.0	Burkina Faso	12.4	Benin	9.4
Import partners (% of imports)	China	19.8	France	8.9	India	6.1

Social indicators

	2010	2015	2023
Population growth rate (average annual %)	2.7	2.5	2.3 [a,b]
Urban population (% of total population)	37.5	40.1	42.2 [e]
Urban population growth rate (average annual %) [k]	4.0	4.0	...
Fertility rate, total (live births per woman)	5.0	4.6	4.2 [a,b]
Life expectancy at birth (females/males, years)	57.4 / 57.2	59.6 / 59.2	62.2 / 60.9 [a,b]
Population age distribution (0-14/60+ years old, %)	41.8 / 4.6	41.4 / 4.7	40.0 / 5.1 [a,b]
International migrant stock (000/% of total pop.) [i,m]	255.6 / 4.0	277.4 / 3.8	279.9 / 3.4 [j]
Refugees and others of concern to the UNHCR (000)	14.2 [n]	22.6	11.2 [b]
Infant mortality rate (per 1 000 live births)	60.2	52.4	43.9 [a,b]
Health: Current expenditure (% of GDP) [o]	4.5	5.0	6.0 [j]
Health: Physicians (per 1 000 pop.)	0.1 [p]	~0.0	0.1 [c]
Education: Government expenditure (% of GDP)	4.1	5.1	4.2 [c]
Education: Primary gross enrol. ratio (f/m per 100 pop.)	120.8 / 133.9	124.9 / 131.2	122.0 / 126.4 [c]
Education: Lower sec. gross enrol. ratio (f/m per 100 pop.)	41.5 / 72.3 [i,q]	... / ...	72.8 / 86.6 [c]
Education: Upr. sec. gross enrol. ratio (f/m per 100 pop.)	17.2 / 41.1 [i,q]	... / ...	35.3 / 47.6 [c]
Seats held by women in the National Parliament (%)	11.1	17.6	19.8 [r]

Environment and infrastructure indicators

	2010	2015	2023
Individuals using the Internet (per 100 inhabitants) [i]	3.0	7.1	35.0 [c]
Research & Development expenditure (% of GDP) [s]	0.2	0.3 [t,u]	...
Threatened species (number)	54	66	129 [b]
Forested area (% of land area)	22.8	22.5	22.2 [j]
CO2 emission estimates (million tons/tons per capita)	2.5 / 0.3	1.5 / 0.1	2.1 / 0.2 [i]
Energy production, primary (Petajoules)	99	112	126 [j]
Energy supply per capita (Gigajoules)	20	17	18 [j]
Tourist/visitor arrivals at national borders (000)	202	273 [v]	482 [v,j]
Important sites for terrestrial biodiversity protected (%)	79.5	79.5	79.5 [b]
Pop. using safely managed drinking water (urban/rural, %)	23.2 / 0.0	31.0 / 6.8	33.9 / 8.1 [b]
Pop. using safely managed sanitation (urban/rural, %)	7.3 / 2.8	7.2 / 3.7	7.1 / 4.7 [b]
Net Official Development Assist. received (% of GNI)	11.85	4.62	4.16 [c]

a Projected estimate (medium fertility variant). b 2022. c 2021. d African Financial Community (CFA) Franc, Central Bank of West African States (BCEAO). e 2019. f Excludes irrigation canals and landscaping care. g Data classified according to ISIC Rev. 4. h Excludes publishing activities, recycling. Includes irrigation canals. i Estimate. j 2020. k Data refers to a 5-year period preceding the reference year. l Including refugees. m Refers to foreign citizens. n Data as at the end of December. o Data refer to fiscal years beginning 1 July. p 2008. q 2007. r Data are as at 1 January of reporting year. s Excluding business enterprise. t Excluding private non-profit. u 2014. v Including nationals residing abroad.

Tokelau

Region	Polynesia	Population (000, 2023)	2 a,b,c
Surface area (km2)	12 d	Pop. density (per km2, 2023)	155.9 a,b,c
Sex ratio (m per 100 f)	99.8 a,b,c	Capital city	Tokelau e
National currency	New Zealand Dollar (NZD)	Exchange rate (per US$)	1.6 c

Economic indicators	2010	2015	2023
Agricultural production index (2014-2016=100)	90	103	112 d
International trade: exports (million current US$) f	~0	~0	~0 c
International trade: imports (million current US$) f	1	1	1 c
International trade: balance (million current US$) f	- 1	- 1	- 1 c

Major trading partners							2022
Export partners (% of exports) f	Poland	93.6	Nigeria	2.7	Singapore	0.4
Import partners (% of imports) f	Samoa	38.6	Germany	21.1	United States	9.5

Social indicators	2010	2015	2023
Population growth rate (average annual %) a	0.9	- 2.7	1.1 b,c
Urban population (% of total population)	0.0	0.0	0.0 g
Urban population growth rate (average annual %) h	0.0	0.0	...
Fertility rate, total (live births per woman) a	3.3	3.0	2.7 b,c
Life expectancy at birth (females/males, years) a	74.6 / 72.8	75.3 / 73.8	76.2 / 74.4 b,c
Population age distribution (0-14/60+ years old, %) a	30.4 / 14.6	30.1 / 14.6	28.5 / 12.9 b,c
International migrant stock (000/% of total pop.) i	1.1 / 99.9	1.2 / 95.0	1.2 / 91.7 j
Infant mortality rate (per 1 000 live births) a	7.8	6.0	4.7 b,c
Education: Primary gross enrol. ratio (f/m per 100 pop.)	... / ...	... / ...	150.0 / 142.4 d
Education: Lowr. sec. gross enrol. ratio (f/m per 100 pop.)	... / ...	... / ...	176.2 / 244.2 d
Education: Upr. sec. gross enrol. ratio (f/m per 100 pop.)	... / ...	... / ...	115.2 / 54.3 d

Environment and infrastructure indicators	2010	2015	2023
Threatened species (number)	41	46	61 c
Forested area (% of land area)	0.0	0.0	0.0 j
Important sites for terrestrial biodiversity protected (%)	0.0	0.0	0.0 c

a For statistical purposes, the data for New Zealand do not include this area. b Projected estimate (medium fertility variant). c 2022. d 2021. e The "capital" rotates yearly between the three atolls of Atafu, Fakaofo and Nukunomu, each with fewer than 500 inhabitants in 2011. f Estimate. g 2019. h Data refers to a 5-year period preceding the reference year. i Including refugees. j 2020.

Tonga

Region	Polynesia	UN membership date	14 September 1999
Population (000, 2023)	107[a,b]	Surface area (km2)	747[c]
Pop. density (per km2, 2023)	164.4[a,b]	Sex ratio (m per 100 f)	97.8[a,b]
Capital city	Nuku'alofa	National currency	Pa'anga (TOP)
Capital city pop. (000, 2023)	22.9[d]	Exchange rate (per US$)	2.3[b]

Economic indicators	2010	2015	2023
GDP: Gross domestic product (million current US$)	371	403	472[c]
GDP growth rate (annual %, const. 2015 prices)	0.8	1.2	- 2.7[c]
GDP per capita (current US$)	3 457.3	3 799.9	4 450.5[c]
Economy: Agriculture (% of Gross Value Added)[e,f]	18.7	19.7	19.9[c]
Economy: Industry (% of Gross Value Added)[e,g]	20.5	18.1	19.4[c]
Economy: Services and other activity (% of GVA)[e]	60.9	62.3	60.6[c]
Employment in agriculture (% of employed)[h]	32.8	32.1	30.2[c]
Employment in industry (% of employed)[h]	27.3	26.1	27.0[c]
Employment in services & other sectors (% employed)[h]	39.9	41.7	42.5[c]
Unemployment rate (% of labour force)[h]	1.5	1.9	2.9
Labour force participation rate (female/male pop. %)[h]	43.3 / 68.5	42.8 / 66.8	42.4 / 65.1
CPI: Consumer Price Index (2010=100)[h]	100	110	113[i]
Agricultural production index (2014-2016=100)	130	106	94[c]
International trade: exports (million current US$)	8	15[h]	27[h]
International trade: imports (million current US$)	159	208[h]	202[h,b]
International trade: balance (million current US$)	- 151	- 193[h]	- 175[h,b]
Balance of payments, current account (million US$)	- 87	- 44	- 31[b]

Major trading partners						2022
Export partners (% of exports)[h]	United States	27.0	Australia	16.6	Republic of Korea	12.8
Import partners (% of imports)[h]	Fiji	27.3	China	21.6	New Zealand	20.7

Social indicators	2010	2015	2023
Population growth rate (average annual %)	0.3	- 0.5	0.9[a,b]
Urban population (% of total population)	23.4	23.3	23.1[j]
Urban population growth rate (average annual %)[k]	0.8	0.3	...
Fertility rate, total (live births per woman)	3.9	3.6	3.2[a,b]
Life expectancy at birth (females/males, years)	73.4 / 67.6	73.5 / 67.9	74.1 / 68.6[a,b]
Population age distribution (0-14/60+ years old, %)	37.6 / 8.2	36.8 / 8.6	34.3 / 9.0[a,b]
International migrant stock (000/% of total pop.)[l]	4.6 / 4.4	4.0 / 3.9	3.7 / 3.5[m]
Refugees and others of concern to the UNHCR (000)	~0.0[n]	...	~0.0[m]
Infant mortality rate (per 1 000 live births)	11.3	10.7	9.2[a,b]
Health: Current expenditure (% of GDP)[o]	4.8	4.5	5.3[m]
Health: Physicians (per 1 000 pop.)	0.5	0.5[p]	1.0[c]
Education: Government expenditure (% of GDP)	...	...	6.6[c]
Education: Primary gross enrol. ratio (f/m per 100 pop.)	107.3 / 109.4	116.0 / 116.7	112.1 / 117.4[m]
Education: Lowr. sec. gross enrol. ratio (f/m per 100 pop.)	103.0 / 106.5[q]	111.6 / 112.1	106.5 / 90.9[m]
Education: Upr. sec. gross enrol. ratio (f/m per 100 pop.)	93.4 / 84.8[q]	76.9 / 64.5	67.6 / 55.7[m]
Intentional homicide rate (per 100 000 pop.)	0.9	0.9[r]	1.0[j]
Seats held by women in the National Parliament (%)	3.1	0.0	7.1[s]

Environment and infrastructure indicators	2010	2015	2023
Individuals using the Internet (per 100 inhabitants)[h]	16.0	38.7	71.6[c]
Threatened species (number)	58	74	120[b]
Forested area (% of land area)	12.4	12.4	12.4[m]
Energy production, primary (Petajoules)	0	0	0[m]
Energy supply per capita (Gigajoules)	16	15	25[m]
Tourist/visitor arrivals at national borders (000)[t]	47	54	~0[c]
Important sites for terrestrial biodiversity protected (%)	26.1	26.1	26.1[b]
Pop. using safely managed drinking water (urban/rural, %)	50.2 / 23.1	50.5 / 23.1	50.8 / 23.1[b]
Pop. using safely managed sanitation (urban/rural, %)	29.3 / 39.4	25.7 / 37.5	22.3 / 35.0[b]
Net Official Development Assist. received (% of GNI)	17.54	15.51	30.75[m]

a Projected estimate (medium fertility variant). **b** 2022. **c** 2021. **d** 2018. **e** Data classified according to ISIC Rev. 4. **f** Excludes irrigation canals and landscaping care. **g** Excludes publishing activities, recycling. Includes irrigation canals. **h** Estimate. **i** 2016. **j** 2019. **k** Data refers to a 5-year period preceding the reference year. **l** Including refugees. **m** 2020. **n** Data as at the end of December. **o** Data refer to fiscal years beginning 1 July. **p** 2013. **q** 2006. **r** 2012. **s** Data are as at 1 January of reporting year. **t** Arrivals by air.

Trinidad and Tobago

Region	Caribbean	UN membership date	18 September 1962
Population (000, 2023)	1 531 [a,b]	Surface area (km2)	5 127 [c]
Pop. density (per km2, 2023)	298.4 [a,b]	Sex ratio (m per 100 f)	97.3 [a,b]
Capital city	Port of Spain	National currency	TT Dollar (TTD) [d]
Capital city pop. (000, 2023)	544.3 [e,f]	Exchange rate (per US$)	6.7 [b]

Economic indicators

	2010	2015	2023
GDP: Gross domestic product (million current US$)	23 352	26 852	24 460 [c]
GDP growth rate (annual %, const. 2015 prices)	3.3	- 0.8	- 1.0 [c]
GDP per capita (current US$)	16 558.3	18 389.5	16 032.5 [c]
Economy: Agriculture (% of Gross Value Added) [g,h]	0.7	1.0	1.0 [c]
Economy: Industry (% of Gross Value Added) [h,i]	49.9	37.9	43.4 [c]
Economy: Services and other activity (% of GVA) [h]	49.5	61.1	55.6 [c]
Employment in agriculture (% of employed)	3.8 [j]	3.4	3.0 [j,c]
Employment in industry (% of employed) [j]	29.9	23.1	26.4 [c]
Employment in services & other sectors (% employed)	66.4 [j]	68.6	70.6 [j,c]
Unemployment rate (% of labour force)	4.0	2.4	3.7 [j]
Labour force participation rate (female/male pop. %)	49.8 / 72.4	49.5 / 70.9	46.9 / 63.1 [j]
CPI: Consumer Price Index (2010=100) [k]	100	134	147 [c]
Agricultural production index (2014-2016=100)	109	89	90 [c]
International trade: exports (million current US$)	10 982	10 756	13 223 [j,b]
International trade: imports (million current US$)	6 480	9 298	6 197 [j,b]
International trade: balance (million current US$)	4 502	1 458	7 026 [j,b]
Balance of payments, current account (million US$)	4 172	2 057	2 900 [c]

Major trading partners

						2022
Export partners (% of exports) [j]	United States	41.6	Guyana	6.7	Mexico	4.3
Import partners (% of imports) [j]	United States	34.6	China	10.5	Mexico	7.0

Social indicators

	2010	2015	2023
Population growth rate (average annual %)	0.7	0.6	0.3 [a,b]
Urban population (% of total population)	54.0	53.3	53.2 [f]
Urban population growth rate (average annual %) [l]	0.1	0.2	...
Fertility rate, total (live births per woman)	1.7	1.7	1.6 [a,b]
Life expectancy at birth (females/males, years)	76.1 / 69.3	77.9 / 71.1	78.2 / 71.3 [a,b]
Population age distribution (0-14/60+ years old, %)	20.8 / 10.7	20.4 / 13.4	19.0 / 17.2 [a,b]
International migrant stock (000/% of total pop.) [m]	48.2 / 3.6	50.0 / 3.7	78.8 / 5.6 [n]
Refugees and others of concern to the UNHCR (000)	0.1 [o]	0.2	31.6 [b]
Infant mortality rate (per 1 000 live births)	19.9	17.2	15.0 [a,b]
Health: Current expenditure (% of GDP) [p]	5.1	6.0 [q]	7.3 [j,n]
Health: Physicians (per 1 000 pop.)	1.7	2.5	3.4 [c]
Education: Government expenditure (% of GDP)	...	3.4	3.0 [c]
Education: Primary gross enrol. ratio (f/m per 100 pop.)	104.4 / 108.0	... / ...	... / ...
Education: Lowr. sec. gross enrol. ratio (f/m per 100 pop.)	97.5 / 97.7 [j,r]	... / ...	... / ...
Education: Upr. sec. gross enrol. ratio (f/m per 100 pop.)	... / ...	... / ...	94.7 / 84.8 [c]
Intentional homicide rate (per 100 000 pop.)	33.5	28.8	29.4 [c]
Seats held by women in the National Parliament (%)	26.8	28.6	28.6 [s]

Environment and infrastructure indicators

	2010	2015	2023
Individuals using the Internet (per 100 inhabitants)	48.5 [j]	65.1 [j]	79.0 [c]
Research & Development expenditure (% of GDP)	~0.0	0.1	0.1 [t,n]
Threatened species (number)	48	65	164 [b]
Forested area (% of land area)	45.3	44.9	44.5 [n]
CO2 emission estimates (million tons/tons per capita)	21.1 / 15.8	20.7 / 15.0	14.9 / 10.6 [n]
Energy production, primary (Petajoules)	1 786	1 557	1 226 [n]
Energy supply per capita (Gigajoules)	591	546	405 [n]
Tourist/visitor arrivals at national borders (000) [u]	388	440	41 [c]
Important sites for terrestrial biodiversity protected (%)	32.0	32.0	32.0 [b]
Net Official Development Assist. received (% of GNI)	0.02		

a Projected estimate (medium fertility variant). b 2022. c 2021. d Trinidad and Tobago Dollar. e Data refers to the urban agglomeration. f 2019. g Excludes irrigation canals and landscaping care. h Data classified according to ISIC Rev. 4. i Excludes publishing activities, recycling. Includes irrigation canals. j Estimate. k Data refer to the Retail Price Index. l Data refers to a 5-year period preceding the reference year. m Including refugees. n 2020. o Data as at the end of December. p Data refer to fiscal years beginning 1 October. q Data are based on SHA2011. r 2009. s Data are as at 1 January of reporting year. t Excluding business enterprise. u Arrivals by air.

Tunisia

Region	Northern Africa	UN membership date	12 November 1956
Population (000, 2023)	12 356 a,b	Surface area (km2)	163 610 c
Pop. density (per km2, 2023)	79.5 a,b	Sex ratio (m per 100 f)	97.5 a,b
Capital city	Tunis	National currency	Tunisian Dinar (TND)
Capital city pop. (000, 2023)	2 327.8 d,e	Exchange rate (per US$)	3.1 b

Economic indicators

	2010	2015	2023
GDP: Gross domestic product (million current US$)	44 051	45 779	46 687 c
GDP growth rate (annual %, const. 2015 prices)	3.5	2.4	4.3 c
GDP per capita (current US$)	4 043.2	3 960.9	3 807.2 c
Economy: Agriculture (% of Gross Value Added)	8.1 f	9.9	10.9 g,c
Economy: Industry (% of Gross Value Added)	31.1 f,h	26.8	24.8 c
Economy: Services and other activity (% of GVA)	60.8	63.3	64.4 c
Employment in agriculture (% of employed)	17.9	14.8	13.9 i,c
Employment in industry (% of employed)	32.3 i	33.1	34.2 i,c
Employment in services & other sectors (% employed)	48.6	52.1	51.8 i,c
Unemployment rate (% of labour force)	13.0	15.2	16.1 i
Labour force participation rate (female/male pop. %)	24.9 / 69.6	26.1 / 68.9	26.4 / 66.5 i
CPI: Consumer Price Index (2010=100)	100 i,j	127 i	192 b
Agricultural production index (2014-2016=100)	85	115	104 c
International trade: exports (million current US$)	16 427	14 073	18 426 i,b
International trade: imports (million current US$)	22 215	20 223	24 832 i,b
International trade: balance (million current US$)	- 5 789	- 6 149	- 6 406 i,b
Balance of payments, current account (million US$)	- 2 104	- 3 924	- 2 781 c

Major trading partners

						2022
Export partners (% of exports) i	France	24.1	Italy	18.5	Germany	12.8
Import partners (% of imports) i	Italy	13.5	France	11.4	China	10.4

Social indicators

	2010	2015	2023
Population growth rate (average annual %)	1.1	1.1	0.8 a,b
Urban population (% of total population)	66.7	68.1	69.3 e
Urban population growth rate (average annual %) k	1.5	1.6	...
Fertility rate, total (live births per woman)	2.1	2.3	2.1 a,b
Life expectancy at birth (females/males, years)	78.6 / 72.6	78.9 / 72.8	77.4 / 71.4 a,b
Population age distribution (0-14/60+ years old, %)	23.8 / 9.8	24.2 / 11.2	24.8 / 13.7 a,b
International migrant stock (000/% of total pop.) l,m	43.2 / 0.4	56.5 / 0.5	60.1 / 0.5 n
Refugees and others of concern to the UNHCR (000)	0.1 o	1.0	9.5 b
Infant mortality rate (per 1 000 live births)	15.6	14.6	13.5 a,b
Health: Current expenditure (% of GDP) p	5.6	6.2 q	6.3 i,n
Health: Physicians (per 1 000 pop.)	1.2	1.3	1.3 s
Education: Government expenditure (% of GDP)	6.0	6.2	...
Education: Primary gross enrol. ratio (f/m per 100 pop.)	107.0 / 107.4	114.6 / 114.5	111.2 / 113.2 c
Education: Lowr. sec. gross enrol. ratio (f/m per 100 pop.)	109.6 / 113.5	103.5 / 101.9	116.6 / 112.0 c
Education: Upr. sec. gross enrol. ratio (f/m per 100 pop.)	84.2 / 67.6	84.9 / 69.1 t	89.8 / 68.9 u
Intentional homicide rate (per 100 000 pop.)	2.6	3.0 v	4.6 n
Seats held by women in the National Parliament (%)	27.6	31.3	26.3 w,b

Environment and infrastructure indicators

	2010	2015	2023
Individuals using the Internet (per 100 inhabitants)	36.8	46.5	79.0 i,c
Research & Development expenditure (% of GDP)	0.7	0.6	0.7 e
Threatened species (number)	75	83	129 b
Forested area (% of land area)	4.4	4.5	4.5 n
CO2 emission estimates (million tons/tons per capita)	23.8 / 2.2	26.1 / 2.3	25.7 / 2.1 n
Energy production, primary (Petajoules)	341	269	207 n
Energy supply per capita (Gigajoules)	39	40	37 n
Tourist/visitor arrivals at national borders (000) x	7 828	5 359	2 475 c
Important sites for terrestrial biodiversity protected (%)	26.0	39.8	39.8 b
Pop. using safely managed drinking water (urban/rural, %)	83.4 / 56.6	83.6 / 61.0	77.4 / 67.1 b
Pop. using safely managed sanitation (urban/rural %)	79.2 / 41.7	84.1 / 51.8	88.9 / 62.9 b
Net Official Development Assist. received (% of GNI)	1.25	1.12	2.40 c

a Projected estimate (medium fertility variant). **b** 2022. **c** 2021. **d** Refers to Grand Tunis. **e** 2019. **f** At factor cost. **g** Excludes irrigation canals and landscaping care. **h** Excludes publishing activities, recycling. Includes irrigation canals. **i** Estimate. **j** Break in the time series. **k** Data refers to a 5-year period preceding the reference year. **l** Including refugees. **m** Refers to foreign citizens. **n** 2020. **o** Data as at the end of December. **p** Data based on calendar year (January 1 to December 31). **q** Data are based on SHA2011. **r** Estimates should be viewed with caution as these are derived from scarce data. **s** 2017. **t** 2011. **u** 2016. **v** 2012. **w** Data are as at 1 January of reporting year. **x** Including nationals residing abroad.

Türkiye

Region	Western Asia	UN membership date	24 October 1945
Population (000, 2023)	85 341 [a,b]	Surface area (km2)	783 562 [c]
Pop. density (per km2, 2023)	110.9 [a,b]	Sex ratio (m per 100 f)	100.4 [a,b]
Capital city	Ankara	National currency	Turkish Lira (TRY)
Capital city pop. (000, 2023)	5 018.0 [d,e]	Exchange rate (per US$)	18.7 [b]

Economic indicators

	2010	2015	2023
GDP: Gross domestic product (million current US$)	776 967	864 314	819 034 [c]
GDP growth rate (annual %, const. 2015 prices)	8.4	6.1	11.4 [c]
GDP per capita (current US$)	10 615.0	10 851.9	9 661.2 [c]
Economy: Agriculture (% of Gross Value Added) [f,g]	10.2	7.8	6.2 [c]
Economy: Industry (% of Gross Value Added) [f,h]	27.8	31.6	34.8 [c]
Economy: Services and other activity (% of GVA) [f]	62.0	60.6	59.0 [c]
Employment in agriculture (% of employed)	23.7	20.4	17.1 [i,c]
Employment in industry (% of employed)	26.1	27.3	26.5 [i,c]
Employment in services & other sectors (% of employed)	50.1	52.3	56.4 [i,c]
Unemployment rate (% of labour force)	10.7	10.2	9.9 [i]
Labour force participation rate (female/male pop. %)	26.9 / 69.5	31.3 / 71.3	34.3 / 71.1 [i]
CPI: Consumer Price Index (2010=100)	100 [i]	146 [i]	542 [b]
Agricultural production index (2014-2016=100)	87	102	120 [c]
International trade: exports (million current US$) [j]	113 883	143 850	254 201 [b]
International trade: imports (million current US$) [j]	185 544	207 207	363 709 [b]
International trade: balance (million current US$) [j]	- 71 661	- 63 356	- 109 508 [b]
Balance of payments, current account (million US$)	- 44 620	- 26 625	- 48 751 [b]

Major trading partners

						2022
Export partners (% of exports)	Germany	8.3	United States	6.6	Iraq	5.4
Import partners (% of imports)	Russian Federation	16.2	China	11.4	Undisclosed	9.5

Social indicators

	2010	2015	2023
Population growth rate (average annual %)	1.3	1.7	0.6 [a,b]
Urban population (% of total population)	70.8	73.6	75.6 [e]
Urban population growth rate (average annual %) [k]	2.1	2.4	...
Fertility rate, total (live births per woman)	2.1	2.2	1.9 [a,b]
Life expectancy at birth (females/males, years)	78.2 / 71.9	79.8 / 73.5	81.5 / 75.4 [a,b]
Population age distribution (0-14/60+ years old, %)	26.7 / 9.5	24.6 / 10.6	23.2 / 12.7 [a,b]
International migrant stock (000/% of total pop.) [l]	1 373.7 / 1.9	4 346.2 / 5.5	6 052.7 / 7.2 [m]
Refugees and others of concern to the UNHCR (000)	17.8 [n]	1 985.3	3 967.9 [b]
Infant mortality rate (per 1 000 live births)	15.3	11.0	7.7 [a,b]
Health: Current expenditure (% of GDP)	5.0	4.1	4.6 [m]
Health: Physicians (per 1 000 pop.)	1.7	1.8	2.0 [m]
Education: Government expenditure (% of GDP)	3.8	4.3	3.4 [m]
Education: Primary gross enrol. ratio (f/m per 100 pop.)	100.6 / 102.0	102.7 / 103.4	95.8 / 97.2 [m]
Education: Lowr. sec. gross enrol. ratio (f/m per 100 pop.)	97.3 / 101.4	100.0 / 98.5	106.5 / 104.4 [m]
Education: Upr. sec. gross enrol. ratio (f/m per 100 pop.)	67.5 / 77.4	102.9 / 109.8	99.4 / 107.1 [m]
Intentional homicide rate (per 100 000 pop.)	4.2	2.8	2.5 [c]
Seats held by women in the National Parliament (%)	9.1	14.4	17.4 [o]

Environment and infrastructure indicators

	2010	2015	2023
Individuals using the Internet (per 100 inhabitants)	39.8 [p,q]	53.7 [q]	81.4 [p,r,c]
Research & Development expenditure (% of GDP)	0.8	0.9	1.1 [m]
Threatened species (number)	150	370	451 [b]
Forested area (% of land area)	27.4	28.1	28.9 [m]
CO2 emission estimates (million tons/tons per capita)	272.3 / 3.7	322.9 / 4.1	395.2 / 4.6 [c]
Energy production, primary (Petajoules)	1 355	1 317	1 826 [m]
Energy supply per capita (Gigajoules)	61	68	73 [m]
Tourist/visitor arrivals at national borders (000) [s]	31 364	39 478	29 925 [c]
Important sites for terrestrial biodiversity protected (%)	2.3	2.3	2.3 [b]
Pop. using safely managed sanitation (urban/rural %)	54.2 / 58.7	63.5 / 67.3	78.0 / 81.1 [b]
Net Official Development Assist. disbursed (% of GNI) [t]	0.23	0.65	1.04 [c]
Net Official Development Assist. received (% of GNI)	0.14	0.25	0.13 [c]

a Projected estimate (medium fertility variant). b 2022. c 2021. d Refers to Altindag, Cankaya, Etimesgut, Golbasi, Keçioren, Mamak, Sincan and Yenimahalle. e 2019. f Data classified according to ISIC Rev. 4. g Excludes irrigation canals and landscaping care. h Excludes publishing activities, recycling. Includes irrigation canals. i Estimate. j Special trade system up to 2012. k Data refers to a 5-year period preceding the reference year. l Including refugees. m 2020. n Data as at the end of December. o Data are as at 1 January of reporting year. p Population aged 16 to 74 years. q Users in the last 12 months. r Users in the last 3 months. s Turkish citizens resident abroad are included. t Türkiye reports support to refugees in Türkiye against type of aid C01 "project-type interventions" instead of H02 "in-donor refugee costs".

Turkmenistan

Region	Central Asia	UN membership date		02 March 1992	
Population (000, 2023)	6 431 a,b	Surface area (km2)		488 100 c	
Pop. density (per km2, 2023)	13.7 a,b	Sex ratio (m per 100 f)		98.2 a,b	
Capital city	Ashgabat	National currency		Turkmen. Manat (TMT) d	
Capital city pop. (000, 2023)	828.1 e	Exchange rate (per US$)		3.5 f,b	

Economic indicators

	2010	2015	2023
GDP: Gross domestic product (million current US$)	22 583	36 052	53 954 c
GDP growth rate (annual %, const. 2015 prices)	16.2	3.0	4.6 c
GDP per capita (current US$)	4 286.9	6 252.0	8 507.7 c
Economy: Agriculture (% of Gross Value Added)	11.5	9.4	11.1 c
Economy: Industry (% of Gross Value Added)	60.0	55.1	44.6 c
Economy: Services and other activity (% of GVA)	28.5	35.5	44.3 c
Employment in agriculture (% of employed) g	31.6	26.9	22.3 c
Employment in industry (% of employed) g	28.5	31.1	34.3 c
Employment in services & other sectors (% employed) g	40.0	42.0	43.5 c
Unemployment rate (% of labour force)	4.0	4.1 g	5.4 g
Labour force participation rate (female/male pop. %) g	50.1 / 48.2	48.4 / 46.2	47.2 / 44.7
Agricultural production index (2014-2016=100)	109	102	116 c
International trade: exports (million current US$) g	3 335	3 670	12 821 b
International trade: imports (million current US$) g	2 400	2 596	3 160 b
International trade: balance (million current US$) g	935	1 074	9 661 b

Major trading partners

						2022
Export partners (% of exports) g	China	71.9	Türkiye	6.7	Uzbekistan	5.1
Import partners (% of imports) g	Türkiye	23.7	China	18.7	Russian Federation	18.2

Social indicators

	2010	2015	2023
Population growth rate (average annual %)	1.7	1.8	1.4 a,b
Urban population (% of total population)	48.5	50.3	52.0 e
Urban population growth rate (average annual %) h	2.0	2.5	...
Fertility rate, total (live births per woman)	2.8	2.9	2.6 a,b
Life expectancy at birth (females/males, years)	71.6 / 64.9	72.2 / 65.4	72.9 / 65.9 a,b
Population age distribution (0-14/60+ years old, %)	30.2 / 6.0	30.4 / 6.8	31.1 / 8.8 a,b
International migrant stock (000/% of total pop.) i	198.0 / 3.9	196.4 / 3.5	194.9 / 3.2 j
Refugees and others of concern to the UNHCR (000)	20.1 k	7.2	4.5 l,b
Infant mortality rate (per 1 000 live births)	36.8	36.1	32.9 a,b
Health: Current expenditure (% of GDP)	3.2	5.1	5.7 j
Health: Physicians (per 1 000 pop.)	2.2	2.1 m	...
Education: Government expenditure (% of GDP)	...	3.0 n	3.1 e
Education: Primary gross enrol. ratio (f/m per 100 pop.)	... / ...	... / ...	114.1 / 116.0 c
Education: Lowr. sec. gross enrol. ratio (f/m per 100 pop.)	... / ...	... / ...	96.4 / 98.1 j
Education: Upr. sec. gross enrol. ratio (f/m per 100 pop.)	... / ...	... / ...	80.0 / 81.4 j
Intentional homicide rate (per 100 000 pop.)	2.0	1.1	...
Seats held by women in the National Parliament (%)	16.8	25.8	25.9 o

Environment and infrastructure indicators

	2010	2015	2023
Individuals using the Internet (per 100 inhabitants) g	3.0	15.0	21.3 p
Threatened species (number)	45	49	60 b
Forested area (% of land area)	8.8	8.8	8.8 j
CO2 emission estimates (million tons/tons per capita)	57.2 / 11.2	59.8 / 10.7	60.5 / 10.0 j
Energy production, primary (Petajoules)	1 982	3 407	3 255 j
Energy supply per capita (Gigajoules)	181	171	170 j
Tourist/visitor arrivals at national borders (000)	8 q	...	...
Important sites for terrestrial biodiversity protected (%)	14.0	14.0	14.0 b
Pop. using safely managed drinking water (urban/rural, %)	91.5 / 72.7	96.4 / 85.1	97.1 / 92.3 b
Net Official Development Assist. received (% of GNI)	0.21	0.07	0.06 e

a Projected estimate (medium fertility variant). b 2022. c 2021. d Turkmenistan New Manat. e 2019. f UN operational exchange rate. g Estimate. h Data refers to a 5-year period preceding the reference year. i Including refugees. j 2020. k Data as at the end of December. l In the absence of official data, the figure reported refers to stateless persons and persons with undetermined nationality identified by UNHCR partner organizations. m 2014. n 2012. o Data are as at 1 January of reporting year. p 2017. q 2007.

Turks and Caicos Islands

Region	Caribbean	Population (000, 2023)	46 a,b,c
Surface area (km2)	948 d,e	Pop. density (per km2, 2023)	48.1 a,b,c
Sex ratio (m per 100 f)	101.4 a,b,c	Capital city	Cockburn Town
National currency	US Dollar (USD)	Capital city pop. (000)	0.1 f

Economic indicators

	2010	2015	2023
GDP: Gross domestic product (million current US$)	687	942	943 e
GDP growth rate (annual %, const. 2015 prices)	1.0	11.3	2.1 e
GDP per capita (current US$)	23 103.9	25 783.3	20 908.6 e
Economy: Agriculture (% of Gross Value Added)	0.6	0.6	0.5 e
Economy: Industry (% of Gross Value Added)	12.4	11.1	18.0 e
Economy: Services and other activity (% of GVA)	86.9	88.3	81.6 e
Employment in agriculture (% of employed)	1.2 g,h,i	...	...
Employment in industry (% of employed)	23.1 g,h,i	...	...
Employment in services & other sectors (% employed)	74.0 g,h,i	...	...
Unemployment rate (% of labour force)	8.3 h,i	...	...
International trade: exports (million current US$) j	16	5	3 c
International trade: imports (million current US$) j	302	410	681 c
International trade: balance (million current US$) j	- 286	- 405	- 679 c
Balance of payments, current account (million US$)	...	154	173 k

Major trading partners

2022

Export partners (% of exports) j	Bahamas	69.3	Togo	17.4	United States	7.3
Import partners (% of imports) j	United States	75.6	Bahamas	10.1	Dominican Rep.	3.3

Social indicators

	2010	2015	2023
Population growth rate (average annual %) b	3.8	5.1	0.8 a,c
Urban population (% of total population)	90.2	92.2	93.4 l
Urban population growth rate (average annual %) m	3.7	2.5	...
Fertility rate, total (live births per woman) b	1.7	1.7	1.7 a,c
Life expectancy at birth (females/males, years) b	79.1 / 73.7	79.6 / 74.5	78.0 / 72.2 a,c
Population age distribution (0-14/60+ years old, %) b	22.9 / 9.5	18.8 / 12.5	16.7 / 15.6 a,c
International migrant stock (000/% of total pop.) n	17.2 / 52.7	22.7 / 63.2	25.7 / 66.5 o
Refugees and others of concern to the UNHCR (000)	...	~0.0	~0.0 c
Infant mortality rate (per 1 000 live births) b	10.5	7.2	11.4 a,c
Education: Government expenditure (% of GDP)	2.5 p	3.1	3.7 c
Education: Primary gross enrol. ratio (f/m per 100 pop.)	84.2 / 77.7 p	74.3 / 74.7	113.8 / 108.7 e
Education: Lowr. sec. gross enrol. ratio (f/m per 100 pop.)	122.4 / 106.4 q	69.7 / 69.9	91.3 / 99.4 e
Education: Upr. sec. gross enrol. ratio (f/m per 100 pop.)	53.7 / 54.6 q	87.1 / 67.4	78.1 / 68.4 e
Intentional homicide rate (per 100 000 pop.)	7.0 q	5.7 r	...

Environment and infrastructure indicators

	2010	2015	2023
Threatened species (number)	34	56	93 c
Forested area (% of land area)	11.1	11.1	11.1 o
Energy production, primary (Petajoules)	0	0	0 o
Energy supply per capita (Gigajoules) j	137	125	117 o
Tourist/visitor arrivals at national borders (000)	281	386	405 e
Important sites for terrestrial biodiversity protected (%)	27.9	27.9	27.9 c
Pop. using safely managed drinking water (urban/rural, %)	46.5 / ...	46.5 / ...	46.5 / 55.7 c
Pop. using safely managed sanitation (urban/rural %)	... / ...	... / ...	33.3 / 43.9 c

a Projected estimate (medium fertility variant). b For statistical purposes, the data for United Kingdom do not include this area. c 2022. d Including low water level for all islands (area to shoreline). e 2021. f 2001. g Data classified according to ISIC Rev. 3. h Break in the time series. i 2008. j Estimate. k 2018. l 2019. m Data refers to a 5-year period preceding the reference year. n Including refugees. o 2020. p 2005. q 2009. r 2014.

Tuvalu

Region	Polynesia		UN membership date	05 September 2000	
Population (000, 2023)	11[a,b]		Surface area (km2)	26[c]	
Pop. density (per km2, 2023)	377.0[a,b]		Sex ratio (m per 100 f)	105.2[a,b]	
Capital city	Funafuti		National currency	Australian Dollar (AUD)	
Capital city pop. (000, 2023)	7.0[d]		Exchange rate (per US$)	1.5[b]	

Economic indicators

	2010	2015	2023
GDP: Gross domestic product (million current US$)	31	36	60[c]
GDP growth rate (annual %, const. 2015 prices)	- 3.3	10.4	1.7[c]
GDP per capita (current US$)	2 975.9	3 327.6	5 370.4[c]
Economy: Agriculture (% of Gross Value Added)[e]	27.3	13.9	9.1[f,g]
Economy: Industry (% of Gross Value Added)[e]	5.7	12.4	16.8[g,c]
Economy: Services and other activity (% of GVA)[e]	67.0	73.7	74.1[c]
CPI: Consumer Price Index (2010=100)	100	101[h]	...
Agricultural production index (2014-2016=100)	94	100	109[c]
International trade: exports (million current US$)[i]	~0	~0	23[b]
International trade: imports (million current US$)[i]	12	12	107[b]
International trade: balance (million current US$)[i]	- 12	- 12	- 83[b]
Balance of payments, current account (million US$)	- 14	- 17	21[c]

Major trading partners

						2022
Export partners (% of exports)[i]	Thailand	82.4	Croatia	9.1	Nigeria	3.9
Import partners (% of imports)[i]	Singapore	33.5	China	20.7	Japan	16.2

Social indicators

	2010	2015	2023
Population growth rate (average annual %)	1.3	- 0.2	0.8[a,b]
Urban population (% of total population)	54.8	59.7	63.2[i]
Urban population growth rate (average annual %)[k]	2.9	2.6	...
Fertility rate, total (live births per woman)	3.5	3.2	3.1[a,b]
Life expectancy at birth (females/males, years)	67.7 / 60.6	68.3 / 60.5	69.4 / 61.1[a,b]
Population age distribution (0-14/60+ years old, %)	32.5 / 8.4	31.6 / 8.9	31.7 / 11.1[a,b]
International migrant stock (000/% of total pop.)[l]	0.2 / 2.1	0.2 / 2.1	0.2 / 2.0[m]
Infant mortality rate (per 1 000 live births)	25.6	21.5	17.6[a,b]
Health: Current expenditure (% of GDP)[n]	15.7	13.5	21.5[m]
Health: Physicians (per 1 000 pop.)	1.2[o]	0.9[p]	1.3[m]
Education: Primary gross enrol. ratio (f/m per 100 pop.)	108.4 / 112.6[q]	97.8 / 101.7	89.8 / 93.3[c]
Education: Lowr. sec. gross enrol. ratio (f/m per 100 pop.)	... / ...	94.8 / 93.3[p]	82.6 / 85.3[c]
Education: Upr. sec. gross enrol. ratio (f/m per 100 pop.)	... / ...	71.6 / 42.1[p]	66.7 / 51.7[c]
Intentional homicide rate (per 100 000 pop.)	9.5	18.4[r]	0.0[i]
Seats held by women in the National Parliament (%)	0.0	6.7	6.2[s]

Environment and infrastructure indicators

	2010	2015	2023
Individuals using the Internet (per 100 inhabitants)[i]	14.6	27.3	71.6[c]
Threatened species (number)	85	93	106[b]
Forested area (% of land area)	33.3	33.3	33.3[m]
Energy production, primary (Petajoules)	0[i]	0	0[i,m]
Energy supply per capita (Gigajoules)	13	11[i]	12[i,m]
Tourist/visitor arrivals at national borders (000)	2	2	~0[c]
Pop. using safely managed drinking water (urban/rural, %)	10.4 / 5.3	10.5 / 5.4	10.5 / 5.4[b]
Pop. using safely managed sanitation (urban/rural %)	37.4 / 51.3	36.3 / 47.4	34.7 / 42.1[b]
Net Official Development Assist. received (% of GNI)	27.27	88.66	42.87[c]

a Projected estimate (medium fertility variant). **b** 2022. **c** 2021. **d** 2018. **e** Data classified according to ISIC Rev. 4. **f** Excludes irrigation canals and landscaping care. **g** Excludes publishing activities, recycling. Includes irrigation canals. **h** 2011. **i** Estimate. **j** 2019. **k** Data refers to a 5-year period preceding the reference year. **l** Refers to foreign citizens. **m** 2020. **n** General government expenditure (GGE) can be larger than the Gross domestic product (GDP) because government accounts for a very large part of domestic consumption and because a large part of domestic consumption in the country is accounted for by imports. **o** 2009. **p** 2014. **q** 2006. **r** 2012. **s** Data are as at 1 January of reporting year.

Uganda

Region	Eastern Africa	UN membership date	25 October 1962
Population (000, 2023)	47 250 [a,b]	Surface area (km2)	241 550 [c]
Pop. density (per km2, 2023)	236.5 [a,b]	Sex ratio (m per 100 f)	98.1 [a,b]
Capital city	Kampala	National currency	Uganda Shilling (UGX)
Capital city pop. (000, 2023)	3 137.7 [d,e]	Exchange rate (per US$)	3 715.7 [b]

Economic indicators

	2010	2015	2023
GDP: Gross domestic product (million current US$)	30 701	29 297	42 661 [c]
GDP growth rate (annual %, const. 2015 prices)	19.9	6.1	6.7 [c]
GDP per capita (current US$)	949.3	781.7	930.4 [c]
Economy: Agriculture (% of Gross Value Added) [f,g]	27.3	23.3	25.2 [c]
Economy: Industry (% of Gross Value Added) [g,h]	26.6	29.4	29.4 [c]
Economy: Services and other activity (% of GVA) [g]	46.1	47.3	45.3 [c]
Employment in agriculture (% of employed) [i]	71.3	67.8	62.9 [c]
Employment in industry (% of employed) [i]	7.4	7.8	9.5 [c]
Employment in services & other sectors (% employed) [i]	21.3	24.4	27.6 [c]
Unemployment rate (% of labour force) [i]	3.6	2.7	4.3
Labour force participation rate (female/male pop. %) [i]	65.4 / 75.0	66.7 / 73.9	67.7 / 72.0
CPI: Consumer Price Index (2010=100)	...	151 [j]	121 [k,b]
Agricultural production index (2014-2016=100)	94	103	125 [c]
International trade: exports (million current US$)	1 619	2 267	3 551 [i,b]
International trade: imports (million current US$)	4 664	5 528	10 243 [i,b]
International trade: balance (million current US$)	- 3 046	- 3 261	- 6 692 [i,b]
Balance of payments, current account (million US$)	- 1 610	- 1 667	- 3 553 [c]

Major trading partners
							2022
Export partners (% of exports) [i]	United Arab Emirates	44.5	Kenya	11.2	South Sudan	8.6	
Import partners (% of imports) [i]	China	16.4	India	11.6	Kenya	9.4	

Social indicators

	2010	2015	2023
Population growth rate (average annual %)	2.9	3.1	2.8 [a,b]
Urban population (% of total population)	19.4	22.1	24.4 [e]
Urban population growth rate (average annual %) [i]	6.1	6.0	...
Fertility rate, total (live births per woman)	6.1	5.3	4.5 [a,b]
Life expectancy at birth (females/males, years)	58.8 / 55.2	63.0 / 59.1	65.7 / 61.5 [a,b]
Population age distribution (0-14/60+ years old, %)	49.9 / 2.6	48.5 / 2.7	44.8 / 2.9 [a,b]
International migrant stock (000/% of total pop.) [m]	492.9 / 1.5	851.2 / 2.2	1 720.3 / 3.8 [n]
Refugees and others of concern to the UNHCR (000)	594.4 [o]	646.5	1 596.3 [p,b]
Infant mortality rate (per 1 000 live births)	51.8	39.4	30.4 [a,b]
Health: Current expenditure (% of GDP) [q]	6.8	5.1	4.0 [n]
Health: Physicians (per 1 000 pop.)	0.1 [r]	0.1	0.2 [n]
Education: Government expenditure (% of GDP)	1.7	2.3 [i]	2.6 [b]
Education: Primary gross enrol. ratio (f/m per 100 pop.)	122.4 / 121.5	103.7 / 101.6	104.1 / 101.3 [s]
Education: Lowr. sec. gross enrol. ratio (f/m per 100 pop.)	... / ...	... / ...	29.8 / 31.3 [s]
Education: Upr. sec. gross enrol. ratio (f/m per 100 pop.)	12.0 / 16.5 [t]	... / ...	7.7 / 12.2 [s]
Intentional homicide rate (per 100 000 pop.)	9.8	12.3 [u]	8.5 [c]
Seats held by women in the National Parliament (%)	31.5	35.0	33.8 [v]

Environment and infrastructure indicators

	2010	2015	2023
Individuals using the Internet (per 100 inhabitants) [i]	4.3	5.8	10.3 [c]
Research & Development expenditure (% of GDP)	0.4	0.1 [w,u]	...
Threatened species (number)	166	188	313 [b]
Forested area (% of land area)	13.7	12.7	11.7 [n]
CO2 emission estimates (million tons/tons per capita)	5.2 / 0.1	6.9 / 0.1	8.1 / 0.1 [n]
Energy production, primary (Petajoules)	599	745	979 [n]
Energy supply per capita (Gigajoules)	20	21	28 [n]
Tourist/visitor arrivals at national borders (000)	946	1 303	513 [c]
Important sites for terrestrial biodiversity protected (%)	72.2	72.2	72.2 [b]
Pop. using safely managed drinking water (urban/rural, %)	28.8 / 3.5	35.6 / 5.7	45.1 / 9.3 [b]
Pop. using safely managed sanitation (urban/rural %)	21.4 / 14.5	21.8 / 15.2	22.4 / 16.2 [b]
Net Official Development Assist. received (% of GNI)	6.44	5.16	6.45 [c]

a Projected estimate (medium fertility variant). b 2022. c 2021. d Data includes Kira, Makindye Ssabagabo and Nansana. e 2019. f Excludes irrigation canals and landscaping care. g Data classified according to ISIC Rev. 4. h Excludes publishing activities, recycling. Includes irrigation canals. i Estimate. j Base: 1 July 2009 - 30 June 2010=100. k Base: 1 July 2016 - 30 June 2017=100. l Data refers to a 5-year period preceding the reference year. m Including refugees. n 2020. o Data as at the end of December. p The estimates represent a rudimentary and unverified/unconfirmed estimate of in situ stateless persons provided by representatives from these unrecognized communities. q Data refer to fiscal years beginning 1 July. r 2005. s 2017. t 2008. u 2014. v Data are as at 1 January of reporting year. w Break in the time series.

Ukraine

Region	Eastern Europe	UN membership date	24 October 1945
Population (000, 2023)	39 702 [a,b,c]	Surface area (km2)	603 500 [d]
Pop. density (per km2, 2023)	68.5 [a,b,c]	Sex ratio (m per 100 f)	84.9 [a,b,c]
Capital city	Kyiv	National currency	Hryvnia (UAH)
Capital city pop. (000, 2023)	2 973.3 [e]	Exchange rate (per US$)	36.6 [f,c]

Economic indicators	2010	2015	2023
GDP: Gross domestic product (million current US$) [f]	136 012	91 031	200 086 [d]
GDP growth rate (annual %, const. 2015 prices) [f]	0.3	- 9.8	3.4 [d]
GDP per capita (current US$) [f]	2 977.3	2 023.7	4 596.3 [d]
Economy: Agriculture (% of Gross Value Added) [f,g,h]	8.4	14.2	12.4 [d]
Economy: Industry (% of Gross Value Added) [f,g,i]	29.3	25.6	27.3 [d]
Economy: Services and other activity (% of GVA) [g]	62.3	60.2	60.3 [d]
Employment in agriculture (% of employed)	16.3 [j]	15.3	14.7 [j,d]
Employment in industry (% of employed)	26.9	24.7	24.5 [j,d]
Employment in services & other sectors (% employed)	56.7	60.1	60.8 [j,d]
Unemployment rate (% of labour force)	8.1	9.1	9.8 [d]
Labour force participation rate (female/male pop. %)	51.9 / 61.6 [j]	50.4 / 63.4 [j]	47.8 / 62.9 [d]
CPI: Consumer Price Index (2010=100)	100	180	381 [c]
Agricultural production index (2014-2016=100)	78	97	114 [c]
International trade: exports (million current US$) [f]	51 430	38 127	44 443 [c]
International trade: imports (million current US$) [f]	60 737	37 516	55 224 [c]
International trade: balance (million current US$) [f]	- 9 307	611	- 10 781 [c]
Balance of payments, current account (million US$)	- 3 016	5 035	8 005 [c]

Major trading partners						2022
Export partners (% of exports) [f]	Poland	15.1	Romania	8.8	Türkiye	6.6
Import partners (% of imports) [f]	China	15.7	Poland	9.9	Germany	8.3

Social indicators	2010	2015	2023
Population growth rate (average annual %) [b]	- 0.4	- 0.3	- 18.4 [a,c]
Urban population (% of total population) [b]	68.6	69.1	69.5 [e]
Urban population growth rate (average annual %) [b,k]	- 0.2	- 0.4	...
Fertility rate, total (live births per woman) [b]	1.4	1.5	1.3 [a,c]
Life expectancy at birth (females/males, years) [b]	75.4 / 65.7	78.4 / 68.2	73.9 / 63.5 [a,c]
Population age distribution (0-14/60+ years old, %) [b]	14.2 / 20.8	15.2 / 22.0	15.4 / 26.5 [a,c]
International migrant stock (000/% of total pop.) [b]	4 818.8 / 10.5	4 915.1 / 10.9	4 997.4 / 11.4 [l]
Refugees and others of concern to the UNHCR (000)	46.4 [m]	1 426.6	6 315.1 [c]
Infant mortality rate (per 1 000 live births) [b]	8.4	6.7	7.1 [a,c]
Health: Current expenditure (% of GDP)	6.8	7.8	7.6 [l]
Health: Physicians (per 1 000 pop.)	3.5	3.0 [n]	...
Education: Government expenditure (% of GDP)	7.4	5.7	5.6 [d]
Education: Primary gross enrol. ratio (f/m per 100 pop.)	99.1 / 98.5	100.1 / 98.0 [n]	... / ...
Education: Lowr. sec. gross enrol. ratio (f/m per 100 pop.)	102.9 / 103.0 [i]	97.7 / 97.1 [n]	... / ...
Education: Upr. sec. gross enrol. ratio (f/m per 100 pop.)	76.4 / 83.6 [i]	89.0 / 96.6 [n]	... / ...
Intentional homicide rate (per 100 000 pop.)	4.4	6.3 [n]	3.8 [d]
Seats held by women in the National Parliament (%)	8.0	11.8	20.4 [o]

Environment and infrastructure indicators	2010	2015	2023
Individuals using the Internet (per 100 inhabitants)	23.3	48.9 [p]	79.2 [d]
Research & Development expenditure (% of GDP)	0.8	0.6 [q]	0.3 [q,r,s,d]
Threatened species (number)	61	87	147 [c]
Forested area (% of land area)	16.5	16.7	16.7 [l]
CO2 emission estimates (million tons/tons per capita)	268.0 / 5.8	189.0 / 4.2 [f]	176.7 / 3.7 [f,d,l]
Energy production, primary (Petajoules) [f]	3 238	2 552	2 329 [l]
Energy supply per capita (Gigajoules) [f]	120	83	79 [l]
Tourist/visitor arrivals at national borders (000)	21 203	12 428	3 973 [d]
Important sites for terrestrial biodiversity protected (%)	57.1	58.3	59.8 [c]
Pop. using safely managed drinking water (urban/rural, %)	90.8 / 71.1	88.5 / 89.6	88.3 / 86.1 [c]
Pop. using safely managed sanitation (urban/rural %)	46.1 / ...	60.8 / ...	68.9 / ... [c]
Net Official Development Assist. received (% of GNI) [f]	0.48	1.53	1.14 [d]

a Projected estimate (medium fertility variant). b Including Crimea. c 2022. d 2021. e 2019. f The Government of Ukraine has informed the United Nations that it is not in a position to provide statistical data concerning the Autonomous Republic of Crimea and the city of Sevastopol. g Data classified according to ISIC Rev. 4. h Excludes irrigation canals and landscaping care. i Excludes publishing activities, recycling. Includes irrigation canals. j Estimate. k Data refers to a 5-year period preceding the reference year. l 2020. m Data as at the end of December. n 2014. o Data are as at 1 January of reporting year. p Users in the last 12 months. q Excluding data from some regions, provinces or states. r Provisional data. s Break in the time series.

United Arab Emirates

Region	Western Asia	UN membership date	09 December 1971
Population (000, 2023)	9 441 [a,b]	Surface area (km2)	71 024 [c,d]
Pop. density (per km2, 2023)	132.9 [a,b]	Sex ratio (m per 100 f)	226.3 [a,b]
Capital city	Abu Dhabi	National currency	UAE Dirham (AED) [e]
Capital city pop. (000, 2023)	1 452.1 [f]	Exchange rate (per US$)	3.7 [b]

Economic indicators

	2010	2015	2023
GDP: Gross domestic product (million current US$)	289 787	358 135	405 468 [d]
GDP growth rate (annual %, const. 2015 prices)	1.6	5.1	3.8 [d]
GDP per capita (current US$)	34 165.9	40 163.6	43 295.4 [d]
Economy: Agriculture (% of Gross Value Added)	0.8	0.7	0.9 [d]
Economy: Industry (% of Gross Value Added)	52.5	43.9	46.6 [d]
Economy: Services and other activity (% of GVA)	46.7	55.4	52.5 [d]
Employment in agriculture (% of employed) [g]	3.8	2.4	1.7 [d]
Employment in industry (% of employed) [g]	26.8	33.2	27.1 [d]
Employment in services & other sectors (% employed) [g]	69.4	64.4	71.2 [d]
Unemployment rate (% of labour force) [g]	2.5	1.8	2.7
Labour force participation rate (female/male pop. %) [g]	42.4 / 89.0	49.4 / 91.4	56.2 / 92.8
CPI: Consumer Price Index (2010=100)	100	109	112 [d]
Agricultural production index (2014-2016=100)	130	98	125 [d]
International trade: exports (million current US$)	198 362	300 479	586 532 [g,b]
International trade: imports (million current US$)	187 001	287 025	424 374 [g,b]
International trade: balance (million current US$)	11 361	13 454	162 158 [g,b]

Major trading partners

							2022
Export partners (% of exports) [g]	China	12.4	India	12.3	Japan	9.3
Import partners (% of imports) [g]	Areas nes	15.3	China	15.0	India	9.2

Social indicators

	2010	2015	2023
Population growth rate (average annual %)	1.1	0.9	0.8 [a,b]
Urban population (% of total population)	84.1	85.7	86.8 [f]
Urban population growth rate (average annual %) [h]	12.3	2.4	...
Fertility rate, total (live births per woman)	1.8	1.5	1.4 [a,b]
Life expectancy at birth (females/males, years)	80.2 / 76.5	81.2 / 77.6	81.4 / 77.7 [a,b]
Population age distribution (0-14/60+ years old, %)	13.7 / 0.3	14.3 / 1.1	15.2 / 3.5 [a,b]
International migrant stock (000/% of total pop.) [i,j]	7 316.7 / 85.6	7 995.1 / 86.3	8 716.3 / 88.1 [k]
Refugees and others of concern to the UNHCR (000)	0.6 [l]	0.8	8.7 [b]
Infant mortality rate (per 1 000 live births)	7.4	6.5	5.2 [a,b]
Health: Current expenditure (% of GDP) [m]	3.9	3.6	5.7 [g,n,k]
Health: Physicians (per 1 000 pop.)	1.4	2.3	2.9 [k]
Education: Government expenditure (% of GDP)	...	1.7	3.9 [d]
Education: Primary gross enrol. ratio (f/m per 100 pop.)	102.1 / 101.1 [o]	111.6 / 114.4	113.2 / 111.5 [b]
Education: Lowr. sec. gross enrol. ratio (f/m per 100 pop.)	85.1 / 85.2	95.2 / 97.8	99.0 / 100.6 [b]
Education: Upr. sec. gross enrol. ratio (f/m per 100 pop.)	... / ...	... / ...	110.5 / 112.6 [b]
Intentional homicide rate (per 100 000 pop.)	0.8	0.7	0.5 [d]
Seats held by women in the National Parliament (%)	22.5	17.5	50.0 [p]

Environment and infrastructure indicators

	2010	2015	2023
Individuals using the Internet (per 100 inhabitants)	68.0 [q]	90.5 [g]	100.0 [d]
Research & Development expenditure (% of GDP)	...	0.9	1.5 [d]
Threatened species (number)	48	48	94 [b]
Forested area (% of land area)	4.5	4.5	4.5 [k]
CO2 emission estimates (million tons/tons per capita)	155.6 / 18.1	187.5 / 20.1	181.9 / 18.3 [k]
Energy production, primary (Petajoules)	7 849	9 995	9 465 [k]
Energy supply per capita (Gigajoules)	351	401	392 [k]
Tourist/visitor arrivals at national borders (000)	7 126 [r,s]	16 842 [t]	11 479 [u,d]
Important sites for terrestrial biodiversity protected (%)	28.6	42.8	51.6 [b]
Pop. using safely managed sanitation (urban/rural %)	98.4 / 98.5	98.4 / 98.5	98.5 / 98.5 [b]
Net Official Development Assist. disbursed (% of GNI) [v]	0.38 [w]	...	0.36 [d]

a Projected estimate (medium fertility variant). b 2022. c Land area only. d 2021. e United Arab Emirates Dirham. f 2019. g Estimate. h Data refers to a 5-year period preceding the reference year. i Refers to foreign citizens. j Including refugees. k 2020. l Data as at the end of December. m Data based on SHA2011. n Data are based on SHA2011. o 2007. p Data are as at 1 January of reporting year. q Refers to total population. r Non-resident tourists staying in hotels and similar establishments. s 2005. t Break in the time series. u Non-resident tourists staying in all types of accommodation establishments. v Data reported at activity level, represent flows from all government agencies. w 2009.

United Kingdom

Region	Northern Europe	UN membership date	24 October 1945
Population (000, 2023)	67 509[a,b,c]	Surface area (km2)	242 495[d,e]
Pop. density (per km2, 2023)	278.1[a,b,c]	Sex ratio (m per 100 f)	97.7[a,b,c]
Capital city	London	National currency	Pound Sterling (GBP)
Capital city pop. (000, 2023)	9 176.5[f,g]	Exchange rate (per US$)	0.8[c]

Economic indicators	2010	2015	2023
GDP: Gross domestic product (million current US$)	2 491 397	2 934 858	3 131 378[e]
GDP growth rate (annual %, const. 2015 prices)	2.4	2.4	7.5[e]
GDP per capita (current US$)	39 697.2	44 996.3	46 541.8[e]
Economy: Agriculture (% of Gross Value Added)[h,i]	0.7	0.7	0.8[e]
Economy: Industry (% of Gross Value Added)[i,j]	20.9	20.2	19.5[e]
Economy: Services and other activity (% of GVA)[i]	78.5	79.1	79.7[e]
Employment in agriculture (% of employed)	1.2	1.1	1.0[k,e]
Employment in industry (% of employed)	19.2	18.7	17.9[k,e]
Employment in services & other sectors (% employed)	79.6	80.2	81.0[k,e]
Unemployment rate (% of labour force)	7.8	5.3	4.0[k]
Labour force participation rate (female/male pop. %)	56.1 / 69.0	57.2 / 68.5	58.7 / 66.6[k]
CPI: Consumer Price Index (2010=100)[l]	100	112	136[c]
Agricultural production index (2014-2016=100)	94	101	99[e]
International trade: exports (million current US$)	422 014	466 296	532 327[c]
International trade: imports (million current US$)	627 618	630 251	822 055[c]
International trade: balance (million current US$)	- 205 603	- 163 955	- 289 728[c]
Balance of payments, current account (million US$)	- 72 121	- 148 708	- 121 382[c]

Major trading partners						2022
Export partners (% of exports)[k]	United States	12.1	Netherlands	8.3	Germany	7.8
Import partners (% of imports)	China	13.4	United States	11.9	Germany	8.6

Social indicators	2010	2015	2023
Population growth rate (average annual %)[a]	0.8	0.7	0.3[b,c]
Urban population (% of total population)	81.3	82.6	83.7[g]
Urban population growth rate (average annual %)[m]	1.3	1.0	...
Fertility rate, total (live births per woman)[a]	1.9	1.8	1.6[b,c]
Life expectancy at birth (females/males, years)[a]	82.3 / 78.4	82.7 / 79.1	83.8 / 80.4[b,c]
Population age distribution (0-14/60+ years old, %)[a]	17.6 / 22.3	17.7 / 23.2	17.5 / 25.2[b,c]
International migrant stock (000/% of total pop.)	7 119.7 / 11.2	8 407.0 / 12.8	9 359.6 / 13.8[n]
Refugees and others of concern to the UNHCR (000)	253.3[o]	155.1	359.3[c]
Infant mortality rate (per 1 000 live births)[a]	4.4	3.9	3.2[b,c]
Health: Current expenditure (% of GDP)	10.0	9.8[p]	11.9[e]
Health: Physicians (per 1 000 pop.)	2.7	2.8	3.2[e]
Education: Government expenditure (% of GDP)	5.7	5.6	5.2[g]
Education: Primary gross enrol. ratio (f/m per 100 pop.)	104.3 / 104.8	101.9 / 102.0	99.5 / 99.8[n]
Education: Lower. sec. gross enrol. ratio (f/m per 100 pop.)	108.1 / 112.2	109.0 / 112.2	114.8 / 115.5[n]
Education: Upr. sec. gross enrol. ratio (f/m per 100 pop.)	99.6 / 96.0	138.5 / 130.2	121.1 / 115.5[n]
Intentional homicide rate (per 100 000 pop.)	1.2	1.0	1.0[n]
Seats held by women in the National Parliament (%)	19.5	22.8	34.5[q]

Environment and infrastructure indicators	2010	2015	2023
Individuals using the Internet (per 100 inhabitants)	85.0[r]	92.0[r,s]	96.7[k,e]
Research & Development expenditure (% of GDP)	1.6[k]	1.6	1.7[g]
Threatened species (number)	73	87	200[c]
Forested area (% of land area)	12.6	13.0	13.2[n]
CO2 emission estimates (million tons/tons per capita)	481.7 / 7.6	398.8 / 6.0	338.4 / 4.9[e]
Energy production, primary (Petajoules)[t]	6 187	4 900	4 894[n]
Energy supply per capita (Gigajoules)[t]	135	116	96[n]
Tourist/visitor arrivals at national borders (000)	28 911	35 149	6 287[e]
Important sites for terrestrial biodiversity protected (%)	80.4	81.0	81.4[c]
Pop. using safely managed sanitation (urban/rural %)	98.9 / 93.6	99.0 / 93.6	99.0 / 93.6[c]

a Refers to the United Kingdom of Great Britain and Northern Ireland. For statistical purposes, the data for United Kingdom do not include Anguilla, Bermuda, British Virgin Islands, Cayman Islands, Channel Islands, Falkland Islands (Malvinas), Gibraltar, Isle of Man, Montserrat, Saint Helena, Turks and Caicos Islands. **b** Projected estimate (medium fertility variant). **c** 2022. **d** Excluding Channel Islands (Guernsey and Jersey) and Isle of Man, shown separately, if available. **e** 2021. **f** Data refer to "Urban area" (Greater London). **g** 2019. **h** Excludes irrigation canals and landscaping care. **i** Data classified according to ISIC Rev. 4. **j** Excludes publishing activities, recycling. Includes irrigation canals. **k** Estimate. **l** Calculated by the UN Statistics Division from national indices. **m** Data refers to a 5-year period preceding the reference year. **n** 2020. **o** Data as at the end of December. **p** Break in the time series. **q** Data are as at 1 January of reporting year. **r** Population aged 16 to 74 years. **s** Users in the last 3 months. **t** Shipments of coal and oil to the Channel Islands and the Isle of Man from the United Kingdom are not classed as exports but as part of UK supply. Exports of natural gas to the Isle of Man are included with the exports to Ireland.

United Rep. of Tanzania

Region	Eastern Africa	UN membership date	14 December 1961
Population (000, 2023)	65 498 a,b,c	Surface area (km2)	947 303 d
Pop. density (per km2, 2023)	73.9 a,b,c	Sex ratio (m per 100 f)	97.7 a,b,c
Capital city	Dodoma	National currency	Tanzanian Shilling (TZS)
Capital city pop. (000, 2023)	261.6 e	Exchange rate (per US$)	2 297.6 d

Economic indicators	2010	2015	2023
GDP: Gross domestic product (million current US$)[f]	31 553	47 379	70 297 d
GDP growth rate (annual %, const. 2015 prices)[f]	6.4	6.2	4.9 d
GDP per capita (current US$)[f]	719.4	927.1	1 136.2 d
Employment in agriculture (% of employed)[g]	70.3	67.5	64.3 d
Employment in industry (% of employed)[g]	5.8	6.4	7.3 d
Employment in services & other sectors (% employed)[g]	24.0	26.2	28.5 d
Unemployment rate (% of labour force)[g]	3.0	2.1	2.9
Labour force participation rate (female/male pop. %)[g]	83.9 / 88.9	80.1 / 88.0	79.3 / 86.8
CPI: Consumer Price Index (2010=100)[h]	100	158 j	209 c
Agricultural production index (2014-2016=100)	77	104	112 d
International trade: exports (million current US$)	4 051	5 854	6 825 c
International trade: imports (million current US$)	8 013	14 706	15 654 c
International trade: balance (million current US$)	- 3 962	- 8 852	- 8 830 c
Balance of payments, current account (million US$)	- 2 211	- 4 477	- 1 122 j

Major trading partners						202
Export partners (% of exports)	India	17.3	South Africa	13.6	United Arab Emirates	11.2
Import partners (% of imports)	China	25.2	United Arab Emirates	15.9	India	12.5

Social indicators	2010	2015	2023
Population growth rate (average annual %)[b]	2.8	3.6	2.9 a,c
Urban population (% of total population)[b]	28.1	31.6	34.5 k
Urban population growth rate (average annual %)[b,l]	5.6	5.5	...
Fertility rate, total (live births per woman)[b]	5.3	5.1	4.7 a,c
Life expectancy at birth (females/males, years)[b]	61.9 / 58.4	67.0 / 62.4	68.9 / 64.7 a,c
Population age distribution (0-14/60+ years old, %)[b]	45.1 / 4.7	44.8 / 4.8	43.4 / 4.7 a,c
International migrant stock (000/% of total pop.)[b,m]	309.8 / 0.7	384.6 / 0.7	426.0 / 0.7 i
Refugees and others of concern to the UNHCR (000)	273.8 n	328.2	248.6 c
Infant mortality rate (per 1 000 live births)[b]	49.5	41.1	31.8 a,c
Health: Current expenditure (% of GDP)[f,o]	5.2	3.6	3.7 i
Health: Physicians (per 1 000 pop.)	...	0.1 p	~0.0 e
Education: Government expenditure (% of GDP)	4.5	4.2	3.4 c
Education: Primary gross enrol. ratio (f/m per 100 pop.)	103.8 / 101.9	87.0 / 82.5	99.0 / 95.4 d
Education: Lower. sec. gross enrol. ratio (f/m per 100 pop.)	38.3 / 46.3	37.0 / 36.2	40.8 / 36.7 d
Education: Upr. sec. gross enrol. ratio (f/m per 100 pop.)	7.4 / 9.8	5.0 / 7.4	5.3 / 6.9 d
Intentional homicide rate (per 100 000 pop.)	8.6	7.1	3.7 i
Seats held by women in the National Parliament (%)	30.7	36.0	37.4 q

Environment and infrastructure indicators	2010	2015	2023
Individuals using the Internet (per 100 inhabitants)[g]	2.9	10.0	31.6 d
Research & Development expenditure (% of GDP)[r]	0.4 s	0.5 t	...
Threatened species (number)	691	1 077	1 591 c
Forested area (% of land area)	56.4	54.3	51.6 j
CO2 emission estimates (million tons/tons per capita)	10.8 / 0.1	14.7 / 0.2	17.7 / 0.2 j
Energy production, primary (Petajoules)	727	785	887 j
Energy supply per capita (Gigajoules)	18	17	16 j
Tourist/visitor arrivals at national borders (000)	754	1 104	923 d
Important sites for terrestrial biodiversity protected (%)	57.2	57.2	62.8 c
Pop. using safely managed drinking water (urban/rural, %)	22.3 / 2.1	23.6 / 2.5	25.5 / 3.1 c
Pop. using safely managed sanitation (urban/rural %)	25.2 / 13.3	29.8 / 16.6	34.4 / 19.8 c
Net Official Development Assist. received (% of GNI)	9.42	5.56	3.88 d

a Projected estimate (medium fertility variant). b Including Zanzibar. c 2022. d 2021. e 2018. f Tanzania mainland only, excluding Zanzibar. g Estimate. h For Tanganyika only. i Break in the time series. j 2020. k 2019. l Data refers to a 5-year period preceding the reference year. m Including refugees. n Data as at the end of December. o Data refe to fiscal years beginning 1 July. p 2014. q Data are as at 1 January of reporting year. r Excluding business enterprise. s Partial data. t 2013.

United States of America

Region	Northern America	UN membership date	24 October 1945
Population (000, 2023)	338 290 [a,b,c]	Surface area (km2)	9 833 517 [d]
Pop. density (per km2, 2023)	37.0 [a,b,c]	Sex ratio (m per 100 f)	98.1 [a,b,c]
Capital city	Washington, D.C.	National currency	US Dollar (USD)
Capital city pop. (000, 2023)	5 264.5 [e]		

Economic indicators

	2010	2015	2023
GDP: Gross domestic product (million current US$)	15 048 970	18 206 023	23 315 081 [d]
GDP growth rate (annual %, const. 2015 prices)	2.7	2.7	5.9 [d]
GDP per capita (current US$)	48 360.5	56 086.2	69 184.7 [d]
Economy: Agriculture (% of Gross Value Added) [f,g,h]	1.0	1.0	0.9 [d]
Economy: Industry (% of Gross Value Added) [f,h,i]	19.7	18.9	18.1 [d]
Economy: Services and other activity (% of GVA) [f]	79.4	80.1	81.0 [d]
Employment in agriculture (% of employed)	1.7	1.8	1.7 [d]
Employment in industry (% of employed)	19.3	19.5	19.2 [d]
Employment in services & other sectors (% employed)	78.9	78.7	79.2 [d]
Unemployment rate (% of labour force)	9.6	5.3	4.6 [j]
Labour force participation rate (female/male pop. %)	57.6 / 69.7	56.0 / 68.4	56.5 / 67.6 [j]
CPI: Consumer Price Index (2010=100) [k]	100	109	134 [c]
Agricultural production index (2014-2016=100)	92	97	106 [d]
International trade: exports (million current US$)	1 278 099	1 501 846	2 062 090 [c]
International trade: imports (million current US$)	1 968 260	2 313 425	3 372 902 [c]
International trade: balance (million current US$)	- 690 161	- 811 579	-1 310 812 [c]
Balance of payments, current account (million US$)	- 432 002	- 408 447	- 943 800 [c]

Major trading partners

					2022
Export partners (% of exports)	Canada	17.2	Mexico	15.7	China	7.5
Import partners (% of imports)	China	17.1	Mexico	13.6	Canada	13.2

Social indicators

	2010	2015	2023
Population growth rate (average annual %) [b]	0.8	0.8	0.5 [a,c]
Urban population (% of total population)	80.8	81.7	82.5 [e]
Urban population growth rate (average annual %) [l]	1.1	0.9	...
Fertility rate, total (live births per woman) [b]	1.9	1.8	1.7 [a,c]
Life expectancy at birth (females/males, years) [b]	81.2 / 76.3	81.3 / 76.4	81.0 / 75.5 [a,c]
Population age distribution (0-14/60+ years old, %) [b]	19.9 / 18.3	19.3 / 20.3	18.0 / 23.4 [a,c]
International migrant stock (000/% of total pop.)	44 183.6 / 14.3	48 178.9 / 15.0	50 632.8 / 15.3 [m]
Refugees and others of concern to the UNHCR (000)	...	491.7	1 787.5 [c]
Infant mortality rate (per 1 000 live births) [b]	6.2	5.9	5.0 [a,c]
Health: Current expenditure (% of GDP) [n,o]	16.2	16.5 [p]	18.8 [m]
Health: Physicians (per 1 000 pop.)	...	...	3.6 [m]
Education: Government expenditure (% of GDP)	6.7	4.9	5.0 [e]
Education: Primary gross enrol. ratio (f/m per 100 pop.) [j]	101.3 / 102.4 [q]	100.3 / 100.3	100.1 / 100.5 [m]
Education: Lowr. sec. gross enrol. ratio (f/m per 100 pop.) [j]	100.0 / 101.6 [q]	100.7 / 100.4	101.7 / 104.1 [m]
Education: Upr. sec. gross enrol. ratio (f/m per 100 pop.) [j]	91.7 / 86.6 [q]	95.6 / 93.9	97.1 / 99.0 [m]
Intentional homicide rate (per 100 000 pop.)	4.7	4.9	6.8 [d]
Seats held by women in the National Parliament (%)	16.8	19.4	29.4 [r]

Environment and infrastructure indicators

	2010	2015	2023
Individuals using the Internet (per 100 inhabitants)	71.7 [s]	74.6 [s,t]	91.8 [j,d]
Research & Development expenditure (% of GDP)	2.7 [u]	2.8 [p,u]	3.4 [v,m]
Threatened species (number)	1 152	1 299	1 960 [c]
Forested area (% of land area)	33.7	33.9	33.9 [m]
CO2 emission estimates (million tons/tons per capita) [w]	5 428.2 / 17.3	5 004.5 / 15.4	4 554.0 / 13.6 [d]
Energy production, primary (Petajoules)	72 292	84 553	90 604 [m]
Energy supply per capita (Gigajoules)	299	282	255 [m]
Tourist/visitor arrivals at national borders (000)	60 010	77 774 [p]	22 100 [d]
Important sites for terrestrial biodiversity protected (%)	43.3	44.4	44.6 [c]
Pop. using safely managed drinking water (urban/rural, %)	96.5 / ...	97.0 / ...	97.6 / ... [c]
Pop. using safely managed sanitation (urban/rural %)	97.0 / ...	97.2 / ...	97.2 / ... [c]
Net Official Development Assist. disbursed (% of GNI) [x]	1.48	0.21	1.00 [d]

a Projected estimate (medium fertility variant). **b** For statistical purposes, the data for United States of America do not include American Samoa, Guam, Northern Mariana Islands, Puerto Rico, and United States Virgin Islands. **c** 2022. **d** 2021. **e** 2019. **f** Data classified according to ISIC Rev. 4. **g** Excludes irrigation canals and landscaping care. **h** Includes taxes less subsidies on production and imports. **i** Excludes publishing activities, recycling. Includes irrigation canals. **j** Estimate. **k** All urban consumers. **l** Data refers to a 5-year period preceding the reference year. **m** 2020. **n** Data are based on SHA2011. **o** Data based on calendar year (January 1 to December 31). **p** Break in the time series. **q** 2005. **r** Data are as at 1 January of reporting year. **s** Population aged 3 years and over. **t** Users in the last 6 months. **u** Do not correspond exactly to Frascati Manual recommendations. **v** Provisional data. **w** Including overseas territories. **x** Development Assistance Committee member (OECD).

United States Virgin Islands

Region	Caribbean	Population (000, 2023)	100[a,b,c]
Surface area (km2)	347[d]	Pop. density (per km2, 2023)	284.2[a,b,c]
Sex ratio (m per 100 f)	87.3[a,b,c]	Capital city	Charlotte Amalie
National currency	US Dollar (USD)	Capital city pop. (000, 2023)	52.3[e]

Economic indicators	2010	2015	2023
Employment in agriculture (% of employed)[f]	2.2	2.1	1.7[d]
Employment in industry (% of employed)[f]	21.0	18.2	17.5[d]
Employment in services & other sectors (% employed)[f]	76.9	79.8	80.7[d]
Unemployment rate (% of labour force)[f]	11.6	12.3	12.3
Labour force participation rate (female/male pop. %)[f]	55.4 / 67.2	49.2 / 69.4	43.0 / 63.6

Social indicators	2010	2015	2023
Population growth rate (average annual %)[b]	- 0.6	- 0.5	- 0.8[a,c]
Urban population (% of total population)	94.6	95.4	95.8[g]
Urban population growth rate (average annual %)[h]	- 0.1	- 0.1	...
Fertility rate, total (live births per woman)[b]	2.5	2.2	2.1[a,c]
Life expectancy at birth (females/males, years)[b]	77.8 / 69.2	80.3 / 69.9	80.9 / 69.8[a,c]
Population age distribution (0-14/60+ years old, %)[b]	20.7 / 20.6	19.5 / 23.9	19.2 / 27.7[a,c]
International migrant stock (000/% of total pop.)	56.7 / 53.4	56.7 / 54.0	56.8 / 54.3[i]
Infant mortality rate (per 1 000 live births)[b]	7.6	6.4	5.3[a,c]
Intentional homicide rate (per 100 000 pop.)	52.8	49.6[j]	...

Environment and infrastructure indicators	2010	2015	2023
Individuals using the Internet (per 100 inhabitants)[f]	31.2	54.8	64.4[k]
Research & Development expenditure (% of GDP)	~0.0[l,m]	...	...
Threatened species (number)	33	53	113[c]
Forested area (% of land area)	52.7	54.7	56.9[i]
Energy production, primary (Petajoules)[f]	0	0	0[i]
Energy supply per capita (Gigajoules)[f]	0	1	1[i]
Tourist/visitor arrivals at national borders (000)	572	642	303[i]
Important sites for terrestrial biodiversity protected (%)	42.8	43.3	43.3[c]

a Projected estimate (medium fertility variant). b For statistical purposes, the data for United States of America do not include this area. c 2022. d 2021. e 2018. f Estimate. g 2019. h Data refers to a 5-year period preceding the reference year. i 2020. j 2012. k 2017. l Partial data. m 2007.

Uruguay

Region	South America	UN membership date	18 December 1945
Population (000, 2023)	3 423[a,b]	Surface area (km2)	173 626[c]
Pop. density (per km2, 2023)	19.8[a,b]	Sex ratio (m per 100 f)	94.0[a,b]
Capital city	Montevideo	National currency	Peso Uruguayo (UYU)
Capital city pop. (000, 2023)	1 744.7[d,e]	Exchange rate (per US$)	40.1[b]

Economic indicators

	2010	2015	2023
GDP: Gross domestic product (million current US$)	40 285	57 081	59 318[c]
GDP growth rate (annual %, const. 2015 prices)	7.8	1.8	4.4[c]
GDP per capita (current US$)	12 015.7	16 774.6	17 312.6[c]
Economy: Agriculture (% of Gross Value Added)[f]	8.0	7.7	7.5[g,c]
Economy: Industry (% of Gross Value Added)[f]	27.3	22.1	20.3[h,c]
Economy: Services and other activity (% of GVA)[f]	64.7	70.3	72.2[c]
Employment in agriculture (% of employed)	11.6	8.8	8.4[c]
Employment in industry (% of employed)	21.4	20.5	18.9[c]
Employment in services & other sectors (% employed)	67.0	70.7	72.6[c]
Unemployment rate (% of labour force)	7.2	7.5	7.9[i]
Labour force participation rate (female/male pop. %)	54.9 / 74.6	56.3 / 74.4	56.9 / 71.1[i]
CPI: Consumer Price Index (2010=100)[j]	100	150	262[b]
Agricultural production index (2014-2016=100)	91	101	98[c]
International trade: exports (million current US$)	6 724	7 670	11 190[b]
International trade: imports (million current US$)	8 622	9 489	12 973[b]
International trade: balance (million current US$)	- 1 898	- 1 820	- 1 783[b]
Balance of payments, current account (million US$)	- 731	- 147	- 2 268[b]

Major trading partners

						2022
Export partners (% of exports)[i]	China	31.1	Brazil	16.3	Argentina	10.0
Import partners (% of imports)	Brazil	19.9	China	18.1[i]	United States	15.8

Social indicators

	2010	2015	2023
Population growth rate (average annual %)	0.3	0.3	~0.0[a,b]
Urban population (% of total population)	94.4	95.0	95.4[e]
Urban population growth rate (average annual %)[k]	0.5	0.5	...
Fertility rate, total (live births per woman)	2.0	2.0	1.5[a,b]
Life expectancy at birth (females/males, years)	80.9 / 72.6	81.4 / 73.4	81.7 / 74.1[a,b]
Population age distribution (0-14/60+ years old, %)	22.3 / 18.8	21.1 / 19.4	19.1 / 20.8[a,b]
International migrant stock (000/% of total pop.)[l]	76.3 / 2.3	78.8 / 2.3	108.3 / 3.1[m]
Refugees and others of concern to the UNHCR (000)	0.2[n]	0.4	32.9[n]
Infant mortality rate (per 1 000 live births)	9.1	7.6	5.8[a,b]
Health: Current expenditure (% of GDP)[o]	7.9[p]	8.3[q]	9.2[q,r,m]
Health: Physicians (per 1 000 pop.)	4.0[s]	...	6.2[c]
Education: Government expenditure (% of GDP)	2.9[t]	4.6	4.5[c]
Education: Primary gross enrol. ratio (f/m per 100 pop.)	110.9 / 114.6	109.8 / 112.2	103.6 / 104.7[m]
Education: Lowr. sec. gross enrol. ratio (f/m per 100 pop.)	114.4 / 107.4	... / ...	116.6 / 115.6[m]
Education: Upr. sec. gross enrol. ratio (f/m per 100 pop.)	104.6 / 79.4	... / ...	135.6 / 112.2[m]
Intentional homicide rate (per 100 000 pop.)	6.1	8.6	8.9[c]
Seats held by women in the National Parliament (%)	14.1	13.1	26.3[u]

Environment and infrastructure indicators

	2010	2015	2023
Individuals using the Internet (per 100 inhabitants)	46.4[v]	64.6	90.1[i,c]
Research & Development expenditure (% of GDP)	0.3	0.4	0.4[m]
Threatened species (number)	80	103	137[b]
Forested area (% of land area)	9.9	11.0	11.6[m]
CO2 emission estimates (million tons/tons per capita)	6.2 / 1.8	6.7 / 1.8	6.6 / 1.8[m]
Energy production, primary (Petajoules)	89	127	132[m]
Energy supply per capita (Gigajoules)	52	63	64[m]
Tourist/visitor arrivals at national borders (000)	2 353	2 773	3 059[e]
Important sites for terrestrial biodiversity protected (%)	12.0	21.5	23.3[b]
Pop. using safely managed drinking water (urban/rural, %)	94.2 / ...	94.5 / ...	94.6 / ...[b]
Net Official Development Assist. received (% of GNI)	0.12	0.05	0.07[w]

a Projected estimate (medium fertility variant). b 2022. c 2021. d Data refer to the department of Montevideo and localities of the departments of Canelones and San José (Cerámicas del Sur and Ciudad del Plata). e 2019. f Data classified according to ISIC Rev. 4. g Excludes irrigation canals and landscaping care. h Excludes publishing activities, recycling. Includes irrigation canals. i Estimate. j Calculated by the UN Statistics Division from national indices. k Data refers to a 5-year period preceding the reference year. l Including refugees. m 2020. n Data as at the end of December. o Data based on calendar year (January 1 to December 31). p Country is still reporting data based on SHA 1.0. q Data are based on SHA2011. r Break in the time series. s 2008. t 2006. u Data are as at 1 January of reporting year. v Population aged 6 years and over. w 2017.

Uzbekistan

Region	Central Asia	UN membership date	02 March 1992
Population (000, 2023)	34 628[a,b]	Surface area (km2)	448 969[c]
Pop. density (per km2, 2023)	81.4[a,b]	Sex ratio (m per 100 f)	100.2[a,b]
Capital city	Tashkent	National currency	Uzbekistan Sum (UZS)
Capital city pop. (000, 2023)	2 490.3[d]	Exchange rate (per US$)	11 215.0[e,b]

Economic indicators

	2010	2015	2023
GDP: Gross domestic product (million current US$)	50 010	86 196	69 239[c]
GDP growth rate (annual %, const. 2015 prices)	9.9	7.2	7.4[c]
GDP per capita (current US$)	1 747.7	2 785.1	2 031.6[c]
Economy: Agriculture (% of Gross Value Added)[f,g]	30.3	31.8	26.1[c]
Economy: Industry (% of Gross Value Added)[g,h]	23.9	24.5	33.5[c]
Economy: Services and other activity (% of GVA)[g]	45.7	43.7	40.4[c]
Employment in agriculture (% of employed)	26.8	26.9[i]	23.9[i,c]
Employment in industry (% of employed)	22.7	23.2[i]	25.5[i,c]
Employment in services & other sectors (% employed)	50.5	50.0[i]	50.7[i,c]
Unemployment rate (% of labour force)	5.4	5.2	6.3[i]
Labour force participation rate (female/male pop. %)[i]	43.5 / 73.0	41.3 / 72.9	39.8 / 73.0
CPI: Consumer Price Index (2010=100)	...	...	214[j,k,b]
Agricultural production index (2014-2016=100)	74	101	109[c]
International trade: exports (million current US$)	11 688[i]	12 871[i]	15 287[b]
International trade: imports (million current US$)	8 680[i]	12 416[i]	28 264[b]
International trade: balance (million current US$)	3 008[i]	455[i]	- 12 977[b]
Balance of payments, current account (million US$)	2 279	896	- 628[b]

Major trading partners

2022

Export partners (% of exports)[i]	Switzerland	22.4	Russian Federation	17.0	China	12.1
Import partners (% of imports)	China	22.4	Russian Federation	21.5	Kazakhstan	11.4

Social indicators

	2010	2015	2023
Population growth rate (average annual %)	1.6	1.6	1.6[a,b]
Urban population (% of total population)	51.0	50.8	50.4[d]
Urban population growth rate (average annual %)[l]	2.5	1.5	...
Fertility rate, total (live births per woman)	2.4	2.5	2.8[a,b]
Life expectancy at birth (females/males, years)	71.8 / 66.7	73.3 / 67.7	74.3 / 69.0[a,b]
Population age distribution (0-14/60+ years old, %)	29.2 / 6.5	28.5 / 7.1	30.2 / 8.6[a,b]
International migrant stock (000/% of total pop.)[m]	1 220.1 / 4.3	1 170.9 / 3.8	1 162.0 / 3.5[n]
Refugees and others of concern to the UNHCR (000)	0.3[o]	86.8	44.9[b]
Infant mortality rate (per 1 000 live births)	25.1	17.1	12.4[a,b]
Health: Current expenditure (% of GDP)	5.3	4.7	6.7[n]
Health: Physicians (per 1 000 pop.)	2.5	2.4[p]	...
Education: Government expenditure (% of GDP)	...	5.5[i]	4.6[c]
Education: Primary gross enrol. ratio (f/m per 100 pop.)	93.1 / 94.7	99.2 / 100.6	97.0 / 99.0[c]
Education: Lowr. sec. gross enrol. ratio (f/m per 100 pop.)	94.9 / 95.3	92.4 / 93.7	97.5 / 99.8[d]
Education: Upr. sec. gross enrol. ratio (f/m per 100 pop.)	82.3 / 81.4	89.6 / 90.4	96.6 / 94.0[d]
Intentional homicide rate (per 100 000 pop.)	3.0[q]	1.6	1.4[c]
Seats held by women in the National Parliament (%)	22.0	16.0	33.6[r]

Environment and infrastructure indicators

	2010	2015	2023
Individuals using the Internet (per 100 inhabitants)	15.9[i]	42.8[i]	76.6[c]
Research & Development expenditure (% of GDP)	0.2	0.2	0.1[c]
Threatened species (number)	50	54	76[b]
Forested area (% of land area)	7.7	8.1	8.4[n]
CO2 emission estimates (million tons/tons per capita)	120.4 / 4.2	94.3 / 3.0	110.6 / 3.2[n]
Energy production, primary (Petajoules)	2 324	2 058	1 730[n]
Energy supply per capita (Gigajoules)	64	56	54[n]
Tourist/visitor arrivals at national borders (000)	975	1 918	1 881[c]
Important sites for terrestrial biodiversity protected (%)	15.4	15.4	17.7[b]
Pop. using safely managed drinking water (urban/rural, %)	86.5 / 46.5	87.7 / 56.5	88.8 / 70.7[b]
Pop. using safely managed sanitation (urban/rural, %)	64.8 / 83.3	64.2 / 84.4	63.4 / 85.9[b]
Net Official Development Assist. received (% of GNI)	0.39	0.52	1.67[c]

a Projected estimate (medium fertility variant). b 2022. c 2021. d 2019. e UN operational exchange rate. f Excludes irrigation canals and landscaping care. g Data classified according to ISIC Rev. 4. h Excludes publishing activities, recycling. Includes irrigation canals. i Estimate. j Base: 2016 = 100 k Calculated by the UN Statistics Division from national indices. l Data refers to a 5-year period preceding the reference year. m Including refugees. n 2020. o Data as at the end of December. p 2014. q 2008. r Data are as at 1 January of reporting year.

Vanuatu

Region	Melanesia	UN membership date	15 September 1981	
Population (000, 2023)	327 [a,b]	Surface area (km2)	12 189 [c]	
Pop. density (per km2, 2023)	26.8 [a,b]	Sex ratio (m per 100 f)	101.2 [a,b]	
Capital city	Port Vila	National currency	Vatu (VUV)	
Capital city pop. (000, 2023)	52.7 [d]	Exchange rate (per US$)	117.2 [b]	

Economic indicators

	2010	2015	2023
GDP: Gross domestic product (million current US$)	701	760	981 [c]
GDP growth rate (annual %, const. 2015 prices)	1.6	0.2	0.1 [c]
GDP per capita (current US$)	2 855.1	2 748.1	3 072.6 [c]
Economy: Agriculture (% of Gross Value Added) [e,f]	21.9	23.1	23.5 [c]
Economy: Industry (% of Gross Value Added) [e,g]	13.0	11.5	10.8 [c]
Economy: Services and other activity (% of GVA) [e]	65.0	65.4	65.7 [c]
Employment in agriculture (% of employed)	63.8	56.8 [h]	48.0 [h,c]
Employment in industry (% of employed)	6.8	6.8 [h]	8.5 [h,c]
Employment in services & other sectors (% employed)	29.3	36.3 [h]	43.5 [h,c]
Unemployment rate (% of labour force)	1.8	1.9 [h]	2.1 [h]
Labour force participation rate (female/male pop. %) [h]	60.3 / 78.3	60.7 / 78.5	60.6 / 78.0
CPI: Consumer Price Index (2010=100)	100	107	126 [i,c]
Agricultural production index (2014-2016=100)	114	98	105 [c]
International trade: exports (million current US$)	46	39 [h]	74 [h,b]
International trade: imports (million current US$)	276	354 [h]	343 [h,b]
International trade: balance (million current US$)	- 230	- 316 [h]	- 269 [h,b]
Balance of payments, current account (million US$)	- 42	- 53	2 [c]

Major trading partners

							2022
Export partners (% of exports) [h]	Thailand	55.0	Japan	18.9	Republic of Korea	6.4	
Import partners (% of imports) [h]	China	22.9	Australia	15.3	Singapore	11.0	

Social indicators

	2010	2015	2023
Population growth rate (average annual %)	2.3	2.4	2.4 [a,b]
Urban population (% of total population)	24.5	25.0	25.4 [j]
Urban population growth rate (average annual %) [k]	3.6	2.7	...
Fertility rate, total (live births per woman)	4.2	4.0	3.7 [a,b]
Life expectancy at birth (females/males, years)	72.1 / 67.6	71.9 / 67.6	73.1 / 68.3 [a,b]
Population age distribution (0-14/60+ years old, %)	38.9 / 5.5	39.6 / 5.6	39.4 / 5.8 [a,b]
International migrant stock (000/% of total pop.) [l]	3.0 / 1.3	3.2 / 1.2	3.3 / 1.1 [m]
Refugees and others of concern to the UNHCR (000)	~0.0 [n]	~0.0	~0.0 [c]
Infant mortality rate (per 1 000 live births)	24.1	23.5	18.8 [a,b]
Health: Current expenditure (% of GDP)	3.5	4.3	4.0 [m]
Health: Physicians (per 1 000 pop.)	0.1 [o]	0.2 [p]	0.2 [j]
Education: Government expenditure (% of GDP)	5.2 [q]	5.6	2.2 [m]
Education: Primary gross enrol. ratio (f/m per 100 pop.)	121.9 / 123.0	107.8 / 110.7	121.9 / 124.1 [c]
Education: Lowr. sec. gross enrol. ratio (f/m per 100 pop.)	70.3 / 64.4	68.6 / 66.9	70.2 / 64.5 [c]
Education: Upr. sec. gross enrol. ratio (f/m per 100 pop.)	43.3 / 51.3	35.4 / 33.7	35.9 / 34.9 [c]
Intentional homicide rate (per 100 000 pop.)	...	...	0.3 [m]
Seats held by women in the National Parliament (%)	3.8	0.0	1.9 [r]

Environment and infrastructure indicators

	2010	2015	2023
Individuals using the Internet (per 100 inhabitants)	8.0	22.4 [h]	66.3 [h,c]
Threatened species (number)	121	137	158 [b]
Forested area (% of land area)	36.3	36.3	36.3 [m]
Energy production, primary (Petajoules)	1	1	1 [m]
Energy supply per capita (Gigajoules)	11	10	12 [m]
Tourist/visitor arrivals at national borders (000)	97	90	22 [m]
Important sites for terrestrial biodiversity protected (%)	2.8	2.8	2.8 [b]
Pop. using safely managed drinking water (urban/rural, %)	55.4 / ...	55.8 / ...	56.3 / ... [b]
Pop. using safely managed sanitation (urban/rural, %)	37.8 / ...	34.5 / ...	29.8 / ... [b]
Net Official Development Assist. received (% of GNI)	16.87	25.07	16.39 [c]

a Projected estimate (medium fertility variant). b 2022. c 2021. d 2018. e Data classified according to ISIC Rev. 4. f Excludes irrigation canals and landscaping care. g Excludes publishing activities, recycling. Includes irrigation canals. h Estimate. i Calculated by the UN Statistics Division from national indices. j 2019. k Data refers to a 5-year period preceding the reference year. l Including refugees. m 2020. n Data as at the end of December. o 2008. p 2012. q 2009. r Data are as at 1 January of reporting year.

Venezuela (Boliv. Rep. of)

Region	South America	UN membership date	15 November 1945
Population (000, 2023)	28 302 a,b	Surface area (km2)	929 690 c
Pop. density (per km2, 2023)	30.9 a,b	Sex ratio (m per 100 f)	97.8 a,b
Capital city	Caracas	National currency	Bolívar (VED)
Capital city pop. (000, 2023)	2 935.5 d,e	Exchange rate (per US$)	10.0 f

Economic indicators

	2010	2015	2023
GDP: Gross domestic product (million current US$)	393 806	344 341	111 813 c
GDP growth rate (annual %, const. 2015 prices)	- 1.5	- 6.2	0.5 c
GDP per capita (current US$)	13 714.3	11 278.9	3 965.0 c
Economy: Agriculture (% of Gross Value Added)	5.7	4.6	5.4 c
Economy: Industry (% of Gross Value Added)	51.0	49.1	48.3 c
Economy: Services and other activity (% of GVA)	43.4	46.3	46.3 c
Employment in agriculture (% of employed)	8.5	6.4 g	13.1 g,c
Employment in industry (% of employed)	21.9	21.4 g	17.5 g,c
Employment in services & other sectors (% employed)	69.5	72.2 g	69.4 g,c
Unemployment rate (% of labour force)	7.1	6.1 g	5.6 g
Labour force participation rate (female/male pop. %)	49.6 / 78.5	48.3 / 75.6 g	41.2 / 66.8 g
CPI: Consumer Price Index (2010=100) h	100	772	801 i,c
Agricultural production index (2014-2016=100)	104	101	86 c
International trade: exports (million current US$)	66 963	37 236 g	4 833 g,b
International trade: imports (million current US$)	32 343	40 146 g	13 841 g,b
International trade: balance (million current US$)	34 620	- 2 910 g	- 9 008 g,b
Balance of payments, current account (million US$)	5 585	- 16 051	- 3 870 i

Major trading partners

						2022
Export partners (% of exports) g	China	17.2	Türkiye	14.8	Spain	12.3
Import partners (% of imports) g	China	30.5	United States	22.9	Brazil	13.5

Social indicators

	2010	2015	2023
Population growth rate (average annual %)	1.3	1.1	1.8 a,b
Urban population (% of total population)	88.1	88.2	88.2 e
Urban population growth rate (average annual %) k	1.6	1.4	...
Fertility rate, total (live births per woman)	2.5	2.3	2.2 a,b
Life expectancy at birth (females/males, years)	77.1 / 68.9	77.2 / 69.0	75.7 / 66.9 a,b
Population age distribution (0-14/60+ years old, %)	30.0 / 8.5	28.5 / 9.7	27.6 / 12.9 a,b
International migrant stock (000/% of total pop.) l	1 347.3 / 4.7	1 404.4 / 4.7	1 324.2 / 4.7 m
Refugees and others of concern to the UNHCR (000)	217.4 n	174.9	3 247.0 b
Infant mortality rate (per 1 000 live births)	14.5	15.5	14.8 a,b
Health: Current expenditure (% of GDP) g,o,p,q	6.8	4.3	3.8 m
Health: Physicians (per 1 000 pop.)	...	...	1.7 f
Education: Government expenditure (% of GDP)	6.9 r	...	...
Education: Primary gross enrol. ratio (f/m per 100 pop.)	101.3 / 104.2	99.8 / 102.0	96.0 / 98.3 f
Education: Lowr. sec. gross enrol. ratio (f/m per 100 pop.)	92.5 / 87.6	100.2 / 96.2	95.2 / 90.8 f
Education: Upr. sec. gross enrol. ratio (f/m per 100 pop.)	77.6 / 66.0	85.7 / 74.7	86.0 / 75.2 f
Intentional homicide rate (per 100 000 pop.)	45.6	51.3	19.3 c
Seats held by women in the National Parliament (%)	17.5	17.0	22.2 s,t,c

Environment and infrastructure indicators

	2010	2015	2023
Individuals using the Internet (per 100 inhabitants) g	37.4	58.0	61.6 f
Research & Development expenditure (% of GDP)	0.2	0.3 u	...
Threatened species (number)	270	312	868 b
Forested area (% of land area)	53.9	52.9	52.4 m
CO2 emission estimates (million tons/tons per capita)	157.5 / 5.5	142.6 / 4.7	55.2 / 1.9 m
Energy production, primary (Petajoules)	8 190	7 390	2 070 m
Energy supply per capita (Gigajoules)	108	86	36 m
Tourist/visitor arrivals at national borders (000)	526	789	427 f
Important sites for terrestrial biodiversity protected (%)	78.8	78.8	78.8 b
Net Official Development Assist. received (% of GNI)	0.01	0.01 u	...

a Projected estimate (medium fertility variant). b 2022. c 2021. d Refers to multiple municipalities and parishes (see source). e 2019. f 2017. g Estimate. h Calculated by the UN Statistics Division from national indices. i Figures in billions. j 2016. k Data refers to a 5-year period preceding the reference year. l Including refugees. m 2020. n Data as at the end of December. o The National Currency Unit (NCU) used for Venezuela data 2000-2020 is the Bolivar Soberano (VES), which replaced the Bolivar Fuerte (VEF) in August 2018 (1 VES = 100000 VEF). Also, WHO is using United Nations' exchange rate for NCU to USD, which differs from the official exchange rate. p Data based on calendar year (January 1 to December 31). q Estimates should be viewed with caution as these are derived from scarce data. r 2009. s Data are as at 1 January of reporting year. t Figures correspond to the legislature elected in 2015 as data for the 2020 election had not been confirmed by the time of reporting. u 2014.

Viet Nam

Region	South-eastern Asia
Population (000, 2023)	98 187 [a,b]
Pop. density (per km2, 2023)	313.3 [a,b]
Capital city	Hanoi
Capital city pop. (000, 2023)	4 479.6 [d,e]

UN membership date	20 September 1977
Surface area (km2)	331 317 [c]
Sex ratio (m per 100 f)	97.6 [a,b]
National currency	Dong (VND)
Exchange rate (per US$)	23 612.0 [b]

Economic indicators

	2010	2015	2023
GDP: Gross domestic product (million current US$)	147 201	239 258	366 138 [c]
GDP growth rate (annual %, const. 2015 prices)	11.6	7.0	2.6 [c]
GDP per capita (current US$)	1 684.0	2 595.2	3 756.5 [c]
Economy: Agriculture (% of Gross Value Added) [f,g]	21.0	18.9	13.6 [c]
Economy: Industry (% of Gross Value Added) [g]	36.7	37.0	41.5 [c]
Economy: Services and other activity (% of GVA) [g]	42.2	44.2	44.9 [c]
Employment in agriculture (% of employed)	48.7	44.0	29.0 [c]
Employment in industry (% of employed)	21.7	22.7	32.2 [h,c]
Employment in services & other sectors (% employed)	29.6	33.3	37.8 [c]
Unemployment rate (% of labour force)	1.1	1.8	1.7 [h]
Labour force participation rate (female/male pop. %)	71.6 / 81.1	72.5 / 82.2	69.1 / 78.4 [h]
CPI: Consumer Price Index (2010=100)	100	145	177 [b]
Agricultural production index (2014-2016=100)	83	101	113 [c]
International trade: exports (million current US$)	72 237	162 017	371 829 [h,b]
International trade: imports (million current US$)	84 839	165 776	380 249 [h,b]
International trade: balance (million current US$)	- 12 602	- 3 759	- 8 419 [h,b]
Balance of payments, current account (million US$)	- 4 276	- 2 041	- 3 812 [c]

Major trading partners

					2022
Export partners (% of exports) [h]	United States	28.8	China	17.2	Republic of Korea 6.5
Import partners (% of imports) [h]	China	33.6	Republic of Korea	17.0	Japan 7.2

Social indicators

	2010	2015	2023
Population growth rate (average annual %)	1.1	1.0	0.7 [a,b]
Urban population (% of total population)	30.4	33.8	36.6 [e]
Urban population growth rate (average annual %) [i]	3.1	3.2	...
Fertility rate, total (live births per woman)	1.9	2.0	1.9 [a,b]
Life expectancy at birth (females/males, years)	78.3 / 68.8	78.7 / 69.1	79.3 / 69.9 [a,b]
Population age distribution (0-14/60+ years old, %)	24.3 / 9.3	23.4 / 10.9	22.4 / 13.8 [a,b]
International migrant stock (000/% of total pop.) [j,k]	61.8 / 0.1	72.8 / 0.1	76.8 / 0.1 [l]
Refugees and others of concern to the UNHCR (000)	12.1 [m]	11.0	35.5 [b]
Infant mortality rate (per 1 000 live births)	18.0	17.2	15.0 [a,b]
Health: Current expenditure (% of GDP)	4.7	4.6	4.7 [l]
Health: Physicians (per 1 000 pop.)	0.7	0.8	0.8 [n]
Education: Government expenditure (% of GDP)	4.0	3.4	3.0 [c]
Education: Primary gross enrol. ratio (f/m per 100 pop.)	103.2 / 108.1	110.1 / 109.7	119.6 / 117.4 [c]
Education: Lowr. sec. gross enrol. ratio (f/m per 100 pop.)	89.1 / 84.9	98.7 / 97.0	106.9 / 103.1 [c]
Intentional homicide rate (per 100 000 pop.)	1.5	1.5 [o]	...
Seats held by women in the National Parliament (%)	25.8	24.3	30.3 [p]

Environment and infrastructure indicators

	2010	2015	2023
Individuals using the Internet (per 100 inhabitants)	30.6	45.0 [h,q]	74.2 [c]
Research & Development expenditure (% of GDP)	...	0.4	0.4 [e]
Threatened species (number)	424	565	933 [b]
Forested area (% of land area)	42.7	44.9	46.7 [l]
CO2 emission estimates (million tons/tons per capita)	132.5 / 1.4	169.0 / 1.8	297.5 / 3.0 [l]
Energy production, primary (Petajoules)	2 747	3 035	2 509 [l]
Energy supply per capita (Gigajoules)	27	35	47 [l]
Tourist/visitor arrivals at national borders (000) [r]	5 050	7 944	157 [c]
Important sites for terrestrial biodiversity protected (%)	31.2	40.1	40.1 [b]
Pop. using safely managed drinking water (urban/rural, %)	74.5 / 41.1	75.0 / 43.3	75.8 / 46.4 [b]
Pop. using safely managed sanitation (urban/rural, %)	40.2 / 36.8	40.5 / 40.4	40.8 / 45.4 [b]
Net Official Development Assist. received (% of GNI)	1.94	1.40	0.15 [c]

a Projected estimate (medium fertility variant). b 2022. c 2021. d Refers to urban population in the city districts. e 2019. f Excludes irrigation canals and landscaping care. g Data classified according to ISIC Rev. 4. h Estimate. i Data refers to a 5-year period preceding the reference year. j Refers to foreign citizens. k Including refugees. l 2020. m Data as at the end of December. n 2016. o 2011. p Data are as at 1 January of reporting year. q Population aged 18 years and over. r Including nationals residing abroad.

Wallis and Futuna Islands

Region	Polynesia	Population (000, 2023)	12 a,b,c
Surface area (km2)	142 d	Pop. density (per km2, 2023)	82.7 a,b,c
Sex ratio (m per 100 f)	92.2 a,b,c	Capital city	Matu-Utu
National currency	CFP Franc (XPF) e	Capital city pop. (000, 2023)	1.0 f
Exchange rate (per US$)	111.9 c		

Economic indicators	2010	2015	2023
International trade: exports (million current US$) g	1	1	2 c
International trade: imports (million current US$) g	35	49	79 c
International trade: balance (million current US$) g	- 34	- 48	- 78 c

Major trading partners						2022
Export partners (% of exports) g	France	37.6	Lesotho	16.9	Singapore	9.3
Import partners (% of imports) g	Fiji	38.2	France	30.6	New Zealand	7.8

Social indicators	2010	2015	2023
Population growth rate (average annual %) a	- 1.9	- 1.0	- 0.7 b,c
Urban population (% of total population)	0.0	0.0	0.0 h
Urban population growth rate (average annual %) i	0.0	0.0	...
Fertility rate, total (live births per woman) a	2.1	2.1	1.9 b,c
Life expectancy at birth (females/males, years) a	78.7 / 72.8	78.5 / 77.4	81.0 / 79.0 b,c
Population age distribution (0-14/60+ years old, %) a	28.9 / 12.7	26.7 / 15.4	22.7 / 19.1 b,c
International migrant stock (000/% of total pop.) j	2.1 / 16.6	2.0 / 16.7	2.0 / 18.1 k
Infant mortality rate (per 1 000 live births) a	14.7	11.9	9.8 b,c

Environment and infrastructure indicators	2010	2015	2023
Individuals using the Internet (per 100 inhabitants)	8.2	9.0 g,l	...
Threatened species (number)	74	88	97 c
Forested area (% of land area)	41.6	41.6	41.6 k
Energy production, primary (Petajoules) g	0	0	0 k
Energy supply per capita (Gigajoules)	29	29	34 k
Important sites for terrestrial biodiversity protected (%)	0.0	0.0	0.0 c
Pop. using safely managed drinking water (urban/rural, %)	... / 69.0	... / 69.0	... / 68.9 c

a For statistical purposes, the data for France do not include this area. b Projected estimate (medium fertility variant). c 2022. d 2021. e Communauté financière du Pacifique (CFP) Franc. f 2018. g Estimate. h 2019. i Data refers to a 5-year period preceding the reference year. j Including refugees. k 2020. l 2012.

Western Sahara

Region	Northern Africa	Population (000, 2023)		576[a,b]
Surface area (km2)	266 000[c,d]	Pop. density (per km2, 2023)		2.2[a,b]
Sex ratio (m per 100 f)	123.2[a,b]	Capital city		El Aaiún
National currency	Moroccan Dirham (MAD)	Capital city pop. (000, 2023)		232.4[e]
Exchange rate (per US$)	10.4[b]			

Economic indicators	2010	2015	2023
Employment in agriculture (% of employed)[f]	25.4	22.9	20.6[d]
Employment in industry (% of employed)[f]	20.9	20.8	21.9[d]
Employment in services & other sectors (% employed)[f]	53.6	56.2	57.6[d]
Unemployment rate (% of labour force)[f]	6.5	7.1	8.3
Labour force participation rate (female/male pop. %)[f]	28.0 / 78.5	29.3 / 79.2	30.4 / 76.9

Social indicators	2010	2015	2023
Population growth rate (average annual %)	3.8	2.8	2.0[a,b]
Urban population (% of total population)	86.3	86.5	86.8[g]
Urban population growth rate (average annual %)[h]	1.9	1.9	...
Fertility rate, total (live births per woman)	2.9	2.5	2.3[a,b]
Life expectancy at birth (females/males, years)	69.4 / 66.0	71.3 / 67.7	73.1 / 69.3[a,b]
Population age distribution (0-14/60+ years old, %)	27.0 / 6.3	26.0 / 7.5	24.3 / 9.4[a,b]
International migrant stock (000/% of total pop.)[f]	4.5 / 0.9	5.2 / 1.0	5.4 / 0.9[i]
Infant mortality rate (per 1 000 live births)	37.9	30.8	23.7[a,b]

Environment and infrastructure indicators	2010	2015	2023
Threatened species (number)	39	39	85[b]
Forested area (% of land area)	2.5	2.5	2.5[i]

a Projected estimate (medium fertility variant). b 2022. c Comprising the Northern Region (former Saguia el Hamra) and Southern Region (former Rio de Oro). d 2021. e 2018. f Estimate. g 2019. h Data refers to a 5-year period preceding the reference year. i 2020.

Yemen

Region	Western Asia	UN membership date	30 September 1947
Population (000, 2023)	33 697 a,b	Surface area (km2)	527 968 c
Pop. density (per km2, 2023)	63.8 a,b	Sex ratio (m per 100 f)	102.1 a,b
Capital city	Sana'a	National currency	Yemeni Rial (YER)
Capital city pop. (000, 2023)	2 874.4 d,e	Exchange rate (per US$)	1 242.0 b

Economic indicators

	2010	2015	2023
GDP: Gross domestic product (million current US$)	30 907	24 819	9 947 c
GDP growth rate (annual %, const. 2015 prices)	4.1	- 36.1	- 1.0 c
GDP per capita (current US$)	1 249.1	870.3	301.6 c
Economy: Agriculture (% of Gross Value Added)	12.1	18.2	19.5 c
Economy: Industry (% of Gross Value Added)	38.7	20.1	20.8 c
Economy: Services and other activity (% of GVA)	49.2	61.7	59.7 c
Employment in agriculture (% of employed)	24.1	30.3 f	28.1 f,c
Employment in industry (% of employed)	19.0	12.7 f	11.7 f,c
Employment in services & other sectors (% of employed)	56.8	57.0 f	60.2 f,c
Unemployment rate (% of labour force) f	12.8	13.8	13.3
Labour force participation rate (female/male pop. %)	10.0 / 68.6	5.9 / 67.8 f	6.4 / 70.7 f
CPI: Consumer Price Index (2010=100) f	100	158 g	...
Agricultural production index (2014-2016=100)	100	100	105 c
International trade: exports (million current US$)	6 437	510	91 f,b
International trade: imports (million current US$)	9 255	6 573	5 275 f,b
International trade: balance (million current US$)	- 2 818	- 6 063	- 5 184 f,b
Balance of payments, current account (million US$)	- 1 054	- 3 026	- 2 419 h

Major trading partners
2022

Export partners (% of exports) f	China	24.4	Thailand	24.3	Saudi Arabia	10.7
Import partners (% of imports) f	Saudi Arabia	19.7	China	18.1	United Arab Emirates	12.4

Social indicators

	2010	2015	2023
Population growth rate (average annual %)	2.9	2.6	2.2 a,b
Urban population (% of total population)	31.8	34.8	37.3 e
Urban population growth rate (average annual %) i	4.6	4.4	...
Fertility rate, total (live births per woman)	4.9	4.3	3.7 a,b
Life expectancy at birth (females/males, years)	69.4 / 65.2	68.9 / 63.0	67.2 / 60.5 a,b
Population age distribution (0-14/60+ years old, %)	43.6 / 4.2	41.7 / 4.1	39.5 / 4.1 a,b
International migrant stock (000/% of total pop.) j,k	288.4 / 1.2	379.9 / 1.4	387.1 / 1.3 l
Refugees and others of concern to the UNHCR (000)	508.6 m	1 540.5	4 386.1 b
Infant mortality rate (per 1 000 live births)	45.7	46.3	46.8 a,b
Health: Current expenditure (% of GDP) n,o	5.2	4.3	...
Health: Physicians (per 1 000 pop.)	0.3 p	0.3 q	...
Education: Government expenditure (% of GDP)	4.4	5.5 q	...
Education: Primary gross enrol. ratio (f/m per 100 pop.)	82.3 / 100.9	89.4 / 106.6 r	87.1 / 99.9 h
Education: Lowr. sec. gross enrol. ratio (f/m per 100 pop.)	42.5 / 66.4	48.2 / 69.1 r	51.5 / 69.2 h
Education: Upr. sec. gross enrol. ratio (f/m per 100 pop.)	24.6 / 41.8	31.6 / 47.2 r	34.5 / 49.5 h
Intentional homicide rate (per 100 000 pop.)	4.4	6.3 r	...
Seats held by women in the National Parliament (%)	0.3	0.3	0.0 s,t

Environment and infrastructure indicators

	2010	2015	2023
Individuals using the Internet (per 100 inhabitants)	12.4	24.1 f	26.7 f,u
Threatened species (number)	269	287	337 b
Forested area (% of land area)	1.0	1.0	1.0 l
CO2 emission estimates (million tons/tons per capita)	22.6 / 1.0	11.6 / 0.4	8.7 / 0.3 l
Energy production, primary (Petajoules)	804	173	164 l
Energy supply per capita (Gigajoules)	13	6	4 l
Tourist/visitor arrivals at national borders (000) v	1 025	367	...
Important sites for terrestrial biodiversity protected (%)	27.9	27.9	27.9 b
Pop. using safely managed sanitation (urban/rural %)	64.3 / ...	61.4 / ...	60.5 / ... b
Net Official Development Assist. received (% of GNI)	2.29	4.33	13.54 l

a Projected estimate (medium fertility variant). b 2022. c 2021. d Data refers to the urban agglomeration. e 2019. f Estimate. g 2014. h 2016. i Data refers to a 5-year period preceding the reference year. j Including refugees. k Refers to foreign citizens. l 2020. m Data as at the end of December. n Estimates should be viewed with caution as these are derived from scarce data. o Data based on calendar year (January 1 to December 31). p 2009. q 2012. r 2013. s Data corresponds to the composition of the House of Representatives elected in 2003. t Data are as at 1 January of reporting year. u 2017. v Including nationals residing abroad.

Zambia

Region	Eastern Africa	UN membership date	01 December 1964
Population (000, 2023)	20 018[a,b]	Surface area (km2)	752 612[c]
Pop. density (per km2, 2023)	26.9[a,b]	Sex ratio (m per 100 f)	97.4[a,b]
Capital city	Lusaka	National currency	Zambian Kwacha (ZMW)
Capital city pop. (000, 2023)	2 646.6[d]	Exchange rate (per US$)	18.1[b]

Economic indicators	2010	2015	2023
GDP: Gross domestic product (million current US$)	20 265	20 859	21 313[c]
GDP growth rate (annual %, const. 2015 prices)	10.3	2.9	4.6[c]
GDP per capita (current US$)	1 469.3	1 283.8	1 094.5[c]
Economy: Agriculture (% of Gross Value Added)[e,f]	10.0	5.3	3.0[c]
Economy: Industry (% of Gross Value Added)[e,g]	34.1	35.3	47.8[c]
Economy: Services and other activity (% of GVA)[e]	55.9	59.4	49.2[c]
Employment in agriculture (% of employed)[h]	66.1	60.5	58.7[c]
Employment in industry (% of employed)[h]	8.7	11.5	8.7[c]
Employment in services & other sectors (% employed)[h]	25.2	28.0	32.5[c]
Unemployment rate (% of labour force)	13.2	8.3[h]	6.1[h]
Labour force participation rate (female/male pop. %)[h]	51.5 / 67.5	51.8 / 66.3	53.9 / 67.4
CPI: Consumer Price Index (2010=100)	100[i]	144	333[b]
Agricultural production index (2014-2016=100)	92	93	125[c]
International trade: exports (million current US$)	7 200	6 607	20 038[h,b]
International trade: imports (million current US$)	5 321	7 934	7 635[h,b]
International trade: balance (million current US$)	1 879	- 1 328	12 403[h,b]
Balance of payments, current account (million US$)	1 525	- 768	1 155[b]

Major trading partners						2022
Export partners (% of exports)[h]	Switzerland	42.1	China	18.9	Singapore	13.5
Import partners (% of imports)[h]	South Africa	31.3	China	12.6	India	6.3

Social indicators	2010	2015	2023
Population growth rate (average annual %)	3.4	3.2	2.7[a,b]
Urban population (% of total population)	39.4	41.9	44.1[d]
Urban population growth rate (average annual %)[j]	4.1	4.3	...
Fertility rate, total (live births per woman)	5.4	4.8	4.2[a,b]
Life expectancy at birth (females/males, years)	58.5 / 54.9	63.5 / 58.8	64.5 / 59.1[a,b]
Population age distribution (0-14/60+ years old, %)	46.6 / 2.7	45.5 / 2.7	42.9 / 3.0[a,b]
International migrant stock (000/% of total pop.)[k]	150.0 / 1.1	132.1 / 0.8	188.0 / 1.0[l]
Refugees and others of concern to the UNHCR (000)	57.9[m]	51.8	105.9[b]
Infant mortality rate (per 1 000 live births)	52.9	46.3	38.2[a,b]
Health: Current expenditure (% of GDP)[n]	3.7	4.4	5.6[l]
Health: Physicians (per 1 000 pop.)	0.1	...	0.3[c]
Education: Government expenditure (% of GDP)	3.4	4.6	3.9[l]
Education: Primary gross enrol. ratio (f/m per 100 pop.)	107.3 / 106.6	101.6 / 101.3	99.9 / 97.5[o]
Education: Lower sec. gross enrol. ratio (f/m per 100 pop.)	63.4 / 71.9	58.3 / 62.0	59.8 / 61.7[o]
Intentional homicide rate (per 100 000 pop.)	5.9	5.2	...
Seats held by women in the National Parliament (%)	14.0	12.7	15.0[p]

Environment and infrastructure indicators	2010	2015	2023
Individuals using the Internet (per 100 inhabitants)	3.0[h]	8.8[q]	21.2[h,c]
Research & Development expenditure (% of GDP)	0.3[i,r]	...	...
Threatened species (number)	67	83	137[b]
Forested area (% of land area)	62.8	61.5	60.3[l]
CO2 emission estimates (million tons/tons per capita)	3.7 / 0.2	6.0 / 0.3	8.5 / 0.4[l]
Energy production, primary (Petajoules)	303	351	405[l]
Energy supply per capita (Gigajoules)	25	25	25[l]
Tourist/visitor arrivals at national borders (000)	815	932	554[c]
Important sites for terrestrial biodiversity protected (%)	46.1	46.1	46.1[b]
Pop. using safely managed drinking water (urban/rural, %)	50.8 / ...	49.5 / ...	45.5 / ...[b]
Pop. using safely managed sanitation (urban/rural, %)	... / 17.4	... / 23.7	... / 30.5[b]
Net Official Development Assist. received (% of GNI)	4.86	3.83	5.64[c]

a Projected estimate (medium fertility variant). b 2022. c 2021. d 2019. e Data classified according to ISIC Rev. 4. f Excludes irrigation canals and landscaping care. g Excludes publishing activities, recycling. Includes irrigation canals. h Estimate. i Break in the time series. j Data refers to a 5-year period preceding the reference year. k Including refugees. l 2020. m Data as at the end of December. n Data based on calendar year (January 1 to December 31). o 2017. p Data are as at 1 January of reporting year. q Population aged 11 years and over. r 2008.

Zimbabwe

Region	Eastern Africa	UN membership date	25 August 1980
Population (000, 2023)	16 320[a,b]	Surface area (km2)	390 757[c]
Pop. density (per km2, 2023)	42.2[a,b]	Sex ratio (m per 100 f)	89.4[a,b]
Capital city	Harare	National currency	Zimbabwe Dollar (ZWL)
Capital city pop. (000, 2023)	1 521.3[d]	Exchange rate (per US$)	80.8[e]

Economic indicators

	2010	2015	2023
GDP: Gross domestic product (million current US$)	12 042	19 963	24 118[c]
GDP growth rate (annual %, const. 2015 prices)	19.7	1.8	6.3[c]
GDP per capita (current US$)	937.8	1 410.3	1 508.0[c]
Economy: Agriculture (% of Gross Value Added)	10.9	9.3	9.4[c]
Economy: Industry (% of Gross Value Added)	23.5	25.0	30.5[c]
Economy: Services and other activity (% of GVA)	65.6	65.7	60.1[c]
Employment in agriculture (% of employed)[f]	67.2	66.5	61.6[c]
Employment in industry (% of employed)[f]	9.3	7.9	11.6[c]
Employment in services & other sectors (% employed)[f]	23.5	25.6	26.7[c]
Unemployment rate (% of labour force)[f]	5.2	5.3	8.0
Labour force participation rate (female/male pop. %)[f]	60.9 / 71.4	60.6 / 72.3	61.3 / 71.9
CPI: Consumer Price Index (2010=100)	100	106	11 077[b]
Agricultural production index (2014-2016=100)	105	101	130[c]
International trade: exports (million current US$)	3 199	3 411	5 958[f,b]
International trade: imports (million current US$)	5 852	6 053	8 082[f,b]
International trade: balance (million current US$)	- 2 653	- 2 642	- 2 124[f,b]
Balance of payments, current account (million US$)	- 1 655	- 1 597	1 096[g]

Major trading partners

2022

Export partners (% of exports)[f]	South Africa	49.3	United Arab Emirates	28.6	Mozambique	8.4
Import partners (% of imports)[f]	South Africa	43.2	Singapore	13.8	China	12.1

Social indicators

	2010	2015	2023
Population growth rate (average annual %)	1.4	2.1	2.1[a,b]
Urban population (% of total population)	33.2	32.4	32.2[d]
Urban population growth rate (average annual %)[h]	1.2	1.8	...
Fertility rate, total (live births per woman)	4.0	3.8	3.4[a,b]
Life expectancy at birth (females/males, years)	52.2 / 48.9	61.6 / 57.3	62.1 / 56.4[a,b]
Population age distribution (0-14/60+ years old, %)	43.2 / 4.6	42.9 / 4.9	40.6 / 4.8[a,b]
International migrant stock (000/% of total pop.)[i]	398.3 / 3.1	400.5 / 2.9	416.1 / 2.8[g]
Refugees and others of concern to the UNHCR (000)	4.9[j]	308.1	22.7[k,b]
Infant mortality rate (per 1 000 live births)	55.0	41.1	37.4[a,b]
Health: Current expenditure (% of GDP)[l]	10.5	7.4	3.4[g]
Health: Physicians (per 1 000 pop.)	0.1	0.2	0.2[g]
Education: Government expenditure (% of GDP)	1.5	6.1[m]	2.1[f,n]
Education: Primary gross enrol. ratio (f/m per 100 pop.)	... / ...	102.8 / 104.9	96.4 / 95.9[c]
Education: Lowr. sec. gross enrol. ratio (f/m per 100 pop.)	... / ...	75.2 / 72.8[o]	... / ...
Education: Upr. sec. gross enrol. ratio (f/m per 100 pop.)	... / ...	38.9 / 43.2[o]	... / ...
Intentional homicide rate (per 100 000 pop.)	5.5	7.4[p]	6.1[c]
Seats held by women in the National Parliament (%)	15.0	31.5	30.6[q]

Environment and infrastructure indicators

	2010	2015	2023
Individuals using the Internet (per 100 inhabitants)[f]	6.4	22.7	34.8[c]
Threatened species (number)	55	60	136[b]
Forested area (% of land area)	46.3	45.7	45.1[g]
CO2 emission estimates (million tons/tons per capita)	11.7 / 0.7	14.1 / 0.8	10.6 / 0.5[g]
Energy production, primary (Petajoules)	372	434	377[g]
Energy supply per capita (Gigajoules)	31	32	28[g]
Tourist/visitor arrivals at national borders (000)	2 239	2 057	381[c]
Important sites for terrestrial biodiversity protected (%)	76.1	81.2	81.2[b]
Pop. using safely managed drinking water (urban/rural, %)	54.4 / 15.2	54.9 / 14.0	55.5 / 12.6[b]
Pop. using safely managed sanitation (urban/rural %)	15.6 / 31.7	33.1 / 31.5	34.7 / 30.4[b]
Net Official Development Assist. received (% of GNI)	5.99	4.02	3.86[c]

a Projected estimate (medium fertility variant). **b** 2022. **c** 2021. **d** 2019. **e** 2005. **f** Estimate. **g** 2020. **h** Data refers to a 5-year period preceding the reference year. **i** Including refugees. **j** Data as at the end of December. **k** A study is being pursued to provide a revised estimate of statelessness gure. **l** Data based on calendar year (January 1 to December 31). **m** 2014. **n** 2018. **o** 2013. **p** 2012. **q** Data are as at 1 January of reporting year.

Below are brief descriptions of the indicators presented in the world, regional and country profiles. The terms are arranged in alphabetical order.

Agricultural production index is calculated by the Laspeyres formula based on the sum of price-weighted quantities of different agricultural commodities produced. The commodities covered in the computation of indices of agricultural production are all crops and livestock products originating in each country. Practically all products are covered, with the main exception of fodder crops. Production quantities of each commodity are weighted by the average international commodity prices in the base period and summed for each year. To obtain the index, the aggregate for a given year is divided by the average aggregate for the base period 2014-2016. Indices are calculated without any deductions for feed and seed and are referred to as "gross" by the Food and Agriculture Organization of the United Nations (FAO).
Source of the data: Food and Agriculture Organization of the United Nations (FAO), Rome, FAOSTAT database, last accessed May 2023.

Balance of payments is a statement summarizing the economic transactions between the residents of a country and non-residents during a specific period, usually a year. It includes transactions in goods, services, income, transfers and financial assets and liabilities. Generally, the balance of payments is divided into two major components: the current account and the capital and financial account. The data on balance of payments correspond to the current account category. The current account is a record of all transactions in the balance of payments covering the exports and imports of goods and services, payments of income, and current transfers between residents of a country and non-residents.
Source of the data: International Monetary Fund (IMF), Washington, D.C., Balance of Payment (BOP) Statistics database, last accessed June 2023.

Capital city and capital city population is the designation of any specific city as a capital city as reported by the country or area. The city can be the seat of the government as determined by the country. Some countries designate more than one city to be a capital city with a specific title function (e.g., administrative and/or legislative capital). The data refer to the year 2023, unless otherwise stated in a footnote.
Source of the data: United Nations Population Division (UNPD), New York, "World Urbanization Prospects (WUP): The 2018 Revision", last accessed May 2018.

CO_2 emission estimates represent total CO_2 emissions from fuel combustion. This includes CO_2 emissions from fuel combustion in IPCC Source/Sink Category 1 A Fuel Combustion Activities and those which may be reallocated to IPCC Source/Sink Category 2 Industrial Processes and Product Use under the 2006 GLs.
Source of the data: International Energy Agency, IEA World Energy Balances 2022 and 2006 IPCC Guidelines for Greenhouse Gas Inventories, last accessed April 2023.

Technical notes (*continued*)

CPI: Consumer price index measures the period-to-period proportional change in the prices of a fixed set of consumer goods and services of constant quantity and characteristics, acquired, used or paid for by the reference population. The index is constructed as a weighted average of a large number of elementary aggregate indices. Each of the elementary aggregate indices is estimated using a sample of prices for a defined set of goods and services obtained in, or by residents of, a specific region from a given set of outlets or other sources of consumption. The indices here generally refer to "all items" and to the country as a whole, unless otherwise stated in a footnote.

Source of the data: United Nations Statistics Division (UNSD), New York, Monthly Bulletin of Statistics (MBS), last accessed May 2023.

Economy: agriculture, industry and services and other activity presents the shares of the components of Gross Value Added (GVA) at current prices by kind of economic activity; agriculture, industry (mining, manufacturing, and construction) and in services and other sectors based on the sections of the International Standard Industrial Classification of All Economic Activities (ISIC), Revision 3, unless a different revision is stated in a footnote.

Source of the data: United Nations Statistics Division (UNSD), New York, National Accounts Statistics: Analysis of Main Aggregates (AMA) database, last accessed April 2023.

Education: Government expenditure shows the trends in general government expenditures for educational affairs and services at primary, lower secondary and upper secondary levels and subsidiary services to education, expressed as a percentage of the gross domestic product.

Source of the data: United Nations Educational, Scientific and Cultural Organization (UNESCO), Montreal, the UNESCO Institute for Statistics (UIS) statistics database, last accessed April 2023.

Education: Gross enrolment in primary, lower secondary or upper secondary education is the total enrolment in the specific level of education, regardless of age, expressed as a percentage of the eligible official school-age population corresponding to that specific level of education in a given school year. Education at the primary level provides the basic elements of education (e.g. at elementary school or primary school). Programmes at lower secondary (or first stage of secondary) education are typically designed to build on the learning outcomes from primary education. Usually, the aim is to lay the foundation for lifelong learning and human development upon which education systems may then expand further educational opportunities. Some education systems may already offer vocational education programmes at this level education to provide individuals with skills relevant to employment.

Technical notes (*continued*)

Upper secondary is the second or final stage of general and vocational secondary education. Programmes at upper secondary education are typically designed to complete secondary education in preparation for tertiary education or provide skills relevant to employment, or both. The programmes offered are more varied, specialised and in-depth instruction than programmes in lower secondary education. Programmes are more differentiated, with an increased range of options and streams available. Enrolment is measured at the beginning of the school or academic year. The gross enrolment ratio at each level will include all pupils whatever their ages, whereas the population is limited to the range of official school ages. Therefore, for countries with almost universal education among the school-age population, the gross enrolment ratio can exceed 100 if the actual age distribution of pupils extends beyond the official school ages.

Source of the data: United Nations Educational, Scientific and Cultural Organization (UNESCO), Montreal, the UNESCO Institute for Statistics (UIS) statistics database, last accessed April 2023.

Employment in agricultural, industrial and services and other sectors: The "employed" comprise all persons above a specified age who, during a specified brief period, either one week or one day, were in "paid employment" or in "self-employment", see ILO's Current International Recommendations on Labour Statistics. The data refer to those 15 years and over, unless otherwise stated in a footnote, who perform any work at all in the reference period, for pay or profit in agriculture (agriculture, forestry and fishing), industry (mining and quarrying; manufacturing; electricity, gas, steam and air conditioning supply; water supply, sewerage, waste management and remediation activities; and construction) and in services and other sectors based on the sections of the International Standard Industrial Classification of All Economic Activities (ISIC), Revision 4, unless an earlier revision is stated in a footnote.

Source of the data: International Labour Organization (ILO), Geneva, Key Indicators of the Labour Market (KILM 9th edition) and the ILOSTAT database, last accessed January 2020.

Energy production, primary, is the capture or extraction of fuels or energy from natural energy flows, the biosphere and natural reserves of fossil fuels within the national territory in a form suitable for use. Inert matter removed from the extracted fuels and quantities reinjected, flared or vented are not included. The resulting products are referred to as "primary" products. It excludes secondary production, that is, the manufacture of energy products through the process of transforming primary and/or other secondary fuels or energy. Data are provided in a common energy unit (Petajoule) and refer to the following primary energy sources: hard coal, brown coal, peat, oil shale, conventional crude oil, natural gas liquids (NGL), other hydrocarbons, additives and oxygenates, natural gas, fuelwood, wood residues and by-products, bagasse, animal waste, black liquor, other vegetal material and residues, biogasoline, biodiesels, bio jet kerosene, other liquid biofuels, biogases,

Technical notes (*continued*)

industrial waste, municipal waste, nuclear, solar photovoltaic, solar thermal, hydro, wind, geothermal, and tide, wave and other marine sources. Peat, biomass and wastes are included only when the production is for energy purposes. See International Recommendations for Energy Statistics (2011) and the UN publication Energy Balances for a complete description of the methodology.

Source of the data: United Nations Statistics Division (UNSD), New York, Energy Statistics Yearbook 2020, last accessed March 2023.

Energy supply per capita is defined as primary energy production plus imports minus exports minus international marine bunkers minus international aviation bunkers minus stock changes divided by the population. For imports, exports, international bunkers and stock changes, it includes secondary energy products, in addition to primary products.

Source of the data: United Nations Statistics Division (UNSD), New York, Energy Statistics Yearbook 2020, last accessed March 2023.

Exchange rate in units of national currency per US dollar refers to end-of-period quotations. The exchange rates are classified into broad categories, reflecting both the role of the authorities in the determination of the exchange and/or the multiplicity of exchange rates in a country. The market rate is used to describe exchange rates determined largely by market forces; the official rate is an exchange rate determined by the authorities, sometimes in a flexible manner. For countries maintaining multiple exchange arrangements, the rates are labelled principal rate, secondary rate, and tertiary rate.

Source of the data: International Monetary Fund (IMF), Washington, D.C., the International Financial Statistics (IFS) database supplemented by United Nations Department of Management (DM), UN Treasury operational rates of exchange, last accessed June 2023.

Fertility rate is the total fertility rate, a widely used summary indicator of fertility. It refers to the number of children that would be born per woman, assuming no female mortality at child bearing ages and the age-specific fertility rates of a specified country and reference period. The data are an average over five-year ranges; 2005-2010 data are labelled "2010", 2011-2015 data are labelled "2015" and 2016-2022 data are labelled "2022", unless otherwise stated in a footnote.

Source of the data: United Nations Population Division (UNPD), New York, "World Population Prospects (WPP): The 2022 Revision"; supplemented by data from the United Nations Statistics Division (UNSD), New York, Demographic Yearbook 2021 and the Pacific Community (SPC) Statistics and Demography Programme for small countries or areas, last accessed July 2022.

Forested area refers to the percentage of land area occupied by forest. Forest is defined in the Food and Agriculture Organization's Global Forest Resources Assessment as land spanning more than 0.5 hectares with trees higher than 5 metres and a canopy cover of more than 10 percent, or trees able to reach these thresholds in situ. It does not include land that is predominantly under agricultural or urban land use. Data are calculated from the forest estimates divided by the land area.

Source of the data: Food and Agriculture Organization of the United Nations (FAO), Rome, FAOSTAT database, last accessed May 2023.

GDP: Gross domestic product is an aggregate measure of production equal to the sum of gross value added of all resident producer units plus that part (possibly the total) of taxes on products, less subsidies on products, that is not included in the valuation of output. It is also equal to the sum of the final uses of goods and services (all uses except intermediate consumption) measured at purchasers' prices, less the value of imports of goods and services, and equal to the sum of primary incomes distributed by resident producer units (see System of National Accounts 2008). The data are in current United States (US) dollars and are estimates of the total production of goods and services of the countries represented in economic terms, not as a measure of the standard of living of their inhabitants. To have comparable coverage for as many countries as possible, these US dollar estimates are based on official GDP data in national currency, supplemented by national currency estimates prepared by the Statistics Division using additional data from national and international sources. The estimates given here are in most cases those accepted by the United Nations General Assembly's Committee on Contributions for determining United Nations members' contributions to the United Nations regular budget. The exchange rates for the conversion of GDP national currency data into US dollars are the average market rates published by the International Monetary Fund, in International Financial Statistics (IFS). Official exchange rates are used only when free market rates are not available. For non-members of the Fund, the conversion rates used are the average of UN Treasury rates of exchange. It should be noted that the conversion from local currency into US dollars introduces deficiencies in comparability over time and among countries which should be considered when using the data. For example, comparability over time is distorted when exchange rate fluctuations differ substantially from domestic inflation rates.

Source of the data: United Nations Statistics Division (UNSD), New York, National Accounts Statistics: Analysis of Main Aggregates (AMA) database, last accessed April 2023.

GDP growth rate is derived on the basis of constant 2015 price series in national currency. The figures are annual rates of growth expressed in percentages.

Source of the data: United Nations Statistics Division (UNSD), New York, National Accounts Statistics: Analysis of Main Aggregates (AMA) database, last accessed April 2023.

GDP per capita estimates are the value of all goods and services produced in the economy divided by the population.

Technical notes (*continued*)

Source of the data: United Nations Statistics Division (UNSD), New York, National Accounts Statistics: Analysis of Main Aggregates (AMA) database, last accessed April 2023.

Health: Physicians includes generalist medical practitioners and specialist medical practitioners, expressed as the number of physicians per 1 000 population. The classification of health workers used is based on criteria for vocational education and training, regulation of health professions, and activities and tasks of jobs, i.e. a framework for categorizing key workforce variables according to shared characteristics.

Source of the data: World Health Organisation (WHO), Geneva, WHO Global Health Workforce statistics database, last accessed April 2023.

Health: Current expenditure refers to all health care goods and services used or consumed during a year excluding capital spending, or rather "gross capital formation", which is the purchase of new assets used repeatedly over several years. These estimates are in line with the 2011 System of Health Accounts (SHA). Current expenditure is expressed as a proportion of Gross Domestic Product (GDP).

Source of the data: World Health Organization (WHO), Geneva, WHO Global Health Expenditure database, last accessed April 2023.

Important sites for terrestrial biodiversity protected shows land which contributes significantly to the global persistence of biodiversity measured as a proportion of which is wholly covered by a designated protected area. Data are based on spatial overlap between polygons for Key Biodiversity Areas from the World Database of key Biodiversity Areas and polygons for protected areas from the World Database on Protected Areas. Figures for each region are calculated as the proportion of each Key Biodiversity Area covered by protected areas, averaged (i.e. calculated as the mean) across all Key Biodiversity Areas within the region.

Source of the data: United Nations Environment Programme (UNEP) World Conservation Monitoring Centre (WCMC), Cambridge, Sustainable Development Goals (SDGs) statistics database, last accessed March 2023.

Individuals using the Internet refer to the percentage of people who used the Internet from any location and for any purpose, irrespective of the device and network used. It can be via a computer (i.e. desktop or laptop computer, tablet or similar handheld computer), mobile phone, games machine, digital TV, etc. Access can be via a fixed or mobile network. There are certain data limits to this indicator, insofar as estimates have to be calculated for many developing countries which do not yet collect information and communications technology household statistics.

Source of the data: International Telecommunication Union (ITU), Geneva, the ITU database, last accessed March 2023.

Technical notes (*continued*)

Infant mortality rate is the ratio of infant deaths (the deaths of children under one year of age) in a given year to the total number of live births in the same year, expressed as a rate per 1 000 live births. The data are an average over five-year ranges; 2005-2010 data are labelled "2010", 2011-2015 data are labelled "2015" and 2016-2022 data are labelled "2022", unless otherwise stated in a footnote.
Source of the data: United Nations Population Division (UNPD), New York, "World Population Prospects (WPP): The 2022 Revision"; supplemented by data from the United Nations Statistics Division (UNSD), New York, Demographic Yearbook 2021 and the Pacific Community (SPC) Statistics and Demography Programme for small countries or areas, last accessed July 2022.

Intentional homicide rate: The rates are the annual number of unlawful deaths purposefully inflicted on a person by another person, reported for the year per 100 000. For most countries, country information on causes of death is not available for most causes. Estimates are therefore based on cause of death modelling and death registration data from other countries in the region. Further country-level information and data on specific causes was also used.
Source of the data: United Nations Office on Drugs and Crime (UNODC), Vienna, UNODC Statistics database, last accessed June 2023.

International migrant stock generally represents the number of persons born in a country other than that in which they live. When information on country of birth was not recorded, data on the number of persons having foreign citizenship was used instead. In the absence of any empirical data, estimates were imputed. Data refer to mid-year. Figures for international migrant stock as a percentage of the population are the outcome of dividing the estimated international migrant stock by the estimated total population and multiplying the result by 100.
Source of the data: United Nations Population Division (UNPD), New York, "International migrant stock: The 2020 Revision", last accessed July 2022.

International trade: Exports, imports and balance show the movement of goods out of and into a country. Goods simply being transported through a country (goods in transit) or temporarily admitted (except for goods for inward processing) do not add to the stock of material resources of a country and are not included in the international merchandise trade statistics. In the "general trade system", the definition of the statistical territory of a country coincides with its economic territory. In the "special trade system", the definition of the statistical territory comprises only a particular part of the economic territory, mainly that part which coincides with the free circulation area for goods. "The free circulation area" is a part of the economic territory of a country within which goods "may be disposed of without Customs restrictions". In the case of exports, the transaction value is the value at which the goods were sold by the exporter, including the cost of transportation and insurance, to bring the goods onto the transporting vehicle at the frontier of the exporting country (an FOB-type valuation). In the case of imports, the transaction value is the value at which the goods were purchased by the importer plus the cost of transportation and insurance to the frontier of the importing country (a CIF-type valuation). Both imports and exports are shown in United States dollars. Conversion from national currencies is made by means of currency conversion factors based on official exchange rates (par values or weighted averages). All regional aggregations are calculated as the sum of their components.

Source of the data: United Nations Statistics Division (UNSD), New York, Commodity Trade Statistics Database (UN COMTRADE), last accessed June 2023.

Labour force participation rate is calculated by expressing the number of persons in the labour force as a percentage of the working-age population. The labour force is the sum of the number of persons employed and the number of unemployed (see ILO's current International Recommendations on Labour Statistics). The working-age population is the population above a certain age, prescribed for the measurement of economic characteristics. The data refer to the age group of 15 years and over and are based on ILO's modelled estimates, unless otherwise stated in a footnote.

Source of the data: International Labour Organization (ILO), Geneva, Key Indicators of the Labour Market (KILM 9th edition) and the ILOSTAT database, last accessed May 2023.

Life expectancy at birth is the average number of years of life at birth (age 0) for males and females according to the expected mortality rates by age estimated for the reference year and population. The data are an average over five-year ranges; 2005-2010 data are labelled "2010", 2011-2015 data are labelled "2015" and 2016-2022 data are labelled "2022", unless otherwise stated in a footnote.

Source of the data: United Nations Population Division (UNPD), New York, "World Population Prospects (WPP): The 2022 Revision"; supplemented by data from the United Nations Statistics Division (UNSD), New York, Demographic Yearbook 2021 and the Pacific Community (SPC) Statistics and Demography Programme for small countries or areas, last accessed July 2022.

Major trading partners show the three largest trade partners (countries of last known destination and origin or consignment) in international merchandise trade transactions. In some cases a special partner is shown (i.e. Areas nes, bunkers, etc.) instead of a country and refers to one of the following special categories. Areas not elsewhere specified (i.e. Areas nes) is used (a) for low value trade, (b) if the partner designation was unknown to the country or if an error was made in the partner assignment and (c) for reasons of confidentiality. If a specific geographical location can be identified within Areas nes, then they are recorded accordingly (i.e. Asia nes). Bunkers are ship stores and aircraft supplies, which consists mostly of fuels and food. Free zones belong to the geographical and economic territory of a country but not to its customs territory. For the purposes of trade statistics, the transactions between the customs territory and the free zones are recorded, if the reporting country uses the Special Trade System. Free zones can be commercial free zones (duty free shops) or industrial free zones. Data are expressed as percentages of total exports and of total imports of the country, area or special partner.

Source of the data: United Nations Statistics Division (UNSD), New York, Commodity Trade Statistics Database (UN COMTRADE), last accessed June 2023.

National currency refers to those notes and coins in circulation that are commonly used to make payments. The official currency names and the ISO currency codes are those officially in use, and may be subject to change.

Source of the data: International Organisation for Standardization (ISO), Geneva, Currency Code Services – ISO 4217 Maintenance Agency, last accessed June 2023.

Net Official Development Assistance received or disbursed is defined as those flows to developing countries and multilateral institutions provided by official agencies, including state and local governments, or by their executive agencies, each transaction of which meets the following tests: i) it is administered with the promotion of the economic development and welfare of developing countries as its main objective; and ii) it is concessional in character and conveys a grant element of at least 25 per cent. It is expressed as a percentage of Gross National Income of either the donor or recipient. The multilateral institutions include the World Bank Group, regional banks, financial institutions of the European Union and a number of United Nations institutions, programmes and trust funds.

Source of the data: Organisation for Economic Co-operation and Development (OECD), Paris, the OECD Development Assistance Committee (DAC) statistics database, last accessed June 2023.

Population refers to the medium fertility projected de facto population as of 1 July 2022, unless otherwise stated in a footnote. The total population of a country may comprise either all usual residents of the country (de jure population) or all persons present in the country (de facto population) at the time of the census; for purposes of international comparisons, the de facto definition is used, unless otherwise stated in a footnote.

Source of the data: United Nations Population Division (UNPD), New York, "World Population Prospects (WPP): The 2022 Revision", last accessed July 2022.

Population age distribution refers to the percentage of the population aged 0-14 years and aged 60 years and older at the mid-year unless otherwise stated in a footnote.

Source of the data: United Nations Population Division (UNPD), New York, "World Population Prospects (WPP): The 2022 Revision"; supplemented by data from the United Nations Statistics Division (UNSD), New York, Demographic Yearbook 2021 and the Pacific Community (SPC) Statistics and Demography Programme for small countries or areas, last accessed July 2022.

Technical notes (*continued*)

Population density refers to the medium fertility projected population as of 1 July 2022 per square kilometre of surface area, unless otherwise stated in a footnote.
Source of the data: United Nations Population Division (UNPD), New York, "World Population Prospects (WPP): The 2022 Revision", last accessed July 2022.

Population growth rate is the average annual percentage change in total population size. The data are an average over five-year ranges; 2010-2015 data are labelled "2010", 2011-2015 data are labelled "2015" and 2016-2022 data are labelled "2022", unless otherwise stated in a footnote.
Source of the data: United Nations Population Division (UNPD), New York, "World Population Prospects (WPP): The 2022 Revision", last accessed July 2022.

Refugees and others of concern to the UNHCR: The 1951 United Nations Convention relating to the Status of Refugees states that a refugee is someone who, owing to a well-founded fear of being persecuted for reasons of race, religion, nationality, political opinion or membership in a particular social group, is outside the country of his or her nationality and is unable to, or owing to such fear, is unwilling to avail himself or herself of the protection of that country; or who, not having a nationality and being outside the country of his or her former habitual residence, is unable or, owing to such fear, unwilling to return to it. In this series, refugees refer to persons granted a humanitarian status and/or those granted temporary protection. Included are persons who have been granted temporary protection on a group basis. The series also includes returned refugees, asylum-seekers, stateless persons and persons displaced internally within their own country and others of concern to UNHCR.
Source of the data: United Nations High Commissioner for Refugees (UNHCR), Geneva, UNHCR population statistics database, last accessed May 2023.

Region is based on macro geographical regions arranged according to continents and component geographical regions used for statistical purposes as at 31 July 2017.
Source of the data: United Nations Statistics Division (UNSD), New York, Statistical Yearbook 2017 edition (60th issue) Annex I - Country and area nomenclature, regional and other groupings (based on Series M49: Standard Country or Area codes and Geographical Regions for Statistical Use), last accessed October 2017.

Research & Development expenditure refers to expenditure on creative work undertaken on a systematic basis in order to increase the stock of knowledge, including knowledge of humanity, culture and society, and the use of this stock of knowledge to devise new applications, expressed as a percentage of Gross Domestic Product (GDP). It is the total intramural expenditure on R&D performed on the national territory during a given period. It includes R&D performed within a country and funded from abroad but excludes payments made abroad for R&D.

Source of the data: United Nations Educational, Scientific and Cultural Organization (UNESCO), Montreal, the UNESCO Institute for Statistics (UIS) statistics database, last accessed June 2023.

Safely managed water and sanitation: population using safely managed drinking water sources is currently being measured by the proportion of population in urban and rural areas, according to national definitions, meeting the criteria for using safely managed drinking water sources (SDG 6.1.1) by using an improved basic drinking water source which is located on premises, available when needed and free of faecal and priority chemical contamination. Improved drinking water sources are those that have the potential to deliver safe water by nature of their design and construction, and include: piped water, boreholes or tubewells, protected dug wells, protected springs, rainwater, and packaged or delivered water. Population using safely managed sanitation facilities is currently being measured by the proportion of the population in urban and rural areas, according to national definitions, meeting the criteria for having a safely managed sanitation service (SDG 6.2.1a) by using a basic sanitation facility which is not shared with other households and where excreta is safely disposed in situ or transported and treated off-site. Improved sanitation facilities are those designed to hygienically separate excreta from human contact, and include: flush/pour flush to piped sewer system, septic tanks or pit latrines; ventilated improved pit latrines, composting toilets or pit latrines with slabs.
Source of the data: World Health Organization (WHO) and the United Nations Children's Fund (UNICEF), Geneva and New York, the WHO/UNICEF Joint Monitoring Programme (JMP) for Water and Sanitation database, last accessed July 2023.

Seats held by women in the National Parliament refer to the number of women in the lower chamber of the National Parliament expressed as a percentage of total occupied seats in the lower or single House, situation as of 1 January 2023.
Source of the data: Inter-Parliamentary Union (IPU), Geneva, Women in National Parliament dataset and the Sustainable Development Goals (SDGs) statistics database, last accessed March 2023.

Sex ratio is calculated as the ratio of the medium fertility projected population of men to that of 100 women as of 1 July 2022, unless otherwise stated in a footnote.
Source of the data: United Nations Population Division (UNPD), New York, "World Population Prospects (WPP): The 2022 Revision"; supplemented by data from the United Nations Statistics Division (UNSD), New York, Demographic Yearbook 2021 and the Pacific Community (SPC) Statistics and Demography Programme for small countries or areas, last accessed July 2022.

Surface area refers to land area excluding inland water.

Technical notes (*continued*)

Source of the data: United Nations Statistics Division (UNSD), New York, Demographic Yearbook 2021 and the demographic statistics database, last accessed July 2023.

Threatened species represents the number of plants and animals that are most in need of conservation attention and are compiled by the World Conservation Union IUCN/ Species Survival Commission (SSC).
Source of the data: International Union for Conservation of Nature (IUCN), Gland and Cambridge, IUCN Red List of Threatened Species publication, last accessed May 2023.

Tourist/visitor arrivals at national borders is any person who travels to a country other than that in which he or she has his or her usual residence but outside his/her usual environment for a period not exceeding 12 months and whose main purpose of visit is other than the exercise of an activity remunerated from with the country visited, and who stays at least one night in a collective or private accommodation in the country visited (see Recommendations on Tourism Statistics of the United Nations and the World Tourism Organization). The data refer to arrivals of non-resident tourists at national borders, unless otherwise stated in a footnote.
Source of the data: World Tourism Organization (UNWTO), Madrid, the UNWTO statistics database, last accessed December 2022.

UN membership date: The United Nations (UN) is an intergovernmental organization whose members are the countries of the world. Currently there are 193 Member States of the United Nations, some of which joined the UN by signing and ratifying the Charter of the United Nations in 1945; the other countries joined the UN later, through the adoption of a resolution admitting them to membership. The process usually follows these steps: first, the country applies for membership and makes a declaration accepting the obligations of the Charter; second, the Security Council adopts a resolution recommending that the General Assembly admit the country to membership and finally the General Assembly adopts a resolution admitting the country.
Source of the data: United Nations (UN), Department of Public Information (DPI), News and Media Division, New York, Member states and date of admission, last accessed May 2018.

Unemployment refers to persons above a specified age who during a specified reference period were: "without work", i.e. were not in paid employment or self-employment as defined under employment; "currently available for work", i.e. were available for paid employment or self-employment during the reference period; and "seeking work", i.e. had taken specific steps in a specified recent period to seek paid employment or self-employment (see ILO's current International Recommendations on Labour Statistics). The data refer to the 15 years and over age group and are based on ILO's modelled estimates, unless otherwise stated in a footnote.

Source of the data: International Labour Organization (ILO), Geneva, Key Indicators of the Labour Market (KILM 9th edition) and the ILOSTAT database, last accessed May 2023 .

Urban population is based on the number of persons at the mid-year defined as urban according to national definitions of this concept. In most cases these definitions are those used in the most recent population census.
Source of the data: United Nations Population Division (UNPD), New York, "World Urbanization Prospects (WUP): The 2018 Revision", last accessed May 2018.

Urban population growth rate is based on the number of persons defined as urban according to national definitions of this concept. In most cases these definitions are those used in the most recent population census. The data are an average over five-year ranges; 2005-2010 data are labelled "2010", 2011-2015 data are labelled "2015" and 2016-2022 data are labelled "2022", unless otherwise stated in a footnote.
Source of the data: United Nations Population Division (UNPD), New York, "World Urbanization Prospects (WUP): The 2018 Revision", last accessed May 2018.

Statistical sources

Food and Agriculture Organization of the United Nations (FAO), Rome, FAOSTAT database, available at http://www.fao.org/faostat/en/#home.

International Energy Agency (IEA), Paris, available at https://www.iea.org/data-and-statistics?country=WORLD&fuel=Energy supply&indicator=Total primary energy supply (TPES) by source

International Labour Organization (ILO), Geneva, the ILOSTAT database, available at http://www.ilo.org/ilostat.

_____, Key Indicators of the Labour Market (KILM 9th edition), available at http://www.ilo.org/global/statistics-and-databases/research-and-databases/kilm/lang--en/index.htm.

International Monetary Fund (IMF), Washington, D.C., Balance of Payment (BOP) Statistics database, available at http://data.imf.org/bop.

_____, the International Financial Statistics (IFS) database, available at http://data.imf.org/ifs.

International Organisation for Standardization (ISO), Geneva, Currency Code Services – ISO 4217 Maintenance Agency, available at https://www.iso.org/iso-4217-currency-codes.html.

International Telecommunication Union (ITU), Geneva, the ITU Database, available at http://www.itu.int/en/ITU-D/statistics/Pages/default.aspx.

International Union for Conservation of Nature (IUCN), Gland and Cambridge, IUCN Red List of Threatened Species publication, available at http://www.iucnredlist.org/about/summary-statistics.

Inter-Parliamentary Union (IPU), Geneva, Women in National Parliament dataset, available at https://data.ipu.org/women-ranking.

Organisation for Economic Co-operation and Development (OECD), Paris, the OECD Development Assistance Committee (DAC) statistics database, available at http://stats.oecd.org/.

Pacific Community (SPC) Statistics and Demography Programme, Nouméa, Population and demographic indicators, available at http://sdd.spc.int/en/.

United Nations (UN), Department of Economic and Social Affairs (DESA), Population Division (UNPD), New York, "International migrant stock: The 2020 Revision", available at http://www.un.org/en/development/desa/population/migration/data/index.shtml. [check]

_____, "World Population Prospects (WPP): The 2022 Revision", available at https://esa.un.org/unpd/wpp/.

_____, "World Urbanization Prospects (WUP): The 2018 Revision", available at https://esa.un.org/unpd/wup/.

United Nations (UN), Department of Economic and Social Affairs (DESA), Statistics Division (UNSD), New York, Commodity Trade statistics database (UN COMTRADE), available at https://comtrade.un.org/.

_____, Demographic Yearbook (Series R, United Nations publication), available at https://unstats.un.org/unsd/demographic-social/products/dyb/.

_____, Energy Statistics Yearbook (Series J, United Nations publication), available at http://unstats.un.org/unsd/energy/yearbook/default.htm.

_____, Monthly Bulletin of Statistics (Series Q, United Nations publication), available at http://unstats.un.org/unsd/mbs/.

_____, National Accounts Statistics: Analysis of Main Aggregates (AMA) database (Series X, United Nations publication), available at http://unstats.un.org/unsd/snaama/introduction.asp.

_____, Statistical Yearbook (Series S, United Nations publication), available at https://unstats.un.org/unsd/publications/statistical-yearbook/.

_____, Sustainable Development Goals (SDGs) statistics database, available at https://unstats.un.org/sdgs/indicators/database.

United Nations (UN), Department of Management (DM), Office of Programme Planning, Budget and Accounts (OPPBA), New York, UN Treasury operational rates of exchange, available at https://treasury.un.org/operationalrates/OperationalRates.php

United Nations (UN), Department of Public Information (DPI), News and Media Division, New York, Member states and date of admission, available at https://www.un.org/en/about-us/member-states.

United Nations Educational, Scientific and Cultural Organization (UNESCO), Montreal, the UNESCO Institute for Statistics (UIS) statistics database, available at http://data.uis.unesco.org/.

United Nations High Commissioner for Refugees (UNHCR), Geneva, UNHCR population statistics database, available at http://popstats.unhcr.org

United Nations Office on Drugs and Crime (UNODC), Vienna, UNODC Statistics database, available at https://data.unodc.org/.

World Health Organization (WHO) and the United Nations Children's Fund (UNICEF), Geneva and New York, the WHO/UNICEF Joint Monitoring Programme (JMP) for Water and Sanitation database, available at https://washdata.org/monitoring/sanitation.

World Health Organization (WHO), Geneva, WHO Global Health Expenditure database, available at http://apps.who.int/nha/database.

_____, WHO Global Health Workforce statistics database, available at https://www.who.int/data/gho/data/indicators/indicators-index

World Tourism Organization (UNWTO), Madrid, the UNWTO statistics database, available at Global and regional tourism performance (unwto.org).

References

Food and Agriculture Organization of the United Nations (2015). Global Forest Resources Assessment 2020, available at http://www.fao.org/forest-resources-assessment/en/.

International Labour Organization (2000). Current International Recommendation on Labour Statistics, 2000 Edition, available at http://www.ilo.org/global/publications/ilo-bookstore/order-online/books/WCMS_PUBL_9221108465_EN/lang--en/index.htm.

International Monetary Fund (2009). Balance of Payments and International Investment Position Manual, Sixth Edition, available at https://www.imf.org/external/pubs/ft/bop/2007/bopman6.htm.

United Nations (1951 and 1967). Convention relating to the Status of Refugees of 1951 (United Nations, Treaty Series, vol. 189 (1954), No. 2545, p. 137), art. 1) and Protocol relating to the Status of Refugees of 1967 (United Nations, Treaty Series, vol. 606 (1967), No. 8791, p. 267), available at https://treaties.un.org/doc/Publication/UNTS/Volume%20189/volume-189-I-2545-English.pdf and https://treaties.un.org/doc/Publication/UNTS/Volume%20606/volume-606-I-8791-English.pdf.

United Nations (1982). Concepts and Methods in Energy Statistics, with Special Reference to Energy Accounts and Balances: A Technical Report. Statistical Office, Series F, No. 29 and Corr. 1 (United Nations publication, Sales No. E.82.XVII.13 and corrigendum), available at http://unstats.un.org/unsd/publication/SeriesF/SeriesF_29E.pdf.

United Nations (2008). International Standard Industrial Classification of All Economic Activities (ISIC), Rev. 4. Statistics Division, Series M, No. 4, Rev.4 (United Nations publication, Sales No. E.08.XVII.25), available at http://unstats.un.org/unsd/publication/SeriesM/seriesm_4rev4e.pdf.

United Nations (2017). Principles and Recommendations for Population and Housing Censuses Rev. 3. Statistics Division, Series M, No. 67, Rev. 3 (United Nations publication, Sales No. 15.XVII.10), available at https://unstats.un.org/unsd/demographic-social/Standards-and-Methods/files/Principles_and_Recommendations/Population-and-Housing-Censuses/Series_M67rev3-E.pdf.

United Nations (2010). International Merchandise Trade Statistics: Concepts and Definitions, Statistics Division, Series M, No.52, Rev.3, (United Nations publication, Sales No. E.10.XVII.13), available at http://unstats.un.org/unsd/publication/SeriesM/SeriesM_52rev3E.pdf.

United Nations (2011). International Recommendations for Energy Statistics (IRES), Statistics Division, available at http://unstats.un.org/unsd/statcom/doc11/BG-IRES.pdf.

United Nations (2013). International Merchandise Trade Statistics: Compilers Manual Revision 1 (IMTS 2010-CM), Statistics Division , Series F, No. 87, Rev.1 (United Nations

Statistical sources and references (*continued*)

publication, Sales No. E.13.XVII.8), available at https://unstats.un.org/unsd/trade/publications/seriesf_87Rev1_e_cover.pdf.

United Nations (2018). Standard Country or Area Codes for Statistical Use, Statistics Division, Series M, No. 49, available at http://unstats.un.org/unsd/methods/m49/m49.htm

United Nations, European Commission, International Monetary Fund, Organisation for Economic Cooperation and Development and World Bank (2009). System of National Accounts 2008, Statistics Division, Series M, No. 2, Rev.5 (United Nations publication, Sales No. E.08.XVII.29), available at http://unstats.un.org/unsd/nationalaccount/sna2008.asp.

World Health Organization (2019), International Statistical Classification of Diseases and Related Health Problems, Eleventh Revision (ICD-11), (Geneva) available at http://www.who.int/classifications/icd/en/.

United Nations and World Tourism Organization (2008). International Recommendations for Tourism Statistics 2008, Statistics Division, Series M, No. 83/Rev.1 (United Nations publication, Sales No. E.08.XVII.28), available at http://unstats.un.org/unsd/publication/SeriesM/SeriesM_83rev1e.pdf.

Related statistical products

The World Statistics Pocketbook can also be viewed online in PDF format as well as an app for Android and Apple devices at http://unstats.un.org/unsd/publications/pocketbook/ and in UNdata at http://data.un.org/en/index.html.

Other statistical publications offering a broad cross-section of information which may be of interest to users of the World Statistics Pocketbook include:

1.   The Monthly Bulletin of Statistics (MBS) in print and the Monthly Bulletin of Statistics Online, available at http://unstats.un.org/unsd/mbs/.
2.   The Statistical Yearbook (SYB) in print and online in PDF format, available at http://unstats.un.org/unsd/publications/statistical-yearbook/.

Both publications are available for sale in print format (see below for instructions on how to order). For more information about other publications and online databases prepared by the United Nations Statistics Division, please visit: https://unstats.un.org/unsd/publications/. For additional information about the work of the United Nations Statistics Division, please visit http://unstats.un.org/unsd. To order United Nations publications, please visit https://shop.un.org or contact:

United Nations Publications
300 East 42nd Street
New York, NY 10017
Tel: 1-888-254-4286 / Fax: 1-800-338-4550 / E-mail: publications@un.org

Please provide the Development Data Section – which is responsible for producing the World Statistics Pocketbook, the Monthly Bulletin of Statistics and the Statistical Yearbook – your feedback and suggestions regarding these statistical products, as well as the utility of the data, by contacting statistics@un.org.